Materials & Techniques

in the

Decorative Arts

An Illustrated Dictionary

MATERIALS & TECHNIQUES

IN THE

Decorative Arts

An Illustrated Dictionary

EDITED BY LUCY TRENCH

JOHN MURRAY

Albemarle Street, London

Typeset in Monotype Modern Extended by Wearset,
Boldon, Tyne & Wear.
Printed and bound in Great Britain
by The University Press, Cambridge

CONTENTS

Contributors   vi

Introduction   vii

Dictionary   1

Bibliography   558

Acknowledgements   570

*Colour plates appear
between pp. 244 and 245*

CONTRIBUTORS

TONY BEENTJES FGA	Metalwork
SANDRA DAVISON FIIC	Glass and enamel
JENNIFER DINSMORE	Stone, plasterwork and other building materials, gemstones
CATHERINE HASSALL	Paint
FRANK MINNEY	Wood, lacquer, ivory, shell, tortoiseshell and amber
SUSAN MOSSMAN	Plastics
STACEY PIERSON	Ceramics
CATHERINE RICKMAN FIIC	Paper
MARY SCHOESER	Textiles
ROY THOMSON FRSC, FSLTC	Leather

INTRODUCTION

This dictionary focuses on the materials and techniques used in the decorative arts. Its aim is to describe and illustrate creative processes, but not to serve as a craft manual. Each technique has its own constraints and possibilities, and each material has its intrinsic properties, whether real or perceived. Jet, for example, is a form of fossilized wood found in small pieces in very limited locations. It calls for special techniques, as it fractures so easily that it cannot be undercut and has to be carved using files and abrasives rather than chisels. Also, our ancestors believed it to be talismanic, and it is hard not to see a trace of this superstition in its use in Victorian mourning jewellery. An understanding of such factors will greatly enhance our appreciation of an art object, and is especially valuable in the modern world when few people have any direct experience of craftwork.

The thorny question of what constitutes a 'decorative' rather than a 'fine' art has occupied many fine minds for many decades. The distinction is a fairly recent one, established only since the 18th century, and this is not the place to resolve it. In any case, from the craftsman's point of view it is irrelevant since most materials and techniques transcend these artificial boundaries. Lost wax casting may be used to make a silver candelabrum, a glass ornament or a bronze statue.

Our approach has been pragmatic, including in the decorative arts those objects and forms of decoration that have a practical purpose but are also prized for their beauty and craftsmanship. Photography has been excluded on the grounds that, while it may serve a practical or an aesthetic purpose, it seldom fulfils both at the same time; on the other hand, a number of building materials have been included, either since they may be used ornamentally or since they are integral to the production of other crafts. The graphic arts have also been admitted as they are so important to design work and book illustration, but they are not treated in detail.

This leaves us with seven major, core materials—textiles, metals, wood, ceramics, glass, stone and paper—as well as minor, but no less important, ones such as gemstones, ivory, lacquer, leather and shell. We have endeavoured to cover a material from its raw state through any processing or preparatory stage, through every possible craft stage, and finally to any surface finishing.

The *Dictionary* follows the precedent of other arts dictionaries in including 'non-Western' arts that are of general interest. Attention is given to materials such as lacquer and jade, which are primarily associated with East Asia but are greatly admired in the West. That said, the prime orientation of the book is to the arts of the West; it is not conceived as a reference work for specialists in ethnographic or Asian cultures. However, one of the fascinating aspects of the subject is that the techniques of, say, weaving or metalworking vary little from culture to culture. Even with very simple tools it is possible to achieve astonishingly sophisticated results. Another point that emerges from this book is the sheer age of many of the processes described. The woodworkers of Ancient Egypt were familiar with most of the techniques used by modern cabinetmakers, while the basic procedures used in glassmaking were known in the first millennium BC. Glass blowing, a relatively late development, emerged around 50 BC.

Of the ten contributors to the *Dictionary*, six are conservators, three scientists and one an art historian. It was Diderot's belief that 'only an artisan knowing how to reason can properly expound his work.' Though patronizing, this claim was founded on experience, as he had spent many hours with reluctant and inarticulate workmen in his attempts to elucidate their craft. The modern conservator, who fortunately is more communicative, combines the fine manual skills of an artisan with a profound knowledge of materials, an appreciation of science and a familiarity with art objects across a wide range of cultures and historical periods. And it is the dialogue between the craftsman and the intellectual— the conservator and the historian—that has done so much to enrich our understanding of art objects in recent decades.

For ease of access, we have assembled the material in fairly short entries, with cross references to help the reader explore a subject. The cross references themselves have been used selectively. They indicate other entries crucial to an understanding of the subject in hand, or point out headings that the reader may not be aware of. The fact that a certain word is not treated as a cross reference does not imply that there is no entry on the subject. Metric measurements have been used throughout. In certain cases, for example paper, they are preceded by imperial measurements since these represent standard sizes.

No apology will be made for the many illustrations that have been taken from Diderot's *Encyclopédie, ou Dictionnaire raisonné des sciences, des arts et des métiers*. In this great enterprise, the clear beam of the Enlightenment was shone on the gloom of the medieval workshop, dispelling many of the mysteries that surrounded the crafts. Much of the 18th-century technology that Diderot depicts has continued to this day in the hands of specialist craftsmen, while the clarity, elegance and precision of his plates are unsurpassed by any modern photograph or computer drawing.

What has changed, of course, is production on a large scale, which is now fully industrialized with complicated machinery and operations that are beyond the scope of this book. Contrary to popular belief, however, the industrial revolution has been a gradual process and one that has not entirely destroyed traditional skills. In textile production, for example, mechanization was widespread by the late 18th century and soon aided by auxiliary power, but handwork continued into the early 20th century. Even now, when the vast majority of fine textiles are factory-made, hand dyeing and weaving are still used commercially, albeit on a small scale. In other areas, industry has simply adapted processes long known to handworkers. Whatever the future holds, it is certain that much human ingenuity will go into the making of beautiful objects, using skills that have been known for several millennia and evolving new ones suited to the computer era.

LUCY TRENCH

THE
Dictionary

Abalone A shell material derived from molluscs of the species *Haliotis refescens* and others, found on rocks at the shores of most warm seas, especially the Pacific. The flattened, ovoid shells can grow up to 30 cm long and 25 cm wide and are used in the manufacture of a variety of decorative objects. The shells are also used as a source material by shellcarvers. The iridescent inner layer provides the material used in most LAC BURGAUTÉ and much japanned ware and papier mâché.

Acacia A hard, strong and elastic wood, known also as robinia in Britain and as locustwood in the USA. Among the several species used in Britain are *Acacia arabica* (babul) from India, *A. formosa* (sabicu), *A. homalophylla* (myall) from Australia and *A. koa* from Hawaii. Acacia is light brown to creamy yellow, with darker markings and usually a straight but coarse grain. It is difficult to season and hard to work and is used for veneers, fencing and cabinetmaking.

Acetate See RAYON.

Acid etching A technique for decorating glass with an acid-resist process. See ETCHING.

Acid gilding A method of gilding ceramics, using acid etching. See GILDING.

Acid polishing The polishing of glass by brief immersion in a mixture of hydrofluoric and sulphuric acids.

Acrylic A synthetic plastic. It has a clear, shiny, glass-like appearance, but is relatively expensive and may yellow with age. A glass-like acrylic resin was first formed by the German chemist Rudolph Fittig in 1877 and was developed by another German chemist, Otto Rohm. In 1928 the German company of Rohm and Haas produced acrylic commercially, and at first the resin was used in coatings for metals and fabrics. Rowland Hill and John Crawford, British chemists working at ICI, produced the harder form of acrylic in 1934. ICI called the transparent form PERSPEX; in Germany the material was called Plexiglas. The sheet (polymethyl methacrylate) is made by heating the monomer methyl methacrylate into a heavy syrup, which is poured between flat glass sheets (giving acrylic its highly polished surface). The glass 'cell' is placed in an oven to complete the polymerization process, taken out and cooled. The glass plates are then removed.

Acrylic sheet is used for domestic items such as furniture, storage units and light fittings. Acrylic can also be cast and machined into sculptural shapes, or moulded by vacuum-forming (see PLASTICS). These techniques have been used since the 1960s to make decorative items such as jewellery and sunglasses.

Acrylic fibres were developed in the 1940s and derived from acrylic resins with 85% or more acrylonitrile. They have

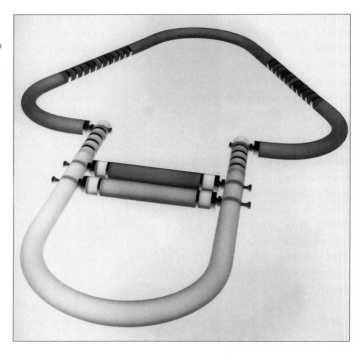

Neckpiece in acrylic and silver, by David Watkins, 1974. Some of the acrylic is self-coloured and some dyed by the designer, using a process originally developed for buttons.

a soft, woolly feel, wash-and-wear performance, pressed-crease retention and wrinkle-resistance. They are often blended with wool to improve the latter's performance, and are widely used in carpeting and knitwear. In 1956 reactive dyes were perfected for use with acrylic fibres, giving brilliant light- and wash-fast colours. Trade names for acrylic and modified acrylics include Orlon, Acrilan and Dynel.

Acrylic paint A generic term for paint in which the pigment is bound in a synthetic polymer medium. More specifically, it refers to a paint based on an acrylic resin. The medium is prepared as an emulsion, with the synthetic material suspended as droplets in water. It is only when the water evaporates, after the paint is brushed on, that the polymer units lock together and form a continuous plastic film. The diluent for the painting process is water, and brushes can also be washed

with water. Acrylics were developed in the USA in the 1920s
for use by the Mexican mural painters, and they are still
much used for the decoration of walls, as long as there is no
problem with damp. In an unsuitable environment the paint
will tend to blister or flake. See also ALKYD.

Adhesive A substance used to bond materials together. It is
usually applied as a paste and sets to a hard film. The most
widely used and effective natural adhesives are gelatinous
substances derived from animal products such as hoofs,
horns, bones and skins. These, which have been used for
several millennia, are also known as glues, the weaker, more
refined ones often being called SIZE. A variety of animal
adhesives are made, variously described as English, Scotch,
French, Cologne, Russian and fish, each of which has particular qualities. To extract the gelatine from the proteinaceous
animal collagen, the source material is cooked slowly in water
and then clarified, condensed and dried. Once sold in cakes or
as beads or powder, these materials can now be obtained only
as beads or flakes. To use, the glue is soaked in water for
twelve hours and then heated in a water-jacketed glue boiler.
Repeated reheating reduces the effectiveness of the glue.
Other adhesives derived from animals include CASEIN (a
protein obtained from milk), blood albumen and egg white or
GLAIR.

A second group of natural adhesives is obtained from
plants. Starch, which is found in roots and seeds, can be
heated with water to form an adhesive paste, while various
forms of resin and GUM have also been used. In the Far East
URUSHI resin has been used as an adhesive for at least 5000
years. Its effectiveness is increased when mixed with a paste
made from rice or wheat flour, when it is known as *nori* or
mugi-urushi. Waxes and mineral adhesives, for example
bitumen, have also been employed to some extent.

Since about 1930 a variety of modern adhesives have been
formulated. These include the urea-formaldehydes, which are
mixed with cold water, rubber-based contact adhesives and a
wide range of water emulsion polyvinyl acetates. The PVA
adhesives can have a variety of properties: they are thermosetting, quick-drying, pressure-setting, water-resistant
and generally easy to use, which makes them particularly
valuable in the woodworking trades. EPOXY RESIN and POLY-
ESTER are also important synthetic adhesives since they form
a strong bond without the use of solvents.

Adze See Woodworking tools.

African red slipware See Roman red slipware.

Agate A form of the quartz mineral chalcedony. It has a strongly banded structure, in which each layer has a different colour and degree of translucency. Agates are formed by silica infilling of gas cavities occurring within igneous rocks, and thus the banding is concentric. Colours range from reds, browns and yellows to greens, bluish white and white; the stones can also be dyed. Onyx and sardonyx are forms of agate with distinctive banding. Moss agates contain oxide inclusions which have formed a dendritic, or tree-like, pattern.

Agate pebbles were collected from river banks, beaches and deserts and used in ancient India and Egypt. There was also an ancient source of agate along the River Achates in Sicily, which is thought to be the origin of the name. The Romans believed that agates had talismanic powers. Forms of agate have been used for making cameos. Locally sourced agates were cut in the Rhineland of Germany from the 15th century and were used in jewellery and to make vessels and boxes. Agates and other stones, such as jasper and granite, were used in 19th-century Scotland to make pebble jewellery. Agates, shaped and mounted in wooden handles, are used as burnishers for gilding; they have also been used to make mortars and pestles.

Agate ware An earthenware or stoneware with marbled decoration, which imitates the striations on agate stone. This effect is created by combining different-coloured clays, glazes or slips, or by spraying or sponging different colours onto the surface of the vessel. Agate ware made from marbled clays is known as 'solid agate ware' or 'scrodled ware'; with surface treatments it is usually known as 'surface agate ware'. Agate ware was made by Josiah Wedgwood but was first developed in Staffordshire *c.*1725 by Thomas Astbury and Thomas Whieldon.

Agba Wood from the moberon, or Nigerian cedar (*Gossweilerodendron balsamiferum*).

Air twist stem See Twist stem.

Ajour See Pierced work.

Alabaster A dense, homogeneous form of the mineral gypsum, hydrated calcium sulphate, which is formed through the evaporation of saline waters from shallow seas. The name alabaster is thought to derive from the Egyptian town

Teapot in solid agate ware,
Staffordshire, c.1740.

Alabastron, which may have been the source for a material of
similar appearance composed of calcium carbonate and
known as calcite alabaster, Egyptian alabaster or ONYX
MARBLE. Alabaster is generally translucent and white, cream
or grey in colour; streaks or mottling of reds and browns can
occur, owing to the presence of iron. Although it is soft
(approximately Mohs 3) and can be carved with a knife,
alabaster can be polished to a smooth, waxy appearance.

The Assyrians quarried alabaster from Mosul and used it
to carve shallow relief panels for the palaces of Nimrud and
Nineveh. In Yemen it was employed for architectural ornament, sculpture and inscriptions from the 5th century BC. In
Europe alabaster is quarried in Castellina in Tuscany and has
been carved in the region since Etruscan times. Religious
carvings are still produced; these are sometimes immersed in
water, which is then brought to the boiling-point in order
partially to dissolve the surface, rendering it white, less
translucent and very similar to marble in appearance.
Alabaster is also quarried in the English Midlands, from
where it was exported widely from the 14th century. This
source was particularly important for the late medieval pro-

duction of small religious relief carvings, which were partly painted and gilded; frequently the flesh areas of the figures were left unpainted to suggest the skin tones. Alabaster has also been used for architectural ornaments such as altarpieces, panelling, columns and balustrades and for tomb effigies (see colour plate xv). Because alabaster is slightly water-soluble it has largely been confined to indoor use, although windows in Mediterranean countries from Roman times were made from thin sheets of alabaster.

Satin-spar, a variety of gypsum with a banded, fibrous structure, is formed by the mineral infilling veins within rocks. It has been used to make decorative stone panelling, beads and cabochons, although its softness makes it prone to wear.

Alizarin The dye material found in MADDER. It was the first of the natural dyes to be synthesized but, although reported by the German chemists C. Graebe and C. Liebermann in 1868, it was not available until 1884, when it was known as Congo red. It is much used in crimson lakes, as it is stronger and more light-fast than madder.

Alkaline glaze A low-temperature glaze with an alkaline flux. Alkaline glazes are composed of glass formers and a high proportion of such alkalis as soda, potassia, lithia and baria, with soda and potassia the most common in historical ceramics. Alkalis are effective fluxes with a high rate of expansion and contraction, which often leads to crazing. They are therefore rather unstable and the glaze fit is often not good.

Alkaline glazes are notable for their ability to produce brilliant colours, such as turquoise from copper pigment (see METALLIC OXIDE), pink from cobalt and blue from iron. These glazes mature at a relatively low temperature (c. 900–1000°C) and are therefore usually applied to earthenwares or as a low-temperature glaze on a pre-fired, high-fired body. Although they have been used in the Far East and in Europe, alkaline glazes are mainly associated with ceramics from Islamic and Near Eastern traditions.

Alkyd A type of paint similar to acrylic in that it is based on synthetic polymers, but prepared in a different way. Instead of being made up into an aqueous suspension, alkyd emulsions are solvent-based. This means that they are slower-drying, that thinners such as white spirit have to be used and that they handle more like oil paint. Alkyds were developed in the late 1960s and have undergone many improvements since to bring them even closer to oils.

Alloy A term traditionally used for a metal composed of a combination of two or more metals, or of a metal and a non-metal. Nowadays, however, the term is used more widely, to include the new range of space-age materials. Bronze (which is a combination of copper and tin) is an example of a metal–metal alloy, while steel (a combination of iron and carbon) is an example of a metal–non-metal alloy. Because most metals are soluble in one another in their liquid state the number of different alloys runs into thousands. An alloy of only two materials is referred to as a binary alloy; an alloy of three materials is a ternary alloy. Metals are alloyed in order to create such properties as corrosion-resistance, hardness, strength or workability, to raise or lower the melting-point, to create special colours or for purely economic reasons. Almost all metals found in the decorative arts are alloys, ranging from precious metals such as the various gold alloys and sterling silver to brass, bronze, pewter and steel.

Alpaca A fibre or yarn derived from the fine, soft, downy fleece of the *Lama pacas*, a domesticated member of the camel family, related to the llama, and native to the high Andean regions of southern Ecuador, Peru, Bolivia and north-western Argentina. The long strands—between 20 and 40 cm in length—are lustrous and elastic, unlike those of the llama, which can be coarse or brittle. Alpaca is seldom used as a warp, which is thus often cotton, wool or rayon.

Alum A generic term for a wide variety of astringent salts, the most common of which is a hydrated double-sulphate of alumina potassium. This was by far the most widely used mordant until the late 17th century; its association with madder dates back to at least 2000 BC.

Aluminium A light metal of a silver white colour with a bluish tinge. The most plentiful metal in the earth's crust, of which it constitutes around 8%, it was not isolated until 1825, by H. C. Oersted. In the 19th century the cost of production was so high it was used to make expensive jewellery, but since the 1930s it has been employed for a vast range of products, including furniture. The most important ore for the extraction of aluminium is bauxite, of which there are significant deposits in Australia, Brazil, Jamaica, Surinam, Guyana and the USA. The bauxite is dissolved in molten cryolite (sodium aluminium fluoride) at a temperature of 1000°C. This solution is put into a carbon-lined bath (cathode), with carbon anodes suspended in the centre. When a very high current (up to 250,000 amperes) is run through this electrolytic cell, pure aluminium is formed on the cathode.

Aluminium is widely used today mainly because of its lightness and corrosion-resistance. It can be worked very easily through hot and cold working, and some alloys have excellent casting and welding properties. Aluminium can be attractively coloured through the process of anodizing.

Amalgam An alloy of mercury with another metal. Most metals, with the exception of iron, nickel, titanium and platinum, will dissolve in mercury to make an amalgam. However, the most common amalgams are those of gold and silver, which can be used for the FIREGILDING of metals, porcelain and glass. When made with tin, amalgam was used as a backing for mirrors.

The term is also used for the naturally occurring alloy of silver and mercury. It probably derives from the Arabic *al-malgham*, meaning 'the assembly'.

Amalgam gilding See FIREGILDING.

Amber A fossilized resin exuded by certain species of now extinct conifers during the Oligocene epoch (30–50 million years ago). It is found most frequently on the beaches of the southern Baltic coast and to a lesser extent in parts of Australia, Burma, Britain, Greenland, Romania, Siberia and Sicily. It occurs as irregular masses and as small, more or less spherical lumps and has been used since prehistoric times to manufacture personal ornaments and amulets. True amber is also called succinite because of the relatively high levels of succinic acid it contains (2–5% by weight). Some varieties, such as Mexican and Sicilian amber, contain no succinic acid and are more correctly referred to as retinite. Amber varies in both colour and transparency, from a cloudy opaque yellow to a rich transparent orangey red, and often contains the remains of fossilized insects. The different varieties of amber are commonly referred to by names that reflect their clarity, origin or a combination of these features. Some of these varieties are described below. Amber can be identified by the pleasant smell it emits and by the static charge that it accumulates when rubbed. It is slightly brittle and will break with a conchoidal fracture under pressure.

Amber is easily worked and can be carved using light and shallow paring cuts. More usually, however, it is worked by scraping and abrasion, using files and shaped abrasive stones.

With care it can be lathe-turned, using turner's scrapers. The turning speed must be kept low and the tools must be sharp and lightly applied, or the workpiece can melt or fracture. Amber is easily polished with mild abrasives. It softens at about 150°C and melts at between 250° and 350°C. Small or waste pieces of the resin can be fused and moulded under heat

Cabinet decorated with amber plaques and carved amber finials and figures, Germany, 16th century.

and pressure to form a material called amberoid, which can be recognized by the presence of more or less parallel flow lines inside and sometimes on the surface of objects formed in this way.

Some natural pieces of amber display a concentric ring construction, reflecting the way in which the original resin was deposited and set. This is known as 'shelly amber'. Pieces in which the layering is not visible are known as 'massive amber'.

Colour and clarity The clarity of a piece of amber varies according to the amount of air, in the form of minute bubbles, formed or trapped within the resin during the solidification process. The more air contained within the piece, the cloudier and whiter is its appearance, and there is a term for each different degree of clouding. Transparent amber is known as 'water clear'; amber with a slight, fine clouding is 'fatty', 'cloudy' or 'flomig'; transparent with some dense whitish, opaque patches is 'clouded bastard'; and completely whitish clouded is 'bastard proper'. Clear amber with swirly cloud formations is known as 'cabbage leaf' or *kapusciak*. Completely yellow-brown clouded amber is *kumst*, and completely white is known as 'pearl', 'bone' or 'osseous'. Some authorities recognize more than 70 different colours and degrees of opacity in various combinations. Colour can be indicative of source: amber found in the Dominican Republic, for example, is often blue or greenish, and Burmese amber can be a distinctive cherry red. These are only rough generalizations, however, and in any case the colour of worked amber changes over time, becoming darker and more reddish. This is a result of atmospheric oxygen acting on the exposed surfaces, a progressive process that works from the outside inwards and penetrates along the lines of flaws and cracks. Amber artefacts retrieved from wet or subaqueous locations, where contact with the air has been restricted, have undergone less colour change than those from dry sites.

Sources The most extensive deposits of amber are currently found in the Baltic states and the Dominican Republic. Others are in New Zealand (a material called ambrite) and the Eocene beds of southern Nigeria (amekite). Burmite is the name given to the material mined in northern Burma. Most of this material was exported for use in China. Chemawinite is a rare, highly fossiliferous type of amber formed in the Cretaceous period and found in parts of Canada. Hachettite is a dull, yellowish translucent form found near Bologna in Italy and once mined in parts of Wales. Loban, also known as the 'balm of Mecca', is said to originate from the area around Mecca. Mexican amber, mined from the Miocene beds in the Chiapas region of that country, is not a true amber and is normally referred to as Mexican retinite. Amber derived from Romanian sources is also strictly speaking a retinite: rumanite (known to have been used by the ancient Romans) is found in various parts of the country, particularly the Oligocene beds in the Buzau district, but other forms include almashite from Piatra and mutenite from Oltenia. Simetite is a type of amber once found on Sicily, as deposits in the River Simeto. Derived from Oligocene beds, it was also known to the ancient Romans and noted for its spectacular colours, said to possess 'all the colours of the spectrum'.

Other resins can be mistaken or substituted for amber. Some of these, such as kaurigum, extensive deposits of which have been mined in New Zealand, have also been fossilized, but at about 1 million years old they are comparatively young. The process of polymerization which transforms a raw resin into amber is thus incomplete and the material is softer than true amber and does not take a sustainable polish. Fossilized resins from yet another group are known as 'copals' and, though even younger than kaurigum, they can be harder and more workable. The distinction between some types of copal and some forms of true amber can be difficult to define. Both find uses in the manufacture of varnish.

Amberoid See AMBER.

Amboyna Wood from the vryabuca or kiabooka tree (*Pterocarpus indicus*), native to South-East Asia. It is orange or reddish brown, with a curled and mottled grain and well-figured burrs and it is used for veneers and furniture (for illustration see page 245).

American whitewood See BASSWOOD.

Amethyst A form of quartz (Mohs scale 7) which contains iron, producing the characteristic range of colours from deep purple through violet to pale mauve; white or transparent areas of quartz may also be present. Amethysts form along the walls of cavities within rocks by the crystallizing out of silica-rich water. Where the rock has eroded, amethyst can be collected from river, lake or beach gravels; where the host rock has remained intact, amethyst is mined. Amethysts may be faceted, carved, cut as cabochons or made into beads.

Amethyst is widely distributed and has been used throughout history. The Egyptians made beads and scarabs from it and the Greeks used it as an amulet to protect against drunkenness, poison and harm in battle. Amethysts have been found among the grave goods of the Aztecs. In Europe there are significant deposits in the Rhineland in Germany and stones from this source were worked from the Middle Ages for jewellery and to embellish reliquaries and book covers. In the late 19th century significant deposits of amethyst were found in Brazil and Uruguay, which substantially reduced its cost.

Anaglypta See LINCRUSTA WALTON.

Ancona A type of Mediterranean WALNUT.

Angora A fibre or yarn derived from the hair of the angora rabbit, originally indigenous from North Africa to France but now raised for this purpose across Europe and North America. It is a fine, soft, fluffy and slippery fibre that requires special handling when spun; the resulting yarn is extremely lightweight and warm. It is often blended in its natural white state with compatible yarns, such as wool and rayon. It should not be confused with the hair of the angora goat, which produces MOHAIR.

Aniline dyes A class of dyes derived from coal tar derivatives and giving pure brilliant colours, the first of which was Perkin's mauve (1856). A.W. Hofmann isolated a bright blue-red 'magenta' in 1859, and blues, violets and greens followed. Known also as basic dyes, they are absorbed readily by animal fibres, especially silk, in a solution of water and acid. In 1862 a patent was registered to fix anilines on cotton, but they were initially much more widely used, commercially, for silks, cashmere and feathers, and as 'amateur' home dyes. Employing benzenes, naphthalenes or anthracenes (all by-products of the manufacture of gas), they had poor fastness on textiles and were replaced by acid and other dyes, but remained important for dyeing paper and leather.

Aniline leather A leather that has been coloured using only dyestuffs and, in particular, clear, non-pigmented finishes. These aniline finishes do not obliterate minor faults present in the skin and therefore result in slightly uneven but very natural-looking leathers. The term derives from the use of aniline-based synthetic dyestuffs developed at the end of the 19th century.

Annealing The heat treatment of a metal to a temperature below its melting-point, to remove internal stress and to soften it for further cold working. (Internal stress is usually the result of cold working such as hammering, stamping and spinning.) After heating the metal to a certain temperature for a particular length of time, the next step is usually quenching or air cooling. Quenching, in which the object is immersed in water to promote rapid cooling, is used for silver, gold and copper. It creates a softer metal, with an improved internal structure for further working. Air cooling, which is slower, is used for steel and brass.

For the annealing of glass, see GLASS.

Anodizing A process by which an oxide layer is formed on a metal by means of electrolysis. This protects the metal from further corrosion and may also allow it to absorb dye. Aluminium and titanium are frequently anodized, but less well-known metals such as magnesium, nobium or tantalum also can be treated. The metal is made the anode (positive) in a bath of diluted sulphuric acid with a lead cathode (negative). Electrolysis creates an oxide layer on the anode, and since this oxide is porous it is capable of absorbing dye. The object is then immersed in a bath containing a brightly coloured organic dye, after which its surface is sealed with lanolin.

Antimony A brittle semi-metal, similar in appearance to zinc, used as a hardening addition in pewter alloys.

Aogai See LAC BURGAUTÉ.

Applied decoration Relief decoration applied to the surface of a ceramic. It is sometimes referred to as 'appliqué' and can be used on almost any type of ceramic. It can be freely modelled by hand or made in moulds such as sprig moulds, into which the clay is pressed before being flattened on the back so that it can be applied easily to the surface of the vessel (see SPRIGGED WARE). The flat-backed appliqué is scored and slipped for ease of adhesion. The most popular forms of applied decoration include modelled figures, moulded patterns or bosses and decorative handles or rings. Other types of applied decoration include JEWELLED DECORATION and LACEWORK. Most applied decoration is attached to the surface of an unglazed vessel, which is then glazed, or it is applied over a glaze and forms biscuit decoration. It is attached to the clay with slip. (For illustration see page 102.)

Appliqué A decorative treatment of textiles created by stitching one fabric to another, with invisible or ornamental stitches. The motif may be cut out in advance and appliquéd, or stitched first, with the surplus being removed as a second stage. Reverse appliqué (or découpé) treats the motif as a 'hole' in the top fabric, which is cut away to reveal the cloth below. Appliqué is an ancient technique known around the world and is associated with patchwork. See also EMBROIDERED LACE and EMBROIDERY.

For appliqué on ceramics, see APPLIED DECORATION.

Aquatint See INTAGLIO PRINTING.

Arbor vitae Wood from a British conifer of the *Cupressus* family, sometimes known as thuya. It is a pale variegated colour and is both durable and strong.

Argillite A fine-grained black stone derived from shale which has become hardened by the pressure of overlying sediments and the introduction of minerals which cement together the grains of stone. Argillite, which can take fine detail and a high sheen, was used by Indians of the Pacific north-west to produce small carvings, such as pipes, primarily for sale to European collectors. Argillite objects are sometimes coated with natural or synthetic varnishes to enhance the sheen.

Armenian bole See BOLE.

Arretine ware See ROMAN RED SLIPWARE.

Arsenic A semi-metal often found in copper alloys, where it is used to increase the hardness and the colouring properties or to give the copper alloy a silvery appearance. Because it is highly toxic, care should be taken when handling arsenic or arsenic alloys.

Art needlework A form of secular embroidery evolved from English ecclesiastical embroidery during the 1860s and 1870s. The term mainly refers to inlaid and onlaid appliqué and the use of silk and crewel threads (or metal threads in church embroideries), and was distinguished from BERLIN WOOLWORK by its freedom in the selection of stitch type, direction and colouring and by the individuality of design.

Artificial stone A general term for a variety of materials and techniques used to simulate building or decorative stone, either for reasons of economy or because of a lack of suitable natural stone. The Egyptians occasionally painted architectural elements carved in limestone to resemble more decorative and costly materials such as granite. The Etruscans imitated coloured marbles using pigmented stucco. The Romans used *opus marmoratum*, a lime- or gypsum-based plaster, mixed with marble powder and worked to a hard smooth surface, to simulate marble.

Materials such as MAREZZO, SCAGLIOLA and STUCCO LUSTRO have been used to imitate white and coloured marbles. In Islamic countries lime plasters were also used, rubbed to a high sheen, to simulate marble. Various mixtures of modified gypsum plasters, such as KEENE'S CEMENT, crushed stone and colouring materials, were patented in the 19th century as artificial marbles, many of which were cast into slabs for interior decoration. One such product, Guattaris marble, was made by treating blocks of the anhydrite form of gypsum with chemicals such as sodium and calcium silicate to harden them, heating to a high temperature and crushing the material to a powder known commercially as marmorite, which could be mixed with water to make moulded ornament; pigments could be added to marmorite to produce coloured casts. Another mouldable artificial marble is made from aluminium ammonium sulphate, mixed with water, bulked with plaster of Paris or talc and coloured with aniline dyes.

From the Middle Ages lines were inscribed into lime-based renders to suggest the ashlar blocks of building stone. A more sophisticated form of this technique was used in 18th- and 19th-century England, where cement-based renders, applied to building façades, were incised with lines to resemble mortar joints, painted and then dusted with sand to imitate building stone. An artificial building stone, used in the construction of the Royal College of Surgeons in London and patented in 1832 as 'Ranger's artificial stone' after its inventor, combined a hydraulic lime with an aggregate such as beach shingle or broken flints and boiling water, which apparently produced a rapid set. In some instances the true nature of an artificial stone was concealed by its manufacturer. COADE STONE, a ceramic material manufactured from 1769 to 1843 to produce architectural ornament and decorative items such as garden furniture, is a convincing simulant for fine-grained, cream-coloured limestone. Its inventor, Eleanor Coade, never acknowledged the ceramic origins of her product.

CEMENT, mixed with sand and crushed stone, and often referred to as cast, reconstituted or reconstructed stone, was widely used from the late 19th century in Europe and North America to produce balustrades, urns, plinths, paves, columns, architraves, arches and tracery windows. A thin layer of neat cement was brushed into wooden or gelatine moulds to take fine detail; the cement mix was trowelled on

Coade stone lion, Stowe, 1778. The fine details on the lion's muzzle and mane would have been carved onto the moulded object before firing. The crispness of these features illustrates Coade stone's excellent resistance to weathering.

top. Large casts were of hollow construction and were internally strengthened with pieces of tile or brick and metal
mesh; thin areas were supported with steel rods or wires.
Various aggregates such as granite and other stone dusts, slag
and crushed brick were used to produce a range of colours
and textures; pigments could also be introduced. These products reduced the cost of construction as they were manufactured in workshops and later in factories, using inexpensive
materials and requiring the less time-consuming skills of
mould-making and casting, rather than carving; once speci-
fied by an architect they could be quickly fixed on site.

Artificial stone can often be distinguished from natural
stone by its appearance and by the fact that the latter is
colder to the touch. More precise identification of the simulant can involve microscopic examination and chemical
analysis of its components.

Ash A very tough and elastic wood from the tree *Fraxinus
excelsior*, found in Europe. It is greyish white in colour, with
occasional yellow markings. It is generally straight but
coarse-grained and is excellent for steam bending; it is thus
used by wheelwrights, chairmakers and for sporting goods
and is one of the favourite woods for the handles of tools that
need to withstand impact, such as chisels. The mottled burrs
are used for ornamental veneers.

The American varieties *Fraxinus americana*, *F. pennsyl-
vanica* and *F. nigra* do not possess the same qualities as the
European ash, and hickory therefore tends to be used in
North America as a substitute.

Ash glaze A high-fired stoneware glaze with a flux made from
plant or wood ash, generally used to produce celadon wares.
Ash glazes are composed of glass formers (see GLAZE) and
organic ashes, which provide strong fluxes. They mature at a
high temperature, approximately 1200°C. Organic ashes
contain high levels of calcia or lime, and as a result ash glazes
are also known as lime glazes. As such, they are usually
coloured with iron oxide (see METALLIC OXIDES) to produce
cool green or blue colours or, when used in high concentrations, black glazes. Ash glazes or pure wood ash can be
applied over another glaze to produce in-glaze effects.

The earliest ash glazes were produced in the 2nd millennium BC in China, probably from ash falling accidentally on
the surface of pots in the firing. The ash fluxed the surface of
the vessel, thus creating a thin, uneven layer of glaze. This

type of glazing continues to be used in Japan. Most often associated with East Asian ceramics, ash glazes are also used by modern potters producing Asian-style ceramics in the West. The early porcelains produced at Bow, east London, were also ash-glazed.

Assaying A process in which a piece is tested to determine the amount of precious metal contained. This is done at an assay office, to ensure compliance with the legal standard. After being assayed the work is officially stamped or hall-marked.

The term derives from the old French word *assai*, meaning 'examination' or 'trial'. The earliest evidence of assaying dates from around 1400 BC. There are several methods of assaying, of which the most well-known, used for precious metals, is to rub the metal over a black fine-grained stone known as a TOUCHSTONE. A streak of metal will be left on the touchstone. The next step is to take a set of gold or silver rods (the composition of which has already been established) and rub them also on the stone. By comparing the colours of the streaks the purity of the alloy can be determined. A refined version of the same process involves applying acids to the streaks on the touchstone: the acid will dissolve the streak left by the test metal if it is not of the same composition as the test rod.

A more scientific method is CUPELLATION. The cupel is a small bone ash crucible in which a precisely weighed scraping of the metal to be tested is placed, wrapped in lead. When heated in a furnace, the base metals and the lead are absorbed in the crucible, leaving the pure metal behind. By comparing the weight before and after heating the amount of precious metal can be determined.

Aubusson A flat, tapestry-woven carpet, named after the manufactory established at Aubusson, France, in 1664. See CARPET-WEAVING.

Aurene An iridescent glass developed at the Steuben Glass Works from 1904 onwards.

Aventurine A quartz with sparkling inclusions of Mica or haematite. This spangled effect was emulated in lacquerware (see VERNIS MARTIN) and also in glass. Aventurine glass is translucent and flecked with metallic particles reminiscent of gold dust. It is coloured with a metallic oxide which, if added in sufficient quantity, is unable to dissolve in the glass and instead forms crystals that reflect light. This glass was first made in Venice in the 17th century and its name derives from the Italian *per avventura* ('by accident'); it was exported in pieces to be crushed and reused by foreign manufacturers. In Venetian aventurine the speckled effect was due to metallic copper particles, resulting from the addition of copper oxide to the batch. In the 19th century chrome or chrome and tin were used to create, respectively, green and pink aventurine.

Axe See WOODWORKING TOOLS.

Axminster A cut-pile, machine-made carpet, closely resembling hand-knotted carpets and capable of being produced in large widths and without any repeating pattern (see CARPET-WEAVING). This form of carpet has been available since the 1880s and (like chenille carpets) takes its name from the English town of Axminster, which from 1755 to 1835 was the site of the manufacture of symmetrically knotted carpets, made on upright looms that were subsequently transferred to Wilton.

Ayrshire work See EMBROIDERED LACE.

Azurite A blue pigment obtained from the mineral azurite, a naturally occurring basic copper carbonate. It was occasionally used in opulent interiors in the 16th century and early 17th, but was then replaced by a cheaper, synthetic copper carbonate blue known as 'blue verditer'.

Back painting See REVERSE GLASS PAINTING.

Baidunzi See CHINA STONE.

Baize See PLAIN WEAVE.

Bakelite A synthetic plastic used in the 1920s and 1930s for a wide range of decorative ware. The name was first used as a trade name by the Bakelite Corporation of America for a particular group of phenolic plastics which are dark in colour. It is now more generally used to describe a variety of early plastic materials, including celluloid, casein and urea-formaldehyde.

The original Bakelite (phenol formaldehyde, or phenolic) plastics were the first truly synthetic plastics. They were invented by Leo Baekeland and first patented in the USA in 1907. Baekeland reacted phenol and formaldehyde under controlled conditions to produce an amber-coloured resin. He combined this with a filler such as wood flour (made of sieved

B

Bakelite ashtray made of walnut-effect phenolic, with 'Michelin' man made of ivory urea-formaldehyde, c.1945.

sawdust or chips, usually spruce or Columbian pine) or cotton flock to produce dark-coloured mouldings. By 1928 this resin could be cast on its own, and moulded into small decorative items such as jewellery, cigarette boxes, light fittings and small radio cases. Cast phenolic objects of this kind were popular in the Art Deco period.

Phenolic products can be mass-produced by compression moulding (see PLASTICS), and phenolic was commonly used for items such as radios and telephones. In recent decades this application has largely been replaced by other plastics such as ABS (acrylonitrile-butadiene-styrene), a plastic with more robust qualities than Bakelite. Phenolics can be brittle and may crack if dropped.

Products made from phenolic resins possess good electrical resistance and mechanical properties. Phenolics are very difficult to ignite and, being thermosets, are ideal for electrical components such as plugs and insulators and for domestic appliances such as thermos flasks, saucepan handles and even electric hot water bottles. Different fillers such as cotton rags, paper or mica can be used to alter the appearance of the material. Sometimes a grained appearance is created to imitate wood. If heated, phenolics give off a smell of carbolic acid (phenol).

Balata A natural plastic similar to GUTTA PERCHA, although streaky brown rather than dark brown in colour. It is obtained from the *Mimosups balata* tree in South America and was used in the 19th century to mould decorative items such as dishes.

Ball clay A highly plastic clay found worldwide and used as an additive in ceramic bodies. As their particle size is too small, ball clays cannot be used on their own to produce ceramics (see CLAY), but their plasticity makes them useful as additives to ceramic bodies which are not normally very plastic. They have a maturing temperature in the range of 1100–1200°C. Ball clays are traditionally dug up in easily transportable balls of up to 13.5 kg in weight. When unfired, ball clays tend to be dark, often grey or black. When fired, they are light in colour.

Bamboo Grasses of the Bambuseae family, found mainly in tropical and sub-tropical regions. The stems are hollow and divided by internodes to form boxlike structures. In their unseasoned form they are used for basketry; seasoned and dried, they can be worked like wood, though with special

Bamboo brushpot carved in high relief, China, Qing period, mid-18th–19th century.

joints sometimes bound with split bamboo. They can also be
shaped by steaming over a form. In addition to its use in basketry, bamboo is widely employed in the East for construction and furniture; fine paper is also made from the pulped
leaves.

Bandalasta ware A trade name used by the British firm of
Brookes & Adams for a range of brightly coloured decorative
table and picnic ware in plastic. It is made from thiourea-
formaldehyde, discovered in 1924 by a British chemist,
Edmund Rossiter, while working for the British Cyanides
Company. By 1929 urea-formaldehyde offered improved
qualities.

Bandalasta plastics could be made in light, bright colours,
and mottled marble, alabaster and stone effects, achieved by
adding coloured powders to the mix, were popular. Although
heat-resistant, they tended to absorb water. However, unlike
phenolics, they did not smell or 'taste' and this made them
suitable for tableware.

Banding A form of wooden inlay, made in a variety of patterns from rare, well-figured or coloured veneers and often
incorporating STRINGING. It is usually narrow (5–25 mm) and
is generally used around the edges of veneered surfaces on
boxes, table tops, drawer fronts and so on.

See also CROSS BANDING.

Bands Raised features on the spine of a book. Raised bands
occur at the spine of a hand bookbinding as protruding ridges
showing the position of the cords, thongs or tapes onto which
the text block is sewn. Because they divide the spine into
compartments, the bands are frequently the focus of decoration. Sometimes false bands are stuck onto the spine of a
book sewn with recessed cords. At the head and tail of a
handbound book, headbands are made to conceal strengthening material (such as a cord or thong ensuring secure board
attachment) finishing the spine. These are embroidered by
hand, using coloured threads, and in fine bindings are frequently made of silk.

Banker See STONECARVING TOOLS.

Bantam An old name for COROMANDEL work, derived from
the Dutch East India Company trading post on the Java
coast from which lacquerware was exported to Europe.

Bargello A canvaswork embroidery stitch in which brightly
coloured wool or worsted and, sometimes, silk yarns cover the
entire surface of the ground cloth in upright stitches of

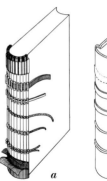
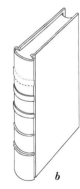

a   *b*

*(a) The spine of a book
sewn by hand on different
types of cores and thongs to
demonstrate a variety of
techniques. The loose ends,
or slips, are used to attach
the text block to the boards of
the book. (b) The finished
book with the cords or thongs
visible as raised bands.*

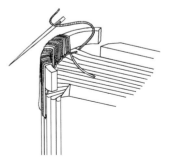

*A traditional headband
being sewn onto the spine of
a book before the binding is
covered. Thread is taken
around a core of leather and
sewn through the folds of the
sections. Note the rounded
shape of the spine at this
stage. The spines of
Western-style books are
hammered into a rounded
shape after sewing to
compensate for the swelling
caused by the sewing thread.*

varying lengths, rising and falling in their positioning to give the effect of flames. It is also sometimes called flame stitch, Irish stitch and Florentine stitch. A related technique is Hungarian stitch (or *point d'Hongrie*), which covers the canvas with small interlocked diamond shapes. Bargello was especially popular in the 17th and 18th centuries.

Bark materials Sheet materials made from tree bark and used in place of paper and cloth. They have been made throughout the world since early times. Unlike true paper, bark papers are made from intact strips of bark, usually inner bark beaten by hand with wood and stone tools on a board to consolidate it into sheets. Bark cloth is made in a similar fashion, by soaking and beating it out to the desired thickness.

Bark sheet materials have been dyed and used as a support for painting and printing, and have even been made into garments, but have only rarely been used for calligraphy. Terms used to designate particular types of prepared bark paper include *tapa* in the Pacific islands, *amatl* in southern Mexico and *huun* in the Yucatán peninsula of Central America, where the Mayans were using the material in the 10th century. North American Indians traditionally painted directly onto pieces of unprepared birch bark.

Barwood See BRAZILWOOD.

Basalt An igneous rock, largely composed of the minerals plagioclase feldspar and pyroxene and formed by lava flows. It is black or grey, or brown when weathered. Most basalts are fine-grained, although some have an open texture where bubbles of gas were trapped during formation. Although it occurs widely, the use of basalt as a building stone is limited. In the Deccan region of India, however, cave temples were carved into basalt formations; it was also used, with other stones, in the construction of Cologne Cathedral. The Egyptians used basalt to make stone vessels from the neolithic period and for stoneworking tools.

Basalt ware An unglazed black fine-grained stoneware developed by Wedgwood in the late 1760s, when it was known as 'black basaltes'. The body was composed of ball clay and slag, which was added as a flux and coloured with iron and manganese oxides. Such a fine-grained body was suitable for casting but not throwing on the wheel. The forms produced were therefore limited to vases, medallions and busts with engine-turned decoration.

Basanite A grey igneous rock of volcanic origin containing a number of minerals, including feldspar and olivine, which has occasionally been used as a building stone. The name basanite has long been used incorrectly as a synonym for TOUCH-STONE, a piece of black stone employed for assaying metals.

Basil A vegetable-tanned, full-thickness sheepskin (sometimes called bazan). The term usually denotes that the skin was tanned using indigenous materials rather than more expensive imported tanning agents. These leathers were used for industrial gloves, shoe linings and the quilted linings of saddles.

Basketry The interlacing of linear materials to make containers and other artefacts. Basket-making is a very ancient craft, known from neolithic times and pre-dating weaving and ceramics; even utilitarian items may be made with great artistry. The materials used include: straw and other cultivated cereal stalks; raffia and other palms; reeds, rushes, grasses and sedges; bamboos and canes; species of osier or basket willow (*Salix*) and occasionally other coppiced woods; and wire, sometimes plastic-coated. Many of the natural materials need lengthy preparation. Willow shoots, for example, are harvested annually, dried (with or without their

A basket-maker at Cleeve Loude, Worcester, using stripped willow in a stake-and-strand construction.

bark), then soaked again before use.

A variety of off-loom weaving techniques are used in basketry. In the stake-and-strand method a framework of radiating or parallel stakes is interwoven with more pliable natural material, built up from the bottom. In frame or ribbed baskets the weaving passes across a rigid frame or hoop over stiff ribs that create a deep, rounded shape. Coiling employs a bundle or rope of fibre (or a single strand), which is coiled and sewn into place. The sewing may cover the coil entirely or be virtually concealed. Cane, raffia, rush or straw is used for the core, and raffia, twine or split wood for the sewing. Plaiting, which is suitable for rushes, employs two or more elements, usually of the same material. These may be worked into a single wide lattice or into narrow braids, which are then coiled and sewn together. Twining uses a warp and weft of a soft or semi-soft material, such as grass or split root. The wefts are worked in pairs, passed alternatively before and behind each warp and at the same time locked together in a twist between the warps; this results in a flexible construction, but one so tight that it can hold water. In another form of twining one weft remains passive while the other binds it to the warps; this technique is used for open, stiff baskets such as fish traps.

The choice of technique will depend on the materials available, and each is therefore often associated with a particular region. In northern Europe the stake-and-strand and framed-and-ribbed methods are most common, for example, while plaiting is associated with the Middle East, coiling with Africa and twining with North America. Decoration is introduced through different coloured materials, the incorporation of feathers, shells and beads, or the use of woven effects such as twill.

Basse taille See ENAMEL.

Basswood A light and soft, but not particularly strong or durable wood produced in Canada and North America and derived from certain species of the *Tilia* genus of American lime or linden (wood from British and European species of linden is called LIMEWOOD.) It is creamy or greyish white to light brown and is sometimes called American whitewood. Even-grained and with a fine texture, it works easily but is prone to warping and shrinkage. It stains and polishes well, is available in large sizes, and is used for plywood, cheap cabinets, containers and carving. The stringy inner bark is used in rope making.

Bat printing See TRANSFER PRINTING.

Bath stone A name given to several varieties of oolitic lime-stone quarried from the area around Bath in south-west England. It is golden to yellow in colour and has a medium- to fine-grained texture. It has been employed from Roman times, both in Bath and elsewhere, as a building stone and has also been used for carving architectural ornament.

Batik A pattern-dyeing technique that employs a hot wax resist, which is positioned by hand-drawing with a TJANTING or printing with a block. The wax prevents the dye from per-meating the cloth and cracks during immersion, giving the crazed lines characteristic of this method. Generally used on cotton cloths, batiks have long been an important product of South-East Asia, particularly Java and Bali, but the tech-nique is also represented in Indian textiles found in 1st-century AD Egyptian tombs and in Pre-Columbian Peruvian textiles.

Bating See TANNING.

Battersea enamel See ENAMEL.

Bazan See BASIL.

Beading A decorative border of tight beads, often found on silverware. The earliest examples were probably made rather crudely by filing the beading out of round wire. Later, a more sophisticated technique involved rolling the round wire between a flat surface and a tool with a semicircular groove. The final development was to stamp the beading between two dies. The latter two methods were described by the German monk Theophilus in the 12th century, in his treatise on metalworking. After it has been shaped, the beaded wire is soldered onto the workpiece.

Beadwork A general term covering a number of embroidery techniques, primarily forms of laid and couched work and knitting, that employed beads, especially beads of glass. The couching of pearls, known from as early as the 12th century, is generally referred to as pearl work. From the 17th century to the 19th, beadwork was popular for jewel cases, shoes, picture and mirror frames, trays, purses and small dressing-table items, and beads were also often incorporated into can-vaswork. Also couched or strung were wampum, North American Indian beads of polished shells used as currency.

Beech A light pinkish or reddish wood from the *Fagus sylvat-ica* tree, found in Europe and sometimes known as red beech.

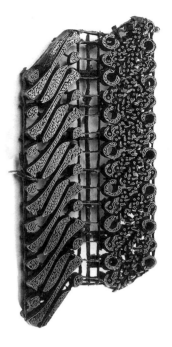

A batik block intended for printing a hot wax resist onto cloth, Java, 19th or early 20th century. The raised areas, representing the design, are created by hammering metal strips into the wooden base.

It has a fine, straight, close grain, is easily worked and will take a lustrous finish. It is very versatile and is used for furniture, tools, bentwork and treen. The various species of so-called New Zealand beech (*Nothofagus*) have a similar range of uses.

Beetle-wing embroidery A form of laid and couched work that employs the wing cases (elytra) of beetles in the family Buprestidae, or jewel beetles, noted for their iridescent appearance. Many varieties are found in tropical regions and were used in embroidery; the practice is thought to have been most long-lived and elaborate in style in India, where, aside from indigenous use, textiles, clothing and harvested elytra were also produced from *c.*1760 to *c.*1930 for European consumption.

Bell metal A pale high-tin bronze used for casting bells, because of its sonorous qualities. Typical compositions range from 76 to 80% copper and from 24 to 20% tin.

Bentwood A name applied to THONET FURNITURE and more generally to any wooden item that is artificially bent. A variety of techniques have been used. All are less wasteful of timber than sawing or carving and produce a piece that is comparatively strong as the grain continues through the bend.

The kerfing technique involves cutting part way through the timber, across the grain, from one or both sides. This allows the timber to be bent to shape, at which point both sides are veneered. Alternatively, concave surfaces are formed by kerfing from one side, bending the workpiece around a form and gluing wooden slips into the kerf to prevent closure. Steam bending involves exposing the timber to steam in a special box, which may be nothing more than a strongly constructed wooden case connected to a source of steam. The workpiece is exposed at the rate of one hour for each inch (2.5 cm) of thickness, after which it becomes very flexible and is removed from the box and bent around a former. The workpiece is sometimes supported on the outer curve by a 'strap' to prevent splitting during bending. This is the method usually used to produce the curved elements of a WINDSOR CHAIR.

Bera See LIGNUM VITAE.

Berettino ware See SMALTINO.

Berlin woolwork A form of canvaswork named after the city where printed patterns were first produced early in the 19th century. Coloured wools were worked on canvas according to a pattern printed on a chart ruled in squares, with each square representing a stitch; the result was criticized in the mid-19th century as too regimented and, often, too realistic in its representation. In the latter part of the century the charts were replaced by printing directly onto the canvas; today's 'needlepoint' kits are latter-day examples of this concept.

Bezel setting See STONE SETTING.

Bicheroux process See FLAT GLASS.

Bidri ware A type of Indian metalwork, in which silver and/or brass are inlaid in a chemically blackened high-zinc alloy. The name derives from the Indian town of Bidar. The zinc workpiece is first cast in sand and then roughly finished. The design is traced and then chiselled out, with the edges having a slight lip to hold the inlay. When large areas have to be chiselled out, these are roughened to hold the sheet inlay better. After the inlay has been positioned, the piece is scraped, filed, polished and finally patinated with a hot

Bidri ware ewer, Deccan, 17th century.

mixture of mud and ammonium chloride. The zinc will turn black, creating an attractive contrast with the silver and brass, which will not change colour.

The earliest surviving pieces date from the late 16th or early 17th century and are influenced by Iranian design and forms. The craft of making bidri ware almost died out at the end of the 19th century but was kept alive by state support and continues to be practised by a few hundred craft workers in the Deccan.

Bird's eye A decorative wood figure common in maple and some other species. It is formed by small depressions in the outer annual growth ring, with later growth following the contours. It appears as a series of small concentric circles on both rotary-cut veneers and plain sawn timber.

See also PEACOCK'S EYE.

Biscuit A partly fired or fully fired but unglazed ceramic body. If it has been deliberately left unglazed, the body is usually a fine porcelain (see BISCUIT PORCELAIN). The term can also refer to a stage in firing when a piece is first fired to a relatively high temperature and then glazed and fired again. Indeed, the word derives from the French for 'twice fired', as a second firing was introduced at Vincennes in the 17th century for the production of soft paste porcelain. In some ceramic traditions a biscuit-fired body is decorated with enamels, to produce 'enamel-on-biscuit' decoration. This method was used especially in China in the late 17th and early 18th centuries. In industrial ceramics the term 'bisc' or 'bisque' is used to describe an initial lower-temperature firing before a higher-fired glaze is applied. A biscuit-fired ware has the advantage of being easier to handle for glazing and setting in the kiln.

Biscuit porcelain Fired porcelain that has been deliberately left unglazed. It was produced first at Vincennes in the 1750s and later also at Sèvres and Derby, and it continued to be popular in England and Europe through the 19th century. Made from a soft paste porcelain body, biscuit porcelain was usually used to produce small sculptures prized for their sugary or marble-like surface texture. In the 19th century a type of biscuit porcelain called PARIAN WARE was produced in England and this was often tinted to resemble marble.

Black figure ware Ancient Greek pottery with black painted decoration. It was first introduced in the 5th century BC. The decoration usually consisted of black figures painted in slip

Soft paste biscuit porcelain figures of Ceres *and* Bacchus, *Sèvres, c.1770.*

on a red pottery ground, sometimes with purple and white additions. The figures were executed in silhouette with incised details such as hair or costume.

The black slip was coloured with iron oxide (approximately 15%) and was very glossy and dense. This slip fused easily, which was essential for the creation of black decoration on a red ground. The firing of black figure ware was carefully controlled. The initial atmosphere was oxidizing, but this was then changed to a reducing atmosphere, which turned the slip black. The slip then fused and vitrified, so that its colour was unaffected by the final, oxidizing atmosphere in cooling. At this time the unslipped area turned red,

A blacksmith at work. The wrought iron is heated until red hot, at which point it is soft and easy to bend with a scroll wrench.

creating the red ground for the black decoration.

At the end of the 5th century a more flexible painting technique was introduced. The wares are known as 'red figure ware', as the designs are reserved red on a black ground.

Blacksmithing The process of hot FORGING, shaping and WELDING iron and steel. Iron is traditionally heated to white-hot in a coal-fired forge, although gas is now also used. In this state the iron is very malleable and can easily be shaped on an anvil, using hammers. Occasionally, for unusual forgings, small specially shaped anvils called swages are fitted in a hole in the main anvil.

Blanc de Chine A white porcelain made in China and exported to Europe in the 17th and 18th centuries (the name translates as 'Chinese white'). It was first made at the Dehua kilns in Fujian province in about the 11th century and is known in China as Dehua ware (for illustration see page 77).

As is typical of southern Chinese porcelains, *blanc de Chine* has a body that is composed mainly of china stone. It is covered with a colourless glaze of similar composition and fired to approximately 1250°C in an oxidizing atmosphere (see FIRING) from which it acquires an ivory tone. The body material is very plastic and thus suitable for producing small vessels and press-moulded figures with moulded and applied decoration. When press-moulded, the figures are usually also modelled before firing.

The Dehua kilns are best known in China for their Buddhist figures, which are still produced today. For the European market numerous small figure groups were produced, usually featuring gentlemen in European dress. The ware was also exported to South-East Asia and small vessels such as boxes and bowls were made specifically for that market. It was copied at many European kilns, including Meissen.

Most *blanc de Chine* ware exported to Europe in the 17th century was undecorated, but in wares produced in the 18th century complicated moulded and applied decoration can often be seen. On ceramics made for the Chinese market, some underglaze painting and overglaze enamel decoration can be found. The wares made for the Chinese market are of considerably better quality than those made for Europe and are exceptionally translucent.

Bleach An agent or chemical compound used either to whiten fibres, yarns or fabrics by removing the natural colouring matter, or to remove colour from a dyed fabric. In its simplest form bleaching is carried out by steeping in an alkaline solution followed by exposure to the sun, a process carried out several times and closely associated with linen and cotton cloths. The development of textile printing in Europe prompted attempts to replace sun bleaching with a series of treatments and, in the mid-18th century, led to the introduction of oil of vitriol (sulphuric acid) in place of buttermilk in the penultimate stage, called souring. This reduced the bleaching time—previously up to eight months—by half. Late in the century chlorine was isolated and by *c.*1810 chlorinated lime (bleaching powder or chemic) was widely available for use on cellulose fibres, reducing bleaching time to about a day and providing the first effective bleach for printers. This and other related improvements, the result of advancements in organic chemistry, greatly improved the ability of mordant and discharge printing works to create strong bright colours adjacent to each other or to white; a good white ground was also essential for some colours, especially clear reds on cotton, and for this reason the highest-quality bleach was long referred to as 'madder bleach'. In the 20th century bleaching agents included chlorine and hydrogen peroxide for cellulosics, and peroxides, perborates and sulphur dioxide for protein fibres.

Blind tooling See TOOLING.

Block printing A method of hand-producing printed textiles and wallpaper, using carved wooden blocks with the pattern area raised, and also sometimes incorporating metal insertions or wooden-edged areas of felt (for illustration see pages 394 and 520). The former technique was in use in Europe from at least 1780. The use of blocks can be detected by the presence of 'pin' marks at regular intervals, which are made by small metal claw-like pins at each corner of the block and guide the printer during production. Technically, there is no limit to the size of the finished design, since numerous blocks can be used in its creation, although for practical reasons the block itself is seldom larger than 40 cm in height or width. It is pressed against a sieve (or tier) floating on the mordant or dye vat, placed on the cloth and tapped with the heel of a weighted wooden mallet; if there is more than one colour, each is printed the length of the piece before the next one is laid on. In craft production between $c.1910$ and $c.1960$ hand-printing was often done with linoleum blocks, generally no more than 20 cm in height or width and without the pins. Block printing is a flexible process, allowing designs to be positioned where required, as in borders, or combined with other patterns, including those made by roller printing or copperplate printing.

Blocking The decoration of a leather or cloth binding by machine to produce an impressed design. It is known in the USA as 'stamping'. It may be intended to imitate hand tooling, or may incorporate coloured inks and metal foils to create a recessed image derived from an artist's design. Blind blocked or stamped panels (without colouring material) were created on European hand bookbindings as early as the 16th century, but blocking a design mechanically onto a cloth binding was a popular technique in commercial book production in the mid- to late 19th and early 20th centuries. Unlike hand tooling, which is carried out on the finished book, blocking could be done on a prefabricated leather or cloth binding (called a case binding) before attachment to the text block. The blocks were made in metal. Initially this was hand-engraved brass, but from the late 19th century the design could be transferred photomechanically to zinc and etched. See also GOLD BLOCKING.

For discussion of blocking as a technique in metalwork, see SINKING.

Bloodstone A dark green, opaque form of the gemstone chalcedony, which contains inclusions of iron oxide or red jasper, which can resemble spots of blood. It is also sometimes called heliotrope. Bloodstones are cut as cabochons and were used in pietre dure.

Blue and white White ceramics with cobalt blue decoration, which can be painted or applied either under or in the glaze. More specifically, the term refers either to porcelain decorated with underglaze cobalt blue painting or to earthenwares with white glazes painted in cobalt blue.

Blue and white porcelain was first made in China in the 8th century AD. It is produced by forming a white porcelain body into the desired shape and allowing it to dry. It is then painted directly with cobalt pigment mixed with a liquid medium. The unfired body is highly porous and the pigment very strong, so mistakes in the painting cannot be erased. Once painted, the vessel is dipped into a colourless glaze and fired to porcelain temperatures. The resulting ceramic has deep blue decoration under the glaze. Blue decoration can also be applied by transfer printing.

Cobalt oxide has been used to paint ceramics since at least the 8th century BC, when it was employed on Egyptian earthenwares. From the 8th century AD it was used in China to paint white porcelain and in the 9th century cobalt was used in Islamic ceramics to paint designs into a white glaze, a technique that was later used on Dutch Delftware. From the 14th century China was the main producer of blue and white porcelain, which it exported in great quantities. The ware was given as tribute to foreign rulers, by Islamic potentates to the doges of Venice, for example, and greatly influenced the production of blue and white ceramics in the Near East and Europe.

Blue John A variety of the mineral fluorspar (calcium fluo-

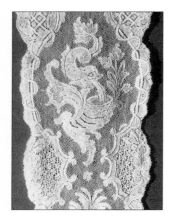

*Detail of a lappet of
Mechlin bobbin lace,
c.1755–65. Recorded as
early as 1657, Mechlin was
made all in one piece with
an integral cordonnet; the
distinctive ground mesh
(with three twists rather
than the more usual four)
is nevertheless
characteristic of bobbin
laces in its apparent
delicacy, a feature that
machine-made nets, such
as 'patent nets' and
bobbinet, attempted to
duplicate in the early 19th
century.*

ride) with distinctive banding of blue, violet and purple, found at Treak Cliff, near Castleton in Derbyshire, England. It has been used since Roman times for the production of decorative objects such as vases, which were shaped on a lathe.

Blueing The chemical or heat treatment of a steel surface to produce an attractive blue colour.

Boarding The process of raising or emphasizing the surface character of a leather by folding it grain side in and working it backwards and forwards under the pressure of a cork board attached to the forearm. The leather was often worked in two or more directions, giving a range of surface effects.

Boar's tusk ivory See PIG IVORY.

Bobbin lace A type of lace characterized by the use of bobbins to tension the threads lightly and to manoeuvre the threads according to the desired pattern (for illustration see page 265). This technique is based on that of plaiting. From the 16th century until 1833 the threads were principally flax; later cotton threads were also used, although metal thread and black, white and blonde-coloured silk bobbin laces were also made (see CHANTILLY LACE and MALTESE LACE). Eastern European bobbin laces often incorporated coloured threads.

The design is pierced on parchment or card and placed on a pillow, into which pins are stuck through the holes; these provide the guides around which the threads are worked. Under magnification solid areas (called *toilé*) appear woven and grounds are plaited or twisted. Most bobbin laces are made vertically in one continuous process, with each area being moved up as it is completed to allow work to begin on another. The exceptions are Milanese, some Flemish, Brussels and Honiton bobbin laces, which have grounds worked around completed motifs (after *c.*1800 Brussels and Honiton motifs were applied, technically creating embroidered lace). Stylistically, until the mid- to late 17th century bobbin lace followed needle lace, having barred grounds; these were then replaced by meshes, which until the mid-18th century were highly decorative and then became net-like and more dominant in the design, before becoming coarser in the mid-19th century, when guipure styles, with bars, were revived.

The place of manufacture can often be identified by a distinctive mesh. Many bobbin laces made in what is now northern France (such as Mechlin, some Binche, Lille, Chantilly and Caen) included a cordonnet adapted from needle lace styles or incorporated other identifying techniques such as an

A demonstration model of a foot-powered bobbinet machine, working with fairly coarse yarns to make the cloth structure apparent.

edging to the *toilé* of minute holes (as with Valenciennes lace) or raised edgings or veining (as in *point d'Angleterre*); Honiton and Bucks bobbin laces, influenced by Flemish laces, also often incorporated a cordonnet.

Bobbinet The first machine-made net, imitating bobbin lace grounds by twisting the wefts (instead of looping, as in the stocking frame) to secure the shape of the mesh. Invented by John Heathcoat in 1808 and modified within a year, the first bobbinet machine was worked by hand or foot. Improvements such as the adaptation to water and steam power (in 1816 and 1824 respectively) and the addition of Jacquard machines (in the late 1830s) allowed the original two-twist hexagonal mesh to be supplemented with many other twists and enabled small motifs to be included. Although generally made in cotton, bobbinet is also made in silk (two-twist silk bobbinet was known as *tulle illusion*) and in rayon and nylon.

In the 19th century plain bobbinets were often attached to edgings of bobbin lace or used as a ground for appliqué and embroidery.

Body colour See GOUACHE.

Bois durci A trade name for a natural plastic used to make decorative mouldings, usually in the form of plaques commemorating famous people. These are frequently stamped with the trade name and a trademark feather. Other uses include inkwells and pen trays, as well as ornamental plaques for furniture and doors. Bois durci (French for 'hard wood') was invented by François Charles Lepage, who patented it in Britain in 1856. Produced between 1855 and the late 1880s, it is a form of wood pulp moulding made from sawdust (from a hardwood such as ebony or rosewood) mixed with egg or blood albumen. The sawdust could be mixed with any vegetable, mineral or metallic powders and the albumen with any other glutinous or gelatinous substance. The powder was soaked in albumen diluted with water, dried and then compressed in a steel mould under steam heat and pressure.

Bois serpent See ZEBRAWOOD.

Bole A red or yellow clay used as a ground for water gilding and sometimes called Armenian bole. Its principal function is to create a cushion for the gold leaf, and because clay crystals are so shaped that they slide over each other, bole can be rubbed smooth with gilders' burnishing tools. A secondary function is to provide a background colour to the gold, with bright yellow clays creating a more glittery finish and dark red clays producing warmer effects. In the 18th and 19th centuries it was quite common to use both colours on the same piece of furniture to emphasize certain details.

Bolster See STONECARVING TOOLS.

Bone A light and strong material taken from the skeletons of the higher animals. It is formed from a mixture of organic and inorganic substances. The organic part is composed mainly of the fibrous protein collagen, and the inorganic portion is composed of hydroxyapatite, a complex of tricalcium phosphate and calcium hydroxide. It is fairly flexible, with good cross-sectional strength. It has always been readily available and is easy to work with simple tools: it can be carved, sawn, filed and scraped, and even tiny shards and other small pieces of bone can be used.

The long bones derived from the limbs are those most often used in manufacture. They have a hollow centre, sur-

A bone decorated with engraved designs, China, Shang period, 13th–12th century BC.

rounded by highly porous material, and the denser bony walls rarely exceed 1.5 cm in thickness in even the largest animals. Because of their size and general structure, the use of even the largest bones is therefore generally confined to the manufacture of small objects, although bones may occasionally be sectioned and jointed to form larger structures.

Bone artefacts tend to be utilitarian in nature but they are often decorated by carving and engraving, and bone is often used as a decorative inlay on wooden objects and furniture. Objects made from bone are among the earliest known man-made artefacts. Broken animal bones are common on Stone Age sites and decorated bone tools have been found at palaeolithic sites such as Courbet, Monastruc and La Madeleine in France and Creswell Crags in England.

Bone china A type of porcelain with particularly good translucency owing to the addition to the body of bone ash, which encourages glass formation. The ash is made from cattle bones, which are calcined to produce calcium phosphate. Bone china bodies are traditionally composed of china clay, feldspar and bone ash (up to 50%). They are prone to warping and are therefore fired on alumina powder for support in the kiln. The body is higher-fired than the glaze and must be biscuit-fired before glazing. The first firing is usually at 1280°C and the second at approximately 1080°C. The body is not very plastic and is thus better suited to slip casting or press moulding than to throwing on the wheel.

Bone ash was first used as a flux in soft paste porcelain bodies at Chelsea and Bow in the mid-18th century. Bone china was probably developed by Josiah Spode in the early 1790s and was produced commercially at Wedgwood from 1799. It is made almost exclusively in England and is often referred to as 'English porcelain'.

Book fittings Metal fittings added to leather bookbindings to protect the binding and hold the book closed. In medieval Europe books were commonly fitted with bosses, clasps and corner pieces made of metals such as copper and brass. Clasps were particularly important for books written on parchment or vellum, because the pages of the closed book might distort if not kept under slight pressure. Fittings were made by gold- and silversmiths and were often ornamented by pressing, chasing and casting processes. Books were stored singly, usually flat, but during the 16th and 17th centuries fittings became less common as books became more numerous and began to be stored upright side by side on shelves.

Book illustration A graphic art form produced to accompany a handwritten or printed text. There are two main types of book illustration: those printed with the text, and those created separately. Before the introduction of PRINTING into Europe, books were illustrated by hand, the arts of decorated calligraphy and illumination reaching their peak in the early 15th century. At the same time woodcuts began to be used for printing on paper and vellum. Metal cuts were introduced briefly in the late 1400s and engraving and etching on metal followed. Wood engraving was developed in Britain chiefly as an illustrative medium in the late 18th century and around the same time lithography was invented in Bavaria. Photographic processes followed in the 19th century and silkscreen printing in the 20th.

Bookbinding The craft of making books, and the name for the cover of a handmade book. Different techniques and styles of bookbinding have evolved to suit various purposes, but they are all intended to hold together the text and/or illustrations of a book in a usable form by a variety of SEWING STYLES and to provide a protective case, which can be highly decorated. The text is usually composed of single leaves or folded sheets of paper or parchment, gathered into groups called sections, gatherings, quires or signatures. The sections are then sewn through the folds with linen thread onto tapes, thongs or cords, which are subsequently attached to a pair of boards which form the book cover. Originally made of wood, the boards are nowadays of cardboard. The boards and the back or spine of the book are then covered with leather, cloth or paper. A book covered in one piece of leather is referred to as 'full-bound'. When the spine and corners of the binding are covered in leather and the rest in paper or cloth, the book is said to be 'half-bound'; when just the spine is leather-covered, it is known as 'quarter-bound'. The tapes, thongs or cords onto which the pages are sewn naturally protrude at the spine of the book, where they may form raised BANDS. Inside the book the text block is protected by endpapers, and these are often made of decorated paper which is pasted down to the inside of the boards. This basic book format is called a codex and came into existence as early as the 1st century AD, when folded and sewn papyrus was used. Because papyrus cracks, however, parchment or vellum was used for this format by the 4th century. Other

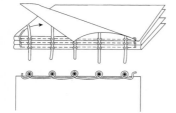

Sewing a book together. Here three sections, or gatherings, of the book have been joined together by sewing to raised cords. The ends of the cords would be attached to a sewing frame during this process to hold them taut.

formats include accordion bindings (concertina-folded) and
oriental styles (see below). Heavy wooden boards and metal
clasps were popular on medieval bindings, because vellum
and parchment tend to distort unless kept under pressure (see
BOOK FITTINGS).

The leather used for bookbindings can be from virtually
any animal, from a rat to a crocodile, but is most frequently
calf-, goat- or pigskin; occasionally sheepskin is also used. Each
has a distinctive grain related to the hair follicle pattern of the
animal. The most durable bookbinding material is alum-tawed
leather, treated with aluminium sulphate instead of vegetable
tannins; vellum and parchment are also used to make flexible,
long-lasting bindings, particularly in the style without boards
or adhesive called LIMP VELLUM BINDING. Certain methods of
tanning and preparation make the leather more prone to deterioration than others: many 19th-century bindings suffered
from 'red rot' caused by pollution of the atmosphere from
sulphur dioxide, while others fall apart because the leather has
been over-thinned ('pared down') to get a neat finish. The
adhesives used to glue the spine and fix leather and paper to
the book boards were generally starch paste and hot gelatine,
but in the second half of the 20th century synthetic polymer
emulsion adhesives began to be used.

*An 18th-century bindery or
bookbinding workshop,
from Diderot's*
Encyclopédie des arts et
des métiers, *showing, from
the left: (a) a worker
apparently consolidating
and rounding the spine of
a book which has been sewn
together but not covered;
(b) a woman using a
sewing frame; (c) another
man trimming the edges of
the sewn leaves in a laying
press, probably using a tool
with a fitted blade called a
plough; (d) completed
volumes placed in a screw
press to prevent warping of
the covering boards.*

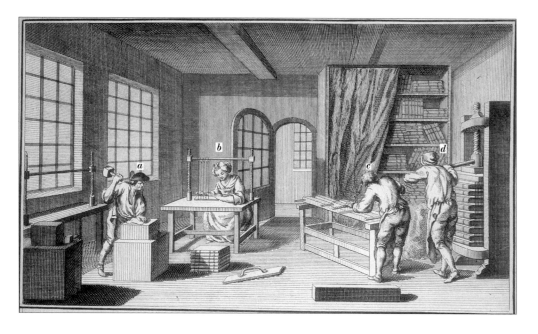

A Western-style book, showing the rounded spine and boards with covering materials extending slightly beyond the text block to form squares: (a) head; (b) text block; (c) fore edge; (d) tail; (e) front cover with leather turned over; (f) square; (g) pastedown. This sheet of unprinted paper, sewn with the text so that one half acts as the pastedown and the other as the endleaf, has yet to be pasted to the inside of the covered board.

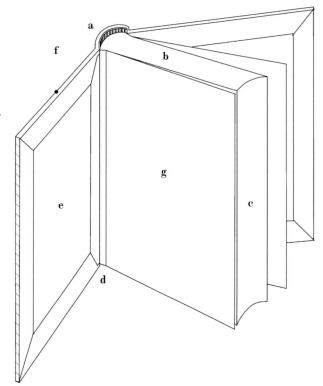

Leather bookbinding by Pierre Legrain, 1920s. Although the book has been bound by hand using traditional materials and techniques, the binder has designed a modern cover incorporating inlays of different types of leather in a mosaic pattern.

The outside of the book is often highly decorated, especially if it is an important leather binding. Decorative techniques include TOOLING, which impresses a pattern into leather (and sometimes cloth or paper) with a variety of small hand tools heated on a stove. The process is also called finishing and can be done to achieve an indented pattern, called blind tooling; alternatively gold leaf, metal foil, inks and other coloured materials can be used to make coloured patterns, including gold tooling. Impressing the binding by machine rather than by hand is called BLOCKING or stamping.

It is thought that at least half of the books produced in Europe between the 12th century and the 16th were bound with coloured leather, but most of the surviving examples are now unrecognizably faded. The leather was stained, probably after binding, with a dye incorporating a mordant: the dyes used included brazilwood or madder for red, indigo or woad for blue and *Rhamnus cathartica* for yellow. Coloured leather and paper, metal bosses, textiles and even precious stones and wrought metals or enamels may also be added to a traditional binding.

Some 19th-century bindings used mother-of-pearl, ivory and velvet for the covers and leather for the spine, which has to flex at the joints. Modern designer bookbindings employ an even wider range of formats and decorative techniques, including inlays and onlays of leather to create a mosaic effect, and local manipulation of wet, adhesive impregnated leather to create three-dimensional decoration. Stains, dyes and marbling or sprinkling to colour the binding are other traditional techniques which have been developed by modern binders.

Chinese- or Japanese-style book.

In contrast to Western practice, books produced in the Far East, which are traditionally printed from woodblocks, usually have paper covers instead of boards. These are stab-stitched at the spine, together with the text or illustrations, to create one unit, instead of being assembled in sections and gathered together by the binding. The stab stitching looks similar to blanket stitch: the thread is passed through holes made through the entire text block close to the spine and is also taken around the spine itself. The coloured silk threads often used are a decorative element in themselves. An additional difference is that the sheets of paper are printed on one side only and folded at the fore edge of the book rather than the spine. It is possible to make this style of book with Chinese and Japanese papers because of their relative flexibility in comparison with European papers. The paper's translucency also makes it desirable to print on one side only, hence the folded leaves. A one-part slip case with the spine side open and covered in paper or cloth is invariably provided and may enclose the several volumes of a single book.

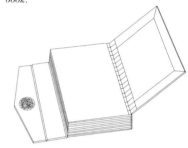

Islamic-style bookbinding.

In the Islamic world books are traditionally leather-bound and are often decorated with gold or blind tooling. At the fore edge there sometimes is an additional flap, which is closed to protect the text block when not in use. The sections are sewn together at the spine with a chain stitch which links the sections to each other rather than to bands, thongs or tape; this allows the book to open flat. Attachment of the boards is with cloth glued to the spine and boards. The boards are less likely to be rigid than in the European styles and the text block is flush with the covering material rather than lying behind projecting board edges. A two-part leather-covered slip case, joined horizontally, is traditionally provided for protection.

Bottle glass An unrefined glass, dark green or brown in colour, used from the early 17th century for making bottles. The colour results from the traces of iron found in the sand used for the batch, though sometimes iron oxide is added to darken the colour.

Bouchard hammer See STONECARVING TOOLS.

Boulle A type of multi-material MARQUETRY used to decorate tables, cabinets and clock cases, developed in the early 17th century and perfected by André Charles Boulle (1642–1732). Thin sheets of two or more materials, such as tortoiseshell, gilt brass, copper and tin, were pasted together and then cut into elaborate arabesque and floral designs (see colour plate III). When separated, the cut-out from one sheet could be laid into the piercing of another so that, for example, brass could be laid into tortoiseshell with accompanying designs in copper and tin. When tortoiseshell is used in thin sheets it becomes semi-transparent and the wooden support and glue are visible. To avoid this, the tortoiseshell was painted or gilded on the reverse: red and yellow were the favoured colours. The colour or gilding was visible from the front and served to enhance the pattern of the tortoiseshell. A sheet of paper was usually applied on top of the paint to avoid disruption during final assembly. Metal on tortoiseshell became known as boulle and tortoiseshell on metal as counter- or contra-boulle.

Bow drill See WOODWORKING TOOLS.

Bower-Barff process A patented process developed in the 19th century by the Englishmen George Bower and Frederick Settle Barff, involving the use of steam and gas to create a protective and attractive black surface on architectural ironwork. The first step in the process is to produce a light layer of surface rust by exposing the iron to steam. The rust is then converted to magnetite by reduction, using gas. The black magnetite is corrosion-resistant.

Boxwood A very hard and tough wood, with an even and close grain. It is derived from the Abbasian, European, Spanish and Turkey box tree (*Buxus sempervirens*) found in central and southern Europe and the Middle East. Boxwood rarely exceeds 12.5 cm in diameter and is used for carving, tool making, superior tool handles, turnery and lines and stringing for inlays. It also is the favoured wood for printing blocks, since it will take very fine lines and detail, especially when worked on the end grain. The name boxwood is often

Netsuke carved from boxwood, Japan, 19th century.

*Aquamanile, southern
Saxony, 13th century. The
aquamanile is cast in brass
by lost wax casting and the
surface decoration
enhanced by chasing.*

applied to other species with similar characteristics, such as
amarillo, blue gum, dogwood and jacaranda.

Braiding See PLAITING.

Branscombe lace See TAPE LACE.

Brass An alloy, essentially of copper and zinc, although some
brasses also contain other metals, such as lead or iron. The
zinc content alters the colour and lowers the melting-point.
With 10% zinc the alloy is a red bronze colour; with 15% it is
a golden colour; and with between 20 and 40% zinc it will be
a range of yellow colours. More than 45% zinc gives the brass
alloy a silver white colour. Until recently most antique
copper alloys were described as bronzes, but modern analyses
have established an increasing number of these so-called
bronzes actually to be forms of brass. The earliest known
brass objects date from 1300 BC and are from Asia Minor.

The main obstacle to making brass in the past was the difficulty in extracting zinc. Zinc occurs in nature only as an ore,
and the volatility of the metal causes a problem because it
boils at 917°C, below the smelting temperature. Instead of
flowing out of the bottom of a furnace in molten form, like
most metals, zinc therefore leaves the furnace as a vapour.
The early brasses were alloyed with zinc droplets which were

sometimes formed as a rare by-product of silver smelting.

Probably during the 1st century BC the cementation process was developed in the West to produce large quantities of brass. This process uses closed crucibles in which zinc ore (calamine) is mixed with finely divided copper and charcoal. When heated, the zinc ore is reduced to metallic zinc vapour, which diffuses into the copper to form brass. The production of brass depended on the cementation process, or on alloying copper with imported zinc metal from the East, until the 18th century, when in 1738 William Champion of Bristol patented a process for distillation of zinc on a large scale.

There are three main types of brass: alpha brass, with less than 36% zinc and with good cold-working properties; beta brass, with 36–45% zinc, and with good hot-working properties; and gamma brass, with over 45% zinc, and with no cold or hot workability. A few well-known brasses are: gilding metal (95%Cu:5%Zn); red brass (85%Cu:15%Zn); yellow brass (65%Cu:35%Zn); Muntz metal (60%Cu:40%Zn); PINCHBECK (88–83%Cu:12–17%Zn); Dutch metal (80%Cu:20%Zn); and tombac (75%Cu:23%Zn:2%Sn).

Brass is a very versatile material and has excellent casting properties. It can therefore be used for free-standing objects such as statues, and parts made from cast brass can also be attached to other objects, by hard soldering, soft soldering or riveting. Brass can also be shaped by spinning and stamping. For decoration, engraving is often used, but the surface can also be embossed and chased to create designs in relief.

Brass rubbing See FROTTAGE.

Brazilwood A mordant dye from trees of the genus *Caesalpina*, used mainly on wool from as early as the 14th century. It produces a reddish brown when mordanted with chrome and a bluish red with aluminium. It was also sometimes used with aluminium acetate as an extract for calico printing and was then called sappenwood. Similar claret-brown dyewoods are camwood and barwood.

Brazing A process for joining metals, using heat and a filler metal with a melting-point above 450°C but below that of the other metals to be joined. Normally the term is used specifically for the process of joining metals with a brass alloy sometimes called SPELTER. See also SOLDERING.

Breccia A term used to describe sedimentary rocks composed of angular fragments of one or more rock types cemented together by other minerals. The sharpness of the fragments indicates that they were not worn or eroded before embedding in the matrix, and breccias were formed following cataclysmic events such as landslides and volcanoes. Breccias generally contain a number of different coloured materials and thus have been used decoratively. Hard and polishable breccias were used extensively in Rome during the Baroque period for decorative panelling, plinths and inlays. The ancient Egyptians made vessels from various breccias.

Brick A building material, used from antiquity, made by pressing a form of clay, called brickearth, into a mould and then hardening it either by sun-drying or firing. The origins of brickmaking are not known, although sun-dried bricks have been found in the remains of neolithic structures at Jericho, and fired bricks were produced in the Indus Valley from the 3rd millennium BC. Historically, brickmaking has often exploited clay from the site of intended construction, involving minimal transport and simple technology. The individual units, of reasonably consistent size and shape, are generally lightweight and small enough to be picked up with one hand, allowing their positioning and setting in mortar to be accomplished by one person. The type of brickearth and additives used, as well as the method of forming the brick and the firing temperature and conditions, influence the colour, texture and durability of the brick produced.

Brickmaking The first stage in brickmaking is to dig the brickearth from river banks or shallow pits. Most brickearths are of recent geological origin and were formed through glacial action or in river estuaries and lakes; some earths, such as loess, were transported and deposited by the wind. A brickearth should ideally contain enough clay to make it mouldable as well as sufficient sand or silt to reduce shrinkage, owing to loss of water, and distortion during drying and firing. Once extracted, the brickearth is prepared for use by prolonged kneading or treading, as was practised in ancient India, to give the material a smooth, even texture. In cold climates brickearths are prepared by leaving them exposed over winter to allow the frost to break down large lumps. If the earth does not have a suitable consistency, additives such as tree sap, fruit juice and animal dung make it more cohesive; chopped straw increases strength and provides inbuilt fuel for firing; additional silt and sand are incorporated to reduce shrinkage if these are not already present in sufficient quantity.

The prepared brickearth is shaped either by rolling it into

A brickmaker about to press a lump of prepared brickearth into a wooden mould, a process designed to eliminate pockets of trapped air which would expand during firing, leading to damage. The looped string at the worker's waist is used to trim excess brickearth from the top of the mould.

a sheet on a flat surface covered with sand and then cutting it into slabs, a method used by the Romans, or, more commonly, by pushing it into a mould. In ancient Egypt this took the form of a wooden frame placed on a reed mat. In Europe from the Middle Ages the clay was rolled into a crescent shape and then lifted over the head and thrown into a wooden mould which had been dusted with sand to facilitate removal; the excess clay was trimmed with a scraper, wire bow or a wooden bat. The throwing process was intended to expel pockets of air which could cause damage during firing. The formed brick could be released from the mould and placed on a small piece of wood, slightly larger than the brick, to be taken away for drying, a technique known as pallet moulding. In the slop moulding method a wetter mix was used so that the brick, once removed from the mould, had to be carefully lifted from the moulding bench onto a sand-covered surface for preliminary drying. As bricks shrink by approximately 8% during drying and a further 6% in firing, they have to be made proportionately larger to produce a finished unit of the desired size.

The drying process removes, through evaporation, much

of the water added to the brickearth to make it workable, in order to reduce the risk of distortion and damage during firing. Drying platforms, or hacks, are made of fired bricks or tiles, stacked approximately 15 cm high, to create a smooth, dry surface. The green, or unfired, bricks are placed in low stacks with space between the rows to allow for circulation of air; they are protected from rain with straw matting. The bricks are turned periodically to ensure even drying. In temperate climates brickmaking is largely confined to the spring and summer months and, depending on weather conditions, drying can take four to eight weeks.

In areas such as Egypt, where fuel is scarce, bricks are placed in the sun to dry and turned regularly to ensure even hardening. Sun-dried bricks, also known as adobe, are durable in areas of low rainfall and have been widely used in parts of Africa, China and Latin America. A similar building material, referred to in England as clay lump, can survive in temperate climates when protected by a projecting roof and an external finish.

Firing, or burning, bricks, produces units that are stronger and more durable than sun-dried material. Kilns were used from the 3rd millennium BC in Sumeria and in the Indus Valley. The simplest form of kiln was a clamp in which fired bricks were used to form a platform, with gaps left as flues. The green bricks were stacked in rows and fuel, such as wood or straw, placed between them. The top was covered with fired bricks and/or clay to reduce heat loss, the fuel lit and allowed to burn over a period of days until exhausted; several more days were required for the bricks to cool. Levels of heat were not even across the clamp, resulting in variations in the colour and hardness of the bricks. Although clamps did not produce consistent bricks, they required only simple technology to construct and use and, as temporary structures, were suited to firing bricks at the site of construction; clamps were in use until the 19th century. Up-draught kilns, used by the Romans, in which the fire was built in a chamber beneath the green bricks, produced more even firing. Down-draught kilns, often circular in plan, in which the heat passed over the bricks and out through a horizontal flue at ground level, achieved greater fuel-efficiency and more control over the firing temperature. A further increase in efficiency was obtained from the continuous kiln, patented in Germany in 1859 by Friedrich Hoffman, which was circular in plan and divided into twelve chambers by a system of baffles, allowing heat to be moved from one chamber to the next so that drying, firing and cooling could be carried out sequentially without moving the bricks or needing to cool the kiln between firings. Rectangular continuous kilns, which were more efficient in the use of space, were developed in the late 19th century and early 20th.

Brickearth containing iron oxides and fired in an oxygen-rich, or oxidizing, atmosphere between 900°C and 1000°C produces red brick; higher temperatures can result in purple, brown or grey brick. Reduced oxygen levels can yield purple or blue bricks. Cream and yellow bricks are produced if the earth contains lime or chalk and is fired in oxidizing conditions.

Industrialized brickmaking, from the 18th century, has involved mechanization of extraction, allowing deeper, harder clay deposits to be used. Pug mills, early versions of which were turned by horses, forced freshly dug clay over a series of knives, to produce a sieved and well-kneaded material, ready for moulding. From the mid-19th century bricks were formed by extruding the prepared earth through a die and then slicing it off with a wire; such bricks often retain striations produced by the wire. A slightly later innovation was press moulding, in which the clay was mechanically compressed into a mould, to produce a dense brick of consistent shape. As the brickearth was forced into the mould, less plasticity, and therefore less water, was required, reducing the drying time. Drying tunnels—heated structures through which the bricks travelled on flat cars on railway lines—were in use by the end of the 19th century and further speeded up the process. Continuous kilns fired to consistent temperatures and produced bricks of even coloration. Mechanized transport allowed greater movement of clays and fired bricks, permitting 19th- and 20th-century architects to create polychrome effects by using bricks from a variety of sources. Virtually all modern brickmaking is mechanized, although some handmade bricks are still produced for restoration purposes.

Bricks for wall construction have generally been rectangular in shape. Standardization of brick sizes was introduced by the Romans, who produced some pyramid-shaped bricks, designed to be set with the apex facing inwards to reduce the amount of material used; they also made large, flat bricks to form levelling courses in rubble walls. Some of the Roman brick sizes were adopted by Islamic architects. In early

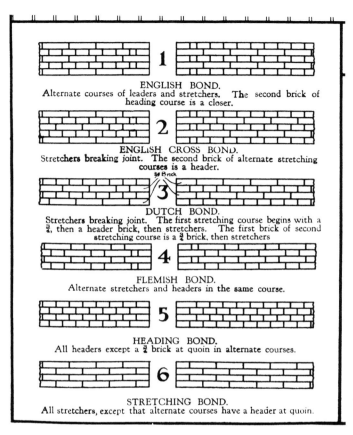

1

ENGLISH BOND.
Alternate courses of leaders and stretchers. The second brick of heading course is a closer.

2

ENGLISH CROSS BOND.
Stretchers breaking joint. The second brick of alternate stretching courses is a header.

3

DUTCH BOND.
Stretchers breaking joint. The first stretching course begins with a ¾, then a header brick, then stretchers. The first brick of second stretching course is a ¾ brick, then stretchers

4

FLEMISH BOND.
Alternate stretchers and headers in the same course.

5

HEADING BOND.
All headers except a ¾ brick at quoin in alternate courses.

6

STRETCHING BOND.
All stretchers, except that alternate courses have a header at quoin.

Bricklaying bonds, from Nathaniel Lloyd's History of English Brickwork *(1925).*

medieval Europe some large flat bricks were produced, probably because the large surface area facilitated drying, but these had the disadvantage of being prone to distortion in firing and unwieldy in use. From the late Middle Ages bricks were made to the generalized proportions of the length equalling twice the width, plus the thickness of a mortar joint, or three times the thickness of the brick, plus two mortar joints. Although the proportions were maintained, the sizes of bricks tended to increase from the Middle Ages to the end of the 19th century, in response to technological changes which aided consistent production. Metric bricks, now used throughout Europe, measure 215 mm × 102.5 mm × 65 mm. The proportions of bricks were used to advantage in brickwork bonds, the overlapping patterns in which bricks were set, with the end (or header) often alternating, either within or between horizontal courses, with the long side (or stretcher). Bonds increased the strength of construction by tying two or more layers of brick together but also had a decorative quality. Such bonds were used in the Islamic world from the 8th century. A wide variety of bonds became prevalent in Europe from the 15th century onwards.

Bricklaying A bricklayer's tools consist of: a pointed metal trowel for applying mortar and tapping bricks in place; a hammer, chisel or saw for cutting bricks; a thin metal pointing tool used to smooth the mortar joints; and plumb rules and lines to establish accurate vertical joints and horizontal course. A hod, a triangular trough open at one end and supported on a pole, is used for carrying bricks to the place where they are to be laid, and a hawk, a small, hand-held wooden platform, carries the mortar. In constructing a brick building a bricklayer first lays several courses at the corners and then, using a line, lays courses between them, applying mortar to the end of the previous brick laid in the course and to the top of the bricks beneath; the next brick is then slid into place.

In Seljuk architecture decoration and calligraphic inscriptions were produced by setting bricks in recessed and raised patterns; this same principle was used to produce raised decoration in Europe from the 17th century. In the Islamic world bricks are also cut into shapes using large chisels, smoothed with hard stones and then set in geometric patterns with gypsum plaster to form decorative panels. In Europe special shapes for window frames, arches or chimneys can be moulded or cut with an axe and then smoothed. From the 16th century soft bricks were produced which could be sawn and then rubbed to a precise shape using a hard brick, called a rubber, allowing tight mortar joints and complex decorative forms to be made. This technique is called carved brickwork. Patterning can also be introduced by using bricks of various colours or GLAZED BRICK.

Bright-cut decoration See ENGRAVING.

Bristol blue A deep blue glass, tending to purple in the thicker sections, that was produced in Bristol and throughout Britain in the 18th century. The colourant was a natural ore of cobalt oxide.

Britannia metal A pewter alloy containing antimony and worked using industrial techniques. A typical alloy consists of 91% tin, 7% antimony and 2% copper. The name derives from the Britannia Metal Works in Sheffield, which pioneered

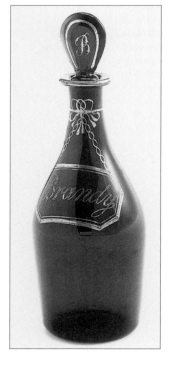

Decanter and stopper in 'Bristol blue' glass with gilding, England, 18th century.

the use of the metal in the late 18th century. The inclusion of copper and antimony rather than lead, which was used in the old cast pewter, produced a hard, strong alloy that could be fashioned using new cold-working techniques such as rolling, spinning or stamping. This made it possible to produce pewter wares much more cheaply. Previously, these had been made by casting all the different parts in expensive bronze or stone moulds and soldering them together.

Britannia silver A silver alloy mandatory in England between 1697 and 1720 and optional after that date. It was introduced after the English Civil War to prevent the melting down of sterling coinage to make silver objects. The composition is 958 parts of silver in 1000. Britannia silver is hallmarked with the figure of Britannia.

British plate Unplated NICKEL SILVER wares made in Britain in the second quarter of the 19th century. They were made from European nickel silver (German silver) and differ from PAKTONG wares made from Chinese nickel silver with a slightly different composition.

Broad glass See FLAT GLASS.

Brocade A cloth with additional decorative threads added by hand-held bobbins. The technique resembles a form of embroidery and is used around the world, although outside Europe the resulting cloths are more generally referred to as having supplementary warp or weft decoration. Correctly, the description of 'brocade' should be paired with the description of its ground cloth, as in 'brocaded damask', 'brocaded satin' or, if a more complex cloth, 'brocaded lampas' (for illustration see page 269).

Brocatelle A cloth with raised areas resulting from the use of too many warp threads to lie together in one plane; the warps are often divided into two sets, one of which remains at the back of the fabric and is often linen. Its construction is related to damask but usually has a satin or twill pattern on a plain or satin ground.

Broderie anglaise See EMBROIDERED LACE.

Broken stripe A type of figured wood-grain, in which ribbon-like markings taper and fade, owing to a twisted grain, and appear broken.

Bronze An alloy of copper and tin, typically containing between 5 and 15% tin, but with up to 24% tin when used for bells and 30% tin when used for highly reflective surfaces such as mirrors. The addition of tin makes bronze much harder and stronger than copper. Bronze is usually cast but some alloys can be wrought. When untarnished, the colour of bronze varies from pale gold to pink. When bronze corrodes, an attractive patina can develop, ranging in colour from dark brown to green.

The first so-called 'bronzes' contained only small amounts of tin (usually not more than 3%) and it is likely that these low-tin bronzes were produced by smelting tin-bearing copper ores. The earliest evidence of these low-tin bronzes comes from Asia Minor around 3000 BC. There are two ancient ways of producing true bronze (with more than 5% tin). The first is by mixing tin ore (cassirite or stannite) with metallic copper and heating this mixture under a layer of charcoal until the tin ore is reduced to metallic tin and absorbed by the copper. The second is to melt metallic tin together with copper to a homogeneous alloy. The first of these true bronzes—weapons and tools from Asia Minor, dating from the 2nd millennium BC—were probably produced using the first of these methods.

As a new metal, bronze had some great advantages over copper: it was more than 70% stronger than copper and much harder. (This hardness could be doubled by WORK HARDENING, hammering the bronze when cold.) Another great

Bronze food vessel (fang ding) cast from piece moulds, China, Shang period, 12th–11th century BC.

Bronze casting in Burma, with clay moulds drying in the sun, c. 1995. The moulds are then turned upside down and filled with molten bronze. After the bronze has solidified, the moulds are smashed to reveal the cast.

advantage was the ease with which bronze could be cast. Although copper was sometimes cast, this proved to be a difficult process, and it was with bronze that casting really took off as a technique for producing and reproducing objects. The first moulds for casting bronze were simple open moulds of sand, baked clay or carved stone. These produced a rough casting that needed much further working, such as hammering. The next step was to use a two-part mould of baked clay or stone, which fitted together to form a closed mould. Later a core of baked clay or stone was placed in the two-part mould to produce hollow castings. This core was held in place, without touching the sides of the mould, by bronze pins. This two-part mould casting was used extensively for casting bronze axe heads. An improvement on the technique was piece moulding, which used a more complicated mould made up of several pieces and assembled like a series of bricks, with the mould pieces locked together by means of mortices and tenons. Piece moulding was used extensively by the Chinese to cast their large bronze ritual vessels.

Another technique used for hollow or complicated bronzes is LOST WAX CASTING. Here a rough model is first made in clay and then covered with a layer of wax, in which the details are modelled. The channels for running the metal are added and the model and runners covered with the mould material, such as clay. When the mould is heated the wax runs out and the resulting cavity can be filled with molten metal. Lost wax casting was brought to perfection by the Greeks and Romans in making their bronze statues.

After casting, bronzes are usually finished by filing,

sanding and chasing (to give detail), followed by polishing. The final stage is usually patination, using chemicals or heat and often a combination of the two. Another way of finishing is FIREGILDING; sometimes a combination of patinated and gilded surfaces can be found on a single object.

In the past the term bronze was used for almost all copper alloys and it is only in recent times, by analysing objects systematically, that a considerable amount of these 'bronzes' have been shown to be of brass or gunmetal (copper alloy with equal amounts of tin and zinc). A good example of this is ORMOLU, often called firegilded bronze but more accurately referred to as firegilded brass. Other early 'bronze' objects often prove to be coppers with antimony or arsenic. Some well-known bronzes are bell metal (76–80%Cu:24–20%Zn), speculum metal (66%Cu:33%Sb:1%Zn) and jewellery bronze (87.5%Cu:12.5%Zn).

Brown oak The rich brown heartwood of the English oak, prized for cabinet work and furniture. The brown colouring may be caused by a fungal infection or, in certain trees, by exceptionally high acid levels, but it does not affect the quality of the wood.

Browning The application of a brown colour to steel, with the aid of chemicals. Browning is carried out primarily to make the shiny steel surface of a weapon less reflective, but it has also been thought to make the metal less susceptible to corrosion. In reality, however, it gives no real protection of this sort.

Brush An instrument used primarily for drawing and painting, made of a bundle of fibres bound together to hold a volume of wet paint or ink. The most primitive brushes are more or less round in section. Until about the late 18th century artists and craft practitioners made their own brushes, but since then brush manufacture has been mostly an independent craft.

Animal hairs are the main fibres used, along with plant fibres and, occasionally, feathers. The ancient Egyptians relied on reeds macerated at the end to make the tuft of fibres. Traditional Chinese and Japanese brushes are made of deer, fox, sheep and horse hair, pig bristle and also palm fibre. The finest European brushes are made today from tail hairs of squirrel, sable and mink: the best are *kolinsky* sable from Russia. Coarser, bristle brushes are made from hogs' hair. The hairs are graded and grouped by hand to shape the brush and it is important that the naturally tapering ends of the hairs should form the tip to ensure a good point. The other end is cut. Once formed into the shape of the brush head, the fibres are bound into a bundle with thread, glued at the cut end and inserted into a ferrule—once the quill of a feather or a strip of leather, now more usually made of metal—which is fitted over a wooden stick forming the handle. In the East this is often made of bamboo.

Brushes used in Japanese SCROLL mounting (*hyogu*) have a rather different structure. Instead of forming a point, the fibres are arranged in a linear fashion and sandwiched into a ferrule or handle made of cypress wood. Traditionally the fibres were bound with cherry bark, secured with bamboo pegs, and stitched into the handle with silk cord.

Brussels A looped-pile carpet, limited to five or six warp colours and with those not in use interwoven in the foundation. Brussels carpets were hand-woven from the 17th century to the mid-19th, in WILTON (from 1720), in KIDDER-MINSTER (from 1749), and in Yorkshire and Scotland (from the early 19th century). Shortly afterwards they began to be made in the United States, where power was first applied to Brussels looms by Horatio Bigelow in 1849, and his patent was acquired by John Crossley & Sons of Halifax, Yorkshire. The name derives from the source of the horizontal loom, often also given as Tournai, which reached Wilton by way of the Savonnerie. See also CARPET-WEAVING.

Buff leather Originally a thick, spongy leather manufactured by an oil tanning process from cattle hides which had had the grain removed. This leather was used widely throughout Europe from the 16th century to the 18th for working gloves and protective jerkins, such as the buff coats worn by both sides during the English Civil War.

The term was used in later periods for full-thickness cattle hide leathers tawed with alum for belts, straps and other military accoutrements.

Bullion work Embroidery, mainly LAID AND COUCHED WORK, with metal threads.

Burato See EMBROIDERED LACE.

Burin An engraver's tool, better known as a GRAVER. The name derives from the Old English *borian*, 'to bore'.

Burl An alternative name for a BURR. The term is also applied to the grain pattern formed around knots and crotches.

Earthenware water jug with burnished slip and incised decoration, West Africa, Hausa, probably early 20th century.

Burnishing The process of polishing a surface by friction and compression, with the use of a burnisher, without removing any material from the surface. The working part of the burnisher is made of a hard, smooth material such as agate, haematite or hardened steel, with a handle attached. It is necessary to work very cleanly and to use some lubrication to avoid scratches.

Burnishing is used to create a high polish on metals, gilding and other materials. In the manufacture of ceramics burnishing takes place before firing, usually on a turntable or wheel. The process smoothes and flattens the suface of the vessel, rendering it semi-impervious to liquid, and is therefore often used on coiled pots and other handbuilt ceramics. Burnishing is also used to polish unglazed ceramics, especially low-fired earthenwares, to brighten up lustre and to fix decoration, whether painted, gilded or slip.

Burr An excrescence formed on most species of tree around the site of an injury or irritation, and consisting of a dense, deformed, gnarled and interwoven mass of woody tissue. On some species, particularly walnut, oak, beech and elm, burrs are large and decorative and valued for veneers.

Cabinetmaking The manufacture of mobile furniture. The term was first used in the late 17th century to distinguish the craftsmen who worked with veneer and marquetry from the joiners who were otherwise responsible for the manufacture of furniture. Cabinetmakers employ many of the techniques of the joiner, though perhaps on a finer scale, but the ornamental use of veneer is usually confined to cabinetmaking. Two distinct sub-groups are the chairmakers and piano makers. See also WOOD.

Cabochon See GEMSTONES.

Cadmium red A brilliant, opaque scarlet pigment. It has been commercially available since *c.*1910 and is very similar to vermilion, which it has now all but replaced. It is stable, light-fast and unaffected by atmospheric gases.

Cadmium yellow A strong, opaque yellow pigment (cadmium sulphide) which comes in a range of hues from fiery orange to pale lemon. In a polluted atmosphere, if it is in an aqueous medium, it can blacken. It is therefore most suitable in oil, although even in this medium it has been known to discolour. The pigment was first introduced for artists' paint in the 1840s but was initially very expensive and it was not much used before the latter part of the 19th century.

Caen stone A pale-coloured, fine-grained limestone quarried near Caen in Normandy, France. It was used extensively in that region from Merovingian times (*c.* AD 500–700) and was also exported in large quantities to south-east England after the Norman Conquest. The trade arose because it was easier to transport stone across the Channel than to bring it from the west of England, and also because it was a familiar material to the French masons who came to England in the wake of the conquest. It was used for major buildings such as Canterbury Cathedral and Westminster Abbey.

Cage cup A glass beaker, with an ovoid base, whose decoration takes the form of a free-standing lattice (see colour plate VIIa). The decoration is almost completely undercut, and is attached to the underlying body only by fine struts. Experiments have shown that this remarkable effect was created by careful grinding into a heavy glass blank. The cage cup (Latin, *vasa diatretum*) appears to have been made in several locations in the Roman empire in the 4th century AD.

Calamander See COROMANDEL.

Calcite alabaster See ONYX MARBLE.

Calico A name given in Great Britain to a plain, bleached

C

cotton cloth heavier than muslin. The word originally denoted a fast-dyed, patterned cotton from India, and it derived from the town of Calicut, a major centre for the export of such cloths. In North America the term still signifies a patterned cloth, generally a small brightly coloured all-over design printed on cotton woven from carded yarns. From the late 18th century to the mid-20th, commercial printing of textiles was often referred to as calico printing, even when the cloths were not all cotton.

Calligraphy Ornamental handwriting. Until the introduction of printing, all books had to be individually written by hand. The surviving European examples are mostly Christian texts such as psalters, gospels and books of hours produced by scribes in religious communities. The cost and significance of these books meant that the calligraphy was usually ornamented (see ILLUMINATION) and this tradition of decorated writing was continued outside monasteries with the production of ceremonial documents, for example those bearing coats of arms, until the present day. In the Arabic world, Asia and the Far East, handwritten texts of spiritual significance are characterized by special styles of calligraphy, and the act of writing is traditionally executed and appreciated as having a religious value in itself (see colour plate XII).

In Europe fine writing has been done since medieval times using pens made of reed, metal or quill, whereas oriental calligraphy is executed with a brush. The tools dictate the shape and style of the letters: sharp-edged when executed with a pen, soft and blurred when done with a brush. The black ink used in Chinese and Japanese calligraphy is made from pine soot and is known in Japan as *sumi*. The red ink seen as stamped seals (*chop*) on oriental scrolls is made of vermilion, which was also used in European manuscripts. In the West iron-gall ink has traditionally been used, but calligraphers are unlikely to choose it today as the ink soon fades and its acidity corrodes the paper. Instead they can use the permanent indian ink, which is made of carbon black and a resin binder, or coloured inks made of water-soluble dyes. Paper (sometimes burnished) and vellum or parchment are the usual supports for calligraphy, but textiles such as silk are not uncommon in Asia.

Camel hair A pure wool fibre or yarn derived from the Bactrian camel of Asia, an ancient cross-breed of the dromedary, with a coat of great heat-resistance, and the original Bactrian camel, with a coat of great cold-resistance. The two features combine in the coat of the Bactrian cross-breed. There are three grades of fineness: the best comes from the soft, lustrous noils in the undercoat, and is used in its natural tan colour for most clothing fabrics; the second grade, longer and coarser, is often combined with it; while the very coarse long hair is used for utilitarian cloths and yarns, such as carpet yarns. Beard hair is used for paint brushes and rugs.

Cameo A form of small-scale, shallow relief decoration, executed in stone, shell, glass or ceramic, in which the subject is frequently shown against a background of contrasting colour. The technique is especially suited to jewellery. It was developed in the Hellenistic period and was used by the Greeks and Romans to produce gemstone portraits and other images in profile which were set into rings and brooches. Roman cameos were highly prized during the Renaissance and were often reset in jewellery of the period (see colour plate I).

Onyx and sardonyx, with alternating bands of light and dark, were ideally suited to the technique but other stones such as chalcedony and sapphire were also used. Carving was carried out with hard stone points, drills and wheels fed with abrasive and water. By exploiting the differences in colour of the banding and by varying the depth of carving the artist could indicate the modelling of forms. By the 16th century the stone to be carved was mounted on a stick and then presented to a rotating iron point, charged with abrasive.

The desire to imitate the banded stones used for cameos may have been an impetus for developments in glass manufacture in antiquity (see CAMEO GLASS). The Romans developed a process for making laminated glass of blue and white layers; this was carved to produce gems as well as vessels, which could not have been made from stone because of the virtual impossibility of finding suitable material with regular, concentric banding. Cast glass cameos were made in the 18th century, using moulds taken from ancient and modern cameos. Cameos have also been carved since the 19th century from the helmet shell (*Cassis madagascarensis*), which has a banded pale brown and white structure, and the giant conch (*Strombus gigas*), which has layers of pale pink and white.

Cameo encrustation A method of embedding a ceramic or metal cameo medallion in clear glass. The cameo, which is usually small, white and opaque, is heated and then covered in hot glass. The vessel is often finished with cut decoration. The process, which is also known as crystallo-ceramie or sulphide, was first used in Bohemia in the mid-18th century and then in France. It was improved by Apsley Pellat in Britain and patented in 1819.

Cameo glass A form of CASED GLASS in which the outer layer, usually white, is cut away from the underlying coloured layer to create a contrasting relief design. It can also be executed on layered combinations of opaque glass, or on clear glass with coloured or opaque glass overlays. The outer layer of glass is cut back by hand- or wheel-cutting (see GLASS ENGRAVING), or by acid etching, and is often translucent against the dark ground. The technique was adapted from cameo carving on natural stones or shells and was developed by the Romans; it is seen to perfection in the Portland Vase (early 1st century AD; British Museum, London). Although widely used in China, it was forgotten in the West until the mid-19th century, when it was rediscovered by English glassmakers.

Cameo glass carving at the Stevens & Williams factory, Stourbridge, 1880s. White overlaid glass is being cut away to varying degrees with sharp styluses, to reveal the coloured glass beneath. Two styluses can be seen lying on the bench in the centre of the picture.

Campeachy See LOGWOOD.

Camwood See BRAZILWOOD.

Cane The outer skin of the RATTAN palm. It is used for basketry and, woven into a mesh, for chair seats and backs.

Cannel coal A black material used from antiquity as an imitation of jet, probably because it occurs more widely. Composed of fossilized plant material, such as pollen and algae, and fine mud, cannel coal does not take as high a polish as jet.

Canton enamel See ENAMEL.

Canvas See PLAIN WEAVE.

Canvaswork A form of embroidery based on counting the threads of the canvas ground cloth, and resulting in the entire cloth being covered with stitches; these include the self-explanatory brick, fern, plaited and fishbone stitches, as well as BARGELLO, GROS POINT and PETIT POINT. A widely known and long-established technique, it appears not to have been used for upholstery until shortly after c.1600, after which it became increasingly favoured for this purpose. BERLIN WOOL-WORK is canvaswork, distinguished by the source of the pattern rather than the stitching techniques.

Carat A unit of measurement of the purity or fineness of gold. Pure or fine gold is 24 carat or 1000 fine, and the amount of pure gold in a gold alloy is cited as parts of 24. For example, 18 carat is 18/24 parts or 75% of gold in the alloy or 750 fine. In North America the term carat is used only for the weight of gemstones (1 carat = 0.2 g); the term karat is used there for the fineness of gold.

Card weaving See TABLET WEAVING.

Carding See SPINNING.

Carpentry The construction of main framing for structures such as houses and barns. Carpenters tend to use timber straight from the saw with little or no secondary finishing such as planing.

Carpet-weaving The production by hand or machine of cut-pile, loop-pile or flat textile surfaces, all on a strong, relatively inelastic ground warp. The development of hand-woven pile and loop carpets is associated with southern Persia from as early as 4000 BC. Middle Eastern carpets are woven on both upright and horizontal looms, with the pile tied in as the creation of the foundation, or backing, of warp and weft progresses. Two main types of knot are used: the asymmetrical knot (also known as the Sehna or Persian knot) and the symmetrical knot (also known as the Ghiordes or Turkish knot).

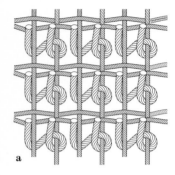

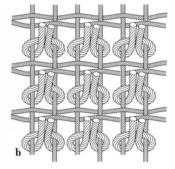

*(a) Asymmetrical carpet knot, which may be angled either to left or right.
(b) Symmetrical carpet knot, with two tufts between every two warps.*

Both are worked around two adjacent threads, the asymmetrical knot producing a tuft between each warp and the symmetrical version producing two tufts between every two warps. Angled to either left or right, the asymmetrical knot produces a closer texture and is worked as a running thread, looped around the finger and cut for a pile or uncut for a loop. The symmetrical knot, which gives a true knotted pile, is almost always found in Turkish, Caucasian and many Persian carpets; it was also used in British hand-knotted carpets. Spanish pile carpets, known from the 8th century, were knotted over a single warp. From the early 17th century the French SAVONNERIE loom (an upright pile carpet loom) used an asymmetrical-type construction but with a bladed rod in place of the fingers; when removed, the blade cut the loops open.

The mechanization of carpet-weaving made further progress in the 18th century. Between 1720 and 1755 the English carpet-making industry emerged in WILTON, AXMINSTER and Kidderminster. Wilton gave its name to the treadle-operated horizontal loom with a bladed rod akin to the Savonnerie, but with a maximum of five colours, each buried in the foundation when not used as a pile weft. This loom was itself a development of the so-called BRUSSELS (or Tournai) loom, which left the loops uncut and had two wefts, as opposed to Wilton's three, in each foundation row. By the 1820s both looms were automated with Jacquard attachments and by the mid-19th century they were power-driven; they produced 27 in. (68.5 cm) body carpet and 18 in. (45 cm) or 22½ in. (57 cm) borders. Axminster gave its name to a group of machines, the first of which was patented by Halcyon Skinner of New York in 1876. Adapted from the French moquette loom (which produced carpet by the yard), it allowed an unlimited number of colours by inserting pile yarns, cut from pre-positioned spools as the foundation weaving progressed, thus eliminating the excess yarns characteristic of the foundations of Wilton and Brussels; it was in use in Britain by 1878. Other methods of making multi-coloured piled carpets were weaving with CHENILLE or with pre-printed warp-pile yarns. These techniques were developed in Glasgow in 1830 and Edinburgh in 1831 respectively and were widely used by the 1840s by hand carpet-weavers; later mechanized, the manufacture of both types declined in the 1930s. Halifax became the British centre for printed-yarn carpets, known as 'tapestry' carpets and the least expensive form of pile carpet. The spool and the chenille techniques came to be called spool Axminster and chenille Axminster because they could imitate the richness of pattern and texture associated with the hand-knotted carpets originally made in that town. A single-colour, loom-woven, warp-pile carpet was, as in weaving generally, termed a velvet.

Flat-woven carpets include those made by hand in the true tapestry technique, such as Aubussons and kelims; those of the Middle East, which use a SOUMAK flat weave; and Scotch, Kidderminster, or ingrain carpets, which by virtue of their warp-faced DOUBLECLOTH construction are reversible. The latter, made on horizontal looms, are like most flat-woven carpets, characterized by simple geometric patterns, especially multicoloured stripes; they were body carpets, that is, produced in 27–36 in. (68.5–91.5 cm) widths to be used singly as runners or seamed together for larger areas. Alternatives were provided by rag and braided rugs, particularly in North America (where factory-made ingrains were locally made from the 1790s); the hand-woven varieties were partly supplanted by machine versions, which became available from the mid-19th century.

Carrara marble A fine-grained white marble, which may contain grey streaking, obtained from the Apuan Alps near Carrara in Tuscany, Italy. It was first quarried in the 1st century BC, when large quantities were used in Rome as a building stone. Although famous as a statuary marble, it has continued to be used as a building stone (for example, at Pisa Cathedral) and for decorative carving, vases, panelling and flooring, often contrasted with coloured stones.

Carrara porcelain See PARIAN WARE.

Carré setting See STONE SETTING.

Cartoon A full-size drawing made in order to transfer a design to a painting, textile, stained-glass panel or plastered surface. It may be coloured or simply have the outlines indicated in strong, clear lines. The design is transferred to the support by tracing, in which the back of the cartoon is chalked over and the lines inscribed from the front; by pouncing, where the lines are first pricked and then dabbed with a charcoal filled bag, which results in dotted lines on the support; or by squaring, in which grids are employed to replicate the image (for illustration see pages 379 and 485).

Cased glass Glass made of two or more differently coloured layers. It is sometimes called overlay glass. The outer layer, which is quite thick, is blown into a mould and subsequent layers are then blown inside it. When the piece is reheated, the layers fuse. Alternatively, in the dip-overlay method, an elongated gather of glass is dipped in molten glass of a different colour and then blown. It seems that only the latter technique, which is akin to that used for flashed glass, was used in antiquity: fusion onto the inner side was a 19th-century development, especially popular in Bohemia.

Casein A protein in the form of a pale solid, obtained from milk. It is made by adding hydrochloric acid to hot skimmed milk, by curdling milk with rennet or by controlled souring. The addition of lime to the milk curd makes a powerful adhesive which is miscible in water but waterproof when dry: on exposure to atmospheric carbon dioxide the lime forms calcium carbonate and the casein returns to its original form as an insoluble binder.

Casein has been used in cabinetmaking and joinery since ancient times, and also as a water-based paint medium, particularly for walls and decorative work. The paint film is brittle but very hard-wearing. It was popular in the late 19th century for stencilling on walls as it dries quickly and has the required matt finish. Furthermore, since it is instantly soluble and does not form a thick layer, elaborate schemes could be built up with four or five overlaid stencil shapes. Casein paints are now sold in powder form or ready-prepared.

When immersed in aqueous formaldehyde, casein hardens to form a semi-synthetic plastic resembling horn or bone. Developed by W. Krische and Adolph Spitteler, this material was patented in 1899 and marketed in Germany as Galalith. In Britain it was called Styrolit (1909) and later Erinoid (1914). Initially it was made from milk curds, but after 1914 skimmed milk became the main base material. Erinoid Ltd produced it using resin in the so-called 'dry' process: the casein was ground to a powder, mixed with water and then, when absorbed, fed into an extruder. The extruded rods were then sliced into button blanks, pen barrels and other items or used for moulding sheet. The sheets (produced in presses) were stamped into the desired form. The casein was then put in the aqueous formaldehyde. Afterwards, unable to be reworked, it could be slightly shaped by hot pressing. Casein could be coloured during its manufacture or surface-dyed, usually after polishing. Fish scales were added to produce a

Art Nouveau mantel clock designed by Josef Olbrich, Austria, 1902. It is made of stained sycamore inlaid with metal, abalone and casein veneer, and the hands are of copper.

pearlized effect.

Casein was employed as a veneer on gramophones, clock cases, fountain pen cases and desk accessories. It was also used to make a variety of buttons in many colours and finishes but, since it distorts in the damp, most buttons are now made of machine-washable plastics such as polyesters and acrylics.

Cashmere A fibre or yarn derived from the hair of the inner coat of the cashmere goat (*Capra hircus*), native to Kashmir and parts of northern India, Tibet, Mongolia, Turkestan, China, Iran and Iraq. Sometimes known as pashmina (an Indian word for cashmere), it is a fine, downy wool and possibly the softest of all fibres. It has dyeing properties similar to wool but does not felt, a feature that makes it especially important to knitters. The fibre is used for only the finest Kashmir and European 'cashmere' shawls (many are partly or entirely wool); in addition, several types of cloth derive their name from the use of cashmere, on its own or combined with other fibres.

Casting The process of forming an object by pouring a liquid or molten material into a mould and allowing it to solidify. An artefact made by this process is known as a 'cast'. Its design may be fashioned directly in the mould, but it is more usual to create a model in a plastic material such as wax, plaster of Paris or clay, and from this to construct a mould.

There are several different forms of casting, the most simple of which is open mould casting, using an uncovered mould of stone, clay, or metal into which the material is poured directly. This method is not suitable for an object to be seen in the round, for which a waste or piece mould is necessary. In waste mould casting the mould is destroyed, or 'wasted', in the process of removing it from the cast; the process is therefore not used for the casting of multiples, for which piece moulding is required. Here a complex mould is taken from a model and assembled like a series of bricks, with each mould piece maled to its neighbour by means of mortices and tenons. The casting material is then poured into the assembled mould to form a hollow or solid positive. Once it has set, the mould is dismantled in sections, freeing the cast. Raised seams, formed by small gaps between the mould pieces, are then removed from the cast. Objects can be cast solid, or around a core.

To make a piece mould the surface of the model must first

be coated with a barrier material such as shellac, oil or soap to facilitate removal of the mould. Its surface is then divided into sections along the lines of undercuts or projecting areas, using thin walls of clay or metal strips. Plaster of Paris is applied to each section in turn and allowed to set. The plaster pieces, numbered and coated with shellac, can be held together by notches cut in adjoining surfaces, with a metal band or with a plaster casing or support mould which holds all the pieces in correct alignment. Piece moulding can also be carried out with flexible materials such as latex and silicone rubbers, which can be easily pulled away from undercut sections and then reused. Another well-known and ancient method, which is used with both waste and piece moulds, is LOST WAX CASTING, in which hot, molten glass or metal displaces a wax model within the mould.

Modern forms of casting metal all use some form of pressure. This forces the metal into the mould to create more detail and a better finish. In die-casting the metal is cast into a metal die or mould. There are two methods: gravity mould casting (known in the USA as permanent mould casting), in which the molten metal enters the die under its own weight; and pressure mould casting, in which the metal is kept under pressure until solidification. The most popular metals used for die-casting are zinc alloys (for toys) but also aluminium and copper alloys. In centrifugal casting the mould is held in a rotating, centrifugal machine which creates extra pressure on the molten metal. This pressure is maintained until solidification to give even detail and better surface finish to a casting. Centrifugal casting is mainly used for small items such as jewellery, usually in combination with lost wax casting.

In slush casting the molten metal is poured out of the mould before total solidification, leaving a thin walled casting. The technique is based on the fact that the cold mould causes the hot metal with which it is in contact to solidify. The procedure is often repeated to build up a casting of sufficient thickness. A similar process, known as SLIP CASTING, is used for the manufacture of ceramics.

See also PRESS MOULDING (for ceramics and glass) and SAND CASTING.

Cast iron An iron–carbon alloy containing more than 1.9% carbon. The first use of cast iron was probably in China around 600 BC, but the technology for casting iron did not

Cast iron tiara, Germany, c.1825. The tiara was cast in sand, finished and patinated.

reach Western Europe until the late Middle Ages. Traditionally, most iron is cast in sand, using simple two-part moulds and sometimes a core (see SAND CASTING). It can be finished by filing, scraping or machining.

Cast iron can be divided into two different categories: grey and white. In grey cast iron, so called because of the grey colour of the fracture surface, most of the carbon exists as graphite, with some silicon. This alloy has very good casting properties and can be machined well. White cast iron has a light-coloured fracture surface; the carbon is mostly in the form of cementite and pearlite, which render it hard and brittle. It is possible to heat-treat white cast iron to convert the carbon to create a malleable cast iron.

Cast iron is used for a very wide range of products, from fine jewellery to firebacks and engineering works such as bridges.

Casting on The process of attaching one or more of the constituent parts of a metal object by casting directly against it. The casting-on technique was sometimes used to cast bronze hilts onto blades but also for the fabrication and repair of large bronze figures. It was usually done by making a wax addition to an existing object; this was then covered by a clay mould and the wax melted out, leaving a cavity into which the molten metal was poured.

Caulking See UPSETTING.

Ceba See KAPOK.

Cedar A common name given to a wide variety of woods, from many different species and including both hardwoods and softwoods, which share particular characteristics. They are usually soft, light, straight-grained, aromatic, easily worked, very durable and resistant to both fungal and insect attack. Species include *Cedrus libani* (cedar of Lebanon or true cedar), *Juniperus procera* (East African pencil cedar), *Shorea macroptera* (Borneo cedar, often sold as meranti), *Thuya plicata* (western red cedar) and *Cupressus lawsoniana* and various *Chamaecyparis*. All are used for many different purposes, including cabinetmaking, box making, fencing and house building.

Ceiba See KAPOK.

Celadon A high-fired green glaze pigmented with iron oxide on stoneware or porcelain, or a ceramic decorated with such a glaze. The use of iron oxide for colouring (rather than copper, which can also produce a green glaze) is an essential feature of celadon wares (sometimes referred to as greenware). Since the glaze is high-firing, they are fired once, rather than being biscuit-fired. Celadon on stoneware is usually an ash glaze with less than 1% iron oxide. The colour varies from green to blue and from olive green to grey green, depending on the firing atmosphere and the presence of any impurities. Titanium, for example, will lend a yellow tone to the glaze. In order to produce green or blue glazes, the ceramics must normally be fired in reduction.

Celadon wares and glazes can be decorated with painting either under or in the glaze. For underglaze painting, copper or iron pigments are painted directly onto the body under a transparent glaze. Such pigments can be painted into more opaque celadon glazes, such as those from the Longquan kilns in China.

Celadons were first produced in China and are still made all over East Asia. The earliest examples are from Zhejiang province and date from the 2nd millennium BC. Subsequently both Korea and Japan began production. From the 14th century AD Chinese potters began to produce celadon glazes on porcelain, using standard porcelain glazes tinted with iron. In the East Asian tradition celadons were fired in wood-

Stoneware temple vase,
with carved decoration
under a celadon glaze,
Longquan, China, 1327.

fuelled dragon kilns, which were considered essential for their successful manufacture since the rapid firings possible in such kilns encourage the formation of crystals in the glazes, a characteristic feature of East Asian celadons. Also, the use of wood fuel is conducive to reduction firings. Some celadons were made in Europe before the 20th century, but since *c.*1920 they have mainly been produced by studio potters working in an East Asian idiom.

Cellonite See SYNTHETIC IVORY.

Cellophane A general term for man-made cellulose film, sheet or strips produced by the viscose process (see RAYON). The film is transparent, lustrous and dyes easily. Slit-film can be

twisted or used flat as a yarn; in the latter form it was sometimes known as viscut. Cellophane was most widely used
from the mid-1930s to the mid-1940s, when other fibres were
first rising sharply in price, and later restricted to war use.

Celluloid A semi-synthetic, highly flammable plastic (cellulose nitrate) available in a range of colours and patterns. It is
very susceptible to heat and light degradation.

A mouldable plastic material made of cellulose nitrate and
invented by Alexander Parkes was exhibited with the name
of Parkesine at the International Exhibition of 1862, held in
London. Later called Xylonite or Ivoride in Britain, by 1870
the material had been renamed Celluloid by the American
John Wesley Hyatt. Although commonly regarded as the
inventor of the material, Hyatt is more correctly identified as
the person who patented the use of camphor as an excellent
solvent and plasticizer for cellulose nitrate (celluloid smells of
camphor when rubbed against cloth). In collaboration with
Charles Burroughs, Hyatt also developed a range of
machinery for the successful production of celluloid, making
it a commercial success.

Celluloid was widely used from the 1870s onwards in the
production of such objects as dressing table sets, jewellery
and lampshades, as well as accessories such as collars, cuffs,
handbags, spectacle frames and even dolls. Elaborate celluloid combs were made by famous designers such as Auguste
Bonaz. In this context the possibilities of creating finishes
imitating ivory, tortoiseshell and mother-of-pearl were
invaluable. Pearlized finishes were made by adding materials
such as lead phosphate to celluloid. The material's popularity
fell rapidly in the 1920s with the fashion for short, bobbed
hair resulting in a much smaller market for hair combs. The
early film industry was dependent on celluloid until it was
replaced by CELLULOSE ACETATE safety film in the 1940s. Now
largely fallen into disuse, celluloid is still used for laminates
on drum kits, table-tennis balls and as parts of mortars
(exploiting its flammable properties). It can also be inlaid
with precious metals and has the advantage that waste can
be reprocessed and reused.

Cellulose nitrate was the first cellulose derivative to be
used in protective coatings. It was used as a constituent of
lacquer to coat cars, aeroplanes and furniture as well as decorative items, textiles and paper. Early First World War aircraft were coated with cellulose nitrate dope to stiffen their

fabric wings. This proved too flammable and the cellulose nitrate dope was replaced by cellulose acetate. Another use of liquid cellulose nitrate was in glues and paints.

Cellulose acetate A semi-synthetic plastic available in a range of colours and patterns. The first cellulose acetate was prepared in 1865 by the French chemist Paul Schützenberger, heating cotton with acetic anhydride in closed tubes at 130–140°C. Techniques were gradually refined for controlling acetylation under less severe conditions. By 1910 the Swiss manufacturers the brothers Henri and Camille Dreyfus had made cellulose acetate photographic film and by 1921 they had made Celanese, a cellulose acetate fibre.

Cellulose acetate was first produced on an industrial scale in the form of dope (cellulose diacetate) dissolved in acetone. This was used to coat the fabric wings of aeroplanes during the First World War, when it replaced the dangerously flammable cellulose nitrate lacquers. Dope is produced by acetylating cellulose to triacetate, which is then treated to produce diacetate. In 1918 a glut of cellulose acetate led to the

Celluloid (cellulose nitrate) objects, late 19th century and early 20th century, including a stiff collar and a handbag and cigarette box in the Art Deco style.

production of cellulose acetate rod, sheet and household products such as lampshades. Owing to its non-flammability, cellulose acetate was used as a glass substitute (in preference to cellulose nitrate) in car window interlayers and goggles. Edouard Fornells, working in the Parisian workshops of René Lalique, used it for decorative boxes. Cellulose acetate jewellery and toys were also made. Produced in a mouldable powder form by 1929, cellulose acetate was then injection-moulded and was the only notable plastic to be injection-moulded until after the Second World War. Designer spectacle frames are still made from the material.

When cellulose acetate is used as a lacquer, it is usually combined with acetic acid. It is also used in paints and varnishes.

Cement A fine grey powder obtained by heating limestone and clay, which sets hard by chemical reaction and is used as a mortar and a render. The Romans discovered that certain materials, such as volcanic earths, when mixed with lime could produce a hydraulic set, without the presence of air (see LIME). Experimentation with similar materials in the 18th century led James Parker in 1796 to patent a hydraulic product, Roman cement, made by firing Septarian nodules, naturally occurring lumps of clay-rich limestone. It is pinkish brown in colour and quick-setting and was widely used by Nash and other British architects as a render. It was also used in North America, for example, at the Beth Elohim synagogue in Charleston, South Carolina, built in 1839, where it was used to produce fluted Doric columns over brick cores.

Further developments in hydraulic technology occurred in the 19th century with the patenting in 1824 by Joseph Aspdin of Portland cement, so called because it was supposed to resemble Portland limestone. It was made by firing limestone to produce lime, which was then crushed and mixed with clay. This was fired at between 1000°C and 1200°C. Although this material was hydraulic, it was not as strong as modern cements because it was manufactured at lower temperatures. In the late 1830s Isaac Johnson took over Aspdin's mill and discovered that overburnt lumps from the kilns produced a stronger, more reliable product with a slower set. His process, patented in 1838, involved heating limestone or chalk to 1300–1500°C, which converted it to quicklime. This then reacted with the clay to form clinker (so called because it is partially vitrified and produces a clinking sound when dropped), which was ground and mixed with gypsum to retard the set. For use it was mixed with water.

The set occurs through the formation of calcium silicates and calcium aluminates in the kiln. These react with water to form starburst-shaped particles which interlock to give cement its strength. Modern ordinary Portland cement is a hard, grey, impervious material which is mixed with sand for use as a mortar and a render (in contemporary building terminology render is defined as cement and sand). Rendered surfaces could be roughcast or dashed by throwing aggregate onto the wet cement with a trowel or made to resemble masonry construction by incised lines. Early 19th-century rendered façades were colour-washed with distemper; oil paint for external walls was introduced around 1840.

Cement, mixed in the proportions of one part cement to two parts of an aggregate such as sand, crushed stone, slag or brick to form concrete, has been used to produce cast ornament and garden sculpture; when mixed with stone dust it is often termed ARTIFICIAL STONE because of its resemblance to stone. The mix is rammed into wooden moulds, treated with oil as a separator, to increase the compressive strength of the material. Tensile strength is enhanced by using iron armatures for large projecting forms. In order to reduce the weight of large pieces of statuary these are modelled with concrete over a hollow core, formed by shaping wire mesh to follow the contours of the figure, attaching it to the armature and then coating the mesh with lime plaster; the concrete is then applied with a trowel to a depth of 5–10 cm.

Centrifugal casting See CASTING.

Ceramics Objects made from fired clay or related silicate materials. A ceramic object is formed or shaped from a body material of wet CLAY, with certain additives, which is allowed to dry and then subjected to heat in a kiln or 'fired'. The heat gradually breaks down the mineral structure of the clay and transforms it into a hard, often glassy substance. Decoration may take place before or after firing.

Body materials The clay from which a ceramic is made is described as the body material. The main types of body material used for ceramics are earthenware, stoneware, porcelain and fritware. Earthenware bodies are low-fired (to $c.1000°C$) with a porosity of more than 5% and come in a wide range of colours and textures. Among the most common are a red earthenware that is often called terracotta, and a cream-coloured body that is used in many ceramic traditions to produce fine domestic wares. (The term 'pottery' is often used to describe earthenware and sometimes ceramics in general.) As this body is porous, it is usually glazed or covered with a SLIP and burnished to seal the surface. The most common clays used for earthenware bodies are red clays, marls or a combination of BALL CLAY, CHINA CLAY and flint or FELDSPAR.

Stoneware bodies are hard, high-fired (to $c.1200°C$ or more) and vitrified. They are not as porous as earthenwares and, when glazed, have an integrated body-glaze layer. Stoneware bodies are usually pale and range in colour from grey to white, although in some ceramic traditions red stonewares are produced. The clays are usually ball clays or, for industrial stonewares, fire clays. These clays are plastic and workable, with a long vitrification period that ensures the bodies produced are dense but not brittle. In East Asia stoneware bodies, particularly celadon wares, are also made from CHINA STONE. As china stone is a primary constituent of hard porcelain bodies, these stonewares are often referred to as 'porcellanous'.

Porcelain bodies are very high-fired (to $c.1400°C$), translucent and fully vitrified. They are often very glassy. When glazed, a very thick body-glaze layer is produced. Porcelain is always white and is usually made from china clay and china stone, which produce a semi-plastic body, although in East Asia some porcelains are made from china stone only. In Western ceramics there are two types of porcelain bodies: hard paste porcelain and soft paste porcelain. The former is traditional porcelain and the latter is a lower-fired version (generally 1050–1100°C) made in imitation of true porcelain from white-firing clays and glass frit, bone ash or other materials.

Another body made in imitation of porcelain is fritware. This is relatively low-fired (to $c.1050°C$), white, usually porous and sugary in texture. The chief component is not clay but quartz, in the form of crushed pebbles and fritted glass. Small amounts of white clay are added to improve workability and strength.

Most ceramic-producing cultures tend to specialize in a particular type of ware, often as a result of the availability there of a particular raw material. China, for example, is known for its porcelain and, as a result, in the West porcelain

Covered bowl, turned and painted porcelain, by Roseline Delisle, 1997.

is often called china. The Netherlands is famous for Delft-ware, Africa for earthenware, Japan for stoneware and Islamic countries for fritware. Certain types of ceramics have been exceptionally influential and have been replicated in many different cultures. Among the most prominent examples are blue and white porcelain and celadon, which originated in China, and lustreware, which was first made in Iraq.

Shaping Ceramic forms are made from wet clay, using a variety of different shaping methods. The choice of method is determined by the clay body to be used, the available techno-logy and the preferences of potters themselves or their patrons. The clay is prepared by wedging or kneading to make it workable and to remove air bubbles, which can cause problems in the firing. From a wedged ball of clay almost any form can then be created. The simplest and earliest shaping method used in ceramics is handbuilding, encompassing pinching, coiling and slab building. Pinched pots are formed by pressing the thumbs around the inside of a ball of clay and gradually raising and thinning the walls until the desired vessel form is created. Coiling employs ropes of clay which are raised up continuously from a coiled or circular clay base. The coils are often painted with clay slip to aid adhesion. When the desired shape is formed, the layered coils are smoothed over to create a continuous surface. Both pinching

A ceramics workshop, with teapots and ewers in various stages of production. The potter is joining a handle to the body of a ewer. Similar handles, known as strap handles, can be seen on trays in the foreground.

and coiling can be aided by using a type of turntable or fabric circle as a base from which the vessel is built up while being rotated. In both these methods of shaping, the finished vessel form is often smoothed and thinned by beating and paddling, evidence of which may be seen on the surface. Pinching and coiling are methods used today in ethnographic ceramic traditions such as those in Africa and South America, as well as by studio potters. Vessel forms can also be made from slabs of clay joined to create a box shape. The edges of the slabs are scored, painted with clay slip and then joined. The joined

edges are then smoothed over. Slabs can also be rolled to form
a cylinder.

Handbuilding techniques are most suitable for simple
forms. Where more complex forms are desired, moulding is
often used. The two main types of moulds used in ceramics
are press moulds and casting moulds. In press moulding the
clay is pressed into or over a mould and then removed. Press
moulds can be used several times to produce identical pieces.
Casting moulds are used to produce hollow vessels with walls
of even thickness. This method is known as hollow casting or
SLIP CASTING. In industrial manufacture, moulds are used to

Blanc de Chine *figure of
Guan di, China, 1610. The
figure was press-moulded
and modelled by hand,
with the head made
separately and luted in.*

produce large quantities of identical vessels. The most common method—used, for example, to produce multiple plate and bowl forms—employs spinning moulds, which form either the outside of a vessel (jolleying) or the inside (jiggering). Clay is placed into or over the mould, onto which a profile is pressed.

The spinning section of an industrial plate mould works on the same principle as a POTTER'S WHEEL, the most sophisticated and versatile means of shaping ceramics. The wheel is a large round disc powered either electronically or by hand or foot so that it is continuously spinning in a clockwise direction. A lump of clay is then centred on the wheel and the hands are used to shape a form outwards and upwards from the lump of clay. The vessel can be made very thin or thick, and tell-tale throwing rings are often left on the finished piece. By using the centrifugal force of the wheel, hollow ceramic forms can be produced quickly and evenly, and a skilled potter can create a number of nearly identical vessels in one sitting. In cases where vessels have to be made in separate parts (for reasons of size or complexity of design), these will be moulded and joined together before firing, a process known as luting.

Decoration, glazing and firing After a ceramic is formed, it is often decorated. Clay is an extremely versatile medium and can be decorated in a number of different ways. In general, ceramics are decorated either before or after firing, although in some instances the process of decoration is carried out in two stages. The simplest way of decorating a ceramic before firing is by impressing or incising decoration into the clay body. Impressed decoration is created by using a solid form, which is then pressed into the clay. This may be a rope, textile, coin, or specially prepared stamp made of fired clay, which can leave repeated patterns of flowers or leaves, for example. A patterned roulette wheel is also used, especially for creating bands of continuous decoration. The most common method of decorating clay before firing is that of incising or carving. Incised decoration is produced by using a sharp tool to cut a design into the surface of the vessel. This is best done when the clay is slightly dry, as this will leave a sharper line. If the line is very deeply impressed, it is usually described as carved decoration. Incised or carved decoration can be further enhanced with coloured slip inlays. This is known as inlaid decoration and is usually produced by apply-

Mug with stamped decoration, Greater Syria, Umayyad period, 8th century AD.

ing slip to an incised or carved vessel and then wiping away the slip on the surface, leaving lines filled in with slip.

The impression of incised and carved decoration can be produced by moulding. An incised mould produces relief decoration if clay is placed over it, or intaglio decoration if the mould is carved in relief. The moulds used for decoration are similar in shape to the finished vessel and are slightly porous so that the clay is absorbed and a sharp impression is left. The most suitable decoration moulds are made from the same body material as the vessel to be decorated, but slightly underfired so as to remain porous. Moulds can also be used to produce a type of marbled decoration (see MARBLED WARE). APPLIED DECORATION can be created using moulds (such as sprig moulds) or can be hand-modelled to give a more sculptural effect.

The most common method of ceramic decoration is painting. Painted ceramics are produced in almost all ceramic-producing cultures (the earliest examples pre-date glazing by thousands of years), and by industrial producers as well as studio potters. The decoration can be carried out before, during or after glazing. Coloured slips or mineral pigments (see METALLIC OXIDES) are normally used under a glaze or without any glaze at all. However, painted decoration can also be applied to a glaze before it is fired; in this case it is incorporated within the glaze layer and is known as in-glaze decoration. Lastly, ceramics can be painted after firing either on top of a fired glaze, in the case of overglaze ENAMEL COLOURS, or on an unglazed but fired surface with coloured slip paints that are not durable. This kind of painted decoration is often found on burial ceramics. GILDING in the form of gold leaf or gold enamel can also be applied after firing, the enamel method being more permanent.

Without glazing, a smooth surface for decorating can be produced by burnishing the surface of the vessel with a rounded tool before firing. Burnishing has a practical function as well, in that it helps flatten and seal the surface of the vessel, making it less permeable to liquids. Burnishing is most suitable for softer ceramics such as earthenwares or lower-fired stonewares.

Porcelain lantern by Adelaide Robineau, USA, 1908. It has been carved, pierced and decorated with coloured glazes.

Glazing is the most effective way of sealing a ceramic vessel and is also a permanent means of decorating a ceramic (see GLAZE). Glazes can be colourless or brightly coloured, opaque or transparent, and may be high-fired or low-fired. High-fired glazes are used on stonewares and porcelains and low-fired glazes usually on earthenwares. Glazes are applied after a vessel has been formed and before it is fired, using a variety of techniques, including dipping, brushing and spraying. They are normally classified according to their fluxes, which have a strong influence on the resulting colour and texture. Some glazes are classified by the pigment (see METALLIC OXIDE) used for coloration. Occasionally, the texture or chemical nature of the glaze is described in the name, as with temmoku or crystalline glaze.

Firing is the final stage in the creation of a ceramic, unless it is to be further decorated with gilding or enamel, and it is through heat that clay is converted to ceramic. Glazes are easily affected by firing temperature and atmosphere, which need to be carefully controlled (see FIRING). The firing process is usually carried out in a KILN.

Certosina See INTARSIA.

Cerulean blue A greenish synthetic pigment produced from cobaltous stannate. Introduced commercially in 1860, it produces a weak colour when mixed with oil. The particles are heavy and thus unsuitable for watercolour washes unless a grainy effect is required. Because the pigment is based on cobalt it is only used for the more expensive ranges of paint.

Chairmaking The specialized craft of making chairs. Chairs were relatively rare items of furniture until the late 17th century and in England they were generally made by either carpenters or joiners. In rural districts the village carpenter, joiner or even the wheelwright continued, on occasions, to make complete chairs to order. Later, however, it was more

*Armchair in the style of
William Kent, c. 1740.
This is a framed mortise
and tenon construction;
reinforcing pegs are clearly
visible at the joints of the
arms. Originally the chair
was gessoed and gilded.*

common for the labour to be divided among the various specialist trades. The chairmaker would make the seat and backstand, but would buy in finished parts from other specialists,
then assemble and finish the complete chair. Jobbing turners
provided turned elements, and carvers decorated such parts
as the cresting rails and cabriole legs. This system continued
into the first half of the 20th century, especially in areas such
as High Wycombe in Buckinghamshire, the centre of manufacture of the well-known WINDSOR CHAIR. Vernacular chairs,
in which the majority of the elements are turned, were made
by turners, while framed chairs were made by the joiners and
later by cabinetmakers or upholsterers.

    From the mid-19th century and throughout the 20th
various methods were developed to simplify and mass-
produce chairs. Many of these systems involved the use of
BENTWOOD elements. Some of the most popular were the
designs of the Thonet family (see THONET FURNITURE), which
were based on the use of turned elements reshaped by steam
bending. Others, created by designers of the Modern Movement, involved the moulding of sheets of plywood to make
graceful organic shapes.

Chalcedony A fine-grained form of quartz with a fibrous, banded structure which ranges from translucent to opaque. It occurs in a variety of colours, such as brown and red, resulting from iron oxide contamination, and green, which contains hydrated nickel silicate. As chalcedony is porous, it may be dyed to produce further colours, a technique known to the Romans. AGATE and BLOODSTONE (or heliotrope) are forms of chalcedony. The Romans made cameos and intaglios from chalcedony (see CAMEO). It is commonly cut as a cabochon; in the 19th century this form was enlivened with facets cut around the edges of a thin cabochon.

Chalcedony glass A glass made by the Venetians, as an imitation of semi-precious stones, by briefly combining opaque glass in the pot.

Chalk A fine-grained limestone which occurs worldwide, composed of almost pure calcium carbonate formed through the deposition of minute marine organisms. Chalk is white to pale grey and generally soft. It has been used for architectural decoration, where its softness permits the production of fine detail, and as a building stone. Chalk has also been used from antiquity for carvings, as a source for lime, as a pigment and graphic medium, and in grounds for painting (see GESSO). As a pigment, chalk is transparent in oil or acrylic and therefore cannot be used as a white in these media, but it is opaque if it is bound in a lean, aqueous medium such as gum or glue. The same applies to *gofun*, the white made from crushed shells (and therefore also based on calcium carbonate) which is still extensively used in Japanese artwork.

Chamois A leather made from the flesh split of a sheepskin, using fish oils. The term derives from the Arabic *sha'hm* and not, as is widely supposed, from the name of the European mountain antelope. The skin is impregnated with the oil and then carefully heated. The oil oxidizes *in situ*, producing complex organic chemicals which cross-link the collagen fibres.

Champlevé See ENAMEL.

Channel setting See STONE SETTING.

Chantilly lace A bobbin lace named after the French town that was its main centre of production from the 17th century until about 1785 and again from 1804. The best-known of the black silk laces, it was originally made of linen until about 1740, when dull grenadine silk was introduced into its manufacture, producing a fine, soft lace. It was worked in naturalistic designs set in spacious grounds and edged with an untwisted, flat cordonnet. White silk was also used during the 19th century, and similar, less fine laces were made elsewhere in France as well as in Barcelona and Buckinghamshire.

Chardonnet silk See RAYON.

Chasing A decorative technique involving the use of various shaped punches and a chasing hammer to model the surface of a metal object. It can take a number of different forms. In flat chasing the metal surface is only incised to give lines. This can look very similar to engraving but involves no cutting away of metal. Flat chasing was the favourite decorating technique on fused or Sheffield plate, because the blunt punches did not damage the silver plating. Cast chasing is used to add detail to the surface of a casting.

Usually, however, chasing is performed on a metal surface that has already been worked from the back (see REPOUSSÉ WORK). Chasing, with finer punches and a small chasing hammer, is used to add the final details. When working with

A silversmith decorating a dish by punching the surface with differently shaped chasing punches and a chasing hammer. The dish is filled with pitch to make a firm support for the work.

sheet metal it is usual to support the object on a resilient surface, commonly a bed of pitch. Another word sometimes used for chased work is *ciselure*.

Chemical lace A type of lace produced through a form of DISCHARGE PRINTING, in which a printed corrosive paste removes unwanted areas of cloth. The process evolved in the late 19th century in tandem with DEVORÉ and relies on the use of mixed-fibre cloths, in which only some of the fibres are removed. Many variants have been developed but they typically call for caustic alkalis to remove protein fibres and acids to remove cellulosics. They are often produced on a Schiffli machine.

Cheney See MOREEN.

Chenille A yarn with a protruding pile on all sides. The term derives from the French word for caterpillar; by the 18th century the term 'snail' was also used. It is made by weaving firmly packed wefts of any fibre (but typically silk, wool, cotton or rayon) on cotton or linen warps bunched in sets of four each. Once woven, the cloth is slit between the bunches, and the resulting group of four-warp threads is twisted to form the yarn. Chenille has been used in machine-made carpets, embroidery, brocading, needle lace (on silk grounds), shawls, and double-faced fabrics called chenille velvet. The yarns are not used as warps and may, owing to their construction, be multi-coloured.

Chenille Axminster A carpet woven with chenille yarn. See CARPET-WEAVING.

Cherry A moderately hard, heavy and strong wood, with low durability. It has a fine and even texture, but its curled grain can be difficult to work and, as it is available only in small sizes, its use is restricted to turnery and cabinet work. The most commonly used species are *Prunus avium*, *P. cerasus* and *P. padus*. *Prunus serotina* (the North American black cherry, also known as cabinet and rum) is pale red to dark reddish brown, with an attractive wavy grain pattern; it is unusual in that it is easily worked.

Chert See FLINT AND CHERT.

Chestnut A moderately heavy, hard and strong, durable wood from the *Castanea vulgaris*, *C. sativa* or *C. vesca*, known in Britain as the sweet or Spanish chestnut. It is easily worked and seasoned and is similar to oak in appearance, but lacks the silver grain. It is used for construction, joinery, furniture, casks, coffins and plywood. The American chestnut

(*C. dentata*) and the Indian chestnut (*C. indica*) are used for cheap furniture, while the Japanese chestnut is highly prized for its elegant watermark figure, caused by a fungus.

The European horse chestnut (*Aesculus hippocastanum*) has a yellowish timber and a close, even grain, with a fine ripple. The wood is soft and light and used little in Britain, except for turnery and dry cooperage.

China blue A method of printing textiles with indigo developed in England by the 1740s, involving printing a paste of finely ground indigo and a thickening agent; the colour develops during alternate immersions of the cloth in lime and ferrous sulphate baths, which respectively dissolve and reduce the colourant. China blue was used frequently in English and French COPPERPLATE PRINTING and was the technique behind a distinct group of so-called 'American blue prints' of the mid-18th century. It remained in use until the end of the 19th century, when it was replaced by improved direct-printing recipes. The most widely used of these is a hydrosulphate process, in which all the chemical reagents are in the print paste and the cloth is steamed after printing, allowing indigo to be printed with other modern vat dyes.

China clay A white firing clay used to produce porcelain bodies. It is also known as kaolin, a name derived from the Chinese clay mine site of Gaoling, and it appears to have been first used in Chinese ceramics of the Shang period (*c.*1700–1150 BC).

China clay is found in both primary and secondary deposits (see CLAY) in China, Europe and America, often in association with coal beds. (In America it is called unaker.) It is composed mainly of the clay mineral kaolinite, which has a layered, plate-like structure that, when mixed with water, forms a semi-plastic clay body. Unlike most clays, china clay is exceptionally stable and pure and is therefore useful for producing both white bodies and vitreous glazes.

China clay is the essential ingredient in hard paste porcelain. Owing to its high alumina content, it is able to withstand temperatures of up to 1700°C and is therefore used in industrial ceramics as well as for the production of fine porcelain vessels. When fired, it is very glassy and hard and usually translucent.

China stone A rock used in the production of porcelain and stoneware. It is also sometimes called Cornish stone or petuntse (*baidunzi*). It is formed from the decomposition of

FELDSPAR and is composed of quartz, mica, feldspar and often kaolinite. Its particle size is small and it can therefore be used to produce a plastic clay body, usually porcelain but also sometimes stoneware.

China stone was first used for porcelain in China in the 10th century AD. Until the 14th century it was used on its own, but then kaolin was added to create an improved body material. At the same time celadons were produced in China with grey stoneware bodies made from china stone.

China stone is high in silica and relatively low in alumina. Used on its own, it will fire to approximately 1280°C. When it is combined with CHINA CLAY (kaolin), the firing temperature can be raised. For use in a porcelain body, the stone is first quarried then crushed, mixed with water and levigated. It is classified as an acid rock but contains sufficient alkalis to be suitable for fluxing. It can also be added to a glaze.

Chiné See IKAT.

Chinese boxwood A wood often used as a substitute for true BOXWOOD.

Chinese white See ZINC WHITE.

Chintz A term used since the 18th century for a glazed cotton cloth of plain weave with a hard-spun fine warp and coarser slack twist weft, whether printed or dyed in the piece. The name derives from *chint*, an Indian term for any printed cotton, itself probably derived from the Hindustani word for 'spotted'. Indian chintzes became known in Europe during the 17th century through their importation by the Dutch, British and French; their popularity, owing largely to their vivid colours, fast to washing, shaped the development of Western printed textiles. In the 18th century the highest-quality European chintzes had patterns derived from woven silks; the bleached white ground and glazing emphasized the similarity between the materials. The glaze takes three basic forms: friction-calendered starch or wax, which washes out; chemical glazes, which withstand washing; and resin schrienering, a modern treatment in which a relatively permanent finish is created by fine scoring of the surface of the cloth, before being pressed flat. From *c*.1840 the term came to be associated with the large floral patterns often printed on the cloth, and in weaving the name was also associated with the use of extra colouring threads in the weft (also called tissuing wefts; see LAMPAS). Between *c*.1850 and *c*.1950 an unglazed printed cotton with a chintz-like pattern was commonly referred to as a CRETONNE.

Chip carving A carving technique used on wood, in which geometric patterns are composed from combinations of triangular and diamond-shaped recesses carved into the surface. One of the oldest of carving techniques, it can be executed with a simple pocket knife, but a blade that cuts at its tip is also useful, as are ordinary chisels. Sets of specially designed chip-carving knives are now available.

Chrome green A strong, yellowish green, synthetic pigment made by mixing PRUSSIAN BLUE and chrome yellow. It has excellent covering power and is very stable: it is resistant to light, atmospheric pollution and very high temperatures. It can be employed in all media, but because of its opacity it is obviously not useful for washes or glazes.

Oak chest decorated with chip carving, England, 1648.

Chrome tannage The preparation of leathers with chromium compounds. The first mention of the process comes from the middle of the 19th century, but it was not until the beginning of the 20th century that it became at all widespread. Two methods have been used: the two-bath process involves impregnating the skin with acid bichromate solutions and then reducing these *in situ* to form the trivalent tanning compounds; the one-bath process employs compounds such as basic chromic sulphate. The process is designed first to achieve penetration of less active compounds and then to adjust the conditions to form strongly active complexes within the skin structure. Today the great majority of all leathers are produced using one-bath chrome tannage.

Chrome yellow A brilliant yellow pigment (lead chromate) which comes in all hues from orange to greenish yellow. The orange end of the series is very similar to cadmium orange, but the pale yellows are more translucent and have less tinting strengths. Like cadmium yellow, there is a slight tendency for it to be blackened by atmospheric gases, especially if it is not in an oil medium. Yellow chromates are used as primers for iron. The pigment first became available in 1814 and was instantly adopted by painters and decorators, as it was much stronger and brighter than any yellow previously on the market. It had an important use in commercially produced mixtures with Prussian blue, creating a range of strong greens that were very popular for exterior joinery and ironwork during the Victorian period. Later it was used as a mineral dye.

Chromium A white, very hard and brittle metal, capable of taking a brilliant polish and highly resistant to corrosion. It was discovered in 1798 but only used commercially from 1925, mainly for electroplating, for furniture and in many alloys. Chromium plating is done for decorative purposes as well as to increase wear-resistance. The thickness of a decorative plating can be as little as 0.0003 mm. The addition of chromium to an alloy can increase its hardness and strength and its resistance to heat and corrosion. The addition of more than 12% chromium to steel will give almost total corrosion-resistance (see IRON).

Chromolithography See PRINTING.

Chrysography Writing in gold ink. The ink is made by mixing powdered gold with water and a suitable binder, such as gum arabic or animal glue.

Cinnabar A mineral ore from which mercury and vermilion are derived.

Cire perdue See LOST WAX CASTING.

Ciselure See CHASING.

Claw See STONECARVING TOOLS.

Clay A soft, sedimentary rock composed of alumino-silicate minerals of crystalline structure and used to produce ceramics. It is an abundant raw material found in most regions of the earth and is formed from the breakdown or weathering of the igneous rocks granite and basalt. Most ceramic clays are formed from granite, which is composed of quartz, mica and feldspar, all silicates or minerals based on silica. Weathering releases these minerals, which can then combine to form clay minerals, which are distinguished by their small particle size and layered structure. The most common clay minerals are kaolinite, montmorillonite and gibbsite. Kaolinite, the main component of kaolin or CHINA CLAY, is formed directly from the decomposition of feldspar.

As clays form, they are either deposited close to the parent rock (granite) or transported elsewhere. Those deposited close to the parent rock are called primary clays and those transported are called secondary (or sedimentary) clays. The particle size of secondary clays is much finer than that of primary clays, and produces a more plastic ceramic body material. This plasticity is a function of the layered structure of the clay mineral. Under magnification, clay crystals appear to be stacked, with stacks of crystals joined at right angles to other stacks. The preparation of clay for ceramic formation through wedging or kneading moves these stacks around so that, when water is added as a lubricant, they slide over one another. Unprepared clay is therefore essentially a mass of dry crystals, which becomes a clay body when water is added. Plasticity increases as particle size decreases, because the smaller the clay particles the more water can move between them and the more easily the particles can slide across one another.

The plasticity of a clay can be improved in preparation. After it has been excavated or recovered from an alluvial site, clay usually needs to be washed and allowed to settle, so that any large inclusions or organic material can be removed as sediment. This process is known as levigation and is usually carried out using a sieve or mesh, through which clay mixed with water is passed repeatedly. For large-scale preparation stepped troughs can also be used to remove unwanted material. In this method larger, heavier particles sink to the bottom and a slurry of fine-particled clay rises to the surface and can be skimmed off. As the clay becomes cleaner and purer, and the particle size is reduced, its plasticity is improved. Plasticity is important for ceramic production, since the clay must be able to stretch and be formed into a shape and then hold that shape during firing. Very plastic clays, however, are not necessarily the most workable, as they tend to be floppy. Non-plastic clays are usually described as 'short' clays and can be friable. During firing all the water is removed from the clay and the clay mineral breaks down. Once this occurs, the clay has been converted to ceramic.

Many different types of clay are used to produce ceramics. The most common are BALL CLAY, CHINA CLAY, FIRE CLAY, red marls, white industrial clays and bentonite. These can be further classified as refractory or fusible clays. Refractory clays such as fire clay or china clay are high-fired clays, and fusible clays such as marls are low-fired. EARTHENWARE is made from fusible clays, and HARD PASTE PORCELAIN and STONEWARE are made from refractory clays.

Cloisonné See ENAMEL.

Cloqué See GAUFFERING.

Close plating An early form of silver plating whereby thin silver foil was soldered to a steel or iron surface. The work-piece was first polished and thoroughly cleaned and then dipped into molten tin to cover it with a thin film of tin. The next step was to cover the piece with silver foil and press the foil hard against the surface, before swiftly rubbing it with a hot soldering iron to solder the foil thoroughly to the base metal. Close plating was used in the 18th and 19th centuries for everyday objects such as knife blades, spurs and buckles.

Cloth binding A book covered in a woven textile. English embroidered bindings on canvas or velvet exist from as early as the 13th century but they eventually went out of fashion in the 18th century. Silk and metal threads were used to create an embossed design covering the boards. The first use of cotton cloth by an English publisher to replace paper or leather as a mass-produced book covering is thought to date to about 1820. Book cloth with a textured grain was subsequently manufactured by embossing calico with heated rollers.

Coade stone A ceramic material used to produce a wide variety of moulded architectural ornament for incorporation into the structure of buildings, for garden and interior furniture, and for statuary and coats of arms. It was devised by Eleanor Coade to resemble a fine-grained, cream-coloured limestone and was manufactured at her factory in south London from 1769 until 1843. The formula, which was lost following closure of the factory and has only been deduced

from recent analysis and experimentation, contained ball clay, powdered grog (previously fired ceramic), sand, crushed flint and soda-lime-silica glass. This material was rolled out into sheets, which were then pressed into plaster moulds. After initial drying the Coade stone was removed from the moulds and details and undercuts were carved into the surface. The pieces were then fired at temperatures between 1100°C and 1150°C over a four-day period, producing a hard, partially vitrified and durable material. Minimal shrinkage and distortion in the kiln, owing to the presence of the pre-fired grog, contributed to the material's commercial success.

Cobalt blue A bright, very pure blue pigment, stable in light, atmospheric gases and heat. It was discovered in 1802. It is one of the more opaque blues and therefore has good covering power. Like cerulean blue, it belongs among the expensive pigments and is generally used only for artists' quality paints and in ceramic glazes.

Cochineal A mordant dye from the dried bodies of the females of the *Coccus cacti* insect, in which carminic acid is the colouring matter. It was introduced to Europe early in the 16th century from the Americas, where its dyeing properties were already well known. On its own it produces purple,

A view of Eleanor Coade's manufactory, by Charles Tomkins, 1798. It shows typical examples of her products, including a coat of arms, sculpture and architectural decoration, such as the urns on the gate posts. (For further illustration see p.15.)

and with alum, iron and copper mordants it gives medium reds. Dissolving in a solution of tin produces the brilliant scarlet for which this dye became known in the 17th century, when it was sometimes known as 'Kuffelar's colour', after the Leiden wool dyer who first used the mordant. Thereafter it gradually replaced kermes and for economic reasons was sometimes combined with lac. It was little used on wool, silk and cotton by the early 20th century, except by craft dyers. The traditional colourant in hunting scarlet (hunting pink), it was also widely used on leathers, in cosmetics and in food. Similar dyes from the insects *Dactyloplus coccus* and *Porphyrophora polinica* were known in Europe and central Asia from the 4th or 3rd century BC and had various names, including St John's blood, Polish grey and Polish cochineal.

Cockling A term used to describe the undulations that occur in a sheet of paper when it is not kept flat. In the West hand-made paper cockles naturally, especially around the deckle edges (see PAPER), while machine-made papers tend to distort when exposed to changes in atmospheric humidity or held under uneven tension by a mounting method.

Cold gilding A method of gilding glassware and ceramics by painting the surface with linseed oil or glue and then applying gold leaf.

Cold painting The decoration of glassware or porcelain with lacquer colours or oil paint, without firing (for illustration see page 413). The colours are easily abraded and have often worn off old pieces. They are best applied to the back of the glass and are sometimes protected by varnish, metal foil or another sheet of glass. The process tended to be used on items that were too large to be fired in the muffle kiln or on forest glass that would not withstand a second firing. Sometimes the painting was also done on glass blanks by craftsmen who had no access to a furnace.

Collage The process of decorating artefacts such as screens with paper ornaments, which are stuck onto a secondary support or substrate, usually paper or a textile.

See also REVERSE GLASS PAINTING.

Collagen The protein which makes up the main three-dimensional fibrous network in a skin. During the tanning process it is modified to produce leather.

Colorcore See FORMICA.

Combed ware A Staffordshire ceramic with combed or feathered SLIP DECORATION. See also MARBLED WARE.

Combing See TRAILING.

Composition A mixture of resin, whiting, size and linseed oil that can be mixed to a dough and then cast in wooden moulds. This substance, which is also known as 'compo', has been used since the 18th century for cheap mouldings on frames and for plaques that can be applied to a flat surface. The term is also associated with a form of papier mâché that includes a high proportion of plaster to paper pulp and was used for architectural ornament.

Compression moulding See PLASTICS.

Concrete See CEMENT.

Copal See AMBER.

Coperta A colourless overglaze used on Italian maiolica. One of the glaze ingredients was potash frit, known as marzacotto, which acted as a flux and gave the glaze transparency. It was made from wine lees, which naturally contain potassium. In early maiolica, marzacotto was combined with the tin glaze that disguised the body material.

Copper The second most commonly used metal, after iron. It has a warm pinkish red colour, is very malleable and ductile, and is one of the best conductors of heat and electricity. Its name is derived from the Roman source of copper, the island of Cyprium (modern Cyprus).

Copper was probably the first metal used by man: the earliest archaeological evidence of its use comes from Asia Minor and dates from between 9000 and 7000 BC. These small objects, such as beads or pins, are made of hammered native copper. (Native copper is relatively pure copper found in nature usually in the form of nuggets.) Copper was also used by the ancient Egyptians to make tools and weapons.

The metallurgy of copper has a long and interesting history. From initially using native copper, man started to extract copper from its ores, of which there are 240 in the earth's crust. It is probable that the ores were first reduced to metallic copper in pottery kilns. Copper ores can be divided into copper oxides and copper sulphides. The former group can be reduced into metallic copper directly by different heat treatments. The copper sulphides must be converted first into oxides through a complex process called roasting.

Because pure copper is difficult to cast, it is commonly alloyed with tin, zinc, lead and nickel. An alloy of mainly copper and zinc is called BRASS; an alloy of mainly copper and tin is called BRONZE; while copper alloyed with substan-

T.457-19.

tial amounts of both tin and zinc is called gunmetal. Bronzes and brasses containing substantial amounts of lead are called leaded bronzes or brasses. An alloy of copper and nickel is called cupronickel.

Copper has traditionally been used to make hollowwares such as cooking vessels. These were usually made from sheet metal, using hammers and stakes, with larger pieces being riveted. Smaller objects are often brazed using brass solder, or soft-soldered using lead solders. To prevent food from coming into contact with the copper the vessels are almost always tinned on the inside, by applying pure molten tin to the surface. Between 1750 and 1840 copper was used extensively as the base material for making fused plate articles. These silver-plated copper-based articles were made by stamping and spinning. Decoration usually takes the form of engraving or chasing.

Copperplate printing A method of hand-producing printed textiles by means of a flat, engraved copper plate. The incised areas of the plate carry the colourant, which is passed to the cloth under extreme pressure, in a rolling press. By the mid-17th century plates were in use with inks for discontinuous printing on silk of designs up to 96 cm square. A century later the technique was in use on continuous lengths of cotton and linen cloth; first recorded in Ireland in 1752, it was employed in London by 1760 and in France by 1770, when copperplate printing on cotton began in Jouy. Generally printed in one colour only (CHINA BLUE or shades of madder), additional colours when required were added by block printing or hand painting. Although floral patterns were printed by this technique, copperplate printing is most closely associated with scenic designs. Such textiles are often erroneously called *toile de Jouy*, since the technique was long thought to be a French invention; the French themselves, however, called scenic copperplate prints *toile d'Irelande*. Although the use of plates for continuous lengths gradually declined with the advent of roller printing, commemorative panels and handkerchiefs were still being printed by this technique as late as the 1860s.

Coral A hard calcareous material secreted as an exoskeleton by a group of medusoid marine invertebrates. There are many species of coral but only one (*Corallium rubrum*) is suitable for use as a material for carving, jewellery and inlay. Known as 'noble', 'precious' or 'jeweller's' coral, it is moderately hard (Mohs scale 3–4) and will accept fine, detailed

OPPOSITE
La liberté américaine, *copperplate-printed cotton designed by Jean-Baptiste Huet, 1783–9. It was printed, in madder, in the Oberkampf royal manufactory, Jouy.*

*Red coral necklace and
hairpin, 19th century.*

carving and a high degree of polish.

The colour and specific shape of the raw material varies according to the source but all corals conform to a generally tree-like, branched structure which widens and thickens towards the base, and most are red or pink in colour. The North African variety is usually light red, with straight, upward-pointing branches. The Tuscan is very convoluted and light red in colour, while the colour of Sardinian coral, a distinctive pink covering a deep cherry red, is often referred to as *rosso scuro*. A blue variety was once common off the coast of west Africa but is rare today.

The Pacific varieties are larger and heavier than the Mediterranean and, unlike the somewhat bushy Mediterranean coral, have a distinct left and right branching structure. A wider range of colours is also available in the Pacific, especially from Japanese waters: a white can be found around Tosa and a rich vermilion in the waters off Kagoshima. Black or brown coral is dead material, gathered some time after the polyps have died. Fresh coral is covered with a friable coating (the sarcosoma) under which a series of parallel tubules are found. These originally housed the living polyps. The outer coating is easily removed by scraping or brushing with a wire brush.

Like shell, to which it is related, coral is carved differently from wood. While carving tools can be used to produce designs, coral is better and more commonly worked using abrasive or scraping techniques, and specially shaped pencils made from abrasive stones, files, scorps and gravers are the tools most commonly used. Deep undercuts and drapery or the piercings of beads are worked using simple reciprocating tools such as the bow drill and Archimedes drill, fitted with spear point or spoon bits. Beads are polished by tumbling in drums loaded first with pumice and then with powdered calcined stag's antlers. Standard graded carborundum and aluminium oxide powders are often used today. Similarly, three-dimensional and relief carvings are polished using cloth or soft leather pads charged with graded abrasive powders such as fine carborundum, pumice, tripoli or rouge, usually lubricated with water. Fine details and undercuts are polished using shaped wooden rubbers dipped in lubricant and then charged with abrasive.

Coral has been used as a decorative and talismanic material since at least the time of the ancient Greeks, by whom it was known as 'the blood of Medusa'. Common and easily harvested in the Mediterranean, it was a popular medium for Roman craftsmen. In the Middle Ages it was believed that coral could detect poison in food, and it was thus often used in tableware. The Tibetans considered it a symbol of longevity. Since the early 18th century European supplies have been supplemented with Pacific varieties, especially from the seas around Japan. It continues in use as a medium for cameos and jewellery throughout Europe, especially in parts of Italy. Typical products are ear-rings, brooches and strings of beads. Larger sections are used for figurines and chess sets. Barely modified pieces are sometimes used as supports for figures carved in other materials such as ivory: one popular subject is an ivory *St Sebastian* against a red coral tree or a similar depiction of the *Crucifixion*. Simply polished stems were also popular as ring stands in the late 18th century and in the 19th. The polished convoluted tips of some of the smaller varieties are used in the manufacture of strings of so-called 'negligé beads', first popularized in the 18th century. In north and west Africa coral is used as jewellery and inlay material. In the Far East it has been used for the manufacture of buttons and beads to ornament costume and hair decorations and as an inlay for lacquerware. Of particular note are the complex interwoven passementerie buttons made from strings of minute coral beads, which were worn in China in the 18th and 19th centuries on the hats of mandarins of the second rank.

Cordonnet Fine silk cords supplied by silk thread merchants for use in chain stitch and other embroidery said, in the 17th century, to be in the Indian style. The term is also used for the multi-stranded edging cord used in needle lace.

Cordovan A very high-quality leather whose name (sometimes corrupted to 'cordwain') derives from the town of Córdoba in southern Spain, where during the early Middle Ages a combination of Moorish tanning techniques and Spanish raw materials led to the production of a distinctive type of fine, soft leather. Although it has always suggested excellence, over the centuries the word has been used for a variety of different products, including: a leather made in medieval times from the skins of Spanish HAIR SHEEP and goats, using a combination of sumac, alum and kermes; GILT LEATHER; and leather made from the shell of a horse hide. This area occurs only in the butt region and is characterized by a layer of very dense compact fibres lying within the thickness of the skin. The resultant product is tough and particularly abrasion-resistant.

Cordwain See CORDOVAN.

Core forming A simple method of making a small glass vessel around a core. A sausage-shaped piece of clay and animal dung is formed around a long metal rod and fired to form a core. It is then dipped into molten glass, which is marvered into shape and decorated by trailing and combing. After annealing, the rod and as much of the core as possible are removed. The technique emerged in the Middle East in the middle of the 2nd millennium BC and was used until the 1st century BC, when it was superseded by blowing.

Cornelian A reddish-brown, uniformly coloured form of chalcedony. The colour is produced by an iron oxide. Although it is distributed worldwide, since the 4th century BC most cornelian has come from India. It also occurs in Egypt, where it was used in antiquity to make beads, amulets, inlays and, occasionally, vessels.

Cornish stone See CHINA STONE.

Coromandel A type of inlaid polychrome lacquerware made in China for export. It was first produced in the 17th century and was known until the early 20th century as bantam. The name (sometimes given as calamander) derives from the site of the British East India Company's trading post in southeast India. The finest coromandel is made by preparing a multi-layered, thick URUSHI paste ground, into which designs are carved. The carvings are then filled with coloured lacquer pastes and pastes made from other media (since urushi reacts with many pigments). Cheaper versions are made by preparing the ground with two or three relatively thick layers of coarse gesso paste. This is ground flat and then coated with lacquer and the design is prepared as above. The most common wares are screens, workboxes and cabinets.

Some authorities assign the name coromandel to polychrome wares and bantam to the Chinese gold decorated black wares. Coromandel is also used for a very hard wood similar to ebony.

Cosmati work A type of mosaic decoration developed in Rome in the early 12th century by marbleworkers called *cosmati*, after the Cosmatus family, who were leading exponents of the technique. It is composed of pieces of glass, coloured marble and other polishable stones such as porphyry (reused from ancient buildings), malachite, serpentine

and alabaster. These materials are used in a variety of sizes and shapes and set in lime mortar. Hence cosmati work differs from true mosaic, which is generally made of square or rectangular tesserae of consistent size. Cosmati, composed entirely of geometric patterns, was used primarily indoors for pavements, decorative panels (as can be seen at St Mark's Basilica in Venice), thrones, altars and columns, and is mainly associated with Italian Romanesque architecture. In 1268 Odoricus, a member of the Cosmatus family, produced a pavement with interwoven bands surrounding roundels and rectangular panels in Westminster Abbey, incorporating Purbeck marble with imported Italian materials such as Carrara marble and coloured glass.

Cotton A vegetable seed fibre made up of almost pure cellulose hairs attached to the seed of several *Gossypium* plants, grown in tropical and warm temperate regions around the world. The word is derived from the Arabic name *qutn* or *quten*. Although it comes in various shades of cream, cotton can also be brown or green, a characteristic which (although not new) was particularly exploited in the late 20th century. The fibres are very fine—the finest are the Egyptian and Sea Island varieties—and their lengths vary from 10 to 26 mm. The distinctive feature of the fibre is a natural twist, which spirals when wet, thus accelerating drying and aiding spinning. It was the mechanization of cotton spinning, in the years around 1770, that spurred forward the development of the Western textile industry, including refinements in dyes and dyeing, and printing. The removal of the cotton seeds (ginning) was mechanized at the end of the 18th century, and in 1844 mercerization was patented by John Mercer. This treatment of cotton yarn or cloth increases its lustre and affinity for dyes; a permanent swelling of the fibre is caused by immersion under tension in a caustic soda (sodium hydroxide) solution, later neutralized in acid. The combination of cellulose, caustic soda and acid formed the basis of the viscose process, used to make cellophane and viscose RAYON.

Counted openwork See EMBROIDERY.

Counted threadwork See CANVASWORK.

Crackle A network of wide cracks throughout the matrix of a glaze which do not permeate the glaze surface and are created deliberately for decorative effect. It is sometimes known by the French term *craquelure*. The technique has been employed in China, Japan and Europe and is frequently used by studio potters.

Glazes crack because they contract more than the body in the firing. When this occurs accidentally it is known as CRAZING. Crackle can be induced by using a glaze with a lower coefficient of expansion than the body. Certain glazes are naturally prone to cracking, such as lime glazes and raku glazes. Stress can also be introduced in the firing to induce cracking (see RAKU). Crackle can be enhanced by staining. This is done while the glaze is still warm, before cooling is complete and the cracks in the glaze have smoothed over. Among the stains commonly used are charcoal ash and ink.

Crackle can be dense or widely spaced, with widely spaced cracks (primary crackle) occurring first, followed by closer ones (secondary crackle). In some Chinese glazes, double layers of crackle are induced by layering the glazes and encouraged by deliberate underfiring.

Craquelure See CRACKLE.

Crazing Cracking in a glaze which results from a glaze fault. It occurs when the glaze fit is poor and the body and glaze contract at different rates (see GLAZE). Both alkaline and lime glazes are prone to crazing as they are rather inelastic, in contrast to lead glazes, which are very elastic. Crazing normally occurs on cooling after firing is complete, but some glazes on earthenware cooking vessels will craze over time, owing to thermal shock. (When this effect is deliberately induced for a decorative purpose it is called CRACKLE.)

Crazing can be prevented by the addition of boric oxide, which makes the glaze more elastic, or by raising the amount of alumina, a craze inhibitor. Careful control of firing can also prevent crazing, as underfiring and overfiring both cause stress. Lead glazes are very elastic and therefore not prone to crazing.

Creamware Lead-glazed earthenware with a cream-coloured body. It was developed by Wedgwood in the 1760s as an alternative to porcelain and was renamed Queen's ware after Queen Charlotte ordered a cream ware tea service. Creamware was one of the most successful Staffordshire ceramic bodies and it is still used today for both tableware and figures.

The creamware body is an earthenware and is composed of ball clay, china clay, flint and Cornish stone. Its recipe is based on a formula developed by John and Thomas Astbury in the early 18th century and results in a body that is pale

Creamware teapot with applied decoration, Staffordshire or Yorkshire, 1770–1830.

but low-fired and therefore economical to produce. Cream-wares were biscuit-fired, then lead-glazed and fired again at a low temperature. They could be left plain or decorated with underglaze painting, overglaze painting, transfer printing, applied decoration and pierced decoration.

Cretonne A group of printed textiles characterized by the presence of an unglazed surface. Its dull, matt appearance is often accentuated by a textured weave and the use of cotton, or cotton and another fibre, for the ground cloth. The term was most widely used from *c.*1850 to 1950; when a printed warp was used to imitate an ikat, the result was called a shadow-warp cretonne.

Crewelwork Embroidery worked with crewel (worsted) threads on a cotton warp, linen weft, twilled fabric, especially associated with late 15th- to early 18th-century large-scale designs for furnishings such as bed-hangings and covers. The technique most often used was stem stitch, a line stitch in which the thread always lies to the right of the needle; from this derived the stitch's alternate name, crewel stitch. As a style, crewelwork is associated with the designs evolved in the second half of the 17th century from European, Indian

Cristallo goblet, Venice, early 17th century. The bowl is clear glass, while the stem is in the form of a dragon formed by an S-shaped, twisted, ribbed rod, with crimped applied decoration between two ribbed nodes.

and Chinese influences, with Baroque leaf forms, often with LAID AND COUCHED WORK fillings, on prominent branches or in Tree of Life designs. American crewelwork was generally lighter and freer in order to make best use of scarce threads.

Crimping See RAISING.

Cristallo A form of soda glass made in Venice from silica (silicon dioxide) obtained from quartz river pebbles, with the ash from the Spanish marine plant barilla as a flux and a small amount of manganese as a decolourizer. Its manufacture was perfected in the mid-15th century. Often a pale smoky grey or yellow colour, the glass can be almost colourless. It then resembles rock crystal, from which it derives its name. It is a thin, fragile glass, unsuitable for decoration except by enamelling, gilding and light diamond point engraving. However, it is highly ductile and can be manipulated into elaborate and sometimes fantastic designs; these became ever more elaborate during the 16th and 17th centuries. Cristallo tends to suffer from crizzling.

See also FAÇON DE VENISE.

Crizzling A defect in glass characterized by surface moisture and a network of fine internal cracks. It is sometimes referred to as 'glass disease', 'sick glass' or 'weeping glass'. The condition is progressive and the glass eventually decomposes. It is caused by an imperfect mix of ingredients in the batch, particularly an excess of alkali, which remains uncombined with the other ingredients and reacts with moisture in the air. Crizzling is commonly found in Venetian cristallo, in early imitations of cristallo and some enamels. It should not be confused with DEVITRIFICATION or with weathering, in which age, moisture and chemical action produce iridescent effects on the glass.

Crochet See LOOPING.

Cross banding A term used by plywood manufacturers for a veneer with the grain placed at right angles to that of the core, in order to resist shrinkage. The term is also used to refer to a veneer border or band in which the grain of the veneer runs across the width of the band (sometimes known as cross-cut banding). This was first used on English furniture in the reign of Charles II.

Crotch A feathered ornamental grain formed at the junction between forked branches and highly valued for cabinetmaking, especially in mahogany. It is sometimes also known as curl.

Crown glass See FLAT GLASS.

Crystal Colourless, transparent glass. Originally the term was used of any clear glass that resembled rock crystal, including Venetian CRISTALLO, Bohemian potash-lime glass (see POTASH GLASS) and English LEAD GLASS, but since 1963 it has been legally confined to high-quality cut glass that contains a minimum of 24% lead oxide.

Crystalline glaze A glaze with crystals suspended in the glaze matrix or on the surface. Crystals grow in glazes during cooling, in a process known as devitrification. Their growth is encouraged by the isolation from the main glaze matrix of certain oxides which act as seeds for the crystals. The crystals in the resulting glaze can create interesting effects such as opacity and optical colours.

The growth of crystals in a glaze is stimulated by 'soaking' or holding the firing at temperature for a period of time, in this case at approximately 800°C. Crystal formation can also be promoted by uneven milling of the glaze ingredients, which causes areas of high concentrations of oxides such as iron in a TEMMOKU glaze or calcia in a JUN GLAZE. Alumina inhibits crystal growth.

Cuenca A term for impressed channels on Spanish tiles which contain fluid glazes. It derives from the Spanish word for 'cell' and refers to a method of glaze control used in Spain from the 15th century on. Tiles were impressed with channels with raised edges, forming a decorative pattern. These channels were then filled with coloured glazes which became fluid when fired. The channels prevented the coloured glazes from running together, thus separating the colours. This technique superseded that of CUERDA SECA, an earlier and less successful method of glaze control.

Cuerda seca A term for grease-resist patterns on Spanish tiles of the late 14th and 15th centuries, used to separate coloured glazes. It derives from the Spanish for 'dry cord'. Grease was mixed with manganese oxide and then used to draw a pattern on the surface of a tile. Coloured glazes were painted between the lines and then fired. During firing, the grease kept the fluid glazes separate and then burnt off, leaving outlines that resembled dry cords.

Cuero cofrado A Spanish term for the decoration of vegetable-tanned sheepskins. The GRAIN side of the leather is pressed against a heated metal plate to produce a slightly burnt design. This type of decoration dates from the 14th century or earlier.

Cuir bouilli A material made from vegetable-tanned leather. It is first soaked for up to twelve hours in cold water until all the fibres are completely saturated, and then allowed to drain until it is uniformly damp but does not exude water when squeezed. In this state it is quite plastic and can be stretched or moulded into complex three-dimensional shapes and decorated by incising or stamping. It is then heated carefully in an oven to between 35° and 50°C. As the leather warms and dries, it becomes firm but resilient, retaining its shape and decorative pattern. If, however, the drying conditions are incorrect the leather shrinks to give a deformed, brittle material.

Some forms of *cuir bouilli* have been made since neolithic times, and examples of fine leather caskets are found from the

Case for a missal, in cuir bouilli, *Italy, mid-15th century.*

early medieval period onwards. The material was also used for the manufacture of protective armour, where its hard but resilient properties were widely exploited. Bottles, flasks, blackjacks, bombards, buckets and other objects required to hold liquids were also widely made from *cuir bouilli*. These usually had their insides waterproofed with a layer of pitch.

Cullet Broken and scrap glass added to the batch as a means of recycling scrap and hastening the melting process. It melts more quickly than new ingredients and therefore saves fuel. Cullet is usually composed of fragments of glass discarded during production, though sometimes out-of-fashion glassware is broken and included. Cullet may be the sole ingredient in the batch, but generally it constitutes only 25–50% of the ingredients.

Cupellation A process for the removal of base metals from precious metals through heating in a bone ash crucible called a cupel. It is used mainly for the removal of lead from gold, silver or platinum during refining and ASSAYING, but other base metals can also be removed by wrapping them in lead foil and putting them in the crucible in a controlled furnace at 1000°C. The base metals are oxidized and absorbed, leaving behind the refined precious metals.

Cupronickel A copper–nickel alloy with 10–40% nickel. A well-known cupronickel containing 75% copper and 25% nickel is used for silver-coloured coins.

Curl See CROTCH.

Currying A term used for the various finishing processes applied to vegetable-tanned leathers. Originally these operations were carried out by a separate group of craftsmen, the curriers. The first operation involves immersing the leather in water or an infusion of sumac leaves, and allowing the leather to drain until it will not exude water when squeezed. It is then shaved to the required thickness with a special knife or, nowadays, by machine. DUBBIN, a mixture of tallow and marine oils, is spread liberally over the hides, which are then piled in a warm room for up to a week. As the moisture rises through the pile and evaporates from the surface, the fatty materials impregnate the fibre structure of the leather, producing a softer, more flexible, waterproof material. This 'stuffing' process is still employed in the manufacture of harness, saddlery and similar thick leathers. After stuffing the leather may be dyed and worked mechanically to give the required softness. Sometimes a surface finish of coloured

An 18th century curriers' workshop and tools, from Diderot's Encyclopédie des arts et des métiers: *(a) trampling on the oiled skins to soften them; (b) shaving the skins to a uniform thickness; (c) flattening the grain with a slicer; (d) boarding to bring up the surface texture of the leather; (e) staking with a moon knife.*

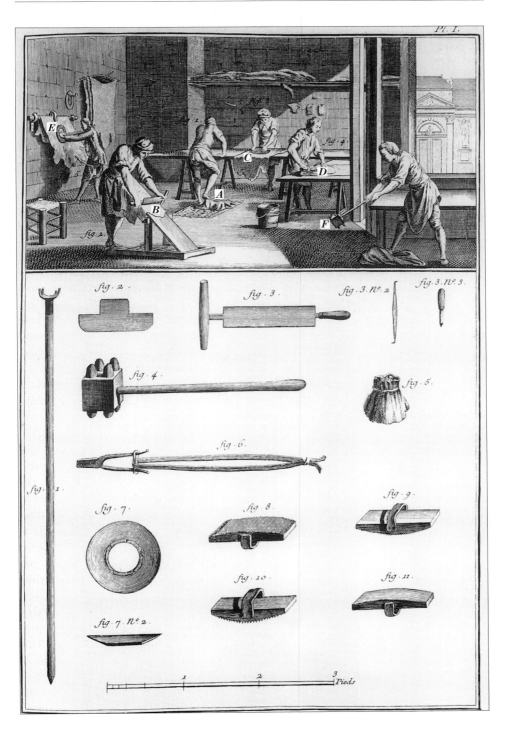

Pl. I.

waxes is applied.

In Britain legislation was introduced in the early 19th century which permitted tanning and currying to be carried out on the same premises. This allowed the two processes to be integrated, which led to rapid technological progress. Today the tanner or leather dresser treats the leather with a range of speciality retanning agents, synthetic dyestuffs and fat liquors to give the required properties. The majority of leathers are also finished with a surface coating consisting of synthetic resins coloured with finely ground pigments.

Cut-card work A decoration of flat metal, sheet-pierced, shaped and soldered or brazed to the main body of an object. This form of relief decoration, usually in the form of foliage or borders, was very popular on silverware in Western Europe around 1700.

Cut glass Glass whose surface has been cut into facets, grooves and depressions with the aid of a large rotating wheel. Glass has been decorated by wheel-cutting since the

A 19th-century glass-cutter at work. The glass is held against a rotating wheel, which cuts the required design into the glass. The wheel is continuously fed with water and abrasive. A rack of cutting wheels can be seen in the background.

8th century BC, but the technique of faceting was perfected only in the 18th century, when the evolution of English lead glass provided a metal with the appropriate softness and refractive qualities.

The process is difficult and expensive. It may be executed 'over hand', with the object pressed down on the wheel, or 'under hand', with it pressed up for more delicate work. First, the design is drawn on the surface of the glass. It is then cut with an iron, carborundum or diamond-coated wheel fed with water or wet sand and smoothed with a sandstone wheel fed with pulverized sand or emery. Finally the glass is polished with wooden or felt wheels aided by a soft powder. Alternatively the item can be acid-polished.

The cutting wheels have three basic profiles: flat for flat facets, V-shaped for grooves, and convex for shallow depressions. The brilliant effect that results is due to the cuts acting as prisms with adjacent cuts. Initially the wheel was powered by foot or water, but the advent of steam in the early 19th century transformed the craft, encouraging deeper, more complex cutting.

Cutwork See EMBROIDERED LACE.

Cylinder glass See FLAT GLASS.

Cypress A moderately soft, light and durable wood from the common cypress (*Cupressus sempervirens*), found throughout Europe and most of the Middle East. It is pale creamy brown, shot with reddish markings, and has a straight, even grain and a fine texture. It is easily worked and is used for general carpentry and joinery purposes. Other species used commercially include Lawson's cypress (see CEDAR) and *Cupressus torulosa* (the Himalayan cypress), which is light brown, mottled with darker patches and streaks, and is moderately soft and light, lustrous and aromatic. With a straight, even grain, the Himalayan cypress is easily worked and is very durable; it is used for interior and exterior joinery and carpentry. Some other timbers which are sold as cypress are in fact other genera: for example, the yellow cypress (*Thuya excelsa*), found in the USA, and the Australian white cypress (*Callitris glauca*).

D

Dalle de verre A technique for creating coloured windows with small slabs of cast glass set in concrete or epoxy resin. The slabs, 20–30 cm square and 2.5 cm thick, may be chipped or faceted on the surface. The system was developed in France in the 1930s and creates windows with a monumental appearance dominated by a dark framework. Unlike stained-glass windows, *dalle de verre* constructions can be load-bearing.

Damascening A process for decorating a metal by inlaying a soft metal into a harder metal ground without the use of heat. The technique is used worldwide by many cultures and has no connection with Damascus steel.

A damascened candleholder, bronze inlaid with copper and silver, eastern Iran, 12th century AD. Here the inlay has been forced into undercut recesses.

There are two main types of damascening. In the first, the inlay is forced into a recess in the workpiece, the edges of which form a slight lip that helps to retain the inlay. This is done by hammering and punching, sometimes followed by filing, sanding and polishing or burnishing. The second type involves cross-hatching the ground to create a rough surface capable of holding the inlay. The thin foil is then hammered into place and burnished. The ground is usually a hard metal such as steel, bronze or nickel. The inlay is usually a soft metal such as gold, silver, brass or copper. This second type of damascening is sometimes called false damascening and was used extensively on armour both in the Far East and (during the Renaissance) in Europe. Other forms of damascening can be seen in TOLEDO WARE in Spain, KUFTGARI in India and *nunome zogan* in Japan, where metal inlay provided opportunities for extraordinary artistry, especially on sword mounts.

Damascus steel An early form of cast crucible steel with a natural, irregular pattern revealed after etching. It was often used for arms and armour and is sometimes also known as 'watered steel' or 'wootz'. The name derives from the city of Damascus, the trade centre through which this kind of steel entered the West from the Far East or India from the 7th century onwards.

Damascus steel is made by heating iron in contact with carbon, some of which is absorbed to produce a wrought iron composed of 1.6% carbon. After solidification, but while still hot, the steel is hammered gently to create a homogeneous steel bar. The bar is then forged into the desired shape, and after finishing the object is etched in a mild acid to reveal the pattern. The 'watered' effect on the surface is the result of an uneven distribution of carbon in the steel.

Damasin See METAL THREAD.

Damask A cloth, often of a single colour, in which, typically, a warp-faced SATIN weave is used in the ground and reversed for the figure (or pattern) so that on the back of the cloth the pattern appears in a satin weave. In single damask the satin weave is tied down by every fifth weft; in double damask this occurs at every eighth weft, creating a firmer, more lustrous cloth. Other weaves may be incorporated and any fibre can be used, although damask is closely associated with silk and linen. (For illustration see page 527.)

Damasquette See LAMPAS.

Davenport's patent glass Glassware decorated in imitation of engraving or etching by a process patented in 1806 by John Davenport, an English glassmaker. The surface of the glass was covered with a powdered glass paste, which was then scraped away to create the desired pattern. A light firing fused the powder onto the glass surface without melting it.

Deal A general term for a particular cut of timber from various species. Different colours can be obtained from trees of the same species or even from within the trunk of one tree, although this is rare.

Decalcomania A form of LITHOGRAPHIC DECORATION on ceramics that was a popular pastime in the 1860s, the term deriving from the Greek *decal* '(off paper)' It is also used more

Glass goblets decorated with sporting subjects by John Davenport, c.1810.

loosely of DÉCOUPAGE.

Decorated paper Paper patterned, textured or coloured by a variety of methods, whether produced for a specific purpose, such as a book or wall covering, or as a decorative object in its own right. Decorative papers date back to the earliest days of papermaking. As with papermaking itself, many of the techniques originate in Asia, and particularly in Japan, where MARBLING, for example, was in use in the early 12th century. Other methods include gilding, resist dyeing, stencilling and a whole range of printing and printmaking techniques. In Japan these include handcraft techniques such as tie dyeing and intricate creasing, which are normally used on textiles. In the latter, which is known as *orizomegami*, or pleat-dyeing, the colours are brushed onto the ridges of tightly folded paper. Two other methods of producing decorated papers which may be unique to Japan are *katazome*

Detail of hand-decorated paper, Japan, 20th century. The paper has been dyed selectively with three different colours by folding the sheet and dipping the points of the folds into dye, which has been allowed to penetrate the paper in a controlled manner. This technique is called orizomegami *('pleat-dyed paper').*

(stencil-dyeing) and *unryushi* (cloud paper). Stencil-dyeing combines resist-dyeing with stencilling techniques. The stencils are cut from handmade paper treated with persimmon juice to make it tough and water-resistant. Projecting details are held in place by an open network of fine filaments, traditionally made of human hair, glued to the stencil. The filaments do not show up on the completed stencil image. The stencil is placed on a sheet of absorbent Japanese paper and an uncoloured starch paste is squeezed through it. The stencil is removed and the paste allowed to dry. Then dye is applied, either freehand with a brush or through further stencils. After drying, the paper is soaked in warm water, which helps to remove the starch paste, leaving white areas where the paste has protected the paper from the dyes. Cloud papers are decorated at the papermaking stage, when clumps of white fibres are placed by hand on one mould and then couched

Detail of hand-decorated paper by Keisuke Serizawa, Tokyo, 20th century. The pattern depicts a rural papermaking village and is made by a combination of stencilling and resist techniques using starch paste. This type of paper is katazomegami *('stencil-dyed paper'). The deckle edge of the handmade paper can be seen at the top and to the right.*

onto a sheet of paper formed in a different colour on another mould. Particles of mica may be added to give a sheen to the paper. A variation on this technique uses fine jets of water to create a filigree pattern in a newly formed, wet sheet of paper in the mould.

The fashion for hand papermaking by amateurs in the late 20th century has produced duplex papers which incorporate materials such as leaf skeletons, pressed flowers and coloured fibres between two layers of paper pulp.

See also GOLD EMBOSSED PAPER and PASTE PAPER.

Découpage A method of producing decorative paper objects by cutting parts of a sheet of paper away, as in the making of a SILHOUETTE. The term is also used to describe a method of decorating furniture or smaller items by pasting cut paper onto the object and then varnishing over it. See also DECAL-COMANIA.

Decoupé See APPLIQUÉ.

Dehua ware See BLANC DE CHINE.

Delftware Dutch tin-glazed earthenwares with cobalt blue decoration. Tin-glazed earthenwares were first made in the Dutch town of Delft in the 16th century, probably in imitation of Italian maiolica, which is of the same ceramic tradition. In the 17th century porcelain from East Asia was imported in large quantities and Delft potters began to imitate the designs and colours of such wares on Delftware. Like maiolica, Delftware was usually decorated with in-glaze cobalt blue decoration, though some other colours were also used, and covered with a colourless overglaze called KWAART. Delftware was imitated in England at kilns in London, where a local tin-glazed earthenware had been made in the early 17th century. Delftwares from both the Netherlands and England were made in a wide range of forms, including tiles, and were used for both domestic ware and decoration (see colour plate X).

Denim See SERGE and TWILL.

Depletion gilding A gilding process whereby an object made of an alloy with a low gold content is treated with acid to remove the base metals from the surface, leaving it rich in gold. This type of gilding has long been used by South American and Mexican goldsmiths. The copper–gold (10–30% gold) alloy generally used is called tumbaga. A low-silver alloy is sometimes substituted.

Devitrification A fault in glassmaking, in which the batch is

heated above the temperature required for VITRIFICATION (*c.*1300–1550°C). The glass liquefies, and if it is cooled too slowly or too long it then becomes crystalline and opaque. Devitrification also occurs naturally during the process of glass deterioration.

Delftware, England, late 17th century. The flower bowl in the middle was made at Brislington, near Bristol, the other pieces in London.

Devoré A group of textiles patterned through a form of DIS-CHARGE PRINTING, in which the printed corrosive paste removes fibres rather than colourants. The term derives from the French for 'devoured'. Developed in the late 19th century along with CHEMICAL LACE, it relies on the use of mixed-fibre cloths, in which only some of the fibres are removed. Many variants have been developed but they typically call for caustic alkalis to remove protein fibres and acids to remove cellulosics. Also described as 'burnt out', this technique is closely associated with lightweight dress velvets of silk–cotton or silk–acetate combinations.

Diamond A transparent gemstone mineral, composed of carbon. It is the hardest natural substance (Mohs scale 10). This property arises from the fact that in diamond each carbon atom is covalently bonded to three other carbons in a tetrahedral (i.e., pyramidal) unit. Covalent bonds are strong and hold the carbon atoms in a tight, regular and repeating pattern within the crystal structure, which is typically octahedral. By contrast, graphite (Mohs scale 1–2), which is also composed solely of carbon, consists of weakly bonded sheets which slide over each other, giving the material its lubricant qualities. Diamonds can also occur in triangular crystals called macles. Unworked diamond crystals are frequently dark grey, with rounded edges. Diamond has a number of unique qualities, including its extreme lustre and optical properties referred to as brilliance and fire. Brilliance, which is enhanced by cutting, is the reflection of light back through the front of the diamond, producing dazzling effects. Fire is the dispersion or splitting of light into the colours of the spectrum, giving rise to the many colours seen within a diamond. Although colourless stones are the best known, diamond occurs in a number of colours, including yellow, red, blue, brown and black, owing to impurities such as nitrogen, boron and graphite.

Diamonds were formed at considerable depth within the earth's mantle approximately 3000 million years ago, in conditions of extreme heat and pressure. They were then carried to the surface by volcanic structures known as kimberlite pipes. Diamonds are found either embedded within the kimberlite host rock or, where this has eroded, in river gravels. When extracted from underground mines, generally all the diamonds are removed because they can be used industrially even if they are not of gem quality. Diamonds are separated from the host rock by passing them over a greased belt: they will adhere to grease, whereas other material is washed away.

From antiquity until the 18th century the principal source of diamonds was the gem gravels of India, where diamonds were described in religious texts as possessing, and conferring on the wearer, powers of strength and invincibility. It was believed that cutting or polishing a diamond would destroy its powers, a prohibition that was carried to Europe and persisted into the Middle Ages. In a 13th-century Spanish text, drawing on Arabic sources, diamonds were described as being both curative and poisonous. In India diamonds were used in their uncut octahedral shape (like two pyramids joined at the base). Although gem diamonds tended to be the preserve of royalty and their export from India apparently tightly controlled, their practical use, as extremely hard cutting tools, was widely exploited, as evidenced by a diamond-cut sapphire cameo produced in Rome in the 1st century AD.

The taboo on cutting diamonds appears to have faded by the late Middle Ages, and combined with an increased trade in gems and technological skill from India, FACETING of diamonds was developed in Europe in the 14th century. The first documented diamond cutting took place in Venice *c*.1330; diamond cutters were established in Paris and Nuremberg by the late 14th century and in Bruges by 1465. The earliest cuts involved enhancement of the natural octahedron, exploiting the fact that diamond can be split along planes parallel to the crystal faces. Further working must be done with tool diamonds or crushed diamond. Cutting is done with a blade formed of crushed diamond embedded in a metal disc. Bruting or shaping involves forcing another diamond against the diamond being worked, and polishing is carried out with crushed diamond on an iron wheel lubricated with oil. Although the technology used is now mechanized, the process does not differ substantially from the methods described by the 16th-century jeweller Benvenuto Cellini. With major finds in the 18th century (Brazil) and 19th century (Australia and South Africa) diamonds have become more prevalent, if still signs of wealth. Styles of cut have been developed to enhance the optical qualities, and the modern round brilliant cut, with a flat top and faceted bottom, involves precise geometry to maximize the fire and brilliance (see FACETING).

Because of the preciousness of diamonds, imitations are common. Historically, PASTE (Mohs 5.5–6) and colourless forms of the gemstone zircon (Mohs 7.5) were the most prevalent simulants. However, when mounted in jewellery both materials are readily abraded and zircon, which is brittle, is easily chipped. In the 1930s synthetically produced white spinels were introduced as diamond simulants and they are still occasionally used in place of small diamonds; spinels can be identified by their relative softness (Mohs 8) and inferior fire. Since the Second World War a number of synthetic simulants, composed of materials such as strontium titanate, rutile and synthetic garnet, have been developed. They can usually be distinguished from diamond by their excessive fire and relative softness. A highly plausible substitute, synthetic cubic zirconium, invented in 1976, is a good optical match for diamond but has a hardness of Mohs 8. A method for producing synthetic gem-quality diamond from other sources of carbon was published in 1976, but the technique is largely confined to the production of diamonds for industrial pur-

Diamond pendant brooch, 1930s, including blue, yellow and pink stones and showing a variety of cuts and settings.

poses. Although diamond can be differentiated from imitations by its hardness, this technique is inherently destructive and other techniques, which exploit unique properties of diamond such as its high thermal conductivity and its attraction to grease, are now widely used.

Diamond point engraving See GLASS ENGRAVING.

Die A term generally used for a form into which a metal is forged, stamped or cast. Dies used for stamping hollowware are usually made from hardened steel. The conical holes in a DRAWPLATE, used for drawing metal wire, are also called dies.

The name is also used for the tool used for cutting external threads on screws, bolts or pipes. This type of die looks like a slotted nut and removes metal rather than forging it.

Die-casting See CASTING.

Die-stamping A process whereby a piece of metal is shaped or impressed with the design cut in a metal die, by the application of pressure. The one or two dies involved in this process are made of a hard metal such as bronze or steel. Because such dies are themselves time-consuming to produce, die-stamping is generally used only when multiple copies of a design are needed. The technique has been used since antiquity to produce gold foil jewellery or to stamp coins and medals between a upper and lower die, first by hand-

A metal sheet is pressed between two dies to form hollowware.

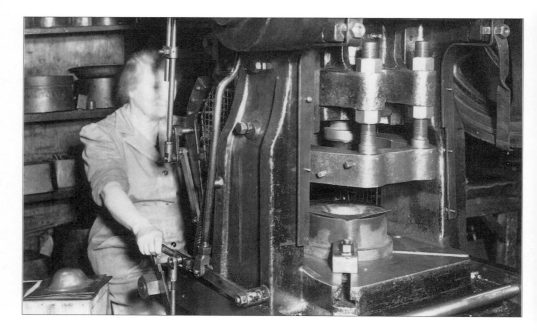

hammering and later using a fly press and drop hammers. It was also used extensively from the late 18th century onwards, especially for inexpensive silverware and fused plate wares. By this time it was possible to stamp large and complicated shapes, because the steel used for dies was much improved and steam technology could produce the immense force needed.

Diluent See THINNER.

Dimity See MUSLIN.

Diorite An igneous rock formed at great depth and composed of the minerals feldspar, hornblende and pyroxene. It is coarse-textured and speckled white and black. Diorite occurs in some European countries, where it has occasionally been used as a building or decorative stone, and in Egypt, where it was used in antiquity for vessels and tools.

Discharge printing A method of producing printed textiles by removing colour from the cloth through printing a reducing agent, which takes oxygen from or adds hydrogen to a reducible dye (see BLEACH). The reducing agent was usually stannous chloride ('tin salt' or 'tin crystals'), which tenderizes natural fibres and thus required sodium acetate in the print-paste. This was replaced in the 20th century by sulphoxylates, often hydrosulphates stabilized with formaldehyde; while hazardous, these were more powerful, cheaper and less harmful to the cloth.

Distemper A general term for paint with a water-miscible binder such as gum, size, casein or egg yolk (see EGG TEMPERA). Most commonly, however, it refers to chalk-based paint bound with SIZE, usually made from rabbitskin glue. For centuries 'soft distempers' were used as cheap house paint, but since the 1950s they have been largely replaced by modern emulsions, and distempers are now mostly used for the restoration of historic interiors. The paint is made up as a slurry with the consistency of cream, and by adding tinting pigments a range of pastel shades can be achieved. It is best applied with broad, long-bristled brushes, which also have the secondary function of keeping the paint stirred and in suspension.

The finish is opaque and powdery, and as it is not as hard-wearing as oil paint or emulsions, distemper has to be replaced more frequently. Oil-bound distempers contain a little oil suspended in the glue as an emulsion, and this makes them more durable. They lack, however, the soft, chalky finish for which distempers have always been prized.

For the use of distemper in the printing of wallpaper, see INK.

Dobby loom A loom with a mechanical attachment (invented in the 1820s but not widely used until the 1850s) controlling, generally, from eight to thirty harnesses, for the weaving of relatively small, generally geometric, all-over patterns. Such patterns were beyond the range of a simple cam loom but too limited to be produced economically with a JACQUARD attachment, of which the dobby loom is a simplification; the resulting cloth is often called dobby weave.

Dolomitic limestone A pale fine-grained limestone composed of calcium carbonate and magnesium carbonate; for this reason it is also called magnesian limestone. It occurs widely in limestone areas and has been used as a building stone (York Minster is constructed from dolomitic limestone) and for architectural ornament. Its softness and texture permit the carving of fine detail, but it is particularly vulnerable to the effects of atmospheric pollution and buildings in urban areas often show severe deterioration.

Doublecloth A cloth with two independent warps and wefts, interchanged at various points and so linked together. Many variations of this technique are known, but the pure form of doublecloth is recognizable by the formation of a reversible patterned cloth with 'pockets' between the interchanges.

Dovetail A group of woodworking joints used first by the ancient Egyptians and later by the Romans. It was reintroduced into Europe in the 16th century, and became widespread with the evolution of cabinetmaking. The dovetail is designed to hold structural elements at right angles to one another and end to end, and specifically to resist pulling apart from front to back or, if used in a vertical fitting, from top to bottom. In its simplest form, the through dovetail, the male part or dovetail of the joint, which is shaped like the spread tail of a dove, is cut with the grain on the end of one piece. The female part or socket is cut across the end of the corresponding piece.

The dovetail is the joint above all others with which the woodworker demonstrates his skill. It is often employed in situations where it can be clearly and easily seen, for example on the sides of drawers, and even the smallest error in construction will be visible. A variety of specific types are used for different constructions. For example, in drawer making,

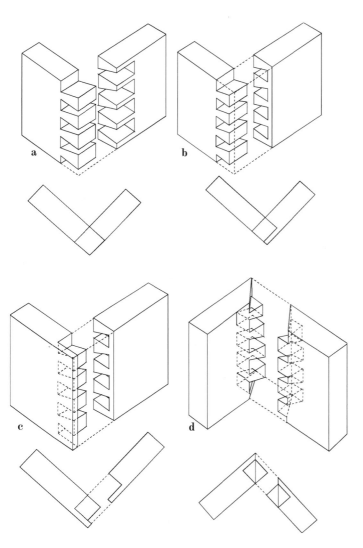

Dovetail joints:
(a) common or through
dovetail, as used on
drawer backs; (b) lap
dovetail, commonly used
on drawer fronts;
(c) secret lap dovetail,
often used in cabinet
construction; (d) secret
mitre dovetail, often used
in box and fancy cabinet
construction.

lapped dovetails are used to fix the drawer front to the sides and through dovetails to fix the back. Dovetail housings, which can be 'through' or 'stopped' may be used to fit shelves and secret mitre dovetails in the best case- and frame-making. When cutting dovetails the pitch of the sides of the joint varies with the type of timber and precise layout, but will normally be between 1 : 6 and 1 : 9. Softwood joints will normally have a greater pitch than hardwood joints, so that they generally look larger than joints cut in hardwood.

Dowel See Wood fixings.

Dragon's blood A resin obtained from *Daemonorops draco* and other species of RATTAN. It is used as a pigment, as a resist for etching, and for varnishes.

Draw loom A loom that allows patterns of (in principle) any width, height and complexity to be woven through the use of cords attached to each warp thread (which itself passes through the eye of a heddle or lease; see LOOM). The cords are lifted as required to divert the passage of ground wefts or introduce supplementary wefts. In practice, the cords were bunched above the loom into groups, each representing the edge-to-edge repeat for each passage of one weft; a leash attached to each bunch was drawn sideways to effect the required lift. The development of such looms, operated by a weaver and draw boy, was associated with silk-weaving areas in China and Western Europe. In China the draw boy sat at the top of the loom, manipulating the leashes from memory. In Europe the leashes run upwards and over pulleys across and down the side of the loom, where they are passed through a perforated board (sometimes called a button board and often positioned against a wall near the loom) in the order of the lifting pattern; this method was perfected *c.*1605 by Claude Dangon, an Italian working in Lyon, France. The key characteristic of draw looms is that the effort is put into the preparation; once the warp is correctly tied and the cords bundled appropriately, the weaving progresses relatively quickly. Weaves associated with this loom include brocade, figured velvet and damask. In the 19th century the draw loom was gradually replaced by looms with a JACQUARD

Draw loom, from Un Recueil de planches sur les sciences, les arts libéraux, et les arts méchaniques *(1772), by Diderot and d'Alembert. The draw boy created the pattern by pulling the cords at the side of the loom, thus raising groups of leases attached to the warps.*

attachment; in England in the 20th century Luther Hooper redeveloped the draw loom for craft weavers.

Drawn threadwork See EMBROIDERED LACE and EMBROIDERY.

Drawplate A flat steel plate with rows of graduated drawholes or dies through which metal wire is drawn to reduce its diameter and alter its shape. In the past these drawholes were made of hardened steel, but they are often now tungsten carbide or even diamond.

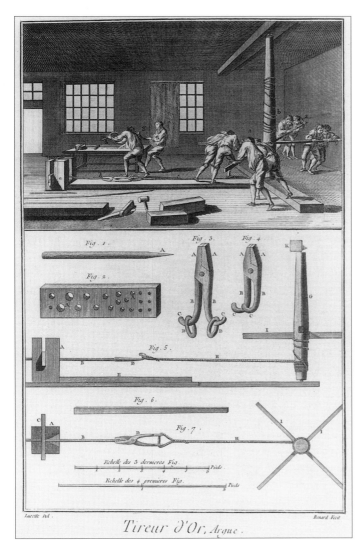

Tireur d'Or, Argue.

Wire-drawing in the mid-18th century, from Diderot's Encyclopédie des arts et des métiers. *The metal wire is reduced in diameter by being pulled through tapered holes in the drawplate, a process requiring considerable force at larger diameters. The drawplate itself is shown in a side view at the left of the illustration and frontally below.*

Drenching See TANNING.

Dresden work See EMBROIDERED LACE.

Drill See WOODWORKING TOOLS.

Drop forging See FORGING.

Dryer A substance added to oil paint to speed the curing process. Dryers are sold as liquids and contain metal salts, such as manganese or lead, which accelerate the oxidation of the oil. Manufacturers add enough to each tube to ensure that the paint is touch-dry within days, but if paint is mixed from first principles, using clear oil and dry pigment, or if extra oil is added to commercial paint, then some drying agent may be needed because oil paint can remain tacky for weeks, particularly if it comes from poppy or walnut rather than the traditional linseed. The use of too much dryer can lead to cracking and discoloration.

Drypoint See INTAGLIO PRINTING.

Dubbin A mixture of tallow and marine oils used in the currying process. Its exact composition depends on the nature of the leather being treated and on the degree of softness and flexibility required in the final product.

Duplex paper See DECORATED PAPER.

Dutch floral paper/Dutch gilt paper See GOLD EMBOSSED PAPER.

Dutch metal A brass with a low proportion of zinc to copper. Also known as *schlagmetal* (German for 'beaten metal'), it is used as a substitute for gold leaf. Different ratios give different colours to the alloy: a high copper content gives a reddish tinge, while a high proportion of zinc produces a greenish shade. Dutch metal tarnishes easily and has to be protected with a layer of varnish or shellac. This, and its poor colour, make it an unsatisfactory alternative to gold. Also, since it can only be applied with a quick-drying oil, it cannot be burnished.

Dye A natural or synthetic colourant capable of impregnating cloth or leather more or less permanently. True dyes should not be confused with pigments or pigment dyes. Since the same or very similar chemicals occur in different natural and synthetic dyes, identifying a dye by its colour alone is difficult; a more accurate guide is obtained by considering the provenance of the cloth and the history of dyes, which has generally seen the replacement of one source with another containing a higher concentration of colourant.

Until around 1900 yellow, red and blue were the three

colours basic to dyeing (see colour plate XVII), and vegetable
dyes were by far the largest group, both in variety and in geographical distribution. The two great dyes—madder for red
and indigo for blue—achieved their position of dominance
not only by virtue of their superior fastness, but also because
they provided strong colours; additionally, they were capable
of dyeing both wool and cotton (and thus silk, flax and many
other of the less common natural fibres; see DYEING). Yellows
and brownish yellows were very fugitive. Although yellows
were available from a very large number of plants, including
nettles and onions, the only one of reasonable fastness in
Europe until the 16th century was weld. Good reds came
from more specialized plants, of which the most important
was madder. The only significant European blue dye was
woad, which contains indigotin, the same colouring agent
that is found, in a higher concentration, in indigo. All other
colours, such as greens and browns, were derived from mixtures of these three colours. Greens were dyed once in blue
and once in yellow; the characteristic bluish green associated
with tapestries is a result of the fading of the yellow. Brownish reds came from dyewoods such as brazilwood; true browns
were more often made by mixing dyewoods with yellow and
madder. Gall nut, a growth from certain oak trees, gave the
only early true black, but was less commonly used than a
mixture of the three primaries. Supplementing the vegetable
dyes were those crushed or squeezed from small living crea-
tures: cochineal, kermes and shellfish purple (which is chemically close to indigo). All three were able to produce good,
strong scarlets and purples.

Dyes, their recipes and their use remained regionally distinctive until migration, international trade and, finally, the
development of empirical expertise in dye chemistry (begun
in earnest in the 18th century) gradually made their use more
homogeneous, at least in the Western world. The first significant change in European colourants came during the 16th
century, when fustic yellow, logwood black and cochineal red
were introduced from the New World, along with more plentiful supplies of brazilwood and indigo. With madder, these
dyes remained important until the end of the 19th century
and provided a richer, more light-fast colour range. Until this
period soluble mordanting dyes were dominant. They were
activated only upon additional treatment with an astringent
or metallic salt (see MORDANT), and altering the mordant

resulted in different shades from the same dye. Soluble transferable (or substantive) natural dyes, with a direct affinity for the fibre, were plentiful but had very poor fastness to light. These dyes included turmeric, saffron and barbary, but probably the most widely known were the lichens, such as orchil, which gave a purple dye for dyeing both wool and silk. Although few in number until $c.$ 1900, of far greater relative importance were the insoluble dyes, which were dissolved chemically before dyeing could begin. Shellfish purple, woad and indigo (similar in colour and each successively replaced by the next) were the principal examples of these so-called vat dyes.

Patterning with dyes is often achieved by resist processes (see RESIST DYEING), but in Europe these have been replaced largely by direct printing (see PRINTED TEXTILES), the result of successive developments between about 1680 and 1840. They include improved methods of treating cotton and cotton mixtures: thickeners for mordants; the use of tin and chrome as mordants (giving far brighter colours, on wool as well as cotton); new methods of printing and spinning; the introduction of chlorine for bleaching (see DISCHARGE PRINTING); the introduction of a 'single' green early in the 19th century; and the discovery of mineral dyes (metals ground to tint solutions, or oxides), which produce much more permanent substantive colours. The main examples of mineral dyes were Prussian blue, iron buff and chrome yellow; Prussian blue was one of the earliest chemical dyes and, like others in this class, was more effective on cotton than on wool.

The emergence of entirely new dyes began with the isolation from $c.$ 1800 of various chemicals, including aniline from indigo (1826), and culminated with Perkin's mauve (1856), regarded as the first product of the modern synthetic dyestuffs industry. During the golden age of synthetic dye chemistry, from $c.$ 1850 to $c.$ 1900, numerous other coal tar or aniline dyes were developed, giving brighter shades than all but a few existing colourants (notably Turkey red). They also provided entirely new colours, especially easy-to-apply secondary and tertiary ones, albeit with poor light- or washfastness. The first synthetics gave violets, magentas and blues and were 'basic' dyes, somewhat like substantive and mineral dyes in that the material to be dyed and the dye itself were treated in the same bath. These were quickly followed by other classes of synthetics, including acid dyes (the first of

which, alkali blue, was introduced in 1862) and soluble azo
dyes containing nitrogen (of which the earliest example is
Bismark brown, introduced in 1862). All were generally like
basic dyes. They were easier to process than natural dyes, but
applicable solely to wool, silk and other protein fibres until
later applied to synthetic fibres. Sulphur dyes, first developed
in 1873, were little used until Vidal black was introduced in
1893. The insoluble azos (the first example of which was a red
dating to 1880) provided direct cotton dyes. These were of
extreme importance for their affinity for cellulose and
included the exact replication of alizarin, the colouring agent
in madder. Natural dyes nevertheless remained the mainstay
of dyeing into the early 20th century and, in the case of
fustic, logwood and cochineal, well beyond. Mordant dyes
continue to be used by wool and craft dyers, and some
natural dyes were also important in other related trades such
as tanning, in which sumac and cochineal have long been
used. The new dyes of the 1880s and 1890s were initially used
on cottons and other cellulosic fibres. The subsequent introduction of new fibres led to disperse dyes (non-ionic, water-
insoluble dyes usually applied from fine aqueous
suspensions), first developed for acetate rayon in the 1920s,
and reactive dyes for acetate in the 1950s.

Synthetic dyes are named according to either their
primary chemical constituent or their means of interacting
with the fibres (and sometimes both); thus direct dyes are a
large, complex group which now includes many important
acid (mainly sodium) dyes for wool. Vat dyes, which set
today's standards for fastness, resulted from the synthesis of
indigo, which was chemically replicated in 1880 and became
commercially available as a synthetic in 1897. Modelled on
natural dyes, most synthetic dyes can be described as insoluble dyes or more permanent soluble transferable colourants;
their interaction with the fibres is the same. The first exceptions were reactive dyes, which obtain a permanent molecular combination between the material and dye (often by
cold-dyeing methods). As early as 1890 dye molecules were
linked to cellulose molecules in cotton by means of an ester
link, but such dyes, which still react with cellulose fibres
under alkaline conditions, were not commercially available
until 1956; with modifications reactive dyes are now available
for all types of fibres.

Dyeing The use of dyestuffs to colour textiles and leather, either entirely or partly. This usually involves immersion in a dye vat, whether of fibres prior to spinning, of yarns prior to weaving or embroidery, or of whole cloths. Resist techniques can be used for partly colouring yarns (see RESIST DYEING) and to create patterns on whole cloths, especially cottons (see PRINTED TEXTILES). Dyeing has been known since the neolithic civilizations of c.7500 BC.

The preparation and application of dyes are complex processes, involving a series of treatments that vary according to the fibre. Wool is the most receptive to dye, followed by silk, and most dyes were readily adapted to both these fibres. Asia and the Mediterranean world became known for the colouring of silk, while the colouring of animal fibres—especially wool—formed the basis of early dyeing techniques in many other areas. Cotton and flax, each respectively more difficult to treat, generally have an affinity for another, separate class of dyes (see FIBRE). The techniques for these developed in the tropical and sub-tropical regions; those for

A mid-18th-century dyer's workshop, depicted in Diderot's Encyclopédie des arts et des métiers, *showing cold and hot methods of silk dyeing. On the left are large, rectangular copper washtubs, and on the right are dye vats, provided with hot running water from the boiler. At the back is a barrel for raising water from the river below.*

Teinturier de Riviere, Attelier et différentes Opérations pour la Teinture des Soies.

cotton are associated with India and Central and South America, those for flax with Egypt.

For most natural dyes and the synthetics developed from them there are two basic aspects of dyeing: immersion and fixing. Most fast-dyeing methods require a chemical agent (see MORDANT) or catalyst to make the cloth receptive to the dye. The mordant may be applied before, during or after the material is placed in the dye-bath, with heat and acids encouraging the dye to pass into or onto the fibre. Since this is a water-based process, it is inevitably reversed by repeated washing. Insoluble dyes, of which INDIGO was the model, are reduced by chemical processes before entering the immersion vat and require oxidation to develop the colour; these give excellent washing fastness. The so-called reactive dyes (since 1956) all form a direct chemical link with the fibre and are therefore very fast; some do so without the aid of heat.

E

Earthenware A low-fired ceramic body that is porous unless covered with glaze. Most clays can be used to produce earthenware (commonly known as 'pottery'), and the main body colours are buff, grey, red and cream. Red earthenware is often called terracotta, particularly when used for flowerpots.

Any ceramic with a maximum firing temperature of about 1050°C is essentially an earthenware. At such temperatures earthenwares are not vitrified and remain porous (see FIRING). The addition of a glaze, however, can render them impervious to liquid. Such glazes are equally low-fired and tend to be lead glazes. Used to create a wide range of goods, including fine tableware and cooking pots, earthenwares were the first ceramic bodies to be produced.

Earthenwares can be formed into almost any shape, as the bodies tend to be very workable. They can be handbuilt, thrown or even moulded. They do not require sophisticated kilns and can even be fired on bonfires, which makes them very economical to produce. Most decorative techniques can be used on earthenware, with the exception of any high-

Earthenware water jars, with applied and unfired painted decoration, Chancay period, Peru, AD 1200–1400.

fired decoration.

Ebonite See VULCANITE.

Ebonizing The staining of timber black so that it resembles ebony. Various close- and fine-grained woods are used, including sycamore and pearwood, and a number of formulae have been employed to achieve the desired effect, one being a strongly alkaline solution of logwood (see STAIN), which was applied hot. When dry, a mildly acetic solution of iron sulphite followed. An alternative was to use a moderately acetic solution of nigrosine (a coal tar dye). Once this had dried, the wood was sanded, then sealed by rubbing into the surface a hot mixture of boiled linseed oil, benzine and japan dryers. Ebonized furniture was popular in the late Georgian period and throughout the Victorian era, especially with Art Nouveau and Arts and Crafts designers.

Ebony The name given to any one of several different woods, characterized as dark brown or green to black in colour, and sometimes marbled or striped. It is usually identified by its place of origin (e.g. Macassar ebony). It is very hard and

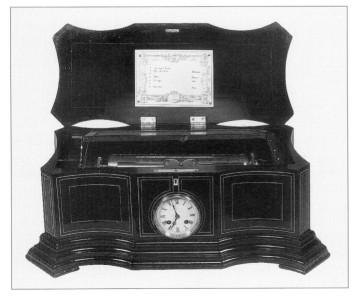

Musical clock in ebonized pearwood case, by Pallard Fils, c.1880.

heavy, with a smooth, fine grain, lustrous and decorative. Most ebony is derived from species of *Diospyros* or *Dalbergia*: Burmese ebony, for example, is from *Diospyros burmanica* and *Dalbergia cultrata*; Ceylon or Indian ebony from *Dios-*

pyros ebenum, *Diospyros tomentosa* and *Diospyros embry-opteris*; East African or Mozambique ebony (also called African blackwood) from *Dalbergia melanoxylon*.

There is considerable variation in colour and quality between the types of ebony. When very stripy or figured it is known by different names, such as arang, blackwood, cala-mander, camagon, khaki, marblewood and persimmon. The logs require special seasoning: they are immersed in water for twelve months after felling, and then the ends are ringed with iron straps to prevent or minimize splitting. Ebony is used for very high-class cabinetmaking, turnery, inlays, mouldings, carving and stringings; in the 17th century it was highly prized for marquetry.

Egg tempera Paint mixed from dry pigment and egg yolk. The paint is thinned with water and applied with small, soft brushes. It dries quickly, and, as it is difficult to blend the brushstrokes, any modelling or shading tends to be carried out with closely hatched brushlines. Large blocks of even colour are therefore hard to achieve, and egg tempera is most suitable for small-scale decoration or ornate detail. Pigments in an egg binder are not as saturated as they are in oil, so the colours are slightly chalky in tone, even after varnishing. Egg tempera is not suitable for covering flexible surfaces such as fabric, as it dries to a brittle film, but it can be used on any rigid support. It is a very stable medium: once dry it is unaf-fected by organic solvents and changes little with time.

In the Middle Ages and early Renaissance, when it was the main painting medium, egg tempera was used almost exclu-sively for altarpieces and other devotional pictures, though it was occasionally also used for the rubrics in manuscript illu-minations, in place of the more usual GLAIR. During the later 19th century, when many traditional techniques were revived, it was sometimes used for the decoration of small items such as boxes, picture frames and musical instruments.

Egyptian alabaster See ONYX MARBLE.

Egyptian faience A vitreous body composed of fritted silica with small amounts of clay and/or alkali. It is glazed with a similar material, coloured turquoise, blue or green by the addition of copper, which may or may not bond interstitially with the grains of the body. Strictly speaking, it is not a glass since it is not homogeneous on a macro-scale. The term 'glassy faience' is often applied when the degree of melting has proceeded to such an extent that the glass phase defines the visual appearance of the material. The term 'unglazed faience' is used to describe a similar body, also produced by the sintering or partial vitrification of silica particles, probably with a fluxing agent and/or colourant added, but without the final glaze layer.

Egyptian faience was made in Egypt from *c.*3000 BC. It seems that a paste of ground quartz or sand was mixed with natron and sintered in an open pan. When soft, it was shaped by hand or in an open mould. It was then heated until the alkali had reacted and fused sufficiently to hold the silica particles firmly together. The final hardness of the material depends on the degree of sintering.

Electroforming The electrolytic deposition of metals on a conducting mould in order to make a metal object. The mould, which is made conductive with graphite or metal powder, is nowadays made of silicon rubber or wax; in the past gutta percha or plaster moulds were used. The plating process is identical to ELECTROPLATING, except that the deposit is much thicker, in order to leave a free-standing object after the mould is removed (generally by dissolution). To create this thick layer the plating process takes much longer than in normal electroplating.

Electroplating The coating of a workpiece with a thin layer of metal by means of electrolytic deposition. Before electroplating the workpiece is first thoroughly cleaned of oxide layers and degreased. It is then immersed in an electrolytic bath

Electroplated tea service designed by Christopher Dresser and made from silver-plated nickel silver by James Dixon & Sons, c.1880. The handles are of ebony.

containing a solution of the salt of the metal being applied. The workpiece will be made cathodic (negatively charged) in this bath; the anode (positively charged), usually at the other end of the bath, may be made of the same metal or of an unaffected conductor such as stainless steel. A low-voltage current is passed through the solution, electrolysing and plating the workpiece with the desired metal.

The thickness of the plating depends on the plating time but also on the current and the solution. Usually the article to be electroplated is a metal, but non-conductive surfaces such as plastics or leather can also be made conductive with graphite or metal powder. The most popular metal platings are gold, silver, chromium, nickel, copper, rhodium and zinc. A relatively recent development is the plating of alloys such as brass, sterling silver and gold.

The origins of electroplating are closely linked to the discovery and development of electricity. It is generally accepted that the Italian scientist G. B. Beccaria was the first to deposit metals by electrolysis successfully, in 1772. He was followed by Luigi Brugnatelli, who made the first decorative plating by covering a silver coin with a gold plating in 1801. In the following decades improvements were made to the supply of electricity as well as to the plating solutions, mostly by British scientists such as Humphry Davy, Michael Faraday and J. F. Daniell. It was only in the 1840s, however, that the British businessmen and cousins George Richards and Henry Elkington filed their first patent for electrogilding. This was followed later by other patents on plating using cyanides. Electroplating rapidly replaced the dangerous firegilding process and within a decade had also wiped out the fused or Sheffield plate industry by virtue of its safety and cheapness.

Electrum A native alloy of gold and silver, containing between 25% and 40% silver, rendering it a pale yellowish white colour. The first coins stamped in Asia Minor in the 7th century BC were made of electrum. The name is also sometimes used for amber.

Elephant ivory A material produced as the incisor teeth or tusks of both the African and the Asiatic elephant. Ivory from the African elephant is normally of better quality (that is, denser and harder) than that from the Asian: the tusks are also generally larger, averaging 23 kg in weight and measuring up to 2 m in length, as against an average 15.5 kg and

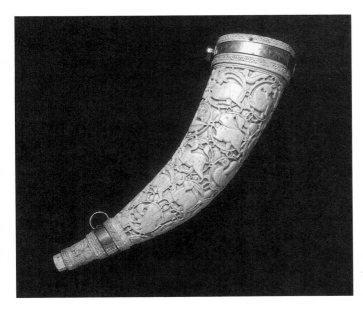

Ivory hunting horn carved from the whole tusk, Italy, late 11th century or early 12th.

1.5 m for the Asian. Tusks weighing more than 65 kg and measuring 3 m in length were relatively common in the past, and one pair of tusks is said to have weighed 208 kg and to have been 8 m long. The tusks are slightly oval in section and are conically hollow for between a third and a half of their length from the jaw (the proximal end). The elephant tusk grows in layers outwards from the central core, so that it becomes thicker as well as longer with age. It does not have the enamel layer found on most other mammalian teeth but does have a cementum layer. This is referred to by carvers and dealers as the 'bark' and is usually removed during carving but may sometimes be retained as a decorative feature.

A distinguishing feature of elephant ivory is the appearance on the end grain or transverse section of two sets of lines, called the lines of Owen and the lines of Retsius. The lines of Owen are formed by the deposition of successive growth layers, similar to those found on wood. If a tusk is cut longitudinally, these lines will be seen generally to reflect the shape of the tusk, growing finer and closer together as they approach the tip and towards the centre of the tusk and wider apart towards the outside. The lines of Retsius are fine lines that intersect spirally to form roughly diamond- or lozenge-shaped patterns, producing the engine-turned effect which helps to distinguish elephant ivory from most other types.

Elm A reddish brown, fairly hard and heavy wood from species of *Ulmus* found in Europe and North America. It is strong, tough and very difficult to split, with good shock-absorption, and it has been used for constructional work (early water mains were made from elm trunks), wheel hubs, furniture and coffins. It has a striking grain pattern, seen in plain sawn timber, but the twisted and interlocking nature of the grain makes it difficult to work. The burrs provide valuable veneers.

Embossing See REPOUSSÉ WORK.

Embroidered lace A category of lace worked on cloth or net. Of those types of embroidered lace worked on cloth, the simplest is cutwork, in which holes are cut and bound by stitches; bars are sometimes incorporated. Cutwork is also known as *broderie anglaise*; Madeira work is also a form of cutwork, often embellished with additional stitches on the cloth itself.

Drawn threadwork and pulled threadwork are two very similar types of embroidered lace: both involve binding groups of threads to create the holes, but in drawn work some are removed and in pulled work they are simply pulled together. Meshes of several kinds can be created in this way

Detail of drawn threadwork cover, linen, Italy or Spain, 17th century. It is made by assembling strips originally made as borders of bed curtains. The patterns are formed from a solid cloth by removing some threads and binding others; the edging is bobbin lace, made in imitation of the Italian needle lace punto in aria.

and threadwork of both types can be found combined, sometimes with the addition of cutwork and/or embellishing stitches. In the late 17th century and during the 18th, the finest, Dresden work, was made with very fine linen and combined varied meshes over the entire surface. More typical in the 19th century was the use of fine cotton, fewer meshes and more embellishing stitches; the best-known example of this widespread style was Ayrshire work. Like cutworks such as *broderie anglaise*, this is a form of whitework, which leaves a good amount of plain cloth and is worked in white on white.

Needlerun or darned laces have threads worked in a zigzag or back and forth over and under an openwork ground to fill in the pattern area. They include filet (or lacis), produced on a hand-knotted square mesh; burato, on a hand-woven square mesh; and others that incorporate a range of off-loom constructions. Other laces in this third group are sometimes referred to as 'imitation' laces and are produced on threads pinned or otherwise held in position, normally radially over a round card. They include Spanish wheel lace, sun lace, Tenerife lace and nandutti, from Paraguay. Nets with plain meshes in hexagonal or other shapes were embroidered in the 19th century after the introduction of machine-made nets such as bobbinet; they formed the basis for new styles of needlerun lace (such as Carrickmacross and Limerick), often using several thicknesses of thread, as well as for styles of tambour work lace, named after their main centres of production (for example, Limerick, Brussels and Coggeshall).

Appliqué laces use outline stitches to connect an upper layer of net or muslin to the net below; the upper surplus is then cut away. Both net and muslin were used in Belgium and the muslin variety was also made in Carrickmacross, where the same method, with needle-made connecting bars in place of the lower net, was known as Carrickmacross guipure. Bobbin lace and needle lace sprays were also applied to hand-made net grounds from *c.*1800 until *c.*1840, which were superseded by bobbinet; some Brussels and Honiton bobbin laces were made in this way (see LACE).

Embroidery The use of a needle and thread to embellish cloth or leather. The practice developed from sewing but is distinguished from it in techniques such as PATCHWORK, QUILTING and SMOCKING by the decorative element it introduces into the finished article. Originally said to have arisen in and spread from the Near or Far East, it is now thought to have evolved independently in most early cultures; by definition allied to the development of needles, in Europe its use can be dated to the early Bronze Age (1500–500 BC) in Denmark and the Iron Age (c.500–100 BC) elsewhere. Embroidery can be carried out with any fibre and can incorporate a wide range of other materials through LAID AND COUCHED WORK; it is always an entirely separate process from the weaving of the ground cloth itself.

From the medieval period, if not earlier, the four basic types of embroidery techniques were fully developed in Europe and the Far East. These are the use of laid and couched work, RAISED WORK, flat running and filling stitches, and counted threadwork. The first two use two elements (thread plus thread or another material) and place the majority of the work on the surface of the cloth; the last two employ a single thread worked more or less equally over both sides of the cloth. The last, counted threadwork, gave rise to a wide range of effects that can be divided into two: those that cover whole areas of the ground cloth, known by various terms around the world and including CANVASWORK in Europe, and those that result in counted openwork, or pulled and drawn threadwork. Counted openwork, especially drawn threadwork, carried out on linen, reveals most clearly the technical meeting point of sewing, embroidery, KNOTTING, and EMBROIDERED LACE; out of the latter came RETICELLA and NEEDLE LACE. This breadth of development is associated

Detail of a whitework cushion cover, probably Germany or Italy, 17th century. It is worked mainly in buttonhole stitch (around the pierced 'dots'), smooth satin stitch and French knots.

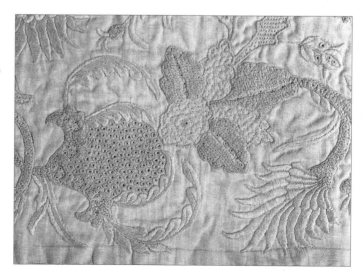

with medieval and early Renaissance Central Europe, especially Germany, Switzerland and northern Italy, although openwork itself was a universally used technique. Counted openwork made use of the distortion (pulled) or removal (drawn) of warp and/or weft threads, with the stitches employed to secure these modifications quickly becoming decorative elements in their own right; the most important of these was buttonhole stitch, a looped stitch forming a firm edge when worked closely together through the cloth, or creating a fixed knot when worked as a detached stitch.

Before embroidery could begin, the ground cloth was stretched on a frame, or tent, composed of four pieces of wood with a series of holes in the horizontal pieces, with pegs fixing them together at right angles in the appropriate dimensions and a cross-brace; the cloth was fixed to these by means of string. The frame provided the tension necessary to produce smooth embroidery. Supported on trestles in professional workshops, frames could accommodate very large items such

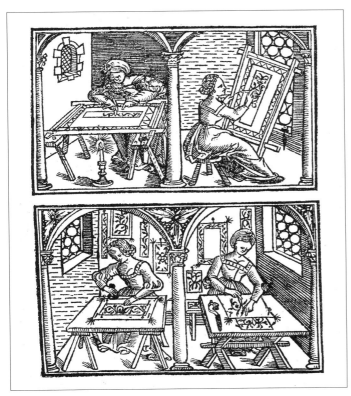

A block-printed illustration from Germany, mid-16th century, showing amateur embroiderers in the various stages of piercing, pouncing, redrawing and embroidering on a small tent or frame.

as altar frontals; only amateurs used small frames held on the knee.

For patterns embroidery relied on either a SAMPLER, a copy book, or a draughtsman, painter or professional embroiderer, who marked out the design ready for work. Copy books were available from the 1520s, first in Germany, then in Italy, France and England; the earliest examples had patterns mainly intended for cutwork or embroidered laces, with true embroidery patterns becoming more important in the 17th century. Prints, herbals and emblem books also provided a source of patterns. The technique for transferring designs remains the same today: a tracing (or a page from a copy book) is pricked with closely set holes, aligned with the cloth and 'pounced' by rubbing through finely ground charcoal or another dark substance (for light-coloured grounds) or French chalk (for dark grounds or, in some cases, white satin), which are then joined together using ink or watercolour. Pattern books and designs were reprinted over long periods; late 16th-century examples are known to have been used throughout the 17th century and a number have been traced in 19th-century English and American embroideries. Late 17th-century patterns were often used in the 18th century, so the style of drawing and, particularly, the costume, cannot be used to date such pieces.

Amateur work can often be distinguished from professional work by two features: the techniques used and the size of the final piece. Canvaswork and patchwork were done by amateurs. Professional embroiderers were responsible for heraldic, ceremonial and armorial trappings and liveries and therefore for APPLIQUÉ and BULLION WORK. Professionals also provided 'kits' and completed amateur work, such as STUMPWORK boxes and frames, or embroidery worked with couched knotting. Large pieces were the province of professional workshops; using appliqué and flat stitches, smaller elements made by amateurs were also assembled by professionals. In the 19th and 20th centuries in particular, amateur work often used a variety of stitches, a feature seldom found in professional work. The stitches favoured by amateurs are flat running and filling stitches, including variations of crossstitch, buttonhole and satin stitch, as well as counted thread work.

Embroidery was highly valued and was often the most costly element of furniture or clothing; crewel hangings of the later 17th century, for example, are recorded as costing ten times the amount charged for a portrait by the painter Sir Peter Lely.

Embroidery machine A generic term describing a number of devices based on mechanizing chain or running stitches, usually accomplished by moving the taut cloth, rather than the embroidering implement. Successful attempts to introduce embroidery machines began at the beginning of the 19th century, during the fashion for embroidered lace, and such machines were widely used from *c.*1850 for muslin appliqué. Many share features in common with the sewing machine, particularly the Cornely, an 1870s' improvement on an 1863 patent (the Bonnaz); both the Cornely and the Bonnaz were foot-powered and used a hooked needle to draw thread from below the cloth, in the manner of tambour work. A second group of machines is characterized by its running stitches and banks of double-eyed needles controlled by a pantograph: it includes the single-thread hand-machine, developed in Switzerland in 1828, and the auxiliary-powered Schiffli machine, which uses two sets of threads to create a lock stitch and which had superseded the hand-machine by the 1880s. By the 1860s the hand-machine made use of borers to create holes, a feature adopted by the Schiffli, which by *c.*1895 was controlled by a JACQUARD. These machines could effectively imitate several types of lace, whereas the single-head Cornely-type machines and the later lock-stitch Multihead (with several heads, each with five needles) had the advantage of being able to embroider shaped pieces.

All machine-embroidered laces can usually be identified by the regularity of stitch or the threads on the reverse, connecting one area of embroidery to another in identical fashion from repeat to repeat.

Emerald A green gemstone composed of beryllium aluminium silicate, with a hardness on the Mohs scale of 7.5. The colour is produced by the presence of chromium, vanadium and iron. Emerald occurs within veins running through limestones, shales and mica schists. Flawless emeralds are extremely rare and many specimens contain fractures and mineral inclusions which can indicate the source of the stone; these flaws are known as the emerald's *jardin*. Emeralds were mined and used in ancient Egypt; this source and another in Austria were used by the Romans and during the Middle Ages. They were also used in ancient India and, although the source of the stones is not known, an ancient Sanskrit text suggests they may have been obtained from Egypt. Despite the fact that various indigenous green gemstones were used in Indian jewellery, emeralds were not found there until 1943. A source of high-quality emeralds was used by the Indians in Colombia, who traded the stone for gold from neighbouring regions. The Spanish brought large quantities of these emeralds to Europe following the conquest of Latin America. From the 16th century the Portuguese led a number of expeditions to Brazil to locate a legendary source of emeralds, but these yielded only other types of green stones, such as tourmaline; in 1964, however, a source of high-quality emerald was found in Brazil. In many cultures emeralds have been thought to possess talismanic and curative properties, effective against many diseases from poor eyesight to dysentery; they were also thought to protect against epilepsy and evil spirits.

Emeralds have been made into beads or cut as cabochons. Faceted emeralds are cut, using diamond dust, in a style known as a trap cut or emerald cut, in which a large, elongated octagonal face is surrounded by narrow facets running parallel to the sides (see FACETING).

Because many emeralds contain fractures, it is a common practice to conceal these by filling the voids with a fine oil, such as cedar oil. This treatment can be difficult to detect until a stone is cleaned or heated, resulting in the removal of the oil and a consequent change in the appearance of the emerald. Emerald simulants, called soude emeralds, are made by sandwiching a green material, such as dyed gelatine or a copper compound, between layers of transparent quartz. The colour of pale natural emerald has been enhanced by applying green paint or coloured metal foil to the back of the stone. From the mid-19th century synthetic emeralds have been made by growing crystals from a solution composed of the natural mineral constituents. Synthetic emeralds can contain inclusions which are similar to those found in natural stones, complicating detection, although they can be identified by their specific gravity, which is lower than that of true emerald.

Emulsion A type of paint in which the pigment and medium are suspended as tiny droplets in another liquid. Once the paint is brushed onto the support, the main liquid phase evaporates and the droplets of paint coalesce to dry as a continuous film. Household emulsion paints are based on acrylics and a variety of other synthetic polymers; artists' emulsion paints include acrylics, alkyds and PVA colours.

Until the 20th century emulsion paints were rarely used, although some artists, particularly in the 19th century, experimented with oil/egg, oil/wax and oil/resin emulsions to produce paints with different textures and degrees of gloss. These were mostly used on easel paintings, but experimental mixtures have been found on wall paintings and furniture.

Enamel A vitreous substance normally applied as a dried frit to a metallic surface such as copper, silver or gold and fused to the metal. The term is also used to describe a material of similar composition employed to decorate ceramics and glass (see ENAMEL COLOURS). It is essential that the enamel fuses to its metallic substrate. Most early enamels failed in this respect. A true enamel must be so formulated as to have a coefficient of contraction roughly equivalent to that of the metallic substrate. Also, to ensure fusion, its melting-point must be approximate to, but lower than, that of its backing. For these reasons most enamels are a lead-soda or lead-potash glass, with or without the addition of colourants and

The enameller Eugène Feuillâtre at his furnace, c.1900. An enamelled vase can be seen at the mouth of the furnace.

opacifiers. On very thin or extensive areas of metalwork, the contraction of the enamel on cooling may be sufficient to cause the metal to warp. To counteract this, the reverse of the object may also be enamelled, a process known as 'counter-enamelling' or simply 'enamel backing'.

Enamels of different composition fuse at different temperatures, opaque enamel usually requiring a lower temperature ($c.300°C$) and transparent and translucent enamels a higher one ($c.850°C$). Hence, they are sometime categorized as *petit feu* and *grand feu* colours. The former scratch easily while the latter are harder and more durable, but all enamels are vulnerable to shock and flexing. The different firing temperatures mean that an object may require as many as a dozen firings. In complicated items any solder has to be protected with plaster of Paris during the firing. All these factors, added to the fact that enamels develop their colours only on firing, make enamelling an exacting process.

Before enamelling the metal is prepared by annealing and immersion in acid to remove any grease or oxides. The frit is ground to a powder, washed and dried, then mixed into a paste with water or, in the case of painted enamel, with oil. It is applied to the metal surface and then fired at a low temperature in an enamelling oven. Where necessary, the surface is polished with fine abrasives when the enamel has cooled.

Translucent enamelling involves the firing of layers of transparent enamel, the fusibility of each carefully matched, onto a metal guilloche surface engraved by hand- or engine-turning. There may be as many as five or six layers of enamel, each fired separately. Sometimes painted decoration, gold leaf or gold foil stamped into tiny stars or rosettes (*paillons*) are incorporated into the design. These are applied to an already fired enamel surface and sealed with a further layer of enamel. The completed enamel is carefully polished with a wooden wheel and fine abrasives and then finished with a buff. The characteristic milky quality of some of Fabergé's translucent enamels was obtained by mixing four to six parts of translucent enamel to one part of opaque enamel, to produce a semi-opaque or opalescent effect.

Types There are several main types of enamel, classified by the manner in which the enamel is attached to the metal (see colour plate v). Usually enamel is applied in such a way as to form a level surface with the surrounding metal, by providing a sunken area into which the frit can be fused.

In the *cloisonné* technique the enamel is placed in compartments (in French, *cloisons*) formed by a network of metal bands soldered onto the surface of the metal object, which is usually copper or gold. The tops of the metal bands remain exposed, allowing the different coloured enamels in the cells to be distinguished. In filigree enamelling, thin wires enclose the enamel in the same manner as the strips of metal. *Cloisonné* is one of the most ancient enamelling processes and probably developed out of the Mycenean and Greek practice of placing precious stones in metal cells with upturned edges. It was much used by Celtic and Byzantine enamellers and was transmitted to China in the 14th century.

In *champlevé*, also known as *en taille d'épargne*, the recesses for the frit are provided for in the original casting of the metal, or cut out with scorpers. They are often left rough to aid grip. The metal may be gold but is more often bronze or copper, sometimes firegilded. It may be engraved or further decorated with *cloisonné* enamel. *Champlevé* (the term derives from the French for 'raised field') was used by Roman, Celtic and medieval enamellers, especially in the Mosan work of the 12th century and Limoges work of the 12th–14th centuries. Surrey enamel, which is usually in black and white, is a form of *champlevé* that is applied to brass objects cast with recesses in low relief. It was made in England in the second half of the 17th century and is found on heavy items such as horse harnesses, andirons and candlesticks.

With *basse taille* (from the French for 'shallow cut') the metal, usually silver or gold, is decorated by chasing or engraving before application of a translucent enamel. The enamel appears lighter over the shallow cutting and darker over the deeper areas, resulting in a rich tonal quality. A refinement of the *champlevé* technique, *basse taille* was first perfected in the Paris enamels of the early 14th century. An almost identical process, *lavoro di basso rilievo*, was developed independently in Italy. A magnificent example of *basse taille* is the Royal Gold Cup (British Museum, London), made in Paris around 1380. Here the different shades of enamel are not divided by metal cloisons; instead the powders were mixed with gum tragacanth and each colour was allowed to dry before the next was placed beside it. The use of translucent enamel over a guilloche background is a form of *basse taille*.

The Royal Gold Cup, in basse taille *enamel, France, c.1380.*

Plique à jour (French, 'against the light') is an exception-ally fragile type, in which the enamel is used without a metal backing, and is held only at the edges in a metal framework. The framework is produced by piercing through a metal sheet, which is then given a temporary backing of mica, or some similar material, to which the enamel will not adhere. A frit, formulated to produce a translucent enamel, is placed in the compartments, fused and cooled. The temporary backing is then removed, thus allowing light to shine through the coloured enamels and producing an effect similar to that of a stained-glass window. *Plique à jour* was known in the Middle Ages and was used in the late 19th century, especially by

René Lalique.

In the *en résille sur verre* technique enamel frit is packed into gold-lined incisions that have been engraved into blue or green glass (the French term means 'in grooves on glass'). It is a difficult technique, only adopted during the second quarter of the 17th century in France, where it was mainly used to decorate miniature cases.

In *en ronde bosse* (French for 'in rounded relief'), opaque enamels are applied to a slightly roughened surface to decorate figures or decorative devices formed in the round. The process is also sometimes called encrusted enamel. It was used in Paris at the beginning of the 15th century on large reliquaries, and probably also in England. The Dunstable Swan Brooch (British Museum, London) is a fine example.

Enamels also can be painted on a metal foundation to produce a picture. The metal is generally copper and slightly domed. The colours, metallic oxides mixed with a glassy frit, are suspended in an oily medium for ease of application with a brush. The medium burns out during firing. The object is first covered with a layer of white opaque enamel and fired. The design is then applied and fired in a low-temperature muffle kiln (*c.*500–700°C). Normally different firings at successively lower temperatures are required to fuse different colours and prevent them from running into one another. The process was invented in Limoges, France, in the late 15th century. Many Limoges enamels are decorated in grisaille, created by painting successive layers of white enamel onto a black ground. Thin layers of gold or silver foil can be inserted between the coats of translucent enamel to provide a warm or cold reflective tonality. In some examples the white enamel is scratched through to the black ground. Another form of painted enamel employed transfers and was first used on the Battersea enamels made in London in the 1750s. A copper-plate engraving was transferred to a white enamelled surface and then painted in translucent enamels.

Saint Mary Magdalene, *painted enamel on copper plaque by Noel Laudin the Elder, 17th century.*

In China a variation known as 'Canton enamel' was practised from the early 18th century. The colours, which include a rose pink derived from gold, are painted onto an opaque, generally white ground. The effect is close to that of *famille rose* decoration on ceramics and was often created in the same factories.

Enamel colours Finely powdered glass (FRIT), coloured with metallic oxides and used for the decoration of glass and ceramics. They are fired at a low temperature and fuse with the glass surface or the ceramic glaze.

For application on glass, the colours are mixed in an oily medium with a flux, which lowers the firing-point to below that of the glass. The resulting thick paste is applied with a brush. The glass is then reheated gradually, picked up on a pontil and fired in a muffle kiln at 700–900°C. This has to be done with great care so as not to overheat the glass. The colours develop in the kiln and are not easy to control. They cannot be blended in the manner of oil paint and several firings may be required to fix the different colours.

The decoration of glass with vitreous enamel colours is an ancient technique, known in Roman times. During the 12th–15th centuries opaque enamelling was used with gilding to decorate Islamic glass in Egypt and Syria. Examples of Venetian enamelling on clear coloured and opaque white glass are known from the late 15th century. From the 16th century enamelling on glass was practised elsewhere in Europe, especially in Germany, where dense bright colours often covered almost the entire glass surface. SCHWARZLOT enamelling was introduced by Johann Schaper. About 1810 the use of transparent enamel, introduced by Samuel Mohn, superseded that of opaque enamel. So-called 'thin' or 'wash' enamel was introduced to England from Germany and the Low Countries. It was especially suited for use on English lead glass and was applied within outlines etched in the glass. This was later superseded by 'dense' enamel. The leading 18th-century enamellers were William and Mary Beilby and Michael Edkins. Enamelling on glass was also practised in China during the 18th century.

Glass jar with lid, painted in enamel, designed by Václav Špála for Artěl, Czechoslovakia, 1921.

In ceramics, enamel takes the form of a lead-based glaze that is applied over a hard, pre-fired glaze. Enamelling is also sometimes called overglaze decoration and is usually applied to porcelain glazes, which are very high-fired, though it can also be used on other glazes. As enamels melt at a low temperature, a wider range of colours is possible than with underglaze paint, which must be able to withstand very high temperatures.

Enamels were first used on ceramics in China in the late 11th century AD. In European ceramics enamel decoration was developed with the advent of porcelain in the 18th century, although they had been applied earlier to imported Chinese and Japanese ceramics in a method known as 'clob-

*Porcelain teapot with
overglaze enamel
decoration, China, Qing
period, 1736–95.*

bering'. The enamel palettes of China and Japan greatly
influenced European porcelains of the 18th and 19th centuries. In China a palette based on transparent green enamels
and called *famille verte* was developed in the 17th century. In
the 18th century a new palette based on pink was created,
which in the West is called *famille rose*. Among Japanese
porcelains, kakiemon ware was very popular in Europe. It
was characterized by red, green, blue, yellow and black
enamel decoration on a translucent, milky white porcelain
ground. The IMARI style of enamel decoration was also
popular in Europe. Enamels can be applied directly to the
BISCUIT, but this method is rare.

Enamel painting See ENAMEL COLOURS.

Enamelled leather Vegetable-tanned cattle hide which has
been treated on the grain side with a PATENT LEATHER type of
finish. Enamelled leathers were often embossed and were in
general more flexible than patent or japanned leathers. They
were made throughout the 19th century and into the early
20th, and were used for the hoods of carriages and early motor
cars and for Gladstone-type bags and instrument cases.

Encaustic A word derived from the Greek for 'burnt in'; it
refers to three unrelated techniques. In painting it describes
the use of coloured wax on a wide range of materials. The
molten wax, mixed with dry pigments, is painted onto a
surface and then heated to 'burn in' the colours. In ceramics
the term refers to the technique patented by Josiah Wedgwood in 1769 for the decoration of basalt and jasper ware in

Encaustic tiles in the chapter house, Westminster Abbey, London, mid-13th century.

emulation of Greek red figure pottery. The pigment was composed of enamel and slip, with a small addition of Cherokee clay from North Carolina. In tiles, encaustic describes a type of inlay widely used in France and England from the early 13th century. A tile in red clay was stamped with a design, the filled with white clay or slip, dipped in lead glaze and fired. The technique was revived on a large scale in the 19th century.

Encrusted enamel See ENAMEL.

End grain The end section of a piece of timber where the tubular structure of wood can be most clearly seen. It often presents difficulty in working, and tools must be very sharp and finely set to achieve a good finish. The end grain of certain very dense species, such as boxwood, can be used for special purposes, such as print block making.

Engine turning Mechanical incised decoration of a ceramic or metal surface using a LATHE. When created with a guide, called a rosette, engine-turned decoration is often referred to

Covered milk jug, red stoneware with engine-turned decoration, by Wedgwood, Brick House site, Burslem, c.1764–9.

as ROSE ENGINE TURNING. The turning of ceramics takes place when the vessels have dried to a leather-hard state, before firing. The technique was employed by Josiah Wedgwood in the 18th century on his new unglazed stoneware bodies, such as basalt ware and jasper ware. These bodies could be cut like glass or stone, and thus engine-turned decoration was very useful for imitating the decoration of other materials on ceramics. The resulting designs are in relief and tend to be geometric.

English porcelain See BONE CHINA.

Engobe A cross between a SLIP and a very stiff GLAZE. The term is sometimes used, more loosely, to refer to a slip that is intended to disguise an inferior clay body.

Engraving The process of cutting or carving lines in a surface, using a GRAVER, in order to produce a decorative design. The first gravers were made from copper, bronze or iron and were used to engrave relatively soft materials such as wood, shell, bone, ivory or stone. Engraving on metal

An engraved silver panel, designed by Eric Gill and made by G. T. Friend to demonstrate lettering and numerals for the 'benefit of the Silversmiths' craft', 1934.

became practicable only with the introduction of steel gravers in the 1st millennium BC. Bright-cut engraving, which was introduced around 1770 by silversmiths in London, involves cutting facets in a metal surface to create a sparkling effect. This was done by tilting the graver, which enabled the workman to cut with the polished side of the tool, producing a much broader cut that resembled the facet of a jewel. Engraving is now often done mechanically, using very fine high-speed rotary tools or a very sharp diamond point to score the lines in the surface of the metal. For the use of engraving in printmaking, see INTAGLIO PRINTING.

See also GLASS ENGRAVING.

En résille sur verre See ENAMEL.

En ronde bosse See ENAMEL.

En taille d'épargne See ENAMEL.

EPBM Electroplated BRITANNIA METAL.

Ephemera A term covering the great variety of decorative items executed on paper and intended for temporary use. Greetings cards and children's games are two categories of ephemera which have been produced with the whole range of printing, drawing, painting and three-dimensional processes. Also included are advertising posters which could be made both large and colourful following the invention of silkscreen printing in the early 20th century, while items printed by photochemical processes such as colour lithography have become increasingly available.

EPNS Electroplated NICKEL SILVER.

Epoxy resin Synthetic thermoset plastic materials, with high resistance to heat and chemicals. They are used as protective coatings, as very strong adhesives (such as Araldite), and with glass fibre to make fibreglass (see GLASS FIBRE REINFORCED PLASTICS). Formed from reacting bisphenol A and epichlorohydrin, epoxy resins were first developed in Switzerland in the 1930s by Pierre Castan and others, and became commercially viable in 1939. Initially, their high production costs compared with polyesters limited their use until production methods were improved.

Etching The creation of a design on a metal or glass surface by means of acid and a resist. Etching was known in the 13th century but became widely used only in the 15th, when it was a popular means of decorating armour. The surface of the object or printing plate is covered with an acid-resistant coating such as wax, pitch or bitumen, which is then partially removed to reveal the ground. When immersed in acid, the exposed ground will be partially etched, thus creating the design. In armour the design was sometimes painted in reverse, in wax, and then etched; details were added by scraping the wax.

A deeply cut, acid-etched design on a jar by Daum, 1920s.

The etching of glass only became widespread in the mid-19th century, following the discovery of hyrofluoric acid in 1771. Wax or varnish is used as a resist, and the acid is usually mixed with potassium fluoride and water. The glass will have a frosted, pitted or deeply carved surface, depending on the strength of the acid and length of treatment. Acid etching can also be used to cut through a layer of glass to expose a different-coloured layer underneath, and even in the creation of CAMEO GLASS.

For the use of etching in printmaking, see INTAGLIO PRINTING.

Etching embroidery/etching work See PRINTWORK.

Faceting The process of cutting flat planes into a gemstone to enhance colour and develop brilliance, properties related to the reflection and refraction of light. Faceting developed in Europe from the Middle Ages; the first gemcutters', or lapidaries', guild was formed in Paris in 1290. Because of the rarity and value of gemstones, the earliest styles of faceting involved polishing the natural crystal faces, thereby reducing the amount of material removed, and examples of such stones, called points, can be seen in ancient Indian and early medieval European jewellery. It was later realized that cutting through the point to produce a flat surface, termed a table, allowed more light to enter the stone. The light is then reflected off the inside surface of the back, or pavilion, and returns to the viewer's eye through the front, creating the brilliance of a gemstone. Nonetheless, early table-cut stones, often placed in closed-back settings, had a dark appearance.

Styles of gemstone faceting: (a) table cut (side view), in which the upper point of an octahedral stone, such as a diamond, has been cut off to allow more light to be reflected back to the eye (in this instance, the point of the pavilion, or back of the stone, has also been cut flat, to enhance the reflectance of light); (b) rose cut (top view), designed to enhance brilliance; (c) side view of the rose cut in figure b; (d) trap or step cut, back view; (e) trap or step cut, front view; this style is typically used with emeralds.

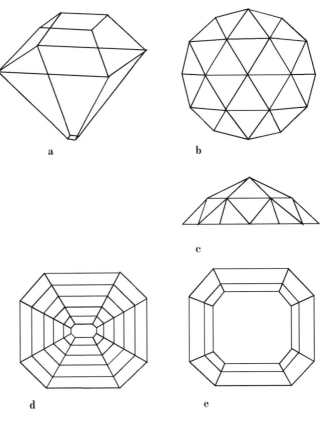

The rose cut, developed in the early 17th century, consisting of a flat back and domed upper surface, cut with triangular facets, produced a more sparkling effect. The rose cut was used for diamonds and also for small garnets, set in clusters, a popular 19th-century style. The trap cut, in which a large, often rectangular, table is flanked by narrow rectangular facets and the pavilion is also faceted, is designed to enhance the colour of stones such as the emerald and the dichroic ruby. The brilliant cut, which is still widely used, particularly for diamonds, was developed in the late 17th century by the Venetian lapidary Vincenzio Peruzzi. It maximizes the brilliance and fire, the splitting of light into the colours of the spectrum, while minimizing the amount of material removed. In the standard brilliant cut an octagonal table is surrounded by 33 facets on the top, or crown, of the stone; the pavilion is cut with 25 facets. The precise angles for diamond used in the modern brilliant were established by Marcel Tolkowsky in 1914; optimal angles of the cutting of other stones have also been calculated.

Before beginning the faceting process the lapidary must examine the stone for flaws and consider its optical properties and the lines along which it can be split. The angles for

Stages in the production of a modern brilliant-cut diamond.
(a) An octahedral crystal; in this state the stone would appear dark grey, as little light would be reflected back to the viewer's eye.
(b) The crystal is sawn above the mid-point to form the table; this style of cut, which somewhat enhanced the fire and brilliance of the diamond, was developed from the mid-15th century.
(c) The stone is shaped into a truncated double cone by bruting, a process that involves forcing one diamond against another.
(d) Top view; at this stage in the faceting and polishing process, carried out by grinding with diamond powder, the table has become octagonal by the introduction of triangular facets around its edge, forming what is termed the bezel; the principal facets of the pavilion, or bottom of the stone, have also been formed.
(e) Top view: a further 24 facets are ground onto the bezel.
(f) Bottom view: the tip of the pavilion is ground flat to reflect more light back to the eye; radiating outward from this are eight five-sided facets and above these are 16 triangular facets, which correspond to those on the edge of the bezel.
(g) Side view of figure d.
(h) Side view of figure e.
(i) Side view of the completed brilliant cut, which has a total of 58 facets, resulting in a loss of 50–60% of the original material, but allowing the optimum fire and brilliance to be achieved.

cutting are marked on the stone, and are designed to retain as much weight as possible while developing the stone's optical qualities. Some stones, such as diamond, can be cleaved, or split along the line of crystal faces by first cutting a small groove, using a piece of tool diamond held in a handle, and placing a blade along the groove. If the groove is correctly aligned when the back of the blade is struck, the stone should split cleanly into two pieces. This permits several faceted stones to be produced from one. Stones are secured for cutting on a handle, termed a dopping stick, using a wax to prevent them from slipping, which would result in misaligned faces. The mounted stone is held in a jig against a rotating metal disc, called a scaife, which is charged with abrasive and oil, as a lubricant. The abrasive is made from a mineral at least as hard as the stone being worked and becomes embedded into the surface of the scaife. Once the facets on the crown have been cut, the stone is released from the dopping stick, inverted and remounted to allow the pavilion facets to be worked. Early faceting machines were treadle-driven. Modern electrically powered equipment incorporates a number of positioning and measuring devices to aid the lapidary in achieving the correct angle of cutting.

Polishing, the final stage of faceting, removes fine scratches introduced by the use of abrasives. Polishing compounds, such as jeweller's rouge (see HAEMATITE), are applied to rotating wheels or laps of wood, leather or, today, soft metals or plastic, to produce a high sheen.

For the faceting of glass, see CUT GLASS.

Façon de Venise Soda glass in the style of Venetian CRISTALLO but produced elsewhere in Europe. It was made from the mid-16th century to the end of the 17th, often by itinerant Venetian craftsmen, and decorated with filigree and elaborate embellishments.

Faience The French term for tin-glazed earthenware. It is also used, loosely, for EGYPTIAN FAIENCE, for glazed TERRACOTTA and for ceramic slabs used as cladding.

False damascening. See DAMASCENING.

Famille rose, famille verte See ENAMEL COLOURS.

Fan A broad, flat device which, when waved gently, creates a cooling draught of air. Hand-held fans are made in two forms: there is the folding fan popular in the West and the single-leaf fan or hand screen of the East. The folding fan was a fashion accessory throughout the 17th, 18th and 19th centuries, and many were made in China for the export market, while the hand screen was in use in China as early as the 6th century.

Folding fans consist of a semicircular leaf which is creased and folded like a concertina and supported on ribs. These are attached to sticks gathered together at the base, where they pivot on a metal rivet. When folded, the fan is protected by the guard sticks at each end of the leaf, which also give it rigidity when in use. The leaf or leaves of the fan are usually made of paper, but textile fans, feather fans and those made of a fine vellum known as 'chicken skin' are fairly common. When made of paper, there are usually two paper leaves stuck either side of the ribs to form a mount. The ribs are generally made of wood with sticks of ivory, bone or tortoise-shell.

Decorative techniques for folding fans include painted or printed designs on the mount, cut paper lacework, mica windows and applied materials such as ivory. Nineteenth-century fans often have a Dutch gilt paper edging to the leaves. The 'gold' is made from zinc and a copper alloy. Sticks were ornamented by carving, inlay, gilding, painting and piqué work (gold or silver pins inlaid in the surface). Early sticks made of precious metals were often reused when a mount wore out. A few examples of mid-18th century Euro-

Fan, China, 1770s. It is painted in watercolour on paper and has fragments of mother-of-pearl as highlights, net and mica insertions for windows, and silk appliqué for the costumes. The guards are carved and painted ivory, the sticks are red lacquer with gold; both are also decorated with mother-of-pearl.

pean fans incorporate articulated design elements in the leaf: part of the design can be made to appear or disappear by operating a metal lever which slides a painted panel in and out of view within an aperture in the leaf.

Screen fans consist of a rigid mount and a handle. Solid materials such as jade, ivory or papier mâché, or paper laminated to make a rigid sheet, might be used for the mount, while paper or a textile would be stretched over an oval or circular wood or bamboo frame to make a lightweight screen which did not pleat or fold. Decorating techniques are similar to those used for folding fans, with the addition of oriental lacquer, gold and silver leaf.

Feather An ornamental figure in wood formed at the junction of branches with the trunk or where branches divide (see CROTCH). The term is also used to refer to a plank reduced in thickness towards one edge, and to a loose tongue used to join two pieces of timber by fitting in a groove on the edge of each of them.

Featherwork Decoration with feathers, used alone or attached to a foundation of cloth, netting, basketwork, leather or wood. There are three main types of feather: contour feathers, which form the bird's outer covering, have a stiff shaft and vane, formed by interlocked barbs; semi-plumes, such as ostrich feathers, which have floppy, less cohesive vanes; and down feathers, which have no shaft and have soft barbs in place of a vane. The wide range of colour effects arise from the presence of melanin and carotenoids in the feathers or by optical effects resulting from the reflection or refraction of light on the keratin. Feathers may be stuck, sewn, woven or tied in place; they may also be dyed and curled with steam.

Feldspar An alumino-silicate mineral used in the production of porcelain. Feldspar is one of the products of the decomposition of granite. Its structure is crystalline and it contains sufficient alkalis to be used as a glaze material. Many Chinese porcelains contain feldspar, either as an additive to encourage glass formation or as a natural ingredient in kaolin or china stone deposits. Orthoclase, anorthite and albite are the most common forms of the mineral used in ceramics. Feldspars are added to both ceramic bodies and glazes as a flux. Porcelains with sufficient quantities of feldspar in the recipe are often described as feldspathic.

Feldspathic glaze A glaze containing a high proportion of

FELDSPAR, which is added as a flux. Feldspar is used in high-fired glazes and can encourage crazing, owing to its high alkali content. Many stoneware glazes are feldspathic and have the characteristic of being stiff and filled with minute bubbles. In traditional Chinese ceramics many porcelain glazes are feldspathic.

Felt A material made from wool, hair, fur or some man-made fibres by a combination of heat, moisture and pressure, without adhesives. It can also be made from cotton or other fibres bound together with adhesives. An ancient material evolved from the natural matting qualities of wool and certain hairs, it has had wide application in hatmaking and for floor and table covers, padding, insulation and industrial uses.

Fettling The trimming of a ceramic after forming and before firing, sometimes also known as 'turning'. After a ceramic is formed, marks of the forming process usually need to be removed or the vessel will need to be thinned. This can be done with any sharp tool, usually while the ceramic is on a wheel for ease of rotation, or even with a lathe. On slip cast ware, fettling is an essential finishing process.

Fettling a vessel at the Wedgwood factory, Stoke-on-Trent. Cast marks, seam marks and other blemishes are removed with the aid of a metal tool.

Fibre A strand used in creating textile yarns, fabrics and structures. Technically, a fibre is defined as having a length at least 100 times its diameter or width. Fibres can be divided into three groups: natural, man-made and synthetic. The processing of each of these types requires different techniques in spinning. The names given to many cloths often indicate their original fibre content.

Natural fibres may be animal, vegetable or mineral in origin. Animal fibres and filaments include ALPACA, ANGORA, CAMEL HAIR, CASHMERE, cow hair, fur, HORSEHAIR, MOHAIR, SILK, VICUNA and WOOL, all essentially nitrogenous substances made largely of keratin and other protein substances. With the exception of silk and horsehair, most animal fibres have scales facing the tip of the hair, enabling them to absorb moisture without feeling wet and giving them a natural tendency to felt: when made into cloths, especially any constructed with loops, holes or piles, or with a brushed finish, they are also, with silk, good insulators. They take natural dyes well, since they are able to withstand acidic treatments, although those with a natural mid-dark colouring are often used in the natural shade.

Vegetable fibres number in the hundreds and include seed hairs such as COTTON and KAPOK, bast or soft fibres such as flax and hemp (see LINEN), jute and ramie, and hard fibres from the leaf or stem, such as RAFFIA, abaca (from the banana plant *Musa textilis*) and sisal, an important crop in Indonesia and East and West Africa. Their composition is mainly cellulose; more inert and damaged by acid solutions, they are more difficult to dye than animal fibres, but dry more rapidly once wet and, as they do not have a tendency to felt, are easy to wash.

Mineral fibres include those obtained from the processing of asbestos and glass, and those used to create types of METAL THREAD. Their chief use is yarns and fabrics for industrial purposes or, in the case of metal threads, for decorative purposes; they are not dyed.

The terms synthetic and man-made are often used interchangeably of fibres and fabrics. However, it is more correct to categorize man-made fibres (also called regenerated fibres) as those made by processing cellulose, or by the chemical treatment of proteins, including soybean and peanut protein, and casein, or milk protein. Such fibres include RAYON and CELLOPHANE. Casein is also used in plastics, and the connection with plastics is even more apparent in synthetic fibres. These are made by modifying natural resins, such as SHELLAC, or by the polymerization of petrochemicals, as in POLYESTER, or acrylonitrile, as in ACRYLIC. Other synthetics include saran and elastomeric yarns, such as LYCRA. The first true synthetic, the polyamide NYLON, was commercially available in 1937, and since 1948 the number of such fibres has grown rapidly, each with specific performance features and, when developed by two or more companies, its own trade name, for both yarns and cloths made from them. Most synthetics can be used in solid, moulded, extruded-thread and staple or tow forms (short or longer lengths cut from continuous threads for spinning); as yarns and cloths most were initially difficult to dye, until it was established that they could take disperse dyes, previously developed for acetate rayon, and, after 1956, reactive dyes.

Fibreglass The common name for GLASS FIBRE REINFORCED PLASTICS.

Fibrous plasterwork A technique for producing large, lightweight, pre-cast sections of decoration for ceilings, patented by the French modeller Leonard Desachy in 1856. The ornament to be reproduced was moulded with gelatine. The moulds were filled with GYPSUM PLASTER, reinforced with canvas or hessian and supported with wooden or metal braces. The cast sections were then fixed to ceiling rafters and the joins between them were plastered. This method provided quick and inexpensive decoration, widely used in theatres, libraries, hotels and houses in Europe and the USA in the late 19th century and early 20th.

Fiddleback An attractive natural figure in wood, giving the impression of a wavy effect on a flat surface. Also known as RIPPLE, it is commonly found on sycamore and maple and is popular for violin backs.

Fiddle drill See WOODWORKING TOOLS.

Figure A generic term for the range of natural ornamental markings found in wood, formed by the arrangement of grain, colour variation and by naturally occurring phenomena such as insect parasites, fungi, wounds and decay. The way in which timber is converted can also influence the grain pattern (see WOOD). Different patterns are known by various descriptive names, such as BIRD'S EYE, BROKEN STRIPE, brown oak, BURL, BURR, CROTCH, curl, FEATHER, FIDDLEBACK, GRAIN, HERRINGBONE FIGURE, LACEWOOD, MOTTLE, PEACOCK'S EYE, PLUM FIGURE, quartering, QUILTED FIGURE, raindrop, RAM'S HORN, RIBBON GRAIN, RIPPLE, ROE, SILVER GRAIN, STRIPE FIGURE and WATERMARK FIGURE.

Filet See LACIS.

Filigrana See FILIGREE.

Filigree [glass] Blown glass decorated with embedded opaque threads, sometimes known as *filigrana* (Italian: 'thread-grained'). The threads may be white (see LATTIMO) or coloured. Although a simple form of filigree had been used by the Romans on the edges of bowls, the technique was developed and perfected only by the Murano glassmakers of the mid-16th century. It was revived in the 19th century but the work of the earlier Venetians remains unsurpassed.

Stages in the making of vetro a fili.
(a) Clear glass canes with a white core are laid, touching each other, on a ceramic plate, before being placed in furnace. They soften and fuse into a single rectangle of glass.
(b) While the canes are still soft, they are picked up on a collar of clear glass, which is attached to one corner of the rectangle and then rolled along the ends of the canes to form a cylinder.

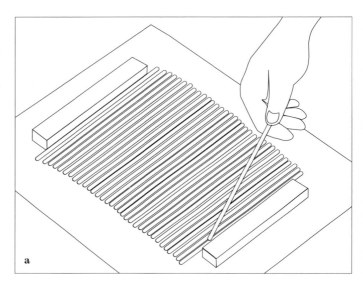

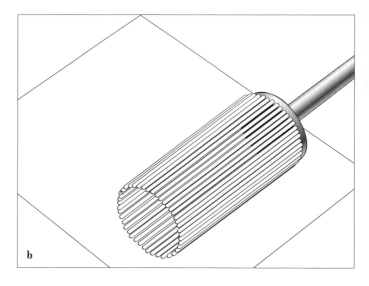

There are various types of filigree. In *vetro a fili* white canes are laid in a grooved ceramic plate. They are then heated until soft and picked up on a gather of glass. As the glass is blown and manipulated into shape the threads remain parallel, although they may be twisted into a spiral or helix form. To produce a more closely packed effect, clear canes with a white core are laid side by side, touching each other, and then melted and compacted into a single sheet of striped glass that can be

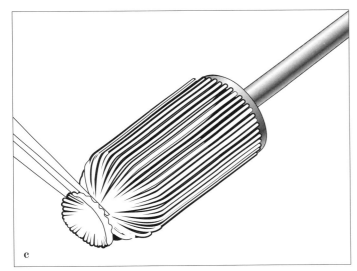

(c) After reheating, the cylinder is closed at one end by constricting the ends of the canes with pincers.

(d) After further reheating, the closed end of the cylinder is held rigid while the blow-pipe is rotated, producing a spiral pattern. Gentle blowing prevents the cylinder from folding or collapsing. Further blowing, reheating, constriction and twisting are carried out to form the foot.

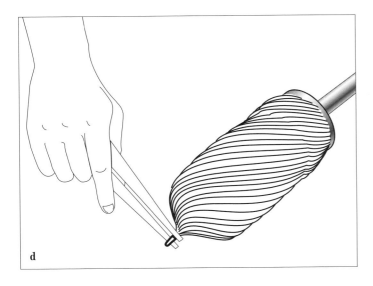

rolled and picked up on a blow pipe. *Vetro a retorti* is a variation on the *vetro a fili* process in which the canes already incorporate helix patterns. This creates a lacy effect.

A more complicated form of filigree, *vetro a reticello*, is characterized by threads crossing at right angles to form a mesh containing tiny air bubbles. This is usually created by blowing a vessel of spiralling *vetro a fili* and then rapidly blowing into it a second layer of *vetro a fili*, spiralling in the opposite direction. As the glass cools, the two layers fuse, and since the canes project slightly from the surfaces, air bubbles are trapped between the layers.

See also TWIST STEM.

Filigree [metal] A form of open or backed wire work, usually in gold or silver and only rarely using other metals. The fine wire is often twisted, plaited and soldered or brazed to form a design.

Goblet in vetro a reticello,
Venice, late 17th century.

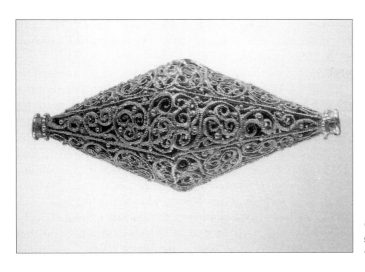

Gold bead, filigree with granulation, Egypt or Syria, 11th century AD.

There are three main types of filigree. The first is openwork filigree without a backing. This is constructed of fine wire units held together by a heavier wire framework. Another type is backed filigree, in which the wires are riveted, soldered or brazed to a backing of sheet or woven wire mesh. The third type of filigree uses enamel or niello to fill the spaces between the wires. This can be done on backed filigree as well as on openwork filigree.

Filigree work was practised widely in ancient times from Mesopotamia to Egypt and Greece and is still used in folk jewellery in Europe, North Africa, the Middle East, Russia, Asia and Mexico.

Fire clay A very heat-resistant clay, usually associated with coal deposits, which is normally high in alumina and thus high-fired. Because it matures or fuses at a very high temperature it is quite refractory and can therefore be used in kiln building, brickmaking or for making grogs. Some of the more refined fire clays are suitable for making stonewares and oven wares.

Fire clays range in colour from white to buff to red, depending on their depositional situation. Those associated with iron deposits are red-firing and are used for bricks. Most fire clays, however, are buff in colour after firing and quite plastic, owing to weathering.

Fire polish The bright, polished surface imparted to a finished piece of glass by placing it in a glory hole. This takes place before the final annealing and removes the dull surface sometimes left by the mould.

Fire stain An oxide layer just below the surface of a silver–copper alloy, caused by unprotected heating and appearing as shadowy grey patches on the surface after polishing. Fire staining can be avoided by covering the entire surface of the workpiece against oxidation with a flux before heating, or by heating in an oxygen-free furnace.

Firegilding A gilding process in which a metal workpiece is covered with a gold amalgam, from which the mercury evaporates upon heating to leave a surface layer of gold. Silver, brass and even tin were sometimes plated in this way, as were ceramics and glass. The process is also called amalgam gilding, mercury gilding or mercury amalgam gilding.

The first evidence of firegilding is found in China (4th century BC), from where it spread to the Roman world in the 2nd century AD. It remained in use as the main gilding process on metals until the invention of electroplating in the mid-19th century. Because of the toxicity of mercury in general, and of the fumes in particular, it is now prohibited in the West, although it is still used in Nepal and some other Asian countries.

The first step in firegilding is to make the gold amalgam by dissolving finely divided gold into mercury until it has the consistency of butter. The surface of the article to be gilded is thoroughly cleaned from grease and oxides and then brushed with mercury nitrate to make it more receptive to the amalgam, which is applied evenly to the surface with a spatula. The workpiece is then slowly heated to drive off the mercury (which has a boiling-point of 357°C), leaving behind a thin layer of gold fused to the surface. Usually the process is repeated to create an even and thick gold plating. The gilding is semi-matt in appearance at this stage and is often then burnished to give a shine.

See also ORMOLU and VERMEIL.

Firing The process of converting wet clay to hard ceramic by heating in a KILN. Only in intense heat in a bonfire or kiln can the clay mineral be broken down and the clay converted to ceramic. This process of ceramic change occurs when water that has been added to clay to aid plasticity is removed, and the clay particles move closer together, melt slightly and eventually fuse permanently. (A dried vessel that has not been fired is too fragile to handle and is therefore not a ceramic.)

The process of ceramic change begins outside the kiln, when formed clay objects are allowed to dry and the added water of plasticity begins to evaporate into the surrounding atmosphere. The air in the workshop or drying area is usually warmed to speed up the drying process. When the vessel is at the right stage of dryness it is described as being 'leather hard'. The drying process needs to be carefully controlled because evaporation causes water to move to the surface of the clay, which in turn causes the clay particles to move closer together. If a vessel is dried too fast it will crack. If it is not dry enough, when it is heated in the kiln too much steam can build up and the vessel will burst.

Once the clay vessels are suitably dried, they are placed in the kiln. The firing then proceeds through several stages as the clay objects are heated to the desired maximum temperature. In the first stage, to about 120°C, excess water in the pores between the clay particles is removed as steam. In the next stage, from 120°C to about 350°C, any additional water is boiled off and vegetable or organic matter in the clay begins to decompose. There is a slight expansion of the vessel at this stage, as the body expands with heat. From about 350°C to 650°C ceramic change begins. The water binding the clay particles is driven off as small amounts of steam, and the clay mineral (see CLAY) begins to break down and is converted to a new crystal, called metakaolin. The clay is no longer soft and has become ceramic, but it is weak because the clay particles are touching but not fused. It is in the next stage of firing, from 650°C to 950°C, that sintering begins, which welds the clay particles together by softening the points of contact between them. Additional heating will encourage vitrification, where the clay crystal breaks down even further, releasing silica which melts and forms a glass. This process of forming glass in effect glues the particles together and forms a permanent bond. A vitrified ceramic is hard and durable and cannot be converted back to clay. When the desired peak temperature has been reached, the kiln is allowed to cool, during which time the ceramic contracts. The finished vessel is therefore usually smaller than the original dried clay version. The complete firing process can take hours or up to ten days with traditional kilns.

An important aspect of firing is the atmosphere created in the kiln during the firing cycle, as fuel is burnt and the kiln heats up. Depending on the amount of oxygen available, the atmosphere can be either reducing or oxidizing. A reducing atmosphere is smoky, with very little free oxygen, and oxygen compounds in the clay and/or glaze are therefore reduced to a lower atomic state. An oxidizing atmosphere is clean, and because oxygen is freely available in the air only a little is extracted from the firing clay. The chemical reactions affect the colour and hardness of the clay and the colour of the glazes. METALLIC OXIDES (iron, for example) will generally produce warm colours (such as red or ivory) in an oxidizing atmosphere and cool colours (such as grey or green) in a reducing atmosphere. The firing atmosphere can therefore be a crucial aspect of ceramic design, determining, for example, whether a porcelain glaze is ivory-toned or bluish white.

The kiln atmosphere is related to both the kiln design and the available fuel. Certain fuels are conducive to particular

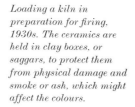

Loading a kiln in preparation for firing, 1930s. The ceramics are held in clay boxes, or saggars, to protect them from physical damage and smoke or ash, which might affect the colours.

atmospheres: wood fuels are best for reduction firings and coal for oxidation. Solid fuels of any type require oxygen for cooling down the kiln or ceramic, so the atmosphere in the final stage of firing will normally be oxidizing. With modern electric kilns the atmosphere is closely controlled and can even be neutral.

Firing can be completed in one stage or in several. Some ceramics, for example, are fired twice. The first firing (BISCUIT firing) is used to remove water and make the vessel strong enough to handle for glazing. In the second firing the GLAZE is matured. Some ceramics with low-fired glazes (such as lead glaze) or enamel decoration will be fired at a lower temperature in the second firing, and others, with high-fired glazes, will be fired at a higher temperature in the second firing. Many Asian ceramics are glazed raw and then fired once. When peak temperature has been reached in a single firing, the ceramics are often 'soaked', or held at temperature for a time, to allow the body and glaze to mature and any bubbles in the glaze to smooth out.

Flambé glaze An imitation JUN GLAZE produced in France in the 19th century.

Flame stitch See BARGELLO.

Flameworking See LAMPWORKING.

Flannel A medium- or lightweight, plain- or twill-woven fabric with a finer warp than weft and a lightly napped or brushed surface. The name is derived from the Welsh *gwlanen* (from *gwlan*, meaning 'wool'). Although generally made from wool, other fibres are also used, especially cotton (the resulting fabric is often called flannelette); the bulkier weft and napping of cotton give a characteristic soft, warm, fuzzy finish.

Flashed glass Clear glass coated with a thin layer of another colour. It is made by dipping the gather of clear glass into molten glass of another colour before it is blown out. The outer layer can be ground through to create a pattern or a cameo effect. The technique was used in particular to dilute the deep colour of ruby glass for use in medieval stained-glass windows.

Flat chasing See CHASING.

Flat glass Glass made in flat sheets, used mainly for windows and mirrors. A number of methods have been used to produce flat, or sheet, glass. Initially the sheets were quite small but since the 19th century various technological developments, culminating in the invention of float glass, have enabled the production of very large sheets.

Crown and cylinder glass, which are now used only in stained-glass windows, were both known to the Romans. The first method was wasteful of glass and only produced small sheets, but the glass was brilliant and very transparent and was thus valued for windows even up to the 19th century. The glass, also called spun glass, was made from a bubble of glass that was transferred to a pontil iron, cut open and rapidly rotated. With repeated reheating and rotation it became a large flat disc, up to 1.20 m in diameter. The glass was then annealed and cut into small, thin, rectangular or diamond-shaped sheets. Crown glass can be identified by its slight convexity and the concentric wavy lines caused by the rotation. Some pieces include the centre boss, or 'bull's eye' mark, where the pontil rod was once attached.

Cylinder glass, also known as 'broad', 'muff' or 'Lorraine' glass, was made from a large bubble that was marvered and swung on the blowing iron to form a long bottle. The ends were cut off and the cylinder that resulted was cut lengthwise with shears. It was then reheated and flattened by a wooden plane or allowed to sink to a flat state. This glass showed

The manufacture of broad or cylinder glass in the mid-18th century. A gather of glass is drawn from the furnace (a) and blown into an elongated bulb (b). It is then opened out (c) and marvered into shape (d) with the help of a special tool (e) to increase its diameter. Finally, the cylinder is cut open (f) with shears (g) and laid on a flat surface to cool.

straight ripples and was not as clear as crown glass, but it came in a bigger sheet, up to 1.50 m in length. Improvements in the 19th century allowed the manufacture of even larger sheets of flat glass, and in 1903 an entirely mechanical process was developed in the USA by John Lubbers, in which a cylinder of molten glass, over 15 m long and 90 cm wide, was drawn from a tank of molten glass by an iron ring.

It was also possible to cast glass into flat sheets. This method had been used on a small scale by the Romans, who

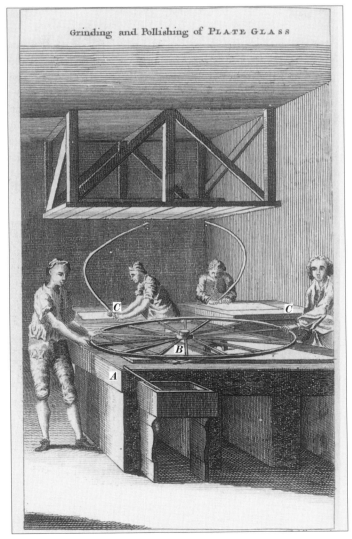

Grinding and Polishing of PLATE GLASS

The polishing of plate glass, depicted in the Dictionary of Arts and Sciences *(1754). Two large sheets of glass (A) are fixed to the spokes of a wheel (B), with emery and wet sand spread between them to grind the glass smooth. Finally the glass is polished with felt buffers affixed to jointed ribs (C) which maintain a constant pressure.*

cast the molten glass into wooden trays, but became widespread only in the 18th century. Plate glass, as it was later called, was the invention of Bernard Perrot, who developed a method of casting glass on iron tables and took out a patent for it in France in 1688. The glass had a dull, rough surface and had to be ground and polished to produce the brilliance required for mirrors and windows. This was a laborious process that often reduced the glass to half its original thickness. The first continuous on-line grinding and polishing was developed in Britain by Pilkingtons in 1923, followed by the development of the twin grinding and polishing process in 1937.

By the early 20th century it was possible to produce flat glass by drawing molten glass out of a tank in a vertical sheet (Fourcault's process), by ladling it onto a casting table and rolling it flat, or by passing it between mechanically driven rollers to form a ribbon (the Bicheroux process). All these methods were superseded when, in 1959, Pilkingtons invented an entirely new process which is now the world's principal method of flat glass manufacture. Float glass is produced as a continuous ribbon of molten glass on a bath of molten tin. It is held on the tin long enough for any irregularities to melt out and for the surfaces to become flat and parallel. It is then slowly cooled and passed through the annealing oven. The glass that results is naturally brilliant, because it has been fire-polished, and very smooth, so that it requires no grinding.

See also NORMAN SLAB.

Flax See LINEN.

Flesh The inner layer of a piece of leather taken from next to the muscle of the animal. A 'flesh split' is produced by cutting the hide longitudinally and removing the GRAIN.

Fleshing See TANNING.

Flint and chert Stones composed of quartz and derived from the redeposition of silica from the skeletons of organisms such as sponges or radiolaria. They formed in the chalk deposits of western Europe (as flint) or in limestones (as chert). Flint, found as irregular blue-black nodules, is hard with a smooth, glassy texture. It fractures conchoidally, forming small concave areas where a flake has been removed. The detached flakes have sharp cutting edges and for this reason the use of flint as a tool material is extremely ancient and widespread. Chert, which can be brown, grey, black or white, was fashioned by the ancient Egyptians into tools, bracelets and vessels.

Flint was used as a building stone in areas such as south-east England, where no other suitable local stone existed. It was used as extracted from the chalk, somewhat smoothed by the action of water when found by the sea, or shaped, or knapped. Knapping involves striking the flint nodule at right angles to the surface with another stone or hammer; the antlers of red deer were traditionally used. Flint can be knapped into blocks or may be kept as nodules with only one worked face. The flints were then set in lime mortar, either on their own or, for decorative purposes, combined in patterns with other types of stone or brick.

Flint glass A synonym for English LEAD GLASS which arose in the early years of George Ravenscroft's experiments in the late 17th century, when he tried calcined flint as a substitute for the pebbles used in Venetian glass. Later, sand replaced the flint, but the term flint glass remained current.

Float glass See FLAT GLASS.

Flock Paper decorated with coloured fibres to imitate textiles such as cut velvets and brocades. A small number of German woodcuts of the mid-15th century have been identified as decorated with flock, but the technique is better-known in wallpaper production. French and English manufacturers began producing flock wallpapers in the mid-18th century, when colour-printed wallpapers were becoming popular. The paper was first woodblock-printed to give the background colour, and then glue, gelatine size or paste was applied from a block in the same way and, while the adhesive was still wet, powdered wool fibres (the trimmings from woollen cloth) were sprinkled on. The glue could also be applied through leather or oiled paper stencils, and the process would be repeated to get a thicker flock. Silk fibres were sometimes used but did not give such a durable paper as wool.

Florentine mosaic A form of mosaic employing hard stones, widely known as PIETRE DURE.

Florentine stitch See BARGELLO.

Flux A substance that lowers the melting-point of a material and aids fusion. Fluxes are used in soldering, ceramic glazes, enamels and glass.

Fly press A type of press which uses a screw mechanism to generate sufficient force to stamp metal. It was probably

developed by the Italian artist Donato Bramante in the early
16th century and was first used to punch and stamp coins and
medals. Later, in the 18th century, the device was also used
to punch designs in fused plate and silverware.

Foil Sheet metal with a thickness of usually not more than
0.1 mm.

Fondi d'oro A term used of engraved gold leaf sandwiched
between two layers of glass. It is particularly associated with
Roman and Byzantine glassware.

Fondporzellan German porcelain with reserved panels and
enamel decoration. The style was developed at Meissen in the
early 18th century, in imitation of Chinese porcelain. It consists of a monochrome ground and reserved white panels
which were filled with enamel decoration. Such porcelains
would have been fired twice, as the enamel decoration is low-
fired.

Fool's gold See MARCASITE.

Fore edge The front of the text block of a book, where the
edges of the leaves can be seen. The fore edge surface can be
decorated in a number of ways, most simply by colouring or
gilding, but also by gauffering with a hot finishing tool which
indents the paper and by marbling. Fore edge paintings were
a feature of some English books in the mid-17th century. A
watercolour painting was made with the leaves slightly
fanned out so that the image could be seen only when the
book was opened again to the same extent.

Forel Parchment made specifically from sheepskins.

Forest glass A rustic form of POTASH GLASS produced in the
forests of northern Europe, using potassium carbonate obtained
from the ashes of burnt beech and other woods. It is light green
or brown in colour owing to impurities such as iron in the raw
materials, although sometimes this effect has been artificially
enhanced. Forest glass was a speciality of the German-speaking
countries throughout the Middle Ages and is often known by its
German name, *waldglas*. It was usually mould-blown and decorated with prunts. See also illustration on page 201.

Forging The shaping or forming of metal by hammering.
Only malleable metals can be worked in this way. Although
most metals can be forged cold, at room temperature, when a
metal (especially a ferrous metal) needs extensive forging it is
usually worked hot (see BLACKSMITHING). As well as shaping
the metal, forging also improves its quality. The coarse
crystal structure in a metal after casting is kneaded, and

*A beaker in green forest
glass, Bohemia, 16th
century. It is decorated in
enamel colours depicting a
game of backgammon.*

blowholes and slag inclusions are usually reduced or disappear after forging to produce a stronger and more ductile metal than the cast counterpart.

Drop forging is the process of shaping metals in dies, using the impact of heavy blows (see DIE-STAMPING).

Formica The trade name for a range of decorative laminates used for veneers for furniture, radio cases, household surfaces and cruise liner interiors. The Formica Insulation Company was formed in 1913. In the 1920s and 1930s dark-coloured laminates were made from cloth or paper impregnated with phenol formaldehyde resins in the core and melamine formaldehyde resin on the surface. The company introduced papers printed with wood-grain designs. New colours and designs arrived in 1931 following the introduction of thiourea-urea-formaldehyde and UREA-FORMALDEHYDE, and finally the tougher MELAMINE-FORMALDEHYDE coloured materials in 1938. A sheet of patterned paper could be impregnated with one of these materials and laminated under pressure onto underlayers impregnated with phenolic resin. The development of these laminates led to easy-care surfaces. To reduce cigarette damage, a foil underlayer was devised by John Cochrane jun. of the Formica Insulation Company.

Colorcore is made in the same way as Formica, but whereas Formica is made from layers of brown paper with a coloured paper surface, Colorcore is a solid colour laminate built up from layers of coloured paper. It does not show the

Hair combs in Colorcore with resin inlay, by Wendy Ramshaw, 1991.

traditional dark line of Formica and other laminates. Promoted within the Formica company by the Design Advisory Board, Colorcore was launched in 1983, with an initial emphasis on architectural, interior finishings and furniture and, later on, jewellery. It has inspired designers such as Frank Gehry and jewellery makers such as Wendy Ramshaw.

Fourcault's process See FLAT GLASS.

Foxing A term used to describe staining on old paper in the form of brown spots. The patches of discoloration may be caused by mould or by the presence of metal particles. They usually indicate that the paper has been damp at some time and that it has a slightly acid pH.

Freestone A term used to describe a sedimentary stone which can be worked equally well across and along the bedding planes.

French ivory See SYNTHETIC IVORY.

French knot stitch See KNOTTING.

French plating An early type of silver plating in which thin leaves of pure silver were rubbed onto a base metal surface. The workpiece—which might be copper, brass or iron—was first thoroughly cleaned and decreased. The thin pure silver leaves (up to six at a time) were then heated and quickly rubbed onto its surface with the aid of a steel burnisher. Up to sixty leaves could be attached to the item before the plating was smoothed down to give a uniform surface. This method, described by Theophilus as long ago as the 12th century, was used by fused plate workers to cover up mistakes or damage on objects.

French polishing The application of successive layers of spirit-based shellac varnish to wood in order to produce a durable finish of more or less high gloss. The degree of shine can vary from a subtle lustre, such as that found on much of the English oak furniture made around 1900, to the deep mirror gloss seen on grand pianos. It is so called because it is believed to have been first used in France, towards the end of the 17th century.

French polishing is a deceptively simple technique, which requires great skill and experience to produce a high-quality, durable finish. Various proprietary products are sold as French polish, usually consisting of an alcoholic solution of shellac resin with a variety of additives intended to ease application or increase brightness. True French polishing is executed using only a pure solution of best shellac in alcohol.

It is applied with a fine lint-free rubber in the form of a pear-shaped pad made from a square of cotton padded with pure cotton wool. The surface of the rubber is kept barely moist and occasionally lubricated with a little linseed oil to prevent sticking.

French ultramarine A deep blue synthetic pigment invented in the early 19th century to replace ultramarine. It is chemically identical to the mineral, and shares its unmistakable blue-red hue, but it does not have the impurities and is naturally much cheaper. It has good tinting strength but has poor drying properties in oil, and in commercially prepared oil paint dryers are added to correct this problem. It is very translucent, and effective both as an oil glaze and as water-colour wash. It is unaffected by light, heat or alkalis and can therefore be safely used to paint walls. By adjusting the chemical composition very slightly, colours other than blue can be manufactured, and ultramarine yellows, pinks and violets are now part of the paint supplier's range.

Fresco A painting technique that involves brushing pigment, mixed with water alone, onto freshly laid lime plaster (calcium oxide). The pigment soaks into the lime plaster, which, as it dries, takes up carbon dioxide from the air to crystallize as calcium carbonate. The pigment particles are thus locked into the network of newly formed crystals, and fresco is therefore one of the most permanent painting techniques. The lime plaster remains wet enough to take the pigment only for about six hours, so large frescos have to be executed in stages, with fresh areas of plaster applied each session; one reason why true fresco is considered so difficult is that the wet paint of one day has to be mixed so that it will eventually match the paler, dried paint of the day before.

Since a chemical reaction is taking place, and as lime plaster is very alkaline, few pigments are suitable for fresco. Historically the ones used are the earth pigments (see OCHRES), carbon black and any white except lead white. However, there is no technical reason why some of the most inert of the modern inorganic pigments should not also be used.

Fretwork A generally elaborate form of pierced decoration cut with the fretsaw into relatively thin sheets of wood. It is produced by holding the workpiece in a special foot-operated clamp, known as a fretcutter's donkey or buhl horse. A design is drawn or traced onto the board and a small hole is drilled

*Treadle-operated fretsaw,
from a watercolour in a
folio album by
A. Boucicault, probably
1870s.*

into the waste material next to each separate design element.
The saw blade is detached from its frame and threaded
through the hole, the frame is reattached and cutting proceeds.

Pierced and cut work has been made since the Roman
period, but the saws used at that time were too wide to have
been used for fine fretwork, which may instead have been cut
by piercing and chiselling. Efficient turning or bow saws
appeared early in the 16th century and while these were primarily intended for the production of curved elements they
could also have been used for relatively coarse pierced work.
Fine fretwork only became possible with the development of
even thinner and narrower steel blades and a suitable frame
for holding them. Towards the end of the 18th century, with
the development of the treadle-operated fretsaw, the production of both fine fretwork and very finely inlaid veneers
became possible. Very efficient electrically powered saws are
available today.

Frit A granular material produced by pre-heating the raw ingredients of glass in a furnace or kiln to $c.850°C$. This initiates glassmaking reactions and drives off volatile reaction products. The material is then placed in water, which shatters it, ground into a powder and washed. The process is known as fritting.

Frit melts more readily than the original ingredients and is added to a glass batch to facilitate fusion. In ancient times, when furnaces could achieve temperatures of only $c.1000°C$, glass was frequently made from frit alone. Also used alone, and coloured with metallic oxides, frit is the basic component of ENAMEL and ENAMEL COLOURS. In the production of ceramics, frits are used as fluxes and stabilizers in glazes. They include lead, feldspar and borax (which is too soluble on its own). Sometimes, certain strong colours are fritted before being added to the glaze recipe. Fritting is also used to neutralize poisonous or unstable glaze and body ingredients.

Fritware A white ceramic body, usually made from crushed quartz, white clay and an alkaline glass frit. It was developed in the Near East in the 11th century to imitate Chinese porcelain and was used for both vessels and tiles. It is related to EGYPTIAN FAIENCE, and is sometimes known as 'stone paste' or 'frit porcelain'. Fritware matures at approximately $1050°C$ and is suitable for moulding, but can be too plastic for throwing on the wheel if much fine white clay is added. A fritware body is most frequently seen in traditional Islamic lustre wares and tiles (see ISNIK WARE) and other Islamic ware, but was also used in Europe as a form of artificial porcelain (see SOFT PASTE PORCELAIN). Fritware bodies normally have transparent alkaline glazes or white tin glazes, as other glazes do not react well with the body.

Frottage The process of creating an image by placing a sheet of paper over a relief surface, where the design stands proud, and taking an impression by rubbing a flat piece of chalk or a crayon over the back of the paper. Brass and stone rubbings are a kind of frottage and rubbings of wood-grain are sometimes made for their decorative value. Thin, flexible Japanese papers are ideal for the work.

Fumed oak Oak darkened by exposure to ammonia. The timber is enclosed in an airtight chamber known as a fuming box or stove and monitored through a window until the desired colour is achieved. Colour tones can vary from an olive green to a blackish brown. An alternative method still used in some places involves exposing the timber or com-

Albarello, fritware with underglaze painted decoration, Syria, late 13th century.

pleted object to the fumes produced in cow barns.

Fundame A Japanese term for a gold or silver URUSHI ground often used as a base for other lacquer techniques (see colour plate XIIIa). Very fine gold or silver powder is densely sprinkled onto a wet ground. Once dry, the metal layer may be coated with a thin layer of clear urushi to leave a lustrous finish resembling gold leaf. Alternatively, it may be left uncoated, either matt or shiny (depending on the method of application).

Furnace A structure in which glass is melted. The GLORY HOLE, for the reheating of glass during manufacture, and the LEHR or annealing kiln are sometimes incorporated into a single structure with the furnace, or they may be constructed separately.

To maintain the very high temperatures required to melt glass, and to withstand the corrosive effects of the metal, furnaces are constructed of FIRE CLAY or stone with a high silica content, such as sandstone. Wood and peat were once used for fuel but they were replaced from the 17th century by coal and, later, by gas or electricity.

There are two types of glass furnace: tank furnaces and pot furnaces. In tank furnaces the glass is melted in a shallow tank, sometimes holding up to several hundred tons at a time. Tank furnaces existed in a primitive form in antiquity but were only developed fully in the mid-19th century. Mainly used for making bottles and window glass, they have been adapted by studio glassmakers for small-scale production.

In pot furnaces, which have been more widely used, the glass is held in pots within the furnace. The pots may be open, or closed with a domed top and side opening. The latter, known as 'crown pots', were first used in Britain in the 17th century and were essential for the manufacture of LEAD GLASS as the sulphurous fumes from the coal-fired furnaces would turn the glass black. The pots are heated in a subsidiary furnace until they can withstand the high temperatures of the main furnace. The difficult process of transferring the pots without a sudden change of temperature is called pot settling.

Early European pot furnaces can be broadly divided into two types. Those in the southern (or Mediterranean) area tended to be circular domed structures in which the bottom section contained the fire, the middle section the pots of

molten glass, and the top section the lehr. A hole in the floor of the lehr allowed the passage of heat upwards from the melting oven. The structure was roughly paraboloid in shape and acted as a reverbatory furnace, in which the heat from the burning fuel was reflected downwards from the furnace crown onto the glass pots for maximum efficiency. The pots were arranged around the inside, and above them were openings in the furnace wall (glory holes) through which the craftsmen inserted the gathering irons to remove the molten glass or reheated the glass as the work progressed.

In northern Europe a different form of furnace developed, first described by Theophilus in the early 12th century. Its salient feature was that the main and subsidiary furnaces were on the same level. The furnace was usually rectangular, with the melting area above or on either side of the central fire. The hottest part of the furnace was termed the seige and its centre was the eye. The annealing ovens were either separate or developed as wings attached to, and deriving the heat from, the melting oven.

In 1615 the used of wood for fuelling glass furnaces was

A view of William Ford's glasshouse erected in 1815, with a cone furnace. It shows glass blowing and vessel formation, with an annealing oven, glory holes and covered pots around the walls.

banned in Britain, and pit coal began to be used instead. This resulted in the development of cone furnaces, with underground flues and a cone-like chimney to produce the powerful up-draught required to burn coal. The interior of the cone provided a spacious working area around the furnace, while annealing ovens and pot arches were built into the exterior walls.

The firing of ceramics also requires specially designed structures capable of reaching and withstanding very high temperatures. For the discussion of these, see KILN.

See also MUFFLE KILN.

Fused plate Silver-plated wares made of copper sheet onto which the silver top layer is fused. The process was invented in Sheffield and used mainly there between the middle of the 18th century and the middle of the 19th; for this reason fused plate used to be known as 'old Sheffield plate'. When silver and copper are heated to near their melting-point, in close contact with each other, the contact surfaces will diffuse. This creates a very thin layer of silver–copper alloy with a lower melting-point which bonds the silver and the copper together without actually melting them.

The process was probably discovered by the Sheffield cutler Thomas Boulsover in 1742. Boulsover is said to have made his discovery while repairing a knife handle composed of both copper and silver. He discovered after overheating the handle that the silver bonded to the copper and, more importantly, that they stretched in the same rate when rolled, without detaching.

To make silver-plated sheet a copper ingot was prepared about 4 cm thick, 6 cm wide and 20 cm long, by scraping it flat and clean. The same thing was done with a similar-sized but much thinner (1 mm) sterling silver sheet. After the two metals had been pressed together with great force, to make close contact, they were bound together with iron wire, usually with some extra iron or copper sheet on the outside to protect the silver from the wire and heat. The whole package was covered in borax and placed in a hot furnace. When the silver in the middle started to show signs of melting, it was time to remove the package quickly from the furnace. Once it had cooled down, the binding wire and the protective iron or copper plate were removed, leaving a block of copper with a perfectly bonded silver top layer. (Later, around 1760, silver was fused on both sides.) The block was rolled to sheet between rolling mills, with the silver stretching at the same rate as the copper and the whole acting like one solid block of silver or copper. In this way sheet articles resembling solid silver objects (but much cheaper) could be made using silversmithing techniques.

The main difficulty in making fused plated wares was to avoid damaging the thin silver surface layer during the manufacturing process. Another problem was to prevent the copper from being visible at the edges. To conceal the copper all kinds of techniques were developed, such as folding the edge over, applying silver solder to the edge, soldering on a silver or silver-plated wire or applying a decorative silver or silver-plated border. These decorative borders were cast or made by die-stamping, filled with molten lead solder and then soldered onto the object.

The pierced decoration in silver that was popular at the time constituted another problem when it was carried out using the traditional silversmith's piercing saw. The fused plate workers overcame the problem of the visible copper edges by punching out the decoration with a fly press so that the punch dragged the silver top layer over the copper core.

Designs for fused plate, from a catalogue of 1780–90.

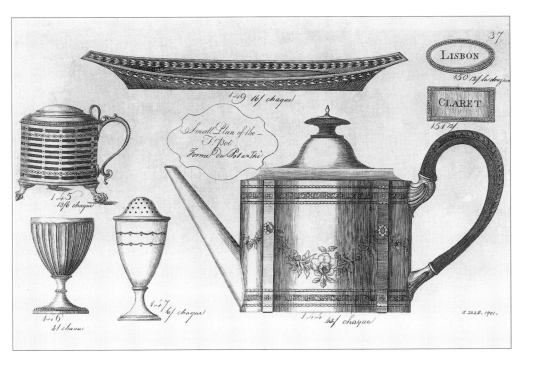

Engraving presented a similar problem, since cutting through the silver surface exposed the copper beneath. This was solved by using an extra thick outer layer of silver plating or, in the case of only a small monogram or coat of arms, by inserting a silver or silver-plated shield. This 'letting-in', as it was known, was done by soldering or brazing and/or burnishing. An alternative to engraving was flat CHASING, which removed no silver but resembled engraving.

Boulsover used his discovery mainly to produce silver-plated buttons, and because he did not patent the process others soon started to produce fused plate. Joseph Hancock, a distant relative of Boulsover, realized its industrial potential and started to make fused plate articles such as saucepans and candlesticks on a large scale. The industry expanded rapidly and fused plate was soon also produced outside Sheffield, for example by Matthew Boulton in Birmingham but also in France and Russia.

Around 1830 fused plate workers began using nickel silver instead of copper as a base. This white metal did not show so much when exposed by wear or damage but it was used for only a short time. Commercial electroplating, introduced by Henry Elkington in 1842, was able to produce silver-plated wares much more cheaply and wiped out the fused plate industry in little more than a decade.

Fustian A term that has changed its meaning several times and which as a result encapsulates significant changes in textile manufacturing. Its earliest known meaning is uncertain but seems to have been a stout soft-surfaced cloth with a linen warp and dominant, worsted weft (see WOOL); the worsted was gradually replaced by cotton from *c.*1600. 'False' fustians such as jean had a twill weave and a brushed or calendered surface, and 'true' fustians had long floats, loops or pile made from an additional weft. By *c.*1735 fustian meant a plain-weave calendered fabric with a linen warp and cotton weft, often used for printing. The older fustian forms were thereafter known by existing alternative names, such as corduroy, thickset, velveret and velveteen (see VELVET) and from *c.*1800 generally became all-cotton cloths. Cotton velvet, originally made with a linen warp, was also a fustian and was known in the 18th century as 'Manchester velvet', after the area in which many fustians were woven.

Fustic A mordant dye wood (*Morus tinctoria* or *Chlorophora tinctoria*) found throughout the Americas. It is regarded as the best natural yellow and largely replaced weld in Europe in the 16th century. Mainly used on wool, it gave a very fast olive yellow to old gold when mordanted with chrome (introduced $c.1800$) and a greenish olive with copper and iron; the latter provided the khaki colourant for British army uniforms. It was also important in combination with logwood, madder and indigo for olive browns and drabs and with indigo alone for greens. It had some limited application in silk dyeing and calico printing, which after $c.1780$ made far greater use of quercitron and chrome yellow; on wool it was in commercial use until the mid-20th century.

G

Galloon See METAL THREAD.

Garnet A group of minerals with a glassy lustre, composed of magnesium, iron or calcium aluminium silicate. They are generally red, but orange, green and colourless forms also exist. Some garnets occur in volcanic rocks and are associated with diamonds in underground deposits or in river gravels. Others, such as the iron-rich almandine garnet, form in metamorphic rocks.

Garnets were used extensively in the ancient world and were sufficiently prized to be traded over long distances: the Egyptians were using Indian garnets in the 3rd millennium BC. In the early Middle Ages garnets were split into sheets and used as an inlay. From the 16th century Bohemian lapidaries produced small rose-cut garnets which were often set in clusters, a form of jewellery popular until the late 19th century. The deep red almandine garnet was cut as a cabochon with the underside hollowed out to lighten the colour, a style which became known as the 'carbuncle', although in antiquity this term was applied to any red gemstone cut as a cabochon. Garnets have been used for cameos and intaglios. Because some types of garnet are hard (Mohs 6.5–7.5) they have been crushed and used since antiquity as abrasives to cut stones such as jade.

Gather A blob of molten glass attached to a gathering iron, blow pipe or pontil. It is then rotated and blown or manipulated into shape.

Gauffering The pressing of cloth with hot metal blocks or engraved cylinders to create a relief design, such as a waffle, crimp or honeycomb, with the effect classing these as cloqué, or blistered, fabrics. The process was patented in France in 1838. Utrecht velvets are pile fabrics with a pattern created by crushing areas of the pile using the same technique.

Gemstones Varieties of minerals and rocks traditionally prized for their rarity, beauty and durability. Gemstone minerals may be individual crystals of spectacular size and beauty; gemstone rocks consist of combinations of minerals. Used throughout history in jewellery and carvings, they have been endowed with protective powers and religious significance and are enduring symbols of wealth and status (see colour plate V).

Properties The rarity of gemstones is related to a number of factors, such as unusual combinations of constituents. For example, topaz is formed by the crystallization of rare elements remaining after the formation of the surrounding rock. In other instances, such as diamond, both the geological processes of formation which occurred millions of years ago within the earth's mantle, and the arrangement of the component atoms of carbon which gives rise to its unique properties of extreme hardness and brilliance, contribute to its rarity. The unusual conditions which favour the growth of large, unflawed and transparent crystals of amethyst and rock crystal, rather than other, more common forms of quartz, also add to rarity. The richness and intensity of colour, prized in opaque stones such as lapis lazuli and turquoise, which occur through highly unusual conditions of formation, make these stones rare and thus valuable. Freedom from inclusions is also rare but the presence of impurities can produce rich colours, as seen in ruby and sapphire, both forms of the mineral corundum.

Flaws, such as those termed the *jardin* of the emerald, can enhance the beauty of a gemstone. Fine, needle-like inclusions, when arranged parallel to more than one crystal face within a mineral, produce an optical effect called asterism, in which a six- or twelve-pointed star is seen when the stone is cut as a cabochon (see below). The optical properties of reflection and refraction of light, plus the hardness of a gemstone, which allows it to be highly polished, contribute to the lustre, or brilliance, of its surface. Transparent and translucent stones, which often reflect and refract light in a similar way to glass, are described as having a vitreous lustre, while the extreme lustre of diamond is termed adamantine. The crystal structure of some gemstones, such as sapphires and rubies, gives rise to an optical effect called dichroism, in which the intensity of the stone's colour appears to change when viewed from different angles. Most gemstones are hard, making them resistant to wear and thus highly durable.

The value of a gemstone is related to its quality (that is, freedom from flaws), to the skill with which it has been cut and to its weight, which is measured in carats. The metric carat, which is equivalent to 200 mg (0.2 g), was universally accepted in 1914. The origins of the carat system are ancient: the Greeks and Romans used seeds of the carob tree (*Ceratonia siliqua*), which have a reasonably consistent weight as a unit of measurement. It is thought that the term carat derives from the name of the tree. Carat weights must be measured on precision scales which are accurate to three decimal places. The weights of set gemstones are estimated by measuring their size and comparing them with published weights of similar stones.

The comparative hardness of gemstones is measured on a ten-point scale, established by the German mineralogist Friedrich Mohs in 1822, in which a stone is given a number on the scale according to its ability to scratch other stones. Hence diamond, the hardest natural material (10 on the Mohs scale), will mark all other minerals, whereas garnet (6.5–7.5) will be scratched by spinel (8) but will in turn scratch opal (5.5–6.5). The scale is non-linear, meaning that the gaps between the values are not of equal size and the gap separating 9, sapphire and ruby, from 10, diamond, is far larger than any other. Although devised to classify minerals, the Mohs system has been applied to other materials, but those with heterogeneous or variable composition are generally assigned a range, rather than a precise designation of hardness. For comparative purposes, a fingernail is normally 2.5 and a steel needle is 6.

Most gemstones form within the earth's mantle or in the overlying crust. Conditions of formation, such as the quantity of constituent elements and the space available, determine the size of the crystals formed. They are then brought to sub-surface or surface regions by volcanic activity or by the formation of mountains. The gem-bearing material may either remain in place or may be eroded, causing the gems to be released from the rock, transported by water and deposited as gravels. Gemstones are extracted either by mining below the earth's surface, by quarrying at the surface or by sifting through gem gravels, which may be found in rivers, on beaches or in extinct river beds, covered with top soil. The hardness of gemstones and their resistance to abrasion enable unflawed stones to survive the weathering process, and gem gravels were the earliest sources exploited, often yielding large amounts of good-quality material, albeit in small pieces.

Working techniques The property of hardness is integral to the ways in which gemstones have been worked. It was recognized from early times that, although some stones were hard, they had planes of weakness along which they could be split. It was also known that stones could only be cut with other stones at least as hard, and thus the Romans used diamond to carve sapphire and the ancient Chinese sawed jade with quartz. As in most stoneworking techniques, the shaping and polishing of gemstones proceeds in stages to avoid removing too much material too early in the process.

In ancient Burma and India many gemstones were used as unworked crystals. In India the tradition of using uncut stones, notably diamonds, continued into the Mogul period, although the stones were often engraved with the name of the owner or various motifs and drilled with small holes so that they could be worn sewn onto a turban. Stones used in pebble form in modern jewellery are polished by placing them in a motor-driven rotating drum, called a tumbler, with water and progressively finer abrasives.

The ancient Indians and Egyptians made gemstone pebbles into beads by flaking or chipping them into shape and then rubbing them against sandstone or quartz blocks to smooth them. The holes were drilled with a flint point mounted on a wooden handle which could be rotated between the hands; an abrasive such as emery, an impure form of the mineral corundum, enhanced the cutting power of the point. After the introduction of copper tools abrasives continued to be used, with the grains of abrasive becoming embedded into the metal. The development of the bow drill, in which the string of a bow is wrapped around the handle of a point, allowed drilling to be carried out at greater speed. A bow drill

A Chinese jade carver using a bow drill. He operates the drill by pulling the bow towards himself, the bow string looped round the drill causing it to rotate with each stroke. The weight suspended from the horizontal beam helps hold the drill in place on the stone. The pot near the worker's left arm probably contains a mixture of abrasive and water, applied to the drill to provide its cutting action.

mounted horizontally functions in a similar way to a modern lathe, with the object to be worked held against the rotating tool; in India beads are still drilled in this manner. Beads could also be shaped by mounting them on a spindle in the bow drill and holding a tool against the surface as it was turned.

The simplest style of gemstone, the cabochon—an oval, round or teardrop shape with a domed top and flat or concave base—is still used for opaque stones. The form of the cabochon appears to have evolved from the natural shape of worn gemstone pebbles; the upper surface was polished with abrasives but the irregular shape was retained. More precise shaping was carried out by temporarily attaching the stone to a piece of stone or wood, for ease of handling, and then pushing it against a rotating disc of wood, copper or iron, charged with abrasive and mounted in a bow drill. The surface could be polished in a similar manner using progressively finer grades of abrasive. Cabochon cuts are used with stones displaying asterism and chatoyancy, an optical effect produced by the reflection of light from fine parallel channels or needle-like structures within the stone.

Intaglio cutting, in which lines and cavities are carved into the surface of a gemstone, has been used since the 6th millennium BC for seal-stones and jewellery. The surface to be carved was first worked smooth, using the same techniques employed for shaping cabochons. The earliest intaglios were carved with flint points mounted in wooden handles. Later, both iron and copper points, used with abrasives, such as emery, mixed with oil, and cutting discs, also made of iron or copper and charged with abrasive, were employed. In the Roman period discs of varied diameter, thickness and section were used to produce differences in width of line and depth of carving. The discs and points were rotated with bows or treadles. For ease of handling the stone was temporarily mounted on a small platform which the lapidary used to hold it against the tool. Diamond points were occasionally used by the Romans to carve fine lines. Similar techniques were employed from the Middle Ages to the early modern period. Modern intaglios are carved with small steel or carborundum burrs, to which diamond powder mixed with olive oil is applied, powered with an electric flexible shaft drill.

Cameos, in which material is removed to form a relief image, often in a colour contrasting with the background, are

made by carving with stone or iron points, the latter charged
with abrasive (see CAMEO).

FACETING, or the cutting of flat planes in a gemstone, was
developed in Europe from the Middle Ages. Early styles followed the shape of the crystal and tried to minimize the
amount of material removed. It was later realized that
further cutting to precise angles could enhance the brilliance
of certain stones, particularly diamonds, by allowing greater
reflection of light from the inside surfaces of facets cut on the
underside of a gemstone and thus justified some further loss.
Faceting is carried out by mounting the gemstone on a stick
which is used to hold it against lathe-mounted cutting and
grinding laps, or discs, charged with abrasive mixed with
water or oil.

*Sawing a diamond. The
stone must be cut across the
grain, using a flexible
sulphur-bronze disc, the
edge of which is
impregnated with diamond
powder and olive oil, added
as a lubricant. The
diamond is held at a preset
angle in a metal dopping
stick. A single worker may
look after as many as 40
machines.*

Polishing, which is the final stage of shaping or faceting a
gemstone, seeks to produce a perfectly smooth surface which
will allow the maximum refraction and reflection of light. It
is carried out with progressively finer grades of abrasive,
mixed with oil or water and applied to rotating laps.
Traditionally leather or felt discs were used; today materials
such as plastic, tin charged with fine diamonds and wax are

common. Research by the British chemist George Beilby in the early 20th century showed that polishing produces, in stones other than diamond, a slight melting of the surface which fills the scratches caused by earlier working.

Identification Because of their rarity and value gemstones have often been reused, placed in a new setting once the old one was no longer fashionable. They have also long been copied or altered. Imitations have been made from a wide variety of materials such as glass (see PASTE) and other stones of similar appearance. The colour of gemstones has been enhanced by dyeing, oiling, heat treatments and by coating, painting or foiling the back surface. Application of materials, such as foils, is the simplest technique and probably the easiest to detect. Many dyes, such as the organic dyes used to stain grey jadeite to a deep green, will fade with exposure to light. More permanent colour change can be achieved by chemical precipitation, such as the deposition of carbon in chalcedony by boiling it in a sugar solution and then treating it with sulphuric acid; a similar technique was used by the Romans. Stones such as lapis lazuli and turquoise, valued principally for their colour, have been rubbed with pigmented polishes or impregnated with wax to improve their colour. Emeralds, sapphires and rubies are often treated with oil to hide flaws and enhance the colour. Heat treatments, which cause a permanent and often almost imperceptible change, work by altering the chemical structure of the stone. Composites, made since Roman times, consist of a small piece of gemstone adhered to a larger piece of less valuable mineral or glass.

The first synthetic gems, industrially produced chemical and optical simulants of natural minerals, were made by Auguste Verneuil in 1902. His technique, which is still used to manufacture rubies, sapphires and spinels, involves controlled feeding of finely ground chemical powders into an extremely hot flame, in which they are fused and then deposited to form a small cone of material. The body of the cone contains a single crystal which can be faceted and polished in the same way as a natural stone.

Many of the methods used to identify gemstones and differentiate them from imitations rely on examination with light in various forms. Even low-powered magnification can detect flaws, areas of abrasion (which can differentiate zircon from diamond) and inclusions such as air bubbles, which can occur in synthetic stones. The refraction of light is characteristic for most minerals and is used for identification. The absorption of light is also characteristic and can be used to distinguish stones and imitations of the same colour. The response of gemstones to ultraviolet light and to X-rays can also be diagnostic. Differences in hardness can also be used to differentiate real stones from simulants, but this will damage cut stones. Uncut stones can frequently be identified by measuring their specific gravity.

For the setting of gemstones, see STONE SETTING.

German silver See NICKEL SILVER.

Gesso A white material made from gypsum or chalk mixed with size. It is used as a ground, especially for gilding and painted decoration, since it fills any irregularities in the base material and can then be worked to a very smooth surface. Before paper became readily available, gesso-covered boards were used as a drawing surface.

Essentially gesso is a form of plaster, with glue added to slow down the setting action and to make the plaster harder when dry. White pigment is sometimes added to make it more brilliant and reflective. The use of gypsum produces a soft gesso, which was preferred in Renaissance Italy, while the addition of chalk results in a harder substance, which was commonly used in northern Europe. A further distinction is made between *gesso grosso*, which is made from burnt gypsum and hide glue, and *gesso sottile*, for which the burnt gypsum is steeped in water and then mixed with parchment glue. *Gesso grosso* is fairly coarse and is used as a base coat, while *gesso sottile* is finer, softer and smoother and is thus preferred for the finish; in some items, such as cassoni, the *gesso sottile* is modelled and carved. Nowadays it is usual to dispense with the layer of *gesso grosso*.

Gilding Surface decoration in gold, silver or other metals. There are various means of achieving a gilded effect, some more durable and versatile than others. The method that is most commonly referred to as gilding is the application of GOLD LEAF. This was employed in Egypt as early as 1500 BC and evolved out of the even more ancient use of thick gold foil nailed to a wooden core. The colour of the leaf can be modified by the addition of other metals. Silver can also be beaten into leaf but, unlike tin leaf, it soon tarnishes unless protected by varnish. Silver with a coating of yellow varnish has been used to emulate gold, as has the brass alloy known as DUTCH METAL. Leaf finishes can be painted with transparent glazes or with opaque paints, which may then be scraped away to reveal a pattern in gold.

Another technique that, like leaf gilding, is permanent is FIREGILDING. Here the object is coated with an amalgam of gold and mercury. When heated, the mercury vapourizes to leave a thin layer of gold. Because the substrate must be able to withstand great heat, firegilding is only employed on metals, ceramics and glass.

Gold paint or lacquer is made by mixing gold powder in the appropriate medium. It has now been largely replaced by paints made from bronze or brass powders, but although cheap and durable, these cannot equal gold leaf or genuine gold paint in appearance. Aluminium-based paints are used in place of silver. The gold powder itself is obtained not by grinding the leaf, which is too plastic, but by heating a mercury amalgam, or by grinding leaf in honey and then washing away the water (see SHELL GOLD). These methods have now been replaced by electrolytic and reduction processes.

Wood and plasterwork are best decorated with leaf. Two methods, water gilding and oil gilding, are used. In water

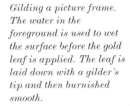

Gilding a picture frame. The water in the foreground is used to wet the surface before the gold leaf is applied. The leaf is laid down with a gilder's tip and then burnished smooth.

gilding the surface to be decorated is first given several coats of gesso, made by blending whiting with glue size. When the gesso is dry, a mixture of Armenian bole, a little wax and parchment or rabbitskin size is applied and allowed to dry. A sheet of gold leaf is placed onto the gilder's cushion and cut into appropriately sized pieces with a knife. Water is brushed onto the part of the surface to be decorated, and a piece of gold leaf is picked up with a special brush known as a 'gilder's tip'. The leaf is transferred to the wet surface, where it settles and adheres to the size. When the gilding is complete the resultant finish is known as matt or dead gold; it may be left in this condition or brightened by burnishing with an agate burnisher. Various shapes of burnishers are used, the most popular and useful of which is the so-called 'dog's tooth'. Water gilding is relatively fragile and cannot be wet-cleaned.

Oil gilding cannot be burnished but can be cleaned with water. Because it is more durable than water gilding, it is used in situations where it will be exposed to wear. The surface to be decorated should be perfectly smooth, and is sealed with a coat of glue size; when this is dry, it is painted with two coats of red, yellow or white oil paint and a coat of 'flatting' to reduce shine. Once these layers are dry, a quan-

Detail of a gilded mirror frame, in the manner of James Moore, England, c. 1720, showing both carved and punched decoration.

tity of thick size is sieved and mixed with oil and a little pigment (vermilion or yellow ochre). It is painted on with a fairly stiff hog's hair brush and set aside to dry. This can take anything from 12 to 30 hours, and it is important to judge accurately the moment at which to apply the leaf. The size should be neither too wet nor too dry, but should be just tacky. The gold leaf is applied with the gilder's tip in the manner described above, ensuring that each leaf slightly overlaps the preceding one.

Once the gilding is complete, the work is gently dabbed or pressed over with a ball of cotton wool, at the same time removing all loose and superfluous material; it may also be stippled with a large hog's hair or cut sable brush to blend any visible joins. A final gentle wipe with a piece of selected chamois leather completes the work. Drying time for the size can be greatly shortened by using japanner's size, which will be ready for gilding in about 20 or 30 minutes or, if mixed with about 33% oil size, in about 2–3 hours. Rich ornamental effects can be created by punching or incising designs into the surface before the gesso is entirely dry. When finished, the work should be painted with a thin coat of the best parchment size to enhance and protect the gold.

Paper and textiles are also gilded with leaf. The surface is first painted, printed or stencilled with size (which may be thickened with pigment to create a raised design) and gold leaf or powder is then applied. Once the size is dry, any superfluous gold is brushed away from around the design. Instructions for applying gold to Japanese marbled papers include directions to brush liquid gold powder onto the surface of the paper while it is still on the drying board. Fragments of gold leaf are also used to decorate Japanese papers. (See also GOLD EMBOSSED PAPER.)

Leather is decorated with gold leaf in a similar fashion by TOOLING or GOLD BLOCKING, while varnished silver leaf was used on GILT LEATHER.

Ceramics and glass are occasionally decorated with leaf. In a method known as 'size', 'oil' or 'cold' gilding, the gold is applied with an adhesive such as linseed oil or animal glue. However, the effect is not permanent and where the leaf has worn away, it is often possible to see a faint pattern or 'bloom' made by traces of the adhesive. A more satisfactory method is to apply gold enamel which is fired on, usually in a low-temperature secondary or tertiary firing. Both of these techniques were used in East Asia.

In European wares a number of other methods were also employed. In gold lacquer, powdered gold was mixed with clear lacquer and then painted on, while in mordant gilding gold leaf or powder was applied to the surface of a vessel in a garlic and vinegar medium, which was heated and then evaporated, leaving a layer of gold behind. Neither of these

Tureen with lid and saucer, hard paste porcelain with firegilding and additional painting, Meissen, possibly by Abraham Seuter, c.1725–30.

methods is very permanent, and both honey gilding and fire- or mercury gilding were preferred. The former method involved mixing gold leaf with honey, painting this on the ceramic and then firing at a low temperature. The resulting effect, while rich and sumptuous, is dull but can be burnished to brightness. This method was superseded by firegilding or mercury gilding, in which the amalgam was painted onto the vessel and fired at a low temperature to leave a gold deposit which could be burnished to brightness. This was cheaper and easier to produce than honey gilding, but the effect is thin, metallic and brassy, quite unlike the dull rich colour of honey gilding.

Some methods are associated with particular manufacturers. At Meissen a complicated technique was developed in the late 18th century using gold powder derived from chloride of gold, which was precipitated with iron. This powder was painted on with turpentine and then fired at a low temperature. The resulting gold decoration, which is known simply as Meissen gold, could be polished and tooled. At Sèvres transfer gilding was used, in which a gold design was printed onto paper with a copper plate and then transferred to the ceramic surface. In the late 19th century the Minton factory began to use acid gilding, in which the surface of the vessel is acid-etched and gold is then applied and burnished.

In ceramics, gilding is usually applied to porcelains. They are pre-fired and usually glazed and the gilding is seen as an overglaze decoration. Certain forms of gilding are only possible on glassware and exploit the unique transparency and ductility of the material. Speckled effects are achieved by sprinkling granular gold dust onto hot glass, or by applying gold leaf to a hot gather of glass, which when blown breaks the leaf into tiny pieces. Gold leaf, perhaps engraved, can be sandwiched between two layers of glass (see FONDI D'ORO, VERRE ÉGLOMISÉ and ZWICHENGOLDGLAS). The gold tesserae used in mosaics are made in this fashion.

In metalwork, gilding has been used not only for decoration but also for economy, and even deception, and to protect an inferior metal from tarnishing. In the past the most widely used method was firegilding (when the gold is restricted to certain areas it is known as PARCEL GILT), but this has now been superseded by ELECTROPLATING.

See also LUSTRE for ceramics and glass, and DEPLETION GILDING for metalwork.

Gilt leather The term now used for the sumptuous material known variously as Spanish leather, CORDOVAN or Guadameci and used widely from the 17th century to the 19th for wall hangings, screens and upholstery and for covering trunks and boxes. Various techniques were employed in its manufacture, but the process generally involved covering the grain sides of vegetable-tanned skins with silver leaf, applied using adhesives based on white of egg. This was treated with yellow or orange varnishes which prevented the silver from tarnishing and gave the rich golden colour from which gilt leather gets its name. This surface was then decorated with punches and moulded into complex patterns, and the design coloured using a range of natural resin- and oil-based glazes or paints. The resins included sandarac and colophony and the oils linseed and possibly walnut. Finally, another layer of clear protective varnish was sometimes applied.

The production of gilt leather appears to have developed in southern Spain during the 13th century, having probably

The manufacture of gilt leather, from Auguste-Denis Fougeroux de Bondaroy's L'art de travailler les cuirs dorés ou argentés: Descriptions des arts et métiers *(1762).*

been introduced there from North Africa. The trade was particularly concentrated in the hands of the craftsmen of Moorish descent, and when these peoples were expelled from Spain in the early 17th century the techniques were spread throughout Europe, particularly to the Netherlands, which at that time was a colony of Spain, and to Venice, a major importer of gilt leather. Soon separate schools of design and manufacturing technique developed in these two new centres. Italian gilt leather continued generally to be made from the skins of goats or hair sheep, using hand punching and glazed designs, often with contrasting silver and gilt patterns. Gilt leather from the Netherlands normally employed larger, heavier calfskins, and often incorporated more heavily embossed patterns and more densely pigmented coloured paints. It was in the Netherlands, at the end of the 17th century, that a process using wooden and metal moulds was developed and gilt leather began to be manufactured on a semi-industrial basis (see colour plate II). The manufacture of gilt leather reached its peak during the 18th century, with colours and patterns following all the latest fashions in interior design. However, by the beginning of the 19th century it had been superseded by wallpapers and, apart from a renaissance during the second half of the century, the manufacture of gilt leather virtually ceased.

Gilt membrane See METAL THREAD.

Glacé kid A fine, soft, white gloving leather made from the skins of goats, hair sheep or sometimes lambs, using the alum TAWING process. The grain surface is rubbed with a smooth stone to give a fine sheen. The term is also used for a flat-grained leather made from chrome-tanned goatskins and employed particularly for shoe uppers during the first half of the 20th century. The surface is given a characteristic smooth, bright, glossy appearance by applying a clear solution of casein and polishing it with a glass cylinder.

Glair Egg white, whipped up and then allowed to settle out as a liquid. It was used in the Middle Ages and early Renaissance as a paint medium for manuscript illumination. Unlike egg yolk, the white dries to a very thin film similar to watercolour, and so works well on flexible supports such as vellum or paper. Glair is also used as an adhesive, especially in gilding.

Glass An artificial, non-crystalline material made by fusing some form of silica (usually sand, quartz or flint) with an alkali (normally soda or potash) and another base (lime) or lead oxide. Usually transparent, it can sometimes be translucent or opaque. Although appearing to be solid, glass is technically a rigid liquid, and it retains the properties and internal structure of a liquid, such as flow. However, the term 'super-cooled liquid' is now considered archaic. At room temperature the flow of common glass can be measured only by extremely delicate instruments.

Some of the terms used to describe vitreous materials have been applied ambiguously or incorrectly. There are four vitreous products: glass, GLAZE, ENAMEL and EGYPTIAN

A 15th-century Bohemian forest glasshouse. To the right a furnace is being fuelled and a worker prepares to remove a gather of glass. In the centre a worker blows and shapes a gather on a flat stone, while to the left annealed glass is removed from the lehr and packed for transport. Behind, a merchant inspects the goods and in the background workers dig sand.

FAIENCE. All four consist of silica, alkali and small amounts of lime. The first three always contain large quantities of alkali, whether sodium carbonate (as in SODA GLASS) or potassium carbonate (as in POTASH GLASS), whereas Egyptian faience is composed of fired silica with very small amounts of clay and/or alkali.

Glassmaking originated in Mesopotamia *c.*3500–3000 BC and probably arose out of local pottery and metalworking traditions. Initially the material was used as a vitreous glaze on stone and ceramic beads, or regarded as a substitute for semi-precious stones. It was first used independently to form glass objects *c.*2500 BC, when furnaces began to achieve temperatures high enough to melt silica. Most of the glassmaking techniques used today were known in the ancient world, with the exception of blowing, which was invented *c.*50 BC, prob-

ably in Syria. With the decline of the Roman empire many
skills were lost, though they survived in the Middle East. As
Islamic power waned, the Venetian glasshouses dominated
the industry from 1400 to 1700. Venetian cristallo was copied
all over Europe and was extremely popular until the late 17th
century, when George Ravenscroft invented lead glass, which
could be cut and engraved. The second half of the 19th
century was a period of enormous inventiveness, in which
older techniques were revived and new ones devised, especially for the coloration of glass.

The batch The silica is the network former and composes
part of the batch. It is usually obtained from sand, taken
either from the sea shore or, preferably, from inland beds
whose sand is free from impurities such as iron and is more
readily ground. In ancient times impurities caused the glass
to have a yellow, green or brownish colour. As glassmaking
became more refined, the sand was washed and heated to
remove calcareous matter, and screened to obtain uniform
small grains. Silica can also be obtained and used in the form
of pebbles or flint. The alkali (sodium or potassium carbonate) is a flux which acts as the network modifier by lowering
the melting- or fusion-point of the silica from $c.1720°C$ to
$c.1300–1550°C$. It is added as a soluble salt, usually soda or
potash, and generally forms about 15–20% of the batch. The
lime, in the form of calcium carbonate (obtained from calcined limestone), acts as a network stabilizer which imparts
stability to the batch and makes it water-resistant. Without
it, the glass would gradually dissolve in water. Originally
introduced unintentionally as an impurity in the raw materials, the importance of lime was realized in the 17th century
and it became a deliberate addition. Lead oxide, which in
some modern glasses entirely replaces the lime, gives the glass
a longer working range and increases its refractive index.

The raw materials are mixed together with other ingredients such as cullet (broken or scrap glass) in a crucible or fire
clay pot. This is heated in a FURNACE (or kiln) to
$c.1300–1550°C$, at which point it forms a molten, glassy (vitreous) substance known as the 'metal'. In the manufacture of
ancient vitreous materials this process was preceded by an
intermediate one known as fritting (see FRIT). In modern
glassmaking there is then an initial phase of heating the
batch in the furnace by founding, when the materials must be
brought up to a temperature of $c.1400°C$. There follows a

maturing (or refining) period of twelve hours, when the molten glass is held at an elevated temperature in order for the larger air bubbles to escape, after which it cools to a working temperature of *c.* 1100°C.

During the process of melting, a scum or gall rises to the surface of the batch and is skimmed off. However, impurities may remain in the glass. In early glass these were unintentional but later they could be used to create deliberate effects. They include stones (specks of foreign matter) and seed (undissolved tiny bubbles of glass that rise to the surface during melting and, if not totally removed, appear as tiny specks in the finished glass objects). To create a decorative effect, a chemical such as potassium nitrate may be injected into the batch. This reacts with the heat to form air bubbles. Cords or striae may appear in glass, again either by defect or design. They are the result of the molten glass not having been a homogeneous mix, for which there are several causes: a variation in the furnace temperature, the unequal density of the raw materials, or some silica in the composition of the pot breaking off and forming with the batch. The resulting product is termed reamy or cord glass. When making high-quality crystal, the formation of cords is avoided by stirring the batch constantly.

Decolourizing agents Until the 17th century glasses were not made to specific recipes. The success of the batch and subsequent glass made from it depended upon the composition of the original materials. These usually contained impurities such as iron, which accounts for the green coloration of many early glasses, especially forest glass. From Roman times a decolourizing agent was sometimes added to the batch to counteract the effect of any impurities, whether leaching from the glass pots or originating elsewhere in the production process. The decolourizing agent acts as a chromatic neutralizer, when it and iron are present in equal quantities, by absorbing the light that the iron transmits. However, if iron and the decolourizing agent manganese are present in too great a quantity, little light can be transmitted, and the glass, if thick, appears grey or black. Manganese dioxide (glassmakers' soap) was used by the Romans in the 2nd century AD. Much later, nickel was used either alone or in blue cullet, producing a bluish coloration to the glass. At the end of the 18th century minute quantities of cobalt were used for decolourizing glass. Arsenic is a constituent, in a very

A glass jar with decorative internal bubbles, by Maurice Marinot, 1920s.

minute quantity, of almost all modern colourless glass, serving to improve the colour, transparency and brilliance. It is introduced as oxide of arsenic, a white powder made by heating minerals containing arsenic in a current of air. In the melting-pot some remains in the molten glass, although some is lost in vapour.

Colouring agents Glass can be coloured by the unintentional presence of METALLIC OXIDES as impurities in the raw materials, or by the deliberate addition of a metallic oxide to the molten glass batch. In general, colours towards the red end of the spectrum are more difficult to produce. Blue is easily made with cobalt or with copper, which in oxidation gives sky blue or turquoise but in reduction a dull red. Green is made by the addition of iron or chromium, the latter giving yellowish greens in an oxidizing atmosphere and an emerald green if the oxygen is reduced. Uranium oxide or silver will give yellow, though in the Middle Ages yellow was made from iron plus manganese. Orange, which is a difficult colour, is made by the addition of selenium. Pale pink and shades of violet and purple are made with manganese, and red with copper, gold, cadmium selenide (a binary compound of selenium) or zinc sulphide. Black will result if any colouring agent is used in excess; an opaque black is made from a combination of iron, manganese and sulphur in a reducing atmosphere. Not all of these metallic oxides were known in antiquity.

Certain red, orange and yellow coloured glasses were produced by dispersing copper, silver or gold metals (rather than their oxides) in the batch. The technology is complicated because of the need to reheat the glass to make the colour appear, or 'strike'. For example, purple of Cassius, a crimson-purple colour, was prepared by precipitating a gold solution by means of chloride of tin and then adding the resultant colloidal gold to the batch; the treated glass became ruby-red when reheated to strike the colour. Dispersed metal colours are known as silver-stain yellow or copper or gold rubies (see RUBY GLASS and SILVER STAINING). The use of a tiny percentage of colloidal metal to the batch can result in the glass having a dichromatic quality (that is, it displays a different coloration when seen by reflected or transmitted light). A famous example of glass displaying this effect is the Lycurgus Cup (see colour plate VIIa), which appears opaque pea-green in reflected light and wine-red by transmitted light. This is

A decanter in filigree glass, striped in alternative opaque white and opaque blue dipped in blue, probably Clichy, c.1850.

due to the presence of gold in the batch, though traces of silver and other minerals may contribute to the dichroic effect.

Opacity can be produced in the glass by the incorporation of tiny bubbles or other dispersed materials, or by the addition of certain agents. Antimony was used in ancient times, tin from the 5th century AD until the 18th (see LATTIMO), and fluorine or lead thereafter. White opaque glass is now produced with arsenic. Glass in imitation of semi-precious stones is made by briefly combining opaque glass in the pot. The ancients used this technique, as did the Venetians in their celebrated chalcedony glass (see also HYALITH and LITHYALIN).

A bottle in mould-blown glass, Iran, 12th century AD. It is yellowish green in colour, with a thread of aubergine glass trailed around the neck opening.

Iridescence may be the result of a natural deterioration in the glass or may be induced chemically. In the latter part of the 19th century attempts were made to emulate the iridescence of degraded ancient glass by artificial means. Thomas Wilkes Webb of Stourbridge invented a method in 1877 in which glass was placed in a closed muffle kiln and exposed to fumes from the evaporation of tin and other metals. Other methods include spraying hot glass with stannous (tin) chloride or lead chloride and then firing it in a reducing atmosphere at the fire. The metallic salts become embedded in the glass surface, producing an optical interference effect. (See also LUSTRE.)

Forming and decoration Glass is plastic when molten, ductile when cooled from the molten state to a temperature at which it can be manipulated, or on reheating, and glyptic when cold. When hot, it will form an instant bond with another piece of hot glass. Molten glass can be freely blown and turned on the blowing iron, then worked with a number of simple tools into a vast variety of shapes, provided these are basically circular in section (see GLASS BLOWING). By blowing the glass into moulds the shapes can be infinitely extended (see PRESS MOULDING and MOULD–BLOWN GLASS). Hot working can also include formative and decorative techniques of applied ornament (see MARVERING and TRAILING). These additions may be from the same batch of metal as the original glass or of a different colour or transparency. Other hot-worked decorative techniques include the inclusion of air bubbles or twists of extended air bubbles (see TWIST STEM) and the manufacture of glass cane. The latter can be employed to create complex filigree designs or mosaic glass and millefiori. Molten glass can be slumped or cast into moulds, or introduced into moulds by the lost wax process

A glass beaker with a view of Osek, north Bohemia, c.1845. It is cut, engraved and painted in ruby.

and press moulding.

When cold, glass can be shaped by cutting, abrading and grinding, and also decorated by hand- or wheel-engraving, acid etching, sand-blasting, lustre painting, enamelling (see ENAMEL COLOURS), cold painting, gilding, transfer engraving and transfer printing.

Some decorative techniques involve both hot and cold processes. In cased glass (or overlay glass), for example, two or more differently coloured glasses are blown inside each other, either free-hand or in a mould. Once hardened and annealed, the top layer(s) of glass are cut away to varying depths, thus producing a cameo effect.

Annealing and other finishing processes After the molten glass has been formed into objects, it retains residual stress and strain owing to the fact that some parts remain hot while others are cooler. The glass is thus prone to cracking or breaking, either spontaneously or when subjected to changes of external temperature. The stresses must be removed by annealing the glass in a lehr. The process involves subjecting the glassware to reheating and subsequent gradual and uniform cooling. Modern-day annealing takes between six and sixty hours, depending on the weight of the glass.

On completion of the manufacturing process but before annealing, the glass surface can be given a brilliant finish, called fire polish, by reheating it in a GLORY HOLE. This controlled reheating is also carried out to affect the basic colour of some glasses, for example to strike gold ruby glass or to produce iridescent effects. Enamelling and gilding have to be fixed by reheating the glass in a muffle kiln after the annealing.

Glass beads Beads formed entirely from glass. They can be made by at least six methods: winding glass threads around a rod; drawing from a gob of glass which has been worked into a hollow; folding glass around a core (the join being visible on one side); pressing glass into a mould; perforating soft glass with a rod; and blowing (though cylindrical blown glass beads are extremely rare). They can be decorated by trailing or by marvering in chips of coloured glass. Mosaic glass and mille-fiori techniques are also used in the production of glass beads.

Glass blowing The manufacture of glass vessels by blowing spheres of hot glass on a blowpipe. Free-blown glass is manipulated into shape with special tools, while MOULD-BLOWN GLASS is blown into moulds. Glass blowing was introduced in

OPPOSITE
Glass vessel manufacture in the mid-18th century, from Diderot's Encyclopédie des arts et des métiers. *Troughs of water for wetting the tools can be seen in the foreground.*
(Fig. 1) Attaching a gather of glass, which will form the foot of a goblet, to a bowl and stem held on the blowing iron.
(Fig. 2) Shaping the foot.
(Fig. 3) Attaching the foot to the pontil rod.
(Fig. 4) Reheating the goblet in the glory hole of the furnace.
(Fig. 5) Trimming the rim of the bowl with shears.
(Fig. 6) Widening and evening the bowl and placing the completed glass in the annealing oven.

Syria in the 1st century BC and revolutionized the production of glass. When combined with mould-blowing, it enabled the rapid industrial manufacture of thin-walled vessels, in shapes and profiles to rival those in metal or pottery.

The process requires great skill, speed and co-ordination. It begins with the craftsman picking up a blob of molten glass (a gather) from the mouth of the furnace on a gathering or blowing iron. In the manufacture of a simple wineglass, this gather is rolled back and forth (marvered) over a flat surface to make it perfectly cylindrical and concentric. It is then blown into a bubble (parison) to form the bowl of the glass. The blowpipe may also be swung through the air to control the shape and thickness of the bubble. Once it is the correct size, the stem and foot are added from small lumps of molten glass. A solid iron rod (the pontil) is then attached to the foot. This enables the blowing iron to be 'cracked off' (or 'wetted off'): the glass is circumscribed with a sharp, wet metal tool and tapped so that it breaks off cleanly. Finally, the glass is held on the pontil while the rim is finished by working with shears or pincers. During the entire process, the glass is taken

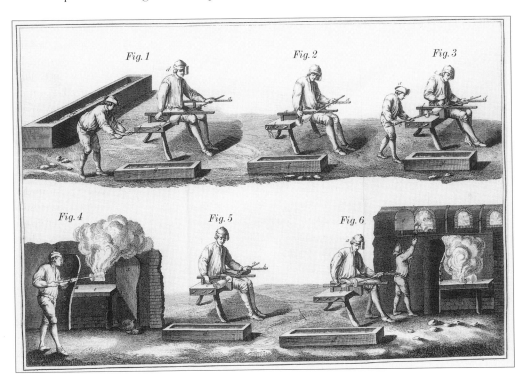

Glassmaking tools, from François Haudicquer de Blancourt's The Art of Glass *(1699). They include an iron blowpipe (A) with a wooden handle, scissors (D), pincers (E), a ladle (F) for transferring glass into small pots for the workmen, a sieve (N) for skimming impurities from the surface of the molten glass, and a shovel (H) for moving the hot glassware.*

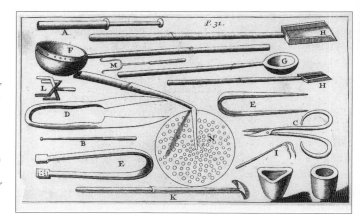

to the GLORY HOLE and reheated to keep it soft and malleable; it is also kept in constant rotation to stop it sagging out of shape. Once the object has finally cooled, the pontil is cracked off. This leaves a rough mark on the foot which in the best glass is polished out.

In more elaborate items blobs of hot glass are used to form handles, stems, rims and so on, while the metal is also worked with various tools to elongate, twist or pinch it into shape. Components can be worked on a pontil and then attached by fusion to other pieces, perhaps a foot or bowl, which are ready and hot in the LEHR.

Many of the hot-working techniques can be carried out by an individual glassblower; however, it is more usual to work around the furnace in a team, called a chair (or 'shop'). The principal glassworker is the 'gaffer', who does most of the skilled and intricate work and controls the working of the team until the objects are completed and sent to the lehr for annealing. The gaffer is supplied with the gather of glass, and assisted in the manufacturing process by other members of the chair, usually numbering five or six craftsmen and apprentices.

The glassmaker has a number of simple tools in addition to the gathering iron, blowing iron and pontil. These include pincers to squeeze the glass into shape, shears and scissors to snip it, a hollow block of wood that is dipped in water and used to form the molten glass into a sphere before it is blown, and a flat wooden paddle, called a battledore, to smooth the underside of items. The 'chair' is a wide bench with arms over which the gaffer rolls the blowing iron. The arms are flat, extended, and slightly sloping so the gaffer can rest the blow-pipe with its attached gather of molten glass. He constantly rotates the gather back and forth with his left hand so that it keeps its symmetrical shape and does not collapse while he works it with his right hand. The marver is a flat surface on which the gather of molten glass is rolled into a cylindrical, symmetrical mass. Originally it was of stone, especially marble (hence the name, from the French, *marbre*), but now it is iron.

Glass cane A slender rod of glass made by drawing out a gather of glass attached to two pontil irons to the desired thinness. There are two basic types of cane used as decorative inclusions in glass: lengths of coloured cane, which are

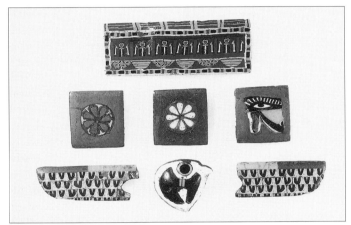

Slices of glass cane, Egypt, Ptolomaic period, 1st century BC. Each pattern is composed of coloured canes, fused by heating and drawn out to produce the desired size. When cold, the resulting block of glass is sliced to be used as inlay. The two pieces to the bottom left and right are mirror images, both cut from the same block.

embedded singly or in groups to form spirals, for example within the stems of wineglasses; and canes patterned in cross-section, which are thinly sliced and embedded in clear glass to reveal their design. The former are made by dipping a gather of coloured glass into clear, molten glass and stretching it out into a cane. If a number of these canes are laid side by side and then picked up on a hot gather of clear glass, stretched and twisted, they will develop vertical spiral patterns (see TWIST STEM and FILIGREE).

Canes to be seen in cross-section are usually made by arranging rods of different colours in a mould, then fusing and drawing out the glass. The cross-section may be a compli-cated geometric pattern or the image of a person or animal. The colours or patterns do not change their relative positions in the drawing-out process and some canes are of such tiny diameter that the motif in cross-section is no larger than a pin-head. In order to make an even more complicated pattern, these canes are drawn, sliced and used as constituents of a new cane. A cane with a spiral cross-section is often used in MOSAIC GLASS. It is made by rolling a flattened gather of opaque white glass, thinly coated in clear glass, around a cane of contrasting colour and then drawing it out.

Profiled canes are cast in moulds and then stretched. By repeating the process with moulds of increasing size, a concentric pattern can be created. This type of cane is used for MILLEFIORI.

Glass disease See CRIZZLING.

Glass engraving The decoration of glass by engraving or cutting. The technique most commonly used is wheel-engraving, using rotating abrasive discs. The same basic processes are used for engraving or cutting (see CUT GLASS), and the difference lies in the size of the wheels, which are large and powerful for cutting but usually small, and therefore sometimes portable, for engraving. The design is drawn on the surface of the glass and the rotating wheels, usually copper fed with abrasives, are used to grind away the glass surface to varying degrees and produce an illusion of modelling and depth.

Both intaglio and relief effects can be created. In intaglio engraving (sometimes known as 'hollow relief' or *tiefschnitt*), the design is executed below the surface of the glass and the

Glass engraving. A sheet of glass is held against a rapidly turning metal wheel continuously fed with water and abrasive in order to cut the design drawn on the glass.

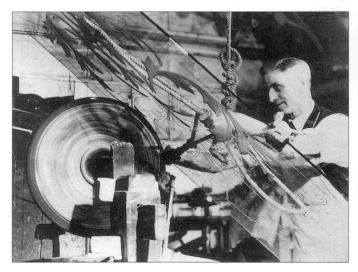

background is not cut away but left as the highest plane of the design (an impression taken from the glass will show the image in relief). The engraving may be polished or left matt. In relief engraving (or *hochschnitt*) the design projects and the ground is cut away, as in cameo carving. The projection may be very pronounced (high relief), or merely distinct (medium relief) or very subtle (low relief).

Wheel-engraving developed out of the work of lapidary workers who saw glass as a substitute for rock crystal. It was used by the Romans but largely died out in Europe through a lack of suitable glass. It became feasible again only in the late 17th century, with the invention of potash-lime glass (see POTASH GLASS). Its development, which is credited to the early 17th-century Prague-based gem cutter Caspar Lehmann, is also linked to the evolution of rotary power.

A plaque in intaglio-engraved clear glass, by Caspar Lehmann, Prague or Dresden, 1602 or 1606. It shows the Elector of Saxony, Christian II.

Goblet, colourless glass cut and engraved in relief, Bohemia, c.1730. The depth of the cutting can be seen in the profile.

Goblet, colourless glass engraved with diamond point, Hall, Tyrol, late 16th century. The lines of the engraving, done by hand, are uneven and the design merely scratched into the glass.

Initially only foot treadles had been available, but by this period water power was in use. Deep relief and intaglio cutting would have been impossible without this extra power.

A simpler option was diamond point engraving. This is occasionally seen on Roman and Islamic glass but re-emerged in Venice in the mid-16th century. The Venetian cristallo was especially suited to diamond point as it was soft enough to take an impression easily and allow free movement to the engraver. Later diamond point engraving was used throughout Europe, especially on glass *à la façon de Venise*, and it became a popular pastime for amateurs. The diamond is held

Goblet, lead crystal glass stipple engraved by Jacobus van den Blijk, Dordrecht, 1775. The design, an Allegory of Freedom, is soft in appearance. Small air bubbles can be seen in the stem knop.

in a pen-like device.

Stipple engraving is a variation of diamond point engraving in which the point is tapped to produce grouped and graded dots. These create the highlights of the design, while the shadows and background result from leaving the polished glass untouched. The technique evolved in the Netherlands in the 1720s and was popular until the end of the 18th century.

See also ETCHING and SAND-BLASTING. For gold engraving, see VERRE ÉGLOMISÉ.

Glass fibre Fibre drawn from molten glass as a thread. When made as a continuous filament it can be drawn out and wound round a spool for use in knitting and weaving. It was known in the ancient world and reappeared in Europe in the 18th century. In 1713 a glass fibre cloth woven by the Venetian Carlo Riva was submitted to the Paris Academy of Science by the French physicist René Réaumur.

Glass fibre reinforced plastics Plastics made of glass fibres bound together with polyester or epoxy resins. 'Low-pressure resins' for reinforced plastics were first used commercially in 1942 in the USA as glass cloth reinforced resin radomes for aircraft. By the late 1940s glass fibre reinforced plastics were in commercial use and in the 1950s designers such as Charles

Tulip *chair, with a glass fibre reinforced plastic shell on a cast aluminium base coated with nylon, designed by Eero Saarinen in 1956. Strong plastics such as this allowed designers incredible freedom in form, which was to be explored, sometimes to extreme lengths, in the 1960s and 1970s.*

Eames began to use the material, leading to the design of the classic glass fibre stackable chair: tough, fairly inflexible and light. Other modern uses include decorative architectural mouldings, furniture, baths, roofing, car bodies and boat

hulls.
Glassmaking tools See GLASS BLOWING.
Glaze [ceramics] A layer of silicate glass applied to the surface of a ceramic vessel in order to seal the surface and decorate or change the surface texture. Most utilitarian ceramics are glazed, with the exception of low-fired earthenware flowerpots or water vessels whose function requires them to be porous. Glazes are made from essentially the same ingredients as a ceramic body (i.e., clay) but with more glass formers or silicates, such as quartz or feldspar, and with fluxes, which are added to reduce the melting-point of the silica from 1700°C. In order to be effective, a glaze must melt so that it can flow over the surface of the ceramic, and then it must cool into a hard glass covering. The melting process must therefore be carried out at temperatures supported by available kiln technology. Accordingly, glazes are generally classified by the type of flux used.

Glazes used on low-fired ceramics include lead, alkaline and tin glazes. On high-fired ceramics the main types are lime, lime-alkali, salt and porcelain glazes, which are also sometimes called acid-rock glazes. These glazes are coloured with metallic oxides, the most common of which are iron, copper, cobalt, manganese, antimony and chromium (see METALLIC OXIDES). Iron is the most abundant metal oxide found on earth and is therefore used more often than other oxides as a ceramic colourant. Most pigments can produce a wide range of colours, depending on the chemistry of the base glaze and the firing atmosphere (see FIRING). For example, copper oxide used in an alkaline glaze produces mainly turquoise colours, whereas in a lead glaze a bright green colour is produced, and in a porcelain glaze fired in reduction a red glaze results. Glazes of one colour (or monochrome glazes) are often named after the colourant, such as copper red or imperial yellow. Glazes can be decorated either before firing, with IN-GLAZE DECORATION, or after firing, with overglaze or enamel decoration (see ENAMEL COLOURS).

Glazes are usually applied as a liquid suspension, either by dipping a vessel in a vat or by spraying or brushing glaze onto the surface. Some of the more unusual types are not applied by hand but rather by adjusting the chemistry of the body material or by manipulating the firing (see SALT GLAZE). Several glazes can be layered to produce interesting decorative effects or to imitate the natural glazing effect of kiln ash,

Red earthenware jug with slip decoration and lead glaze, England, probably Harlow, c.1630–60.

as in some Japanese stonewares. Glazes can be applied to both unfired or pre-fired ceramics (see BISCUIT). When applied to unfired ceramics, the vessel must be handled and dried very carefully, as the glaze can overwet the body and damage it. A biscuit-fired vessel is easier to handle but the glaze fit is not as good as with once-fired glazed vessels. Ideally, the glaze should be compatible with the ceramic body in terms of expansion and contraction, so that it does not peel off, blister or crack (see CRAZING), although cracking is sometimes induced deliberately for decorative effect (see CRACKLE). When a glaze is fired with the body, particularly with high-fired ceramics, an integrated layer forms where the glaze soaks into the body slightly. This layer, often very thick in the case of porcelain, acts as a buffer which absorbs shock and can prevent glaze faults. This is also where layers of crystals can form which reflect light back through a glaze, making it appear luminous (see CRYSTALLINE GLAZE and JUN GLAZE).

Glaze [paint] A layer of translucent coloured paint which acts like a sheet of tinted glass, enriching and deepening the colour of the material over which it is laid. Thus a blue glaze laid over an opaque red base coat will produce a purple far more intense than a simple red and blue mixture. Almost all paint can act as a kind of glaze if it is brushed on sufficiently thinly, but watercolour, oil and oil/resin paints are the most effective, particularly when used with pigments of low opacity. Pigments vary in covering power from the completely opaque ones such as titanium white or cadmium red (which would obviously not be useful for glazing) to very translucent ones such as ultramarine or viridian. The most translucent of all are the LAKE pigments.

Glazed brick Brick with a smooth, vitreous coloured layer on its surface. Although glazed bricks were produced by the Babylonians and Assyrians from the 9th to the 6th century BC, their manufacture was not widespread until the 19th century. Three glazing techniques were developed. A brown glaze, which was used on bricks for utilitarian purposes, was produced by throwing salt into the kiln when the temperature had reached 1200°C. The production of other colours was more elaborate. For the dry-dipped method, previously fired bricks were first dipped in a mixture of clay slip (a suspension of clay in water) and crushed flint. After this dried, a second layer containing the same mixture plus a metallic oxide colourant, such as copper for green, chromium for pink or cobalt for blue, was then applied and left to dry. A final layer containing sodium, potassium and calcium carbonate was applied before the unit was fired for the second time, producing a vitreous surface. A simpler process, the wet-dipped method, which involved applying the three layers to unfired brick, was more economical as it required only a single firing but resulted in a less durable product.

Glory hole A hole in the side of a furnace through which the workman picks up the gather of glass or reheats it as work progresses. In modern glassmaking the glory hole is often a separate furnace, perhaps with multiple openings, used exclusively for reheating. Mould-blown glass is often fire-polished at the glory hole to remove imperfections remaining from the manufacturing process.

Glue An ADHESIVE based on the gelatine extracted from animal products.

Gobelins stitch See GROS POINT.

Gold A yellow precious metal that is soft, extremely malleable and has a high density. The purity or fineness of gold is expressed in carats (US, karats): 24 carats is pure gold and an 18-carat alloy contains 75% gold (see CARAT). Gold has always been one of the most valued materials, partly because of its rarity but also because of its nobility. Gold jewellery and artefacts have been made for more than 6000 years, and gold is still the principal metal in jewellery. Gold as a medium of exchange has a history going back as far as 3500 BC.

Gold is found in nature, as a native metal, in two forms: as small pebbles in gravel and riverbeds, where it is known as placer gold, or in veins of quartz, where it is called vein gold. Nuggets are gold found in pebble form and can vary in size from tiny particles to large lumps weighing over 100 kg. Gold can also be found in a natural alloy with silver, called electrum. Most gold ores contain very little gold ($c.5$–15 g per metric ton) but some gold-rich ore in South Africa can contain up to 30 g per metric ton.

Gold can be found in small amounts in most countries but the main modern producers are South Africa, the former USSR and Canada. It is extracted from its ore first by grinding the ore to fine particles and then dissolving the gold in mercury or cyanides. This produces an impure gold containing silver, some copper and other base metals which can be removed by oxidation. The final refining is done by electrolysis, which produces a 99.99% pure gold. Methods of working gold are similar to those used for SILVER.

The largest consumer of gold is still the jewellery trade, where the metal is almost always alloyed to improve its working properties and colour, but also to moderate the price. Pure gold is too soft to use and is usually alloyed with silver and/or copper; silver gives a pale yellow to greenish colour to the gold, while copper renders it reddish. A white-coloured gold can be produced by alloying gold with nickel or palladium. Other large modern users of gold are the electronics industry and dentistry. Gold is also used as a decorative and protective coating (see GILDING) and in colouring glass.

Gold blocking A method of decorating leather, in which a gold leaf design is applied using a heated block in a press. It is thought to have been introduced to Europe from Persia by the late 15th century. For the finest work the pattern is first impressed into the grain surface. The embossed area is then coated with size or glair. Gold leaf is then placed over the surface and the same block is used again. This melts the size and sticks the gold leaf to the leather. Once cool, the excess gold can be brushed off.

The preliminary blind embossing stage can be by-passed by treating the whole of the leather surface with size or other suitable materials. Some leathers are sold by the tanner in this already prepared condition. Plastic films to which gold or substitute mixtures have been electro-deposited are now obtainable, which will stick to leather under the combined effects of heat and pressure.

Gold embossed paper Paper embossed and gilded to resemble a textile. It is also known as 'Dutch gilt' and 'Dutch floral' paper but was actually manufactured in Germany and Italy. It was produced on a roller press similar to that used for etchings, but the copper plates were thicker (about 6 mm) and were deeply engraved and gouged. The imitation gold leaf (a copper–zinc alloy called DUTCH METAL) was laid on the heated plate. Above this was placed the sheet of dampened and sized paper, and finally a sheet of felt. The whole sandwich was then turned through the roller press. The leaf in the areas of the plate which were incised did not adhere and could then be brushed away, leaving the desired pattern. The papers were used for book endpapers and wrappers from about 1700 and remained in production through to the 19th century.

Gold lacquer Gold leaf mixed with lacquer and painted onto the surface of an object.

Gold leaf Gold beaten to gossamer-thin sheet for use in GILDING. For centuries leaf has been made by passing a gold ingot between steel rollers to give a long ribbon that is then cut into squares. These are interleaved with sheets of parchment and repeatedly beaten and folded into a pack of leaves 80 mm square. They are then divided into sections of 25 leaves and formed into a 'book' between sheets of rouged tissue. In recent times transfer gold has been made by pressing leaf onto tissue paper, or spluttering it onto waxed paper. Foil is made by vapourizing the gold onto a polyester film.

Gold paint See GILDING.

Goncalo alves A wood, also known as zebrawood, with a very varied grain pattern and colour, from the *Astronium fraxinifolium* tree.

Gouache Watercolour paint that has been made opaque and given a more solid texture. Traditionally this was done by mixing watercolours with white chalk or, since the 1830s, zinc white and, since the 1930s, with titanium white. These pigments work well in aqueous paint, unlike traditional lead white (which has a tendency to turn black). Ranges of gouache are now sold in tubes which have good covering power, yet have no white added. Additives such as bulking agents give gouache a consistency similar to oil paint when it is squeezed from the tube, and since it does not soak into the paper, as watercolour does, it can be used to create blocks of colour with a uniform, matt finish. Because it is so useful in creating simple fields of colour it has been much used by designers of textiles and wallpapers in creating artwork. It is sometimes called body colour.

Graffito See SGRAFFITO.

Grain [leather] The outer layer of a piece of leather from which the hair or wool has been removed. The 'grain split' is a leather composed of the grain side only, separated longitudinally from the 'flesh split'.

Grain [textiles] An alternative name for KERMES, the most expensive dye in the Middle Ages. Its cost gave rise to the phrase 'dyed in the grain' to indicate the highest quality of fastness. The term 'grained' refers to stick LAC when the twigs have been removed.

Grain [wood] The pattern produced by the arrangement of the various elements that make up wood, to some extent interchangeable with the term FIGURE but usually confined to those features that affect the way in which the timber can be worked. Grain that runs parallel to the length of the timber is called straight grain. Interlocking grain is a spiral wood-grain that varies in pitch and direction. The spirals are opposed in different growth periods. Timber with interlocking grain is difficult to work and split.

Graining A painting technique used on furniture and architectural woodwork made from cheap timber such as pine to make it resemble another wood. Oak and walnut are the most commonly imitated, but experienced grainers can duplicate the effect of any exotic hardwood. The practice goes back to the 17th century, but the methods used today are based on the skills developed in the 19th century, when graining was in high fashion. Seventeenth-century graining was very stylized, with bold brushwork and solid colours laid on in a single layer. A more naturalistic effect was achieved in the 18th century, but the technique was still quite simple, and specific woods were only loosely imitated. It was not until the 19th century, when grainers started using multiple superimposed glazes, that the deceptively realistic effects common today first became possible.

A uniform base coat of oil paint, in an appropriate colour, is laid over the surface to be grained—dull yellow for oak, reddish brown for mahogany, and so on—and the dark streaks of the wood-grain are feathered over this with soft, long-haired brushes and comb-shaped tools. The process is completed with translucent glazes to adjust the colour, and the graining is then varnished to give it the sheen of highly polished wood.

Granite An igneous rock, formed at great depth, composed of distinct crystals of quartz, feldspar and mica. It has a coarse- to medium-grained texture and is usually pale grey or pink with black flecks produced by the mica, although a blue-grey variety is quarried in Sardinia. Granite is hard, dense and resistant to weathering. It occurs throughout the world and has been used for utilitarian structures such as bridge piers and harbour walls, where its strength and imperviousness are valued. It has also been employed as a building stone, often in places where no other suitable stone was available, but also elsewhere as an impressive, monumental material, and for columns, sarcophagi, basins, plinths and as a facing material. Because of its hardness granite is generally carved into broadly rounded forms with few undercuts.

The ancient Egyptians used granite extensively and probably obtained it from boulders, rather than by quarrying, until at least the Middle Kingdom. The high tensile strength of granite allowed them to produce large structures, such as obelisks, from single blocks. The ancient Indians probably quarried hard stones such as granite by heating them with fires and then suddenly cooling them with water to promote cracking. Granite was shaped by the Egyptians by pounding with hand-held stones, cutting and drilling, with quartz sand applied to metal saws and water as a lubricant; polishing was also carried out with sand or emery, an impure form of the mineral corundum, and water. With these materials a high, durable sheen could be produced. The Aztecs also cut granite with copper saws and sand.

These techniques were not known in medieval Europe, where granite was obtained from outcrops and roughly shaped into blocks. Low relief carving was used to decorate some granite buildings, such as the church of St Mary Magdalene in Launceston, Cornwall, and the cavalry memorials of Brittany. Granite carving was a slow process carried out with a chisel, which was blunter and thicker than chisels used on softer stones, held at right angles to the surface. When struck, the point of the chisel crushed the stone underneath, resulting in a slightly pitted surface. Complex working of granite was not possible until the development of power tools in the 18th century. Today granite is widely used in the form of thin highly polished panels as cladding on steel-framed buildings.

Other related but chemically separate rocks, such as granodiorite, a medium- to fine-grained grey igneous rock, and diorite, are often erroneously referred to as granite.

Granite ware A type of cream ware produced by Wedgwood in the 18th century to resemble natural stone. It is related to AGATE WARE, with surface decoration involving the application of two different coloured slips to give a mottled appearance. For granite ware, a light-coloured slip was splashed all over a grey-blue glaze surface to create a speckled background. As this was usually applied to an unfired glaze, it was a type of in-glaze decoration. Like agate ware, granite ware often featured engine-turned decoration and was made in the neo-classical style.

Granulation A decorative technique used in jewellery, whereby a metal surface is covered, with the aid of heat but without

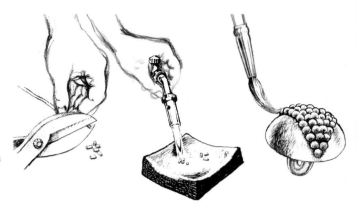

Granulation. The wire is cut into small pieces, heated with a blow torch on a wooden block and stuck to the metal surface with gum.

the use of solder, with minute gold or silver granules. The name derives from the Latin *granulum* (a diminutive of *granum*, 'grain'). The earliest examples of granulation are from Mesopotamia and date from 3000–2000 BC, but the real masters of granulation were the Etruscans, followed by the classical Greeks. The technique remained in use in Asia and Russia but entirely disappeared in the West, to the extent that it had to be reinvented in the 19th century by revivalist jewellers such as the Castellani family, who moved to London from Italy.

The first step in granulation is to make the granules by cutting the gold alloy (65–75% gold) into minute pieces. These are dispersed in a crucible filled with charcoal powder and the crucible is heated until the metal melts and contracts to granules. Examples as small as 0.14 mm can be found on Etruscan jewellery. After cooling, the granules are applied to the surface of the metal workpiece. This can be done in two ways. In the first, metals are heated until their surfaces start to melt and diffuse with each other, so that they form a bond after cooling down. The second method uses a mixture of copper salts and an organic adhesive to aid in the bonding. The mixture is applied to the workpiece with the arranged granules. When heated, the copper compounds form an oxide while the adhesive carbonizes. This carbonization reduces the copper oxide to metallic copper, which alloys with the gold or silver and establishes the bond.

Graphic media Materials used for drawing. Charcoal and white chalk, together with red earth pigments, are ancient graphic media still in use today. Media comprising pigments formed into convenient sticks—such as crayons, pastels, chalks and graphite pencils—rely on the binding together of the finely ground pigment with an adhesive-like substance such as an oil, wax, resin or gum. See also INK.

Graver The main engraver's tool (also called a burin), made of a hardened steel rod attached to a wooden handle and used for cutting grooves, usually in metal. Gravers can have a variety of cross-sections, according to their engraving purposes.

Gravity mould casting See CASTING.

Greenstone A common name for NEPHRITE, one of two minerals known as jade. The term has also been applied to a metamorphic stone containing hydrous magnesium silicates and iron minerals found in Virginia, USA.

Greenware An alternative name for CELADON.

Grisaille A brownish enamel paint made with iron oxide and used to define details in painted glass windows. The term is also used of any form of monochrome painted decoration in other media.

Grog A coarse material consisting of crushed pottery, added to very plastic clay bodies to improve workability. It also increases strength in open firings (such as bonfire firing or uncovered pit firing) by creating steam channels in the body and helps to ensure even drying and firing. Quartz and sand can also be used for similar purposes. As well as improving the texture of wet clay and making it easier to handle and form, grog also opens the clay, which reduces shrinkage and warping and in the case of soft-fired grogs allows very sticky clays to be handled for biscuit firing. It is also sometimes known as 'temper'.

Gros point The name of a canvaswork embroidery stitch (also known as Gobelins stitch) which leans to the right by one ground thread and rises up by two, or for canvaswork made with this stitch. Saint-Auban describes both *gros point* and PETIT POINT as having designs drawn in ink and then stitched over with coloured silks to indicate the shades to be used. The term is also used for a form of needle lace.

Ground A coat of paint or gesso laid over an object to seal it, and to give it the texture and colour that the painter wants as a background for his work. Gesso grounds are also used under gilding to seal the wood and provide a smooth surface for the application of gold leaf. The material of the ground has to be appropriate for the support, so that gesso grounds, based on chalk and animal glue, work well on rigid supports such as wood, where they fill the hollows of the grain and create a good working surface, but they are too brittle for fabric, which needs the flexibility of an oil ground. The ground also has to be compatible with the paint, so that oil grounds are used as a base for oils and acrylic grounds for acrylics. On impermeable surfaces such as glass, stone, composite wood, plastic or metal, the sealing function is unnecessary, and a ground is applied only when a specific background colour is wanted.

Gu embroidery See NEEDLE PAINTING.

Guadameci See GILT LEATHER.

Guarea The common name for three types of wood. *Guarea marinheiro* is a type of mahogany from Central America. It is reddish brown, moderately hard, heavy and strong. Straight-grained, smooth and easily worked, it is used as a substitute for true mahogany. *Guarea cedrata* is a Nigerian timber also known as scented guarea, pearwood, bossé and obobonufua. Moderately hard, heavy, strong and stable, it has a closely interlocking grain and roey figure. It is easily worked and is used for high-class joinery, furniture, flooring, turnery and veneers. *Guarea trichilioides*, or trompillo, is a Central American timber resembling mahogany. It is greyish pink to mahogany brown, and is sometimes streaked. It is moderately hard, heavy and strong, and is straight-grained with a roey figure and some rays which can be accentuated by quartering. It is also highly fragrant and is used for high-class joinery and furniture making.

Guattaris marble See ARTIFICIAL STONE.

Guipure embroidery See RAISED WORK.

Guipure lace A term used of any lace without a mesh ground, its motifs joined only by threads, or 'brides'. The name is generally applied only to bobbin and embroidered laces, such as Carrickmacross, that adopted these features in imitation of needle laces.

Gum A substance exuded in small lumps from the bark of certain trees and shrubs. Gums form solutions or mucilages with water, which on evaporation leave an adhesive film. They are used as adhesives, binders and sizes, and sometimes to aid the adhesion of a glaze to a ceramic body. Gum arabic, which is soluble and is used as a medium for watercolour, is obtained from *Acacia senegal* and other acacia species native to northern Africa. Gum tragacanth, which forms a gelatinous mass with water, comes from the *Astragalus* genus, found in the Middle East.

Gunmetal See COPPER.

Gutta percha A dark brown natural plastic closely related to rubber. It is exuded mainly from the Malaysian palaquium tree, and can be shaped by softening over heat and pressing into cold moulds or by extrusion, producing tubes or other profiles.

In 1845 the Irish chemist Henry Bewley and the English artist and inventor Charles Hancock set up the Gutta Percha Company. Bewley adapted equipment used for rubber extrusion to produce gutta percha tubes, which were used to cover the earliest submarine cables, exploiting the material's excellent insulating properties. In the 19th century gutta percha was popular for decorative mouldings, ear trumpets and golf balls (known as 'gutties') and was also used for dental fillings, picture frames and (less successfully) for furniture. However, its poor durability means that few objects have survived.

Engraving of a gutta percha sideboard exhibited at the Great Exhibition in 1851, from the Illustrated London News. *Unfortunately this was not a successful use of gutta percha, as a contemporary observer reported that the pendulous fruit on top of the sideboard cracked and fell off.*

Gypsum A mineral composed of hydrated calcium sulphate, formed by the evaporation of saline waters. It can occur either as the homogeneous rock alabaster or as crystals, known as selenite. Coloration is due to impurities such as clay, limestone and iron oxides. Gypsum is extracted from open quarries or mines. Although alabaster is used decoratively, the principal use of gypsum is to manufacture gypsum plaster.

Gypsum plaster A plaster composed of hydrated calcium sulphate, obtained by heating gypsum, alabaster or selenite to moderate temperatures to drive off most of the water contained in the crystal structure. For use it is mixed with water, when it reacts rapidly to regenerate needle-like crystals of hydrated calcium sulphate. Gypsum plaster may contain contaminants such as limestone, clay or iron oxides. Its more pure form is known as PLASTER OF PARIS.

H

Haematite An opaque, black and dense form of iron oxide which has a metallic lustre. It was used by the ancient Egyptians to make beads and amulets and has also been used to make cameos and intaglios for seal-stones. The Romans believed that haematite had occult powers and used it for magic gems. Haematite can be faceted or cut as a cabochon and has been used to imitate black diamond and black pearl. Finely ground haematite is the polishing compound jeweller's rouge.

Hair sheep Varieties of sheep which grow hair rather than wool. These generally originate from warmer climates such as Brazil, North Africa, the Middle East and some areas of the Indian subcontinent. The leather from these animals has a smoother, finer grain and is much tougher than that from wool sheep. It is used particularly for making gloving leathers.

Hallmark A stamp applied by a legally appointed official to a precious metal article after ASSAYING, to denote its fineness or quality. In certain countries no article made of gold, silver or a platinum metal is marked before it has been assayed and found to conform to the legal standard. The name derives from Goldsmiths' Hall in London, where since 1300 precious metals have been assayed and 'hallmarked'. In most countries nowadays producers of precious metal objects are allowed to stamp, in addition to their own maker's mark, a mark denoting the quality of the metal, and this too is generally called a hallmark.

Several different hallmarks can be found on a single object. A maker's or sponsor's mark, denoting the person or company responsible for the manufacture of the article, is usually applied by the maker before sending the article out to be hallmarked. A hallmark or assay office mark, also known as a 'town mark', identifies the office where the assaying and hallmarking were done. The quality mark guarantees that the alloy meets legal standards. The date letter is a letter of the alphabet denoting the year in which the article was hallmarked.

The current system of hallmarking in the Western world was developed in the 13th and 14th centuries, although in Roman times precious metal bars were marked and in Byzantium there was also a system of marking precious metal objects. Hallmarking is the oldest form of consumer protection, since the system is designed to enable the assayer and maker of an article to be traced back, in the event of its proving to be below standard.

Hand-coloured print A print coloured by applying water-based paint by hand with a brush. Until the invention of chromolithography in the late 19th century printmaking in the West was primarily a monochrome process. To make a print with more than one colour was laborious, requiring the production by hand of a separate woodblock or metal plate for each colour and very careful registering during printing. Consequently, hand-colouring was sometimes a cheaper option. Early examples of the technique included the relatively crude colouring of 15th-century woodcuts such as playing cards and religious images using glue-based media, while in the 18th century there were some outstanding examples of the skilful tinting of popular prints with water-colours.

Harateen See MOREEN.

Hard paste porcelain Very high-fired porcelain made from china stone and china clay. It is white, translucent and resonant and is fired at 1250–1400°C. The earliest hard paste porcelain was made in China in the 6th century AD. The first European attempts to imitate this material led to the invention of SOFT PASTE PORCELAIN, but true porcelain was not produced in the West until 1709 at Meissen. Hard paste porcelain traditionally has a thin, transparent glaze made from body material plus glaze ash and is fired once to mature the body and glaze. It is sometimes referred to by the French term *pâte dure*.

Hardwood Timber derived from deciduous, broad-leafed, evergreen trees or dicotyledons. The timbers are generally harder than those derived from the conifers but there are many exceptions. Indigenous hardwoods in common commercial use include ash, beech, birch, chestnut, elm, hornbeam, lime, oak, poplar, sycamore and willow.

Hare's fur glaze See TEMMOKU.

Harewood Figured sycamore or sometimes maple wood treated with ferrous sulphate to produce a silvery grey finish. The term can also refer to San Domingo satinwood, which is yellow when cut but seasons to a silver-grey, sometimes with greenish markings. With a roe and mottle figure it is used in cabinetmaking, veneers and the production of fancy goods.

Harigaki An engraving technique, used to delineate designs on Japanese MAKI-E lacquer It is sometimes known as *hikkaki*.

A candelabrum in hard paste porcelain, with the figure of Diogenes, Meissen, c.1760. It epitomizes the strength combined with delicacy that is possible with hard paste porcelain.

Heartwood The core or inner part of the tree, which does not normally contain living cells. It is sometimes called true-wood, and it is usually harder and heavier, more durable and less permeable than SAPWOOD. The proportion of heartwood to sapwood varies from species to species and generally increases over time.

Table, by Verena Wriedt, Hamburg, 1996. The top is constructed from solid myrtle wood and uses to decorative effect the strong contrast between the heartwood and the sapwood.

Heliotrope See BLOODSTONE.

Hematite See HAEMATITE.

Herringbone figure An artificial figure pattern in wood formed by matching silver grain veneers so that adjacent pieces radiate in opposite directions.

Herringbone weave See TWILL.

High-temperature colours Pigments used in high-fired glazes and ceramics. See METALLIC OXIDE.

Hinterglasmalerei See REVERSE GLASS PAINTING.

Hippopotamus ivory An ivory derived from six teeth set in the lower jaw of the hippopotamus. Of these, four are too small to be of anything but limited use; they provide solid material up to only 10 cm long and 4 cm in diameter. The two canines are much larger but are sharply curved and more or less triangular in section, and they are covered with a very hard enamel layer which is difficult to remove, even with modern tools. It is usually dissolved away using dilute mineral acid. The ivory is hard and white, and can be polished to an almost porcellanous shine. Being denser and harder than elephant ivory, the material does not stain as readily, and objects made from it will tend to stay white longer. Objects made from hippopotamus ivory are smaller than those made from elephant ivory, are often somewhat triangular in section and are more or less curved longitudinally, reflecting the shape of the unworked tooth. Examination of the end grain will usually reveal traces of the distinctly triangular pulp cavity.

Hiramakie See MAKI-E.

Hochschnitt See GLASS ENGRAVING.

Hollie point An English NEEDLE LACE made in a continuous strip with straight rows of minute buttonhole stitches worked from side to side; the design is formed by gaps left in this process. The lace is recorded as being in use between the 16th century and the early 19th, for inserts, especially in christening sets and babies' clothes.

Hollow cutting See SILHOUETTE.

Hone stone A generic term for a stone, often slightly gritty in texture and containing silicate minerals, used for sharpening edged tools (see WOODWORKING TOOLS). The term has been applied, mistakenly, to the fine-grained limestone Solnhofen stone.

Honey gilding A form of GILDING used on ceramics and glass, in which gold leaf or powder is mixed with honey and then lightly fired. See also SHELL GOLD.

A selection of inlaid horn or hoof brooches, late 19th century. Dyed horn as well as shellac and vulcanite were used as substitutes for rarer or more expensive materials such as jet.

Horn A natural plastic based on keratin, derived from the horns of animals such as rams and goats. Probably first used for drinking horns, and later knife handles and spoons, by the 1620s it was employed for decorative goods such as medallions. It was also used in thin sheets for lanterns and as a cheap substitute for glass. By the 18th century London was a major horn-moulding centre, with makers such as John Obrisset producing elaborately moulded snuff boxes. Comb-manufacturing was one of the material's most important applications, particularly between 1770 and 1880. Many techniques which were traditionally used to form objects from horn, such as pressing into flat sheets and moulding into simple shapes, were later adapted to shaping semi-synthetic plastics.

See also RHINOCEROS HORN and illustration on page 516.

Hornbill A material taken from the large excrescence on top of the beak of the helmeted hornbill. Known as the casque,

this excrescence provides a material as dense as elephant ivory but rarely exceeding 6 cm in length, 4 cm in height and 2 cm in width. It ranges from deep creamy white to pale orange in colour.

Horsehair Hair from the manes and tails of horses. It varies from 20 cm to 1 m in length and is very lustrous. Although generally black, it is also used in all other naturally occurring colours. The shortest hairs were curled and used for stuffing furniture and mattresses, while slightly longer hairs were used for brushes. The longest were employed in fabrics, known generally as haircloths; these are stiff, glossy, wiry cloths made with horsehair in the weft and with a warp of cotton, or occasionally silk, for upholstery fabrics, and a warp of linen, cotton or mohair for the open fabrics used to retain shape in tailored clothing and for women's hats. The fabric width is limited to the length of the hair and its manufacture requires a special loom. For use as upholstery, for which it was popular in the late 18th century and the 19th, it was woven in plain, satin and small all-over patterns, although more elaborate patterns were possible. Thick monofilament viscose rayon was formerly called artificial horsehair. It replaced real horsehair in interlinings, millinery and transport upholsteries after about 1920, when the combination of heavy losses during the First World War and the Russian Revolution, combined with the development of the car, greatly reduced the horse population.

Hot printing See TRANSFER PRINTING.

Hungarian stitch See BARGELLO.

Hyalith A dense, opaque glass in jet black or sealing-wax red invented in the early 19th century in Bohemia by Count von Buquoy. It was used to imitate Josiah Wedgwood's rosso antico and black basalt stoneware and was often decorated with fired silver and gold.

Ice glass Glass with a rough, irregular outer surface resembling crackled ice. It was made in Venice from the 16th century and became popular again in the 19th century. Originally two different processes were used. In the first, a partially blown, white-hot parison was plunged into cold water and immediately reheated with great care so as not to fuse the cracks caused by the sudden cooling. It was then blown fully to enlarge the network of fissures. This was repeated several times to give a frosted appearance. In the second process the gather was marvered on a hot table covered with fine glass splinters or chips (sometimes coloured). When slightly reheated, these fragments fused to the glass surface.

A third method was developed in Murano in 1933 and made a form of ice glass called *vetro corroso*. Here the surface of the glass is covered with a resin which cracks as it dries. The glass is then dipped in hydrofluoric acid, but only the cracks are attacked by the acid. The resulting surface has irregular patches of lines and rough spots.

I

Bucket in ice glass, Venice, late 16th century or early 17th. The decorative effect was produced by plunging the hot, finished object momentarily into cold water.

A silk patola, or double ikat, Gujarat, India, late 19th century or early 20th. It shows the effect of weaving with pre-patterned yarns in the striations that appear on all sides of the geometric patterns.

Ikat A Malay/Indonesian word for the RESIST DYEING process on yarns, which are tied in areas that are not to be coloured, a process that can be repeated over several dye-baths, one for each colour (see colour plate XIa and b). The word is now used to indicate a cloth woven from such yarns, which produce a 'shadowy' effect around the design; an alternative name is *chiné*, although this latter term is usually restricted to multicoloured floral patterns woven in silk. Single ikat has the dyed yarns in the warp only; double ikat, or patola (an Indian term associated with silk yarns), has dyed yarns in both warp and weft. Matmee (or matmi) is a South-East Asian term for weft ikat. In many countries ikat is associated with indigo.

Illumination The embellishment of a handwritten book or of a single manuscript sheet with illustrations to the text and patterns worked around the lettering. The decoration may take the form of an outline drawing with a water-based medium, or a miniature painting in egg or glue tempera, often enhanced with gold leaf and precious pigments such as lapis lazuli. The supports are parchment, vellum or paper, and are sometimes covered in burnished gold leaf. Illumination achieved what many regard as technical and artistic perfection in 15th-century Europe, just before the introduction of printing, when books of hours (private prayer books) were commissioned by wealthy patrons. In addition to miniature paintings, sections of the calligraphy and page borders were embellished. Headpieces, initials and margins all provided opportunities for ornament. Earlier European devotional books with decorative calligraphy (for example the Lindisfarne Gospels, dating from the 7th century) were produced by monastic communities, but from the 12th century the work began to be taken over by independent workshops.

The calligrapher, artist and bookbinder were brought together in a similar way in the production of illustrated Islamic manuscripts of the 14th to 16th centuries, which were often bound in albums (see colour plate XII). Besides the Koran, the most popular themes under the Moguls in Iran, for example, were usually poetry and history. Like the late medieval illuminated manuscript in Europe, these books were an opportunity for exquisite miniature paintings framing and enhancing the text. The supports were laminated paper, burnished and often sprinkled or patterned with gold leaf, while the medium for the painting was glue.

Illustration See BOOK ILLUSTRATION.

Imari Japanese porcelain decorated with overglaze enamels and gilding. It is named after the Japanese port of Imari, from where porcelains made at Arita in Hizen province began to be exported in the 17th century. The earliest ware produced at Arita was blue and white, but from the 18th century Arita porcelains with overglaze enamel decoration and gilding were produced. These were very popular in Europe and were imitated at many porcelain-producing centres. Imari ware was also imitated in China: such examples are described today as 'Chinese Imari'.

Imari ware is characterized by rather crowded decoration based on textiles and brocades, with a palette in which strong dark colours predominate. It usually features underglaze blue decoration as well as overglaze enamels and (from 1658) gold enamel gilding. Such wares are hard paste porcelains and therefore usually fired three times: for the body, the enamels and the gilding.

Impasto Paint that is applied so thickly that it stands in relief. Ceramics are sometimes decorated in this fashion. In Chinese porcelain the *famille rose* palette often features areas of yellow enamel in impasto. Impasto decoration may also be found on the surface of a tin glaze, in Italian maiolica or Isnik tiles for example, often with slip. In some cases underglaze decoration is also applied in impasto.

Imperial purple See SHELLFISH PURPLE.

Imperial yellow A warm yellow glaze made with iron pigment, one of the most common monochrome glaze colours used in Chinese ceramics. It is usually a low-fired lead-based glaze, applied over a high-fired porcelain glaze and fired in oxidation.

The colour yellow is traditionally associated with the Chinese emperor and is one of the monochrome colours for porcelains that were required in the Ming period (1368–1644) for state ceremonies to represent the Four Altars. In the Qing period (1644–1911) porcelains with auspicious colours were no longer used and other colours emerged, including a citrus yellow based on antimony and stannate. This is often erroneously called imperial yellow.

Impressed decoration See CERAMICS.

Incised decoration See CERAMICS.

Indian boxwood A wood with similar, if inferior, properties to true BOXWOOD. It is from a different species (*Gardenia lati-*

folia) but is often used as a cheap substitute.

Indigo A vat or reduction/oxidation dye derived from the leaves of a large number of plants of the genus *Indigofera*, especially *Indigofera tinctoria*. A synthetic indigo was first produced in 1880 and became commercially available in 1897. With natural indigo the leaves are soaked in water, enzymic hydrolysis changes the colouring matter indican into indoxyl (a leuco-derivative also called indigo white) and glucose, and vigorous whipping encourages the introduction of oxygen, causing indoxyl to convert to indigo, sometimes called indigotin. During oxygenation the water is made alkaline, traditionally by the introduction of wood ash or lime; the water is drained to leave a blue paste. This pigment dye paste, damp or dried, is insoluble; it is dissolved and reduced in a warm alkaline solution in a vat, adding hydrogen and returning the liquid to the indigo white stage. Fibres or fabrics are then immersed and raised clear of the vat, and with each contact with the air oxidization converts the deposited yellowish green microscopic particles into blue (see colour plate XIc); the more times this is done, the darker the colour becomes. The dye bath is referred to as a fermentation vat if the breaking down of the indigo dye paste is done by the introduction to the vat of organic matter, which can include a wide range of fruits, liquors and beer, honey, wheat bran, sesame oil and urine. Inorganic fermentation was explored in the 16th–17th centuries and by the 1730s the first cold inorganic vat was introduced, using ferrous sulphate and slaked lime or potash; this so-called 'copperas' vat was joined in the mid-19th century by a zinc-lime bath, and both were replaced *c.*1900 by a sodium hydrosulphite and caustic soda or ammonia bath, capable of reducing both natural and synthetic indigo and suitable for most fibres.

Indigo, whether natural or synthetic, is fast to light and washing (although since deposited in layers, darker colours will rub away) and dyes all fibres directly, although the alkaline bath must be weaker for protein fibres such as silk and wool. To slow rubbing-off, cloth is sometimes finished with starch or gum arabic, or calendered. In some cultures, for example among the Solomon Islanders, indigo has long been chewed and spat onto bark cloth, for use as a finger paint. Since it is difficult to print directly, indigo is associated with resist dyeing. (See also CHINA BLUE and PRINTED TEXTILES.)

In-glaze decoration Decoration applied to an unfired glaze.

Because ceramics with opaque glazes are difficult to decorate—underglaze decoration is not visible and overglaze decoration often does not complement the colour of the base glaze—decoration is sometimes applied to the unfired glaze so that during firing it becomes incorporated within the glaze. In Chinese ceramics in-glaze decoration appears to have been used since the 1st century AD. It was used most commonly on Jun ware, which has an opaque blue glaze. The technique was also used in early Islamic ceramics with tin glazes. Here cobalt pigment was applied to the unfired tin glaze surface, resulting in a blue and white ware when fired. This technique was subsequently used on maiolica, Delftware and faience. The most effective in-glaze techniques utilize strong, high-fired pigments such as cobalt, copper and iron, or stains and strongly coloured glazes. Slips can also be used for in-glaze effects. In-glaze decoration is often erroneously called on-glaze decoration.

Ingot A metal casting, to be processed further by hot- or cold-working techniques such as rolling, forging or stamping.

Ingrain carpeting See KIDDERMINSTER.

Ink A liquid suspension or solution of colouring material in an aqueous, oily or resinous binder, called a medium, which holds together the coloured particles on drying. Inks differ from paints in that they generally have finer pigment particles.

Inks used in the decorative arts fall into two main categories: printing inks, of which the majority have an oil or varnish medium, and drawing and writing inks, which usually have a water-soluble medium. For example, the traditional printing ink for Western text and monochrome prints is made of carbon black pigment ground in linseed oil.

In the East printing, writing and drawing were traditionally more likely to be done with water-based inks made from carbon in the form of soot combined with gum, animal or fish glue and moulded into sticks for drying. To reconstitute the ink, the stick would be rubbed on an ink stone with water. Western drawing and writing inks are usually made from a suspension of pigment in water or water-soluble dyes, many of which are not light-fast, combined with a medium such as gum arabic. Iron-gall ink, the most popular writing and drawing ink from medieval times until the early 20th century, was made from gallotannic acid derived from oak galls, combined with ferrous sulphate and with the addition of dyes. Virtually black when first applied, it fades to pale brown and also has a tendency to corrode paper, owing to its acid content. The more stable, waterproof Indian ink may have contained shellac in the past but is today made of carbon with a synthetic resin binder, which is not water-soluble once dry.

Wallpaper printing in colours from wooden blocks, as practised in Europe in the 18th and 19th centuries and as continued today to a limited extent, used distemper (sometimes known as sedimentary ink). This is a combination of water-soluble animal glue and finely ground pigments and is suitable for printing pale colours which would otherwise be darkened by an oil medium. Oil colours were occasionally used for printing wallpaper in the mid-18th century, especially for black outlines to designs and the chiaroscuro papers of John Baptist Jackson, making them less susceptible to damage by moisture. In the mid-19th century oil-based colours were again used in England to produce so-called sanitary papers, which could be cleaned with water.

Inlaid decoration Decoration which has been inlaid into a ceramic body before firing. It is related to incised decoration in that the clay body is carved or incised with a pattern and then slip or clay is wiped or pressed into the incisions. The object is then glazed and fired. Traditionally, inlaid decoration appears on earthenware and stoneware but modern potters such as Lucie Rie have used the technique on porcelain.

Inlays can be produced using slip or different coloured clays. When using slip, a slip of a colour different from the body clay is wiped onto the surface and allowed to soak into the decorative incisions; the excess is then wiped off. When using clay, an area is usually removed from the clay body and then an insert of a different colour is put into position. This is a common way of producing marbled decoration. Thin clay designs which have been cut out can also be rolled onto the surface of a clay slab to produce 'rolled inlay'.

The earliest inlaid decoration can be seen on Chinese ceramics of the mid-11th century from the Cizhou kilns and then in Korean ceramics of the mid-12th century. In both traditions it was made in imitation of earlier metalwork with silver and gold inlays. In France a white earthenware with inlaid slip decoration was made in the 16th century at Saint-Porchère. This was imitated at Minton in the 19th century.

Inlay A form of decoration in which part of a surface is removed and a contrasting material inserted into the space. For its use in wood, see BANDING, INTARSIA, MARQUETRY and STRINGING.

Inlay patchwork See PATCHWORK.

Intaglio The decoration of a hard substance by cutting the design into the surface (in Italian the word *intaglio* means carving). The process is the opposite of CAMEO carving and has been applied to GEMSTONES, glass, ceramics and metals.

Intaglio printing A general term for printmaking processes that involve the transfer of ink from depressions in a metal plate to dampened paper under pressure. The name derives from the Italian word for carving, because the image is carved onto the plate by various forms of engraving and etching.

The Art of Etching and Engraving.

Engrav'd for the Universal Magazine for J. Hinton at the King's Arms in St Paul's Church Yard London 1748.

The engraving of lines in metal for printing on paper was developed in Italy and Germany in the second quarter of the 15th century from the metalworker's technique of creating linear patterns, while etching is derived from a method of decorating weapons and came into use soon after 1500. Engraved printing plates are incised with a metal tool called a burin which, with practised control, can be used to gouge out fine lines and dots in a copper sheet. In etching, the design on the printing plate is bitten out in an acid bath. The plate is first coated with a wax ground, which is removed in the desired areas by drawing with a needle, and the strength of a line is then determined by the length of time it is exposed to the acid. After the plate has been cleaned, stiff ink (traditionally made of carbon and linseed oil) is applied with a leather or cloth pad and then wiped away with dry cloths and the palm of the hand from all but the incised lines. The PRINTING PRESS passes the inked plate, the paper (slightly damp) and woollen blanket padding between two rollers. To prevent the metal plate from cutting the paper, its edges are bevelled; they thus create a characteristic 'plate mark' on the finished print where the paper is impressed, while the printed lines stand up where the paper has been squeezed into the incisions.

Over the centuries a variety of tools and techniques have been developed in the West for creating texture, as well as lines, in an etched or engraved design, primarily to imitate original drawing and painting effects in reproduction. Stipple engraving renders tone by covering the plate with dots; in mezzotint the whole plate is first evenly pitted with a special tool called a rocker in order to hold the ink, and the image is then created by selectively removing the resulting burr with scraping and burnishing tools; drypoint uses lines incised in the printing plate with a sharply pointed tool; aquatint creates tone on etchings through the use of sprinkled resin as an acid resist.

Intarsia The art of inlaying wood in wood (as opposed to overlaying a carcass with an inlaid veneer) and the technique from which MARQUETRY was derived. It is believed to have originated in Italy in the 13th century. Early examples that have survived are geometric mosaics that may have been intended to imitate stone originals, and often incorporate shell, ivory and ebony. This early style of intarsia was known in some countries as Certosina or Certosian mosaic after the

A book-plate printed from a hand-engraved metal plate, by Vladimir Fuka, Czechoslovakia, early 20th century.

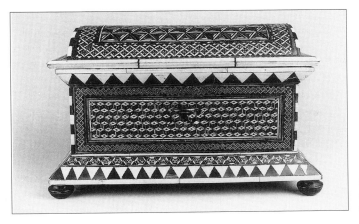

Certosina casket in wood and ivory, Italy, 15th–16th century.

Certosa di Pavia, the Carthusian monastery where some of the best examples were made. Another major centre of production was Venice, but the finest pieces were made in Siena and were normally of light wood laid into a dark ground in arabesque and intertwined botanical designs. In the early period many of the craftsmen were monks or laymen bound to monasteries and churches, and the work produced, such as panelling and choir stalls, was for ecclesiastic use.

From these early prototypes a more pictorial style emerged, incorporating the rules of perspective. By the 15th century designs depicted street scenes and buildings in full perspective. Others showed half-open doors, through which the contents of a cupboard or an open courtyard could be seen. Sand scorching, pokerwork and coloured stains were used to add detail and shading to provide a full *trompe l'oeil* effect. Some of the designs were developed from cartoons produced by notable artists of the time. By the middle of the 16th century the art had spread to northern Europe, where it was used to decorate furniture, panelling and architectural features. However, technological innovation around the same time allowed the development of marquetry, which soon superseded intarsia as a method of decorating furniture.

An idea of the tools and techniques used to produce the designs can be derived from a panel produced by the late 15th-century Sienese *intarsoro* Antonio Barili. The panel is a self-portrait of Barili at work, and it shows that the tool used to outline the designs and begin the process of excavating the recesses to receive the design elements was a short-bladed knife fitted with a long shoulder stock. The knife is shown held in Barili's left hand with the stock braced against the left shoulder, while the right hand guides the blade with a short rod. Other tools shown are a gouge, which was probably used to finish the recesses, a folding knife and the small knife used to cut inlay elements.

Interlocking grain See GRAIN.

Iridescent glass See GLASS.

Irogane A collective name for patinated Japanese copper alloys with a range of attractive colours, such as SHAKUDO and SHIBUISHI. The colour of the patinated metals depends on the alloy and the patination treatment, called *nikomi-chakushoku*. After being cleaned and degreased, the metal is boiled in a colouring solution of verdigris, copper sulphate and alum. This process colours the surface of *shakudo* purplish black, and *shibuishi* a greyish or whitish brown.

Wrought-iron screen from Avila Cathedral, Spain, c.1520–30. The scrolls have been bent hot and joined with collar joints.

Iron A silver-greyish white metal which is ductile, malleable and attracted by magnets. About 5% of the earth's crust consists of iron, and in its many forms this is the metal most used by mankind. Iron is almost always found in nature as an ore, except in some meteorites, where almost pure iron can be found alloyed with nickel. The main iron ores used are haematite, limonite, siderite and magnetite. Meteoric iron was used for making the first iron artefacts as early as the 3rd millennium BC, but iron objects began to be made on a larger scale from iron ore in Asia Minor around 2000 BC. The first articles were jewellery but soon iron was used for making weapons and tools.

Pure iron has a melting-point of 1539°C, and as this high temperature could not be produced until the 18th century it was not possible before then to smelt iron directly from the ore. Instead, iron ore was reduced to iron with the aid of charcoal at a temperature of 1200°C. This reduced iron, or bloom, is a brittle mixture of solid iron, slag and charcoal, and was turned into solid iron by careful hammering to a homogeneous mass known as wrought iron. This is a ductile and malleable iron that can be forged and welded but not easily hardened and is used where tensile strength is needed, for example in gates, buildings and bridges. When iron ore is

Wassily *chair in bent tubular steel, by Marcel Breuer, 1925.*

heated sufficiently for a prolonged period, it can absorb enough carbon to form a very hard and brittle metal which melts at 1150°C and is suitable for casting (see CAST IRON).

Around 1000 BC it was discovered that iron with a small amount of carbon (0.45–1.7%) could be hardened by quenching (immersion in water to promote rapid cooling) after heating, usually followed by a slight reheating (TEMPERING) to reduce the brittleness. This steel can be divided into two groups: carbon steel, composed of iron and carbon, and alloy steel, which is iron with other metals such as chromium and nickel. The best-known alloy steel is stainless steel, in which iron is alloyed with chromium and nickel to create resistance against corrosion. The most corrosion-resistant stainless steel consists of 18% chromium and 8–10% nickel.

Ironstone china English stoneware made in imitation of porcelain. It was first made in 1813 by the Staffordshire potter Charles James Mason and was known as 'Mason's ironstone'. It was said to have contained iron slag and was often decorated with blue printed decoration or overglaze enamels. Like other Staffordshire stonewares of the period, ironstone china is quite hard and opaque and very pale-bodied.

Isnik ware A type of fritware produced at the Isnik (or Iznik) potteries near Istanbul from the end of the 15th century. Tiles and ceramics were produced in imitation of the Chinese porcelains that had been exported in large quantities to the Near East, many of which ended up in collections in Turkey, where they were much admired. The earliest examples of Isnik ware are blue and white but soon coloured underglaze decoration was added, with red, black, blue and green the predominant colours. The red decoration was made from a fine ferruginous earth called BOLE. Both vessels and tiles were made using this palette. The decoration was inspired by both Chinese designs and traditional Ottoman textile patterns.

Tile, Isnik ware with blue and turquoise decoration, Turkey, c.1530–40.

Isnik ware was made from the fine white local clay and white sand, covered with white slip or tin glaze. It was decorated with fritted coloured pigments (iron, cobalt and copper) and then glazed with a colourless, lead-alkaline glaze. It was usually fired once, to about 900°C. Isnik tiles were formed in wooden moulds.

Istrian stone A hard fine-grained limestone, usually creamy grey in colour, quarried since Roman times from Istria in Croatia. Istrian stone was widely used in Italy, particularly in Venice, for carved decoration. Its dense texture permits the production of fine detail which is more resistant to weathering than other types of limestone.

Ivoride/ivorine/ivorite See SYNTHETIC IVORY.

Ivory A hard, fine-grained, creamy white material derived from the modified teeth or tusks of various animals. It is similar in appearance to bone and is chemically identical to it. More fibrous than bone, ivory is a form of modified dentine. It is a very dense material, and its close, compact pores, filled with a gelatinous substance, make it both tough and elastic. When freshly cut, a variety of grain patterns in transverse or longitudinal section is visible, depending on the species from which the ivory is taken.

The most familiar type is ELEPHANT IVORY, often referred to as 'true ivory'. Other types are HIPPOPOTAMUS IVORY, MAMMOTH IVORY, NARWHAL TUSK, PIG IVORY, SPERM WHALE TEETH and WALRUS IVORY. Most elephant ivory derives from the tusks of the African elephant, generally from the central and eastern parts of the continent. Ivory carvers recognize different qualities of hardness, colour and opacity in ivories from different sources. West African ivory is hard and difficult to cut, and it may be more prone to cracking than that from the east, which is soft and more easily worked. However, the harder types will take a much higher, almost porcellanous polish and are less prone to discoloration over time.

Ivory is one of the most ancient of carving materials and ivory objects have been found that are more than 20,000 years old. Its fine grain and dense structure make it an ideal material for the carver, turner and engraver. The tools and techniques used are the same as or similar to those used by woodworkers. It can be sawn, carved with chisels and gouges, drilled, filed and worked with scrapers, and it can be fixed with pins, screws or glue. Its density makes it suitable not only for very fine carved or engraved detail but also for a high degree of surface finish. It is reasonably malleable and can generally be worked down to a very thin cross-section without breaking. Thin sections of ivory can be shaped either by steam-heating or by immersion in a solution of phosphoric acid, which can render ivory so flexible that it can be knotted. After rinsing in water and drying, the ivory retains the shape into which it has been bent. If the piece is later immersed in water, it will become flexible once more. A drawback of this technique is that it can weaken the ivory and

Ivory netsuke, the details stained black and the buttons inlaid with horn, Japan, 18th century.

spoil the finish.

Apart from power tools, the techniques and instruments used by the modern carver are broadly similar to those employed since the development of metal tools. Fine-bladed saws with tensioned blades, such as coping, fret and piercing saws, are fairly recent additions to the carver's kit, but other tools, such as handsaws, hacksaws, chisels, gouges, gravers, files, drills and abrasives differ from traditional ones only in the materials from which they are made and in the number of types available.

Ivory is often carved in the round, following the general shape of the original tusk or portion of tusk. The end of the tusk which is embedded in the jaw (the proximal end) is hollow and has been used in the manufacture of bangles, armlets and circular boxes. Otherwise the ivory is first prepared by sawing out a blank in the shape of a block or slab that will accommodate the required design. The design is then drawn onto the blank: in the case of a three-dimensional carving the design should be drawn right around the blank. Preliminary shaping is achieved by sawing away any large unwanted areas. This is followed by rough carving, using chisels, gouges and knives, to produce the main features of the design. The chisels and gouges are rarely, if ever, struck with a mallet or hammer; generally hand pressure alone is used to produce a paring cut. Deep undercuts such as those found in drapery are produced by drilling out the majority of the waste and are then finished by carving. The main features are finished by further, but more restrained, carving and then polished with a succession of increasingly fine abrasives, the finest of which are lubricated with a little vegetable oil. Lastly, fine details such as hair or textile patterns are cut using simple points or engravers' tools such as burins and gravers.

Simple pierced work can be produced by merely drilling out a series of holes to produce a design, but more complex work, such as scrolling foliage, is produced by drilling a small through hole to allow access for the blade of a frame-saw. A coping saw is used for coarse work or a piercing saw for fine work.

Turned work can be produced using simple machines such as the bow lathe or more sophisticated technology such as the ornamental lathe (see LATHE). The tools employed in hand turning are often the same as those used by the wood turner

1. *A Roman sardonyx cameo depicting the Emperor Augustus. The carver has exploited the alternating brown and white bands in the stone to create dark areas in the foreground and background. The gold diadem was added in the Middle Ages and restored in the 18th century. It contains several cameos, the central one carved from sardonyx or a similar banded stone.*

11. *Gilded and painted leather panel, Netherlands, mid-18th century. The leather, probably calf, has been silvered and varnished in yellow to simulate gold. It was embossed with a heated metal plate.*

III. *Boulle marquetry. The top of a* bureau Mazarin, *France, 1690.*

IV. (above) *Chinese wallpaper, painted in watercolour, Saltram House, Devon, c. 1700.*

v. (right) *Jewellery and enamel work from various periods. The gold necklace is hung with intaglio-carved cabochon scarabs in turquoise, opal, amethyst, lapis lazuli and various forms of quartz. Within it is an 18th-century paste buckle and a brooch from the 1920s by Verger Fils, which makes use of the different colours, reflectance and textures of amethyst, emerald, diamond, pearl and amber. The brooch to the left has an antique amethyst cameo in a 19th-century gold setting. The 17th-century gold ring to the right has a lapis lazuli cameo in a bezel setting. Below the necklace is a pair of 19th-century gold ear-rings with filigree decoration.*

In the lower tier are a 17th-century pendant painted in enamel with The Crucifixion, *cuff links in pink* guilloche *enamel by Fabergé, and a 19th-century brooch by Castellani with a sardonyx cameo, simply faceted rubies and a baroque pearl. Below is a pair of ear-rings by Falize in blue* cloisonné *enamel set with tiny diamonds. Between them lies a Dutch pendant of c.1640 in en ronde bosse enamel, in which are set table cut diamonds and rubies; the dark colour of diamonds set in this fashion is evident. The gold knife is decorated with* champlevé *enamel.*

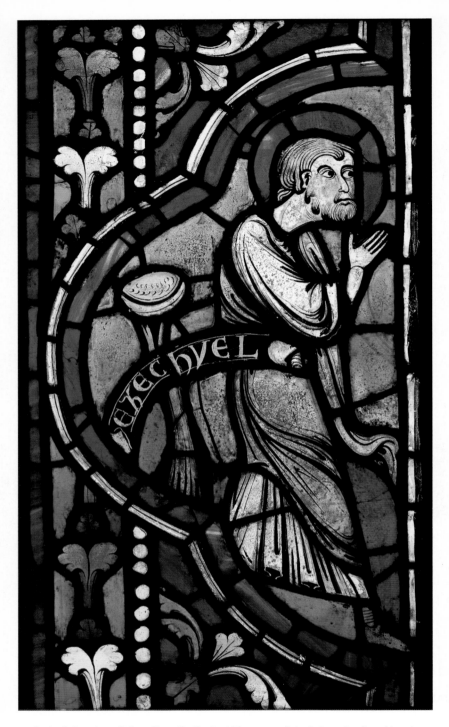

VI. *Stained glass from Sainte-Chapelle, Paris, 13th century. It includes ruby glass, blue glass coloured in the batch ('pot metal'), silver staining to render yellow, and painting in brown enamel.*

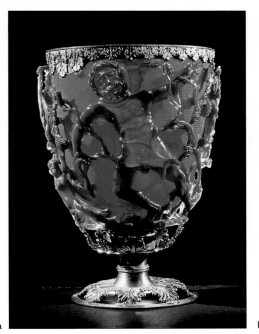

a

b

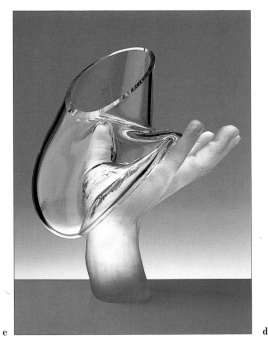

c

d

VII. *(a) Glass. The Lycurgus Cup, perhaps Rhineland, 4th century AD, with 17th- or 18th-century mounts.
It is made of dichromatic glass and appears to be deep red in transmitted light but pea green in reflected light.
This type of heavily carved beaker is known as a cage cup.*
(b) Drinking glass with air twist stem, England, c. 1750.
*(c) Single-handed vase by Bruno Romanelli, 1997. The vase is free-blown and the hand is cast in a resin mould,
then etched with acid.*
(d) Detail of a leaded glass shade, Tiffany studios, c. 1900.

VIII. *Three porcelain bowls, by Lucie Rie, 1979–80. Rie brushed her glazes on to unfired pots. For the bronze rim she used manganese oxide mixed with copper carbonate, allowing it to bleed into the glaze.*

IX. Vase hollandais, *painted by Louis-Denis Armand the elder, Sèvres, 1758. Soft paste porcelain with enamel decoration and fired gilding.*

x. *An 18th-century Frisian pottery for the manufacture of Delftware, depicted in tiles by the firm of Tichelaar in Makkum, 1978, after an original from the Bolsward pottery of 1737, now in the Rijksmuseum, Amsterdam. The ground floor has a horse-driven pug-mill, a lift to convey the prepared clay to the floor above, another mill to crush the glaze, and the decorator's room, where stacks of painted dishes await a second firing. The first floor is the throwers' loft, where the potter works at a wheel while assistants place his work on drying racks. The top floor is the tilemakers' loft with stacks of tiles drying near the kiln. The wood-fired kiln, which rises through three floors, is a building within a building, with walls a metre thick. The heat is drawn from the fire through holes into the chamber above, where the firing takes place. The articles are moved in and out of the chamber through a large door, which is bricked up during the firing.*

XI. *(a) Preparation for ikat weaving, Andhra Pradesh, India, 1992. The woman is tying rubber strips around the warps to prevent dye from penetrating the fibre in those areas. (b) Ikat weaving, Orissa, India, 1994. The weaver is untying the dyed warp bundles and setting up the warp on the loom. (c) Dyeing a printed cloth with indigo at Bagru, India, 1994. The greenish, reduced dye can be clearly seen. (d) Lacquer workers in Burma, c. 1995. Wooden table tops are rubbed with a paste made of green pigment and a lacquer obtained from* Melanorrhea usitata. *The paste is then wiped clear of the surface but remains in the engraved decoration. In the background are trays to be similarly decorated.*

XII. *An artists' workshop, or* kitabkhana, *in Mogul India, by Sanju, 1590–95. The painting is executed on paper in opaque watercolour, gold paint and ink. The gold paint was made by grinding gold leaf, mixing it with gum. A team of artists and craftsmen is shown painting and making bookbindings. The scribes' pose, with the folio for writing or painting placed on a board and supported on one raised knee, is typical of both Iranian and Indian artists' portraits of the period.*

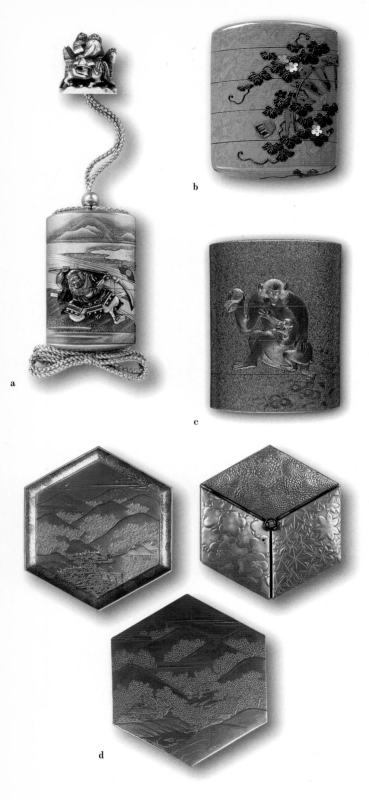

XIII. *Japanese lacquerwork.*
(a) Inrō by Hara Yōyūsai,
19th century. Gold and silver
maki-e, *including* togidashi,
hiramakie *and* takamakie, *on*
a fundame *ground, with further*
decoration inlaid in gold, silver,
shakudō *and* shibuishi.
(b) Inrō by Zonsei, early 19th
century. Mokume-ji *with*
details in rubbed green, black
and brown lacquer, with
additional mother-of-pearl
and pewter.
(c) Inrō by Koma Kansai II
and Masaharu, 19th century.
Nashiji *ground with decoration*
inlaid in shibuishi, *copper*
and gold detailed with gold
and silver hiramakie *and*
takamakie.
(d) Kōjubako, 19th century.
Bright kinji *ground with*
decoration in gold hiramakie
and details in gold foil,
kirikane, koban, keuchi, *red*
lacquer, togidashi *and* ōhirame.

XIV. *The Spanish Room at Kingston Lacy, Dorset, 1838–55. The early 17th-century ceiling probably came from the Palazzo Contarini in Venice. The gilded leather on the walls is also Venetian and has been tooled and painted in the manner of a bookbinding. The pendant garlands on the chimneypiece are carved in a strongly veined Italian marble and fitted into black marble. The carpet is an early 19th-century Axminster.*

XV. *The Marble Hall at Kedleston, Derbyshire, designed by Robert Adam, 1760s and 1770s. The columns are made of a locally quarried alabaster and were fluted in situ. The papier mâché panels on the walls were supplied by Henry Clay of Birmingham.*

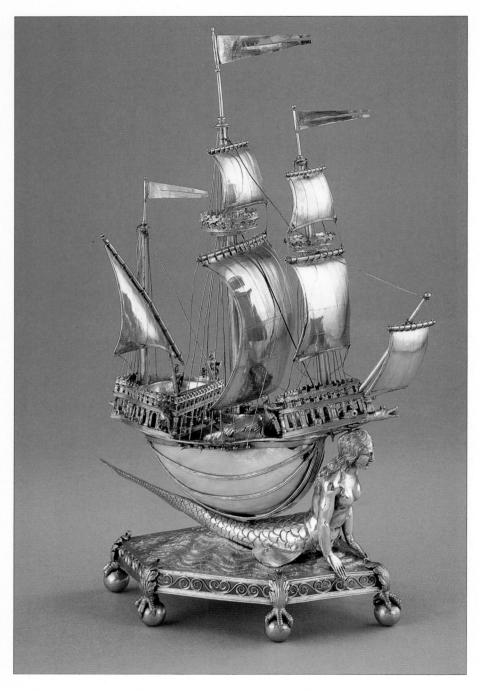

XVI. *The Burghley nef, nautilus shell mounted in silver and partially gilded, by Pierre le Flamand, Paris, 1482–3.*

XVII. *Block-printed cotton, England, c.1808–15. The pattern was created by immersion in three dyes: Prussian blue. madder and a yellow, probably quercitron. The print pastes were a complete resist (for white); a resist-red, containing a block against the Prussian blue and a mordant for madder (after which the blue was dyed); a mordant for madder where needed on white areas (the red was then dyed); and finally the mordant for the yellow, which over blue and red created green and brown respectively. Because of the use of resist-red in a pin-dot ground this method of dyeing came to be known as the 'lapis style'.*

XVIII. *Detail from a pietra dura cabinet with lapis lazuli columns; the panels were made in France, c.1650, the cabinet in northern Europe, c.1690. This example shows the richness of colour that can be achieved with stones such as lapis, jasper, rosso antico and quartz. It also illustrates how modelling, texture and pattern are possible with careful selection of the stone and precise cutting.*

A corner cabinet veneered
in amboyna wood with a
panel of ebony and ivory
marquetry, Jacques-Emile
Ruhlmann, 1916.

(see TURNING), particularly when working on spindlework
between centres. Owing to its density, however, ivory is especially suited to the use of scrapers. These tools resemble
turning chisels, but whereas a chisel cuts with the sharp edge
on its end, a scraper cuts with a fine burr formed on either the
end or the side. There are seven main designs: the straight,
the round, the half-round, the point, the bead and the left-
and right-side scrapers. A wide range of special profile scrapers is also used to produce fixed patterns which mirror their
cutting edge. In faceplate turning, as in ornamental work,
only the scrapers are used.

Sheets of ivory and ivory veneers are usually produced by
sawing the tusk longitudinally, but transverse and radial sections of elephant and walrus ivory are also occasionally used,
putting the effects seen on the end grain to good use. Rotary-
cut veneers have been made since around 1850. These are
done on special machines which peel the tusk and can
produce uniform sheets of considerable length and width.

For ivory substitutes, see BONE, HORNBILL, SYNTHETIC
IVORY and VEGETABLE IVORY.

Iznik ware See ISNIK WARE.

J

Jacquard An attachment to a weaving, knitting, carpet-weaving or lace machine that allows patterns of (in principle) any width, height and complexity to be woven through the use of cords attached (by means of a heddle) to each warp thread (see LOOM). The cords are lifted as required to divert the passage of ground wefts or to introduce supplementary wefts. They are bunched above the plain loom into groups representing one (of one or more) edge-to-edge repeat; the leashes are attached to each bunch and topped with a metal rod, then pushed against a stiff card that admits or denies the rods by the presence or absence of holes, thus controlling the lift. One punched card is needed for each pass of the weft in the vertical repeat; laced together to form a continuous belt, the cards can be lifted off, replaced with another set and returned when required.

The device was a significant improvement on the DRAW LOOM since it could be operated by a single weaver. It was perfected by Joseph-Marie Jacquard, who exhibited it in Paris in 1801, although it was not widely adopted in France and Great Britain until the 1820s; its application became common elsewhere only during the 1830s and 1840s. Its first use was with hand-operated machines to produce luxury goods; it was only in the mid-19th century that it was incorporated into auxiliary-powered machines. The principle of belts of punched

Hand-loom with a Jacquard machine, 1810. The Jacquard 'engine' above a hand-powered loom shows the form in which it was known in London by 1820, with two sets of cards: the larger set controls the leashes below, through which every warp passes; the smaller set controls the ground-weaving harnesses and is related to the dobby mechanism in its scale and relative simplicity. The Jacquard cards, two of which can be seen clearly, are laced into a continuous loop; each band of numerous holes represents one throw of the shuttle. Metal-tipped cords are pulled up against one downward-facing card at a time and raise their connected warp or warps (one for each width-ways repeat) where the card is perforated.

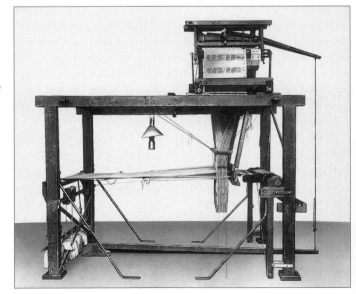

cards had widespread subsequent application, leading to a diverse range of binary devices, including pianolas and computers, as well as other shedding-control mechanisms, such as the DOBBY LOOM, which uses similar principles to control entire harnesses rather than individual warp threads. (For further illustration see page 527.)

Jade A term used to describe two minerals, NEPHRITE and JADEITE, renowned for their green colour, which have a similar waxy, translucent appearance. The difference between these minerals was not recognized until 1863 and thus the term jade, derived from the Spanish name *piedra de hijada*, used by the conquistadors to refer to the green stone they found in Central America, was applied to both. Nephrite, the jade of the ancient Chinese and the Maoris, which has a hardness of Mohs 6.5, ranges from green, produced by the presence of iron, to buff, resulting from a low iron content. Jadeite, used by the Mayans and the Chinese from the 18th century, has a hardness of Mohs 6.5–7 and occurs in a wide range of colours from green, caused by the presence of chromium, to white, pink, brown, red, yellow, mauve, blue and black, produced by other minerals such as iron and manganese.

Both nephrite and jadeite can be found as water-worn pebbles or boulders. In this form the outer surface is often weathered to a brown skin owing to the oxidation of iron. Both minerals are tough, permitting the carving of delicate forms, such as thin-walled vessels. Nephrite has a fibrous structure in which the needle-like crystals are interlocked, and it can be polished to a smooth, greasy sheen. Jadeite consists of granular, interlocking crystals that give the material its

Nephrite carving of a recumbent horse, China, late Ming period, 17th century. By this time the Chinese were using the hard mineral corundum for the working of jade, which permitted the carving of the deep undercut below the horse's head and the fine, sinuous lines of its mane.

characteristic 'orange peel' texture except when polished with diamond abrasive.

Large pieces of jade were traditionally sawn into sheets, a fact reflected in the planar format of many early carvings. Where pebbles were used, this also influenced the form of the object produced and many carvers also retained some of the brown skin as a decorative element. Because of the hardness of jade most early carvings have gently rounded contours with minimal undercutting. Early cutting techniques employed abrasives, such as thin sheets of sandstone, quartz sand (Mohs 7) or crushed garnet (Mohs 6.5–7.5), applied to a wooden or stone tool with water or oil as a lubricant, a laborious process that became faster with the use by the Chinese from the 15th century of corundum abrasive, embedded in metal cutting wheels. The use of this harder material (Mohs 9) allowed the production of more intricate carvings of greater depth. The Chinese applied abrasives to bamboo rods for drilling holes, while the Maoris used flint or obsidian points with quartz or sand as an abrasive. Modern jade carving employs carborundum (silicon carbide) or diamond-tipped grinding tools mounted in power-driven lathes or flexible shaft drills. Jade is used for carvings, beads or cabochons.

Nephrite objects from archaeological sites in China, referred to as 'buried' jade, from their burial in yellow loess clay, have developed a yellowish brown colour; some changes in composition may also have occurred. The same type of colour change can be caused by heating, or calcining, nephrite. Nephrite can be distinguished from jadeite by the difference in their specific gravity, which is approximately 3 for nephrite and 3.3 for jadeite. A number of materials, including serpentine, green garnet, dyed chalcedony and opaque glass, have been used to simulate jade.

Jadeite A translucent mineral, one of two known generically as JADE, composed of sodium aluminium silicate. Although best known in its green form, produced by the inclusion of chromium, jadeite occurs in a variety of colours. It is found in Burma, from where it was exported to China in the 18th century for carving, and also in Guatemala, which is thought to be the source used by the Mayans, who carved ritual masks from it.

Japanned leather See PATENT LEATHER.

Japanning A term for European techniques used to produce imitations of Far Eastern lacquerwares. A variety of formulations were used for the varnish layers, including mixtures of sandarac, copal and other resins, but by far the majority were finished using various types of lac, including alcoholic solutions of SHELLAC. There were also various different methods and qualities of groundwork preparation. The best-quality wares were constructed using methods that closely followed Far Eastern techniques but used materials with which the European craftsmen were familiar. The method outlined below is for high-quality English black japan work of the late 17th century, but similar techniques were used to produce different coloured grounds. A bright red was produced using vermilion mixed with seedlac, while a deeper red was made with dragon's blood. Other colours were produced using watercolours mixed in isinglass or gum arabic. At that time seedlac was considered superior to shellac.

The surface of the wooden carcass was sealed with glue size

Bureau bookcase in green japanning, England, c.1710.

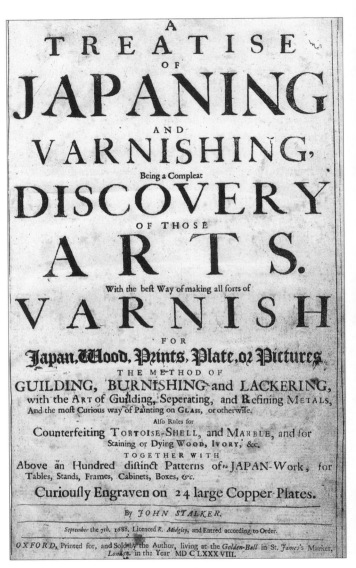

The title-page of A Treatise of Japanning and Varnishing (1688), by John Stalker and George Parker. The instructions in this book enabled European craftsmen for the first time to emulate the effects of oriental lacquerwares.

or lac, and when this had dried a layer of hemp or linen cloth was glued on and smoothed. Next, nine or ten layers of gesso would be applied, each thoroughly smoothed before the next application was made. When the gesso coatings were completely dry they were thoroughly smoothed again. The gesso layer was sealed with three layers of shellac and various lac coatings were then applied, each being allowed to dry completely before the subsequent coating was painted on. The base coats of colour were then applied. Seedlac varnish was mixed with sufficient lampblack to obscure the gesso with one coat. Three applications of this mixture were made. This was followed by three more layers of the same composition, each layer smoothed with rushes when dry. Then seedlac solution was mixed with a little Venice turpentine and just sufficient lampblack was added to colour the mixture very slightly. Nine applications were made of this mixture, followed by twelve layers of a solution of the best-quality seedlac, barely tinted with lampblack. A drying and resting period of five or six days was then allowed before polishing. The surface was first smoothed with rushes and then given a fine polishing using finely sieved tripoli powder. A soft, well dampened cloth was dipped into the tripoli powder and rubbed over the surface using moderate pressure and elliptical strokes, occasionally broken with smooth, straight strokes. As the work progressed, more water was used and less tripoli. Any remaining tripoli was washed off with water and the surface rubbed dry with clean soft cloths. Finally a thin mixture of lampblack and fine oil was rubbed carefully over the surface and then removed with a succession of clean cloths, the last one of which would be soft and closely woven.

Areas of raised design were produced with a paste made from gum arabic solution, bole and whiting. The mixture was laid over a drawn design using a sharply pointed stick, each application being allowed to dry before subsequent layers were applied. The raised areas were then painted with watercolours and coated with at least three coats of clear seedlac. Any gilding could be done before or after the application of the seedlac, depending on the desired effect. Raising was sometimes done on a surface that was already coloured and polished, in which case the design would be lightly cut into the surface to expose the underlying gesso coats. This method gave a better result than raising on the gesso layer or immediately after the first painting. *Maki-e* effects were achieved using finely chopped metal wires applied and finished as in VERNIS MARTIN.

Imitations of coromandel work were made by preparing a fully polished surface as above and then cutting the design into the surface and painting the exposed gesso with layers of powder pigment in gum arabic solution. Lower-quality work was made by applying a gesso coat of only one or two layers. This was rubbed smooth when dry and the design was painted on using watercolours; two or three coats of shellac were applied, often without polishing the intermediate coats.

From about the middle of the 18th century similar techniques, with the addition of shell inlay, were used to decorate furniture and other objects made from papier mâché, and in some areas the word 'japan' or 'japanned' became synonymous with papier mâché. The term is also applied to a type of decorated tin plate first produced in Staffordshire in the late 17th century (see PONTYPOOL WARE).

Jasper A hard (approximately Mohs 7), fine-grained, dense form of opaque quartz. It occurs in a range of colours caused by impurities: reds and yellows are due to iron oxides, greens to the mineral chlorite; clays can produce white or grey jasper with a porcelain-like texture. Jaspers are sedimentary or metamorphic in origin and occur as infilling of cavities. They are found worldwide and have been used for beads, carvings, vessels, inlays and mosaics (see colour plate XVIII).

Jasper ware Coloured unglazed stoneware made at Wedgwood from the 1770s (for illustration see page 459). It was one of the most popular of the many new ceramic bodies developed by Wedgwood, and has a fine stoneware body that is sometimes translucent. The body material is similar to artificial porcelain (see SOFT PASTE PORCELAIN) but contains significant quantities of barium sulphate to render it a fine stoneware. The body is naturally pale but was stained with various oxides to produce such monochrome colours as blue, lilac, green and yellow. Jasper ware was often decorated with neo-classical relief decoration in white slip that was applied on top of the coloured body. The forms included busts, dishes, plaques and vases, some of which were designed by John Flaxman.

Jean See FUSTIAN and TWILL.

Jersey A plain knitted fabric, characterized by the lack of any prominent ribs. It can be made of any fibre, but when made of silk it is sometimes called milanese or tricot.

Jet An opaque black gem material composed of fossilized wood which can be carved and given a high, permanent polish. It is a fairly soft (Mohs 2.5–4) and fragile material which fractures readily. Significant deposits of jet at Whitby in Yorkshire were worked from the neolithic period. In this area the hardest jet was quarried from oil-bearing limestone sea cliffs, where it occurs in lens-shaped pieces. Smaller, softer pieces, rounded by water erosion, were obtained from beaches

A jet plaque from a bracelet, England, late 19th century. The shallow forms and high polish are characteristic of the working of jet, while the damage on the right edge shows the conchoidal fracture also typical of this material.

where they had washed out of the cliffs. Jet, which is also found in France and Spain, where it was used to carve small figures for pilgrims to the shrine of Santiago de Compostela, was highly popular in the 19th century for mourning jewellery. Because of its tendency to fracture, jet was cut with knives, files or metal discs and abrasives rather than carved with chisels. In Iron Age Britain it was polished with small particles of jet mixed with oil; later polishing was carried out using jeweller's rouge.

The small size of pieces of jet, the frequent presence of flaws and its talismanic powers, believed to provide protection from the evil eye, all contributed to the high cost of the material. From antiquity imitations of jet, such as lignite and cannel coal, were used; glass, hard rubbers, such as vulcanite, and plastics have also been used as simulants. The sheen of polished jet, its warmth to the touch and its ability to produce static electricity when rubbed can help distinguish it from imitations. Radiography can be used to identify jet and to study the ways in which it has been worked.

Jewelled decoration Overglaze decoration made in imitation of precious stones. The technique was invented at Sèvres in France in the late 18th century for use on porcelains and is

Detail from a Sèvres saucer, soft paste porcelain with fired gilding and jewelled decoration, c.1785. The painted cameo portrait is of Benjamin Franklin.

characterized by enamel decoration, which is applied to gold or silver foil and fused. The foils are then placed on fired porcelains and fired again to fix them to the surface. The decoration is extremely fragile and thus few examples survive, but it was used on a wide range of vessel forms at Sèvres and was copied in the 19th century at various English factories, including Worcester and Spode.

Genuine jewelled decoration is not unknown on ceramics. Some Chinese porcelains in Near Eastern collections have glass 'jewels' which have been embedded into the surface of the vessels. As this type of decoration damages the surface, it is suitable for use only on extremely hard ceramics.

Jeweller's rouge See HAEMATITE.

Jiggering A technique for shaping CERAMICS.

Joinery The manufacture, fitting and finishing of fixed components in houses, shops and offices, especially window frames, doors, panelling and fitted furniture. The majority of timber used by joiners will have undergone secondary finishing to provide smooth surfaces and may be given tertiary treatments such as the application of mouldings, paints and polishes.

In Britain the joiners' company, the Brotherhood of the Guild of St James Garlickhythe, was first established as a guild in 1375. The work of the joiner was differentiated, by decree, from that of the carpenter and the turner, and was then limited to the production of beds, chairs, stools, tables and chests. In the late 17th century it was further distinguished from the work of the cabinetmaker, who specialized in the use of veneer. Little joinery has survived from any period earlier than the Renaissance; most of that which has is ecclesiastical and includes church panelling, seating and particularly rood screens and choirs.

Jolleying A technique for shaping CERAMICS.

Jun glaze An opalescent blue glaze used on stoneware produced in Jun in northern China between the 11th century and the 15th. The ware was sometimes decorated with copper inglaze decoration. The Jun glaze is a type of lime glaze that is deliberately coarsely prepared and underfired to encourage the growth of crystals, the formation of numerous tiny bubbles and a brilliant blue colour that is largely optical in nature. In order to ensure the opalescence and blue colour, the glaze must be very slowly cooled and the firing temperature limited to approximately 1220–1250°C. The glaze is composed

Dish, Jun ware with in-glaze copper red decoration, 12th–13th century AD, China, Henan province.

of local clay, which was used for the body material, powdered feldspathic quartz rock, lime and plant ash. Owing to its chemistry, this glaze is classified as a phase-separated glaze, because it splits in the firing into droplets of glass suspended in the main glaze matrix. These are so small that they reflect only blue light, thus contributing to the optical blue colour of the glaze. On traditional Chinese Jun wares the glaze is separated from the body by a thin white layer of anorthite crystals which reflect light back through the glaze, making it appear exceptionally bright.

Modern potters also produce Jun glazes (sometimes called chun glazes), but they differ from the traditional Chinese form in that they are based on modern glaze recipes, which often include whiting, colemanite and talc. They therefore do not have the same texture as Chinese Juns and are difficult to control. Imitation Jun glazes (such as flambé glaze, produced in France in the 19th century) also usually contain cobalt and manganese oxides, which are used to imitate the colours produced by phase separation in a true Jun glaze.

See also CRYSTALLINE GLAZE.

K

Kakiemon See ENAMEL COLOURS.

Kamassi boxwood A South African wood from the species *Gonioma kamassi*, with characteristics similar to BOXWOOD.

Kantha work See QUILTING.

Kaolin An alternative name for CHINA CLAY.

Kapok A light, lustrous and brittle unicellular seed-pod fibre from the kapok tree, *Ceiba pentandra*; mainly produced in Java, it is moisture-resistant, resilient and buoyant and is thus used for stuffings and for temperature and sound insulation. Alternative names for the fibre include silk cotton, silk floss, ceba and ceiba.

Karat See CARAT.

Kaurigum See AMBER.

Keene's cement A type of interior wall plaster obtained from gypsum. In a process patented in England in 1838 by R. W. Keen (*sic*), a sculptor and inventor, and J. D. Greenwood, gypsum is heated above 170°C to form anhydrous calcium sulphate [$CaSO_4$] in which all water incorporated into the crystal structure is removed. This material will set when mixed with water but the reaction is very slow and therefore alum (potassium aluminium sulphate) is added as an accelerator. The mixture is then reheated to 400–500°C and ground to form a plaster. Because Keene's cement sets more slowly than gypsum plaster it is easier to use; it does, however, set more rapidly than lime and produces a hard, smooth finish which can be painted or wallpapered within a few hours of application. Keene's cement has also been used to make casts of ornament, to be fixed to interior walls, in wax, plaster or metal moulds.

Kelim See CARPET-WEAVING and TAPESTRY.

Kerfing See BENTWOOD.

Kermes A mordant dye from the dried bodies of the females of the insect species *Kermes vermilio* Planchon, which live on the kermes oak, native to the eastern Mediterranean and Middle East, and contain a colouring matter of kermesic acid. It is said to have been discovered by the Assyrians and in use in Armenia by the 7th century BC, but it was particularly important during the Middle Ages, when it replaced shellfish purple as the dye used for the most brilliant scarlets and reds. It was the most highly taxed wool dye during this period and was also known as 'grain' (although there is some indication that these terms were not exactly parallel) and as 'little worm'; it was from vermicular, or worm-shaped, that vermilion, the term for bright red, was derived. In the 16th century it was generally replaced by cochineal, derived from another species of the shield-louse family.

Kidderminster A reversible DOUBLECLOTH carpet without a pile, made in Kidderminster from about 1735 and from there introduced to weaving towns in southern Scotland and North America by the 1790s. It has subsequently also been known as Scotch or ingrain carpeting. In the second half of the 18th century Kidderminster weavers also began producing BRUSSELS and later WILTON carpets. See also CARPET-WEAVING.

Kiln A closed oven-like structure used to fire clay objects and transform them into hard ceramics (see FIRING). Low-fired utilitarian wares can be fired in a bonfire or open pit, a method that is suitable for unglazed earthenware. Pit firings are more efficient than bonfires because the heat is partially contained and thus a higher and more constant temperature can be maintained. In order to produce hard, high-fired ceramics a different structure is required, one in which the fire is contained and the ceramics separated from the fire in a chamber where the heated air can pass over and around them. This type of closed structure for firing ceramics is called a kiln (from the Latin *culina*), and traditional kilns are usually classified by the type of draught or current of warmed air that passes through the structure. The main types are up-draught, down-draught and cross-draught kilns. Modern kilns are often classified by the type of fuel used (wood, electricity or gas). Traditional kilns are usually constructed from bricks made from refractory clays such as fire clay. Modern kilns generally have metal casings.

The earliest true kilns were up-draught kilns, usually consisting of a fuel box or firebox, a grated floor or layer of bricks on which the ceramics were placed, and a domed outer wall which contained the firing chamber and directed the warm draught over and around the pots, up and out through a hole in the roof. The earliest excavated examples of this type of kiln come from ancient Mesopotamia and date to around 6000 BC. They are similar in design to Romano-British kilns. Up-draught kilns are not permanent structures and were usually rebuilt after each firing. In the 18th century a sophisticated version of this type of kiln—called a bottle kiln, after its tapering shape—was in use at Stoke-on-Trent. The earliest up-draught kilns could reach only low stoneware temperatures (up to 1050°C), but the small, almost bottle-shaped kiln used at Meissen in the early 18th century could reach the high temperatures (1250–1400°C) at which hard paste porcelain is fired.

Down-draught kilns first appeared in China around 1500 BC. They were usually round or rectangular in shape and had a firebox at the side (or sometimes two fireboxes), flue holes beneath the firing chamber and a flue leading to a chimney (or two chimneys in some cases). They were more efficient than up-draught kilns because they produced higher temperatures (early Chinese examples could reach 1200°C, and later ones 1350°C) and the heated air was distributed more evenly. Down-draught kilns were more often used in Europe from the 18th century onwards.

Kilns with a draught that flows across the firing chamber were and are very common in the Far East, where they were first used in the 3rd century AD, and are known as cross-draught kilns. They come in various designs and include bank or cave kilns, single- or multi-chambered climbing kilns which snake up a hillside and are therefore often called dragon kilns, and the egg-shaped or beehive kilns used in modern industrial ceramic production in China. These kilns can usually reach temperatures of 1200°C or more. European brick kilns are of similar design. Each of these cross-draught

Kilns for the firing of ceramics.
(a) 'Primitive' or simple kiln used for low-temperature firings; the top is rebuilt after each firing.
(b) European up-draught pottery kiln.
(c) Multi-chambered climbing kiln, used in East Asia for firing celadons.
(d) Bank kiln, an early closed kiln design that relies on the slope of the hill for the draught.

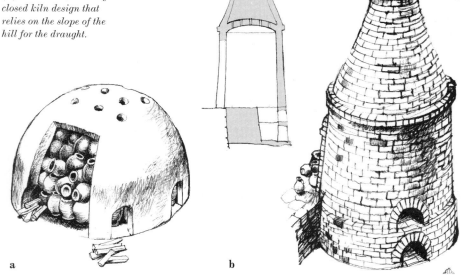

a   b

kilns has the feature of a sloping firing chamber, with either no chimney at all or one large one at the opposite end to the firebox. The kilns are very long and have the disadvantage of requiring constant fuelling and inducing rapid coolings. For Asian celadons, however, such conditions are essential (see CELADON). The multi-chambered kiln is somewhat more efficient, as the heat from one chamber is used to warm up the next one and so on. Multi-chambered kilns are also self-supporting and require little insulation. Each chamber is, in effect, a single down-draught kiln. A type of tunnel kiln that is also in effect a cross-draught kiln is used in modern large-scale industrial production. These tunnel kilns, which were first used in 18th-century France, are loaded by carts which convey the pots to the heated central part of the tunnel and then out towards the cooler end. Such a loading system can enable continuous production.

Most of the above kilns use traditional solid fuels, such as coal or wood for the sloping kilns. These fuels produce ash, which must be collected in an ash pit through a grate. Coal is useful for high-temperature firings and wood is most suitable for reduction firings (see FIRING), as much smoke is produced during combustion. Unless readily available, solid fuels can prove quite expensive and labour-intensive. In modern ceramics cheaper and more easily accessible fuels are preserved. Wood is still found today in small craft studios, as is oil, but the most common flame-producing fuel is gas, which is inexpensive and easy to control. Gas-burning kilns are single-chambered and are classified as up-draught kilns. The most practical kiln and the easiest to use, however, is an elec-

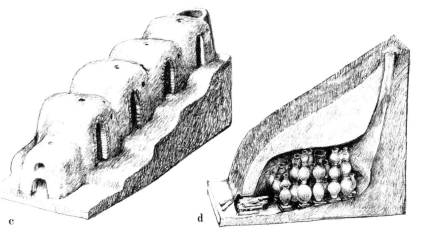

c   d

tric kiln, which does not produce flames. Such kilns are small, single-chambered and top- or front-loading. They run automatically but are normally used only for oxidation firings. One type of kiln can use various different fuels including coal, wood or gas. This is a salt glazing kiln, which consists of a single, domed chamber and a large chimney; it was first used in Germany in the 16th century. More specialized kilns include raku kilns, for producing Japanese RAKU ware, or the small and well-insulated muffle kilns used for enamelled wares. (The muffle is in fact the inner lining of a kiln which protects fragile wares from direct heat or flames.)

When ceramics are put in a traditional kiln for firing, they are usually placed on a support, which is then positioned on the kiln shelf or floor or in a protective clay box or SAGGAR. Supports are often made of high-fired clay and come in many different forms, including ring setters, spurred setters (which have cone-like projections on which the ceramic rests), pegs, trivets, stilts or other footed supports, clay pads or discs. All of these supports are known by the collective name kiln furniture. Alternatively, the ceramics may be supported on a bed of sand or other refractory material laid in the bottom of a saggar. In gas and electric kilns unglazed ceramics are placed directly on shelves or bats for firing.

The manufacture of glass also requires specially designed structures capable of maintaining very high temperatures, in which the glass is melted, reheated and annealed. For discussion of these, see FURNACE, GLORY HOLE and LEHR.

King's yellow See ORPIMENT.

Kingwood A type of rosewood from *Dalbergia cearensis*, a native of Central and South America. It is a rich, variegated, chocolatey brown-black in colour, and is smooth and lustrous. It is available only in small sizes, and is used for veneers, decorative inlays and turnery. See also ZEBRAWOOD.

Kinrande Chinese porcelain decorated with overglaze enamels and gold leaf. (The name is derived from the Japanese for 'gold brocade'.) Kinrande ware was produced in Jingdezhen specifically for the Japanese market. Trade with the Japanese began very early in Chinese history, but Jingdezhen porcelains were first exported to Japan in the 14th century. In the 16th century Chinese porcelain was very much in vogue in Japan and thus porcelains were made to Japanese taste and in forms that would appeal to that particular market.

Kinrande wares are characterized by monochrome coloured grounds such as dark blue, apple green or iron red, with scrolling gold leaf decoration applied either directly to the surface of a high-fired glaze or on an enamel ground. The forms include bowls, jars and figures, with small bowls the most common. Some related wares feature other colours, including turquoise, with the gold decoration applied to the red areas. Kinrande ware was superseded by domestic Japanese enamelled porcelains (see IMARI).

Knitting A method of making fabric from a single strand of yarn by means of LOOPING. The yarn is manipulated with the aid of one (flexible) or two or more (rigid) long blunt needles. Numerous varieties of stitch have been developed; those basic to cloth production are 'knit' and 'purl'. An important characteristic of knitting is that the continuous strand provides for movement within each loop, allowing the construction to stretch, even when made of elements that are inherently non-stretchy. Knitting was the earliest means of fabric formation to be mechanized (see STOCKING FRAME).

A late 19th-century illustration of knitting, from Thérèse de Dillmont's Encyclopedia of Needlework. *It illustrates the knit stitch, made by looping the free yarn anti-clockwise over the tip of the right-hand needle and withdrawing it back through the opened loop.*

Knotting A wide range of textile techniques characterized by the use of one or more elements locked together by working with the leading end, that is, drawing the entire element through the previous or current stitch; these techniques include tatting, MACRAMÉ and NEEDLE LACE. More specifically, the term refers to the use of knotted thread or cord in LAID AND COUCHED WORK, a practice known in late medieval Europe but not in general use until the mid- to late 17th century. It is thought to have been popularized by the Dutch, who had extensive trading links with China, where this technique had been long established. The cords were knotted by amateurs but often couched by professionals; the latter themselves appear to have developed the alternative and still widely used French knot stitch, in which the knot is worked as part of the securing stitch itself.

Kossu A Chinese term (sometimes spelt *k'ossu*) used for silk cloths constructed in the hand-woven TAPESTRY technique.

Kraak porcelain Chinese blue and white porcelain made for the Dutch market. At the end of the Ming period in late 16th- and early 17th-century China, trade with overseas markets such as Portugal and the Netherlands flourished. The Dutch in particular imported huge quantities of Chinese porcelain, and in the Wanli period (1573–1620) Kraak porcelain was the prevalent style. Decorated with underglaze cobalt blue, the designs and patterns were usually quite dense, separated into radiating panels containing various decorative devices at the rim and a central, main motif. Two kinds of Kraak ware were produced: very fine, thin-bodied examples, which are among the highest-quality porcelains made in this period, and second-quality wares with standard patterns.

The name is probably derived from the word for the Portuguese ships used to carry the porcelain to Europe (carracks). However, it has been suggested that the name might derive from the Dutch word for break (*kraken*) or from the name of shelves in Friesland (also *kraken*) used to display blue and white. The production of Dutch Delftware was very much influenced by Kraak porcelain.

Kraft paper Paper made from wood pulp broken down with sodium sulphate. The process was first used in the USA in 1909 and gives a paper that is brown in colour, with strong fibres.

Kuftgari A type of DAMASCENING practised in India, involving the inlay of silver wire in a cross-hatched steel surface. Pure silver wire is hammered into the grooved steel ground; the excess silver is then cut away with a chisel. The main attraction of kuftgari is the contrast between the bright silver and the dark blue steel. This is accomplished by heating the workpiece over a charcoal fire, which at a certain temperature (290°C) gives the steel a deep blue colour. The silver inlay is not affected by the heat and therefore remains bright.

Kwaart A lead-based, low-fired, colourless glaze used on Delftware or tin-glazed earthenwares. It produces a glossy finish and is applied to pre-fired, tin-glazed and decorated bodies which are then fired again at a lower temperature. Italian maiolica has a similar second glaze, known as coperta.

L

Laburnum A brown to dark green wood with a strong figure, from the *Laburnum vulgare*, *L. anagyroides*, *L. alpinum* and *L, cystisus* species found in Europe and North America. It has very distinct rays and is only available in small sizes. It is difficult to work, but is used for oyster veneers, inlays and small turned items. The Indian laburnum, *Cassia fistula*, is lustrous and seasons to a dark purplish brown; it is hard, heavy and strong, and is used for cabinet work, turnery and veneers.

Lac A mordant dye from the insect *Coccus lacca*, which has a colouring matter of laccaic acid, giving a bright red similar to kermes and cochineal; also the resin from the same source from which the dye is extracted. The crude resin often includes the twigs that support the insects and is known as stick lac; cleaned of these it was 'grained' and fused into moulds, giving the form known as caked lac. It was used in combination with cochineal, which was more expensive, and from the late 17th century it was usually applied with a tin mordant; in the 18th century it was introduced into British East India Company printing. See also SHELLAC.

Lac burgauté Mother-of-pearl inlaid URUSHI lacquerware characterized by the use of very thin, iridescent layers of shell. The ware is said to have been developed in China as early as the Song period (960–1279). No Chinese examples pre-dating the Ming period (1368–1644) have been positively identified,

Black dish in lac burgauté, *China, believed to be late Yuan or early Ming period, 14th–15th century* AD.

but Korean examples dating from the late Koryo period (12th–13th century) are known. The technique is said to have been introduced to Japan by the artist Chobei in about 1620.

Known in China as *ping-tuo*, the ware is called *aogai* in Japan and *najon ch'ilgi* in Korea. The production technique was refined and developed by the Koreans and became the main type of decorated urushi in that country. The usual substrate for shell inlay is wood, but papier mâché, metal and ceramic have also been used. Several different species of shell are used, the most attractive of which is ABALONE, known in Japan as *awabi*. A highly iridescent blue-green, it can be cut into sheets so thin that twelve sheets together are less than 0.01mm thick. These can be easily cut with knives or chisels. Where large numbers of repeat patterns are required, small cutting punches can be used to produce individual design elements which are pasted onto a prepared ground to produce mosaic pictures using the iridescence of the shell to simulate shading effects. Once the design elements are fixed in place, successive coats of urushi are applied until the spaces between the design elements are filled and the shell is covered. The final process is a graduated polishing, which is continued until the shell inlay is exposed, leaving deposits of urushi in the previously engraved details.

Lace A general term for a large number of decorative openwork fabrics differentiated by the shape of the surrounding holes and the manner of creating them. The name derives from the Latin *lacqueus* ('noose'). The holes in the fabric may be formed into a regular pattern (known as the mesh, ground, *fond* or *réseau*) used to surround motifs; to create tonal values within motifs; or, in guipure lace, to provide open areas (stabilized by plain or decorative bars called bridges or brides) around meandering or geometric designs. Until the second quarter of the 19th century lace was principally made from fine flax threads, but silk, metal threads, cotton and other fine, strong, pliable threads have also been used. Braids were often called laces since the metal thread varieties especially were often supplied by the same tradesmen that sold lace; also, the sides of braids were finished with similar loops or other free-floating extensions.

Laces can be divided into five basic categories: EMBROIDERED LACE, NEEDLE LACE, BOBBIN LACE, machine-made lace, and lace-like structures made by knitting or knotting (including tatting and crochet). However, a combination of

A Buckinghamshire lacemaker, using a pillow and bobbins in the making of bobbin lace, 1898.

categories may sometimes be used: 'mixed' laces include those with bobbin motifs and needle-made grounds or insertions (for example, Mixed Brussels and some Honiton types), TAPE LACE and those worked on BOBBINET. Although some of these techniques are known around the world, the making of the full range of laces was concentrated in Europe, especially Italy, France, Belgium and Britain, and flourished from the 16th century to the 19th.

Machine-made lace evolved from the plain weft- and warp-knitted nets made on the hand-powered STOCKING FRAME in the 1760s and 1770s and the invention of Bobbinet in 1808. Warp frames using silk threads were adapted in the 1820s (in Lyon, France) and 1830s (in Nottingham, England) to the production of patterned laces by the addition of a JACQUARD machine. The lace produced was characterized by vertical chains, the loops made by needles. However, warp frames were little used from *c*.1840 until *c*.1940, when a similar technology was applied in Raschel machines, used largely for synthetic-fibre lace. In the intervening period their place was taken by powered machines such as the Pusher and the Leaver, invented in 1812 and 1823 respectively. These, and the Nottingham lace or Curtain machine that was developed in 1846, evolved from bobbinet machines, in which the warps were secured in a traversed twisted position, distinguishing them from stocking and warp frames, which employ a looping action. Once Jacquards were added to the Pusher machine in 1839 the latter could be used to make shawls, especially of wool, and good imitations of Flemish bobbin lace, including Valenciennes, Mechlin, and Chantilly and other silk laces; however, the outlining thread (lacer) was still run-in by hand. By the 1830s the Leaver machine developed untraversed warps, giving it its characteristic verticals in the solid areas of a pattern, and from 1841 it incorporated a form of Jacquard (with wooden knobs in place of holes) to insert lacers. The Leaver could produce a very wide range of imitation bobbin laces, including those that themselves imitated needle laces. The Curtain machine was similar in its operation but made far fewer types of grounds, although with much larger repeats (the Leaver was restricted to $c.30$ cm $\times$ 30 cm). Its grounds tended to be square, rather than hexagonal or round (as with the Leaver), and it produced bobbin-style laces, many original in design, as well as imitation embroidered laces, such as filet. Tape lace and geometric-style bobbin lace braids up to 20 cm wide can be effectively imitated by the Barmen machine, developed in Germany in 1858, which has bobbins placed in a circle to facilitate the necessary cross-twisting action. Imitations of all types of laces, including chemical lace, were also produced by types of EMBROIDERY MACHINE.

Lacewood The wood of the PLANE tree when quarter-cut and selected for its wavy figure.

Lacework A type of applied decoration found on European porcelain figures, made from actual lace which has been dipped in slip. The slipped lace is applied to the figure, which is then fired. The lace burns away in the firing to leave a pattern on the porcelain. Used mainly for costumes, the technique was invented at Meissen in the 1770s and is associated with figures by Michel-Victor Acier. Lacework can also be found on 19th-century figures from Derby and Sèvres.

Lacis A needle-run or darned EMBROIDERED LACE, also called filet.

Lacquer A generic and imprecise term for a more or less glossy, decorative and protective varnished finish and also

for the material used to create it. The word derives from the
Indo-Persian *lac*, best known in the West as SHELLAC, which
is one of the materials found in Middle Eastern and European
lacquerwork; the word is now used to describe any one of the
many different varnished finishes, irrespective of their
origins. The term is also applied to many of the modern
materials used to achieve a flat decorative or protective
surface, such as the celluloses and melamines which are often
applied by spraying.

Some finishes referred to as lacquer are in fact only varnished; that is to say, the varnish has been simply brushed on
and allowed to dry with little or no refinishing. A true
lacquered finish requires careful preparation of the ground,
which is usually wood, with layers of intermediate groundwork made from hard-setting pastes. This is followed by
numerous applications of thin coats of varnish, each carefully
rubbed down with fine abrasives when dry. The final appearance can be anything from a deep lustrous shine to a semi-
matt finish. A lacquer finish can be applied to many
materials, including wood, papier mâché and basketry, as
well as (less commonly) metal, ivory and horn (see colour
plates XId and XIII).

There are four major schools of lacquerware, the origins of
which are differentiated both geographically and by the lacquers used. The Far Eastern school is based on URUSHI
resins. The main Middle Eastern school is based on spirit-
soluble resins such as sandarac and shellac with vegetable oils
such as linseed, walnut and poppy; a secondary technique
employed in Turkish work, in some types of Persian work and
in Indian flat wares uses only shellac. The European school
(see JAPANNING) is based mainly on Middle Eastern materials
and techniques, with some methodology derived from the Far
Eastern schools.

Laid and couched work A group of embroidery techniques,
all involving securing an outlining or filling thread by stitching with a second thread. The secured thread is 'laid', that is,
always remains on the surface, while the couching thread
penetrates the supporting fabric and, often, creates a pattern
at the same time. If, at its turning point, the laid thread,
usually metal, is just pulled through the cloth by the couching thread, it is called underside couching. In addition, a wide
variety of decorative elements can be laid and couched; these
include pearls, spangles, glass discs and beads, feathers,

*Lacquered comb, Iran,
Qajar period, late 19th
century. Middle Eastern
lacquerwares were painted
in watercolour or oil paint
and then sealed with
several coats of varnish.
Shellac or sandarac resin
in linseed oil were the
usual varnishes.*

insect cases, shells, metal threads and plain or embroidered cloth or leather motifs (known as APPLIQUÉ). See BEADWORK, BEETLE-WING EMBROIDERY, KNOTTING, OPUS ANGLICANUM, OR NUÉ and QUILLWORK.

Laid paper See PAPER.

Lake A type of pigment made by locking a soluble dye onto a colourless powder, known as the 'substrate'. The term derives from the Latin word *lacca*, used in the Middle Ages to denote both lake pigments and the LAC dye. Barium sulphate is used for cheaper lakes, but the most common substrate is aluminium hydroxide, which not only bonds to the dye very strongly but is also highly translucent, a fact that is important because lake pigments are mostly employed as a GLAZE.

The technique of making lakes was well known by the 14th century, using colours extracted from natural materials such as berries, flowers and roots. Lakes were important in the Renaissance for the illumination of books. The colours were bright and suited to fine detail, and were protected from the damaging effects of light, but once the era of manuscript illumination came to an end many organic pigments ceased to be used. Among those that disappeared were Tyrian purple from the murex shellfish, reds, blues and purples from the turnsole flower, and yellow from saffron. Other organic pigments were more colour-fast and continued to be part of the palette until the end of the 19th century, the most important of which were reds from the bark of the brazilwood tree and from lac insects, blue from woad and indigo plants, and yellow from buckthorn berries.

The manufacture of rose madder lake at the Winsor & Newton works.

The most successful lakes have been the crimson ones, first from kermes beetles, then from Mexican cochineal beetles, and finally from the madder root, once the technique for its colour extraction was perfected in the 18th century. In the late 19th century the chemical industry discovered synthetic equivalents of madder and indigo and went on to produce a range of new ones from coal tar derivatives. These and many of the bright new pigments introduced in the 20th century have all been manufactured as lakes. The only paint company still to use a natural material is Winsor & Newton, which produces rose madder from crushed madder roots, using original 19th-century lake-making equipment.

Lakes are used wherever translucent colours are needed. Sometimes they are employed on their own, for example on 18th- and 19th-century glass painting, or they are used as a glaze over opaque underlayers. They have had an important role since the Middle Ages in the glazing of tin, gold and silver foil, for details of polychrome sculpture, church ornaments, furniture, jewellery, horse trappings and armour. Wonderfully preserved crimson and yellow lakes have been used to glaze silver leaf on 17th- and 18th-century embossed leather hangings.

Lamelle A method of decorating leather by thonging strips of silver, brass or other metal through a series of slits cut into its surface.

Lamination The act of fixing together several layers of wood veneer to make a stronger coherent whole, such as plywood or 'laminboard'. The term is also used for a method whereby circular or serpentine cabinet work is constructed from numerous blocks and then veneered.

Lampas A French term denoting a figured fabric with additional warps or wefts, used in the patterned areas to create extra colours and, when not required, woven into the back of the cloth. Some English firms distinguish between specific

Brocaded tissue (or lampas), in silk and metal thread, early 18th century. At the upper-right, the reverse of the fabric shows the characteristic areas of supplementary brocading wefts, added by means of a hand-held bobbin solely where additional colours are required.

types of lampas weaves: the term 'tissue' is used for cloths with an extra colouring weft; lisère (contrary to its French meaning, 'selvedged') denotes a figured weave with a striped additional warp; while damasquette indicates a damask with an additional single-coloured warp which usually matches the weft, so that a pure unblended colour can be created where they interact on the surface.

Lampblack A pigment made by burning oil or wax and collecting the black soot. The powder is extremely fine and one of its most important uses is in the manufacture of so-called Indian ink or Chinese ink. It is a useful pigment if a very dense, opaque black is required.

Lampworking The manipulation of readily fusible glass rods and tubes over a flame or gas burner. The practice (also sometimes called flameworking) was known to the Romans and in

Lampworked group of a shepherd with his flock, attributed to Nevers, early 18th century. Such figures were often supported by a copper wire armature.

recent centuries has been used to make beads, small animal and human figures, and other knick-knacks. Lampworking is also used to heat moulded parts before their attachment to the body of a vessel.

Lapis lazuli An opaque blue rock with a hardness on the Mohs scale of 5.5, containing various silicate minerals, principally lazurite plus small amounts of calcite, which is evident as white patches, and specks of pyrites, which are gold-coloured. It generally contains other minerals such as hornblende, augite and mica; hornblende may make lapis difficult to work as it has a fibrous texture. The blue coloration (see colour plates V and XVIII), which can be deep or pale, greenish or nearly purple, is produced by sulphur contained in one of the minerals. Pale lapis can be dyed to enhance the colour.

Lapis lazuli is formed during the metamorphic process which converts limestone to marble. The distribution of lapis is limited, owing to the rare conjunction of materials and conditions necessary for its formation, and its principal source is the Badakshan region of Afghanistan. Lapis is extracted from mines by heating the stone and then rapidly cooling it with water, which causes cracking of the surrounding material, allowing pieces approximately 5 kg in weight to be removed. It was sufficiently prized for trade in lapis to exist in antiquity and it was used in Sumer and pre-dynastic Egypt for beads, amulets and inlays. The name is derived from the Persian word *lazhward* ('blue'), suggesting that the Persians were involved in the trade. It was transported to the Far East, where it was used for carvings, and to Europe, where it was used for jewellery, intaglios, vases and other decorative items and for PIETRE DURE; it was also ground to obtain the pigment ultramarine. Lapis was worked with abrasives, applied to discs or saws. In 1939 a source of lapis was found in a remote area of the Chilean Andes. Stones from this source are a deep blue and contain more calcite and pyrite than Afghan lapis.

Because of the rarity of lapis lazuli, simulants, including blue glass seals from Sidon dating from the 13th century BC, are common. So-called 'Swiss lapis' or 'German lapis' is made by treating jasper with potassium ferrocyanide and ferrous sulphate, which produces blue pigmentation. These imitations can be detected by their lack of pyrite inclusions. Owing to the heterogeneous nature of lapis, convincing synthetic stones are extremely difficult to produce, although some attempts were made to do so in the 1970s.

Lapis style See RESIST DYEING.

Lapping The process of polishing a flat metal surface by holding it against a rotating flat rigid polishing disc of felt, wood or leather.

Latex See RUBBER.

Lathe A machine used for the manufacture, by TURNING, of generally circular items such as wooden bowls, platters and poles. It can also be used to decorate wood, ivory, ceramic or metal items with incised lines (see ENGINE TURNING).

A number of different lathes are used throughout the world, all of which consist in their simplest form of a horizontal bed and a pair of stocks, one of which is usually movable, and between which the workpiece is held. The workpiece is made to rotate towards the operator, either mechanically or by hand. A cutting tool, either a gouge or chisel, is manipulated against the periphery of the workpiece to produce the desired shape.

The simplest types of lathe are the pole lathe and the bow lathe, both of which have been used since the Graeco–Roman period. The bow lathe is a simple development from the bow drill (see WOODWORKING TOOLS), which is known to have been used in ancient Egypt. Both types are still used extensively: pole lathes were employed to produce the legs and spindles for chairs made at High Wycombe, England, in the 1960s. The motive power for the bow lathe is provided by a small bow held in the left hand of the operator, with its string wrapped around a spindle to which the workpiece is attached. The power source for the pole lathe comes from a springy, greenwood tree branch (for illustration see page 504). The branch is fixed above the bed of the lathe, and a string is attached at one end to the tip of the branch, wrapped around the workpiece and attached to a treadle at the other end. Depressing the treadle causes the workpiece to rotate and draws the springy branch down; when the treadle is released the branch springs back, raising the treadle for the next action. The advantage of the pole lathe over the bow lathe is that it leaves both of the operator's hands free to control the cutting tools, but the motion is still reciprocating, limiting the cutting action to the forward stroke. The treadle lathe converts the power of the operator's leg into rotary motion via a rod that connects the treadle to a flywheel; this in turn is connected to the headstock by a circular belt or cord. The motion of the workpiece is always towards the operator, making regular use of the cutting tools possible.

Powered lathes have been available since the invention of the steam engine in the 18th century and have improved and developed with each advance in motive power. Most modern lathes are powered by integrated electric motors, enabling

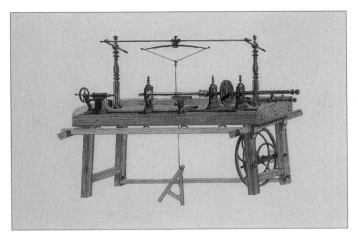

A treadle-operated bow lathe, from a watercolour in a folio album by A. Boucicault, probably 1870s. The fly wheel appears to be superfluous.

much higher turning speeds and allowing heavy workpieces to be turned with ease. Modern holding and chucking systems facilitate high-quality finishes with minimal remounting of the workpiece.

The ornamental lathe is a complex machine that enables the production of intricate surface patterns and elaborate profiles. It uses a series of interchangeable gears, cambs and faceplates, with fixed cutters in mobile tool holders, coupled with elliptical, oval, eccentric, epicycloidal and rose cutting frames. The workpiece, though usually static, can be made to rotate, reciprocate or move laterally, while the cutter can be moved in any direction.

Relative simple ornamental lathes (also sometimes called rose engines) were in use in the 16th century and are mentioned by Joseph Moxon (1696) and Charles Plumier (1701). More sophisticated examples were incredibly expensive, a factor that limited their use to costly materials such as ivory and imported hardwoods. A good-quality machine with a complete range of attachments cost about £1500 in 1838 (equivalent to about £200,000 today). However, they were very finely and durably constructed. The aristocracy and gentry were soon attracted to ornamental turning, and the works and machines of Peter the Great, Prince August of Saxony and Louis XVI can be seen in museum collections.

The ornamental lathe was brought to its ultimate development by the Holtzapffels, a German family of engineers. In about 1782 John Jacob Holtzapffel established a workshop in London. The best craftsmen of the day, such as Joseph Whitworth, were employed and the company remained in production until 1914. In 1843 the family began publication of the monumental and highly influential *Turning and Mechanical Manipulation*. Started by Charles Holtzapffel and finished by John Jacob II, volumes 4 and 5 were not published until 1883; the proposed volume 6 was never completed.

See also ROSE ENGINE TURNING.

Latten A term sometimes used confusingly in old literature to refer to hammered brass or special brass alloys.

Latticino An outdated term for glassware decorated with embedded white threads (see FILIGREE and LATTIMO).

Lattimo An opaque white glass invented in Venice in the late 15th century in imitation of Chinese porcelain. The original opacifying agent was probably tin oxide. Lattimo was often decorated with enamelling and was also much used in FILIGREE glass and in trailed decoration.

Lavoro di basso rilievo See ENAMEL.

Layout paper See TRACING PAPER.

Lead A white or bluish grey metal which is soft, very malleable, and has a low melting-point. Lead was used extensively in antiquity for water pipes, baths and sarcophagi. (The Latin word for lead is *plumbum*; hence, a plumber was originally a worker with lead.) Later its use was extended to architectural features such as roofs, spires, cisterns and garden ornaments and statues. The main source in nature is the ore galena, which is reduced to lead with the aid of carbon and carbon monoxide. Ancient sources for lead were Britain and Spain.

Lead can be worked easily because of its softness, and its low melting-point facilitates welding, soldering and casting. One important use is in alloys and especially with tin, to form 'soft' or lead solders. These low-melting solders can be used for joining most metals, including copper, iron, zinc and tinplate. Lead must be handled with care because of its toxicity; the fumes are especially dangerous.

Lead glass Glass that contains a large amount of lead oxide. Present-day lead glass (crystal) must contain at least 24% lead oxide. It is sometimes called half-lead, and glass with 30% lead oxide is called full lead or *crystal supérieur*. It has a brilliance, softness and strength that make it ideal for facet cutting and engraving. Vessels emit a characteristic ring when struck lightly on the rim.

Lead glass was invented in 1676 by the English glassmaker

George Ravenscroft in his attempts to find a replacement for the fragile CRISTALLO glass then being made in London. Initially he used flint and potash instead of the pebbles and barilla ash used by the Venetians. However, the glass was inclined to crizzle. Ravenscroft then discovered that by reducing the proportion of potash and adding oxide of lead (to around 30% of the batch), he could eliminate crizzling and make a glass that was similar in appearance to natural rock crystal. The formula continued to be modified and English glass enjoyed enormous success during the 18th century.

See also FLINT GLASS.

Lead glaze A low-fired glaze fluxed with lead.

Lead tin yellow A pale yellow pigment sometimes known as 'massicot' or 'masticot'. It was too expensive for use in house painting but was important in easel painting until the mid-18th century.

Lead white A white synthetic pigment (lead carbonate) made by exposing strips of metallic lead to acidic vapours and carbon dioxide. It has been an enormously significant pigment since pre-classical times and still plays an important role in oil painting. Unlike any other pigment, it forms a chemical link with the drying oil, giving the paint properties that cannot be reproduced using the modern whites titanium white and zinc white. When used from the tube it has excellent brushing qualities, and in domestic house paint it has always been admired for the way it becomes soft and silvery with age. Health and safety regulations mean that in many countries it is banned completely, but in the United Kingdom it is still allowed for artists' oil paint, and special dispensation can be obtained for its use in the restoration of Grade I listed buildings. It has never been successfully used in aqueous media because of a tendency to blacken in contact with polluted air.

Leading up See STAINED GLASS.

Leather A material made from the hide or skin of a mammal, fish, bird or reptile by a series of operations which renders it non-putrescible even under warm, moist conditions. A true leather will retain this fundamental property after repeated wetting and drying. (Leather-like materials can be prepared from skins by careful drying, the use of salt, or by treating them with alum in the TAWING process. The effects of these treatments are, however, reversed by immersion in water and the skins rapidly revert to the raw condition, in which they

Finishing persians for
hatband leathers, 1861–2.

are susceptible to biological deterioration.) Although leather generally dries to give an opaque, relatively soft, flexible handle, it can be hard or soft, flexible or rigid, stiff or supple, thick or thin, limp or springy, depending on the nature of the skin used and the processes employed.

The visual appearance of leather is due primarily to the pattern of small holes that remains when the hair, wool, feathers or scales are removed during processing. Factors determining this pattern include the type of animal, its age and sex, and the part of the skin from which the particular piece of leather originates. Calf leather, for instance, has a smoother, finer, more uniform grain pattern than that of a more mature cattle hide. The grain of a goatskin is more pronounced and this characteristic is often emphasized, as in the production of Morocco leathers. Sheepskin leathers, on the other hand, often have a coarser, softer grain pattern. The arrangement of hair follicles is generally tighter and more uniform along the back than in the belly region.

The physical properties of a piece of leather are also fundamentally dependent on the same factors. Sheepskins will give a softer, more flexible and less dense leather than cattle hides, making them suitable for clothing and gloving purposes. Calfskin and goatskin leathers are tough and abrasion-resistant and are therefore used for footwear and bookbindings. Bull hides are coarser and thicker than cow hides and were traditionally used for making textile machinery components.

The characteristics of leather taken from the shoulder of a hide are very different from those taken from, say, the belly region. For this reason larger hides are often rounded or cut into smaller pieces which are tanned in a different way to produce entirely different products. Some leathers are manufactured in such a way as to emphasize these natural effects. Others are processed in an attempt to produce a uniform, smooth surface. It has been the aim of the tanner throughout the ages to make a product with just the right combination of aesthetic and physical properties for any given end use.

The conversion of a hide into a leather involves first a series of pre-tanning operations, in which the unwanted components of a skin structure are removed chemically or mechanically. The remaining network of collagen fibres is then treated with tanning materials, which react chemically to convert them into leather. These materials can be divided into three groups: mineral tanning agents, such as alum, used in the tawing process, or chrome tanning salts; vegetable tanning materials; and reactive oils and fats, such as those used to produce chamois leathers, together with the more recently introduced synthetic chemicals (for further information see TANNING). The leathers are then finished out to produce the required handle and appearance in a series of operations, such as the CURRYING process. Today an extensive range of speciality dyes and chemicals is employed to give the wide variety of leathers required by the modern consumer.

It is the three-dimensional woven structure of the fibres within a piece of leather that imparts its unique combination of aesthetic and utilitarian properties. Pieces of leather, particularly vegetable-tanned leather, can be cut and moulded into a variety of shapes, joined together by stitching and gluing, and tooled or decorated using a wide range of techniques. The raw, cut edge of a piece of leather will not fray and the fibre structure allows the edge to be 'skived' or pared to a uniform chamfered cut. This can either be turned

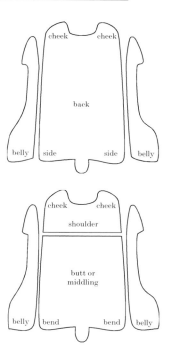

The parts of a cattle hide. Each of the various ways of cutting the hide gives a different type of leather.

over and stuck, or sewn to produce a neat effect, or joined to another skived edge to produce a scarfe joint. For the same reason leather can be pared or thinned down by cutting shavings from the flesh side more or less horizontally, using a sharp knife or a spoke shave.

If a vegetable-tanned leather is dampened it becomes malleable and can be moulded and decorated using a range of techniques. These include tooling, in which the design is outlined into the grain surface with a fine agate or ebony tracing point. The background is then either flattened, leaving the design in raised relief, or given a contrasting punched effect. Incising involves cutting the design at right angles into about two-thirds of the thickness of the leather. The cut is opened on one side only, pressing the grain into the incision. With the repoussé technique the dampened skin is worked from the flesh side to raise the design on the grain and bring it into relief. The indentations are filled to prevent the leather from flattening. BLOCKING, TOOLING and stamping involve the use of metal tools to impress patterns into the grain surface. These methods have been used individually or in conjunction with each other since prehistoric times.

Since it is an organic material, leather is liable to deterioration caused by a wide range of agents. Storage in damp atmosphere will result in attack by moulds, and prolonged immersion in water will strip the tanning materials, leaving the skin open to bacterial attack. On the other hand, the material is remarkably resistant to insect pests, and burial in anaerobic waterlogged conditions can preserve leather objects for thousands of years. The major cause of deterioration of vegetable-tanned leathers is acidic atmospheric pollution, particularly that of sulphur dioxide, which causes the 'red rot' so often apparent in leather bookbindings from the late 19th century.

Lehr An oven used for annealing glassware. Early lehrs were connected to the main furnace but the heat and smoke made them unreliable. In the late 18th century a long, brick-lined, separately heated tunnel was developed through which the glass was slowly drawn. Within the tunnel the temperature decreased from just under melting temperature at the receiving end to ordinary room temperature at the other. In modern production the glass passes through on a conveyor belt and the process is controlled automatically.

Letter carving The inscribing of writing onto stone, practised throughout history and in all cultures, to serve as memorials, records of achievement or durable versions of religious texts. Letters or pictograms can be carved or incised into the stone so that they are recessed below the surface and thus more protected from weathering, or the background may be removed, leaving the letters in relief, a technique used in some Egyptian and Mayan hieroglyphic inscriptions.

Inscriptions have often been carved in fine-grained stone so that the texture of the material does not interfere with the legibility of the inscription. Before an inscription could be carved a smooth surface would be produced by sawing, splitting (used with materials such as slate) or working the stone flat with chisels. As it is impossible to correct mistakes of spacing, size of letters or spelling in a carved inscription, the letter carver had to set out his work carefully. From antiquity horizontal guidelines were transferred to the stone by snapping a taut string, charged with chalk or pigment, against the surface. Egyptian texts were painted on the stone by a scribe as a guide for the carver. In ancient Greece the letters may have been drawn on the stone with charcoal or chalk. From the 1st century AD in Rome drawn letters were then painted over with a chisel-edged brush. The variations in the thickness of line produced by the brush were followed in the carving, resulting in the characteristic changes in width of Roman letter forms; the serif is also believed to have evolved from painted letters. The Romans also used compasses and other measuring tools for laying out inscriptions.

Stones such as marble, limestone, sandstone and slate were carved with iron or steel chisels with a thin blade; modern

A letter carver at work on a memorial. She uses a chisel with a narrow blade, struck with a metal mallet to produce V-cut letters. The words have been laid out in pencil before the carving begins, a process usually carried out in a standing position, with a strong, directional light to enhance the legibility of the letter forms while work is in progress.

letter-carving chisels are narrower than those used for other purposes. Some inscriptions from the Roman republican period (509–31 BC) were incised with a pointed tool producing a line which is rounded in section. From the 1st century AD the Romans used chisels with square corners to the blade held at a constant angle to the surface and perpendicular to the stem of the letter being carved. This produced a V-shaped cut which is widely used in contemporary letter carving. Before the development of power tools harder stones were inscribed using bow-driven wheels and drills and other abrasive cutting tools (see STONECARVING TOOLS). Letter carving in stones such as granite is now carried out by shot blasting through a rubber stencil, which can be cut by a computer-guided laser.

Roman letters were often painted red or were gilded or filled with metal inlays. Lead was widely used to fill the letters in 19th-century gravestone inscriptions.

Levant The skins of goats, sheep or seals vegetable-tanned so as to 'draw' or shrink the leather, producing a characteristic uneven grain pattern. This is then emphasized by BOARDING the leather. This type of leather was produced during the second half of the 19th century and in the early 20th, for making wallets, handbags and other small leather goods, and for covering boxes and document cases.

Levigation See CLAY.

Lias A group of coarse- to medium-grained limestones which occur in the English Midlands and south-west. They contain clays and iron, which produce a range of colours from pale cream, reds and browns to greens and greyish blues. In Hornton stone, a type of lias, blues, greens and brownish oranges can be found in a single block of stone. The lias limestones have been used for building since Roman times. Blue lias was occasionally used for column shafts in medieval churches, for example at Wells Cathedral. Because of their iron and clay content, lias limestones can be calcined to obtain hydraulic lime.

Lignite A form of coal derived from peat, used from antiquity to imitate jet. Unlike jet, it will not take a high polish.

Lignum vitae A very hard and heavy, tough and durable wood from the *Guaiacum officinale* and *G. sanctum* species (the Guayacan or Congo cypress) of Central America, sometimes known as bera. Olive green to dark brown in colour, with a distinct waxy feel and a very fine interwoven grain, it is very difficult to work but turns well using scrapers and takes a fine polish. It produces an oily secretion which acts as a lubricant. The wood is used for machine bearings, hand tools (especially mallets and formers), castors, bowl turning and other sophisticated turnery, and is usually marketed under the name of its source (e.g. Bahamas, Cuba, Jamaica or Nicaragua). Similar woods derived from other species, such as SANTO WOOD and VERAWOOD, are considered inferior.

Lime A white powder made from limestone. It is used as a mortar, a render and interior wall plaster, for moulded and modelled decoration and as the basis for fresco decoration. It is also an important component in cement and is used in the manufacture of glass. Lime is obtained by a process known as calcining, in which a material containing calcium carbonate is heated in a kiln to temperatures between 700°C and 900°C; the most common source is limestone, but other materials, such as shells and coral, have been used in Sri Lanka and the Persian Gulf. Traditional batch kilns are cylindrical structures lined with blocks of limestone in which the stone to be heated is arranged in a vault-like shape and a fire lit beneath this; additional stone to be calcined is placed on top of the vault. The calcining process can take several days, during which the temperature must be maintained, and drives off carbon dioxide from the calcium carbonate [$CaCO_3$]. The resulting strongly caustic material is calcium oxide [CaO], or quicklime.

For use the quicklime must be 'slaked' by adding it to water, a process traditionally carried out in a lime pit set into the ground. Water becomes incorporated in the crystal structure to form calcium hydroxide [$Ca(OH)_2$]. Prolonged slaking, for several months or years, produces a smooth, plastic putty which is mixed with an aggregate for use. Lime sets by reaction with carbon dioxide in the air to form calcium carbonate, chemically the same material as the original limestone. This process, called carbonation, is very slow as the air must reach each molecule of calcium hydroxide; once carbonation has occurred at the surface it reduces the porosity, thus further slowing the reaction.

The addition of highly reactive forms of silica and alumina, such as volcanic earths, ash or rock (such as tuff or pumice), brick dust, or ground iron slags, produces a hydraulic set in which the lime does not set by carbonation, but instead forms calcium silicates and aluminates by reaction with these additives and can solidify rapidly even under water. Materials which induce this effect are called pozzolanic additives, after the town of Pozzuoli, near Naples, where the Romans extracted volcanic earths for this purpose. The principles of the hydraulic set were discovered around the 4th century BC, and the Romans used hydraulic mortars to build piers, bridges and aqueducts. Hydraulic lime can also be made by calcining limestones such as lias, which have a high silica content.

Lime glaze A high-fired glaze fluxed with calcia or lime. See ASH GLAZE.

Limestone A sedimentary stone composed largely of calcium carbonate. Limestones occur extensively and exist in a wide range of colours, textures, densities and porosities. They were formed through one of several processes. Calcium carbonate, if present in high concentrations, can be precipitated from ground water (see TRAVERTINE and TUFA) or sea water, where it forms in small spheres, called ooliths, around a minute fragment of sand or shell. Limestones can also be formed from the fossilized shells or skeletons of sea animals or corals which may be whole or fragmented. The remains of weathered, pre-existing limestone can also be deposited to form a new limestone. Over time the sediments become more compact and are cemented together with further calcium carbonate or with silica, clay or iron. The type of cementing material and the extent of compaction, along with impurities, will affect the colour, texture and hardness of the limestone.

The formation process may result in the presence of pronounced layers or beds which can influence how the stone can be worked. A limestone in which narrow, soft beds alternate with taller beds of harder, workable stone facilitates the removal of good-sized blocks from the quarry. In contrast to the homogeneous nature of many marbles which can be quarried in large blocks, limestones are generally extracted in long blocks that are limited by the height of the bed. For external use limestones are most resistant to weathering when the beds are positioned horizontally, that is, in the same orientation they had in the quarry. This protects softer layers from penetration by rain water, to which they could be exposed if placed vertically, eventually causing the outer worked surface to be lost.

Many limestones are affected by sulphur dioxide pollution produced by the burning of fossil fuels, notably coal. By reacting with water and oxygen in the atmosphere sulphur dioxide is converted into sulphuric acid, which can then react with the calcium carbonate of the limestone to form calcium sulphate. This material, chemically identical to the mineral gypsum, is somewhat water-soluble and is washed away from areas of the stone regularly exposed to rain, resulting in the eroded appearance of the carved elements of many limestone buildings. In sheltered areas the gypsum can accumulate and, over time, absorb soot and dirt from the environment to form disfiguring black accretions.

Most limestones are reasonably soft and easy to work, and many can accept fine detail. They have been used from antiquity for building, architectural carving and sculpture. Limestones have frequently been painted, either with or without a ground layer. However, as most limestones are porous the surface of the stone was usually sealed with a material such as a gum or glue to prevent the paint or ground medium from being too readily absorbed, leaving the pigment underbound. Hard limestones, capable of taking a polish and often richly coloured and patterned with fossils, are widely referred to as marbles (see MARBLE and VERONA MARBLE) and have been employed decoratively. Limestone is also heated to obtain LIME.

Limestone lectern, England, c.1180. It is carved from a limestone known as 'Wenlock marble', which takes and retains fine detail and crisp edges. The hardness of this type of limestone would limit the depth of undercutting.

Limewash A paint with no added binding medium. It is sometimes called whitewash. Calcium oxide (quicklime) is made up as a slurry in water, and brushed directly onto the wall. As the water evaporates, the calcium oxide takes up carbon dioxide from the air and crystallizes as an insoluble layer of calcium carbonate. Limewashes are quite hard-wearing and have long been used for exterior finishes. It is possible to tint the paint, using chemically inert pigments such as ochres and umbers, but limewashes are usually white.

Limewood A soft and stable, but non-durable, wood from species of linden (*Tilia vulgaris, T. cordata, T. parvifolia, T. platyphylla*) found in Britain and Europe. It is ivory white, sometimes with a reddish tinge, and has a fine, close grain with a very faint ripple. It is easily worked, and is used for carving, for musical instruments, for artificial limbs and for turnery. Wood from American species of linden is called BASSWOOD.

Limewood clock with gilding and silver gilding, by Ignaz Michal Platzer, Bohemia, c.1790.

Liming See TANNING.

Limp vellum binding A book cover made of VELLUM alone, without rigid boards and lacking ornamentation. Such bindings have been used for various purposes in Europe since the 14th century. Originally used as inexpensive but durable covers for account books, limp vellum bindings were used for private press publications in the 19th century and are now considered appropriate for conservation rebinding of medieval books which have lost their old bindings. The books are sewn on raised thongs which are laced into the cover (coloured sewing threads can sometimes be seen in the 19th-century bindings), and the vellum is folded back on itself for strength at fore edge, head and tail. Occasionally vellum has been cut or pierced to give a patterned binding through which a coloured textile shows.

Lincrusta Walton The name of a relief-decorated wallpaper produced from the end of the 19th century in England in imitation of ornamental plasterwork. The paper was patented in 1877 by the inventor of linoleum, Frederick Walton. It was made from a mixture of cotton fibres and linseed oil which, formed into a sheet, was passed between two metal rollers. The pattern was raised on one roller and recessed on the other, so that the material was forced into relief. Lincrusta Walton was usually painted with oil-based paint in one colour and often hung between the skirting board and dado rail to make a very durable lower wall covering. Anaglypta was a cheaper and more lightweight alternative made on a base of paper pulp.

Linden A common name for the lime tree. Wood from American species of linden is called BASSWOOD; that from British and most European species is called LIMEWOOD.

Linen A fibre and fabric made from flax (*Linum usitatissimum*), a slender, soft-fibred annual bast plant that grows to 1 m in height and is also cultivated for its seed (the source of linseed meal and oil). The oldest textile fibre known, it is very long, fine, flexible and extremely strong and lustrous, although inelastic. It is difficult to dye, but its natural colours range from a pale yellowish white to silver grey, bluish green and brown. There is some indication that the use of wax resist printing developed simultaneously with linen processing, for the flax plant can also support substantial beehives. It can be bleached to a pure white and washes well; early household cloths such as towels, table DAMASK and sheets were made from linen, as were the finest shirts and undergarments, made in plain weaves such as lawn and cambric. However, its processing by hand was arduous and cotton began to replace linen once cotton spinning was able to produce a strong alternative warp yarn (see also FUSTIAN). For the same reasons, linen was superseded by cotton as the basis for most lace production in the early 19th century.

A greetings card printed in black from a linocut, by František Koblíha, Czechoslovakia, 1928.

Linocut A relief printmaking technique which uses LINO-LEUM rather than wood. It was developed in the mid-20th century. Like other relief printing processes, the linoleum is cut away from the areas that are to remain blank, and ink is rolled onto the remaining surface for transfer to paper. Only light pressure is needed to print. Woodcutting and engraving tools (gouges) can be used, but fine lines are not possible with the linocut and the linoleum itself is not durable. It is therefore rarely used for large editions or extensive patterning.

Linoleum A composite material made from colour pigments and linseed oil, mixed with fillers such as cork, wood, flour, tree resins or limestone, and applied to a jute canvas backing. Generally used as a floor covering, it was patented in Britain in 1861, since when it has been variously improved. Scrap linoleum can be recovered and reused in plain linoleum and is biodegradable.

Linotype See TYPESETTING.

Lisère See LAMPAS.

Lithographic decoration Printed ceramic decoration created from paper-backed lithographic sheets. The prepared sheets can have many colours on one sheet and are applied directly to a biscuit-fired ceramic. When first used in the 19th century in England, the lithographs were applied to a varnished ceramic which had a sticky surface, and the paper was then removed and the piece fired a second time. The modern method of lithography eliminates the need for a varnish, as the lithograph is printed on plastic-backed paper and the paper is removed by sponging with water. The plastic is allowed to burn away in the firing.

Lithography is a simple and versatile method of decorating ceramics, as it can be applied either under or over a glaze. The technique is related to transfer printing but is less labour-intensive.

Lithography A printmaking process which relies on the principle that oil and water will not mix and which requires no mechanical or chemical deformation of the printing surface. Originally the surface was a slab of densely grained limestone on which the image or design was drawn with a greasy medium. The stone was then wetted and oil-based ink applied, which would be attracted only to the intended design and could subsequently be transferred to paper by pressure. To print, the paper was laid on the stone in a flat-bed press. Above it was placed some spare paper for protec-

A lithographic stone inked ready for printing, with the inking roller, 19th century.

tion and then a hinged sheet of brass or zinc, called the tympan. A lubricated scraper blade was positioned on the edge of the tympan and held rigid while the stone and tympan were cranked along beneath it from one edge to the other.

Lithography was the first of the planographic printing processes. The technique was invented by the Bavarian Aloys Senefelder in 1798 and first used for music publishing, but has subsequently had wide applications in the decorative and fine arts. Colour lithography was available from 1820, paving the way for the poster designs of Toulouse-Lautrec in the 1880s. All forms of lithographic printing require a separate plate, stone or roller for each colour. Metal plates have now replaced stone for most commercial lithographic printing. Offset lithography, where the image is transferred from a plate or stone to a rubber-covered cylinder roller and thence to paper on a powered machine, makes possible high-speed printing for publishing, packaging and decorative purposes.

Lithyalin An opaque glass with marbled striations in imitation of semi-precious stones. It is most effective when cut to reveal the marbling. True lithyalin evolved out of HYALITH and was produced in Bohemia from 1828 to 1840 by Friedrich Egermann, but imitations were made elsewhere.

Lloyd loom Furniture with a BENTWOOD frame and a painted covering of woven fibre fabric made from steel wires bound in KRAFT PAPER. The furniture was first made by the Lusty

A vase in green lithyalin glass, probably St Louis, USA, c.1850.

Company in Britain in 1922, using the invention of the American Marshall B. Lloyd.

Locustwood See ACACIA.

Logwood A mordant dye from the wood of the tree *Haematoxylin campeachianum* and also known as campeachy wood, bluewood and blackwood. It contains the colouring matter haematoxylin and haematin and is one of the easiest natural dyes to apply. Logwood provided the first good black dye in Europe, when it was introduced from Central America and the West Indies in the early 16th century. When mordanted with alum it gave a blue of poor fastness and for this reason its use was banned in England from 1581 to 1662. However, in a copperas or ferrous sulphate vat, it gave a good black. In the early 19th century this was replaced by a chrome mordant, giving a dye of such fastness that although superseded by aniline black with an iron mordant for cotton, it was not replaced for wools until some time after synthetic chrome black was isolated in the 20th century. It has remained in use for specialist purposes, such as dyeing silk and in the hat trade. Logwood was the basis for 'weighting' silk, that is, increasing the volume of the silk fibre through swelling by as much as 400%, resulting in a proportional loss of strength; a widespread practice in the second half of the 19th century, it has continued to this day.

Loom A general term used to describe a diverse group of weaving machines characterized by the incorporation of an automatic shedding device, which lifts or depresses selected warps (fixed to the loom under tension) to allow the passage

A backstrap loom in Sarawak, Malaysia, late 19th century or early 20th. The woman, a Sea Dayak or Iban, is using her own weight to tension the loom. Typical of those used around the world but most closely associated with South-East Asia, the loom has a single heddle, shedding sticks and a continuous warp, looped around the breast and back beam. It thus produces a cloth twice the length of the loom.

of wefts. Some looms are classified by the position of the warp: upright (also called vertical or high-warp), as in many ancient and more recent tapestry and carpet looms, or, more typically, horizontal (called low-warp in tapestry weaving). The means of applying tension also often determined the name of the loom: the tension may be supplied by weights, which was the case in Greek and Roman vertical warp-weighted looms; by the weaver leaning backwards into a strap connected to the breast (front) beam, one of two bars around which the warp is connected, as in the various back-strap looms associated with nomadic and semi-nomadic cul-tures; or by staking the warp (back) and breast beams to the ground to create a horizontal ground loom.

In these and other looms, cloths longer than the distance between the two beams are made by carrying additional warp on rotating warp and breast (or cloth) beams fixed into a rigid and permanent loom structure, as occurs in the majority of Western looms. In many of these, the method of creating a shed and/or introducing wefts gives its name to the loom. The main shedding devices are represented by tablet looms (see TABLET WEAVING), rigid heddle looms (in which the warp passes through a single board, with slits alternating with holes) and heddle looms (with eyes or loops through which warp threads are passed). The first two types are used only for narrow fabrics of limited length and to produce simple

A double-heddle loom used by a Bambara weaver in Burkina Faso to make a weft-faced cotton band. It is so called because of the pair of string heddles that control the basic shed opening. Clearly seen are the shedding stick, turning 90° to insert the weft-float patterning yarns; the reed, for aligning the threads and 'beating up' the weft; and the shuttle, held in the weaver's right hand.

weaves (although tablet looms can create doublecloths), but the third forms the basis of the majority of shedding devices, which take two general forms. The first is the heddle rod, to which, for example, all the odd-numbered warps are connected by loops that, when raised or, in vertical looms, pulled forward, separate these warps from their even-numbered alternates; this principle is used in upright tapestry looms. The second is the harness system, in which two or more shafts are suspended perpendicular to the warp and contain heddles (or leases in draw looms); as a shaft is raised, the warps entered through its heddles are raised, and the order of entering the warps and lifting or lowering the shaft (or shafts) creates the weave structure. Shaft or harness looms are the basis of treadle looms (using foot pedals), typically used in the hand-weaving of cloth, and the mechanically powered cam (for simple weaves) and dobby looms.

However powered, the making of 'fancy' weaves was achieved by combining shafts with another device, which also typically gave its name to the loom. The most important of these were: the Dutch or engine loom, in widespread use by the 17th century for the making, side by side, of a dozen or more 'small wares' (ribbons, loom laces, garters, edgings); its mid-18th century successor the swivel loom, with small localized bobbins moved simultaneously to insert identical areas of supplementary wefts and also used for making loom-width cloths; the swivel's counterpart, the tappet loom, in which the localized bobbins inserted supplementary warps; and, for larger or more complex patterns or weave structures, the DRAW LOOM and JACQUARD.

Looping A wide range of textile techniques characterized by the use of a single element, interlooped by various simple tools at the point nearest to the previous stitch, and including KNITTING (vertical interlooping), some needle lace and crochet (vertical and lateral interlooping).

Lorraine glass See FLAT GLASS.

Lost wax casting A method of casting metal or glass using a wax model. It is also known by its French name, *cire perdue*. When a wax model is invested in plaster or clay, a one-piece mould is formed around the model (see illustration on page 53). The mould is then heated gently to melt out the wax and so create a cavity. This cavity can then be filled with molten metal or glass. Once the cast is cool, the mould is removed and any excrescences on the cast are removed.

The advantage of lost wax casting is that there is no real limit to the shape of the model. The main disadvantage is that both the model and the mould can be used only once, whereas with open and piece mould casting the mould and sometimes the model can be reused. The solution is to make a reusable piece mould around a wood or clay model. The mould is then carefully removed and lined with wax. It is reassembled with a core of refractory material and the object is cast in the standard way.

Lost wax casting dates back to at least the 3rd millennium BC and was brought to perfection by the Greeks and Romans. It declined, but never entirely disappeared, after the fall of the Roman empire and was revived in Italy during the Renaissance. Since then it has been widely used in the production of fine sculpture and sculptural objects.

See also CASTING.

Lost wax casting. (a) A figure is modelled in wax over a clay core and fitted with sprues and risers in wax to allow air to escape as the hot metal is poured in. (b) A plaster mould is fitted around the figure. (c) The mould, strengthened with wire, is smoothed. It is then fired to burn out the wax. (d) The mould is embedded in a box of sand and filled with molten bronze. (e) Once the metal has cooled, the mould is chipped away. (f) The sprues are removed from the figure.

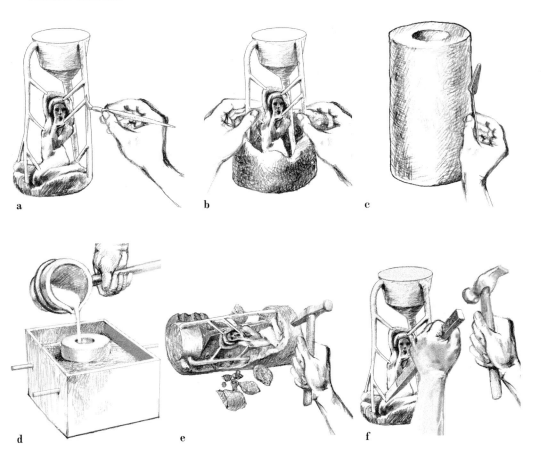

a   b   c

d   e   f

Low-temperature colours See METALLIC OXIDE.

Lurex See METAL THREAD.

Lustre Metallic decoration applied to glass and ceramics through precipitation. Salts of silver, gold or copper are dissolved, mixed with an organic medium and painted onto the glass or onto pre-fired ceramic glazes. The ware is then fired at a low temperature in a reducing atmosphere, smoky and rich in carbon monoxide. During the firing the medium burns away and the salts are converted to a thin, iridescent, non-palpable metal film. Careful control of firing is essential as lustres can easily be ruined by excessive temperatures. After cooling, the film can be burnished. Some metallic compounds can be fired in oxidation because they contain natural reducing agents.

Each oxide makes a different colour. Copper is the most popular metal, as it produces rich gold and ruby colours. Silver gives a straw-yellow, gold also a ruby colour and platinum a silver effect. The lustre may cover the entire surface of the object, or be applied in a design.

When used on ceramics, lustre is a type of overglaze decoration. It can be used as a surface lustre or an in-glaze lustre. Surface lustre is the traditional method, whereas in-glaze lustres are more modern and can be fired at higher temperatures. Traditional Islamic lustrewares have surface lustres which are applied to a white tin glaze on a fritware body. After an initial glaze firing at $c.1050°C$ in oxidation, lustre paint was applied in the form of crushed silver (for yellow lustre) or copper ore mixed with vinegar and ochre. The vinegar helped create a metallic salt and the ochre was used to aid application. The lustre designs were often scratched through with scrolling patterns while still wet.

Lustre decoration was invented in the Near East, where it appears on Islamic 'lustrewares' of the 9th century AD. The technique spread with Islamic culture to Spain, where it appears on Hispano-Moresque wares. It was then adopted in Italy, where it appeared on ceramics from Gubbio and Deruta in the 16th century. In the 19th century the English potter William De Morgan began to develop lustrewares, and the technique is still used by potters today. Commercial lustres are available which use bismuth, and tin lustres can be seen on raku wares. At the Leeds pottery in the 19th century platinum was used to create silver lustre decoration, often combined with resist patterns.

Luting The process of joining together separate parts of a ceramic with slip before firing. Ceramic vessels are often made in separate parts because they are too big or complicated to throw in one piece or because additional elements need to be attached, such as handles or spouts. In such cases the basic form is made and the attachments are added by scoring their edges, painting with slip and then applying to the main part. The slip acts as an adhesive and the scoring helps the slip to adhere. Luting can also be used to affix applied decoration or sprig-moulded decoration, or to join slabs. Luted parts usually leave obvious join lines which can be removed by turning.

Lycra A trade name for the spandex (elastane) fibre or yarn developed by the Du Pont firm in 1958 as a substitute for Neoprene synthetic rubber, itself invented by Du Pont in 1930. Its chief characteristics are its elasticity, resistance to wear from rubbing, acceptance of heat and perspiration without damage, and ease of washing. Cloths cannot be made from pure Lycra and are combined with a supporting thread in several ways during the spinning or twisting processes.

A tile painted in lustre, Kashan, Iran, 12th century AD.

M

Macramé A textile technique using four or more elements, two of which alternately are knotted, while the other two are passed or looped through the knot. The most typical knots used are the clove hitch, the vertical granny knot and the square knot. The name comes from the Arabic *mucharram*, meaning 'lattice' or, more generally, 'fringe'.

Late 19th-century illustration of macramé, from Thérèse de Dillmont's Encyclopedia of Needlework. *It shows the characteristic passage of two passive yarns at the centre of the flat double knots.*

Madder A mordant dye from the roots of the *Rubia tinctorum* bush and related to quinine and wild madders, all of which produce a red dye when mordanted with alum (see colour plate XVII). True madder was the most important natural red dye for all fibres. Native to all tropical and temperate zones, it was also cultivated in large quantities in central and northern Europe from *c.*1400 to *c.*1890. A fine brown powder made from ground roots, potash and cow dung was fermented in sealed containers before use; combining with alum in varying degrees of strength gave pinks to deep reds, iron gave purple to black, and iron with alum produced chocolate browns. By printing with these mordants a range of colours developed in one dye-bath; mordant printing, a process recorded by Pliny the Elder in AD 70, was so often done with madder that it was later called the 'madder style'. Because a good white ground was fundamental to the production of good printed or discharged reds on vegetable fibres the highest-quality bleach became known as 'madder bleach'. A brilliant red was obtainable only by the TURKEY RED method.

See also ALIZARIN.

Madeira work See EMBROIDERED LACE.

Magnesian limestone See DOLOMITIC LIMESTONE.

Mahogany A hard and heavy, durable and very stable wood.
Between 60 and 70 different types, from various countries,
are marketed as mahogany but only three species—*Khaya
mahogoni* (Cuban mahogany), *Entandrophragma mahogoni*
(Spanish mahogany) and, especially, *Swietenia mahogoni* —

are recognized as true mahoganies. Most so-called mahoganies are of West African origin. Other timbers sometimes sold
as mahogany include Australian or rose mahogany (*Dyxo-
phyllum   mahogoni*),   Borneo   mahogany   (*Calophyllum
mahogoni*) and seraya, also sometimes called Borneo
mahogany or cedar (*Shorea macroptera*). The qualities of the
different timbers vary greatly. True mahogany, which has
been a favoured cabinet wood since the late 17th century and
was popularized in the 18th by, among others, Thomas Chippendale, is a rich reddish brown flecked with chalky deposits;
it darkens with age. It has an interlocking ribbon grain dis-

*Mahogany tea chest, from a
design by Thomas
Chippendale, c.1760,
exploiting the hardness
and attractive figure of the
wood.*

playing both roe and ripple figuring, and it is easily seasoned and worked. One of the most favoured woods for cabinet making, it is also seen in superior joinery and has been used to make the patterns from which loam or sand moulds are taken for metal casting.

Mahogany was known in England by the 1660s, when it was mentioned as an import from Jamaica, and it was being used for furniture making in the Americas by the 1690s. By the early 18th century its use in England for furniture making and joinery was becoming common. In 1724 John Gumley and James Moore supplied the royal household with a mahogany dining table and two side tables, and by 1730 large and regular shipments were being received. The use of mahogany did not have a significant impact on the design of furniture before about 1750. The great width of mahogany boards allowed the construction of wide elements such as table tops and cabinet sides to be constructed in one piece, and its cross-sectional strength allowed the inclusion of delicate features such as pierced frets and the slender and thin sections of chair splats. While mahogany remained popular with furniture makers throughout the 18th century and into the early 19th, it was to some extent superseded for small furniture by satinwood and other pale timbers in the 1770s and by rosewood in the Regency period.

Maiolica Tin-glazed earthenware with polychrome decoration, produced in Italy in the Renaissance period. Tin-glazed earthenware was first made in the Near East in the 8th century AD. From the 9th century such wares were decorated with lustre. This technique spread to Islamic Spain, where it was adopted for Hispano-Moresque ware. These ceramics were exported to Italy through the island of Mallorca. Italian potters copied the technique and for a time all such ceramics were called maiolica. In the 16th and 17th centuries the term came to signify Italian earthenwares with polychrome painted decoration. The term is now used specifically to refer to the tin-glazed earthenwares produced in Italy during the Renaissance. They were decorated with in-glaze painting which was often, though not always, covered with a transparent overglaze called COPERTA, which gave a glossy surface.

A wide range of pigments was used for maiolica. The earliest wares have copper green and manganese purple decoration, whereas in later examples lead-antimonate yellow and tin oxide white were used on their own and mixed

Maiolica dish, Caffaggiola, Italy, 1514. The brushwork can be clearly seen in the background.

with other oxides to produce such colours as orange and lime green. The transparent overglaze helped to fix the pigments by sandwiching them between two glazes. The tin glaze layer was often stained to produce a dark blue (cobalt) or purple ground (manganese) for painting. The body material used for maiolica was a local high-lime clay which was light-fired. The tin glaze was made from similar materials and thus the glaze fit was good. Maiolica could be thrown, but moulding was the favoured forming method. Some vessel forms were piece-moulded. Textual references state that the formed ceramics were biscuit fired to 1000°C and then dipped in tin glaze, painted and glazed with a colourless glaze. The ceramic was fired a second time to 950°C, and sometimes a third firing was necessary for lustre decoration. The pieces were placed face down in saggars on spurs which left marks on the insides of dishes. They were fired in wood-burning kilns.

Majolica The name used by the Minton factory for their lead-glazed earthenwares produced in the mid-19th century. The term is sometimes used erroneously as an anglicized version of MAIOLICA. Majolica wares are characterized by coloured, transparent lead glazes and often have relief and applied decoration. The majolica body is cane clay, a refined fire clay

which was ideal for relief decoration and modelling and which
was fired to a light straw or cane colour.

Maki-e A group of Japanese lacquer techniques in which pictures are built up by sprinkling various sizes, shapes and
colours of metal powders and flakes (*fun*) onto a wet or
partially dried design drawn with URUSHI (see colour
plate XIII). The designs are drawn using a special brush made
from rat hair, and the powders and flakes are sprinkled
through a tubular sieve. Approximately 20 different alloys of
gold, silver, tin and copper are used, produced in 5 shapes
(*keshi-fun, nashiji-fun, hirame, maru-fun* and *hiragoku-fun*)
and up to 15 sizes. In addition, 13 colours of dried ground
urushi (*kanshitsu-fun*) are produced in 3 grain sizes, and fine
powder pigments and charcoal dust can be used for shading.
Parts of the design are produced free-hand but the main pictorial elements are usually painted onto a paper transfer
using a specially prepared slow-drying urushi, and then
'printed' onto the prepared urushi foundation.

There are four classes of *maki-e*. In *kiji-makie* the powders
used to form the design are sprinkled onto a plain wood (or
sometimes ivory) surface. In *togidashi-makie* the design is
formed, then painted over with urushi coatings until it is
completely buried. The surface is then carefully polished
back using charcoal blocks until the design is exposed, now
completely embedded in a flat ground. *Hiramakie* is a form in
which the design is raised above the ground by the thickness
of the urushi layer used to delineate the design, and in *takamakie* the design is raised substantially above the surface. In
cheaper wares the raising is achieved by building the design
with layers of urushi paste (*sabi*) or a mixture of glue and clay
powder. On finer-quality objects the design is delineated with
urushi and then sprinkled with finely ground charcoal
powder, and the process is then repeated until the desired
thickness is achieved, at which point the decorative coatings
are applied. The designs are drawn with *e-urushi*, a mixture
of *suki-naka-urushi* and *benigara* (red iron oxide pigment).
This is used in three grades: medium, which is relatively fresh
and is used for drawing the outlines of designs; soft, which is
also relatively fresh but is mixed with a small amount of oil of
camphor, and is used as an adhesive for the sprinkled
powders; and hard, which is thickened with age, highly prized
and reserved for painting fine detail.

In the finest wares the first part of the design is sprinkled onto a wet ground using the selected grade of powder or powders. In a landscape this would be the background, the development of which is called *maki-bokashi*. When dry, one or more coats of transparent urushi are applied and the surface is polished. Another coat of urushi is applied and the next part of the design is sprinkled on, then painted over and polished. The process is repeated until the design is complete. The final application of gold may be left unpainted or it may be coated and polished. The polishing process cuts through some of the powder grains, leaving bright spots of polished metal. The final result is a surface decoration of great clarity and almost tangible depth.

Makoré A fairly hard and heavy, durable and stable wood from the mimusops tree (*Dumoria heckelii*), sometimes known as cherry mahogany, aganokwe or baku. Its source is Nigeria, and it is a medium reddish brown, with a straight, fine, inter-locking grain with roe and mottle figure. It works fairly easily and polishes well, and is used for cabinetmaking, veneers and high-class joinery. The fine dust is a respiratory irritant.

Makrana A white marble obtained from north-western India and used in the construction of the Taj Mahal at Agra. It was also used to carve pierced screens and window grilles (for illustration see page 301).

Malachite An opaque green mineral composed of hydrated copper carbonate with pronounced, and often concentric, banding. It is formed by the deposition of copper within rock cavities and is often found in conjunction with other copper-containing minerals such as azurite and chrysocolla. The finest and most plentiful malachite is found in the Ural Mountains in Russia, although it is also mined in Australia. Malachite is hard enough (Mohs scale 4) to take a polish and has been used to make beads, cabochons, decorative items and PIETRE DURE. It is also ground to make a green pigment.

Maltese lace A bobbin lace developed in Malta in the 1830s, with patterns derived from early Italian bobbin laces but distinguished by the incorporation of a Maltese cross and, often, the use of natural-coloured silk. Its popularity inspired the development of Bedfordshire Maltese lace, which was less angular in detail and omitted the cross; it was mainly made in white cotton. Black silk was also used in both laces. Maltese-style lace was also made in Genoa.

Mammoth ivory An ivory derived from excavated tusks of the woolly mammoth. The most common source is the Siberian tundra but substantial quantities have also been found in parts of Alaska. After it has been worked, mammoth ivory is almost impossible to distinguish from elephant ivory. The end grain displays an engine-turned effect similar to elephant ivory, but the lozenge shapes formed by the intersecting lines may be somewhat finer.

Frozen since burial, much of the material is in very good condition and large quantities have been exported to Europe and the Far East. Large amounts were discovered in the late 19th century, and it is probable that in the 1890s more mammoth ivory was sold on the London market than any other type. It is sometimes found stained and mineralized by contact with mineral deposits during burial. A bright turquoise blue form called odontolite is found among the deposits in Alaska, and a mottled nutty brown type in Siberia. Mammoth ivory carvings display the same features as elephant ivories but tend to age to a distinctly yellowish cream colour and display a more opaque surface finish.

Manchester velvet See Fustian.

Manganese blue A bright, sky blue pigment, introduced *c.*1935 and used in all media. It is inorganic and extremely stable to light, atmospheric gases and heat. It appears the same colour whatever the illumination, unlike some blues, which change when viewed in different light. Painting conservators use the pigment for in-painting damaged areas of blue, knowing that the repair will remain invisible in all conditions.

Maple Wood from the numerous widespread species of acer, but mostly those found in North America and Europe. There is great variation in the character and quality of the wood from differing species, but it is generally pale brownish white, hard and compact, fairly heavy and strong, and lustrous, with a fine, straight grain. It is used for kitchen implements, plywood, furniture, cooperage, turnery and joinery. Well-figured examples such as Bird's eye maple are used as veneers.

Marble A metamorphic stone, composed mainly of calcium carbonate, which has formed through the action of heat and/or pressure on limestone. During the metamorphic process the marble becomes crystalline and may develop translucency; all fossils present in the original limestone will be destroyed. Pure calcium carbonate will produce a white marble but other constituents in the limestone, such as iron or clay, will also be altered, giving rise to the great range of coloured marbles.

Marble occurs worldwide and has been used throughout history for building, architectural ornament and sculpture. It often denotes status and wealth because of the beauty of the material, the delicate detail which it will take and, particularly in the case of coloured marbles, the difficulty and expense of obtaining it. Many white marbles, such as Carrara, can be quarried in large blocks, the size being influenced by the purpose for which the marble will be used and the ease of transport. Coloration in marbles is often unevenly distributed within a quarry and frequently occurs as streaks, veins or mottling. Therefore the stone must be extracted in such a way as to obtain the desired colour and patterning; this entails much wasted material and increases the cost.

In ancient Greece the exploitation of marble was facilitated by the development of iron, rather than bronze, tools. The Greeks often painted architectural marble to provide a contrast with white figurative sculpture placed on the building, although sculpture was also frequently painted. The Chinese also painted white marble sculpture and used marble panels as a support for painted decoration. The Romans used coloured marbles sourced from many parts of their empire, such as ROSSO ANTICO from Cape Matapan in Greece and giallo antico, a yellow marble quarried in North Africa, in conjunction with the pure white of Carrara marble. The tradition of using combinations of coloured marbles continued in Italy, as can be seen in the inlaid floors of Siena Cathedral and the develop-

Makrana screen, Mogul, 19th century or earlier, showing the crisp detail that could be produced in this fine, white Indian marble.

ment of PIETRE DURE in 16th-century Florence. During the Baroque period the taste for richly coloured marbles, for columns, panelling and ornament, led to the frequent reuse of stone from ancient Roman buildings. For decorative purposes coloured marbles were sawn with wire saws, fed with abrasives. Slabs of coloured marble, cut from the same block, were sometimes positioned so that the patterning of one piece appeared as the mirror image of the other, a technique known as book matching owing to the resemblance to the symmetry of pages of a book. In the Islamic world marble is used for building, for architectural elements such as pierced screens and for inlaid decoration (see MAKRANA).

Many materials referred to as marble are, in fact, hard limestones which will take a polish (see VERONA MARBLE) or other types of dense, polishable stones, such as breccias (see BRECCIA). The technique used in the production of SCAGLIOLA, which employs coloured mixes of gypsum plaster and small chips of stone, was developed to imitate the rich colours of pietre dure.

Marbled ware Ceramics with clays, glazes or slips that have been combined to suggest the striations of hard stones. Such wares have been produced in many different ceramic traditions. The marbled appearance can be created in a number of ways, essentially by combining two different coloured clays, slips or glazes. With marbled clays, small slices from tubes of different coloured clays are arranged together in a mould and then smoothed to produce a marbled effect. Alternatively, different coloured clays can be thrown together on the wheel. Marbled slips can be created by applying one slip on top of the other and then running a sharp tool or comb through them to create a striated pattern. This is often described as 'combed ware' and was made in Staffordshire in the 17th and 18th centuries. Marbled glazes can be created in a similar fashion.

Another technique for producing marbled ware, which was used in China in the Tang period (AD 618–907), involves rolling together two different coloured clays and then cutting the resulting rolls into small pieces which are then placed in a mould and pressed together. This creates a very complex marbled pattern which runs throughout the piece. Another method is inlay, which was also used in Chinese ceramics. Discs of marbled clays were inlaid into a finished vessel or headrest, which was then glazed and fired.

The most popular form of marbled ware produced in

Dishes with slip decoration, England, possibly north Staffordshire, late 17th century. They were manufactured by press moulding and the left-hand dish is painted with feathered and marbled slip.

Europe was AGATE WARE from the Wedgwood factory. Modern potters usually stain and combine two different clays and then throw them on the wheel to produce a softer effect than traditional marbling.

Marbling [paintwork] A technique developed to imitate the appearance of polished marble or other decorative stones on a wood or plaster substrate. The Romans imitated simple marble veneers in their frescos, but these wall coverings were not meant to deceive, and the term tends to be used more commonly to refer to the techniques developed in the 18th and 19th centuries. As with GRAINING, 18th-century marbling is fairly stylized and simply painted, but 19th-century techniques, involving multiple interactive layers, produced finishes that are indistinguishable from the real thing. Marbling can be carried out on any inert material, but because the surface has to be very smooth for the impression to be effective, it is usual to build up a base coat in three or four layers, each one carefully sanded down. Oil or oil/resin paints are generally used and, depending on the stone to be imitated, the colours are applied in different ways: stippled and spattered to reproduce granites and porphyry, or laid on with threads and fine, soft brushes for thinly veined marbles. As in graining, the colour is adjusted with translucent glazes and the surface sealed with a glossy varnish. The brushes and tools employed for marbling are all specific to the particular technique being used.

See also SCAGLIOLA.

Marbling [paper] A technique for decorating paper with

marbled or varied patterns by the transfer of colours floated on a tray of water. Each paper is unique. In the traditional European method a water bath is prepared, with a gum such as agar or tragacanth. Drops of paint, to which ox-gall has been added, are then released from the tip of a brush or stick held above the water surface. There they spread slightly with the aid of the ox-gall and remain caught in the surface tension with the help of the gum. The colours are then gently blended with a stylus and sometimes combed, brushed or blown upon to create the desired pattern. A sheet of damp paper, which may be pre-treated with a mordant, is then lowered onto the tray. The pigments remain on the paper as it is lifted off the bath and are subsequently left to dry. The technique reached Europe in the 17th century via Persia and Turkey, where it was used for ornamenting books and manuscripts.

Marbling with oil colours. The paint floats on a size extracted from carragheen moss. In the foreground is a comb for producing feathered patterns in the paint.

A variation, known as *suminagashi*, was in existence in Japan in the 12th century. *Suminagashi* differs from Western marbling in that a thickening agent is not always added to the water and the inks are based on *sumi*, made from pine

soot. A dispersant is added to the colours, which are spread in typically flowing, asymmetrical patterns, sometimes with a figurative element. Classic *suminagashi* papers often provide the background to masterpieces of calligraphy.

In the 20th century individual artists and bookbinders took up making marbled papers. The productions of the Cockerell workshop in England in particular achieved a uniformly high standard with papers intended for bookbinding. In the 1930s sheets marbled with oil colours were made by Tirzah Garwood (wife of the British printmaker Eric Ravilious), proving that the results of oil marbling could rival that of traditional water-soluble media floated on a vegetable mucilage, although the oil colours are harder to control.

Marcasite A form of iron sulphide, the mineral pyrites, which is used as a gemstone. In mineralogical terms marcasite is actually another form of iron sulphide with a different crystal structure. The gemstone marcasite is an opaque yellow with a metallic lustre, earning it the name fool's gold, and has a highly reflective surface. It was used in antiquity by the Greeks, in jewellery, and by the Incas for mirrors. Since the 19th century it has been faceted and set in clusters to produce inexpensive jewellery.

Marezzo A material used to imitate marble, produced in panels by a technique similar to that used in the production of SCAGLIOLA. Moulds of wood, plaster or glass (to allow the underside to be seen while work is in progress) are used. Strips of silk or flax fabric or skeins of threads are knotted at one end and coated with a slurry of coloured KEENE'S CEMENT or GYPSUM PLASTER and arranged in the mould to suggest the pattern of veining in marble; the knotted end is draped over the side of the mould. A fluid mix of plaster, animal glue and pigments (if a coloured marble is being copied) is then dripped on top of the threads to imitate mottling. Before the plaster has set completely the strips are pulled out by the knotted end, leaving the pattern in place. The mould is then filled to the desired depth with plaster. Once removed from the mould, the surface is polished with pumice stones. As the mould creates a reasonably smooth surface, the polishing process is not as lengthy as that for scagliola and thus marezzo is easier to produce.

Marmorite See ARTIFICIAL STONE.

Marquetry A wood inlay technique, derived from the art of INTARSIA (for illustration see pages 515 and 540). Marquetry

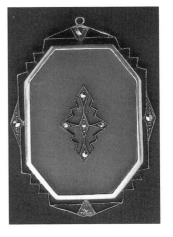

Marcasite pendant, 1920s. The small fragments of marcasite, cut with facets to enhance the stone's reflective qualities, are combined with other materials such as enamel, quartz or paste, to produce inexpensive pieces.

differs from intarsia in that it is produced by overlaying two
or more sheets of VENEER of contrasting colours and cutting
through all of the sheets at the same time to produce closely
interlocking designs. The technique was made possible by
two developments, both of which seem to date from the early
16th century. The first, which made it possible to cut very
thin veneers, was the ability to manufacture broad but thin
strips of steel for use in frame saws. The second was the redis-
covery of the bow fretsaw, which, along with the ability to
manufacture thin, narrow steel blades, made the saws ideally
suited to the cutting of tight curves and allowed the accurate
cutting of such designs. For some time bow fretsaws were
known as Buhl saws, *Buhl* being the German version of *boulle*,
a type of multi-material marquetry (see colour plate III).

*A fretcutter's donkey, from
André-Jacob Roubo's*
L'art du menuisier
*(1772). The treadle
depresses the lever, which
clamps the veneer in place.*

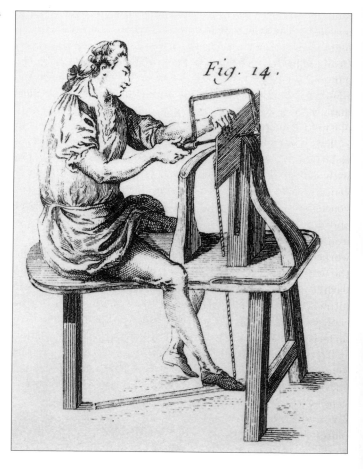

Fig. 14.

Around the middle of the 18th century, when even narrower blades were being produced, a treadle-operated saw known as the fretcutter's donkey was developed. This device substantially reduced the time required for the production of marquetry panels (and therefore the cost), thereby increasing the output of inlaid furniture. Throughout the later 19th century the development of various powered mechanical saws further increased production, and in the early 20th century die-cutting became possible on an increasing scale.

A simple transfer technique was used to produce fast and accurate copies of designs. First a full-scale drawing was made on stiff, durable paper, and the outline traced with a 'prick wheel', a device that produced lines of small, evenly spaced holes around each individual element. Then the pierced design was laid onto a sheet of clean paper and 'pounced' over with a bag containing finely ground graphite or some other coloured powder. The powder penetrated the holes in the traced design, forming a series of dots on the clean paper. The individual design elements could then be cut out and pasted to the verso of the selected veneer, which could then be cut to shape. The original pattern could be used many times before it needed replacing, so that a large number of copies could be produced.

Two methods were used to fix veneers to the support. Relatively small surfaces (up to about 1 sq m) could be laid with thin veneers, using the technique known as hammer veneering. A layer of glue was applied to the support, the veneer or marquetry panel was dampened with warm water and quickly laid onto the glued support, and a heated flat iron was passed over the surface. The veneering hammer was worked rapidly over the surface, working from the centre of the workpiece outwards towards the edges following a zigzag path, squeezing out excess glue and pressing the veneer into intimate contact with the support. Because the animal glues cooled and set fairly rapidly, this method could only be used on larger pieces if the veneer was applied in small sections.

To get around this problem and to enable easier handling of veneers with erratic grain (such as burrs), which have a tendency to cockle when wet, or larger areas of thicker saw-cut veneers, the technique of 'caul veneering' was developed. This involved the use of a veneering press fitted with a pair of press plates or cauls slightly larger than the workpiece. For flat work, the lower or base board was flat while the upper or press board was slightly convex. Both cauls were faced with a thin sheet of zinc or sometimes brass. The cauls were warmed, the workpiece was laid onto the base board, glue was applied and the dampened veneer or marquetry panel was laid in place. Sheets of paper (to prevent adhesion to the press plate) were laid over the veneer and the press plate was put in place. Hand clamps were tightened around the edge of the cauls, pulling the press plate flat and squeezing out excess glue. When dry, the surface of the veneered panel cleaned up with scrapers and abrasive paper. This technique is still used in small workshops and much modern large-scale production is just a modification of it.

To avoid the separation of the individual elements of a marquetry panel, paper was glued onto the top face after cutting and left in place until the panel was laid. Best practice demanded the application of a balancing or counter veneer to the verso of the support, to avoid warping caused by shrinkage of the top veneer as it dried.

In the past the favoured adhesives for veneers and marquetry panels were hoof and hide glues, made by processing animal by-products, and the more refined but weaker glues made from rabbit skins, fish skins and bones. Although these are still used by restorers and some specialist manufacturers, they have been replaced in commercial furniture manufacture by various quick-setting and convenient synthetic adhesives, such as the PVAs and epoxies. During the 1930s some manufacturers started to use high-frequency radio waves to heat the workpiece, and today microwave heating is used to activate thermoplastic resin adhesives for mass-produced furniture.

Martin's cement An interior wall plaster obtained by soaking gypsum in a strongly alkaline solution of pearl ash (potassium carbonate) in water. A small amount of sulphuric acid is added. The mixture is then heated to produce a plaster which can be worked to a hard, smooth finish and coloured by adding metallic oxide pigments to the mix. The process, patented in 1834, was the first of a number of industrially produced, modified gypsum plasters.

Marvering The process of rolling a hot gather of glass on a flat surface to shape it or to pick up gold leaf, coloured glass powder or other embellishments. See GLASS BLOWING.

Marzacotto A glaze used in Italian maiolica. See COPERTA.

Massicot/masticot See LEAD TIN YELLOW.

Matmee/matmi See IKAT.

Matting The application of a texture or pattern to a metal surface, generally by using a punch.

Mazak A zinc die-casting alloy used from around 1900, mainly for toys and decorative castings. The name derives from the initials of its components: magnesium, aluminium, zinc and 'kopper'. (In the USA the term zamak is used.) Mazaks made from around 1950 on contained only zinc (94–96%), aluminium (3–4%) and copper (1–2%).

Medium-density fibreboard A composition board made by bonding wood fibres and pulp with an adhesive bonding agent under high pressure and at high temperature. Commonly known as MDF, it was developed in the 1970s as an improvement on hardboard: not only was it stronger, but it was also available in a greater range of thicknesses. It is stable, strong and available in widths of up to 2.5 m. It forms an ideal support for veneers or painted finishes, and since the 1980s it has been widely used in the manufacture of cabinet furniture, table tops and work surfaces.

Meissen gold A method of gilding ceramics using chloride of gold. See GILDING.

Melamine-formaldehyde A thermoset amino plastic produced by condensation polymerization. Melamine was first isolated by Baron Justus von Liebig in Switzerland in 1834. Melamine-formaldehyde polymer was patented in 1935, and commercially produced in 1939 by the American Cyanamid Company. Melamine-formaldehyde is both more water-resistant and tougher than urea-formaldehyde, with improved heat and chemical properties, and it can be brightly coloured with pigments, making it very suitable for a range of attractive tableware. It is transparent and so can be used to impregnate patterned papers for the surfaces of decorative laminates such as Formica and Warerite.

Meranti Wood from the *Shorea* and *Hopea* genera, commonly known as lauana, red seraya or red meranti (nemesu), and found in the Philippines, Borneo and Malaya. It is soft and light but neither strong nor durable and it is prone to woodworm. Meranti is coarse-grained and displays conspicuous rays and resin canals on worked surfaces. Available in reasonably large sizes, it is easily worked and takes a fine polish. The most common uses are as a substitute for mahogany and for producing veneers, cabinet work and joinery.

Mercerization See COTTON.

Mercury A silver white metal. It is also sometimes called quicksilver, and is the only metal found in a liquid state at room temperature. It can form alloys with most metals except iron and platinum (see AMALGAM). It is toxic and should be handled with care. Mercury is found in nature in the form of a red mineral called cinnabar, which is reduced to mercury by roasting and distillation. The main source was and continues to be Italy but Spain and North America are also important. Mercury was used for barometers and thermometers and for FIREGILDING .

Mercury gilding See FIREGILDING.

Metal thread A narrow filament of metal, such as aluminium, bronze, copper, gold and silver, used in embroidery, embroidered laces and weaving. It is sometimes called tinsel yarn. The earliest examples in ancient Chinese and Egyptian cloths took the form of flat strips or drawn wire. By the late Middle Ages the finest-quality gold thread was associated with Milan and the finest silver thread with Genoa. Since then, increasingly, 'gold' threads have been made of gilt silver and 'silver' threads have been made of copper with a covering of silver.

Metal threads are used in many different forms: plate (flat strips), passing (smooth and wire-like, around a silk core), crimped passing, purl (like a coiled spring), square purl and flat, convex or concave spangles (like sequins). When incorporated into a cloth, the fabric is generally referred to by type: for example, cloth of gold (a substantial silk and metal

Detail of a ceremonial cloth, embellished with metal threads, spangles, pearls and semi-precious stones, north India, c.1900. The most extensively used thread is coiled spring-like purl. All the elements are held in place by laid and couched work.

thread fabric, worn solely by the nobility since the Middle Ages), cloth of silver (usually a sheer or gauze fabric), damasin (brocade with metal threads), galloon (narrow close-woven braids of metal and silk threads) and orris lace (a bobbin lace fashionable in the 17th and 18th centuries). In about 1870 Japanese gold thread, a gilt paper wrapped around a silk core, was introduced in the West. With the advent of cellophane, metal filaments were encased in plain films; in 1952 this process, producing a so-called 'gilt membrane', was largely replaced by Lurex, a trade name for a non-tarnishing flat metallic yarn of plastic-coated aluminium.

Metallic oxides Compounds in which a metal is chemically combined with oxygen. Metallic oxides are used as colouring agents in GLASS, CERAMICS, ENAMEL, ENAMEL COLOURS and LUSTRE. Some oxides act as a natural flux in glazes, while tin oxide is also used as an opacifier (see TIN GLAZE and GLASS). The metals used include antimony, arsenic, barium, cobalt, copper, gold, iron, lead, manganese, nickel, silver, tin and uranium. The colours that are created depend on the firing conditions (whether oxidizing or reducing), the concentration of oxide and the composition of the base material.

In ceramic manufacture the oxides can be mixed with the clay or glazes, or applied directly to unfired glazes for in-glaze decoration. The oxides are usually ground to a powder and mixed with a liquid medium for ease of application. Some oxides are used as stains. These are modified metal oxides, such as chromium-tin oxide, which creates a pink stain.

The primary oxides used in traditional wares include cobalt, copper, iron, antimony and manganese. Each of these produces different colours, with copper and iron the most versatile. Some oxides (such as cobalt and iron) are suitable for use in high temperatures, whereas others (for example, antimony and manganese) are used to produce low-temperature colours. Copper is particularly versatile as it can be used as both a low-fired and a high-fired colour. It can produce green colours in a lead glaze or turquoise in an alkaline glaze, both fired in oxidation. When used in a high-fired porcelain glaze, a red colour results if fired in reduction. Variable concentrations of iron oxides can also produce a wide range of colours, from yellow to brown, black and red when fired in oxidation and cool blues and greens when fired in reduction. Cobalt is almost always blue and manganese is usually used to produce purple tones. When saturated with metallic oxides, some glazes produce unusual effects such as spotting or streaking (see OIL SPOT GLAZE and TEMMOKU).

In glassmaking the oxides are added to the batch. They may either disperse in the molten glass rather like a dye in water, moving with the current and with the stirring action of escaping gases to give the glass an even colour throughout; or they may be dispersed in the same way but remain in colloidal suspension as opaque particles reflecting their colour. The colour that results depends upon the nature of the glass itself, the purity of the ingredients and the furnace conditions (that is, the degree of heat and the existence of an oxidizing or reducing atmosphere). For example, under oxidizing conditions the addition of copper (cuprous oxide) to the batch produces a green glass, whereas under reducing conditions, red glass is produced.

Metals A group of chemical elements showing similar properties: good conductivity of heat and electricity, good reflection of light, malleability and ductility, high density and (with the exception of mercury) solidity at room temperature. The name derives from the Latin *metallium* ('mine' or 'metal'). Semi-metals or metalloids are chemical elements showing some but not all of the properties of metals. Two well-known semi-metals are antimony and arsenic.

Some metals, such as gold, silver, copper and platinum, can be found in nature in pure or native state, but more commonly metals are found in a combined state as ores. Generally metals can be separated from the non-metals in the ore by heating (called smelting), which is usually followed by further refining. Metallurgy, the science of metals, includes extracting metals from their ores, purifying, alloying and fabricating. Metals are often combined with other metals and non-metals to form an ALLOY. This is usually done to improve their appearance, working properties, strength, corrosion-resistance and conductivity, but also for economic reasons.

Metals are generally divided into two main groups: ferrous and non-ferrous. Ferrous metals are iron and iron alloys such as steel, which is essentially an alloy of iron and carbon. Non-ferrous metals are divided into precious (or noble) metals and base metals. Precious metals include gold, silver and the platinum six-metal group (platinum, palladium, rhodium, iridium, osmium and rhuthenium). These precious metals are chemically very stable, very corrosion-resistant and rare, which makes them suitable for coinage and jewellery but also for decorative and protective coatings. Well-known base metals include copper, lead, aluminium, tin, nickel and zinc. Sometimes other classifications are used; for example, light metals (including aluminium, magnesium and titanium), heavy metals (such as lead, mercury and copper) and refractory metals, or metals with high melting-points (such as the platinum group, nobium and titanium).

The first metals to be used were those which can be found in pure, native form in nature. Gold and silver, because of their rarity, were used almost entirely for decorative purposes. Copper was also originally confined to small decorative items, but around 5000–4000 BC it was employed also for tools. Normally copper is too soft for this purpose, but it was discovered that the hardness of the metal could be increased by hammering. This WORK HARDENING can also render the metal too brittle for further working unless it is reheated to soften the metal again, a process called ANNEALING. Later the copper was hardened by alloying, first with arsenic or by using arsenic-rich copper ore, and later with tin to form bronze. Iron is usually not found in native form in nature, but there was a source of almost pure iron in the form of iron meteorites. This meteoric iron has a high nickel content and

A gold- or silversmith's workshop in the mid-18th century, from Diderot's Encyclopédie des arts et des métiers. *The illustration shows the whole silversmithing process from casting an ingot to hammering an article. The first stage is to melt the silver on the forge and pour it from a crucible into a mould (a). The ingot is then hammered on an anvil into sheet (e), which is fashioned into hollow ware by raising (b) or sinking (c), followed by planishing (d).*

is very strong and was used as early as the 3rd millennium BC. Later iron was extracted from the ore, and subsequently it was discovered that by introducing carbon into the iron a harder metal could be made. This alloy, known as steel, could be made even harder by heating and quenching or cooling, often followed by TEMPERING.

There are two main ways of fashioning metals: casting the metal when molten into the desired shape, using models and moulds, or shaping sheet metal into an object by techniques such as hammering, bending and stamping. Often metal objects are created by a combination of these techniques; for example, the body of a vessel might be made by hammering and the handles then cast and soldered onto the body.

Mezzotint See INTAGLIO PRINTING.

Mica A type of mineral composed of aluminium silicate. It is a constituent of many rocks, such as granite and schist, and also occurs in deposits of large crystals. Micas are characterized by their metallic lustre and ability to split perfectly into thin sheets. They are brown or dark grey in colour and translucent or transparent when in thin sheets.

The ancient Egyptians used mica as a gem material and to make mirrors. In Europe it was employed as a window glazing material and is sometimes found set into cut-out windows in 18th- and 19th-century fans. In the Far East crushed mica is sometimes added to paints to produce a shimmering effect. Alternatively, it is powdered and sprinkled on pasted paper to give an iridescent sheen to fans and Japanese woodblock prints.

Milanese See JERSEY.

Millefiori Glassware in which slices of multicoloured GLASS CANE, with concentric rosette or flower-like designs, are embedded in clear glass or picked up on a gather and blown. Millefiori was known to the Romans and was revived in Venice in the 16th century. (The word means 'a thousand flowers' in Italian.) In the 19th century it began to be used for making paperweights in Murano and in Bohemia. The finest examples, however, were made in France by Baccarat, Clichy and St Louis. The term is sometimes used of MOSAIC GLASS.

Mineral dye A metal ground to a tint solution, or an oxide. Mineral dyes were important in the development of printed cottons in the first half of the 19th century (see RESIST DYEING). The most significant was PRUSSIAN BLUE, but

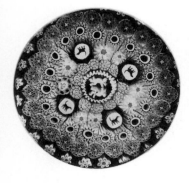

Millefiori paperweight, with coloured glass canes enclosed in clear glass, by Baccarat, 1847.

another early mineral dye of importance was iron buff (using oxides produced by soaking old irons in vinegar and through ageing, giving characteristic 'iron mould' on linens) and, after *c.*1810, yellow/orange antimony, chrome (lead acetate and potassium bichromate) and manganese colours. The most long-lived was manganese bronze, introduced into Britain in 1823 by Thomas Mercer and popular until 1880; it was developed by observing a ceramic manganese glaze, while Mercer's yellow derived from the CHROME YELLOW pigments previously used in carriage painting.

Mirror A flat or slightly convex polished surface of glass with a metal backing, providing a reflected image. In ancient times and right up to the medieval period mirrors were usually made of polished bronze, silver or SPECULUM METAL. In the Middle Ages rock crystal backed with foil made a highly prized mirror, and small mirrors of crown glass were backed with lead, tin or other metals. Convex mirrors were made in Nuremberg in the 15th century by blowing a metallic mixture with resin or salt of tartar into a hot glass globe. Mirror-making on a commercial scale began in the mid-16th century in Venice with the use of cristallo broad glass backed with amalgam or mercury. This backing was later applied to plate glass until, in 1835, the German chemist Justus von Liebig discovered a means of using silver or platinum instead. In this process, known as silvering, a silver-ammonia compound is reduced chemically to metallic silver and deposited

Mirror-making in the mid-18th century, from Diderot's Encyclopédie des arts et des métiers. *On the left (fig. 2) workers polish sheets of glass. On the right (fig. 3), the glass is slid onto a sheet of tin foil coated with mercury. It will then be weighted with rocks. When the excess mercury has been squeezed out, the mirrors are propped upright to drain further (fig. 4) and harden. The rim around the table on the right prevents the liquid mercury from running off.*

on the glass.

Mirrors can be decorated on the front or rear by enamelling, gilding, acid etching and other techniques. In back-painting, the amalgam is scraped away before the painting takes place.

See also FLAT GLASS.

Mirror black A high-fired, glossy black glaze used on Chinese porcelains from the 18th century. Black iron glazes have been used on Chinese stonewares since at least the 3rd century AD, but in the 18th century, during the Qing period, new monochrome colours were developed at the Imperial kilns for use on porcelains. These included a dense, glossy monochrome glaze known as 'mirror black' because of its exceptionally shiny surface, which was often gilded initially with gold leaf decoration. The glaze itself contains iron oxide but also cobalt and manganese oxides, which give a richer black colour as well as traces of copper. In areas where the glaze has run thin, a faint blue line can often be seen revealing the presence of cobalt.

Modelled leather A raised decoration on the boards of a bookbinding. In some very early bookbindings (7th–8th century) this was made by pasting and moulding leather over a substrate, possibly cords. Later binders cut and indented the leather (*cuir ciselé*), while in the 19th century it became fashionable to model moistened leather with hand tools to create a raised design. The thick, wet leather was cut or impressed following the outlines of the pattern and retained the modelling once dry. Moulded papier mâché-covered boards in imitation of modelled leather are found on 19th-century books.

Modelling The shaping of three-dimensional forms from clay, plaster or wax. In ceramics the term is used to describe two different processes. First, and most commonly, it refers to the shaping of pre-moulded forms after removal from the mould to enhance relief decoration (see BLANC DE CHINE) or to the forming by hand of elements of APPLIED DECORATION. (By extension, any ceramic sculpture created by hand can be said to be modelled.) Alternatively, modelling can refer to the creation of ceramic models for moulds.

For modelling, a plastic clay is required and care must be taken to ensure that the clay does not dry out during shaping. The process can be aided by special modelling tools, which are used to push and shape the clay.

Mohair A fibre or yarn derived from the long, white, lustrous hair of the angora goat, native to Asia Minor, although farmed in various other parts of the world. The fibres range from 10 cm to 30 cm in length, and are usually made into compact, resilient, sleek yarns through the Bradford system of spinning (see WOOL). The term is also used for a cloth made of this yarn, often employed for upholstery pile fabrics.

Mohs scale See GEMSTONES.

Moiré A cloth with a watered effect created by passing a folded, ribbed fabric through high-pressure cylinders. The term has been applied to this treatment on cloths of silk, cotton, viscose, some synthetic fibres and acetate (the only fabric on which the treatment is permanent). Before the 18th century the word was also used to refer to lustrous gold, silver and silk fabrics. Cloths of hard-spun worsted or cotton yarns finished with a watered effect are called MOREEN.

Moiré paper Paper with a watered pattern made by embossing the paper with heated cylinders. Moiré papers were first made in 1806 and are used in bookbinding.

LEFT Mokumé gane *bowl in white metal and copper, by Alistair McCallum, c.1980. The bowl is shaped by raising a sheet of soldered* mokumé gane; *after finishing the surface is artificially patinated.*

Mokumé gane A Japanese process of laminating different metals and then working them to create a wood-grain pattern on the surface. (In Japanese *mokumé* means 'wood-grain' and *gane* 'metal'.) Several combinations of metals can be used, ferrous as well as non-ferrous, as long as their melting-points and malleability are similar. The most popular are copper, shakudo, gold, silver and shibuishi.

There are two main methods of creating the laminate: a solder can be used to bond the metals, or the metals can be

ABOVE Mokumé gane. *Once the differently coloured metal layers have been fused together, they are distorted by punching or cutting. When abraded or flattened, the surface will show a woodgrain pattern, which is usually enhanced by patination.*

fused together without solder, using heat and pressure. When two metals with similar melting-points are heated to a temperature near those points, a bond is formed at their contacting surfaces, a process called diffusion. Once the different metals have been laminated to form a sandwich, a pattern is created by hammering, chasing or cutting through the different layers. When the laminate is flattened by rolling or planishing, the structure of the different layers is distorted and eventually a wood-grain pattern emerges, especially when the metals vary in colour or react differently on patination. There are other forms of *mokumé gane* in which the edges of the laminates are used to create a mosaic or a twisted pattern. The technique has been used in Japan since around 1700, particularly on sword fittings. Today it is also used outside Japan for jewellery and hollowware.

Mokume-ji A type of finish used in Japanese MAKI-E lacquer. Various gold powders and finely ground powder pigments, or *kanshitsu-fun*, are sprinkled onto a finished black ground in imitation of wood-grain. (The name is Japanese for 'wood-grain ground'.) The pattern is delineated using a mixture of red ochre and a slow-drying, hard-setting form of lacquer known as *seshime*, which is obtained from branches or twigs. Coloured powders are then sprinkled over the delineations while they are still wet.

Monotype See TYPESETTING.

Moquette See VELVET.

Mordant A metallic salt used to create permanent colours from many natural dyes, since it is able to form a relatively insoluble chemical bridge with both the fibre and the dye. Also known as 'colours' or 'drugs', the most common mordant until the 18th century was ALUM. Other widely used mordants were tin, aluminium, tannic acid (an astringent that also occurred naturally in gallnut and catechu—the latter was introduced as a dye *c*.1806—and gave brown shades) and iron; tannic acid and iron eventually cause the cloth to disintegrate. Iron was often combined in the form of filings with vinegar to create the mordant for blacks and purples, but was replaced, mainly by wool dyers in Europe, by ferrous sulphate in the 18th century and by chrome in the early 19th century. Printing several mordants to create different colours in one dye-bath was a technique associated with MADDER.

Mordant gilding Gold leaf applied to a ceramic or glass vessel in a garlic and vinegar medium. When heated, the medium evaporates to leave a layer of gold behind.

Moreen A weft-ribbed worsted cloth finished with a watered (see MOIRÉ) or wavy patterned effect by hot pressing. It is closely related to—and may be synonymous with—harateen and cheney; the three together were widely used as furnishing fabrics from at least *c*.1650 until the 19th century, when cotton moreens were introduced. Small floral or other patterns were sometimes impressed on them, and their embossing by cylinders is documented from as early as 1750.

Morocco Vegetable-tanned goatskin which has a uniform, raised grain pattern produced by boarding the skin in four directions. Morocco leathers were traditionally said to have been produced from goatskins from sub-Saharan Africa, where they were processed using indigenous tanning materials. The skins were then transported by camel to North Africa, where they were dyed and finished. It was considered that the combination of mechanical action caused by the camel's motion and the heat of the desert journey distributed the natural fats through the skin, giving an especially fine, soft handle to the leather. Morocco-type leathers were thought to have been introduced into southern Spain by the Moors in the early Middle Ages. Until the mid-18th century, when a tannery in Paris started its own production, Morocco leathers were imported into Europe from North Africa or the eastern Mediterranean.

Morocco leathers dyed red with natural vegetable dyestuffs were widely used in the 19th century for upholstery purposes. The disadvantages of using small skins were overcome by disguising the joins in the folds produced by the deep buttoning techniques introduced during that time. Today Morocco leathers are used particularly for bookbindings and the manufacture of small leather goods. Morocco-type patterns are now often embossed onto sheepskin and other leathers.

Morse ivory See WALRUS IVORY.

Mortar A material used to bind together brick, ashlar blocks or less regular pieces of stone to construct a wall; it is also used as a matrix in which to set mosaic tesserae. A mortar may be made of clay, used in ancient Egypt in conjunction with mud bricks; gypsum plaster, also used in Egypt and Islamic countries up to the Middle Ages; or lime putty and sand. Lime and sand mortar was widely used with or without other aggregates throughout Europe from the Roman period until the advent in the 19th century of Portland cement (see

CEMENT), which is now employed throughout the world. In addition to its adhesive functions a mortar is used to fill, or point, the gaps between the blocks to help make the building stable and weatherproof. The thickness of the pointing is dependent on the shape of the blocks being joined: small, irregular pieces of stone require large amounts of mortar to hold them together, whereas precisely cut ashlar can be pointed with only a thin layer of mortar. The colour of the mortar can be altered to match the adjacent masonry, by the addition of stone dusts, or to contrast with it, as some 19th-century British architects did by adding ash to their mortar to produce blacking pointing.

Mortise and tenon A group of woodworking joints used in framing, construction and furniture making. They were first used by the ancient Egyptians. A tongue or tenon is cut and sized on the end of one member to fit into a slot or mortise on another. The various types used for specialist purposes include bare-faced, box, chase, closed, double, dovetail or fox-wedged, shouldered, stub, tusk and twin.

Mosaic A technique for decorating floors and walls, in which square or rectangular pieces of stone, glass or ceramic of consistent size, known as tesserae, are set in a mortar. It developed from the use of pebbles to make decorative pavements, in which patterns were produced by using stones of varying colours and sizes. This type of flooring was made by the Assyrians in the 9th century BC, although the technique of embedding materials in a plastic medium is much older. From the 4th millennium BC the Sumerians set small pieces of stone and ceramic cones into clay walls, both as decoration and to protect the clay from erosion. At Ur, around 3000 BC, wooden columns were decorated with pieces of stone and shell set in bitumen. By the 3rd century BC in Italy and Greece tesserae of regular shape were made by cutting stone into slabs and then into square or rectangular rods, using toothless metal saws with an abrasive such as quartz sand and water as a lubricant (see STONE). Individual tesserae were then snapped off the rod by placing the end over a hardie (a chisel blade set in a block of wood) and hitting it with a hammer with two cutting edges. These tools, along with trowels, spatulas, rulers, squares and compasses, are the basic equipment of the mosaicist and have remained largely unchanged since antiquity. Ceramic tesserae were cut from bricks, tiles or fragments of pottery; glass tesserae were

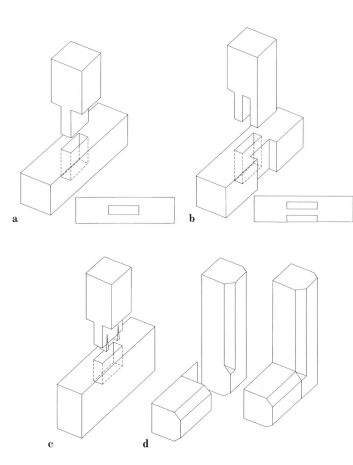

Mortise and tenon joints:
(a) common mortise and
tenon; (b) double
barefaced tenon; (c) the
fox-wedged blind mortise;
(d) the mason's mitre, a
corner mortise joint.

salvaged from glass vessels.

By the Roman period the use of mosaic pavements in public buildings and private villas was widespread. Throughout the empire local stones were used, supplemented by some imported pottery, glass and brightly coloured stone. From the middle of the 1st century AD opaque glass tesserae were produced by fusing together silica, obtained from quartz sand, a flux such as potassium carbonate or sodium carbonate, obtained from plant ash and added to lower the melting-point of the silica, and metallic oxide colourants; cobalt oxide produced blue, and various copper oxides yielded reds and greens. The materials were melted together in a crucible at 900°C and the molten glass was then pressed between marble slabs to form a disc approximately 1–2 cm thick and up to 30 cm in diameter. The disc was placed in an annealing chamber, an insulated container which allowed slow cooling to reduce the possibility of internal stresses forming in the glass, which could cause crumbling when the tesserae were cut. Modern glass tesserae are manufactured in the same manner, although fusion is carried out at higher temperatures, designed to expel impurities and gas bubbles and so produce a more uniform product. The Romans made gilded tesserae by using mastic to sandwich gold and silver leaf between thin layers of glass.

In the construction of Roman floor mosaics, where the ground was not sufficiently firm, a foundation of progressively finer stones and gravels, surmounted by layers of coarse lime mortar, was prepared. The tesserae were set in a layer of lime mixed with marble powder, known as the bedding layer. In some instances red ochre underdrawings were used as a guide for positioning the tesserae directly in the mortar. Working on site, the mosaicist cut the tesserae and placed them close together in sequence to create the outlines of the image and then filled in the forms. Shading was indicated by carefully grading the colour of adjacent tesserae. Once the pattern was complete, mortar would be rubbed between the tesserae to hold them firmly. This technique, known as the direct method, required considerable skill as changes in the composition could not be easily made once the tesserae were set in the mortar. With the indirect method, thought to have been used from the Roman period for complex designs, the mosaicist constructed the image in

A modern re-creation of a Byzantine mosaic, using the indirect method. The outline has been drawn onto thick kraft paper and water-soluble glue is used to stick the tesserae face down. Once assembled, the mosaic will be picked up and placed on a bed of adhesive. The paper will then be removed to reveal the front of the design.

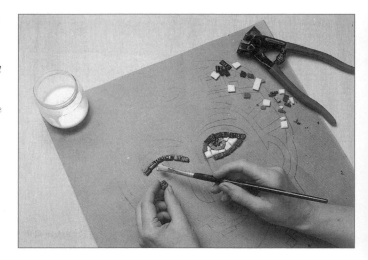

reverse on a cartoon drawn on fabric or a bed of sand in the workshop; when using sand, fabric would then have been attached to the backs of the tesserae to allow the completed work to be picked up. The prefabricated unit, which might form the central panel of a large mosaic, was then transported to the site and set into the mortar. This technique allowed for more adjustment of the design before setting.

Mosaics were widely used in Byzantine architecture for floor and wall decoration. Wall mosaics were constructed in a similar manner to pavements, although the fact that they were not subjected to the same pressures from feet and furniture meant that more glass could be used; as glass is lighter than stone, it was also easier to fix onto a vertical surface. The wall was prepared with at least three layers of lime mortar; the final layer was applied in sections corresponding to the area that could be covered with tesserae in one day. The working drawing for the mosaic was applied either to the wall or to one of the mortar layers; a more detailed drawing was often executed on the bedding layer using fresco technique. Slabs of coloured glass were cut into rods and then into cubes on site. As with Roman floors, the mosaicist first outlined the figures and then filled them in; finally the background was set in straight or undulating rows. Glass and stone tesserae of the same colour were often used in close proximity to create a range of tonalities between the translucent and opaque materials. Gold and silver tesserae were made by applying the metal leaf to glass and then covering it

A detail of mosaic from the Albert Memorial in London, designed by J. R. Clayton and executed by Salviati of Venice, 1866–8. It shows how the mosaicist can indicate shading and form, designed to be viewed from a distance, by the selection and positioning of individual tesserae. The artist has also varied the size of the tesserae to produce the delicately tapering fingertips.

a

b

c

with powdered glass, which was vitrified by firing in a kiln. From at least the 6th century AD these tesserae were set into the mortar at a 30–45° angle to increase the reflection of light from the surface. This technique was also practised in the Islamic world, where mosaics with geometric designs were used extensively for wall decoration.

Forms of stone inlay and decorative paving, such as COSMATI WORK and PIETRE DURE, developed in Italy from the Middle Ages. In the late 18th century a technique was developed in the Vatican workshop for making mosaics composed of minute tesserae, approximately 1–2 mm square. Known as micromosaics, these were made from fine glass canes with a high concentration of colourant, which were heated in a flame and pulled into thin filaments with tweezers. The tesserae were placed, using the tweezers, on a piece of glass or copper coated with a resin, and the spaces between them were filled with wax or a form of mortar; in some instances the grouting material between the tesserae was painted to match the glass. Micromosaics were used to decorate jewellery, snuff boxes, vases and furniture.

The Mayans and Aztecs made mosaics using small tesserae of turquoise, jade, malachite and other gemstones, as well as gold and shell, which were set into pitch or gum on a stone or wooden substrate. This technique was used to make masks and other ceremonial items.

In the 19th and 20th centuries mosaics, often made of industrially produced glass tesserae, were used to decorate building interiors and exteriors. Antoni Gaudí used fragments of glazed ceramic tiles, scavenged from manufacturers and cut into irregular shapes, to embellish the buildings and sculptures of his Park Güell in Barcelona.

Mosaic glass Glassware made from slices of multicoloured cane fused together. There are two methods of making true mosaic. In the first, the slices are placed closely together on a flat clay surface, given a rim of glass cane, then softened in the furnace and slumped over a clay mould. In the second, they are arranged in a shaped mould, held in place by an adhesive or by another mould, and fused in the furnace. These techniques were used by Hellenistic glassmakers. In the 16th century the Venetians developed another method, sometimes known as 'mosaic inlay' or MILLEFIORI, in which the sliced cane was embedded in clear glass and blown into shape.

Mother-of-pearl A generic term for the hard iridescent lining of certain marine mollusc shells such as the oyster, ABALONE and mussel; of these, the great pearl oyster (*Meleagrina margaritifera*) produces the most workable and plentiful material. The colour varies from a silvery pale grey to pink, blue or green, depending on the waters from which the shell is obtained. Its iridescence is a result of the way in which light is reflected from the very thin overlapping sheets of calcium carbonate which form the lining. When mother-of-pearl is exposed to sunlight this iridescence is lost and the material becomes 'blind'. The material is sometimes also called nacre.

The shell may be worked from the inside or the outside. When carved from the outside, a pattern can be created by leaving the hard outer layer in place or partially grinding it back to form a distinctive feature. Sometimes acid etching is employed to remove the outer layer, with a wax resist to protect those areas that are to be retained. This is cheaper and easier than carving, but tends to damage the iridescence.

OPPOSITE
The making of a mosaic glass bowl.
(a) Sections of patterned cane, about 6 mm thick, have been formed into a disc and fused together by heating in a kiln. A hot twisted cane is quickly wrapped around the edge of the disc, which may require reheating during the process. (b) While hot, the disc is draped over a hemispherical shape to form a bowl. It is then replaced in the furnace to allow the glass to slump down over the form. (c) Before cooling, any folds that form around the rim are pressed flat with tools. Later the glass is freed from the form with a few sharp taps on its base, and after annealing and cooling one or both sides of the vessel are ground and polished.

Detail of an ebony cabinet, inlaid with abalone, oystershell and silver, by Süe et Mare, France, 1927.

Mother-of-pearl has a long history of use as a decorative inlay in the Far and Middle East and has been employed in the West for several centuries in a similar way as an inlay on boxes and furniture. It is still used to manufacture buttons, decorative penknife cases and jewellery.

Mottle A descriptive term applied to figure in wood and used to describe patterns that appear broken and uneven. It is often used in conjunction with other descriptive terms so that, for example, fiddleback becomes fiddle-mottle.

Mould-applied decoration See SPRIGGED WARE.

Mould-blown glass A form of glass produced by blowing molten glass directly into a mould (for illustration see page 205). This can be a one-piece dip mould, open at the top, or a piece mould in two or more sections (see CASTING). The mould is usually wetted so that its surface and that of the glass are protected by steam. Early moulds were made of fire clay, carved wood or stone; later, metal was used. The mould may be quite plain, simply to form the basic shape of the item, or it may have a raised or indented pattern on the inside which will be transferred to the surface of the glass. This results in 'pattern-moulded' glassware, which is sometimes reheated and blown further to soften, twist or enlarge the pattern. In industrial glass production mould blowing is the principal means of manufacture.

Mould-pressed glass See PRESS MOULDING.

Muff glass See FLAT GLASS.

Muffle kiln A low-temperature kiln (700–900°C) used to fire glass or porcelain that has been decorated with enamels or gilding. The items are enclosed in a fire clay box, known as a muffle, to protect them from the flames and smoke.

Muntz metal See BRASS.

Murex See SHELLFISH PURPLE.

Muslin A firm, plain-weave cotton varying in weight from semi-sheer book muslin to heavyweight sheeting, although when associated with window curtains from *c.*1790, the word indicates the sheerest type. In the initial decades after the development of machine-spinning the term was applied both to very fine, strong white cotton yarns and to any cloth made from them, including those with simple woven 'spot' patterns or stripes, such as dimity.

N

Nacre See MOTHER-OF-PEARL.

Nail See WOOD FIXINGS.

Namban Japanese export lacquerware first produced in the 16th century. Examples include gilt and polychrome screens and black lacquered cabinet work, densely decorated with gold and shell inlay, often depicting European and Christian motifs.

Nandutti See EMBROIDERED LACE.

Naples yellow A warm, opaque yellow pigment, similar in colour to a mixture of ochre and white. It probably originated as a by-product of the glassmaking industry. Its earliest use has not been determined, but it is thought to have been developed towards the end of the 17th century, and by around 1700 it had replaced lead tin yellow as the main bright yellow on the artist's palette. Despite its expense, Naples yellow was important throughout the 18th century, and was even used in house paint. It was much less used after the invention of more brilliant pigments in the 19th century, but it is still available today in a narrow range of tones. It is reliable as long as it is not used in contact with metal, particularly iron, or mixed with natural organic pigments such as indigo or crimson lake. In these circumstances it has been known to blacken.

Nappa Originally a full-thickness, chrome-tanned sheepskin leather treated with a heavily pigmented finish and used for gloving, clothing or handbags. More recently the term has come to be used for any sheepskin or lambskin grain clothing leather.

Narwhal tusk A form of ivory obtained from the narwhal or Arctic whale. The highly developed left canine forms one spirally formed conical tusk up to 2.5 m long but rarely more than 9 cm in diameter. The right canine is of similar form but rarely exceeds 18 cm in length. Both tusks are hollow for most of their length and, although they are occasionally carved or made into staffs and walking sticks, they are generally only of curiosity value.

Nashiji The Japanese name for one of the grounds used in MAKI-E lacquer and for the metal powders (*nashiji-fun*) or flakes used to produce it (see colour plate XIIIc). Named after the speckled appearance of the skin of the Japanese pear (*nashi*), the so-called pearskin ground was imitated in European work as the aventurine finish perfected in the VERNIS MARTIN technique.

Nautilus A shell material derived from five species of mollusc
of the genus *Nautilus* (see colour plate XVI). Related to the
ancient ammonites and to the squid and octopus, the nau-
tiloids inhabit the Indian and eastern Pacific oceans. The
smooth, coiled shell of the nautilus can grow up to 28 cm in
diameter. It has a nacreous MOTHER-OF-PEARL lining and is
composed of a series of separate chambers divided by septa.
These are pierced by a tube called the siphuncle, through
which the animal moves gas and liquid to regulate its buoy-
ancy.

Nautilus is often used as source material by shellcarvers,
who use its varicoloured layers in the manufacture of cameos.
Alternatively, the shell can be used whole. The hard outer
layer is scraped off or stripped by immersion in acid. The
exposed nacre is then burnished to a beautiful lustre with
diluted alcohol or decorated with carved, etched or engraved
designs. The engraving may be left 'blind' (uncoloured) or
brought out in black with powdered coal mixed with wax or
oil. In the Baroque period the shell was often supported in an
elaborate mount and used as a goblet.

Needle lace A category of lace made mainly of fine flax threads.
Needle laces (sometimes called needlepoint laces) evolved
from embroidered laces and are based on variations of the
buttonhole stitch (loops or knots over a foundation thread).
With the exception of HOLLIE POINT, they are assembled in
units rather than being made in one process from left to right
or top to bottom. RETICELLA, although classed as a needle
lace, is an intermediate form, being cutwork with large areas
removed, and the emphasis placed instead on the decorative
infill.

Needle laces are made on a parchment or waxed paper
pattern to which outlining threads (the cordonnet) are
tacked; buttonhole stitches fill the design area and constitute
the meshes or bars placed at random angles which hold the
whole together. When a section is complete, the tacking is
removed and the pattern used again. The cordonnet is therefore an integral part of the technique and played an important role in the changing styles of needle lace. Initially, in the
late 16th-century and early to mid-17th century forms, such
as *reticella*, PUNTO IN ARIA or *point plat*, it was inconspicuous
or replaced entirely by flat tape (see TAPE LACE). It was then
padded to create features in mid- to late 17th-century Venetian needle laces such as *gros point*, rose point and *point de*

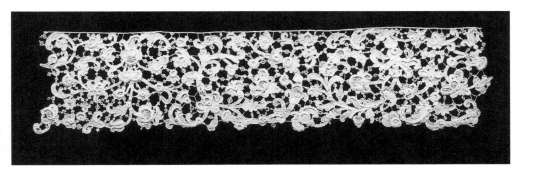

Gros point *needle lace, Venice, c.1625–50. This example incorporates the dominant raised cordonnet characteristic of this period and the short connecting brides which, when used in bobbin, appliqué and machine-made imitations of needle lace, identify these latter as guipure-style laces.

neige, and later revivals such as the Bayeux needle lace *point de Colbert*. The next and last important development in needle lace techniques was a modest cordonnet combined with a mesh ground, initiated in the 1660s as *point de France*. Grounds may be twisted or buttonholed, according to the place of manufacture, and with time they became lighter and the motifs more recognizably floral; the late 19th-century Flemish *point de gaz*, for example, had tiered rose petals. A form of *point de France* was revived in 1846 in Ireland as Youghal lace.

Needle painting A term referring to an embroidery technique that uses fine stitches to create an appearance similar to a painting. It has been used to describe embroideries created as early as the 10th century AD, although the term itself may not date back that far and may instead have originated from the description of medieval embroiderers who were members of the Antwerp Guild of St Luke, which described them as *acu pictores*, or 'painters with needles'. The technique is also called Gu embroidery.

Needlepoint A general term, formerly used widely, and especially in America, for CANVASWORK. It can also denote NEEDLE LACE.

Nephrite A green to buff-coloured mineral, often called greenstone, composed of calcium magnesium aluminium silicate and iron (for illustration see page 247). If a large proportion of iron is present, it produces a rich green; with lower levels the mineral is buff-coloured. Nephrite was the JADE known to the ancient Chinese, who from neolithic times used it for blades, carvings and gemstones; their principal source of nephrite was Khotan. It occurs in many parts of the world and is either quarried at the place of formation or gathered as river boulders or pebbles. The Maoris used nephrite pebbles to make talismanic carvings known as *tiki*; the shape of the pebble is reflected in the form of the object. Nephrite crystallizes in needle-like forms which felt together, producing an extremely tough material that is traditionally worked with abrasives.

Netting See BOBBINET.

Nickel A silver white metal which is malleable, ductile, harder than iron, magnetic and capable of taking a very high polish. The name derives from the German *kupfernickel* ('Devil's copper'), a name given by 15th-century miners to a poisonous ore found in Saxony. Later it was discovered by the Swede Axel Cronstedt in 1751 that the ore was a compound of arsenic with a new metal, which Cronstedt named nickel.

Although nickel was therefore isolated in 1751, it had been used long before that date in alloys such as PAKTONG. It can also be found in prehistoric tools made from meteoric iron, which can contain up to 15% nickel. Until 1865 nickel ores were found in small amounts only in Germany and Scandinavia, but large deposits were found that year in New Caledonia and later also in Canada. The metal is extracted from the ore by a complex method, although today it is also refined by electrolytic processes.

The main use of nickel in the decorative arts has traditionally been in nickel silvers and as decorative plating. Today it is still used decoratively but mainly in stainless steel (with chromium) and other special steel alloys, where it is valued for its corrosion-resistance. Other uses are in protective electroplating, NICKEL SILVER and CUPRONICKEL. Nickel enhances the heat-resistance, strength, hardness and toughness of most of its alloys.

Nickel silver A generic term for brass with nickel added to change the colour and improve other properties. A nickel content over 18% gives a white colour to the alloy and improves the mechanical properties and the corrosion-resistance. Despite its name, nickel silver does not contain any silver but only resembles it in appearance. The first use of nickel silver was around 170 BC in Bactrian coins, which typically used an alloy of 42% zinc, 38% copper and 20% nickel. There is no other recorded use of nickel silver in the West until the end of the 17th century, when a nickel silver called PAKTONG was imported from China, where there was a long history of its use. It was not until around 1820 that nickel silver could be produced in Europe. Known as German silver, it had a composition of 55% copper, 25% nickel and 20% zinc. One of its first uses, developed in Germany and Britain, was as a base for fused plate: unplated wares were called British plate. With the introduction of electroplating around 1840, nickel silver became a very popular base, mainly because areas where the plating has worn are hardly discernible. A popular alloy for this electroplated nickel silver (EPNS) is 65% copper, 18% nickel and 17% zinc.

Niello A black inlay in a metal surface, consisting mainly of the sulphides of silver, copper and lead. Niello can be applied to precious metals, ferrous metals and copper alloys. It is now produced by heating silver, copper, lead and sulphur together in a crucible; when all the ingredients are properly mixed the molten niello is poured out on a flat surface. It is allowed to cool before being crushed to a powder with a pestle and mortar. This niello powder, mixed with some borax and water, is then applied to hollows in the metal surface, which may be made by engraving or chasing or may be already present in the casting. The article is heated until the niello starts to melt and flow, thus filling the hollows. When cooled and solidified, the surface is finished by filing, grinding and polishing to reveal the contrast between the dark niello and the bright base metal. Because niello is actually fused, like a solder, to the underlying metal, the hollowed-out area of the metal surface can range in size from very fine lines to a large expanse.

Niello is mentioned by Pliny, and several examples of Roman niello work survive. It continued to be used extensively in Western Europe until the Renaissance, and in Eastern Europe, Russia and the Middle East it is still common: the Russian town of Tula is famous for its niello, which is therefore sometimes referred to as 'Tula work'.

An étui, *or small case, silver and niello, Italy, c.1450–1500.*

Nipt diamond ware Glassware with a large, open, diamond-shaped design on the exterior. The term was first used in the 17th century by George Ravenscroft and is now universal. The effect is produced by making a glass with parallel ribs in a dip mould and then pinching the ribs together in an alternating fashion while the glass is still hot. The glass is then inflated. A simpler method is to blow the glass into a mould with a diamond pattern on its interior.

Non-impact printing See PRINTING.

Non-woven fabrics Any of a number of fabrics made without intertwining or interlooping, including felt and bark cloth. These cloths, including the modern non-wovens, are generally produced by applying pressure to soaking or previously soaked fibres or materials.

Norman slab A window glass made by blowing a gather of molten glass into a mould shaped like a square-sided bottle. When cold, the glass is cut into five flat panels. Whole panels can be recognized by their thin edges, as it is impossible to blow an even thickness of glass into the extremities of the mould. The technique is suited only to the production of small panels. It was used in Roman times but is now employed only for special orders, usually in connection with stained-glass windows.

Nubuck A leather which is finished by buffing the grain surface with fine abrasive papers.

Nylon A tough, chemical-resistant synthetic plastic. It was discovered in the 1930s by a team based at the firm of Du Pont, Delaware, USA, led by Wallace Hume Carothers. Du Pont initially concentrated on a form of nylon known as nylon 6,6. Other types which have since proved commercially successful include: nylon 6; nylon 6,10; and nylon 6,11. The numbers refer to the number of carbon atoms in the nylon monomer(s) which condense to form the repeating unit in the polymer.

Nylon was patented in 1935 and first displayed in 1938 as bristles on the Miracle Tuft toothbrush. Nylon stockings were first made in the USA in February 1939. In 1939 Du Pont licensed ICI to develop nylon in Britain and the Common-wealth. ICI and Courtaulds formed British Nylon Spinners in 1940. For the next five years production was dedicated to wartime needs such as parachutes. In the USA too, nylon was taken out of commercial production in 1942 for dedication to military purposes.

Very strong but light, nylon is wear-resistant, springs back into shape, and is not prone to fungal or insect attack. Ther-moplastic, it can be injection-moulded, rotational-moulded and extruded. The moulded variety is very tough and light so that, with its low coefficient of friction, it can be used to make zips and curtain rails.

O

Oak A very durable, hard and heavy wood obtained principally from the *Quercus pedunculata*, *Q. robur*, *Q. sessiliflora*
and *Q. petraea* species found in Britain and Europe. Many
other species from different parts of the world (and with
varying qualities) are also used, but the English oak—of
which alone there are 300 varieties—is considered to be the
best. It is generally a rich light brown colour, and it becomes
even harder, and darker in colour, with age. When quarter-
cut and rift-sawn it reveals a very attractive figure. It can be
difficult to work owing to its hardness, especially in old
samples, but has been put to many uses, particularly in situations where strength and durability are paramount, such as
building, cooperage, ship building and flooring, as well as furniture, carving and turnery; it is also used for making
veneers.

Oak was the main timber used for European medieval furniture and building; others were employed but, being less
durable, have not survived. By the close of the 17th century,
however, the use of oak in the manufacture of fashionable
furniture was becoming restricted to carcass work and drawer

*A carved oak chest of
panelled construction,
France, c.1480.*

linings. Oak from the Baltic states has been imported to England since at least the 13th century. Softer and straighter-grained than the majority of English oak, it was favoured for cladding and panelling (wainscoting) and became known as 'wainscot oak'. Before the adoption of large, two-man saws in the 16th century, most oak was converted by splitting and quartering. Quartered timber displays the medullary rays in the so-called SILVER GRAIN pattern and is both more attractive and stable than straight sawn boards. As sawn boards became more common, quarter cutting was reserved for prime timber but the majority was prepared by plain 'through and through' sawing. This method gave a surface better suited to the even absorption of the glues and varnishes used in the preparation of veneered and japanned work, which became increasingly popular throughout the 17th century.

Obsidian A shiny natural glass formed by the rapid cooling of lava. It is usually black, but red, yellow and brown obsidian also exist. Obsidian occurs widely, notably in areas of recent volcanic activity. It fractures readily in a conchoidal form, producing sharp edges, and was used as a tool material from the Stone Age. Obsidian was used for seal-stones in the ancient Near East, for the inlaid eyes of Egyptian mummies, as a gemstone by the Greeks and Romans and for mirrors and masks by the Aztecs, for whom it was a sacred stone. Obsidian is of medium hardness (Mohs 5) and can be worked with harder materials such as quartz and corundum. It is used to produce beads and cabochons and for these purposes is obtained mainly from North America.

Ochres A group of pigments varying in colour from red to brown to light yellow. Natural ochres are minerals combining clay and iron oxide: the colour of the ochre is determined by the proportion of iron oxide present. Ochres have a major function in preparing surfaces for gilding (see BOLE), but are also an important type of pigment as they are chemically inert and therefore completely reliable on all surfaces and in all media. They have a high oil absorbency and so in oil there is a tendency for them to 'sink' or become matt, which can lead to uneven finishes if they are used to cover large surfaces.

Red ochre is coloured by large amounts of iron oxide. The pigment has acquired many names over the centuries, such as Venetian red, Indian red and Spanish red, according to where it is quarried. These names are still used, but they are now purely historical, because the material sold today is almost all synthetically produced iron oxide, made in a range of tones from bluish purple to orange. Synthetic ochres are rich in colour and predictable in hue, but painters appreciate the spread of tones and the translucency that come with the finer qualities of native ochres, so these can still be bought from specialist suppliers, some of whom continue to grind the pigment using the traditional windmills. Native yellow ochres have also not been completely supplanted by synthetic iron oxides, because the French ochres which have always been prized for their colour and purity are still quarried in large quantities.

See also SIENNA and UMBER.

Odontolite See MAMMOTH IVORY.

Off-loom constructions A broad range of textile techniques made without the benefit of an automatic shed-formation device. Their categorization has been the subject of detailed research which has failed to provide a consensus; they may be classed by the resulting basic structure or by the specific method of construction (for example, KNOTTING vs. tatting and MACRAMÉ; LOOPING vs. KNITTING and NEEDLE LACE; PLAITING vs. BOBBIN LACE). Since many of the same structures may be produced through a number of methods of construction, (see, for example, BOBBINET), a useful distinction can be made between primary methods, which need only very simple implements, if any, and advanced methods, which use a fixed and tensioned warp.

A second method of categorization divides the constructions into those using one theoretically continuous element, or strand, and those using two or more, some of which may be discontinuous. Among the former are crochet, and KNITTING; the latter are encompassed by the general term PLAITING. Knotting can be done with one or more strands.

Offset lithography See LITHOGRAPHY.

Oil gilding A form of GILDING in which gold leaf is applied to a gesso surface that has been sized and painted with oil. The term is also sometimes used of COLD GILDING on glassware and ceramics.

Oil paint Paint made by mixing pigment with a drying oil. Whether an oil dries or not depends on its chemical structure, and there are half a dozen that are suitable as a paint medium. The most commonly used is linseed oil from the flax plant, as this dries most rapidly, but it is slightly yellow, and painters who want to maintain the purity of their whites sometimes choose to work with poppy or walnut oil. Of all the traditional paint media oil paint creates the most saturated and most translucent colours, and is therefore best suited for glazing techniques. It can be used on all impervious surfaces and on porous ones, provided these have been sized or prepared with some kind of ground.

Oil spot glaze A Chinese black iron glaze with silvery spots on the surface, first produced in the Song period (960–1279) in north China and still used on tea wares. In traditional Chinese ceramics iron is a popular glaze pigment which can be used to produce a wide range of colours. One of the most common is a black glaze which usually contains approximately 5–6% iron oxide, the amount which the base glaze can easily dissolve. If extra iron is added, either as an additional layer of a higher iron glaze or as additional pigment painted onto the glaze surface, the glaze will be saturated with pigment and any undissolved iron will rise to the surface and crystallize in the cooling process. With an oil spot glaze, the excess iron collects on the surface in globules which have been reduced to metallic iron and thus appear silvery or oil-like. In some very rare cases, the spots appear to be iridescent blue, which is probably a result of phase separation in the glaze (see JUN GLAZE).

On-glaze decoration See IN-GLAZE DECORATION.

Onyx A form of the banded quartz gemstone AGATE, in which bands of white alternate with bands of dark brown or black; the white and brown form is also known as sardonyx. Cameos were made with these stones by cutting into the white layer to produce a relief portrait in profile against the darker layer (see colour plate I).

Onyx marble A translucent, crystalline, banded form of calcium carbonate, also known as calcite alabaster or Egyptian alabaster, which has a similar appearance to gypsum alabaster. Its earliest known source was probably the town of Alabastron in Egypt, from which the word alabaster derives. The name onyx marble derives from the material's resemblance to onyx, a banded form of quartz. Onyx marble forms in shallow lakes or in cave deposits through the precipitation of calcium carbonate from mineral-rich waters; it is thus not a true marble formed through metamorphism (see MARBLE), but rather a limestone. The material is also referred to as 'stalagmitic calcite', owing to its formation within caves, but it is not obtained from stalagmite or stalactite columns. The banding can vary in degree of translucency and colour, ranging from white to reds, browns and black, owing to the incorporation of iron and manganese salts. Onyx marble has a hardness of approximately Mohs 3 and can be polished to a smooth, waxy appearance. It was used by the ancient Egyptians as a building stone and for vessels, such as canopic jars, and has also been used for decorative carving and panelling. The Aztecs considered it a sacred stone and used it for temples and sacrificial vessels.

Opal A mineral composed of silica chemically combined with water. This material forms minute spheres, rather than crystals, which, if arranged in a regular pattern, give rise to iridescence. This effect is combined with colours ranging from white, grey, pink and black to striking blues, greens and oranges in gem-quality opal; other opals lack iridescence. Opals range in hardness from Mohs 5.5 to 6.5. They are found within cavities in igneous and sedimentary rock.

The Romans used opal obtained from mines in Slovakia which were subsequently worked until the 19th century. The Aztecs acquired opal from Honduras. In the Middle Ages it was believed that opals could predict disaster and also had curative powers; however, they became unpopular in the 18th and 19th centuries because they were thought to bring the wearer bad luck. Major finds of opal were made in Australia in the late 19th century and this remains the principal source. Opals are generally cut as cabochons, which often include a thin layer of the host rock to give them added strength and, in some cases, to enhance the iridescence; similarly, thin slices of opal may be backed with common opal, glass or silk fabric.

Opal simulants have been made from glass and plastic. Synthetic opals, in which the structure is imitated with minute silica spheres, were first produced in the 1950s.

Opaque glass See GLASS.

Opus anglicanum Fine medieval English ecclesiastical embroidery in which the entire surface of the ground cloth was often embellished with stitches, especially underside couching (a form of LAID AND COUCHED WORK), and closely packed split-stitch, worked to follow the contours of the face to give sculptural form. The name is Latin for 'English work'. The finest examples were made c. 1250–1350 in workshops that exported both finished articles and embroiderers to continental Europe.

Opus sectile A pictorial panel composed of pieces of coloured glass embedded in resin or mortar. Each piece of glass may be plain-coloured or may contain a design or image made in the manner of glass cane. The overall effect resembles a stained-glass panel but is of course opaque, since it is intended as a wall covering. The technique was known in ancient times and was used in 19th-century Britain by Whitefriars Glassworks to form, for example, interior church memorials.

Or nué A form of LAID AND COUCHED WORK in which drawn gold wire or metal threads form the background to silk couching threads that, by their placement (close together or further apart) create the illusion of chiaroscuro shading. It is often used to depict drapery or folds in garments. Although principally associated with 15th-century Italian and Flemish

A sample for the Sir Stuart Coats chasuble, designed by Sir Ninian Comper and worked in the Sisters of Bethany convent embroidery workshop, 1921. It is worked in silk floss split stitch (the face and hands), and floss and metal thread patterned couching (background) and or nué.

embroidery, the technique was revived at the end of the 19th century by the Anglican community the Society of the Sisters of Bethany, London, in concert with the architect–designer Sir Ninian Comper.

Ormolu A term for decorative objects or furniture mounts, made in the 18th and early 19th centuries, in cast brass, chased and gilded by the FIREGILDING process. The name derives from the French *or moulu* ('ground or powdered gold'), and is often wrongly used for gilt bronze in general. Recent analysis has shown that most ormolu objects are of brass rather than bronze, which is not surprising since brass is

A clock in gilded and patinated bronze, by Antoine Ravrio, Paris, c.1810. The ormolu mounts are cast in brass, chased and firegilded. To create the contrast between the matt and polished parts the gilded mounts were lightly etched and selectively burnished.

easier than bronze to cast, chase and firegild. The finest examples of ormolu were produced in France in the second half of the 18th century, when famous makers included Pierre Gouthière, Charles Cressent and the Caffiéri brothers. The best ormolu from this period shows, apart from superb chasing, a delicate play of matt and burnished gilding. Some very fine ormolu was also produced in Birmingham by Matthew Boulton between 1768 and 1782.

Ornamental lathe See LATHE.

Orpiment A yellow sulphide of arsenic used as a pigment and sometimes known as 'King's yellow'. It is poisonous and evil-smelling and was therefore rarely used for wall decoration, although it can be found in early manuscript painting.

Orris lace See METAL THREAD.

Overglaze decoration See ENAMEL COLOURS.

Overlay glass See CASED GLASS.

Ox blood red See SANG DE BOEUF.

Oyster veneer See VENEER.

P

Padauk A hard and heavy, very strong and durable wood from the species *Pterocarpus dalbergiodes*, found in the Andaman Islands, *P. macrocarpus* from Burma and *P. soyauxii*, from Africa. It is also known by such names as Andaman redwood, Burmese rosewood, corail and Indies mahogany. A dark crimson red, padauk darkens on seasoning to almost purple with darker stripes. It is stable and resistant to insect attack, with a smooth, heavily interlocking grain. Used for joinery, cabinet work and flooring, it is difficult to work and polished surfaces must be carefully grain-filled. Burmese padauk is the best variety.

Paint Liquid colour that dries to a permanent finish. Since earliest times man has used colours to decorate himself and his environment. Neolithic painters used muds and charcoal applied without any additives to the cave walls, and the paint stuck because of the clay content and the roughness of the stone surface; usually, however, paint contains a binder to make it adhere to the support. The choice of binder not only dictates the permanence of the paint but also affects the handling properties and its ultimate appearance.

Detail from a painted sideboard by William Burges, 1862. It is decorated with a scene depicting a contest between the wines and the beers, painted by E. J. Poynter.

In classical and pre-classical times paints used for wall and object decoration were mostly watercolours, distempers and caseins. One exception was the use of encaustic, or molten wax, a technique practised in classical Roman times, particularly in Egypt. During the Middle Ages and early Renaissance egg was a very important binder, the yolk being used for decorating wooden surfaces and the white, or glair, for manuscript illumination (see EGG TEMPERA). Painters in the south of Europe explored the possibilities of true fresco for the decoration of walls, while in the north they were experimenting with oil. Oil was used initially for walls and for metals but from the 13th century it began to be used on wood, and by the end of the 15th century it had become the prime painting medium for the whole continent. The development of oil paint in the 16th and 17th centuries was linked to mastering dryers and diluents and producing quick-drying paint in textures ranging from liquid washes to thick paste.

Until the end of the 17th century all painters made their own paint, grinding pigment to a fine powder on a slab and mixing it with binder just prior to painting. By the 18th century paint of all types was being made and sold by colour merchants, and the practice expanded to industrial proportions in the 19th century. Packaging became important: the introduction of the collapsible aluminium tube for oil paint in the early 19th century meant that painters were no longer so firmly tied to the workshop. But factory-made, pre-mixed paint was no longer a simple combination of pigment and binder; instead, additives were introduced to increase shelf life, bulk out expensive pigments and improve brushing. Artists became concerned about the quality of paints, but controls were only instituted at the end of the century, when the situation came to a head after a range of pigments introduced in the 1860s and 1870s were found to fade severely. In England painters and chemists collaborated in testing materials, and the Russell Abney report of 1888 marked the beginning of proper standardization.

The early 20th century saw the invention of synthetic binders. The first use of acrylics was by mural painters in South America, but the paint is now used for all surfaces. Acrylics began to be used in house paint just before the Second World War, but only became important for this purpose in the 1950s. Acrylics, alkyds and PVA paints now form a very large part of all paint ranges, and have an important role for amateur painters and in schools, but they have never managed fully to displace oil. Most developments in paint in the late 20th century have been in expanding the range of synthetic organic pigments, which have now largely replaced the traditional palette.

Paktong A Chinese nickel–silver alloy containing 40–50% copper, 35–45% zinc and 5–15% nickel. This white alloy was used in China from the 16th century for household utensils and coinage, and was exported from the late 17th century to Europe, where it was used between 1680 and 1820 mainly for the manufacture of domestic wares such as candlesticks. Paktong wares may be cast as well as being made out of sheet. The import of paktong ceased when Europeans succeeded in making NICKEL SILVER. The name derives from the Chinese *baitung* ('white copper').

Palm leaf A sheet material made from the leaves of palm trees. According to the 1st-century AD Roman naturalist Pliny, it was the first sheet material to be used for writing. Pliny was referring to the practice of the ancient Egyptians, but palm leaves were used as a support for calligraphy in India and Sri Lanka until recent times. Varieties of palm and other tree leaves have been used, dried and cut into strips about 5 cm wide, usually joined with cords strung through holes pierced in the leaf and protected with painted wooden boards. The writing instruments were styluses, brushes or quills. Characters incised with a stylus would have ink rubbed into them.

Paper A sheet material made from matted plant fibres. It is used for books, pictures, design work, packaging, fans, decorative artefacts and even clothing. The earliest surviving paper known today was found in the Great Wall of China and dates from about AD 150, by which time paper had begun to replace silk as a writing material in China. In Europe papermaking was introduced into Spain by the Moors in the 12th century, and soon afterwards paper was being manufactured in France and Italy. By the end of the 15th century it was in great demand for printing. Paper was made by hand, with various mechanical aids, until the 19th century, when the first patent for a papermaking machine was taken out in 1806 by Henry Fourdrinier.

Whether made mechanically or by hand, paper is formed by creating a sheet out of a liquid pulp of cellulose fibres suspended in water. The fibrous raw plant material is initially

A papercut showing the arms of the 4th Earl of Orrery, by Nathaniel Bermingham, early 18th century. Papercutting, using scissors and a sharp knife, was largely an amateur pastime, although Bermingham was a professional artist and was also known as a pastellist.

broken down by cutting and pounding or maceration (called beating) and then by cooking, followed by further processing. The type of fibre used and the extent of preparation will determine the fibre length, quality and type of paper produced. The resulting pulp is poured or scooped onto a woven mesh called a paper mould, through which the water drains away, leaving a film of more or less randomly arranged fibres. The type of mould (see below) determines the surface appearance of the paper and its qualities in transmitted light. The newly formed paper sheet is squeezed between woollen felts to extract water and consolidate the fibres, and allowed to dry thoroughly. Various additions, such as gelatine size, may be made to the paper either before or after sheet-forming. Other processes, such as applying pressure by machine (calendering) or hand burnishing, may be carried out to modify the paper surface, depending on the use to which the paper will be put: for example, paper for marbling must be flexible and uniform; for machine printing it must be smooth, even glossy; for intaglio printing by hand a rougher paper is satisfactory, but it must be strong and flexible when dampened.

Raw materials Papermaking fibres of many origins have been tried over the centuries, but cotton and wood are the two most important modern sources. Only natural cellulose is capable of forming a true paper sheet because, unlike synthetics, the fibres have the potential to bond by enmeshing within the sheet without the aid of adhesives. The various processes of purifying and pulping the plant material are all intended to produce fibres capable of bonding in this way. Rags from discarded clothing and linen were the main sources of paper fibre in Europe until the 18th century, when wood was suggested. The bulk of industrially manufactured paper is now made from wood pulp, while Western hand papermakers continue to use cotton, linen, hemp and other fibres which, unlike wood, need less chemical processing to produce a good-quality pulp. For a durable paper, lignin must be removed from the wood pulp, since it will otherwise break down over time, causing discoloration and acid degradation of the cellulose, as happens with newsprint. Excessive processing of any papermaking material, such as bleaching or prolonged beating, will also shorten and weaken the cellulose fibres. However, to produce very fine and translucent paper, such as tracing paper, it is necessary to beat the pulp thoroughly.

Because of the quantity of clean water needed for paper-making, and later for power, early paper mills were sited by rivers and streams, those in chalk and limestone areas giving superior, durable paper owing to the alkaline content of the water. The best-known trade mills in Europe by the 18th century were Fabriano in Italy, Arches in France and Whatman in England.

Handmade paper Until the beginning of the 19th century all paper was made by hand. Although various processes were introduced before then to mechanize the preparation of the pulp, such as the water-powered stamping mill, the sheets of paper themselves were until that time formed by hand on individual moulds, a practice that now survives only on a small scale. The moulds are operated by a 'vatman', who dips the flat mould in a tank of pulp (the 'vat'), ensures even distribution of the matted fibres on the mould by skilful manipulation, and then 'couches' the newly formed sheet by removing the deckle (frame), turning the mould face down and pressing it onto a woollen felt. A double thick (or 'duplex') sheet can be made by couching two sheets on top of each other. Couching felts and sheets of paper are alternated in a pile to form a 'post', which is then compressed in a hand-operated screw press (or usually nowadays a hydraulic press) to extract water. The new paper, still wet, is then peeled away from the felt and dried, either by hanging over a string or on a rack in a naturally ventilated drying loft, or by the use of artificial heat on a metal plate. If a sizing material has not been added to the vat, the dried sheets are then treated with gelatine to give the paper some water-resistance and finally they are pressed again. Asian papers are made by the same principles, with some differences (see below), and

Forming a sheet of handmade paper at Barcham Green & Co., 1980s. The vatman has just dipped the mould into the watery pulp.

papers from the Indian subcontinent are finished with a coating of starch paste rather than gelatine size. Asian papers are traditionally dried in the sun on wooden boards.

Handmade paper can usually be distinguished from machine-made imitations by the 'deckle edges', if these have not been trimmed off, or by the lack of grain direction (see below). Modern Western handmade papers are sometimes described as 'all rag' or 'rag' papers, but this does not necessarily mean that they are made from recycled cotton and linen clothing; they are more likely to have been made from cotton fibre than wood pulp.

While commercial hand papermaking has dwindled in the second half of the 20th century, amateurs have taken up the craft, recognizing its decorative potential.

Machine-made paper Mechanization has made possible not only rapid and plentiful paper manufacture, but also the creation of seamless lengths of paper, impossible to make by hand. The first machine designed to form paper on a continuous conveyor belt of flexible wire mesh was developed around 1800 in France by Nicholas-Louis Robert. In England the London stationers Henry and Sealy Fourdrinier financed the construction of a similar machine, which came to bear their name, and by 1807 a range of machines was being manufactured. At the same time the supply of rags for papermaking had become insufficient, and alternative fibres—including esparto grass and wood, among others—were eventually made available.

By 1830 machines were capable of making paper about 75 cm in width at a speed of 18 m per minute. At the same time heated drying cylinders had been developed, so that the newly formed paper did not have to be cut into sheets for drying but could be left as a continuous roll. The principle of forming paper from pulp drained on a mesh and then transferred to felt remains the same in industrial papermaking as in hand papermaking.

Although machine-made paper can be as strong and durable as that made by hand, given suitable fibres and preparation, it has the drawback of 'grain direction'; in other words, most of the paper fibres are aligned parallel to the machine direction. Machine-made paper is weaker along the grain than across, and it also expands more across the grain when wet. This is an important consideration in bookbinding, or in the creation of any artefact for which the paper has to be folded, flexed or wetted.

Even before the Fourdrinier machine was invented, other machines to prepare the paper pulp were already in use. The most notable of these was the Hollander beater, developed by a Dutch papermaker in the late 17th century as a more efficient alternative to the water-powered stamping mills, which had themselves replaced the primitive pestle and mortar.

Eastern traditions In Japan the traditional form of paper (*washi*) is handmade, using bast fibres from the inner bark of the paper mulberry plant, *Broussonetia papyrifera*. Other plant fibres such as *gampi*, *mitsumata*, wood, straw and cotton are used to a lesser extent. Pulp preparation and sheet forming are similar to those in European hand papermaking, but there are some important differences between the sheet-forming techniques of East and West. In Eastern traditions, instead of a wire mould, the paper is formed on a flexible bamboo screen and the wet sheets are placed directly on top of each other, rather than interleaved with felts, before pressing to remove excess water. Instead of gelatine size, a vegetable mucilage is added to the pulp and the resulting product is more absorbent than European paper. The fibre length is also longer, giving a strong, translucent but very flexible paper. This is used for many purposes other than writing, painting and printing: in Japan clothing, packaging, window panes and string, for example, have also been made from paper.

The early example of paper found in 2nd-century China was made from rags, perhaps offcuts from the woven textiles previously used for writing on. Today bamboo fibre and rice straw are the predominant fibres in Chinese handmade paper. The papermaking techniques used are similar to those in Japan, but the resulting paper has different qualities because bamboo and straw give shorter fibres. The paper is fine-textured, absorbent and has little strength when wet, but it is well suited to drawing and painting with a brush and to woodblock printing. It is also traditionally used to make offerings for the dead, called spirit papers, which range from imitation banknotes to clothing and even large, ingeniously crafted artefacts such as motor vehicles. Chinese handmade paper is sometimes mistakenly referred to as 'rice paper'.

Moulds One universal item of papermaking equipment is the paper mould, consisting of a flat, rectangular mesh onto which the macerated paper pulp in a watery suspension is scooped or poured and allowed to drain. The appearance of a sheet of paper is largely determined by the kind of mould on which it is formed. The dimensions of a handmade sheet of paper are also closely related to the mould.

The earliest moulds were probably made of woven cloth stretched on a wooden frame, onto which the pulp was poured and left to dry. This type of mould is still used in parts of Asia. However, the need for mass production led to the development in the East, and much later in Europe, of moulds from which the wet sheet of paper could be transferred. In China this was accomplished early on by making a flexible mat of split bamboo held in a rigid frame. The mat could be removed from the frame and the paper couched. The raised pattern of threads which held the split bamboos together gave rise to the so-called 'laid' type of paper, as the threads and bamboo strips created tiny variations (now known as 'chain lines' and 'laid lines' respectively) in the thickness of the layer of fibres deposited over them. This pattern was imitated in the earliest European moulds, even though they were made from a rigid mesh of metal wire, usually brass. Wove paper, which is smooth, is formed on a mould with a uniform pattern, like a plain weave textile, the

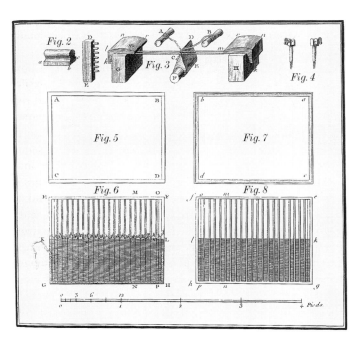

An 18th-century illustration of paper moulds, from Diderot's Encyclopédie des arts et des métiers. *This type of mould was in general use in Europe until c.1800 and is still employed in hand production. The front and back of the mould (figs. 6 and 8) are shown side by side, with the deckle (figs. 5 and 7) above and the wire mesh in the process of being attached. The mould is made with a hardwood frame bound with brass strips and corners and with wooden ribs, wedge-shaped in cross section. The frame supports the mesh of brass wire on which the paper is formed. The wire is stitched together in a 'laid' or 'wove' pattern (laid in this case, as the wires form distinctive parallel lines). The watermark has not yet been added.*

mesh being woven on a loom. In the West wove moulds were not made until the mid-18th century, in response to demand for a smooth printing paper.

The Western paper mould differs from the Eastern one essentially in its rigidity: the mesh is fitted permanently to a robust wooden frame, over which rests a second, detachable frame (called the deckle) which retains the wet pulp. On lifting the mould from the vat, the papermaker removes the deckle in order to couch the sheet, leaving a slightly wavy edge of variable thickness where some fibres have caught under the deckle. This is called the deckle edge. It can be imitated on machine-made paper but will be more regular than the genuine deckle edge.

Watermarks can be created by machine in various ways, but traditionally they were formed from metal wires laced on

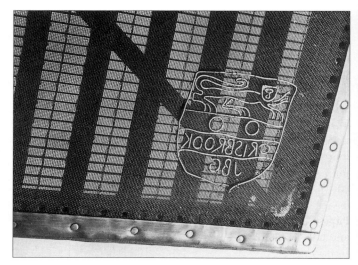

The watermark for a 20th-century, handmade wove paper by the firm of Barcham Green & Co. at Hayle Mill in Kent, England. The picture shows the corner of the paper mould with a wire pattern stitched on to the wove mesh. The layer of paper fibres deposited over the watermark pattern will be slightly thinner than elsewhere in the sheet, thus giving the mark its translucency. The brass-bound edges of the mould are visible because the deckle is not in place.

to the mould and they appear in the finished paper as a slightly translucent outline, usually recording the date and place of manufacture by a symbol. The first watermarks were simply trade marks, which featured on Italian papers towards the end of the 13th century. By the 19th century watermarks had become so elaborate as to be an art form in themselves. European and American hand papermakers' moulds and their watermarks are appreciated today in their own right, for their intricate designs and fine craftsmanship.

Sizes The dimensions of handmade paper sheets are obviously limited by the practical size of a mould, which ideally has to be handled by one person in order to form a perfectly even layer of fibres. Some oriental moulds have divisions intended to form several sheets on one dipping; the larger moulds are sometimes handled by two people and can also be suspended from above with strings or wires to support the weight. This is only possible because of the detachable screen on which the paper is formed. A common paper size in Japan would be 58 × 159 cm, while in China the largest hand-mould size ever used is thought to be 123 × 213 cm. In Europe a range of sizes has been in use over the centuries, and many have been designated with special names referring to their use or their watermark. Among the standard sizes are Antiquarian (the largest, at 31 × 53 in., or 79 × 135 cm), Crown (15 × 20 in., or 38 × 51 cm), Foolscap (13½ × 17 in., or 34 × 43 cm), Imperial (22 × 30 in., or 56 × 76 cm) and Royal (19 × 24 in., or 48 × 61 cm).

The terms folio, quarto and octavo (and occasionally twelvemo and so on) refer not to precise paper sizes but to the number of times a given sheet of paper is folded after printing to form the pages of a book or pamphlet. The terms have been current since the end of the 15th century. Generally speaking, folio means a book or manuscript about 30 cm in height, or a sheet of paper folded once where two pages were printed on each side of the sheet; quarto measures not more than 32 × 24 cm and has the paper folded twice, into four leaves giving eight pages; octavo describes a book 13–15 cm × 19–24 cm, where the paper is folded into eight leaves.

Papier mâché A material made from paper, either pulped and bound with glue and other substances, or laminated. The term derives from the French *mâcher* ('to chew') but first appeared in England in the early 18th century. The use of papier mâché is naturally linked to papermaking, which itself emerged in China. In the Far East moulded paper pulp has been used as a support for lacquer since around AD 600 or earlier, and the Tibetans made pasteboard at an early date. However, papier mâché became widely known in Europe only in the late 17th century. Gradually it evolved from a material of limited use into one of great strength and versatility that could be employed for buttons, small decorative items, furniture, architectural mouldings and imitation plasterwork.

Early European papier mâché was made of waste rag paper boiled in water, mashed into a paste and bound with gum arabic or glue; later, specialist suppliers provided paper pulp and unsized paper sheets for large-scale production. The resulting paste was then moulded into small articles such as mirrors and sconces. The moulds were made of wood, with a drainage hole, or metal, and had to be greased to release the item. Alternatively, pasteboard sheets were made by passing the pulp through rollers and then drying it slowly. An improved pasteboard was patented by Henry Clay of Birmingham in 1772 (see colour plate XV). Ten layers of paper were laid and glued in a metal mould, then waterproofed by immersion in linseed oil and dried at high temperature. The finished boards could be cut with a saw, or turned with a lathe, and made into furniture with moulded trims. Die-pressing was introduced in the late 18th century to shape heavy panels, and in 1847 the firm of Jennings & Betteridge, also of Birmingham, took out a patent for steam pressing. This softened the board and made it pliable, enabling it to be die-pressed into more elaborate shapes.

Since papier mâché was naturally grey or brown in colour, it was desirable to paint the finished article. This was done by means of JAPANNING or, in France, with vernis Martin. Both techniques used varnishes made from blends of resins to replicate the effects of oriental lacquerwares, and indeed papier

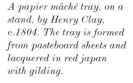

A papier mâché tray, on a stand, by Henry Clay, c.1804. The tray is formed from pasteboard sheets and lacquered in red japan with gilding.

mâché became virtually synonymous with japanning. Henry Clay's panels proved ideal for the stoved finishes used on PONTYPOOL WARE since, unlike wood, they could withstand great heat and did not warp. Most japanning was in black, but red, green and yellow grounds were also possible. Designs were painted in oil paint or in metallic powders, including Dutch metal. Gold leaf was used in the better wares, and mother-of-pearl decoration became popular in the mid-19th century. Thin slices of shell were stuck to the prepared surface and then covered with many layers of stove-dried lacquer. Finally the lacquer was rubbed down with a pumice stone to reveal the shell once more.

Papyrus A laminated sheet material used as a support for writing and painting, and made from the plant *Cyperus papyrus*, a variety of sedge which originally grew along the River Nile in Egypt. The stems were cut into thin strips and hammered together in layers at right angles to each other; they then bonded with their own sap, with wheat flour paste sometimes being added between the layers. Papyrus was used in Egypt in ancient times and in southern Europe until at least the 10th century.

Parcel gilt A partly gilt surface mainly used for decorative purposes and often found on silverware. It is applied by firegilding, whereby the surface is partly coated with a gold–mercury amalgam. The object is then heated and the mercury evaporates off, leaving only the gold.

Parchment A material made by stretching a wet skin, which has been unhaired using lime, on a framework and allowing it to dry in the untanned condition under tension. It is used as a writing surface, for bookbinding and for the painting of miniatures. Often the grain layer is scraped away, using a special knife, and the surfaces are then treated with hot water, chalk and other materials to remove grease and give a more uniform substrate. Parchments are generally prepared from calf-, deer-, goat- or sheepskins, but it is possible to use other raw materials. See also VELLUM.

Pargeting A form of incised, moulded or modelled ornament, executed in lime putty or mixtures of lime and gypsum plaster, used in south-east England in the 15th–16th centuries to decorate the exterior of timber-framed buildings. Incised decoration was made by drawing a wooden tool or a wooden comb through wet plaster applied either to infill panels between the timber members or over them (for illus-

A parchment maker, from Das Hausbuch der Mendelschen Zwölf Brüderstifting zu Nürnberg (1395).

tration see page 373). Repeated patterns were often produced in this way. Relief decoration, thought to have been inspired by the stucco panels created by Italian artists at Nonsuch Palace in the 1540s, was made with wooden or beeswax moulds or was modelled by hand. Animal hair was added for strength and tallow was sometimes used as a plasticizer and a water-repellent. The surface of the pargeting was frequently limewashed; occasionally linseed oil or wax was used as a protective coating.

Parian cement A plaster used for interior stucco decoration and obtained from gypsum plaster. In a process patented in 1846 by J. Keating, a London maker of scagliola, the plaster is first soaked in a solution of borax (sodium borate) and cream of tartar (potassium hydrogen tartrate) in water and then heated. The resulting plaster has good tensile strength and can be painted two days after setting, a great advantage over lime-based stucco. It is also used for sgraffito.

Parian ware A biscuit porcelain resembling white marble. It was invented in the 1840s at the Copeland factory in England and was made from china clay and china stone but fired only to approximately 1200°C, so it was not hard enough or translucent enough to be classified as true porcelain. Its manufacture followed the fashion in France for biscuit porcelain, which was used to make ceramic figures and sculptures. Most Parian figures were white but some were tinted with metallic oxides to resemble other stones, such as malachite or porphyry. They were produced by slip casting. A type of Parian ware was made in America and also by Wedgwood in England, where it is sometimes called Carrara porcelain.

Parkesine See SYNTHETIC IVORY.

Parquetry A decorative surface formed in wood by laying variously coloured or patterned thin blocks or veneers into closely fitting geometric patterns. It is often used on floors.

Pashmina See CASHMERE.

Passementerie A term covering a broad range of decorative textile trimmings principally made by plaiting. The word is derived from the French *passement* ('braid').

Paste Glass faceted and polished in imitation of gemstones, especially diamonds (see colour plate v). Although various forms of paste have been used since antiquity, the term is usually applied to strass, a brilliant lead glass developed in the 1730s by Georges-Frédéric Strass. Strass is a borosilicate of potassium and lead, with small additions of alumina and arsenic. It is soft and highly refractive and can be modified with metallic oxides to represent coloured gemstones.

Paste paper A decorated paper made by coating paper with pigment bound in a starch paste adhesive. While the mixture is wet, hand tools such as brushes, spatulas and combs can be used to create a unique pattern by partly scraping away the pigment to expose the paper. Woodblocks or small rollers cut with a design can also be impressed into the paste. The colour of the pattern will be more intense where the block has created thicker layers of paste at the edge of the motifs. The pattern is fixed as the starch paste dries, giving a slightly translucent effect. Paste papers have been used since the late 16th century as coverings for small items such as books and boxes. The technique flourished in Germany (where it was called *kleisterpapier*) in the second half of the 18th century

Paste paper printed in ochre on handmade laid paper, Venice, 20th century. The soft vertical lines indicate the edges of the blocks.

and the first quarter of the 19th. It requires little equipment and has been successfully revived in the 20th century.

Coloured starch paste was used as an alternative to printer's ink in 18th-century Italy by the company of Remondini e Figli to print from pearwood blocks. The sheets of handmade paper, about 35 × 46 cm in size, were first brushed with a background tint. The patterned blocks were about 20 × 30 cm and repeated twice or more on each sheet, using two to four different colours. Metal pins or brass strips driven into the blocks printed fine dots and lines. Remondini's blocks were reused by the firm of Rizzi to print decorated papers by the same techniques, using starch paste, into the mid-20th century.

Pastel See GRAPHIC MEDIA and WOAD.

A small casket with pastiglia decoration, partially gilded, Italy, 16th century.

Pastiglia A method of decorating small gilded items with mouldings made from a white powder obtained from lead. The ground lead was exposed to vinegar vapour in a closed jar and so converted to a powder. Mixed with egg white, it became a malleable paste that could be cast in small lead moulds and then applied to a gilded surface with animal glue. The decoration was left white, or painted and gilded.

Pastiglia was used in Renaissance Italy on small caskets. Too fragile to be applied to larger items, it is not to be confused with the gesso decoration that was common on large Italian cassoni.

Patchwork A group of embroidery techniques that employ pieces of fabric cut out and shaped in such a way that, when sewn together, they form a complete, and usually regularly patterned, flat cloth. The techniques are associated with bed covers and QUILTING and are also sometimes called inlay patchwork to distinguish them from onlay patchwork, which is a form of appliqué.

Pâte de verre A glass produced from a paste of ground glass to which a flux has been added to lower the melting-point. The mixture is pressed or poured into a mould and fused by heating. When cold the glass has a matt surface. This can be polished smooth or refined by carving. Sometimes the matt effect is exaggerated by placing asbestos or ceramic fibre inside the mould.

Pâte de verre (the name is French for 'glass paste') was first used in ancient Egypt, at least as early as the mid-2nd millennium BC, to form small objects. It was revived in 19th-century France and is still popular with glass artists. It has also been used to imitate semi-precious stones.

Pâte dure See HARD PASTE PORCELAIN.

Pâte sur pâte See SLIP DECORATION.

Pâte tendre See SOFT PASTE PORCELAIN.

Patent leather Vegetable-tanned leather which has been finished with multiple layers of linseed oil based varnishes, usually containing Prussian blue, lampblack and plasticizing agents such as castor oil. The varnishes were designed to give a very bright, smooth, mirror-like, water-resistant finish which completely obliterated the leather surface. The flesh split (see FLESH) was very often used. The original patent was awarded to the Englishman John Bellamy in 1794, but finishes of the type he described appear to have been widely used some years before. The major innovations which allowed manufacture of patent leathers (sometimes referred to as 'japanned leathers') to develop so rapidly in the first third of the 19th century were the inclusion in the formulation of catalysts such as Prussian blue and the introduction of heated stoves. These both accelerated the drying process significantly. Large quantities of patent leather were used for carriage covers, harness work and military accoutrements. Modern patent leathers are made using polyurethane-based finishes.

It has been suggested that the term 'patent' or 'japanned' was originally used only for leather that had been finished on the FLESH side or for which a flesh split had been used, to distinguish it from enamelled leather, which is treated on the GRAIN side. It is probable, however, that the terms have always been used for treatment on either side of the leather.

Patination The chemical alteration of a metal surface, resulting in a change of colour. The recoloured surface, or patina, can be produced by natural or artificial means. A natural patina is formed as the result of a reaction between the metal and its environment. Artificial patination can be carried out with the aid of chemicals or heat or a combination of the two. Copper alloys are well known for their patinas, with colours ranging from deep black and purple to brown and green.

Patola See IKAT.

Pattern welding The process of hammer-welding together strips, wires or rods of low-carbon steel to create a piece of steel with an intricate surface structure or pattern. The strips, wires or rods are twisted together, heated and forge-welded by hammering. The technique probably originated in Germany in the 3rd century AD and remained in use in Europe until the 11th century, mainly in the production of swords and other weapons. It used to be thought that pattern welding was carried out primarily to increase the strength and sharpness of these weapons but nowadays it is generally accepted that the main purpose was purely decorative.

Pattern-moulded glass See MOULD-BLOWN GLASS.

Pavé setting See STONE SETTING.

Peacock's eye A descriptive term applied to figure in wood, comprising small circular markings similar to BIRD'S EYE, but with a halo that fades out from the centre.

Pearl A form of organic gem material, often spherical, obtained from various species of double-shelled mollusc. The formation of a pearl occurs in response to an irritation (usually a parasite) within the shell of the animal. This causes it to excrete nacreous material, the lustrous substance which lines the inside of the shell, in order to surround the irritant and protect itself. Blister pearls are formed around alien material, such as a piece of grit, adhere to the inside of the shell and are often hemispherical in shape. Spherical or encysted pearls develop inside sacs which form within the muscle of the animal. Pearls that develop an irregular shape owing to the presence of an obstruction, such as muscle or other tissue, are referred to as baroque (or 'barrok'); very small pearls are termed seed pearls (see colour plate 00). The nacreous material, which builds up in thin layers, consists of aragonite (a form of calcium carbonate), conchiolin (a proteinaceous material) and water. The aragonite forms as thin,

HH Rajah Singh of Khetie,
1907. His rich costume
includes rows of enormous
pearls, diamond rings and
gold embroidery.

overlapping plates arranged at right angles to the surface of
the pearl. The characteristic lustre of pearl, known as its
orient, is produced by the diffraction of light by the edges of
these plates and by the interference of light by the thin
layers; the same effect can be observed in a thin film of oil on
the surface of water.

The production of cultured pearls, developed commercially in Japan in the early 20th century, involves the same process: a nucleus, usually a sphere of shell, is inserted into the animal, which then produces a nacreous coating. The Chinese had, however, discovered a technique for producing a cultured blister pearl in the 13th century which involved placing a foreign body on the inside of the shell. They used it to coat small objects, such as tin figures of Buddha, with nacreous material; once the coating was formed the figures were sawn off the interior of the shell. Pearls are generally creamy white but also occur in a variety of colours, including pink, yellow, blue and black; the cause of such coloration is not known. For use as beads pearls are drilled from either end with a needle mounted in a bow drill.

The most significant source of natural pearls for jewellery is the pearl oyster, *Pinctada radiata*, which has been gathered by divers from the Persian Gulf since *c*.300 BC; it is also found in the Gulf of Manaar, between India and Sri Lanka. The adult oysters of this species live in clusters and breed by depositing eggs or spermatozoa into the surrounding water. A fertilized egg will begin to develop a shell within 24 hours. After a week it will attach itself to a hard surface and will grow rapidly for two years. The shells are collected for their potential pearls when they reach 60 mm in diameter. Other types of seawater animal, such as the *Haliotis* and the giant conch, also form pearls. *Haliotis* pearls are hollow and have a strongly coloured iridescence; conch pearls can be pink or white and do not have a nacreous surface.

In ancient India pearls were used in jewellery and as amulets. The Greeks and Romans wore pearl jewellery and also used them to embellish clothing and furniture. The Chinese imported Red Sea pearls from around the 5th century BC and, in addition to ornamentation, used them medicinally. The Chinese also gathered freshwater pearls from a species of mussel, as did North American Indians, who used them as grave goods. Freshwater pearls have also been exploited in Europe since the 1st century BC. Freshwater pearls do not have the same lustre as seawater specimens. Pearls have been used throughout European history for jewellery and, at times, to decorate clothing and hair. Flat pearl buttons are made from shell.

Pearls have long been imitated. The Chinese and, from the 17th century, the French used fish-scale essence to line the inside of glass beads as simulants. In Renaissance Europe imitations were moulded using crushed glass, egg white and snail slime. Modern imitations have been made by coating glass, plastic or vegetable ivory beads with an iridescent material.

A number of analytical techniques are used to differentiate natural, cultured and imitation pearls. Natural and cultured pearls have a slightly rough surface, owing to the build-up of the nacreous material, which can be detected by drawing the pearl over the teeth; imitation pearls are, by contrast, smooth. More sophisticated tests involve the measurement of specific gravity; imitation pearls have a low specific gravity, whereas the specific gravity of cultured pearls is higher than natural pearls because of the density of the implanted nucleus. Radiography can detect the structural differences between natural, cultural and imitation pearl. Because pearls are composed of calcium carbonate they will react with acids, even those present in minute amounts on the skin. This can etch the surface and destroy its lustrous appearance.

Pearl work See BEADWORK.

Pearwood A fairly hard and strong, stable but not durable wood from the European pear tree (*Pyrus communis*). It is similar to limewood but harder, and displays distinct annual rings and large mottled figure. Available only in small sizes, it is easily worked, and is used for drawing instruments, carving, small furniture and cabinet work. The Chinese pear (*P. sinensis*) resembles yellow boxwood and is similarly used for fancy turnery and printing blocks. Various other woods, some of which are not true pear, are known by such names as white pear (*Apodytes dimidiata* from Kenya), hard pear (*Olinia cymosa* from South Africa) and the dogwood pear (*Pomaderris apetala* from Australia).

Pen A writing or drawing instrument based on a hollow tube with a reservoir for ink and a tip (nib) shaped to form the desired line. The modern steel pen has been in use only since the mid-18th century. Before that time virtually all writing and drawing in the West were done with a quill: goose and turkey wing feathers were the most suitable, and the nib was cut by the user (hence 'pen knife'). For larger writing, reed pens (often made from bamboo) have been in use since ancient times. Like the quill, the end of the reed is cut to an oblique angle to form the nib and the tip is slit parallel to the shaft to direct the flow of ink when pressure is applied. Both reed and quill pens can be made to hold more ink by inserting a thin metal loop inside the shaft and behind the nib. Nevertheless, this type of pen has to be dipped frequently in ink, and this prompted the development in the 19th century of fountain pens with refillable reservoirs higher up the shaft. The first was patented in 1884 by Lewis E. Waterman.

Other pens capable of prolonged use without refilling were developed in the second half of the 20th century. Unlike ballpoint pens, which use a greasy, viscous ink, felt tip pens (or, more accurately, porous pointed pens) use dyes with quick-drying solvents which flow easily from the fibrous nib and are now commonly used by artists and designers. A rod of compacted wool felt was used in the original pens of the 1940s and 1950s, nylon or polyester fibres were introduced in the 1960s, and nibs have subsequently been made of extruded plastic or plastic granules. Reservoir materials rely similarly on technological developments in synthetic materials to control ink flow. Unfortunately, the inks used in these pens frequently fade, owing to their non-lightfast dyes.

Pentelic marble A hard cream-coloured marble in which weathering of iron and mica impurities produces a golden patina. It can also contain pale grey mottling owing to the presence of iron pyrites. It was quarried from Mount Pentelikon, north-east of Athens, and was used to construct the Parthenon and other buildings in Greece and Rome, such as the Arch of Titus.

Penwork A technique for decorating japanned furniture, popular in Regency England. The surface was first painted black, then a design was applied in white japan (pigment in a spirit varnish medium) and the details overpainted in black indian ink with a fine quill pen. Alternatively, the design could be executed in black ink on a pale wood ground.

Perkin's mauve A bright purple dye first produced by W.H. Perkin as he attempted to synthesize quinine, in 1856. Used on silk and wool, and fashionable for a decade, the dye itself was named 'mauvine' by the French and the colour became known in England as 'Perkin's purple'. For many decades after it was replaced by faster dyes, mauve remained the colouring matter for the British penny stamp. See also ANILINE DYES.

Persian A type of vegetable-tanned leather made from the skins of HAIR SHEEP originating from the Indian subcontinent. It was manufactured particularly in England during the late 19th century and early 20th, for small leather goods (for illustration see page 276).

Perspex A trade name for clear ACRYLIC, registered by ICI on 16 November 1934. It is derived from the Latin verb *per-spicere* ('to see through'). Perspex was sold commercially by 1936.

Petit point A canvaswork embroidery stitch, leaning to the right and rising by one ground thread to produce a strong, flat surface covered with small stitches. The name also refers to canvaswork made with this stitch. The *petit point* stitch is sometimes also called tent stitch; a 'tall' tent stitch is Gobelins stitch, or GROS POINT.

Petuntse See CHINA STONE.

Pewter A tin alloy which can contain small amounts of lead, copper, antimony and bismuth. Apart from a pewter flask found in Egypt, dating from *c.*1450 BC, there is little evidence of the use of pewter before Roman times, when it was used extensively for tableware. In England the composition of pewter was carefully defined and guarded by the Worshipful

A pewterer, from Das Hausbuch der Mendelschen Zwölf Brüderstifting zu Nürnberg *(1395). He is casting part of a flagon by pouring molten pewter from the ladle into the mould. The separate cast parts are then soldered together and finished on a lathe.*

Company of Pewterers in London from the 15th century onwards. Three alloys were allowed. For flatware (plates and dishes, also called sadware) only an alloy of almost pure tin with 1–2 % copper was allowed, called fine metal. Hollowware (bowls and vessels) could only be made using an alloy of fine metal with a maximum 4 % lead, called trifling metal or trifle. The third pewter, which could not be used for food or drink, could contain up to 15 % lead and was called lay (or ley) metal. From the second half of the 17th century antimony was sometimes added to fine metal to make a harder alloy, called superfine hard metal (or French metal). In England pewter wares were usually kept plain, with WRIGGLEWORK engraving as the only decoration. On the Continent, especially in France and Germany, highly decorated pewter ware was cast with a low relief in the Renaissance style. Until the end of the 18th century the only way of making pewter ware was to cast the different parts in stone or metal moulds and solder them together before finishing on a lathe.

In the last quarter of the 18th century producers started to make objects from pewter sheet containing antimony and very similar to superfine hard metal, by using the new techniques of the fused plate industry, such as stamping and spinning. Pewter wares produced using these techniques and alloyed with antimony are called Britannia metal wares. This BRITANNIA METAL was much harder and stronger than the old cast pewter and made it possible to work with less metal. It therefore enabled manufacturers to produce cheaper and more elaborate wares than had the old method of casting in expensive moulds. Cast pewter wares continued to be produced, but on a smaller scale, usually for pub measures. At the beginning of the 20th century there was a short revival of pewter in the Art Nouveau and Art Deco styles through such well-known trade names as Liberty (for whom various firms manufactured an Art Nouveau pewter sold under the trade name Tudric), Kaiserzinn and the Württembergische Metallwaren Fabrik.

Phase separation See JUN GLAZE.

Phenolic plastics See BAKELITE.

Photogravure, photolithography, photomechanical printing
See PRINTING.

Pickling The removal of oxides and vitrified flux from metal by immersion in a diluted acid. After hard soldering or brazing precious metals or copper alloys, an oxide layer and a

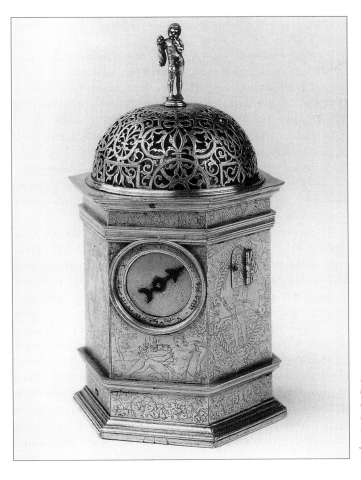

A table clock in firegilded brass with a pierced work dome, France, 1560. The case is decorated with engraving, while the small figure on top has been cast by the lost wax process.

glazed layer of flux are formed on the metal surface. This surface can be cleaned by immersion in a solution of 10% sulphuric acid in water. The solution is called pickle.

Piece moulding See CASTING.

Pierced work A type of decoration found on precious and non-precious metalwork, achieved by perforating the metal sheet. It is cut out with a piercing saw, or punched out with a FLY PRESS, and is sometimes called ajour. For pierced work in wood, see FRETWORK.

Pietre dure An Italian term (meaning 'hard stones'), used in Italy to describe any sculptural or decorative use of hard gemstones. Elsewhere the term has been applied specifically to a type of mosaic developed in Florence in the 16th century, composed mainly of hard stones, which is also known as

'Florentine mosaic' or *commesso di pietre dure* (see colour plate XVIII).

The Florentine technique grew out of earlier forms of intarsia work, a type of inlay used from antiquity in which pieces of coloured stone (and sometimes wood) were set into recesses chiselled into a sheet of stone, which formed the background. In 1588 Ferdinando I de' Medici founded the Grand Ducal manufactory in Florence devoted to pietre dure; it functioned until 1859 and produced table tops, altar frontals, panels to be inset in cabinets, cameos, vases, sculpture and decorative schemes. On flat surfaces foliage patterns and pictorial scenes were produced; three-dimensional work emphasized the colour and patterning of the stone.

The technique involves the use of opaque, richly coloured stones such as jasper, bloodstone, cornelian, lapis lazuli, malachite and rosso antico, most of which have a hardness of Mohs 6–7, allowing them to be highly polished. For two-dimensional work a full-size working drawing is prepared as the basis for selecting the stones and determining the shape of the pieces. Paper cutouts, traced from the drawing, are glued to pre-cut slices of stone. The slice is placed in a vice and cut with a bow saw strung with an iron wire. With each stroke an abrasive paste, containing diamond or ruby dust or metal powder, depending on the hardness of the stone, is applied to the wire. The cut pieces are assembled face down on a flat surface and the backs worked smooth with abrasives. Molten beeswax and colophony resin are poured over the back and a sheet of slate placed on top to form a firm support when inverted. The front surface is then polished with progressively finer grades of abrasive.

Outside Italy, centres for pietra dura work were established from the 16th century in Prague and in France. In Mogul India a similar technique was practised, probably influenced by Italian styles and involving the use of coloured stones to form foliage patterns set into white marble backgrounds. A technique which imitated the appearance of pietre dure was developed in Derbyshire in the 19th century, in which pieces of coloured stone were set into recesses in the local black carboniferous limestone.

Pig ivory Ivory obtained from the canines of the wild pig and from some domestic varieties of pig. These develop as very heavily curved tusks which sometimes form complete circles up to 10 cm in diameter but are rarely more than 2 cm thick.

A tough enamel layer covers the entire tusk but is usually worn through at the tip. Objects manufactured from pig ivory are always small in diameter and usually triangular in section. Because the ivory is so dense, no grain is visible, even under moderate magnification. The term 'boar's tusk ivory' is sometimes used.

Pigment A coloured powder which, unlike dye, is insoluble. When they are mixed in large amounts with a clear binding medium, pigments become paint, but they can also be added in small quantities to fluid materials to act as colouring agents. Lacquers and varnishes are traditionally tinted with

Trade card showing a horse-mill for the preparation of paint, late 18th century. The pigments and oil were fed through funnels to be ground between two horizontal stones. The firm claimed that 'One Pound of Colour ground in a Horse-Mill, will paint twelve Yards of Work, whereas Colour ground any other Way, will not do half that Quantity.' Later, steam power was used to increase production.

organic pigments, as these are light and remain in suspension, but inorganic pigments can also be used so long as the glaze or varnish is brushed out thinly. A limited range of pigments, including ochres, umbers and some inorganic pigments such as cobalt blue, chrome green and chrome yellow, can be used to colour lime mortars, concrete and plaster. The same set would also be suitable for colouring clay that is to be fired.

By the end of the 16th century a painter had access to a range of about fifteen fairly reliable inorganic pigments from three different sources. He had the ochres, umbers and other earths that had been in use since earliest times and which still form the core of today's palette. For his brightest colours he used crushed semi-precious stones such as blue lapis lazuli and azurite, green malachite and yellow orpiment, and he had access to a few synthetic pigments requiring simple chemistry: vermilion, blue smalt, green verdigris, lead white, red lead and lead tin yellow. To supplement this range he also used the less light-fast organic pigments, usually made up as lakes.

The Western pigment trade was centred on Venice. Some of the more exotic materials, such as lapis lazuli, yellow gamboge and red lac from the East, were very costly by the time they reached the far corners of Europe and could be used only for the most prestigious commissions. A few new pigments became important in the 17th century, such as Naples yellow and asphaltum, but the main impact on painters was the fact that as trade links improved, the old geographical distinctions became eroded. One of the most significant changes to the palette occurred in 1704 with the invention of Prussian blue. This cheap, reliable blue revolutionized the colour menu: lapis, smalt and azurite could be dropped; blue could be used in large amounts; and strong, reliable greens became a possibility for the first time.

The ability of 19th-century technology to purify metal ores meant an explosion of new pigments: brilliant yellows, reds and oranges based on cadmium; chrome yellows and greens; cobalt blues and greens; zinc, barium and strontium yellows; and French ultramarine. These inorganic introductions more than trebled the pigment range and introduced colours of unparalleled intensity and clarity. They were matched at the end of the century by a set of synthetic organic pigments that expanded the red and purple end of the spectrum. The 20th century saw a few important additions to the inorganic range, particularly cadmium red and titanium white, but the most important development was the expansion of synthetic organic lakes, dyes and stains.

Most pigments are processed on an industrial scale and are ground to a uniform size by steel rollers. Historic pigments from natural sources such as earths or minerals, or made by traditional methods by specialist suppliers, are ground less finely because particle size influences the depth of colour and even the actual hue.

For discussion of the colouring agents used in ceramics and glass, see METALLIC OXIDES.

Pigment dye A colour that is not fully absorbed, but is bound to the cloth by incorporation into an emulsion. Indigo in its paste state is a pigment dye.

Pillow lace An alternative name for BOBBIN LACE.

Pinchbeck A low-zinc, gold-coloured brass said to have been invented by Christopher Pinchbeck (1670–1732), a London watchmaker. It was used for jewellery and watch-cases and has a typical composition of 83–88% copper with 17–12% zinc.

Pine A very large and widespread group of important softwoods from the *Pinus* genus, of which there are 25 species in North America alone. They are normally distinguished by a qualifier such as Scots, blue, Austrian, Norway or sugar. The timbers can be generally characterized as being soft and light, stable and fairly durable. Their uses are as varied as their species but include building, furniture making, turning, musical instrument making and toy making. Pine can be polished very smooth and is therefore suitable as a base for gilding.

Tortoiseshell box with silver piqué inlay, France, early 18th century.

Pipe clay A white clay found in deposits with fire clay and traditionally used in France to make tobacco pipes and fine earthenwares. In the 18th century, at the ceramic factory at Luneville, pipe clay was combined with lime phosphate and used to make biscuit figures as an inexpensive substitute for biscuit porcelain. Pipe clay can be easily refined and vitrifies at approximately 1000°C. Sewer pipes are also said sometimes to be made from pipe clay but are in fact usually made from fire clay.

Piqué work A technique for decorating tortoiseshell or ivory objects by piercing them with small, profiled (often star-shaped) gold or occasionally silver rods to give the surface a spangled appearance. It was originated by the mid-17th century Neopolitan jeweller Laurentini and brought to perfection in late 17th-century France. The craft was then introduced by Huguenots into Britain, where it was popular in the 18th and 19th centuries.

A variation of the technique involves carving small recesses into the surface of ivory objects, which are then inlaid with metal spangles held in place by minute rivets. Tortoiseshell can be inlaid in a similar fashion, but the recesses are formed by laying the spangles onto the surface, which is softened, and then placing the shell in a press and allowing it to cool.

Pith paper A lustrous white sheet material made from the inner pith of the plant *Tetrapanax papyriferum*, cut spirally

A watercolour on pith paper, Canton, c.1900.

by hand to give sheets up to 30 cm square, with a slightly spongy texture. It has traditionally been used by the Chinese as a painting support and to make artificial flowers. Paintings on pith paper were predominantly made for export to the European and American market in the 19th century and depict Chinese costumes or trades and natural subjects such as butterflies and flowers, with a limited but brilliant palette of intense colours based on mineral pigments. They were often mounted on Chinese paper with a blue silk ribbon surround and bound into albums.

The pith is very brittle when dry or aged, but it becomes flexible with wetting. It has a superficial resemblance to the culinary rice paper, and is sometimes erroneously referred to as 'rice paper'.

Plain weave A weave in which the yarns in the warp and weft are spaced at equal intervals, and the weft passes from selvedge to selvedge in an over–under sequence, reversing to under–over on its return journey. A plain weave (sometimes called tabby weave) is identical on both sides. A wide range of cloths are made in this way. The names of plain and some twill cloths distinguish the weight and density of the fibre or the finish of the cloth; these include taffeta (crisp, closely woven cloths of silk or silk-like fibres), MUSLIN, canvas (strong, firm and closely woven, usually of cotton), baize (loosely woven wool with a napped, or brushed finish) and some tweeds. See also FLANNEL and FUSTIAN.

Plaiting A wide range of off-loom textile constructions characterized by the use of more than one element, and including wrapping, coiling, twining and braiding. Although these techniques are widely associated with basket-making and passementerie, they have a wide range of applications and are capable of producing an enormous variety of fabrics, including BOBBIN LACE. Wrapping, coiling and twining are related in that they utilize an active (binding) element and a passive (warp or core) element, making the results similar to some also produced on looms (see SOUMAK). In wrapping, the active element is taken around a passive element that runs at right or oblique angles to it; in coiling, the passive element is generally at right angles to the binding threads. Twining creates a twist; at its simplest, it uses two strands placed on either side of a core, twisted, placed over either side of an adjacent core, twisted, and so on. It is the basis of SPRANG.

Plaiting and braiding are often used interchangeably;

however, plaiting as a specific term refers to a method of two-dimensional intertwining, done in two or more directions (the characteristic hexagon opening in caned chair seats is made by plaiting in three directions). Braiding, or diagonal plaiting, whether flat, square or tubular, indicates that the outcome is much greater in length than in width or circumference.

Plane A moderately hard and light wood, with distinctive broad rays, from species of plane tree (*Platanus acerifolia*, *P. orientalis*, *P. occidentalis*, *P. racemosa*). It is sometimes called lacewood, and is used for veneers and cabinetmaking. For discussion of the plane as a tool, see WOODWORKING TOOLS.

Plangi A widespread and ancient RESIST DYEING method in which cloth is bound up with raffia or threads, a process that sometimes traps small objects such as seeds or stones. The technique is often combined with TRI-TIC, a combination of treatments known under the collective term *shibori*.

Planishing The light hammering of sheet metal supported on a stake with a planishing hammer. It is usually carried out after RAISING to remove rough hammer marks. A planishing hammer is lightweight, with highly polished, slightly domed or flat faces. When planishing is done properly, it leaves a smooth surface with a texture of evenly distributed hammer marks.

Planography A group of printing techniques, particularly the varieties of LITHOGRAPHY, which have no variation in the level of the printing surface and impart no physical impression to the printed paper.

Plaster A generic term used for various powdered substances, based on CLAY, GYPSUM or LIME, that become plastic when mixed with water and then set hard. In its plastic form plaster can be used for moulding and casting; it can also be trowelled onto walls as a surface finish or modelled *in situ* to form decorative elements. Aggregates, plasticizers, accelerators and retardants of set may be added to alter the workability and structural properties of the plaster. Clay is probably the most ancient and widely used form of plaster. It requires little processing and the addition of only plant or animal fibre, to reduce shrinkage, and an organic plasticizer, such as blood or dung.

Gypsum plaster is obtained by heating the hydrated calcium sulphate [$CaSO_4 2H_2O$] minerals, gypsum, alabaster or selenite, to temperatures between 130°C and 160°C. This process drives off 75% of the water incorporated in the crystal structure to form calcium sulphate hemihydrate [CaSO$_4$½H$_2$O]. The plaster, in powder form, reacts rapidly with water to reform needle-like crystals of hydrated calcium sulphate. Gypsum plaster, which is stronger than clay and sets more rapidly, was known to the ancient Egyptians and Mesopotamians and has been used for renders and mortars. Its rapid setting necessitated great skill in handling when used as a wall plaster. As it is slightly water-soluble, its use in temperate climates was largely confined to interior decoration, as a finish for walls and ceilings, although it was occasionally used, on its own or mixed with lime, for external work such as PARGETING or as an infill in timber-framed buildings. In such situations the surface had to be worked to a smooth finish and protected by effective roofing. In the Islamic world gypsum plaster was widely used, although lime did have applications in humid areas, where gypsum would

Pargeting on the façade of the Ancient House at Clare, Suffolk, 15th century. The decorative techniques used include freehand modelling (as seen on the upper floor elevation), freehand drawing of a tool through wet plaster (to the left of the window) and the use of wooden combs to form the incised patterns (to the right of the door).

have deteriorated, and for the production of hard, polished ornament which resembled marble. PLASTER OF PARIS is a pure form of gypsum plaster originally obtained in Paris. The material was first employed as a wall plaster but has had wider use in the production of cast ornament, sculpture and mould-making.

The production of lime plasters involves the heating of limestone to high temperatures (700–900°C) over a long period and thus requires the technology of building and operating kilns. Scarcity of fuel for such a procedure is thought to be the reason why the Egyptians did not use lime until the Roman period. Lime was, however, used in the Middle East as early as c.6000 BC for making sculpture and was used by the Minoans (3000–1500 BC) as a wall plaster on which frescos were painted. The Romans used lime extensively as a mortar, for relief decoration, and as a ground for wall painting.

The set of lime is very slow and requires the presence of carbon dioxide. Also, without additives the plaster is weak and prone to shrinkage and cracking. For mortar, sharp sand is added; stone dusts can also be included to tone in with adjacent masonry. For wall plaster, animal hair gives the lime and sand greater toughness and cohesion; in medieval work gypsum plaster was frequently added to lime as an accelerator of set. Additives to provide water-repellency, such as tallow or linseed oil, or to entrap air and thus improve the set, such as urine or beer, were traditionally used. For hand-modelled ornament gypsum was added, with a retardant such as glue, sour milk or wine, to allow a long working time. Marble powder was added as an aggregate because it permitted the rendering of fine detail. Lime plasters were commonly used in Europe, both internally and externally, but their long setting time of several months made decoration with paint or wallpaper difficult.

MARTIN'S CEMENT and KEENE'S CEMENT, both patented in the 1830s, involved the modification of gypsum plaster through heating and chemical treatments to produce a material which reliably set more slowly than gypsum but more rapidly than lime. This obviated the problems of difficulty in working and delay before decoration could be carried out.

See also PLASTERWORK.

Plaster of Paris A pure form of GYPSUM PLASTER used for moulding and casting and for the decoration of walls and ceilings (see PLASTERWORK). The name derives from the medieval quarrying of large gypsum deposits in the tertiary strata of Montmartre in the Paris basin. It was first imported into Britain in the 13th century, although similar gypsum plasters were soon produced from local sources such as the Trent Valley, where the gypsum mineral alabaster was quarried for sculpture.

Plaster of Paris is produced by heating the minerals gypsum, alabaster or selenite, which are composed of hydrated calcium sulphate [$CaSO_42H_2O$], i.e., calcium sulphate in which water is incorporated in the crystal structure, to 150–160°C. Early kilns consisted of a chamber filled with small pieces of gypsum with a fire lit at the bottom. Heating to this level chemically alters the material by removing 75% of the incorporated water, producing calcium sulphate hemihydrate [$CaSO_4\frac{1}{2}H_2O$]. For use the dry, powdered product is sprinkled into water and mixed to a creamy consistency. The amount of water used is important: the theoretical quantity of water necessary is 18% by weight; however, in practice up to 35% is commonly used to ensure that sufficient water is available for the reaction. If too much water is used, the resulting solid will be weak.

Plaster of Paris cast in flexible moulds for sections of ornament. In working on the restoration of Uppark House, Sussex, the plasterer is using 18th-century techniques to produce repetitive decorative elements. Here he is repairing imperfections in the cast with plaster applied with a spatula.

The plaster reacts rapidly with the water to form needle-like crystals of hydrated calcium sulphate which interlock with each other, giving plaster of Paris its strength. The set is rapid (approximately 30 minutes) and heat is evolved, producing a temporary expansion of the material. This is beneficial in casting as the plaster pushes into all areas of the mould. When the set is complete the plaster returns to its original size, thus facilitating the removal of the cast from the mould.

Plaster of Paris has been widely used to make anatomical casts, life and death masks, and copies of sculpture and architectural ornament for study purposes. Large-scale models for coins were often formed in clay and then cast in plaster. The surface of the subject would be covered with a release agent such as a wax, oil or resin varnish. Casting of simple forms could be achieved by waste mould casting, in which the surface is covered in plaster, pulled off when set. Plaster is then poured into the resulting mould, which is broken away once the cast has set. More complicated, undercut forms would require piece mould casting (see CASTING), in which the object is moulded in sections along the lines of undercuts so that the pieces can be lifted free of the surface once the plaster has set; this also allows the production of more than one cast.

Because plaster of Paris is pure white and highly porous, the surface is readily soiled and therefore casts were often coated. Materials such as tea, gum arabic, waxes, shellac, lime wash and oil-based paints have been used as coatings. Plaster of Paris is also frequently painted and oil-gilded. A sealant, such as animal glue, gum arabic or shellac, is applied first to reduce the porosity of the plaster. Distemper and oil-based paints are commonly used.

Plasterwork Architectural finishing or decoration executed in plaster. Plasterwork is used both internally and externally and can provide insulation, weatherproofing, embellishment and a degree of fire-resistance. The term STUCCO can also be used to describe all forms of decorative plasterwork.

Renders in clay and gypsum plasters were used in ancient Egypt, India and China to produce a smooth surface over rough stone or mud brick walls. The finished surface was often painted or decorated. The Minoans (3000–1550 BC) and Myceneans (1400–1100 BC) used lime plasters for covering masonry and wooden walls, as a basis for painted and low

relief decoration. Etruscan tombs dating to *c.*700 BC contained stucco decoration, sometimes pigmented to imitate coloured marbles. Mixes of lime and gypsum plaster were used during the Gandharan period (1st–3rd centuries AD) in Pakistan to produce moulded and modelled figurative decoration. The Romans used mixtures of lime and sand to build up preparatory layers over which finer applications of gypsum, lime, sand and marble dust were made; pozzolanic materials were sometimes added to produce a more rapid set (see LIME). They developed great virtuosity in handling the material, which could be coloured, polished to a high sheen or applied in a slurry by brush to suggest thin folds of drapery. Modelled stucco was employed throughout the Roman empire and plaster decoration continued to be used in Europe during the Middle Ages. Clay or lime was applied to interwoven twigs, reeds or wooden slats in wattle and daub construction. Renders, composed of lime and sand, and applied in one or more layers, were used externally, from the early

Plasterwork at Ditchley, Oxfordshire, 1725. It was executed by an Italian team, comprising Francesco Vassalli and the brothers Adalbertus and Francesco Serena Artari. The decoration was constructed in stages, using several techniques, including dragging a template through thick plaster to produce mouldings, the application of pre-cast elements such as the putti and the central plaque, and free-hand modelling to form the foliage.

Middle Ages, over rubble and other forms of masonry walling, as well as over rammed earth and timber-frame construction. Incised lines could be used to imitate ashlar or the surface could be roughcast or harled, by mixing sand, gravel or stone chippings into the lime and throwing it onto the wall with a brush or trowel, to give a rough texture and enhanced weather-resistance. From the Middle Ages surface decoration on building exteriors was produced by incising patterns into wet plaster or by moulding and free-hand modelling (see SGRAFFITO, PARGETING and illustration on page 373).

Following the fall of the Roman empire the addition of marble dust to plaster to allow the production of fine detail and a hard, smooth finish in hand-modelled and moulded decoration was not used until the Renaissance. It was then revived by Raphael and Giovanni da Udine, who discovered Roman stucco remains from excavated buildings and through experimentation prepared a mix containing marble dust which was used in the decoration of the papal palace. Stucco was widely exploited by Mannerist and Baroque artists throughout Europe because it allowed the production of elaborate high relief but lightweight figurative decoration. Stucco decoration was introduced into Britain by Italians working at Nonsuch Palace, built for Henry VIII in the 1540s, but was not widely used until the early 18th century.

Although there was wide variation in the composition of stucco used in the 17th and 18th centuries, lime and sand mixes prevailed, with gypsum added to accelerate the set; if the set was too rapid to allow for detailed working of the surface, glue and water were used to retard it. Various materials were used to increase pliancy, including curd, glue and almond oil. Marble dust was used where it was available.

In 17th- and 18th-century Italy, Germany and Austria plaster was applied to the underside of brick, stone or wooden ceilings by means of scored wooden blocks or mats of reeds fixed to the surface. The lowest layer, containing coarse aggregate, created a key to the substrate; the upper layer or layers, with finer aggregate, in proportions of three parts fine lime plaster to one part aggregate, would be worked to a smooth, flat finish. The innovation of lathing in the 16th century had allowed for plaster decoration to be applied to timber ceilings as well as walls. When applied to laths (narrow, parallel strips of wood nailed to the joists or studding behind), the first coat of plaster was pushed through the

*Freehand modelling of
lime plaster decoration at
Uppark House, Sussex.
The work is guided by the
pounced underdrawing
and grid lines, applied by
pushing chalk or pigment
through holes pricked in a
cartoon.*

laths to form wave-shaped keys to anchor the plaster to the
wall. Progressively finer layers of lime plaster, sometimes
reinforced with hair, were applied. Preliminary sketches of
the intended decoration were transferred to the prepared
surface with red chalk, using grid patterns to enlarge them to
full size. The relief forms were then produced by modelling
with fingers and wooden spatulas and by moulding. In
common with fresco technique, the work proceeded in
giornate, units corresponding to the area which could be
decorated in one day while the plaster was still wet. From the
16th century repeated ornament was made by pressing lime
plaster into wooden or metal moulds, dusted with marble
powder as a release agent and then attaching the casts with a
thin layer of a plaster containing gypsum. Hollow casts of
figures were made using gypsum plaster or lime and gypsum
mixes; as these casts were lightweight they did not require
the support of armatures. Details such as hair could then be
modelled in plaster. Support was required for lime plaster,
which could be applied in as many as ten layers, and armatures made of wood and metal rods, nails or wires (which, by
the 18th century, were threaded through the laths) were
used.

Plaster mouldings were produced by running a metal or
wooden template along a layer of wet plaster. An 18th-
century plasterer's tools included leaf-shaped metal trowels

and rectangular wooden floats, templates, various brushes for wetting the walls and coating finished work, a straight edge, and a hawk, a hand-held wooden platform for holding the mixed plaster.

PLASTER OF PARIS was used from the 18th century to cast repeat decoration for walls and ceilings. Pattern books, such as those which illustrated the neo-classical ornament developed by Robert Adam in the 18th century, were used as a guide for making clay models of decorative elements. Moulds were taken with a flexible material such as beeswax or resin, and then filled with plaster. Once removed from the moulds, the casts were fixed in place on a prepared surface with a layer of plaster of Paris. This process, which allowed for the ready reproduction of ornament in a workshop, required less time and skill than free-hand modelling on site. A further advance in the prefabrication of ornament was the invention of FIBROUS PLASTERWORK in the mid-19th century, in which large sections of lightweight ornament could be quickly produced and fixed in place.

In Islamic countries lime is used for roofing plasters and for hard, highly polished ornament. Slaked lime is mixed with marble powder and applied in two or three layers, each of which is pounded into place and then rubbed repeatedly with pumice and brushes. Gypsum plaster is extensively used for painted and carved decoration, often with an excess of water so that it sets slowly. Plaster window grilles are made by applying gypsum thickly to a board and then cutting in openings with a knife.

Exterior stucco can be painted using the FRESCO technique, in which the pigments become incorporated into the plaster during the setting process, or with oil-based paints. Some stucco decoration, notably in the Renaissance, was left unpainted, with the surface compressed through repeated rubbing to produce a smooth, polished surface. Surface decoration can also be achieved with SGRAFFITO, which involves the application of contrasting layers of coloured plaster; a design is then scratched through the upper layer to reveal the lower colour. Interior work of the Baroque period was frequently painted using watercolour, fresco or oil paint; metal leaf was attached with oil- or water-based adhesives; coloured glazes were applied on top of leaf to produce lustre work. Plain plastered surfaces were often painted using distemper, a mixture of whiting, dry pigment and parchment size or

another proteinaceous glue. The rich appearance of coloured
marbles and the intricacy of pietre dure were imitated with
SCAGLIOLA, in which pigments were mixed with gypsum
plaster, then built up in thin layers and rubbed down to
produce a hard, polished surface. Plastered surfaces could
also be decorated by pressing objects such as shells, pieces of
glass and mirrors, and pebbles into the plaster while wet, a
technique referred to as grotto-work.

Plastics Natural, semi-synthetic or synthetic materials which
can be moulded or shaped into different forms under pressure
and/or heat. (Non-plastic materials, by contrast, have to be
worked.) All plastics are polymers, substances composed of
long chains of repeating molecules (monomers) mainly composed of carbon and hydrogen atoms. Under the right conditions these monomers can be made to join up into chain
structures. Oxygen, nitrogen, chlorine, silicon or other elements may also be found in some polymers.

Certain plastics, including celluloid, polystyrene and polythene, are known as thermoplastic materials. These set into a
certain shape; if reheated they can flow into another form,
owing to their molecular structure, which consists of long
chains of molecules held together by weak intermolecular
forces. Polythene can be shaped by extrusion and blow-
moulding, processes used by the Cascelloid Company in the

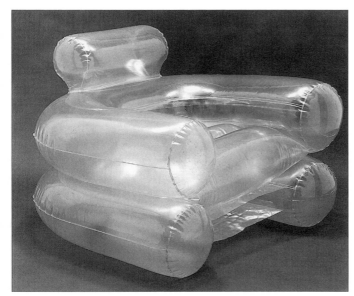

*Blow chair made of PVC,
designed by Scolari,
Lomazzi, D'Urbino and De
Pas, and manufactured by
Zanotta Poltrone, Italy,
1967. It was assembled by
high-frequency welding
and was the first inflatable
chair on the European
market. Unfortunately, it
was prone to deflation
caused by cigarette burns
and punctures.*

1950s to make the first polythene bottles. A small finger-shaped piece of plastic called a parison is extruded, then put in a mould and gas-injected, blowing the parison into the shape of the mould. Today bottles may also be blow-moulded and/or injection-moulded.

Thermosetting plastics include phenolics (see BAKELITE). These are manufactured by compression moulding, the first plastics production process developed on a large scale and still in use today. The material is heated in a mould and pressed into shape by a hydraulic press. This process is best suited to thermosetting plastics, because the setting reaction takes place in the mould and the moulding can be taken out while hot. Once moulded into a shape, thermosets remain in that form, and normally cannot be changed by further heating. At a molecular level, a two-step polymerization process eventually causes their molecules to form a three-dimensional structure with cross-linked bonds which do not break down on heating. At very high temperatures they will break down irreversibly.

Vacuum-forming (developed from thermoforming) is a process used to mould sheets of thermoplastics such as acrylics into a particular shape. Thermoforming was first used with natural plastics such as horn and then celluloid. In this process the sheets of horn or celluloid were shaped with heat over a form. In vacuum-forming the sheets are heated and then clamped over the mould; the air is then removed, forming a vacuum. This causes the sheet to form into the shape of the mould. Thin sheeting is formed under atmospheric pressure, but compressed air is required to form heavier-duty plastic sheet such as that found in acrylic baths. This method was extensively developed in the Second World War in military applications such as aircraft canopies made of Perspex. It is now used to make a variety of items ranging from architectural models to spectacle lenses.

The most widespread plastics moulding method used today is injection moulding. Dr Arthur Eichengrün produced an injection-moulding machine in Germany in 1921, and the first machines for commercial production were made, also in Germany, in 1926 by Wallace Eckert and Professor Karl Ziegler. In injection moulding the polymer is melted in a cylinder and injected into a mould, where it sets. In the case of thermoplastics the mould is at a temperature lower than the setting temperature of the thermoplastic. With thermosets the mould is heated to a degree that ensures that the thermosetting plastic hardens by cross-linking. The mould is then opened and the moulding removed. Originally hand-operated, by 1939 the process was fully automated. Plastics can now be tailored for almost any purpose by a suitable choice of monomers, or by combining them with other materials to form composite plastics.

The common view is that plastics last for ever. This is certainly not true of the earliest plastics, such as celluloid. Indeed, most older plastics are particularly sensitive to heat and light, and a combination of these factors will speed their degradation. It is advisable to keep 19th- and early 20th-century plastic items—such as vulcanite, celluloid, casein and bakelite—in a cool environment with low light levels, ideally less than 50 lux. In certain cases (for example, with respect to cellulose and cellulose acetate) good ventilation will prevent a build-up of acidic vapours. Plastics should also be stored separately by type of material, rather than allowing different types to be mixed together. Ideally they should be stored in/on conservation standard materials, such as Plasta-zote, an expanded polythene foam. Storage or contact with wood or metal should be avoided, particularly in the case of celluloid and cellulose acetate.

Plate A term correctly used only for wares made of silver, although it is often used more loosely to include gold. The name derives from *plate* or *platte*, the old French word for silver.

Plate glass See FLAT GLASS.

Plating The deposition of a thin coating of metal on another metal or a non-metal, whether for decorative or protective purposes. Plating can be done mechanically, chemically and electrolytically. Well-known metals used for plating include gold, silver, copper, bronze, tin, zinc, nickel and chromium. See also ELECTROPLATING, FIREGILDING, FUSED PLATE and GILDING.

Platinum metals A family of six white metals with similar properties and which are almost always found together in nature. The name derives from the Spanish *platina* ('little silver'). Besides platinum itself, the other members of the family are iridium, osmium, rhodium, palladium and rhuthenium. The platinum metals can be divided into two groups, with palladium, rhodium and rhuthenium forming one group and platinum, iridium and osmium the other. The latter group has almost twice the density of the first and also a higher melting-point. Iridium and osmium are the metals with the highest densities among the stable metals. The use of platinum metals began relatively late, as it was not until the 19th century that it was possible to create temperatures high enough to reach their melting-points, which range from 1554°C to 2700°C. Platinum was the first metal of the group to be used, c.AD 500, in South America, where the metal can be found in riverbeds as small pebbles or nuggets. This native platinum is usually alloyed with other metals of the platinum family such as palladium and rhuthenium. Because these nuggets could not be molten on their own, they were often mixed with other precious metals such as gold and silver to form alloys with lower melting-points. Although platinum was mentioned in 1557 as a white infusible metal found in silver mines in Mexico, it was only taken seriously in Western Europe from the middle of the 18th century, and in 1741 it was recognized as a separate metal. Palladium was discovered in 1803 and was soon followed by the other platinum metals. All of them are highly corrosion-resistant and reflective, and were used for making jewellery from the end of the 19th century. Other uses, especially for rhodium, are as a protective and decorative coating.

Plique à jour See ENAMEL.

Plum figure A term for more or less circular, irregularly spaced patches of variation in grain pattern and lustre seen on the surface of converted timber.

Plush See VELVET.

Plywood A wood material made by gluing together under pressure several veneers, each with its grain at right angles to the succeeding layer. Since wood tends to split and warp with the grain, the alternating cross-grained structure resists these actions. The resultant multi-ply sheet is equally strong in all directions and resistant to warping. Plywood intended for furniture making will usually be finished on one face with a high-quality, visually attractive veneer such as mahogany, ebony, satinwood or yew.

Pochoir See STENCILLING.

Point d'Angleterre See BOBBIN lace.

Point d'Hongrie See BARGELLO.

Point de Colbert See NEEDLE lace.

Point de France See NEEDLE lace.

Point de gaz See NEEDLE lace.

The first plywood chair, produced by Charles Eames, USA, 1946, and made from five moulded elements.

Point de neige See NEEDLE LACE.

Pokerwork Designs formed on wood by controlled scorching with heated metal rods or needles. Heated sand is sometimes used for shading. Today electrically heated tools are often used.

Polish cochineal/Polish grey See COCHINEAL.

Polyester A general term for a group of condensation polymers (see PLASTICS), including resins and fibres. The first polyester resin (polyglycerol tartrate) was produced in 1847 by the Swedish chemist Jön Jakob Berzelius. A range of polyester resins now exists, made by a variety of processes, including reacting a glycol with a dicarboxylic acid. One common use is to bind together glass fibres in the production of glass fibre reinforced plastics. Clear unsaturated polyester resins (also known as alkyds) have been used as weather-resistant coatings on cars, to embed objects such as zoological specimens, in sculpture and also for small ornamental items. Unsaturated polyester resins also provide the basis for many hard-gloss paints, making the paint flexible.

Polyester fibre was invented by John Whinfield and

J.T. Dickson of Britain's Calico Printers Association in 1941 and first produced in America from 1946 by E.I. Du Pont de Nemours & Co., who developed it under the brand name Dacron. It is crease- and abrasion-resistant, quick-drying and aids shape retention in garments, for which it is often combined with other fibres. For sheeting it is combined with cotton; alone it has many applications, from clothing to industrial uses. It has been extensively developed and other trade names include Fortrel, Kodel, Terylene and Vycron.

Polyethene The systematic chemical name for POLYTHENE.

Polyethylene The former systematic chemical name for POLYTHENE.

Polystyrene An intrinsically brittle synthetic plastic which can be brightly coloured. Initially it was used to make decorative boxes, jewellery, food containers, picnic ware and electrical insulators.

In 1866 Pierre Eugène Marcelin Bertholet showed that polystyrene could be made from styrene. In 1930 the German company IG Farben produced polystyrene on a commercial scale. In 1937 polystyrene was made in America. Early polystyrene soon cracked and crazed, but it was then found that it could be strengthened by incorporating butadiene to produce high-impact polystyrene. Owing to its optical clarity, polystyrene is used today in medical and industrial probes. Expanded polystyrene is an excellent packaging material and insulant.

Polythene A trade name used by ICI for a synthetic plastic (polyethene) used in the production of such everyday items as Tupperware and plastic bags. It was first marketed in the United Kingdom by ICI under the name Alketh, then Alkatheine.

Polythene was discovered by chance at the ICI plant at Winnington, Cheshire, on 24 March 1933 during a research programme into high-pressure reactions of aromatics with olefins. In an experiment reacting benzaldehyde with ethylene, a leak in the high-pressure reactor meant that more ethylene gas was fed in. This acted as a catalyst, converting some of the ethylene into polythene. It took a long time to establish the cause before the experiment could be repeated, producing low-density polythene. The first 100 ton-per-year polythene plant went into production in 1939 on the eve of the Second World War, after which all polythene went into military applications such as insulation for radar cables.

Brooch made of pearlized pink polystyrene in the form of a woman's head, with a red flower in her hair and painted red lips, c.1945. Polystyrene can be coloured brightly and became popular after the Second World War for eye-catching but inexpensive jewellery.

After the war ICI developed new uses for their product, such as washing-up bowls, buckets and babies' baths. By the 1950s decorative blow-moulded bottles and dolls were made from polythene (see PLASTICS). This low-density form of polythene is still manufactured.

A more rigid, high-density form of polythene was first produced by the German chemist Professor Karl Ziegler in 1953. It is still used for dustbins and stackable boxes, and even for hip replacements. The more recent American Phillips Standard Oil (Indiana) process produces very high-density polythenes. High-density polythene (HDPE) is produced using catalysts permitting lower pressures and temperatures than those used for the ICI high-pressure process. It is stiffer and more temperature-resistant than the low-density form, and not flexible. New generations of polythene are now being developed, based on metallocene catalysts.

Polyvinyl chloride A synthetic plastic polymerized from the monomer vinyl chloride and capable of being produced in a range of hardnesses. First recorded in 1835 by the French physicist and chemist Henri Victor Regnault, polyvinyl chloride (now commonly known as PVC) was polymerized in 1872 and made in a soft plasticized form by I. Ostromislensky in Moscow in 1912. By 1928 it was being manufactured in America and by 1939 it was produced in Britain.

During the Second World War PVC played a significant role in electrical insulation and as a substitute for rubber in aircraft, radio and electrical goods. In 1948, under the name Vinylite, commonly referred to as 'vinyl' (a copolymer of vinyl chloride and vinyl acetate developed by Union Carbide), it was used to make gramophone records, and within five years it had largely replaced shellac. PVC has a variety of modern uses, from waterproof raincoats and fruit bowls to designer wear and inflatable chairs (for illustration see page 381). It is used for structural applications such as pipes, guttering and windows, and for wipeable wallpaper and packaging.

Pontil See GLASS BLOWING.

Pontypool ware The name for japanned tin plate wares in general but often used more specifically for the wares from the Pontypool japanning factory. The technique was first used at Bilston in Staffordshire towards the end of the 17th century but is mainly associated with the high-quality wares produced at Pontypool, Monmouthshire, in the 18th century.

Pontypool (tole) ware coffee pot, USA, 19th century, made from tinned iron sheet, soldered together and japanned.

It involved coating tin plate products such as trays, water jugs and buckets with a black asphaltum varnish which was dried in heated stoves. The shiny black surface was then decorated with gilt or polychrome designs. Some of these were derived from oriental originals but the commonest patterns are more reminiscent of contemporary Dutch still-life paintings of fruit and flowers. Similar wares made in America are called tole ware, from the French word *tôle* ('tin plate').

Poplar A soft and fairly light wood from the poplar genus (*Populus*), a widespread member of the willow family. Different species are usually referred to by a geographical qualifer or a descriptive term such as black, white or yellow. The timber is white to light greyish brown, with darker streaked markings, and it has a close, smooth grain and even texture. It does not split but shrinks heavily in seasoning. It is used for toy making, turnery, match making, clog making, cooperage, plywood cores and some cabinetmaking.

Porcelain See HARD PASTE PORCELAIN.

Porcellaneous stoneware A fine white stoneware often confused with porcelain. Like porcelain, stoneware is a hard, often vitrified ceramic. Stoneware bodies come in a wide range of colours, including white, which is very similar to porcelain in appearance. Unlike porcelain, however, these white porcellaneous stonewares are usually not translucent. In traditional Chinese ceramics the term 'porcellanous stoneware' is used to describe some high-fired white wares that are made from kaolin but are not always translucent. They are not soft paste porcelains because they contain less glassy material.

Porphyry A group of igneous rocks defined by their structure, in which large, distinct crystals are embedded in a fine-grained matrix. Porphyries occur in many parts of the world but the most famous are imperial porphyry, in which crystals of white and pink feldspar are set into a reddish purple material, coloured by manganese, and green porphyry, which

A covered vase of red Egyptian porphyry, France, 1760–65. This example is made in three sections—lid, vessel and foot—with gilded bronze mounts. The extreme hardness of the stone and the difficulty of working with it are indicated by the plain, shallow mouldings.

contains green feldspar crystals in a dark green matrix. The name porphyry is derived from the Greek word for purple. Imperial porphyry could only be obtained from Gebel Abu Dakhan in the eastern desert of Egypt. Although the Egyptians made limited use of the stone before the Roman occupation, it was the Romans who quarried and exported it in large quantities to make columns, flooring inlays, urns and basins. As a hard stone it was cut and shaped with abrasives. After the end of the Roman empire and the closure of the quarry in 5th century AD, porphyry was obtained by reusing ancient material; for example, ancient porphyry columns from Constantinople were incorporated into the west front of St Mark's Basilica in Venice. The uneven contours of these columns attest to the hardness of the stone and the difficulty in working it. Interest in carving porphyry revived during the Renaissance, and Giorgio Vasari describes how Cosimo de' Medici's patronage led to the production of a herbal distillation used to temper steel chisels hard enough to work the stone. Vasari may have been attempting to deflect the attention of rivals from the fact that the only feasible method of working porphyry was with abrasives.

Green porphyry, found in Greece, was also used extensively in Rome and is sometimes mistakenly described as serpentine.

Portland stone A hard, fine-grained oolitic limestone obtained from quarries on the Isle of Portland and neighbouring areas in Dorset. It is initially cream-coloured but becomes white through weathering. Some varieties of Portland stone contain distinct fossils but most have a homogeneous texture. Portland stone was used by the Romans and, although some was transported to London and Exeter in the 14th century, it was not until the later 17th century, when some degree of mechanization was available for cutting, that it was widely used. Christopher Wren chose it for the rebuilding of London churches following the great fire of 1666 because it was quarried in large blocks. It was subsequently used throughout London and exported to other countries.

Potash glass Glass in which potash (potassium carbonate) is the principal alkali. It was made from the 10th century in response to a shortage of soda (see SODA GLASS). In the FOREST GLASS of northern Europe the potash was derived from the ash of beechwood, oak and other timbers, while in the *verre de fougère* of France it was made from the ash of fern

and bracken. Other sources of potash include saltpetre
(nitrate of potash) and the burnt lees of wine. It is now made
commercially from potassium chloride.

Potash glass passes from the molten to the rigid state more
quickly than soda glass. This makes it difficult to manipulate
into elaborate forms and more suited to simple, sturdy
shapes. When lime is added to the batch, the glass becomes
brilliant and cools slowly. This enables it to be blown into
heavy forms that can be facet-cut and wheel-engraved (see
GLASS ENGRAVING).

Potter's wheel A flat round disc that is placed on a vertical,
rotating shaft and used to form ceramics rapidly through centrifugal force. The rotation is powered either manually by
hand or by foot pedal, or mechanically with an electric
motor. The earliest potter's wheels were simply turntables
that were rotated by hand and are known as 'slow wheels'.

*A potter in east Gujarat,
1980s. He turns the wheel
with a stave set into the
outer rim.*

These have been found in China, dating to *c.*4000 BC, and in Egypt, dating to *c.*2400 BC. The addition *c.*3500–3000 BC of a 'fly wheel' below the rotating wheel disc enabled faster, more mechanical rotation and these wheels are known as 'fast wheels'. An early form of fast wheel is known as a 'kick wheel' because it is rotated by kicking. Such wheels can also be powered by the use of a stick inserted in a notch in the head wheel, where the stick is used as a treadle for spinning. In Europe the wheel was used for fine ceramics in ancient Greece and Rome and again in the late Middle Ages (*c.*12th–13th century). However, most ceramics in these periods were probably handbuilt or moulded, as they consisted mainly of crude tableware. Traditional, manually powered wheels are still used in many ceramic-producing regions. The most modern wheels are powered electrically and have a motor instead of a fly wheel.

The action of forming ceramics on a wheel is known as throwing and the forms produced are usually spherical, with sides of even thickness. A large number of similar, consistent pieces can be produced rapidly through the mechanical action of the wheel, making it one of the most useful tools for forming both industrial and studio ceramics.

Pottery See EARTHENWARE.

Pouncing A method used to transfer designs, in which the lines on a paper pattern or cartoon are pricked with a needle or perforating wheel. The paper is then placed on the support, which may be a wall, canvas or cloth, and the lines are dabbed with a bag filled with powdered chalk or charcoal. This leaves a faint indication of the design on the surface below.

Press moulding A technique used in the production of ceramics, whereby clay is pressed into or over a single mould and then removed (for illustration see page 303). Alternatively two moulds are used and the clay is pressed into both and then joined. The resulting single vessel is removed from the moulds and the join smoothed over. Press moulds can be used several times to produce identical pieces.

A similar technique is used in glass manufacture, employing either soft, hot glass or PÂTE DE VERRE. However, in the context of glass, the term press moulding generally refers to the use of a metal mould with a plunger to form the inside shape. In contrast to MOULD-BLOWN GLASS, the surfaces can be intricately patterned with a high degree of definition; also,

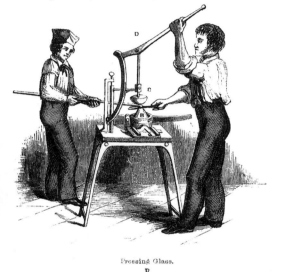

AMERICAN PRESSED GLASS.   121

Glass vessels, by placing a hot prepared cameo, of the usual composition, upon the hot manufactured vessel; a small piece of liquid Glass is dropped on it, and becomes welded; and, if rubbed while hot, the upper coat of fused Glass will be spread as thinly as possible upon and around the cameo, behind which are driven any air bubbles that may be entrapped; thus completely isolating the device between the two Glasses. These incrustations require very careful annealing.

AMERICAN PRESSED GLASS.

Pressing is a mechanical operation, unknown to the

Pressing Glass.

R

An early press moulding machine, from Apsley Pellatt's Curiosities of Glass Making *(1849). A gather of molten glass (B) was cut off the blowpipe and forced into a mould by a plunger (C), depressed by a lever (D).*

the interior form is quite independent of the exterior. The technique was perfected in the USA in the 1830s and made possible the cheap, speedy manufacture of imitation cut glass. Initially, it required a team of two: one to cut the measured gather of hot glass from the pontil rod and drop it into the hot mould, the other to lower the plunger by means of a lever and force the glass into the pattern. Later the process was automated and adapted to mass production. Early pressed glass was marred by its poor surface finish and mould lines. These faults were often disguised by acid etching or a background of closely stippled dots, giving the so-called 'lacy style', until later in the century they were overcome by a new method of fire polishing.

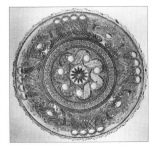

Pressed glass bowl, probably by the Boston & Sandwich Glass Co., c.1830.

Pricked work A decoration on metal, formed by carefully arranged small dots on the surface. This needlepoint decoration was popular on silverware in the 16th and 17th centuries.

Printed textiles Textiles in which the pattern is applied to the surface of the cloth in the form of dyes and other colourants. Because the design is an addition to the cloth, rather than part of the structure (as it is in weaving), its size need not be related to the cloth width and it can be unevenly dispersed over the fabric. Printed textiles emerged, undoubtedly, from the practice of painting or impressing pigment or staining colourants on cloth or skins. However, true printing involves the creation of a pattern with a relatively fast colourant, that is, a pigment that has good adhesion to the cloth or a dye that impregnates the fibre or fibres from which the cloth is made. Far fewer printed than woven textiles have survived from the ancient to late medieval periods, making the history of the early developments in printing much more difficult to chart. All fibres can be printed, but the early development of this technique is predominantly associated with regions such as

Hand-block resist printing, Bagru, India, 1994. The cloth is first soaked in the juice of myrobalan, which contains tannic acid. An iron solution, produced by soaking horseshoes and other pieces of iron in a mixture of water and molasses, is made into a printing paste by adding gum as a thickener. This is applied to the pre-treated cloth with wooden blocks, and the iron reacts with the tannic acid mordant to form a dark, almost black colour. This is very colourfast, but the tannins may eventually damage the cloth fibre.

the Indian subcontinent and South-East Asia, in which cotton was the main fibre. Numerous devices for printing are known, although the principal methods in the past have used wooden blocks, copper plates or screens.

Printing processes can be divided into four basic types. Direct printing involves the use of a block or other stamping device to deposit the colourant for the pattern onto the cloth. mordant printing deposits the mordant as the pattern, which appears once the cloth is immersed in a dye-bath and cleared; this latter process removes any superfluous dye from unmordanted areas. Resist printing (see RESIST DYEING) uses some means to prevent colourant from contacting or binding with the cloth, so that the pattern appears where no resist has been applied. DISCHARGE PRINTING is a means of creating patterns by removing colour already present in the cloth. Direct, mordant-dyed and resist printing techniques are also used on yarns (see IKAT).

Of these four techniques, direct printing was the simplest but the least permanent until 19th-century developments in dyes and dyeing; discharge printing also remained little used until the isolation of chlorine, which provided an effective bleach for printers by c.1800. Resist and mordant printing, which were the most effective processes until the end of the 18th century, form the basis of the ancient and non-Western dye-patterning styles. These include wrapping or folding the cloth to prevent impregnation (see PLANGI and IKAT), as well as stamped or painted resist work, which is closely associated with indigo dyes and BATIK. Mordant printing, which can also be seen as a negative resist technique, is linked to the development of BLOCK PRINTING and, from there, to the industrialization of printed textile production.

Western printing processes emerged during the 17th and 18th centuries and were modelled on the techniques used in Indian printed textiles (see CHINTZ). The Indian method combined painted resist indigo for blues with negative resist mordant dyes; the most important of these was madder, which gave a range of brownish blacks to pale reds, purples where these fell over the indigo, and greens where over-mordanted and dyed with yellow. Because true dyes were used rather than pigment dyes (as was then the case in Europe), Indian patterned cottons were fast to washing. Generally speaking, the introduction of complex methods of block printing to apply the resist or the mordant was a Western addition, although the use of stamping devices made from a variety of substrates appears to have been a universally understood technique. The critical development in the West was the perfection of thickening agents to foster the adhesion of the colourant to the block during transfer from its container to the cloth, a process understood by the mid- to late 17th century. Similarly, the use of hand-drawn blues, or 'pencil blue', was introduced in England in the 1730s; this was made possible by slowing the oxidation of indigo by adding orpiment (an arsenic trisulphide) to a ferrous sulphate indigo vat thickened with gum senegal and could also be used with blocks, although this appears to have been uncommon (see also CHINA BLUE). The existence of the blocks themselves (and thickening agents to a less certain degree) was derived from paper and book-printing practices; so too was the introduction of copper plates, used on silk for direct printing before their introduction in the mid-18th century for mordant printing on cotton and linen (see COPPERPLATE PRINTING). Together these two methods of impressing patterns—colourants held on the surface of the tool, as on a block, or contained in the depressions of the tool, as in plate printing—formed the basis of Western printing techniques until the end of the 19th century. Block printing was mechanized shortly before 1800 by the introduction of wooden rollers (surface printing) and at about the same time copperplate printing spawned copper cylinder printing; both surface and cylinder printing were known as ROLLER PRINTING.

Resist printing of a mechanical nature was introduced from Japan to the West in the late 19th century through the importation of paper and cloth coloured by STENCIL PRINTING, which itself evolved into hand-screen printing and, by mid-20th century, into machine (or rotary) SCREEN PRINT-

Calico printing at the Swainson Birley cotton mill, near Preston, Lancashire, c.1834. This illustration shows roller printing machines and, far right, a block printer and assistant (or tierer).

ING; the last two are now the dominant methods in craft and industrial printing respectively. During the same period direct printing, whether with blocks, hand-screens or machines, became widespread owing to the introduction of increasing numbers of direct dyes; it largely replaced resist styles (the printing of a resist was superseded by the use of the screen as a barrier), except in craft-based production. Discharge printing remained throughout a specialist process, capable of producing a range of seemingly disparate effects, including DEVORÉ and CHEMICAL LACE.

Hand and machine methods co-existed in the printing industry until the mid-20th century; during the 19th century, particularly, rollers were used to lay down one or more madder shades while the remaining colours were added by hand-block printing. In the mechanization of the use of blocks, plates and screens, two limitations consistently occurred. The first was the reduction of the size of the vertical repeat to the circumference of the cylinder on the machine; the second was the elimination of the overlapping of two or more colours, since the speed of mechanical printing does not allow time for colourants to dry, without which underlying colours would be transferred back to the printing surface.

Printing A generic term for the production of multiple images, repeat patterns and text by transferring ink from a worked surface to another surface, usually paper. The earliest prints are thought to have been taken from Buddhist sutras (scriptures) carved in stone in ancient China, and it was from China that the WOODCUT process reached Japan by the 8th century. In Europe among the earliest examples of printing on paper are woodcuts dating from the 15th century. Other RELIEF PRINTING processes which, like wood- and stonecuts, use a raised image or pattern are wood engraving, linocutting, potato printing and relief etching. INTAGLIO PRINTING uses an indented printing surface and planographic processes, such as LITHOGRAPHY, employ a flat printing surface. SCREEN PRINTING is a stencil process, which relies on masking out areas of the printing surface. Almost all these printing techniques invert the original design, so the text or illustration has to be originated as a mirror image.

The printing of text began in Europe with woodblocks on paper or vellum, but the block for each page had to be laboriously cut by hand. Movable type, with individual letters cast in metal which can be set together, cleaned and reused, is more versatile. The Chinese probably invented movable type made from clay and glue in the 11th century and the Koreans were using movable metal type by about 1400. This eventually led to the introduction of book printing into Europe by 1450, when the Gutenberg Bible was produced in Germany. In 1476 William Caxton established the first printing office in London. A fount (or set) of movable type, containing individual letters and spaces cast in metal which could be set in a frame, meant unprecedented flexibility in printing text. Metal and woodcuts were introduced for illustrations in the late 15th century, but were soon superseded by engraving and etching on metal. Wood engraving, using blocks of stan-

Title-page of A Midsummer Night's Dream, *illustrated by Arthur Rackham, 1908. It was probably printed by the line-block process, which was especially suited to the reproduction of line. A photograph of the artwork was transferred to a metal block coated with a sensitized emulsion. The block, which was usually zinc, was then etched to leave the design in relief.*

dard thickness which could be set alongside the type, was developed in Britain in the late 18th century, chiefly as an illustrative medium, and in 1798 lithography was invented in Bavaria. (For illustration see pages 139, 400 and 410.)

In the late 19th century a variety of processes were introduced which use a photographic image, including photogravure, photolithography, line-block and screen printing. These eventually made colour printing an economic option; up to this period images had been coloured by hand (see HAND-COLOURED PRINT). The photomechanical printing processes rely on the principle that light-sensitized gelatine hardens when exposed to light; in areas that are kept unexposed it can be softened and washed away. The gelatine thus acts like the wax coating on an etching plate. Photogravure, invented in 1869, was the first of these processes and was used in fine books of the early 20th century to reproduce watercolour illustrations by artists such as Rackham and Dulac. The originals were photographed through a screen which broke the image up into fine dots capable of reproducing tone as well as line, and the pattern of dots was then etched onto a plate. The dots, or hollows in the plate, were filled with ink and the surface cleaned like an etched or engraved plate. Where the plate was mounted on a roller for printing by a rotary press machine, inking and wiping were automated. With the perfection of the cross-line screen in the 1880s, photogravure could be combined with the colour separation process, developed at the end of the 19th century.

The colour separation process also made subtle colour reproduction possible by photographing the image through filters of the three primary colours of light: red, green and blue. In this process, sometimes called chromolithography, printing plates were made for each colour, plus black, with the red filter negative corresponding to the printing plate for cyan ink, green to magenta and blue to yellow.

In the late 20th century a number of non-impact printing methods were introduced for computer-generated images. These included processes such as electrophotography, laser printing, ink jet and thermal imaging. Increasingly used in graphic design and commercial art, these methods no longer rely on the traditional mechanical means of creating multiple images by contact between a printing surface (such as a block or plate) and the print support (such as paper or plastic). Instead they use digital signals to prompt the transfer of ink

Poster designed by Henri de Toulouse-Lautrec and printed by chromolithography, 1892.

or powder (toner) for the development of an image.

Printing press A device used to transfer an inked image from a woodblock, metal plate, stone or roller to a support, such as paper. The simplest way to make an impression is to use hand pressure, and in European wood engraving and oriental woodblock printing this is still done, using a smooth, slightly curved tool (like an old spoon or the Japanese *baren*) to rub the back of thin paper placed on top of the block. Early European woodcuts of the 14th and 15th centuries were printed in the same way as textiles, by forcing the inked block face

The use of a roller press to print copperplate engravings, as depicted in Vittorio Zonca's Novo teatro di machine ed edificii *(1621). Paper is placed in contact with the inked plate on a supporting bed, covered with a blanket. This is then passed between a pair of rollers by winding the wheel on the left.*

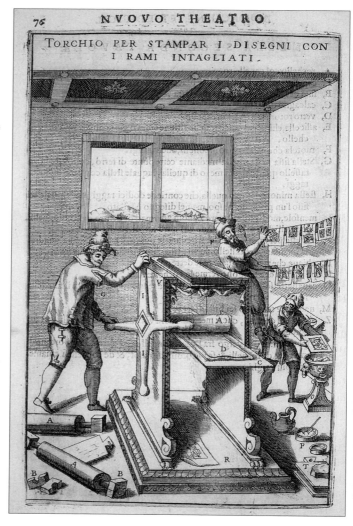

down onto the paper. The various types of mechanical press which subsequently developed are based on one of these two principles: either the paper sandwiched with the inked printing plate is passed between rollers like an old-fashioned mangle, or the inked surface is pressed into contact with the paper by vertical pressure from a platen, screwed down from above or operated with a lever (for illustration see page 507). The lithographic and screen printing processes developed since the 19th century work rather differently, as they rely on a scraping action to get the ink onto the paper. Most modern industrial printing presses are rotary offset machines, where the printing plate is formed around a revolving cylinder. It is inked from another roller and the image is transferred repeatedly via a further cylinder to a continuous length of paper.

Printmaking See PRINTING.

Printwork Black thread or hair embroidery copying prints or worked directly over copperplate printed silk taffeta or satin. It was popular from *c.*1760 to *c.*1820 and was revived in the last quarter of the 19th century, when it was known as etching work or etching embroidery.

Prong and claw setting See STONE SETTING.

Prunt A blob of glass on the surface of a glass vessel, often applied in a series or pattern. In the 16th and 17th centuries prunts were much used on drinking vessels, especially in Bohemia and Germany, to provide a grip for greasy hands. They are available in various forms. Some are pinched into a spiky tip; others are impressed with a pattern and are known as 'raspberry' prunts.

Prussian blue A deep blue synthetic pigment invented at the beginning of the 18th century and later used as a mineral dye. It is a metallo-organic compound (potassium ferric ferrocyanide) with a complex chemical formula that was not understood by the chemists of the period. The blue was discovered accidentally by a paintmaker using materials contaminated with bull's blood, as he attempted to make a red lake. The true chemical nature of the pigment was not properly appreciated until about 50 years later.

Prussian blue was the first cheap and stable pigment to replace the costly minerals azurite and lapis lazuli, and as such had a huge effect on the painter's palette: suddenly blue did not have to be reserved for small and important details but could be splashed over the whole work. It has tremendous tinting strength: 1 part Prussian blue to 700 parts of white will still produce a good tone, and mixed with a strong yellow such as chrome it makes a powerful green. However, many of its functions have been replaced by pthalocyanine blue, which has the same working properties but is more stable and has a brighter hue. Prussian blue is partly organic and will thus fade in strong light, and in alkaline conditions it can become brown. It is therefore inappropriate to use it on plaster walls, or on leather that has been treated with lime.

The pigment was introduced as a mineral dye by P.J. Macquer in 1749 and improved during the second half of the 18th century (see DYE). Prussiate of potash was combined with an iron salt, with the prussiate acting as the dye and the iron as a mordant. More brilliant than indigo, on wool it turned greenish drab in contact with an alkali; on cotton it was very light-fast (see colour plate XVII).

Pthalocyanine green and blue Synthetic pigments developed from the dye industry and introduced into paints around 1935. As they are metallo-organic compounds, they combine the virtues of both organic and inorganic pigments. Their powerful tinting strength and very fine particle size means they are as useful in ink as they are in acrylics. They are resistant to light, pollutants and heat, and have a huge importance in industry.

Puering See TANNING.

Pug mill A mill used for preparing a clay body. It is shaped like a small cannon and provides a mechanical means of compressing clay to remove excess air and water, by replicating on a much larger scale the action of kneading by hand and wedging. It thus helps to create a homogeneous, prepared clay body for forming.

Pumice A pale grey igneous stone ejected from erupting volcanoes, containing numerous cavities. It was generally crushed and used as a polish for other stones of moderate hardness. Pumice can be added to LIME to obtain a hydraulic set.

Punto in aria The earliest known guipure needle lace. Used mainly as an edging, it was made in coiling or geometric patterns with free-hanging motifs or points at the outer edge. The name derives from the Italian, meaning 'stitches in the air'.

Purbeck marble A fossiliferous limestone quarried from the Isle of Purbeck and neighbouring areas in Dorset, and worked from the Middle Ages in the nearby village of Corfe

Castle. The large volume of freshwater snail shells makes the stone sufficiently hard for it to accept a high polish, conferring on it the common name of marble. The sheen, the fossil patterning and dark greenish-grey to brown colours made it a decorative material, first used by the Romans in the 1st century. Purbeck was widely used from the 12th century, for example at Salisbury Cathedral, to produce column shafts which contrasted strongly with paler limestones, and was also exported to northern France. It was also used to carve tomb effigies (for illustration see page 466).

PVC See POLYVINYL CHLORIDE.

Pyralin See SYNTHETIC IVORY.

Q

Quartering One of the cuts used in timber conversion. The log is cut radially to improve the figure of the finished timber. This is especially effective with species having pronounced medullary rays, such as oak.

Quartz A mineral composed of silicon dioxide which occurs as a constituent in many types of building stone, such as granite and sandstone; as large crystals, such as the gemstones amethyst and rock crystal; or as a fine-grained crystalline material, such as chalcedony, jasper or flint. Quartz is universally distributed and, as a hard mineral (Mohs 7) in the ubiquitous form of sand, was often used as a cutting abrasive.

Quartzite A hard fine-grained stone composed of grains of quartz sand cemented together with quartz. The term properly describes the character of the stone rather than the process of formation, which may be igneous, sedimentary or metamorphic. Quartzites range in colour from white, grey and black to brown and yellow, depending on the presence of impurities. They have been used as building stones in India, Egypt, and the British Isles. The hardness of quartzite has limited carving to the production of smooth, rounded forms, shaped with abrasives.

Queen's ware See CREAM WARE.

Quercitron A mordant dye from the inner bark of the quercitron oak, native to North America. It was discovered and patented in 1775 by Edward Bancroft and, cheaper than weld, became a fashionable colour for calico printing from the 1780s (see colour plate XVII). When mordanted with aluminium it gave a yellow dye much brighter than fustic but not as light-fast; with chrome it produced an olive brown, with tin an orange, and with iron a greenish yellow. As a result of its orange tinge, it was often mixed with cochineal. It was gradually replaced by the mineral dye chrome yellow, introduced in the 19th century.

Quicksilver See MERCURY.

Quillwork A form of LAID AND COUCHED WORK used by North American Indians, in which porcupine or bird quills were secured to birch bark or hides by sinew threads. In Europe the term was also used in the 17th century for decorative posies of leaves and flowers made from bird quills and feathers, and in the 19th century, in Central Europe, for the use of these materials for decorative purposes, often with artificial flowers or foliage.

Quilted figure A term applied to highly figured veneers that

Snuff bottle in smoky quartz with needle-like inclusions of tourmaline, China, Ming period.

Watercolour showing a
lady quilting stockings,
China, late 19th century.

give the appearance of folds, waves and blisters.

Quilting A universal embroidery technique, involving stitching two or more fabrics together over their entire surface, to make a single, thicker fabric, often padded for warmth or as a protection against abrasion, for example in garments made to wear under armour. The stitches may—but need not—fall into patterns. The technique probably developed in India or the Far East. Surviving 14th- and 15th-century pieces have wadding or cord introduced through the back fabric after the decorative running or back stitching had been done; later called trapunto, this and general quilting were important elements in Western clothing and furnishings from the late 17th century to the late 19th. In Western cultures quilting is associated with PATCHWORK, but it also has a long worldwide history of use with recycled fabric patched randomly, as in Bengali *kantha* work.

Quinacridone A range of red, violet and purple synthetic, organic pigments invented in the 1950s. They are all cool colours and the ones in the crimson range are able to replace the more traditional crimson lakes, particularly as they are more colour-fast.

R

Racinage A method of decorating vegetable-tanned leather by spraying it with a potassium bichromate solution and then immediately with a mixture of hydrochloric and oxalic acids to give a marbling effect. This style of patterning was introduced into Britain from Europe in the late 19th century, but the use of these materials has a strongly detrimental effect on the long-term stability of the leather and few examples of skins treated in this manner survive intact.

Raffia A fibre from the leaf stalk of the raphia palm, *Raphia ruffia*, grown in Madagascar. It occurs in strips about 1000 mm by 75–150 mm; in this form it can be used in off-loom techniques, mainly plaiting, for items such as chair seats, baskets, hats and mats; the strips can also be separated into finer fibres for these uses or for making cloths.

Rag paper See PAPER.

Raised work A general term for a number of embroidery techniques that give a three-dimensional effect by working over cotton wadding, wool, string, card, paper, felt or wooden moulds. The last two paddings, in particular, were associated with stumpwork, thought to have originated *c*.1300 in continental Europe, where it was initially used mainly for ecclesiastical embroidery; by the 17th century stumpwork was particularly popular for secular items such as needlework boxes and frames and often incorporated folds of needle-made fabric to represent garments. Raised areas made from sculpted piles, known as plush stitch, were used in 17th- and 19th-century canvaswork embroidery; otherwise cord, string and card raised work remained most widely used in ecclesias-

Raising a bowl. (a) A flat disc is hammered into a shallow depression in a tree trunk. (b) The rim is crimped on a wooden crimping block with a mallet. (c) and (d) The workpiece is hammered against a raising stake to bring it into shape.

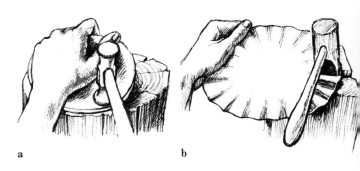

a   b

tical embroidery, giving surfaces varying from medium to low relief. Cardwork over parchment or vellum is also called guipure embroidery and resembles repoussé.

See also QUILTING.

Raising The shaping of a flat metal sheet into a hollow form by hammering the metal on a raising stake or anvil to bring the sides up gradually. First a slightly concave form is created from sheet metal by 'blocking'. Then the shape is hammered over a wooden block and crimped around an anvil. This crimping process, also called creasing, involves making radiating grooves or creases, which are smoothed out later. A narrow-faced hammer, such as a crimping or neck hammer, is used to shape the sheet metal on a wooden form with a grooved depression or a special similar-shaped steel stake called a valley stake. Finally the piece is hammered against a convex raising stake until the desired form is obtained. Usually the metal is annealed several times during the different stages of raising, because the hammering causes work hardening of the metal. Raising was the principal method of making hollowwares until spinning, which was more suited to mass production, became widespread in the early 19th century.

For discussion of the raising of leather, see TANNING.

Raku A low-fired ceramic traditionally made in Japan, with a heavily crackled lead glaze. It was first made in Japan in the late 16th century, possibly in imitation of imported Chinese tea bowls (see TEMMOKU). The glaze is deliberately crackled, an effect induced by stress caused by firing (see

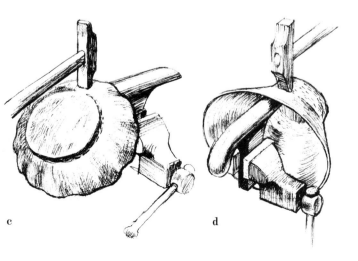

c   d

Water jug, raku ware with crackled white glaze, by Hasegawa Keiko, 1985.

CRACKLE). Raku wares are traditionally fired in pits and then removed when red hot and plunged into water and/or straw, so that they move very quickly from oxidation to reduction. This extreme stress causes cracking of the glaze and lends a rough quality to the ware that appealed to the Japanese aesthetic. Initially, the raku technique was used for making tea bowls, which were usually formed by pinching or handbuilding and were made very thick for ease of handling.

In order to achieve successful raku wares, an open-textured, high-fired body that is resistant to thermal shock is required. Tempers such as grog are added to the body, which is biscuit-fired before glazing. The glazes can be white or tinted with metallic oxides. The colour of the glaze is affected by the body colour and this is usually taken into consideration by the potter. The effect is sometimes enhanced by applying a coloured slip layer under the glaze. The most common colours for traditional Japanese raku ware are black and red, but modern potters can create a much wider range, including lustres.

Ram's horn A variety of ripple or fiddleback figure in wood, in which relatively short rays curve across the surface.

Rattan Palms of the *Calamus* and *Daemonorops* genera, native mainly to South-East Asia, Malaysia and Indonesia. Their trailing, vinelike stems can grow to 120 m. The outer skin is stripped off and used as CANE, while the inner stem, or reed, is used for WICKER furniture.

Ravenscroft glass See LEAD GLASS.

Raw hide A hide or skin that has been dried out under carefully controlled conditions to give a tough, semi-rigid but resilient material. The term is also used for a translucent material prepared by drying out a hide which has had the hair removed by the liming process.

Rayon A term adopted in the mid-1920s for viscose and then for all man-made fibres regenerated from pulped cellulose, until then variously known as 'artificial silk', 'wood silk', 'vegetable silk' and 'glos'. The development of such fibres derived from attempts to duplicate mechanically the production of fibre by the silkworm. The first significant development was a nitro-cellulose process patented by Count Hilaire de Chardonnet in France in 1885 and known from 1889 as Chardonnet silk. This was overtaken by a cupra-ammonium process patented by Depaissis in 1890, and then by the viscose process, patented in England by C.F. Cross,

E.J. Bevan and C. Beadle in 1892 and available in commercial quantities by the early 20th century.

Viscose rayon is chemically exactly like cotton, and is therefore dyed in the same way; it is made from wood pulp or cotton linters, which give a high absorbency rate of colourants, good draping qualities and superior strength. Its manufacture involves several stages, the main ones being steeping in a caustic soda (sodium hydroxide) solution, blending with carbon disulphide (producing cellulose xanthate, or regenerated cellulose), blending again with sodium hydroxide, and extrusion from an acid bath. The last of these processes developed separately from the Cross and Bevan patent. The so-called 'viscose process' has produced variant fibres, designed to serve a range of purposes from clothing to tyre cords, and the extruded filaments can also be cut into staple fibres and spun individually or with other fibres.

The main alternative rayon is acetate, composed of cellulose acetate and an acetic acid-based process. In appearance similar to silk, it was very difficult to dye and so, although produced from *c*.1900, was less widely used until developments in reactive dyes in 1956 (see DYE). It is resistant to wrinkling and is principally used in clothing. For many years it was also known by the British trade name Celanese.

Reamy glass Glass with cords or striae, the result of the molten glass not having been a homogeneous mix. This produces glass of different hardnesses and therefore of different refractive indices. The effect is often unintentional but may be deliberate.

Red figure ware See BLACK FIGURE WARE.

Red lead A pigment made by heating lead white in air. It is almost obsolete in the West because of its toxicity, but as with other lead-based paints there are dispensations for its use in the conservation of historic artefacts. Its main use in the last 200 years has been as a primer for ironwork, and some red lead is still used in marine paints. It is an opaque, red/orange colour, unmatched by modern equivalents.

Red zebrawood A dark red wood with yellow markings, from the Burmese lacquer tree (*Melanorrhea laccifera*).

Relief printing A generic term for printing processes which use a raised surface to transfer ink to paper. Woodcuts and wood engravings are the most widely known relief prints, and their printed image is the reverse of the worked printing surface. Relief processes were the most suitable book illustra-

THE MAGPIE.

PIANET.

(Corvus Pica, Lin.—La Pie, Buff.)

ITS length is about eighteen inches : Bill ſtrong and black ; eyes hazel ; the head, neck, and breaſt are of a deep black, which is finely contraſted with the ſnowy whiteneſs of the breaſt and ſcapulars ; the neck feathers are very long, extending down

A wood engraving from Thomas Bewick's History of British Birds *(1797). Bewick achieved exceptional quality with this method of printing through his fine work with the burin on end grain wood. The technique is capable of conveying tone as well as line by subtle variations in the depth of cut, which vary the pressure on the block in printing.*

tion methods until the photomechanical innovations of the late 19th century (see PRINTING), because the woodblock can be made the same thickness as type to achieve a level printing surface and both letterpress and wood engraving are printed in one operation with the same kind of press.

Renaissance lace See TAPE LACE.

Repoussé work The decorative technique of beating out sheet metal, mainly from the back, using punches, hammers and snarling irons. This is usually followed by CHASING with finer punches from the front to give the final details. When worked from the back, a raised surface, or boss, will appear. (Embossing is another word to describe the repoussé technique.) Usually the workpiece is supported to allow it to

*Silver gilt lidded tankard.
Augsburg, c.1600. The
body of the tankard has
been raised and chased
with low relief repoussé
work.*

stretch in a controlled manner. The usual ground is chaser's
pitch, but other resilient materials such as leather, wood and
lead can be used as a support.

The term is derived from the French verb *repousser* ('to
push again'), and is sometimes also used to describe a similar
process applied to LEATHER.

Resist/reserved decoration Decoration on ceramics produced
with a wax, grease or paper resist. It is also commonly called
reserved decoration. To produce resist decoration a design
can be drawn on a formed clay body with wax or grease. The
vessel is then dipped in glaze, which does not adhere to the
waxed or greased areas. When the piece is fired the resist
burns away, leaving unglazed or biscuit decoration. In some
Chinese celadons, the reserved areas reoxidize at the end of

Porcelain bowl, with copper red glaze and reserved and slipped decoration, China, Ming period, 1506–21.

the firing and turn reddish as a result of iron impurities in the body. The red decorative areas create an interesting colour contrast with the cool green glaze.

Paper can also be used to produce resist decoration. On Cornish ware paper dots are applied to tablewares, which are then sprayed with blue slip. When the paper is removed, cream-coloured dots are left in reserve against a blue ground. Paper resist can also be used on glazes. On Jizhou wares from south China, cut paper designs were placed on a dark base glaze and then a light ash glaze was flecked over the surface of the vessel with a brush. The paper was then removed, leaving dark decoration against a mottled ground. In some cases, the paper was allowed to remain and burn away in the firing.

Both paper cuts and wax resist were used to produce matt designs on a lustre ground in the 'resist ware' that was made at Staffordshire in the 18th century. Grease resist can also be used to control fluid glazes, as can be seen on CUERDA SECA tiles.

Resist dyeing A method of producing a pattern on cloth or paper by dyeing after printing or painting it with a resist (for illustration see page 394). This may be a mechanical resist such as wax (see BATIK), clay or starch-paste, or a chemical resist such as an acid. Alternatively, a physical resist such as stitches, binding, wrapping or tying is used (see IKAT, PLANGI, SHIBORI and TRI-TIC). The 'lapis style', developed in the early 19th century, involved printing a resist paste (called resist-red) containing a mordant for madder; the cloth was dyed Prussian blue and then madder red, resulting in precise juxtapositions of areas of these two colours (see colour plate XVII).

Reticella An intermediate technique between embroidery and needle lace and used primarily as an insertion. It was fashionable from the mid-16th century to the early 17th and involved the removal of threads from linen cloth to leave voids 13–75 mm square; these were then filled with densely set buttonhole stitches worked on diagonal base threads connected to the frame of cloth.

Reverse glass painting The decoration of glass by painting on the reverse side. Especially popular in Europe from the 16th century to the 18th, the technique is sometimes known by the German term *hinterglasmalerei*, or as 'back painting'. It is

Colourless glass dish, with a cold-painted portrait on the underside, Venice, 17th century.

generally used on a sheet of glass or mirror, which is then held in a frame. The brilliance and freshness of the work derive from the transparency of the glass and the use of translucent paints. Various media have been used—oil, enamels, tempera, gum arabic, glue, lime and casein—and gold leaf sometimes adds to the effect. The work is often backed with a protective coating, perhaps of linseed oil mixed with dry pigments, or of cloth, paper or wood veneer. The images were often taken from woodcuts and engravings and naturally had to be executed in reverse, starting with the highlights and finishing with the background, with any script also painted in reverse. Reverse painting can also be seen on Chinese snuff bottles.

Confusingly, the term is also used of a technique, which originated in England in the second half of the 17th century, of mounting a paper print on the back of a sheet of glass and colouring it from behind (see TRANSFER ENGRAVING).

See also COLD PAINTING.

Rhinoceros horn The single, curved horn of the rhinoceros, highly prized in China for drinking cups and other items. It is composed of tightly packed, hairlike filaments of pure keratin, and ranges in length from 10 cm to 1 m. Yellowish grey when fresh, it may develop fine black or brown markings or a golden honey colour. It is cut with knives or chisels and polished to a high sheen.

Ribbon grain A roe or stripe figure seen in rift-cut timber with interlocking grain.

Rice grain decoration Pierced decoration on Chinese porcelain. The body material used for Chinese porcelain from the Imperial factory at Jingdezhen was very strong and could withstand piercing and reticulation without warping or collapsing. In the Wanli period (1573–1620) small porcelain cups were often decorated with pierced designs in patterns taken from architectural ornament or textiles. The piercing was done by hand and described by potters as 'devil's work'. In the 18th century the piercing became more standardized, with a simple floral pattern used for each bowl. This pattern consisted of pierced holes that were shaped like rice grains and filled with glaze, unlike earlier examples which were often glazed without filling in the pierced decoration. In order to fill the holes with glaze, repeated glaze applications were necessary. This type of decoration was also used in Persia in the 17th and 18th centuries on Gombroon ware, which was made from a translucent white frit body that resembled Chinese porcelain.

Rice paper See PAPER and PITH PAPER.

Rio rosewood See TULIPWOOD.

Ripple A descriptive term sometimes used by cabinetmakers to describe the figure that violin makers refer to as FIDDLEBACK.

Roan A high-quality, full-thickness, vegetable-tanned sheepskin originally tanned only with sumac. This type of leather was widely used for less expensive bookbindings and for covering items such as trinket boxes and manicure sets.

Robinia See ACACIA.

Rock crystal A colourless, transparent form of quartz which occurs within types of igneous rock and as infilling in cavities and fissures. The ancient Greeks believed that it was ice, permanently frozen by the gods, and its transparency was highly valued before the development in the late 15th century of transparent glass of consistent quality. Rock crystal is more useful as a gem material than glass as it is harder (Mohs scale 7, compared to 5.5–6, the hardness of most glasses used as gemstone simulants) and can therefore take and retain crisper facets and a higher sheen. It is found worldwide, although the principal sources are the French and Swiss Alps, Brazil, Japan, the USA and Australia. Rock crystal has been used as a gemstone, usually cut as a cabo-

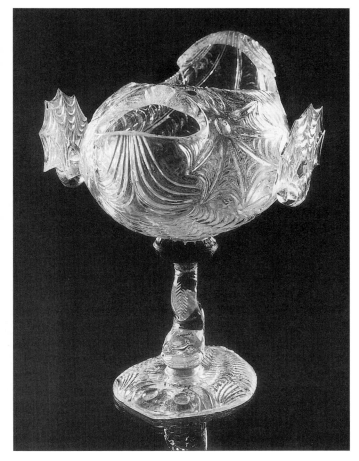

Cut and engraved rock crystal vessel, Prague, early 17th century, showing some of the problems inherent in using the material.

chon or as beads, carvings, crystal gazing balls, mirrors and
vessels, and is worked with cutting discs and the abrasive
corundum powder.

Although rock crystal does occur in large single crystals,
flaws and inclusions are common and therefore some objects,
such as stemmed vessels, are assembled from several pieces,
held together with decorative metal mounts. The hardness
and brittleness of rock crystal, compared with a material
such as jade (Mohs 6.5–7), mean that thin-walled vessels
cannot be produced and that carved forms and incised lines
tend to be angular rather than smooth. However, because of
the similarity in working techniques, both materials were
probably worked by the same craftsmen in Mogul India.

Rock crystal can be differentiated from glass, which has
been used as a simulant, by its comparative hardness and
coldness to the touch and by an optical property whereby a
dot, when viewed through rock crystal, will appear doubled.

Roe Short ribbon or stripe figure in quarter-sawn decorative
hardwoods.

Ro-iro A Japanese urushi (lacquer) technique. Iron acetate
or iron filings are mixed with raw urushi (*ki-urushi*) to make a
black lacquer used for the deep mirror-black finish characteristic of some of the finest Japanese wares.

Rolled inlay See INLAID DECORATION.

Roller printing A group of mechanized methods of producing
printed textiles, comprising machines with wooden rollers
(surface printing), engraved copper rollers (cylinder printing)
or a combination of both (mule printing). The first surface
and cylinder printing machines were installed in Lancashire,
England, in the 1780s and had an average circumference and
therefore pattern height of 30 cm; many were 'pinned', that
is, wooden rollers with metal insertions. Cylinder printing
was usually in one colour, with additional colours added by
block printing. About three years after the development in
1805 of the mule came the engraving of small all-over designs
(known as 'milled' patterns) by impressing the length of the
copper cylinder several times with a small raised-steel cylinder. This, together with the increase in circumference to
50–55 cm and improvements in dye chemistry, especially
steam-fixed dyes, made cylinders the source of the bulk of
single- and multi-colour printed cottons from *c.*1825 to
*c.*1940. Fine lines, hatching, stippling and subtle shading are
characteristics of the engraved (and, from *c.*1834, etched)

A copper-roller printed cotton from the Mulhouse region, Alsace, c.1905. The mottled ground results from the use of stipple engraving.

cylinders; a 'syrupy' unevenness of colour is indicative of surface printing.

Rolling mill A device for reducing the thickness and/or altering the shape of a piece of metal. It basically comprises two or more rollers, with an adjustable space between them, held in a rigid framework. By engraving the rollers with a pattern it can also be used to decorate metal. The origins of the rolling mill are unclear, but it appears first to have been used for iron plate in the 17th century in England, and for precious metals around 1700. Before this time sheet metal was made by hammering ingots, which was time-consuming and less efficient.

Roman red slipware Red earthenware decorated with glossy red slip that was produced in the Roman territories from the 1st century BC. As the earliest examples came from Arezzo, this ware is also often called Arretine ware. It is also sometimes called terra sigillata. Roman red slipware was a

A stem cup in terra sigillata, with red slip and moulded and applied relief decoration, Arezzo, probably 1st–3rd century AD.

development from earlier black slip wares which were fired in reduction. Like the black slip ware, the red version also had a fine clay slip applied to the local, calcareous clay body, but this was fired in oxidation which produced a red colour rather than black. The slip is vitreous and glossy and is often confused with a glaze.

Roman red slipwares were fired to approximately 1050°C in woodburning up-draught kilns. The forms were usually vessels which were created in moulds with relief decoration taken from the mould or applied by stamping to produce similar repeated motifs. Many examples also have sprigged decoration. This type of ceramic was very successful in the Roman territories and was copied in Africa, where it is usually called African red slipware. Examples produced in ancient Gaul are often called Samian ware.

Rose engine turning A mechanical process used to produce an engraved surface pattern of eccentric curved or wavy lines. This pattern was first produced around the 16th

century on soft materials such as ivory and wood but subsequently appeared also on metals. Initially it was produced on
an ornamental LATHE, but this was superseded by a plain
turning lathe with a special attachment, and then by a
purpose-built mechanism used exclusively for surface rose
engine turning. The technique was very popular for decorating boxes in the 18th and 19th centuries, and was also used
extensively for the guilloche metal ground employed in
translucent enamelling.

Rose point See NEEDLE LACE.

Rosewood A hard, heavy, strong and durable wood from
species of *Dalbergia*. It is widespread in the tropics, and individual varieties are normally distinguished by a geographical
prefix, such as Indian rosewood. The name is also applied to
other woods which resemble the true rosewoods, such as Australian rosewood (*Dysoxylum fraserianum*, sometimes called
Australian mahogany) and Burmese rosewood (*Pterocarpus*;
see PADAUK). It is dark purplish brown in colour, often variegated with darker or black veining, with a close grain displaying ribbon figuring, and it is sweetly aromatic when worked.
It is somewhat difficult to work but polishes well, and it is
used for superior cabinetmaking and joinery, carving,
parquet floors, fancy turnery and veneers.

Rosso antico [ceramics] The name of a red stoneware made
by Wedgwood in the 18th century, in imitation of Greek and
Roman red pottery (see ROMAN RED SLIPWARE). The body
material was made from a local red clay and the wares were
usually unglazed. This body was adapted from a red ware
recipe invented by the brothers David and John Philip Eler,
who set up a pottery in Hammersmith, London, *c*.1690 before
moving briefly to Staffordshire, where they produced red
stoneware until 1698. They were trying to imitate the Chinese
Yixing ware that was imported by the Dutch. Yixing teapots
were highly prized for their heat-retaining properties and
were initially copied in the Netherlands in 1672. In England
red ware was first made non-commercially at Fulham,
London, by John Dwight, who registered a patent in 1684.
The Eler brothers had worked for Dwight, and it is believed
that their red ware recipe was an imitation of his.

Some of the Wedgwood red wares have imitation Chinese
marks, but most of the later examples have neo-classical decoration, which was either modelled by hand and applied or
engine-turned. Before 1776, when Wedgwood named his red

ware rosso antico, the decoration was more Chinese in style. The forms were usually slip cast, owing to their complexity, with teapots being made in several parts and then luted together. Handles and finials were often press-moulded.

Rosso antico [stone] A uniformly coloured marble which may range from pale pink to an intense red and has been obtained since antiquity from quarries at Cape Matapan in Greece. It can be highly polished and was used decoratively, notably in PIETRE DURE (see colour plate XVIII).

Rubber A natural plastic (also known as latex or caoutchouc) collected as sap from the *Hevea brasiliensis* rubber tree, native to Brazil. The sap is immersed in acid to extract the water, producing a solid which can be rolled into sheets, dried and cured. Extrusion is currently replacing this water evacuation process. After further processing, rubber is compres-

Natural rubber moulding from South America, mid-19th century. Native rubber toys and mouldings such as this frequently made their way to Britain mixed in with shipments of natural rubber.

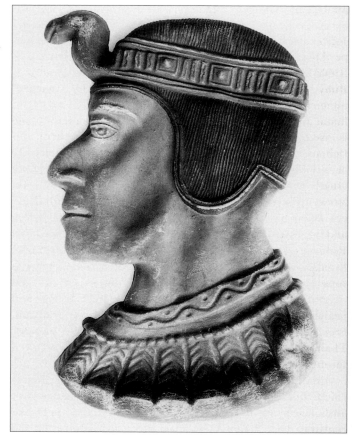

sion-moulded, extruded, cut into shapes or calendered (put through rollers). Natural rubber is malleable, becoming sticky when hot and rigid when cold.

Rubber was introduced into Britain in the late 18th century, and first used by draughtsmen as erasers. In the early 19th century it was used for double-texture waterproof cloaks known as macintoshes, invented by the Scottish chemist Charles Macintosh. In the 19th century machinery was developed to produce a variety of rubber goods. For example, Thomas Hancock's masticator cut up rubber into smaller pieces, using spiked rollers, to produce a doughy, workable mass which could then be moulded. Hancock, an English inventor and manufacturer, also patented a method for modifying the properties of rubber by the addition of sulphur, a process known as vulcanization (see VULCANITE). Fully synthetic rubbers have been produced since the 1930s and are chemically different from natural rubber, with the exception of all cis-polyisoprene rubbers, which only make up 1–2% of all synthetic rubbers as they are uneconomic to produce.

Rubbing See FROTTAGE.

Ruby A red gemstone composed of aluminium oxide, the mineral corundum, second in hardness (Mohs scale 9) to diamond. Its distinctive colour—and that of sapphire, which is also composed of corundum—is caused by impurities; the rich reds found in rubies are produced by chromium. The crystal structure of rubies and sapphires produces an optical effect called dichroism, which results in the intensity of the stone's colour appearing to change when viewed from different angles. This property must be recognized when cutting and mounting the stone, in order to maximize its colour. Rubies are formed in metamorphic or igneous rocks and are usually found in river gravels, often now submerged under topsoil, at a distance from the place of formation.

In many cultures rubies have been seen as talismans of health and good fortune. They were mined in Burma from the Stone Age. Other ancient and still significant sources are Thailand, Cambodia and Sri Lanka. Rubies are generally faceted, using either crushed corundum or diamond for cutting. The colour of pale stones was enhanced by placing coloured metal foil on the back, a process described by the 16th-century goldsmith Benvenuto Cellini. In the late 19th century a technique for making synthetic ruby was developed, the first such process to reproduce chemically a natural mineral.

Ruby glass A deep red glass coloured with gold or copper (see colour plate VI). The metal is dispersed as minuscule particles (colloids) throughout the glass. In ancient times an opaque red glass was made with copper (cuprous oxide) in a reducing atmosphere. The use of copper continued throughout the medieval period when, since the glass is too dense to transmit light, it was often flashed over a clear glass (see STAINED GLASS). It was not until the end of the 17th century that ruby glass became consistent in quality. This was due to the work of the German alchemist and glassmaker Johann Kunckel, who perfected the use of gold chloride. The process is complex since the glass is grey and only develops its colour when reheated or 'struck'. Also, gold is a powerful colouring agent and a proportion as low as 1:100 will produce a very strong colour. In the 20th century it was discovered that cadmium selenide and zinc will also give a deep ruby colour.

Rush A variety of plants with cylindrical stalks or leaves, found in marshy sites in temperate regions. Rushes can be dried and woven, or twisted into rope for basketry.

Russia leather Originally a leather tanned with birch, willow, poplar and larch bark and curried using mixtures containing birch oils. This process gave leather with a deep red colour and a characteristic smell. The grain was often boarded to give a long grain pattern. These leathers were exported into Europe both overland and along sea routes from medieval times until the 19th century. Russia leathers were used for bookbindings, upholstery, covering trunks and luggage, and for the manufacture of wallets, handbags and other small leather goods.

Imitation Russia leathers were produced using suitably dyed vegetable-tanned skins by finishing them with mixtures of oils scented with birch tar.

Sacrificial red See SANG DE BOEUF.

Saggar A clay box used to protect delicate or sensitive clays and glazes during firing from smoke, heat and ash, which could damage the ceramics or adversely affect their colour (for illustration see page 168). Usually made from fired refractory clay, saggars are an essential part of kiln furniture. They are generally used in conjunction with solid fuel kilns, as modern electric kilns provide a clean, well-controlled environment for firing. Saggars can be stacked to form dividing walls in a kiln, a practice frequently used in Asian dragon kilns.

The shape of the saggar depends on the shape of the vessel to be fired. Bowls, for example, can be fired in cone-shaped saggars or in vertical box-shaped ones, whereas more complicated forms may require special designs.

St John's blood See COCHINEAL.

Salt glaze A stoneware glaze created by the efflorescence of salt on the clay surface. The glaze is made by throwing salt

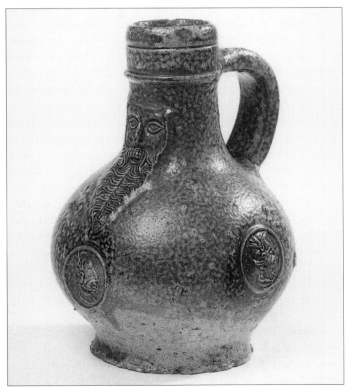

Stoneware bellarmine jug, with salt glaze and moulded decoration, Cologne, probably 17th century.

into the kiln when it reaches maximum temperature (1000–1100°C). The salt then splits into a chloride vapour and sodium oxide, which is deposited on the surface of the vessel and reacts with the body to form a thin, glassy glaze. This method of glazing is relatively simple but rather different from other glazing methods in that the resulting glaze is not smooth and even and usually has a pin-holed appearance.

Glazes made from salt were first used in Europe on medieval German stonewares. This development coincided with the introduction in Germany of a horizontal kiln that had a low stoking area and could reach high temperatures. The salt-glazing technique was taken up in England in the 17th century, and several modern British potters specialize in this type of glazing. Traditional salt glazes are usually grey or brown as they take the colour of the clay body, but some modern potters create green and blue salt glazes with slips and stains (which give a better result with salt glazes than simple oxide pigments). Most salt-glazed wares are decorated with incised and applied decoration, though some Dutch salt-glazed wares have underglaze cobalt blue painted decoration. Unlike other metallic oxides, cobalt reacts well with the salt glaze. In 18th-century Staffordshire fine white stonewares with salt glazes were made, and these were often decorated with overglaze enamels.

In order to produce a successful salt glaze, the salt should be dampened with water and applied several times in the course of firing. Owing to the amount of vapour produced, salt glazing is potentially dangerous and requires good ventilation. The most suitable clays for salt glazing are those high in silica, such as fire clays. Salt glazes have been used industrially for sewage pipes and acid containers, but this practice has been phased out.

Samian ware See ROMAN RED SLIPWARE.

Sampler A collection of embroidery stitches worked together on one panel. The oldest surviving examples date from the early 16th century, but samplers are known to have been made throughout western Europe before that date. Until the late 17th century they served, as their name suggests, to keep a record of stitches, but the stitches gradually came to be ordered into decorative rows and worked to demonstrate proficiency, rather than for reference purposes.

Sand-blasting A means of decorating glass by projecting fine grains of sand, crushed flint or powdered iron onto its surface in a jet of air at high velocity. This leaves a greyish, matt finish and a design can be created by masking the glass with a metal stencil or a wax or rubber resist. Variation in the quality of the sand, the force of the jet and the duration of the blast will create a wide range of effects. The process was invented in the USA in 1870 and is most suited to the decoration of large glass panels, though it has been used for deeply cut vessels.

Sand casting A method of casting metal, using a sand mould, which is held within a wooden or metal frame called a flask. The sand mould usually consists of two parts, which key into each other. One flask is filled with sand, into which the model or pattern is pressed half-way. The other flask is then placed on top of the prepared half, still containing the model, and is also filled with sand. After the two flasks are taken apart, the model is removed and sprues are cut in the sand to enable the molten metal to reach the cavity left by the model. The two flasks containing the sand mould are put back together again and the molten metal can be poured into the mould from an opening in the side of the flasks.

The sand used for sand casting is usually an extremely fine-grained silicate with a low proportion of clay, and it is used slightly damp to enable it to hold together. Sand casting is mostly used to create relatively simple shapes, because the two-part sand mould does not allow any undercuts. It is a relatively inexpensive method of casting because the sand as well as the model can be reused.

Sandstone A sedimentary stone composed of grains of quartz sand, deposited following the erosion of older rocks, held together by a cementing material and compacted by the weight of overlying sediments. The cementing material may be calcium carbonate, quartz, clay or various forms of iron. The nature of the cementing material and the degree of compaction affect the hardness, colour, texture and durability of the stone; the size of the quartz grains and the presence of other minerals also influence the character of the sandstone. Sandstones cemented with clay tend to be soft and friable, more easily worked but more vulnerable to weathering than ones in which quartz is the cementing material. Some fine-grained, well compacted sandstones such as Vosges, quarried in north-eastern France and used to build Strasbourg Cathedral, will accept finely carved detail. Others, such as some of the sandstone from southern Egypt, are too coarse and lack the tensile strength to retain a crisp edge. Conversely, some Egyptian and Indian sandstones are hard enough to take a polish. Because all sandstones contain a high proportion of quartz, which has a hardness of Mohs 7, they can readily wear down steel chisels with a hardness of approximately Mohs 6 and therefore tools must be regularly sharpened. Sandstones occur in a number of colours, including white, yellow, red, brown, blue and grey. As they are formed from successive deposits of sediments, they have a bedded or layered structure which may be subtle or pronounced in appearance.

Sandstones are found in most parts of the world and have been used extensively for building, tiling and paving (see YORK STONE) and for carving. Because of its gritty texture sandstone has also been used as an abrasive: the Chinese used it to shape jade and the Egyptians used small blocks of sandstone as erasers.

Sandwich gold glass See FONDI D'ORO, VERRE ÉGLOMISÉ and ZWISCHENGOLDGLAS.

Sang de boeuf A high-fired, copper red glaze. It is ideally almost a cherry red colour but the pigment is notoriously difficult to control (see METALLIC OXIDES) and can often turn grey or disappear. The viscosity of the base glaze is important because successful copper reds depend on the ability to spread the pigment evenly throughout the glaze without clumping or reaching the surface and volatilizing.

Copper red glazes were first developed on Chinese porcelain in the Song period (960–1279). The most successful examples were those produced in the 15th century at the Imperial kilns in Jingdezhen. They are often known as 'sacrificial red' because of the auspicious nature of the colour in that period.

The technique for producing copper red glazes eventually died out in China but was reintroduced in the late 17th century. At this time the glazes contained less copper than the 15th-century reds and the base glaze was more fluid, often resulting in shading of colour at the rims of vessels. Some of these reds have a liverish tone and it was these that were known as 'ox blood' reds or *sang de boeuf* in Europe, where Chinese porcelains were collected. A similar copper red glaze was adopted by French potters in the 19th century.

Santo wood Wood from the Central American pau santo tree (*Zollernia paraensis*). It is brown to greenish black in colour, and is often variegated. It is frequently used as a substitute for LIGNUM VITAE.

Sapele A hard and heavy, strong, stable and fragrant wood from the sapele mahogany (*Entandophragma cylindricum, E. utile*), also known as the Gold Coast cedar, acajou, sapelli, penkwa and tiama. Some species of *Guarea* are also sometimes referred to as sapele. It is a light gingery brown colour, with a close interlocking grain and roey mottled figure. It is usually quarter-sawn and is easily polished, and it is used for joinery, cabinetmaking, veneers and plywood.

Sapodilla Wood from the Sapotaceae family, which provides gums and resins such as GUTTA PERCHA and chicle as well as heavy, fine-grained ornamental timbers used mainly in turnery.

Sappenwood See BRAZILWOOD.

Sapphire A gemstone form of the mineral corundum, aluminium oxide. (Ruby is also corundum.) The blue of sapphire is produced by iron and titanium impurities. Yellow and green sapphires also exist, owing to reactions between the constituent elements. Star sapphires, in which a thin white star is seen within the stone, are caused by alignments of needle-like inclusions. The crystal structure of sapphires and rubies produces an optical effect called dichroism, which results in the intensity of the stone's colour appearing to change when viewed from different angles. This property must be recognized when cutting and mounting the stone, in order to maximize its colour. Sapphires are formed in igneous and metamorphic rocks and are generally found in gravels where they have been deposited by erosion of the rock. Like rubies, they have been found in Burma, Thailand and Sri Lanka. Kashmir was also an important historical source. Sapphires are generally faceted, although star sapphires are cut as cabochons since faceting would destroy this optical effect.

Sapwood The outer, living layers of a tree trunk. The proportion of sapwood varies with species and often diminishes with age. It usually contrasts strongly with the HEARTWOOD of the tree, being less durable and more prone to insect and fungal attack, but it is nonetheless often specifically selected for certain purposes.

Sardonyx See ONYX.

Satin A weave structure in which a closely set warp floats over more than one weft (in warp-faced satins) or a closely set weft over more than one warp (weft-faced satins) in a random

Satinwood tea caddy with sand-shaded scallop inlays, cross banding in tulipwood and stringing in ebony and boxwood, England, late 18th century.

order, so that the face threads appear to cover the entire surface. Any fibre can be used in its construction, but on its own it is associated with the soft sheen that results from employing silk; in combination with other weave structures, it is associated with DAMASK, BROCATELLE and TABARET.

Satin-spar See ALABASTER.

Satinwood A pale, silky wood with a distinctive, satin-like ripple figure. It became popular in the 1770s, when it to some extent superseded mahogany as the timber of choice for small furniture. Almost always used as a veneer, it was often employed as a contrasting cross banding with darker timbers. A large group of timbers from many different species are referred to as satinwood, including *Murraya exotica* (also known as Chinese boxwood or myrtle), *Phebalium billardieri* and *Euxylophora paraensis* (also known as sateenwood and pao amarello).

Savonnerie A cut-pile carpet, with loops hand-knotted over a sharp-edged iron rod extending across the loom, the withdrawal of which cuts the loops. The technique is attributed to Pierre Dupont, active in the 1590s, and the resulting style of carpet is named after the disused soapworks near Paris that was the centre of production from 1620 to 1825, when the machinery was transferred to the Gobelins tapestry factory at Beauvais.

Saw See WOODWORKING TOOLS.

Scagliola A material composed of gypsum plaster, animal glue and pigments, used to imitate coloured marbles and pietra dura ornament and furniture. The name is derived from the Italian word *scaglia*, meaning 'scale', which refers to the small chips of stone sometimes added to the mix.

Although scagliola has ancient antecedents in lime-based techniques for imitating marble (see PLASTERWORK), it was invented by stuccoists working in Bavaria in the 16th century. Italian artists working in Germany introduced Italianate designs and later transported the technique to Italy, where the reproduction of the highly prized and expensive pietre dure was further developed.

To imitate coloured marble, gypsum plaster is mixed with either rabbitskin glue or parchment glue, which retard the set of the plaster and also help produce a hard surface. The mix is then made into individual cakes which are each coloured with dry pigments to produce the range of tones found in the marble. Veining is mimicked by dusting the surface of the cakes with dry pigments. The cakes are then sliced in half and arranged on a prepared surface to imitate the random patterning of the stone. Chips of alabaster or marble can be pressed into the surface. The surface is then smoothed with a metal scraper. Once the plaster has set, the long process of polishing the surface with pumice stones and filling any voids with a plaster slurry is carried out. Finally the surface is rubbed with oil to produce a high sheen. This material can be used to make columns, which are constructed on a wooden framework around an iron or stone core, and wall coverings,

Scagliola table top, Italy, c.1690, designed in imitation of pietre dure and showing the intricate patterning possible with this technique.

applied over a substrate of lime plaster, and panels.

Inlaid scagliola, which resembles pietre dure, uses the same materials, applied over a rigid support such as slate. A solid background colour is laid down and the shapes to be inlaid are gouged out. Coloured plaster is then pressed into the voids to build up the desired image and the surface is polished and oiled.

Schiffli embroidery A form of embroidery named after the type of EMBROIDERY MACHINE on which it was made. It can also imitate a wide variety of embroidered lace.

Schist A metamorphic stone, characterized by a structure consisting of numerous fine layers, which may contain a number of minerals, although mica is the most common. Schists are grey with green or blue tones, often with a sparkling, metallic lustre produced by the mica. They split readily along the layers, producing thin panels of stone more suited to relief carving than building. Schist was used extensively in Gandhara (Pakistan) in the 1st to 3rd centuries AD for figurative and ornamental carving on Buddhist temples.

Schwarzlot A technique of painting glass or porcelain with black or sepia-brown translucent enamel (see ENAMEL COLOURS). The literal translation of the term is 'black lead'. The paint is applied with a fine brush in a linear style, sometimes in emulation of engravings. Gilding, iron-red enamel and sometimes a wider palette of colours may be added to the design and details are scratched out with a needle. The technique, which was popular in Austria and Bohemia in the 17th and 18th centuries, allows for more subtle tonal gradations than are possible with opaque enamel. Its development is linked to the use of enamel on stained glass, and indeed its finest practitioner, Johann Schaper, was a stained-glass painter by training.

The schwarzlot painter Abraham Helmback depicted in an engraved and etched self-portrait, c.1680. He holds a beaker that is typical of the craft.

Scotch carpeting See KIDDERMINSTER.

Scraper See WOODWORKING TOOLS.

Scratchwork See SGRAFFITO.

Screen A self-supporting panel or set of panels articulated by hinges; also generally a movable item of furniture. Screens made of wood and paper are part of traditional architecture in the Far East, where they form doors, walls and movable barriers which present surfaces for decoration. In the Japanese tradition the sliding panels (*fusama*) and folding screens (*byobu*) are part of the stock-in-trade of the professional mounter, since he uses a similarly constructed moveable

panel called a *karibari* board to stretch a scroll painting
during lining. The board is made of a latticework of lightweight wood, usually cedar, covered with layers of paper,
which are waterproofed with fermented persimmon juice
(*Diospyros lotus*) in the case of the *karibari* board or used as a
support for a painting in the architectural context. The back
of a folding screen or sliding panel is often decorated too, with
gold leaf, for example, and the edges covered with silk
brocade.

Screens, both folding and hand-held (see FAN), are less
often made of paper in the West but in the 18th and 19th centuries the folding screen as a support for a collection of prints
became popular, especially among amateurs. Screens of two
or more panels, constructed of paper with a woven textile
lining nailed over a wooden framework, were decorated with
pasted-on engravings or, later, colour lithographs covered
with a protective layer of varnish.

Screen printing A printing process in which ink is forced
through a sheet material from which a design has been cut
out and which thus acts as a stencil. It is used on both paper
and textiles. STENCIL PRINTING, from which screen printing
evolved in the early years of the 20th century, is limited by
the need for every element of the design to be interconnected.
Screen printing overcomes this problem by supporting the

*Hand screen printing at
Stead McAlpin & Co.,
Cummersdale, England,
early 1950s. Here the final
colour is being printed on
the 1951 Stead design* The
Wilton.

stencil on a framed woven mesh screen, through which the ink or dye can pass. The colouring material is transferred through the screen by a squeegee blade; in stencilling a brush or sponge is adequate.

In textile production, screen printing was employed in the inter-war years primarily as a hand-powered technique for high-quality printed textiles. Flat screens were used, the width of the printing table, which required two printers to pass the squeegee from side to side. The process was initially mechanized by powering the movement of the flat screens and the squeegee, but in the mid-20th century a mesh cylinder was developed. Today this is often of solid metal, etched into mesh only where colour must pass through. Hand screens are still much used in craft printing; they have no design height restrictions, while their mechanized counterparts can produce designs up to only about 1 m high.

Screw See WOOD FIXINGS.

Scrimshaw A folk art in which whale teeth, whale bone and sometimes walrus tusks are engraved or lightly carved with a variety of designs. The earliest scrimshaw dates from the late 17th century but most pieces were worked between 1830 and 1870. The art form is generally attributed to whalers and other seamen, but many examples were in fact carved on land, sometimes by carvers who had never been to sea.

Scrimshaw is largely associated with America but was also practised by British, Australian and New Zealand carvers. The tools employed were simple: saws, files, chisels and gouges were all used, but not lathes. Pictorial designs were 'pricked' through a paper image (sometimes a contemporary print) onto the surface of a tooth or piece of bone, then deeply scratched and darkened with indian ink.

Scroll A roll of a sheet material such as paper, used as a support for painting and writing. In Asia the craft of making rolled manuscripts and paintings primarily for use in religious ritual has evolved with a sophistication which parallels bookbinding in the West. Early Chinese Buddhist banners, dating from the 7th century, are thought to have been the prototypes of these later hanging scrolls and to have been derived from Indian banner paintings.

In the East there are two main categories: hand scrolls and hanging scrolls, known in Japan as *makimono* and *kakemono*. The hand scroll functions as a support to an illustrated written narrative, similar to a book but unrolled from right to left by the reader; it thus has a horizontal format. The hanging scroll, which is in a vertical format, has a more pictorial function and is meant to be displayed, for example during the Japanese tea ceremony.

The painting or manuscript is first executed independently by an artist or calligrapher, using silk or handmade paper as a support, and a scroll mounter then puts together the finished artefact using the appropriate materials and style. Both types of scroll are constructed from laminates of paper, or silk and paper, stuck on with starch paste, and attached at each end to wooden rods around which they can be rolled. In the case of the *kakemono* the upper rod is used for hanging. Hanging scrolls are sometimes remounted several times in their history as parts of the structure wear out. The traditional skills and tools of the scroll mounter (*hyogushi*) are highly regarded in Japan. Scrolls are generally kept in a box or textile wrapping when not in use.

Secco Painting on dry plaster with pigment bound in a medium. The term is used to distinguish this wall-painting technique from that of FRESCO. Traditionally the medium has been egg, oil or animal glue, but casein, acrylics and alkyd paints are more commonly used today, and indeed acrylics were developed specifically for mural paintings.

Before starting to paint on plaster it is quite common to size the plaster with a product such as animal glue, so that the surface is not too absorbent, or even to give it a ground. Most English murals dating from the Middle Ages are on a limewash base, regardless of the medium used for the painting, but from the 17th century it became more common to prepare for oil paint by applying an oil ground. With secco painting, unlike fresco, there are few restrictions on the selection of pigments that can be used, but if there is no ground or sizing layer then the alkalinity of the plaster means that organic pigments and Prussian blue are at risk.

Sedimentary ink See INK.

Serge A generic term for a wide variety of warp-faced twill weaves used from as early as the 12th century for both upholstery and clothing fabrics. The fibre originally used is indicated by the Latin derivation, *serica* (meaning 'silk') and later the Italian *sergea* (meaning 'wool mixed with silk'). Like many cloths, by the 17th century serge incorporated cotton, of which it was subsequently entirely made; the most notable examples of this mutation were *serge de Nîmes* and serge denim (the British imitation of the French cloth); at the beginning of the 18th century both were worsteds, but they slowly evolved into the all-cotton cloth denim.

Serigraph A term used to denote an original artist's print, as opposed to a commercial screen print. The word was first used in the USA in 1940. By then the screen printing method had become popular for advertising and signmaking because it did not require expensive metal plates or elaborate presses.

Serpentine An igneous rock, containing hydrated magnesium and iron silicate minerals, which is formed through the alteration of other igneous rocks. It is heavily veined, green to black in colour, and its name derives from the fact that its mottled appearance is said to resemble a serpent's skin. Serpentine can be highly polished and has been used decoratively in panelling, flooring (such as cosmati work) and fireplaces. It weathers to a dull grey and is not suitable for external ornamental use. The word is sometimes used, erroneously, for green porphyry.

Sewing machine A lock-stitch machine perfected in 1846 by the American Elias Howe, who sold his patent (which expired in 1860) to William Thomas of London. Meanwhile Isaac Merritt Singer was making improvements and he subsequently took out an American patent; Singer's machine was available in Scotland from 1856. After an upsurge of sewing-machine production in the 1860s, hand- and machine-stitching were used together in garments well after 1900.

Sewing styles Various stitches used to join together the pages of a handmade book (see BOOKBINDING). The sewing joins the groups of folded paper or parchment sheets by thread passed through the folds and around a series of BANDS made of cord, leather thong or linen tape placed at right angles to the folds. The ends of the bands (known as 'slips') are secured to the boards by passing through holes ('lacing in') made for the purpose, or by glueing. Until about the 15th century in Europe many different book structures and sewing styles were tried, while in the Near and Far East the chain and stab stitch respectively have remained in almost constant use up to the present day. Although various stitches are possible, sewing in the finished codex or traditional European-style book is rarely visible on the outside of the binding, and except for the bands it is not usually exploited for its decorative potential.

Sgraffito A decorative technique used in various media, also

Lead-glazed earthenware dish with painted and sgraffito decoration, Perugia or Città di Castello, Italy, 1500–1520. This ware is known as bianchetto *or* mezza maiolica *because, without a tin glaze, it is not true* maiolica.

known as graffito or scratchwork, in which layers of contrasting colour are applied to a surface and a design is scratched through the upper layer to reveal the colour beneath. The technique was practised in antiquity and was described by the Renaissance art historian Vasari as being a quick and durable method for decorating building façades. In the Renaissance lime plaster, tinted with ash, was used as the under layer, and then covered with white lime plaster; the design was transferred to this surface by pouncing. Italian artists carried the sgraffito technique to Germany in the 16th century, combining it with modelled stucco decoration. In the 19th century the lowest, levelling layer consisted of Portland cement, above which a layer of cement coloured with earth pigments was applied. The final layer for indoor work was Parian cement; Portland cement was used externally.

With all materials the layers are allowed to dry but not set completely before the design is cut in with an iron stylus or knife, used to peel away the upper layer. After the plaster or cement has set fully, areas of the design can be oil-gilded.

For sgraffito on ceramics, see also SLIP DECORATION.

Shagreen A leather made from the skins of certain species of sharks, rays and dogfish, in particular the stingray (*Hypolphus sephen*). These skins have spines or papillae in the grain surface formed from a hard cartilage-type material, and these are not coloured by the usual dyestuffs employed for leather. If these papillae are ground down and polished, a characteristic surface effect is produced in which the hard white nodules contrast with the dyed leather. Blue, red and, in particular, green shagreen leather were used in the late 18th century and throughout the 19th to cover such small articles as jewel boxes, needle cases and opera glasses. A form of shagreen in which the nodules were allowed to remain proud of the leather surface was used to cover sword hilts, where the uneven surface served to improve the grip.

Shakudo A Japanese alloy of copper with a small amount of gold (between 1% and 5%) and usually a very small amount of silver (up to 1%). It sometimes also contains arsenic. The metal has the appearance of copper but after patination (see IROGANE) the surface becomes an attractive purplish black (see colour plate XIIIa).

Shale A fine-grained sedimentary rock composed of thin layers, formed from clays and sand which were deposited in streams or lakes and slowly compacted. Shales can be brown, grey or black and are readily split along the layers. They were used from the Bronze Age to make jewellery, such as bracelets, and larger decorative objects.

Shantung See SILK.

Sheet glass See FLAT GLASS.

Sheffield plate See FUSED PLATE.

Shell A material secreted as a calcium-rich liquid by the mantle tissues of molluscs. There are three main layers. The nacreous inner layer, called MOTHER-OF-PEARL, is a mixture of a crystalline form of calcium carbonate known as aragonite and the protein conchiolin. (Under certain circumstances the same material builds up around a speck of foreign matter and becomes a PEARL.) The middle layer is built up of prismatic calcium carbonate crystals and the thin outer layer is wholly organic and made from conchiolin.

Shells have been used as a source of decorative material since prehistoric times. Their role as currency and trade objects is also very ancient and continued in tribal societies until the 19th century. A wide range of marine shells have been used, according to availability and the intended purposes. The helmet shell (*Cassis madagascarensis*), the giant conch (*Strombus gigas*) and the NAUTILUS are especially suited to CAMEO carving because of their coloured, banded structure; ABALONE is used for inlaid lacquerware; and smaller shells such as cowries are used intact in jewellery, decorative items and shell pictures. Shells have also been incorporated in stucco and plasterwork in the decoration of grottoes.

The carving of marine shells has a long history. Engraved shell inlays and intaglio carved seals have been found on Babylonian sites, and cameos have been popular since Roman times. The term 'carving' is somewhat inaccurate, however, when applied to shell. The material is too brittle to

Shellwork group, Naples or Genoa, c.1840.

withstand the forces applied to other carved materials, such as wood or stone. The process used is therefore more akin to engraving, and many of the tools employed are those originally developed for metal engravers, such as scorps and gravers. Files and scrapers are also used and 'pencils' or shaped blocks and rods of pumice and other abrasive stones are employed. A knife point is sometimes used to produce certain types of design, but with a distinct scraping action rather than cutting.

Layers of shell have also been used as inlays. These were usually saw-cut and sometimes enhanced by drilling or engraving. Shell inlays have been found on the site of Ur, and inlaid furniture, boxes and cosmetic implements have been found in the tombs of ancient Egypt. By the 12th century AD the Chinese had perfected a method of producing very thin layers (as little as 0.01 mm) of iridescent shell, from which minute repeat patterns could be produced with cutting punches or a resist technique using weak acids. These were inlaid into lacquered surfaces to produce the LAC BURGAUTÉ techniques that were later copied in the West in the production of certain types of japanned ware and papier mâché.

Shell gold A term once used of gold leaf ground in honey. The mixture was kept in mussel shells, and for use as a paint it was then mixed with gum arabic or another suitable medium. In the 19th century small drops of dried watercolour made in this fashion were sold as 'shell gold'.

Shellac One of the forms of the LAC resin. Shellac has been used for many centuries in the preparation of spirit varnishes and polishes and in a variety of craft and industrial processes. Since it is a natural plastic it can also be moulded with a fine level of detail, or it can be used in a solid form and melted onto the object being decorated.

Lac is extracted and refined from a deep brownish red protective secretion deposited by the females and larvae of certain species of insects, the most important of which is *Coccus lacca*, which parasitize certain shrubs and trees in parts of India, Thailand and Burma. The resin was originally obtained as a by-product during the extraction of the bright red dye known also as 'lac' (from which the English term 'lake' is derived). Today the dye is a by-product of lac production, which commences with the harvesting of the resin-encrusted twigs. These are dried and the resin broken off. The largest pieces are washed to remove the red dye and then

placed in calico bags. The lac is warmed before a fire and squeezed out onto flat plates. The resulting sheets are cooled and broken into flakes for sale. Three grades of resin are produced: shellac, seedlac and button lac. Each is formed at a different stage of the refining process and has characteristics suited to specific forms of decoration.

In alcoholic solution shellac is employed as a medium for pigments, and it is the only resin used in good-quality FRENCH POLISHING. The lac resins are also the principal materials used in some of the LACQUER techniques of the Near and Middle East and Europe.

In the 19th century shellac was used as a natural plastic to make decorative goods, including mirror backs. After mixing with a number of different fillers, such as wood flour and slate dust, the shellac was pressed into a heated mould, and when the mould had cooled the object was released. Shellac union cases were popular as containers for daguerreotype and ambrotype photographs. These cases were decorated with

Collection of shellac union cases, mirrors and seals, c.1860–80. Shellac was a particularly good material for decorative uses because of the intricate moulded detail that could be obtained.

geometric patterns produced using a rose lathe. Sometimes very skilled die-engravers produced designs based on famous contemporary paintings. The earliest shellac gramophone records were made in 1897.

Shellfish purple A reduction/oxidization dye extracted from shellfish of the Muricidae and Thaididae families and with a chemical composition that differs by one or two bromine atoms from indigo. The precise process used to transfer this dye to cloth is not known, but it paralleled that for indigo, since the dye substance was a photo-sensitive secretion extracted from the minute hypobranchial glands of the shellfish. About 10,000 shellfish yielded one gram of dye, which had several shades from reddish purple to bluish purple. It was extremely expensive and because of its consequent association with aristocrats in Phoenicia, Rome and Byzantium, it acquired the alternative names royal purple, imperial purple and Tyrian purple (Tyre produced the best quality). Both shellfish purple and indigo are known to date back to the 3rd millennium BC, but the use of the former died out in 15th century AD, following the Turkish conquest of Constantinople in 1453.

Shibori The collective Japanese term for RESIST DYEING techniques based on gathering, binding, tucking, stitching or folding, such as IKAT, PLANGI and TRI-TIC. These techniques are known to have been in use in Japan in the 8th century, but blossomed in the Edo period (1600–1868). The term (from the Japanese for 'squeezed') is also used for West African cloths treated in a similar way.

Shibuishi A Japanese alloy of copper with typically 25% silver (*shibuishi* is Japanese for 'a quarter'). Before patination (see IROGANE) the metal looks like copper, but after colouring an attractive greyish white colour appears on the surface (see colour plate XIIIa and c).

Sienna A yellow ochre pigment originally obtained around the Italian town of Siena. It can still be obtained in its natural form, but most paint and pigment sold under this name is a mixture of synthetic iron oxides. When burnt or calcined, sienna is a warm, reddish brown colour. Burnt and raw sienna are prized for their translucency and warmth; they make wonderful glazes in oil and are therefore used as stains for woodwork and in wood-graining. Their transparency also makes them suitable for watercolour washes. Like all earth pigments, the siennas are colour-fast, stable and chemically inert.

Silhouette A depiction of the outline form of an object or person. Silhouettes were a cheap and popular form of portraiture throughout the 18th century and into the mid-19th, until the invention of photography. The image, which was usually in black, was painted on a ground of plaster, card, ivory, porcelain or even glass. Alternatively, it was cut out of black paper and mounted on a contrasting background of white paper. Hollow cutting followed the same process in reverse, with the white paper forming the surround and the dark background the image. An accomplished silhouettist such as the French artist Auguste Edouart could cut a profile portrait free-hand in paper or thin card, but a number of mechanical devices were invented for tracing a profile and then reducing it to size.

The art, which was practised by both professionals and

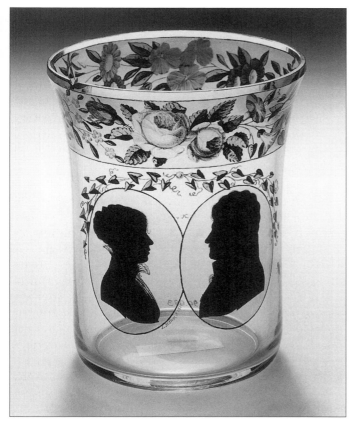

Beaker in colourless glass decorated with black portrait silhouettes and enamel decoration, Dresden, c.1810.

amateurs, was named after Etienne de Silhouette, finance minister under Louis XV, who was renowned for his economies and enjoyed papercutting as a recreation.

Silicone A synthetic material consisting of molecules made up of a repeating silicon–oxygen backbone with organic groups attached by silicon–carbon bonds to a significant proportion of the silicon atoms. Silicones can be produced in liquid form for furniture polishes, paints, coatings, resins, sealants and water-repellent glues and in mouldings ranging from solid, rigid substances to soft gels. Initially explored by Professor Frederick Kipping of Nottingham University, England, in the early 20th century, the applications of silicone were developed in the USA by the Corning Glass Company and the Dow Chemical Company in 1931. This resulted in the formation in 1943 of the Dow Corning Corporation for the commercial production of silicones.

Silicone rubber A synthetic rubber consisting of an inorganic chain molecule backbone made of silicon and oxygen atoms with organic groups attached. To produce elastomeric (rubbery) properties silicone polymers of appropriate weight must be cross-linked. Silicone rubbers are used as sealants in architectural applications and also for implants such as heart valves, ears and noses as well as for gaskets and sealing rings. Liquid silicone rubber is used for coating wire and cable. The material is valued for properties such as its heat-resistance and ability to function over a wide range of temperatures, making it useful, for example, in making the moulds used by sculptors and replica makers.

Silk A continuous protein filament produced by silkworm larvae, especially those of the moth *Bombyx mori*. Secreted by the caterpillar as a viscous fluid and hardened by a secreted gum, it is used by the insect to create its cocoon. In silk production the cocoon is immersed in warm water, the filament is reeled off and the gum is removed by boiling-off, when the silk becomes white and soft; throwing (see SPINNING) completes the production of silk threads, which are exceptionally lustrous, strong and take dye readily. Many varieties of silkworm exist, the others of significance being the undomesticated tussah *Antheraea paphia*, which produces a coarse, light brown silk, more irregular in texture and dye-absorbency, duller and stiffer than filaments from domesticated silkworms, and the undomesticated *Bombyx croesi*, which produces a rich yellow silk known as nistri or wild silk, giving the

characteristic colour and uneven texture to the plain weave cloth shantung. For the weighting of silk, see LOGWOOD; for attempts to replicate silk, see RAYON.

Silk production in Assam, India, 1995. The woman on the right is unreeling silk from the cocoons while the man reels it onto a bobbin.

Silk cotton/silk floss See KAPOK.

Silk throwing See SPINNING.

Silkscreen printing See SCREEN PRINTING.

Silver A white noble metal. It is very malleable and ductile (surpassed only by gold) and is the best conductor of heat and electricity. It is also the whitest of all metals and has the highest reflectivity. Although silver exists as a native metal in nature, it is usually found as an ore, as silver chloride or sulphide. There is a naturally occurring gold–silver alloy called electrum which contains 25–40% silver. The first objects made from silver date from *c.*2500 BC and were found in Asia Minor. These early objects are of such high quality that it must be assumed that they are the result of a long tradition of metalworking. The extraction of silver was carried out by the cupellation process, using a silver-rich lead ore called galena. The metal was first extracted from the ore by smelting, and then heated in a crucible made of bone ash, called a cupel. During heating a draught of air was passed over the molten alloy, oxidizing the lead and any other base

metal in the alloy so that they ran off or were absorbed in the
bone ash, leaving the silver behind in the cupel.

Today most silver is extracted as a by-product from the
refinement of lead, gold, copper and zinc. When silver is

extracted directly from silver ores, processes such as smelting, amalgamation, cyanidation and electrolytic refinement are used to create a pure silver. This pure silver is usually too soft to use, however, and is often alloyed with copper to create a harder metal. The most well-known silver alloy is STERLING SILVER, a legal silver standard which consists of 92.5% silver and 7.5% copper. The only other legal silver alloy in Britain is BRITANNIA SILVER, which consists of 95.8% silver and 4.2% copper.

A silversmith may use a whole range of techniques to work silver. Silver sheet can be wrought into hollowware by hammering techniques such as raising and sinking, usually followed by planishing to create a smooth surface. Spinning and die-stamping are more modern ways of shaping silver sheet. After shaping, the article can be decorated by embossing, which involves repoussé work and chasing. The surface can also be worked by such processes as engraving, etching, enamelling, niello, piercing, filigree, granulation and gilding. Other ways of fashioning silver are casting and electroforming. Often a combination of techniques is used; for example, a vessel may be created by hammering and then decorated with cast ornaments and handles, which are soldered onto the vessel. The last step in finishing a piece is polishing, which can be done by hand (burnishing) or on a buffing machine.

Silver, like gold, has a long history of use for coinage and there was always a direct link between gold and silver plate and their monetary value. This explains why there is such a long history of hallmarking (see HALLMARK), whereby the silver content in the alloy was guaranteed. This oldest form of consumer protection has been in use in Britain and some other European countries for more than 700 years. Non-decorative uses of silver include electroplating, dentistry and photography.

For silver plating, see BRITISH PLATE, CLOSE PLATING, ELECTROPLATING, FRENCH PLATING and FUSED PLATE.

Silver grain The distinctive figure formed by rays in quarter-cut timbers such as oak.

Silver staining The application of a silver compound, usually silver nitrate (or silver sulphide), to the back of glass to produce a yellow colour. The effect of the silver stain depends on the composition of the glass to which it is applied, the amount of stain, the number of applications and the temperature to which it is fired. Introduced early in the 14th century

OPPOSITE *Set of three silver tea caddies in a mother-of-pearl case, by Edward Darville, London, 1762. The silver has been cast, chased and openworked by piercing.*

and frequently used on stained-glass windows (see colour plate VI), silver stain was initially confined to a yellow-on-white combination, but was extended in the 15th century to produce a green tint by applying the stain to blue glass. The generic term stained-glass windows is derived from silver staining, although it is not a major feature of such windows.

Silvering See MIRROR.

Singed leather Sheepskin decorated with the aid of hot metal plates or hand tools to give a slightly burnt effect. Singed leathers were used in the 17th and 18th centuries to make protective covers for furniture when it was not in use.

Sinking The creation of a hollow form in sheet metal by hammering on the inner concave surface while supporting the workpiece on a wooden block, sandbag or metal surface. With sinking, or blocking, the metal is stretched, whereas in raising the metal is compressed.

Size Animal glue dissolved in water. Collagen is extracted from the skin of animals such as rabbits or sheep by boiling it for many hours, and is usually stored as leaves of gelatine or powder. If made up in concentrated form it acts as a powerful adhesive, and it was the standard glue for furniture and woodwork until replaced by PVAs in the 20th century. In diluted form it is used to seal porous surfaces. For instance, gilders seal gesso before water gilding and seal wood before oil gilding, and house painters seal lime plaster walls before painting in oil. It has also been used as a protective layer, to cover gilding and occasionally paint.

Size has been a painting medium since pre-classical times, usually for wall painting (see DISTEMPER) but also for textiles, miniatures, manuscripts and panels. It shares many of the qualities of watercolour, but because it is less translucent it can also create areas of dense matt colour like gouache. It is much less readily soluble than watercolour and therefore makes a hard-wearing medium. One of the difficulties of working with a size paint is the need to keep it warm to prevent it from gelling.

Size gilding Gold leaf attached with animal glue or linseed oil as an adhesive, used on ceramics and glass.

Skiver The thin layer, including the GRAIN surface, which is obtained when an animal skin is split longitudinally. The term is particularly used with reference to sheepskin. Skiver is generally vegetable-tanned to produce a material used for covering desk tops and for binding small books such as diaries.

Slab building See CERAMICS.

Slab glass See DALLE DE VERRE.

Slate A fine-grained metamorphic rock formed through the exertion of great pressure on sediments of clay, volcanic ash or shale. It is predominantly grey, although red, green and blue tones are caused by the presence of mineral impurities. Slates will split readily at right angles to the direction of the metamorphic pressure. Slate is a hard, durable material that is easily worked and will take and retain fine carved detail; it can also be polished. It has been used occasionally in blocks as a building stone, but much more widely in thin sheets for inscriptions, gravestones, roof tiles, paving and relief carving. In Germany and other European countries slates are shaped and hung on the exterior of buildings to from elaborate patterns. Occasionally, hung slates are colour-washed.

Slip Liquid clay used in the manufacture of ceramics. It can

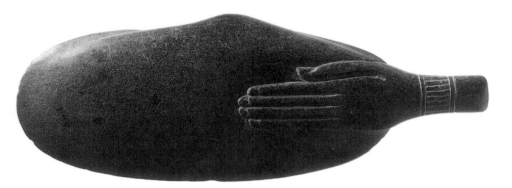

be made from any clays, with water being added to achieve the desired liquid consistency, and is employed for a variety of purposes, including SLIP DECORATION, moulding (see SLIP CASTING) and LUTING. In pre-modern ceramic traditions, slip was often used to disguise an inferior clay body. In this case, slip is often described by the French name *engobe*. In some ceramic traditions very glassy slips were used instead of glazes (see ROMAN RED SLIPWARE). In ancient Greek pottery, for example, the black designs on BLACK FIGURE WARE are made from very fine-particled slips high in illite, which vitrifies on firing to form a hard, glaze-like layer. The particle size in slips can be reduced by levigation (see CLAY). As liquids, slips can be applied by dipping, pouring and brushing. As

Slate cosmetic dish in the form of a hand holding a mussel shell, Egypt, New Kingdom, 1391–1295 BC. Slate, which has a fine-grained texture and tends to split into thin sheets, lends itself to the production of shallow, delicate forms such as this.

with glazes, metallic oxides can be added to slips to impart colour.

Slip casting A method of forming ceramics using slip and a porous mould. The slip should ideally be sufficiently fluid for pouring, dense and finely textured, with small even particles. The moulds for casting are made by taking an impression of a finished vessel in a casting box which when finished consists of two halves of the impression. These two halves are joined together and the slip is poured in and allowed to set as it coats the walls of the mould. The excess is then poured out, leaving a thin-walled hollow form. This is allowed to harden

Slip casting at the Wedgwood factory. Liquid clay is being poured into plaster piece moulds, held together by a band of wire.

and the mould is removed; the form is then finished by turning and can be fired as usual. The moulds are made from porous clay or, most commonly, gypsum plaster and can be in one piece for simple forms or several pieces for more complicated objects.

The advantage of slip casting is that it makes it possible to produce ceramics with thin, even walls and to make complicated forms without modelling. The technique was primarily used in European ceramics from the 18th century, for example at Staffordshire, where it was employed for elaborate teapot designs, often with salt glazes.

Slip decoration Decoration produced by applying slip, or liquid clay, which can be painted on, inlaid, marbled, combed, sprayed and, once dry, cut. Slips can be coloured like clays and are generally created with contrasting colours. In China slip was used to produce sgraffito decoration by applying a dark slip over a light one and then cutting away a design to reveal the light slip underneath. The process can be reversed to show a light slip design on a dark ground. Sgraffito designs can also be produced by incising a design through a slip layer to reveal the body underneath. In Staffordshire ceramics, combing was used to create feathered or marbled decoration in slip, and in several ceramic traditions, including those of China and Korea, slip was used to create inlaid designs (see INLAID DECORATION).

Lead-glazed earthenware dish with trailed slip decoration under the glaze, by Thomas Toft, Staffordshire, c.1662–85. The slip was applied with a device resembling an oil can.

Among the best-known ceramics with slip decoration are those made by Thomas Toft in Staffordshire in the 17th century. These were lead-glazed wares with trailed slip decoration in a folk style. Such ceramics are often called slipware. Slip-trailed decoration also appears on Chinese ceramics from northern blackware kilns in the Song period (960–1279). In the 15th and 16th century slip-trailed designs were applied to Chinese *fahua* ('bounded designs') ware to contain very fluid coloured glazes. A more complex form of slip decoration was created in France, known as *pâte sur pâte*. This was a type of porcelain decoration which used successive layers of white slip to build up a design in relief which could then be carved. The design appeared white on a coloured ground. A similar technique was used in China in the 16th and 17th centuries and at Meissen in the 19th century.

Most ceramics with slip decoration have a transparent glaze applied over the slip, which both fixes and enhances the decoration underneath.

Slipware See SLIP DECORATION.

Slumping A glassmaking process in which a sheet of glass is heated in the furnace and then laid over, or into, a shallow mould, cooled and annealed.

Slush casting See CASTING.

Smalt A pigment made by fusing cobalt oxide, potassium carbonate and white quartz and grinding them to a powder. It was discovered in the late 16th century by Christoph Schürer in Bohemia and used to colour glass a deep blue.

Smaltino A pale blue tin glaze used on early maiolica. Traditional maiolica ware often has polychrome painted designs on a coloured ground. The ground colour is usually dark blue or purple, but some factories produced other ground colours. In the 16th century potters in Venice made ceramics with a pale blue to lavender glaze, called smaltino, which appears to have been coloured with a fritted cobalt. Such wares are known as 'berettino' and were usually decorated with freely painted polychrome figurative designs or scrolling floral and vegetal motifs. At Faenza berettino wares featured opaque white enamel decoration on a lavender ground.

Smart materials systems A generic term for combinations of materials designed to be sensitive to their external environment, for example by responding to heat, mechanical force, deformation, light or electricity. These systems use a combination of different materials to produce their responsiveness. They include the shape-memory alloys used to make 'bendy' spectacles, which return to their original shape after being distorted, and heat-sensitive plastics used for children's toys, T-shirts and responsive spoons, which change colour when touched.

Smocking A universal embroidery technique that employs stitches to control fullness by means of closely set tucks that leave the gathered material on the surface of the cloth. The stitches are often decorative or coloured, but need not be so. The technique is mainly used in garments.

Snakewood A very hard and heavy timber from the species *Brosimum aubletti* (*Piratinera guianensis*) and various species of *Colubrinia*. It is sometimes called leopard wood, tortoise-shell wood, letter wood, West Indies greenheart, ironwood and soldierwood. It is a light reddish brown with darker patches, and is strong and durable, with a very close grain. It is difficult to work but is sometimes used in cabinet work and turnery, in building work and for railway sleepers.

Snarling iron A long iron or steel bar with a curved end, used inside a hollow metal object to emboss its surface. The iron is clamped in a vice and the curved end is inserted in the hollow workpiece. The iron is then hit with a hammer at a point somewhere between the vice and the workpiece, and starts to vibrate. This vibration makes the iron hammer against the inside of the piece, thus stretching the metal outwards. The snarling iron is normally used for vessels with narrow openings not easily accessible to a hammer.

Soapstone See STEATITE.

Soda glass Glass in which soda forms the alkali. Because it also contains lime it is often called soda-lime glass. The basic proportions are 60% silica, 25% soda, 15% lime. Soda was the principal source of alkali for glass until the development of potash glass in the 10th century. Now both types are made, but soda glass is the more common.

In antiquity soda was usually obtained from natron, a naturally occurring form found as a surface deposit in dried-out lakes in Egypt. Later it was made from the calcined ashes of salt-marsh plants, variously known as glasswort, roquetta (in Egypt) or barilla (in Spain and elsewhere in the Mediterranean). Kelp, a type of seaweed, was used in England, Normandy and Scandinavia.

In comparison with potash glass, soda glass is lightweight and lacks resonance. However, it remains plastic over a wide range of temperatures and therefore lends itself to elaborate manipulative techniques. It is the glass of Venetian CRISTALLO and its substitutes (see FAÇON DE VENISE).

Soda-lime glass See SODA GLASS.

Soft paste porcelain Artificial porcelain made with white clay and ground glass. Unlike true or hard paste porcelain, it does not contain kaolin but rather a fine white clay and ground glass frit, which results in a translucent white body that

Vase in cobalt blue soda glass, Venice, first half of the 16th century. The trailed decoration around the neck and the fluid handles were applied while the vessel was still hot.

matures at the relatively low temperature of 1050–1100°C.

Imitation porcelain was first made in Europe in the 16th century and was known as 'Medici porcelain'. In the early 18th century the French factories of Vincennes and Sèvres (see colour plate IX) specialized in soft paste porcelain (known as *pâte tendre*), but this was soon replaced by true porcelain when kaolin deposits were discovered in Europe. The soft paste body was not very strong, had a short firing range and was difficult to throw, but it was ideal for moulding and slip casting. Its whiteness and smooth texture made it suitable for the production of BISCUIT PORCELAIN figures.

Softwood Timbers derived from coniferous, needle-bearing trees, or gymnosperms. Despite the name, some softwoods are in fact harder than many of the hardwoods. Those commonly used throughout Europe include Douglas fir, cedar, hemlock, kauri, pine, pitch pine, spruce, tamarack and yew.

Soldering The joining of metals, using heat and a filler metal or alloy that has a melting-point below those of the metals to be joined. There are two types of soldering: 'soft' soldering, using alloys of tin, lead and bismuth, which melt below 450°C; and brazing or 'hard' soldering, using silver solders and brass solders with a melting-point above 450°C. Brazing gives a much stronger joint than soft soldering. Soft soldering is done with soldering irons or gas torches, while the high temperatures needed for brazing can only be achieved with gas torches. The silver solders contain silver, zinc and copper with melting-points normally between 700° and 800°C. The brass brazing rods usually have a composition of 50% copper and 50% zinc, with a melting-point of 850°C. This alloy is sometimes called spelter.

The first step in the process is thoroughly to clean the surfaces to be joined, since any dirt will weaken the joint. Flux is then applied to help the solder flow and to protect the metal from oxidation. When the workpiece is then heated to the required temperature, the solder is applied and will start to flow into the gap between the metal surfaces to be joined. Sometimes, in particularly precise work, small pieces of solder, called paillons, are placed near the gap before heating. When solder melts, it flows into the gap through capillary attraction and diffuses into the surface of the base metal, thus forming a strong bond. After soldering the remains of the flux are removed by pickling or rinsing.

The usual flux for soft soldering is hydrochloric acid saturated with zinc, rosin or stearine, and since most of these fluxes are corrosive they have to be removed thoroughly by rinsing. The traditional flux for brazing or hard soldering is borax, which glazes upon heating and can be dissolved in warm water or pickle (a solution of 10% sulphuric acid in water).

Solnhofen stone A fine-grained, buff-coloured limestone obtained from the area surrounding Solnhofen in southern Germany and used for carving inscriptions, for making models for metal castings, and, in medieval Europe, for making moulds for the fabrication of lead or tin hat badges. Solnhofen stone is often incorrectly identified as hone stone; however, it is not sufficiently abrasive to be effective for tool sharpening.

Soumak A Caucasian term for weft wrapping, a form of plaiting, but done on a loom. The wrapping may run at right angles, diagonally, or parallel to the warp.

Spalted timber Timber affected by fungal infection. The fungi produce stains and patterns resembling watermarks, and these can sometimes be coloured. If the wood has not been degraded by the fungus, its value may be enhanced.

Spanish leather See GILT LEATHER.

Speculum metal A high-tin (more than 20%) bronze often used for mirrors because of its silver colour and highly reflective surface when polished. A typical composition consists of 70% copper, 25% tin and 5% lead. Speculum metal, sometimes called white bronze, is very similar to bell metal.

Spelter A brass solder used for brazing copper, brass and iron. The name derives from *spiauter*, an old Dutch word for zinc. The term is also used for the zinc alloys used for casting decorative objects such as statuettes. These castings were made as cheap substitutes for bronzes by bronzing the surface. When used for die-casting these alloys are now better known under the name MAZAK or zamak.

Sperm whale teeth A form of ivory derived from the sperm whale, which carries between 30 and 45 teeth set in its lower jaw. Each of these can be up to 20 cm long and 8 cm in diameter. Approximately half of the tooth is hollow, but the tip traditionally provided much useful material. Sperm whale teeth were one of the most popular media for SCRIMSHAW work, in which the entire tooth was generally used.

Spinel A transparent mineral with a hardness of Mohs scale 8, composed of magnesium aluminium oxide and used as a gemstone. It occurs in a range of colours produced by replacement of the magnesium or aluminium with other elements such as chromium, which results in red, or iron, giving blue or green. Spinels occur in metamorphic rocks and may be mined but are more frequently found in river gravels resulting from the erosion of the parent rock. Early and still significant sources of spinels are Burma and Sri Lanka; they are now also obtained in small quantities from Tanzania, Kenya, Pakistan and Vietnam. Red spinels have often been confused with rubies and were known as balas rubies, a name probably derived from Balakshan in Afghanistan, another early source. In Mogul India spinels were used in pebble form, without shaping but with the name of the owner inscribed. In ancient Burma unworked crystals of spinel were set in rings and ear-rings.

Spinning [metal] The process of shaping metal sheet into a hollow form on a spinning lathe, by pressing it, as it rotates, against a wooden or metal form. These forms, called chucks, have the shape of the desired metal article. The metal disc is fixed against the chuck with a spinning tool that looks like an oversized burnisher. Spinning can be done with most malleable metals, although many will need to be annealed several times during the spinning operation. Although most articles made by spinning are circular, it is possible to spin oval shapes on specially equipped lathes.

There is some evidence of spun wares dating from Roman times, but spinning on a large scale was introduced only around 1800, when lathes first became sufficiently powerful. Since it was much quicker than raising, it was particularly suitable as a process in mass production.

For the spinning of ceramics, see CERAMICS.

Spinning [textiles] The action of making thread or yarn by drawing out (drafting) and twisting fibres, usually prepared first by combing (aligning) or carding (cross-combing) into long, soft, rope-like 'rovings'. The nature of the resulting yarn is determined by the tension and intensity of twist between the roving and the spindle, which rotates, winding on at the same time. All natural fibres need to be spun with the exception of silk, which, after being reeled from a cocoon, is twisted with six or more other strands, a process called throwing. Man-made and synthetic fibres can be extruded as continuous filaments or made into staple (cut) fibres, for spinning. The combination of two or more spun yarns into a

OPPOSITE *Various stages of yarn preparation in the mid-18th century, as illustrated in Diderot's* Encyclopédie des arts et des métiers. *The girl on the left (fig. 1) is spinning, inexpertly, with a spindle and distaff. Her implements are shown in greater detail below. The spinning wheel shown (figs. 2 and 10) is of the Saxony type, with a foot treadle. It stretches and twists the roving in one action, the stretch being provided by resistance from the spinner.*

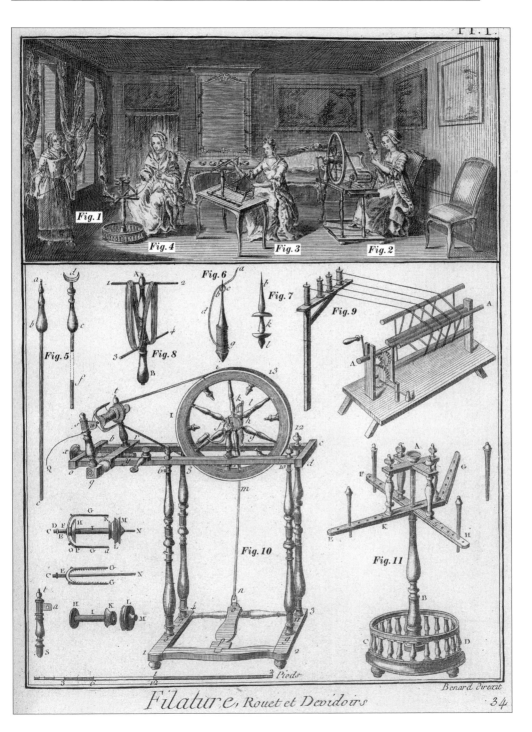

Filature, Rouet et Devidoirs

Benard Direxit

34

single strand is achieved by twisting in the direction opposite to that of the spin, and is called plying. The direction of spin or ply is referred to as 'S' (clockwise) or 'Z' (anti-clockwise). (See also WOOL.)

Spinning can be achieved by three mechanisms: the suspended or drop spindle, which uses its own weight to draft the fibres as it falls; hand-operated spinning wheels; and multi-thread spinning machines. Hand wheels can be divided into two types. Jersey (or muckle) wheels are turned by hand and the spinning is discontinuous, with drafting and twisting being done first, followed by winding on; the smaller Saxony wheel, a 16th-century improvement, has a crank and foot treadle and the spinning is continuous, by the use of a flyer. The flyer is an inverted V-shaped device (said to have been invented by Leonardo da Vinci) placed above the rotating spindle, with roving passing through one arm and the resulting drafted and twisted thread wound on to the bobbin below. Machine-spinning evolved in England by grouping spindles in frames; the earliest known attempt was patented

A reconstruction of James Hargreaves's hand-powered spinning jenny, c.1764. It shows drawing out (or drafting) the first action in discontinuous spinning machines. From bobbins in the lower rack the roving is passed through wheeled clasps, now at the back of the frame, and is thus stretched; next, the strands are twisted, the clasp-filled frame is moved forward and the finished yarn is wound onto the front bobbins.

in 1678, and mechanical power was first applied to a single wheel by Lewis Paul in the 1730s.

The first successful multi-thread machine was the jenny, developed by James Hargreaves c.1764 on the Jersey principle and using hand power to move a row of roving-filled bobbins away from the spindles. It initially had between 8 and 16 spindles and produced a coarse weak thread suitable only for wefts, yet it was widely used in cotton spinning from *c.*1770 until the 1820s, by which time it held up to 130 spindles. The hand-driven spinning mule, with a moving carriage rather than a rigid frame, was patented by Samuel Crompton in 1779 and had up to 144 spindles. It drafted twice via rollers, and made a fine, strong thread, important in the production of muslin and other high-quality cotton yarns, and also long used for spinning wool. Like the Jersey, which it effectively replaced, it was discontinuous in action. Water power and steam power were common by the 1790s for pulling out (drafting), and by the 1830s the self-acting mule, a virtually automatic machine with a powered return (winding on) towards up to 600 spindles, was in general use.

In 1769 Richard Arkwright applied water power to Saxony-type spinning: his 'water frame' (later known as the 'flyer frame') produced a coarse thread strong enough for a warp. Arkwright also patented an improvement to Paul's patents of the 1740s for hand-powered carding. An improve-

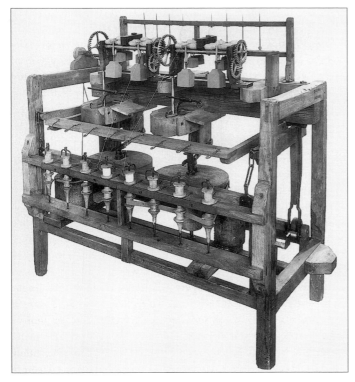

Richard Arkwright's water frame, an improved model made in 1775. It spins in one continuous motion, with the drafting and twisting both taking place as the yarn progresses towards the eight spindles. The vertical spindles that hold the roving and the horizontal drafting rollers can be seen at the top of the machine.

Mule spinning at the Swainson Birley cotton mill, near Preston, Lancashire, c.1834. The spinners use a self-acting (powered) machine based on the 1779 patent of Samuel Crompton. It worked on the same principle as the Jersey wheel and spinning jenny, first drawing out and then twisting, but also had drafting rollers, adapted from the water frame.

ment on the water frame, the throstle frame (named after the noise it produced, like that of a throstle or thrush) was in use by the 1790s; both were characterized by drafting rollers (the feature adopted in the mule, so-called for its combination of two principles), vertical spindles and flyers, and the spinning was continuous, dispensing with the need for the pulling out and return of a carriage. The flyer was replaced by a stationary ring, patented in 1828 in the USA by John Thorp; by the 1840s ring spinning had become dominant there, but not in Britain (where as late as the 1950s some 50% of yarns were still mule-spun). Ring-spun yarn, stronger but less resilient than mule-spun yarn, can therefore identify most cloths produced before the early 20th century as American-made.

Sponged ware Staffordshire pottery to which decoration has been applied using sponges dipped in coloured glazes or pigments. These ceramics were produced for the mass market in the 19th century, but the technique was not new, as it had been used in the 18th century by Thomas Whieldon to create tortoiseshell style decoration on lead-glazed wares. Sponged decoration tends to be mottled and fairly uneven and is usually applied under a glaze.

Sprang A general term for several related off-loom textile constructions in which the warp is fixed between two bars and twisted or interlaced at one end, producing the same structures in mirror image automatically at the other end; the work progresses towards the middle, where it must be fixed. Sprang produces a highly elastic fabric and is similar in appearance to diagonal plaiting and other related techniques. The technique is ancient; the word itself is of Swedish origin.

Sprigged ware Ceramics to which decoration produced in a sprig mould has been applied. A sprig mould is used to produce decoration in relief with a flat back that can be scored and slipped for application (a process known as 'sprigging'). The term 'sprigged ware' usually refers to Staffordshire ceramics with sprigged decoration, but the technique was also used in Chinese ceramics. The sprigged decoration is often of a different colour from the body or ground colour, as in Jasper ware.

In Western ceramic traditions, hand-modelled applied decoration is sometimes described as 'sprigged'. A related form of decoration is found on some examples of Staffordshire ceramics where the mould is pressed directly onto the

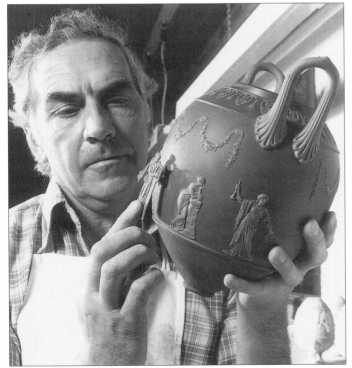

Sprigged decoration being applied to jasper ware at the Wedgwood factory.

clay and the decoration released. This technique is known as 'mould-applied decoration' and the marks of the mould edges are usually visible.

Springing The use of coiled wire springs to stuff upholstery. Springs were used in the 18th century for special items such as exercise furniture, but they were made of iron and cylindrical in shape, which gave a lumpy, uneven effect. In the mid-19th century, with improvements in metal production, biconal (hour-glass) steel springs were introduced. These were stronger and more elastic. Springs are either sewn in place by hand or pre-assembled in a steel box unit.

Stain A dye or colourant used to alter or enhance the colour of wood. Stains may be oil-, water- or spirit-based. Since the mid-19th century a wide range of aniline dyes, originally extracted from coal oil, have been used. Other methods of staining often involve boiling the wood, usually in the form of veneers, in various solutions. Black was produced from a LOGWOOD solution, followed by one of crushed nut galls in copperas (ferrous sulphate), brown was produced using potassium permanganate and magnesium sulphate solutions, and vermilion was made by first dyeing black and then soaking in oxalic acid solution.

Stained glass Coloured and painted window glass that has been assembled to form a decorative panel. The term is slightly misleading, since the majority of these windows contain little SILVER STAINING. The overall colour results either from colourants introduced at the glass-melting stage, or from flashing a clear glass with a thin layer of colour (see FLASHED GLASS), or from ENAMEL COLOURS applied to the cold glass and fused for permanence. Therefore a more accurate term might be 'painted glass'.

The earliest surviving stained-glass windows are the *Prophet* windows from Augsburg, dating to *c*.1130. It is clear from these, however, that the technique was already fully developed; fragments of earlier glass suggest that it was known to the Byzantines and also practised in northern Europe in previous centuries. In the Middle Ages the glass, made by the crown or cylinder method, was used in small pieces (see colour plate VI). It was coloured in the batch ('pot metal') or flashed, usually with a copper-derived ruby glass over clear glass. Colourless glass was also employed. Initially the only way of introducing detail to facial features and so on was by painting with a brownish enamel made with iron oxide. The paint could be applied in a linear fashion, or more sparingly in parallel brushstrokes (smear shading) to tone details such as drapery, or stippled to create the effect of minute points of light all over the glass. Alternatively, the pigment could be applied very thickly and scratched through to the ground. Sometimes the enamel was used on clear glass to give a grisaille effect.

Silver stain, which was introduced in Paris around 1310, made it possible to have two colours in one piece of glass. It was applied to the back, either on clear glass to give a yellow–white combination, or on blue glass to make a green. By abrading away the surface of flashed glass and applying yellow stain to the resulting clear glass, the interpretation of heraldry was simplified, as it obviated the need for complex leading-up.

The gradual introduction of enamelling from the late 15th century transformed stained glass and made it more pictorial in character. First a brownish red akin to silver stain was used for flesh tints, then vitreous enamel in blue, violet and green appeared. Eventually the window came to be treated as a canvas, with large rectangular panes of clear glass painted in polychrome enamels. This approach was abhorred by the artists of the Gothic revival, and in the 19th century there was an attempt to return to medieval practices, with NORMAN SLAB glass introduced to give a less regular effect.

Stained and painted glass, with the figure of Winter, *after a design by Martin Vos, Netherlands, early 19th century. It is executed with silver stain and enamel colours.*

The process of creating a traditional stained-glass window has hardly changed since medieval times and is still carried out in small workshops. First, the design is conceived and sketched. Then a full-size drawing (the cartoon) is produced, on which the colours are indicated and also the vertical and horizontal bars that will support the glass in the window. From this the cut-line, a tracing of the lead-lines, is taken. The centre of each lead-line is carefully drawn so that glass pieces placed over the tracing can be accurately cut to size. The glass is chosen and cut to the required shape. In the past this was done with the tip of a red-hot iron, but now a steel-wheeled or diamond-tipped cutter is used. Minor adjustments may have to be made by nibbling away (grozing) the edges with a grozing iron. The pieces are then assembled on a sheet of glass painted with the lead-lines and held down with beeswax or plasticine. This panel is checked against the light and the pieces of glass are then painted in enamel colours and silver stain. Finally, the colours are fused for permanence in a muffle kiln at 450–650°C. Sometimes many firings are necessary, with the silver stain, which requires a lower temperature, treated last.

The glass pieces are then leaded-up in a lattice of lead cames to form panels. A series of panels is combined to create large windows. Individual small panels or larger windows are cemented into the stonework of a window aperture and supported at intervals by being tied-in to horizontal metal glazing bars (ferramenta).

See also DALLE DE VERRE.

Stakes Anvil-like steel tools with many different profiles against which sheet metal is hammered into shape. Unlike an anvil, stakes are usually held in a vice or a special stake-holder. A professional sheet metalworker such as a silversmith usually owns an extensive array of stakes which enables him to make a wide range of articles.

Stamping An American name for a technique for decorating leather (see BLOCKING). The term also refers to a process used to shape or impress metal (see DIE-STAMPING).

Steatite A dense, homogeneous form of the mineral talc, hydrous magnesium silicate. Steatite is soft, greenish grey, brown, red or yellow and has a greasy or soapy lustre, from where derives its common name, soapstone. It can be carved with a flint or metal knife and was one of the first materials used by the ancient Egyptians to make scarabs. The Egyptians also developed techniques of firing steatite, once carved, to make it harder and of glazing it; for this they probably used a glass frit, a mixture of alkaline materials, silica and malachite. Unfired and fired steatite were also used in the ancient Near East to make cylinder seals and stones. The Chinese made ornamental carvings and vessels from steatite, and it was used in India for architectural carving. Steatite carvings are also made in Canada, by the Inuit, and in Zimbabwe.

Steel See IRON.

Stencil printing A method of hand-colouring textiles and paper by resist printing, using a stencil of waxed card, from which the pattern to be coloured is cut out. The resulting designs are characterized by the lines left by the bars needed to stabilize the stencil.

In textile production stencil printing with oil-based colours is recorded in North America during the early 19th century, when it was known as 'theorem painting'. By *c.*1860 improved direct dyes were in use and mechanized spray painting through stencils had been perfected; both techniques remained in use until the 1920s or 1930s. The process was greatly influenced by Japanese art prints and stencilled indigo, resist-dyed cloths, circulating in Europe from the mid-19th century. Their stencils, stabilized by inconspicuous strands of silk or hair, led to the substitution of a fine silk screen in place of individual strands (see SCREEN PRINTING).

On paper, stencils have been used to colour prints and for book illustration (especially in France, where the technique is known as *pochoir*) and for decorated and PASTE PAPER.

Stencilling The decoration of a flat surface using masking shapes, or stencils, as a guide for paint. The stencils are made from a sheet of impermeable material such as card, plastic or metal, with cut-out areas through which the paint can pass. They are held against the item to be decorated and paint is brushed, air-brushed, sprayed or rolled across them.

Stencilling is an ancient technique especially suited to small repeating patterns. For instance, it was often used in conjunction with gilding on medieval and Renaissance polychrome sculpture to duplicate the effect of damask or embroidery. However, it was not much used for walls until the 18th and 19th centuries. In the late Victorian period stencilling became very fashionable, and elaborate schemes involving complex overlays were used to cover the interiors of entire buildings.

Stencilled decoration at the American Museum in Britain, Claverton Manor, Bath. The walls, from a house in Connecticut, were decorated in the early 19th century by a journeyman artist working with casein paint and stencils cut from thick paper.

Quick-drying paint such as casein was preferred in such schemes, whereas oil paint was more common for furniture.

Sterling silver A silver alloy of legal standard composed of 925 parts silver in 1000. Sterling silver has been used in England to make silverware for more than 700 years continuously, except for a short period between 1697 and 1720, when the higher-quality BRITANNIA SILVER was compulsory. The name probably derives from *easterlings* ('those who live eastwards'), an old English name for Germans.

Stick furniture Furniture of rustic appearance made from unmodified branches and small trunks of trees. Because the bark is left in place, objects tend to be made from smooth-barked trees or the younger growths of coarse-barked species. Elements are fitted together using circular mortise and tenon joints, which are usually reinforced by nailing or pegging. Joints may also be strengthened or decorated by ornamental binding with string, cane or flexible twigs.

Stipple engraving See INTAGLIO PRINTING and GLASS ENGRAVING.

Stocking frame A hand-powered knitting machine with needles mounted horizontally. The folded-back tips (beards) of the needles, when pressed against an indentation in the needle stem, hold the passing 'weft' thread within the fold while being drawn back through the previous loops, which drop over the closed needle to form a new row of loops. The stocking frame was perfected by the Englishman Richard Lee in 1589 for knitting coarse woollen plain weft-knitted cloth, and was adapted in the 1590s for finer cloths of silk. It was in this form that it became widespread in Western Europe by the 1620s. The frame was further adapted in the mid-18th century to make lacy knits from cotton yarn and, in 1768, to make a weft-knitted silk net by transferring loops in diagonal cross-over motions. This was followed by several frame-knitted nets, known collectively as 'patent nets' and all of silk until the early 19th century, when cotton was introduced. By the 1820s the diaphanous frame nets were being

Illustration of a mid-18th-century knitting workshop, from the Universal Magazine *(1750), showing a stocking frame, in which the needle-tips were pressed in by means of foot-operated levers. The woman on the left is plying four threads into the required yarn, while the one in the centre is winding yarn onto a bobbin.*

The Art of STOCKING-FRAME-WORK-KNITTING.

Engrav'd for the Universal Magazine 1750, for J. Hinton at the Kings Arms in St Pauls Church Yard LONDON.

superseded by BOBBINET. In the 1770s experiments began with warp knitting, used to make solid and, later, openwork fabrics; these have no hand-knitted parallel, and can be recognized by the separate threads running lengthwise down each wale (vertical ridge). By about 1800 this development contributed to the production of warp-knitted JERSEY, TRICOT and machine-made laces. A modification to a latched needle in 1847 did not prevent the decline of warp knitting. The principle was revived in the mid-20th century with the Raschel machine, which by then had increased the single or double set of warp threads to 30.

Stone A material of universal distribution, formed through geological processes and used in the construction and ornamentation of buildings, for inscriptions, sculpture, decorative objects and jewellery. It is broadly classified by its process of formation; within those classifications rocks are further defined by composition and texture. Stones are formed of one or more minerals, crystalline materials with an ordered atomic structure and a consistent chemical composition. There is wide variation in the hardness, durability, colour and texture of stone, and this has influenced the ways in which it has been used and the appearance of the completed object. For example, the crisp edges and undercut forms of a Corinthian capital would be impossible to produce in a hard, coarse-grained stone such as granite, whereas the even texture of marble, which will take and retain fine detail, is ideally suited to this form.

Formation Igneous rocks are formed through the solidification of molten material. The rate of cooling determines the texture of the rock: rapid cooling, such as when volcanic lava reaches the air, produces fine-grained stones such as basalt, obsidian and pumice. Slow cooling, far beneath the earth's crust, produces coarse-grained rocks such as granite and diorite.

Sedimentary rocks are formed through the build-up, compaction (caused by the weight of overlying material) and cementing together of loose sediments. Sediments such as sand and clay, which arise through the weathering of other rocks, produce sandstone and shale. Plant and animal material, which become fossilized through the replacement of tissue and skeletal structures with minerals, produce limestone and cannel coal. Sedimentary rock can also form through precipitation from mineral-rich waters; gypsum and travertine are

A incised memorial in Purbeck marble, England, 1310–25. The fine texture of the stone permits the incising of the delicate lines, which have been carved with a chisel.

examples of this type of formation.

The type of sediment and the nature of the cementing material, which may be calcium carbonate, silica, clay or iron oxide, will influence the character and durability of the stone. The composition, colour and texture of the sediments, as well as the rate of deposition, may vary over time, producing a layered structure known as bedding. Where the sediments have been undisturbed by the flow of currents or movements within the earth, the bedding is parallel to the direction in which the sediments are laid down. Soft beds between layers of harder material can facilitate the removal of stone from a quarry, and the thickness of the beds can determine how a stone is used. A sedimentary stone that can be worked equally well both along and across the bedding planes is termed a freestone; a ragstone is too friable or irregularly bedded to accept straight edges and is only suitable for rubble.

Metamorphic rocks are formed through the alteration of pre-existing rock by heat and/or pressure, causing changes in mineral structure, texture and colour. Events such as the formation of mountains can generate heat and exert great force on limestone, converting it to marble. Such pressure causes the realignment of minerals at right angles to the direction of force, producing a banded structure which can be subtle, as in marble, or pronounced, as in schist and slate. Stones with this structure, which are termed fissile, can be split by striking them parallel to the banding.

Identification Rocks and minerals are identified by geologists using a variety of optical examination techniques. Features such as colour, texture, the presence of certain minerals, such as the large feldspar crystals found in granites, the occurrence of specific fossils or other structures, such as ooliths, can be studied in small samples under low magnification, allowing the stone to be classified according to type (i.e., igneous, sedimentary or metamorphic). It is often possible for a geologist to identify specific stones by this method. This type of examination may be complemented by certain chemical tests and the measurement of hardness. More detailed analysis of components or more precise identification is carried out at higher magnification with a microscope, using prepared samples of stone, called petrological thin sections, ground to a thickness of 30 microns. At this thickness light can pass through many minerals and the ways in which each mineral responds to ordinary and polarized light (light restricted to specific directions of movement) is characteristic. The thin section also reveals the shape and colour of minerals, which can be diagnostic, and can show the effects of weathering on the stone. Minerals such as gemstones are often identified by examining the ways in which they refract light when viewed through a device called a refractometer, which contains a prism. X-ray diffractometry, a technique in which a beam of X-rays is fired at a small sample and the angles at which they are scattered by the material produces a characteristic pattern, can be used to identify the component minerals of a stone.

Knowledge of characteristics, such as rock type, composition, texture and the identity of any fossils present, can help locate a rock within a geological context, giving an indication of its age and place of origin; certain fossils can be used to identify and date a rock precisely. It may be necessary to confirm the provenance of a worked stone by comparison with a sample of known origin and a study of documentary evidence, such as records of extraction from a specific quarry. The quarry source of some marbles has been identified by looking at the isotypes of carbon and oxygen in the rock. (Isotypes are variant forms of atoms, containing a different number of neutrons, or electrically neutral particles, from normal.) In a test sample the ratio of such isotypes to the levels of the standard form of carbon and oxygen is compared with the ratios found in samples of known origin.

Quarrying Quarrying is the extraction of stone for use. This generally involves removing stone from its place of formation, although some stones—such as boulders, used in certain types of construction, or gem gravels—have been transported by water or glaciation from their original location, allowing them to be collected with minimal equipment. In some cases, such as rock-cut dwellings and temples (see BASALT), quarrying was carried out to produce a usable space. Quarries may be sited in cliffs or hillsides or in underground tunnels, and extraction exploits, as much as possible, planes of weakness such as soft beds and vertical faults. The topsoil is removed to expose the stone, which is extracted by freeing a block of the desired size on three sides and then breaking it off from the rock beneath. In order to quarry limestone the Egyptians made channels in the stone with stone or copper chisels and then released the block by driving in wooden wedges which were wetted, so that on swelling they would crack the stone; the Indians caused cracking of hard stones by heating them with fire, followed by rapid cooling with water. Wedges are still widely used for splitting stone, either for extraction or during working. A common method employs long metal wedges, known as 'plugs', which are placed in a series of holes drilled in the stone between a pair of thinner, softer pieces of metal, called feathers, inserted in each hole to protect the stone from crushing. Striking the plugs in sequence produces a vertical crack through the stone. Cutting wire, used with abrasive and water, for hard stones, was a 19th-century invention. As quarrying of a cliff or hillside progressed, a series of terraces would be formed. Hoists, levers and other equipment were used to lift the stone from the quarry.

Before the advent of mechanized transport stone was often obtained from local quarries, although there were exceptions, where stone of a particular colour or quality was sought or where no suitable stone was available locally. At many periods in history stone was obtained by reusing previously worked stone, either for reasons of economy or lack of technological capability or as an expression of wealth and religious supremacy, as in the case of the use of older stone columns in early Islamic mosques; reused ancient columns can also be seen on the west front of St Mark's Basilica in Venice.

Design transfer A variety of techniques has been used to communicate an intended design from the architect or designer to the craftsman. In many instances, for example in ancient Egypt, strict rules of proportion meant that a stonecarver would need to know only the size and type of ornament to create the desired product. Details such as hieroglyphic inscriptions were painted on the stone by a scribe as a guide for the carver. In the Islamic world architects made detailed drawings with a superimposed grid to permit scaled fabrication of decoration.

In ancient Rome and medieval Europe carvers often worked by eye from rough sketches to produce complicated ornament; this technique was quicker and more adaptable than taking measurements from a drawing. In Rome mouldings were worked by copying a vertical strip of the desired forms, carved into blank blocks by the head carver. In the Middle Ages the profile of a moulding was conveyed by positive and negative wooden templates which could be traced

An illustration of various processes involved in the working of stone in the mid-18th century, from Diderot's Encyclopédie des arts et des métiers. In the foreground (a), a young man, probably an apprentice, uses a saw to cut slices through a block of dense limestone or marble; the long-handled spoon would be used to feed water and abrasive onto the blade. In the background (b), a carver uses a bolster to work flat the top of a sarcophagus. In the workshop (c), a letter carver is at work on an inscription. To the left, a foreman sets out another piece of work using a compass and straight edge. In the lower left, amid the products of the yard, are examples of the carver's tools.

onto the end of a block or drawn along the carved surface to check for accuracy as work progressed. The complex geometry of Gothic tracery was worked out through full-size drawings on plaster tracing floors in which the master mason would inscribe lines with compasses and other measuring tools. With the increasing availability of paper from the late Middle Ages onwards, measured drawings became more common and architects produced detailed specifications for all carved elements.

Shaping, carving and polishing Much of what is known about the working of stone has been deduced from studying tool marks and from depictions of stonecarving practice. Stone can only be shaped by removing material; the way in which this is done is determined by both the nature of the stone itself and the types of tool material available. The earliest working techniques involved using hard stones to pound and roughly to shape softer ones or to remove flakes to produce a cutting edge, the method used to make flint knives. The knowledge that a hard stone will cut stone at least as hard as itself was widely exploited in areas which did not have hard metals such as iron and steel. Abrasives, in the form of blocks of sandstone, quartz sand mixed with water and trickled on metal saws and core drills, or crushed garnet applied to cutting discs have been used in ancient Egypt to shape granite, in China to cut jade and in Pre-Columbian Latin America to work various igneous stones. Only very soft stones, such as chalk, were cut with toothed saws. For all other types of stone, saws consisting of metal strips, fed with abrasive, were used to cut thin sheets of stone for decorative techniques such as pietre dure and mosaic. A sawn surface is generally smooth, although it will often retain scratches produced by abrasive particles. Modern production of stone cladding also employs abrasive cutting.

Although abrasive cutting is slow, it can provide a good degree of control over the rate of stone removal. Shaping by striking the stone with a chisel driven by a mallet can be less precise, and therefore work generally proceeds in stages with a different tool being used for each stage. Whether producing an ashlar block, with square corners and straight sides, or a Corinthian capital, the carver would first rough out the whole form before introducing details and creating a surface finish. This approach, which a carver would learn from his earliest training, avoids removing too much material too soon in the process.

The first stage in preparing stone for construction purposes often involves splitting quarried blocks to obtain pieces of approximately the desired size; this can be done with wedges or with a pickaxe. In many instances the rough shaping of blocks is carried out at the quarry to reduce the weight of the stone to be transported. A squared block is obtained by working one face flat and then using it as a guide to ensure that the other five faces are at right angles to it.

Mouldings and ornament can then be carved into the prepared block. In ancient India and Rome the block was fixed in place on the building and then carved; in Europe from the Middle Ages the blocks were often carved in a workshop before fixing.

Hard stones such as granite and quartzite are carved with an iron or steel point held at right angles to the surface. This causes localized crushing and entails the slow removal of stone and the production of broad, shallow forms with a rough surface which can only be worked smooth with abrasives. Soft stones, such as the fine-grained limestones of Egypt, were carved with copper alloy tools until the 5th century BC. The chisel would have been held at an oblique angle to the stone and tapped with a wooden mallet. Using the corner of the cutting edge, the carver could incise fine

A stonecarver at work on a marble frieze for Spencer House, London. He uses a fine tungsten-tipped chisel and a small brass-headed mallet to form the tail of a cherub. The fronds to the left of the cherub are roughed out but uncarved.

lines which would be legible on the smooth, cream-coloured stone. The same techniques were employed for carving limestones and soft sandstones, using iron or steel tools, in the construction and decoration of the Gothic cathedrals of northern Europe. The development of iron tools in the 5th century BC facilitated the carving of marble, a fine-grained stone with a high tensile strength which can take crisp detail. To avoid bruising, which results in small white friable areas, marble is carved with the chisel held at a low angle to the surface; this also allows material to be removed in stages, with accuracy and speed. On unpolished marbles and on limestones and sandstones it is often possible to see the individual passes of the flat chisel used for the definition of detail in the final stage of carving. Very soft materials such as alabaster and chalk are carved with woodcarving chisels or knives. Drills are used for working into deep undercuts, for creating channels and for producing holes as part of an ornamental form. (See also STONECARVING TOOLS.)

Worked stones are joined with mortar, metal cramps or ties, or with molten lead poured into channels cut into adjacent blocks. Units in a complicated structure, such as the voussoirs comprising an arch, are inscribed with position marks to ensure that they are assembled in the correct sequence.

Hard stones, such as marble, granite and various dense limestones (see, for example, PURBECK MARBLE), can be polished to a high sheen by using progressively finer grades of abrasive. Sand, sandstone, emery (an impure form of the mineral corundum) and diamond, for very hard stones, have been used for this purpose, mixed with water as a lubricant. Abrasives can be applied selectively to create variations in texture on the finished work. Softer stones are worked smooth with a chisel or by dragging a blade across the surface. Where paint is to be applied, the surface can be roughened with a rasp or claw to provide a key. Before painting, porous stones are sealed with glues, gums, casein or drying oils to prevent the medium being absorbed into the stone, leaving the pigment unbound. Ground layers, containing materials such as calcium carbonate, calcium sulphate and red lead pigment, have been found on stonework. Oils, casein, lime, egg and glues have been used as paint media for interior and exterior work; oil size is used for external gilding.

Polychromy was also introduced by the use of coloured stones. In Italy from Roman times marbles, hard limestone and gemstones were used to produce panelling, columns, and inlaid decoration such as MOSAIC, COSMATI WORK and PIETRE DURE. In Mogul India a technique probably influenced by Italian methods and used for decorating walls, columns and other surfaces involved creating patterns of foliage and geometric forms by cutting recesses into white marble. Brightly coloured stones were set into the recesses, using a mortar, and the surface polished. Coloured marble panels and columns are prevalent in Islamic architecture.

Stone rubbing See FROTTAGE.

Stone setting The permanent fixing of a gemstone, usually for decorative purposes, in a metal or other setting. There are four main types of stone setting. Bezel setting derives its name from the French *biseau*, meaning 'sloping or bevelled edge'. In its simplest form a vertical strip of metal (the bezel), soldered onto a backing, surrounds the stone around its widest part, the girdle. The bezel (sometimes also called a collet) is carefully pressed against the stone to secure it. This is done with a burnisher, a special bezel pusher, punches and a hammer or with an automatic hammer handpiece attached to a flexible shaft drill. A bezel setting is normally used to set cabochons.

Faceted gemstones, which need an open setting with a lot of light, are usually mounted in an elegant prong and claw setting. The gemstone is held by four or more slender claws and set by pressing the ends of these prongs just over the girdle

Types of stone setting.
(a) In bezel setting the stone is dropped into the metal setting and the edges, or bezel, are pushed over to hold it in place.
(b) In prong and claw setting, the seating for the stone is cut into the setting with a burr, file or graver. The stone is positioned and the tips of the prongs are pushed over the girdle of the stone with a stone setter.
(c and d) In carré setting a hole is drilled in the setting and a seating made for the stone with a burr or graver. Small spurs are then made with a graver. The stone is placed in the setting and the spurs pushed over the girdle to secure the stone.

a *Bezel setting*

b *Prong and claw setting*   **c** *Carré setting*   **d** *Carré setting (section)*

with a prongsetter or pusher.

Carré setting (also called pavé setting) is often used to decorate the whole surface of a piece of jewellery with gemstones. A number of holes are drilled in the metal to receive the stones and in each a 'shoulder' is made to seat the stone. The stone is placed in this hole and, with the aid of a graver, corner spurs are lifted slightly over the girdle of the stone to secure it. These spurs, of which there are usually four, are formed into beads with a beading tool and the surplus metal is removed with gravers. Often the edge of a carré setting is decorated by milligraining, which produces a row of half beads. This is achieved by rolling over the edge a milligraining tool which holds a wheel at the working end. The beading pattern is produced by a series of semicircular indentations in the wheel.

In a channel setting, specially cut gemstones (called calibré cut) are set in a channel or in parallel races. These stones are placed end to end in the track so they are held only by the metal bezel at each side.

Stonecarving tools Implements used for shaping, carving and finishing stone which function either by striking or abrading the surface. The earliest and simplest tools were pieces of stone, such as flint, which were at least as hard as that being worked. These were hand-held and struck against the surface to remove chips of stone. In antiquity hard stones such as granite were worked with abrasives, applied to saws or drills, or in the form of blocks of rough-textured stone. The design of carving tools has remained largely unchanged over time, although the materials used to make them have altered. The ancient Egyptians and early Greeks employed stone, copper and then bronze; iron tools were used from the 5th century BC. Copper and stone tools were also used in Pre-Columbian Latin America. The development of power tools in the 18th century allowed harder stones to be worked with greater facility. Today hard stones, such as granite, are carved with tungsten carbide-tipped chisels, driven by compressed air. Compressed air (or pneumatic) tools allow stone to be worked with greater speed and less physical effort than hand tools and are widely used in modern stonework, although they are unsuitable for soft stones or for the producing of fine detail, owing to the force of their action.

Stonecarving tools are used in sequence, first to rough out forms and then to introduce detail. Shaping and carving stone is carried out on a banker, a strong work bench. Axes were used both for quarrying and, in parts of Europe until the 16th century, for shaping stone. An axe with a pointed tip was used perpendicular to the surface to remove small chips of stone; one with a vertical or horizontal blade would be used in long strokes to remove more material. Tools held in one hand while being struck with a wooden, bell-shaped mallet or rectangular metal hammer held in the other provide greater control. A pitcher, which has a flat end and blunt edge, is used to eliminate excess material quickly. A point, or the slightly blunter punch, tapers to a pyramidal cutting edge and is used to rough out forms. A claw, a tool with a serrated edge at the tip, produces a fairly even surface, with further definition of form, which can then be worked smooth with a bolster (or boaster),

A selection of stonecarving tools including metal hammers and wooden mallets, gouges and pitchers (lower left), points, chisels and bolsters (centre), and rifflers and set squares (top). A carving of a hand shows how the small circular metal hammer used for letter carving is held.

which has a wide, tapering blade. The claw can also be used to create a slightly roughened surface texture. Finishing and detailed carving are done with a chisel which has a narrow tapering blade; grooves are cut with gouges, chisels with concave tips. LETTER CARVING is carried out with a chisel which has a smaller, narrower blade than an ordinary carving chisel. Edged steel tools require regular tempering and sharpening.

A textured surface can be obtained by hitting the stone with a bouchard (or bush) hammer, which has a rectangular metal head with pyramidal points on the striking faces. Holes were made with strap, staff or bow drills which rotated stone or metal points. Today electric or pneumatic drills are used with drill bits with a V-shaped tip. Saws, either with metal teeth for very soft stones, or abrasive-fed, long metal strips, pulled across the stone by a handle at each end for harder stones, were primarily used, until recently, for cutting thin panels of stone for decorative purposes. Gang saws, which have a series of parallel blades, were in use from the 18th century, driven by windmills. Power-driven abrasive sawing is now used for squaring blocks before carving as well as for the production of cladding panels. Files, rasps and abrasives are used to give a smooth, polished surface to hard stones. Masons and carvers employ straight edges, set squares and plumbs to produce accurate lines and angles. Wooden or zinc templates are used as guides for carving mouldings.

Stonepaste See FRITWARE.

Stoneware A hard, high-fired ceramic body which, because of its high firing temperature (usually above 1200°C), is dense and relatively non-porous (for illustration see page 423). Stoneware clays come in a wide range of colours, from white and grey to buff and red. Natural stoneware clays include tempered ball clays and fire clays, but in China and Korea stoneware bodies for celadon wares were made with China stone.

Stonewares were first produced in Mesopotamia around 3000 BC; later, in medieval Europe, stonewares with salt glazes were produced in Germany. The clays used here were naturally high in alumina which, in conjunction with long, high-temperature firings, encouraged the growth of strengthening mullite crystals in the body. In England a wide range of stonewares was produced by Wedgwood, including cane ware, JASPER WARE and black BASALT WARE. These bodies were quite hard and dry and thus ideal for engine-turned decoration. Most stonewares are glazed with ash glazes or salt glazes, but many are simply tinted with metallic oxides and left unglazed. When glazed stoneware is fired, an integrated body-glaze layer is formed, which contributes to its strength.

Straight grain See GRAIN.

Straw The dried stalks of grasses, especially cereals. Twisted into rolls and bound with bramble, split withy or twine, straw has been used in many societies for cheap furniture. Strawwork is the term used for the boxes and other small items that were decorated with split and pressed strips of straw in 18th-century England and France. The stalks of wheat, barley, oats, and above all, rye were most suited to the work; sometimes these were dyed. The straws were applied directly to the surface of the item, or stuck onto sheets of paper that

Straw-work gaming box made by French prisoners of war, late 18th century or early 19th.

were later cut into shape and pasted down. The latter technique is a form of marquetry.

Stringing A form of narrow wooden inlay. It is generally no more than 3 mm wide and is produced as 1 m strips of solid wood, often boxwood or ebony. It is usually laid around the edges of veneered surfaces but is sometimes set into solid timber.

See also BANDING.

Stripe figure Ribbon grain in quarter-cut timber caused by interlocking grain.

Stucco A term used broadly to describe all forms of decorative PLASTERWORK, although it refers specifically to relief decoration modelled and moulded in lime and aggregate (often marble dust) mixes, with or without the addition of gypsum plaster. These mixes can take fine detail and be worked to a hard, smooth finish. The word also has regional variations: in Italy it is used to describe a range of pliable materials which can be shaped; in Britain and the USA it can refer also to cement and sand renders, which from the late 18th century were used on building façades to imitate stonework.

Stucco lustro A form of imitation marble (sometimes called stucco lucido) used from the 17th century, in which a thin layer of lime or gypsum plaster is applied over a scored support

of lime. While the plaster is still wet, pigment is scattered on
the surface and then dragged across it with a brush or comb to
suggest veining. The surface is then polished to a high sheen
with a hot iron. Although this method does not make as faith-
ful a reproduction of marble as scagliola, it has the advantage
of being quicker to produce and does not require the use of
scraping tools, which are difficult to employ on curved surfaces. Stucco lustro was used to produce the early 18th-century
twisted columns of the high altar in the church at Osterhofen

*Twisted column in stucco
lustro, Osterhofen,
Germany, 1731–2.*

in south-eastern Germany.

Stuffing See CURRYING.

Stumpwork See RAISED WORK.

Succinite See AMBER.

Suede A leather finished on the flesh side by abrading the surface to produce a fine nap, or a leather from a flesh split produced by cutting the hide longitudinally and removing the grain. The middle layer is then treated to produce a fine nap.

Surrey enamel See ENAMEL.

Swaging The process of moulding sheet metal between shaped rollers or in a hinged die, called a swage. Swages were in use by the 18th century to make moulded rims on salvers and dishes, in silver as well as fused plate. In metalworking they were later replaced by swaging machines. These are

The use of a swage in the manufacture of fused plate dishes, from F. Bradbury's A History of Old Sheffield Plate *(1912). The worker is holding the dish between the jaws of the swage clamped in a bench vice. By hitting the top part of the swage and gradually rotating the article, he shapes the rim of the dish.*

similar to rolling mills but have rollers of different profiles to shape the metal, rather than reduce its thickness.

Sweating See TANNING.

Sycamore A fairly hard and heavy, strong and stable wood from the sycamore maple (*Acer pseudoplatanus*) or Scotch plane (*Platanus occidentalis*) found in Europe and North America. It is creamy white to pale brown and is smooth and lustrous, but with poor durability. It has an even, slightly interlocking grain with distinct rays and some roey or wavy figure. It is easily worked and frequently used for the production of kitchen equipment and work surfaces, musical instruments, plywood and turnery. Chemical treatments are used to produce HAREWOOD, and quarter cutting produces the lacewood figure.

Synthetic ivory An artificial plastic produced to imitate ivory. The first mouldable plastic, CELLULOID, was invented by the Englishman Alexander Parkes and marketed in 1865 as Parkesine. In 1866 Parkes launched the Xylonite Company, producing synthetic ivory. John and Wesley Hyatt of New York then developed a similar material which they marketed in 1877. In 1899 Xylonite and the Hyatt Company merged to form the British Xylonite Company. (This company is still in existence as BXL Plastics Ltd.) Similar substances were manufactured under the trade names of Cellonite and Pyralin. Celluloid was particularly successful at imitating ivory grain, and in the 1920s and 1930s similar materials were developed and manufactured under a variety of names, such as Ivoride, Ivorine, Ivorite, French Ivory and Genuine French Ivory. These were essentially similar to the earlier products but contained plasticizers which made them more versatile. They were dissolved by solvents such as acetone, however, and easily melted or burnt. Nowadays epoxy and polyester resins are used to make reasonable facsimiles of ivory. These can be identified by the fact that they are easily marked with a hot needle, and never display the end grain seen in elephant and mammoth ivory.

T

Tabaret A compound weave with stripes made in different weave structures, often satin and a vertical rib. The stripes may, but need not, be of different colours.

Tabby weave See PLAIN WEAVE.

Tablet weaving A method of weaving in which the warp runs through cards punched with holes near their edges and sitting parallel to the warp. When rotated by 90–180° the cards form varying sheds. The technique is also sometimes called card weaving.

Taffeta See PLAIN WEAVE.

Takamakie See MAKI-E.

Talc See STEATITE.

Tambour work A form of chain-stitch embroidery done with a steel-ended needle. See also EMBROIDERED LACE.

Tanning The series of processes employed to convert a raw hide or skin into leather. These can be divided into three main groups: the pre-tanning operations, in which unwanted hair, flesh and other materials are removed and the three-dimensional interwoven collagen protein network is cleaned up; the tanning process itself, in which the collagen is treated with various tanning materials which chemically cross-link the protein chains to give a material resistant to bacterial attack; and the post-tanning stage, where the desired thickness, colour, softness and other properties are imparted.

The pre-tanning operations commence with a thorough soaking and washing, which removes blood, dung and similar impurities. The hair is then loosened and unwanted materials are removed from the collagen fibre network. In the past this was achieved using naturally occurring bacteria in the 'sweating' process or with the aid of lime or other alkaline materials in the 'liming' process. In the latter method the hide was immersed in a suspension of lime, though other alkalis such as wood ash were also sometimes used. Lime liquors were often used over and over again, as the breakdown products retained in the solution had a beneficial mellowing effect. The hair and flesh were then scraped off mechanically. Traditionally the unwanted hair and epidermal layer were removed using a blunt two-handled knife. Today hair is pulped chemically and washed off the skin. Unwanted subcutaneous membrane from a skin, together with the adhering fat layer and any remaining muscle, is removed by 'fleshing'. In the past this was done with the aid of a sharp two-handled knife, but in the 19th century

Removing unwanted flesh with a two-handled knife, from Eygentliche Beschreibung aller Stände . . . mit kunstreichen Figuren *(1568), by Jost Amman and Hans Sachs.*

machines were developed to carry out the task.

Unwanted materials sited within the collagen network are then broken down and dissolved using further alkalis or by enzymatic action. Traditionally the 'drenching' (or 'raising') process has been used, in which enzymes produced by fermenting barley or other grains are employed to dissolve the remaining lime and break down the non-collagenous materials. The active ingredients in the raising liquor are naturally occurring enzymes together with a mixture of organic acids produced by the breakdown of the starches from the grains. Alternatively, the bating (or 'puering') processes were used. In bating, the skin was treated with an infusion of dog dung, an operation which resulted in a softer, fine-grained leather. Puering was akin to bating but used chicken, dove or pigeon dung in place of that of dogs. It was employed mainly for softer, looser-natured pelts, such as those of sheep or lambs. The noisome materials used in these processes have now been replaced by proprietary products based on pure enzymes. It is only after this series of operations has taken place that the tanning processes themselves can commence.

Some form of tanning was carried out systematically by Neanderthal man. By the pre-dynastic Egyptian period the three main techniques of tanning were being undertaken on a semi-industrial basis. These were: the use of brains, marrows and other fatty materials, often in conjunction with smoke; impregnating the skin with a mixture of alum, salt and fatty materials in what has become known as the TAWING process; and VEGETABLE TANNAGE, in which the skins are steeped in infusions prepared from the leaves, fruit, twigs, barks or roots of specific plants.

These three basic forms of tanning are still represented in modern industrial leathermaking methods. Marrows and brains have been replaced by the fish oils used in the production of chamois leathers. Chromium chemicals are now widely used in place of alum, and are employed for the production of over 80% of leathers (see CHROME TANNAGE). The vegetable tanning process, now utilizing materials specifically grown and harvested for the purpose, is used for the manufacture of products such as shoe soles and equestrian leathers.

From early medieval times until the late 19th century the large majority of leathers were tanned by the vegetable tanning process, which for cattle hides would have involved immersion in pits containing infusions of tanning materials for one to three years, after which the hides were dried. In the past, in Europe, tanners were required to display their leather in this rough dried condition in an open market and to sell it to a completely separate group of tradesmen who carried out the various post-tanning CURRYING operations. In this way it was not possible for a tanner to disguise poor workmanship with cosmetic finishing operations, and an enforced quality control step was introduced into the manufacturing process.

The laws insisting on separation of the different trades were repealed in the early 19th century. This, combined with the gradual introduction of improved chemical and mechanical processes throughout the century, speeded up the operations. In particular, splitting the skin by cutting it longitudinally into layers, thus producing two or more thinner sheets of usable material, enabled the tanning materials to penetrate the hide much more rapidly. The top layer is generally termed the grain split and the bottom the flesh split. In the case of sheepskins the top layer is termed a skiver and the bottom the flesher. The first splitting machines were patented by William Powers in 1768, and improvements were made throughout the following century. Today, using carefully controlled chemical and mechanical processing techniques, the time taken to convert raw hides to finished leather is measured in days and weeks rather than months and years.

Tapa See BARK MATERIALS.

Tape lace A straight-edged lace made from hand-woven or bobbin lace narrow tapes manipulated into curves and simplified floral patterns; these are joined by bars and filled with bobbin and/or needle lace stitches. The tapes may be plain or, if made by bobbins, may incorporate a variety of widths and fillings. It was made across Europe in the 17th–18th centuries, although it was especially associated with Italy. Italian tape laces were imitated from *c.*1850 to *c.*1930, when they were known as Renaissance lace. These were generally made by amateurs and used machine-made tape or braid and buttonhole stitch. From the late 19th century original patterns were also developed using this technique, especially in the variant known as Branscombe, which sometimes used crochet in place of needle-made bars.

Tapestry A heavy hand-woven textile panel, in plain weave, with the warp entirely covered by the weft; also, fabrics con-

Tapestry weaving at the Edinburgh Tapestry Company. Here the cartoon is placed behind an upright loom, a change from the traditional arrangement of cartoon, weaver and loom, with a mirror used to view the design. The individual bobbins needed for each colour can be seen. Just above the weavers' heads (not seen) is the rigid heddle or shedding rod, from which the swathe of cords attach to every other warp; the alternate warps normally stand proud, and by slipping the left hand through a group of cords the recessed warps can be pulled forward.

structed in this way, such as *kossu*. During the weaving the weft is wound on individual bobbins, one for each colour, and worked back and forth over the warp only where required. Where each colour turns back on itself a slit is created and this may be left open, or closed by various means of interlinking.

A widely used and well-documented technique, tapestry is not restricted by the mechanisms required for pattern weaving. The image is therefore non-repetitive and unlimited in size. European pictorial tapestries are usually worked from a CARTOON; they can be made on a number of different looms but are generally woven sideways and so hung with the weft running vertically. This feature gave rise to the term 'tapestry carpet', in which a pile warp is printed before weaving; machine-made imitation tapestries also generally have their patterns created by multiple continuous warps.

Tatting See KNOTTING.

Tawing The production of a soft, white, leather-like material by kneading a paste of alum, salt, flour, olive oil and egg yolk or other fatty material into a pre-tanned skin. Alum-tawed skins are not resistant to the action of water and so cannot be considered true leathers. They were used from medieval times onwards for the production of white gloves and purses. Alumtawed pigskin has been used as a strong, flexible bookbinding material, as it is particularly resistant to both mechanical abrasion and chemical attack by acidic atmospheric pollutants.

Tea dust glaze A Chinese glaze of greenish colour with dark iron specks. It is essentially the same as the deep black iron glaze found on Chinese stonewares at a certain stage in their firing, when crystals of iron and lime appear on the surface of the glaze. These provide the greenish tone that give the glaze its resemblance to powdered tea. In the Qing period (1644–1911), and especially in the 18th and 19th centuries, the tea dust glaze was adapted for porcelain; its appearance is somewhat more even than that of the earlier stoneware glaze. The tea dust glaze technique is also sometimes applied to a very white body, which makes it appear greener and more intense.

Temmoku A Chinese black glaze with reddish iron streaks on the surface. The term derives from the Japanese name for a black glazed ware produced at the Jian kilns in south China in the Song period (960–1279) and known in China as 'Jian' ware. The glaze is often described as a 'hare's fur' glaze because it has numerous iron streaks on its surface, giving a fur-like appearance.

The Jian kilns specialized in producing sturdy tea bowls with thick bodies that retained heat, initially made for monks

Stoneware bowl with temmoku ('hare's fur glaze'), Fujian province, China, 11th–13th century.

at a monastery near the Tian Mu mountains. At this time tea drinking was an important part of Buddhist ritual. Japanese monks who visited the monastery admired the tea bowls, and took examples back to Japan. These had a strong influence on native Japanese ceramics, including tea wares and raku ware.

Temmoku is related to other unusual black glazes from China, such as oil spot glaze and tea dust glaze. It is applied to a body made from a local clay that is highly ferruginous, with a chocolate brown colour and a rather coarse texture.

In order to produce the hare's fur streaks, excess iron pigment was added to the standard black ash glaze used locally. The dark brown body also contributed additional iron to the glaze. In many examples of Jian ware, it appears that a reddish iron slip was painted onto the rims of bowls before firing, thus forming reddish streaks in the glaze as it melted. The resulting glaze is viscous and very shiny, with the reddish areas providing a matt contrast to the glossy black base glaze. Some exceptional examples in Japanese collections have bluish streaks, which are caused by localized phase separation (see JUN GLAZE).

Temper See GROG.

Tempera See EGG TEMPERA.

Tempering The heat treatment of metals to remove internal stress or to make them less brittle. After steel has been hardened, by heating it until it is red hot and subsequently quenching it, it is too brittle to be useful and needs tempering. When the cleaned and hardened piece of steel is slowly heated, the surface starts to change colour, and this change in colour can be used as an index not only of temperature but also of the internal structure and hardness of the metal. According to the specific purpose for which it is to be used, therefore, the steel is heated until it turns a certain colour and then quenched. The tempering colours of carbon steel range from pale straw yellow (very hard) to deep blue (very tough). The heat treatment of silver alloys to increase their hardness is also called tempering.

Tent The name used in the 16th–18th centuries for a plain-woven fabric with evenly spaced yarns of hemp, jute or linen. It was often used as the strong base cloth for what became known as canvaswork, where its stable weave provided a suitable 'grid' for counted threadwork. Tent gave its name to tent stitch (see PETIT POINT) and was also an alternative term for the professional embroiderer's frame. Related to it are the terms tenter hook and tenter frame, both devices for holding fabrics to a given width under tension during weaving or finishing.

Terra sigillata See ROMAN RED SLIPWARE.

Terracotta A decorative building material made by moulding and/or modelling clay and then firing it to obtain a hard and durable product that can be coloured with paint or glazes. The fired units can then be incorporated into the structure of a building. The materials and techniques used to make terracotta are similar to those used in the production of BRICK, and the history of these products is closely related. Distinctions can be made between them, in that the clay used for terracotta is generally more plastic than the raw material of bricks. Additionally, terracotta is often of hollow construction, while brick is solid; the surface of terracotta is frequently fettled, or worked to remove excess clay, before firing, whereas bricks are generally moulded and fired without further refinement or are carved after firing. The term faience is used to describe glazed terracotta, although it can also refer to ceramic slabs used as cladding.

Terracotta was used by the Babylonians from 1400 BC, the Indians from the 1st millennium BC, and the Chinese, who produced decorated hollow stoneware blocks during the Han period (206 BC–AD 221). Painted terracotta ornament was used by the ancient Greeks and Etruscans in conjunction with wooden construction. The Romans used low relief panels as decorative cladding over brick. Although the use of terracotta in building declined in Europe following the end of the Roman empire, it continued to develop in Turkey, Persia and Mogul India. The influence of Islamic techniques, and notably the use of glazes opacified with tin, led to the reintroduction of terracotta into Europe, where it was widely used for the production of ornament from the 14th century.

From the mid-18th century until the 1850s forms of ceramic similar to terracotta, such as Coade stone, were used to imitate stone. Industrially produced terracotta and faience became popular in Europe and North America from the early 19th century until the 1930s as inexpensive, lightweight, fireproof building materials which could be attached to steel-frame construction, using iron or steel fixings secured to the inside of the unit with concrete. Terracotta and faience are also valued for their resistance to the effects of atmospheric pollution.

The clays used to make the terracotta are generally fine-grained so as to accept detail. As with brickearths, after extraction the clay is exposed to weathering to break down large particles and to wash out impurities which might affect the durability of the fired product. Sand or crushed fired clay, called grog, is added to reduce shrinkage and distortion during firing, and the mixture is kneaded thoroughly. The clay is either modelled by hand or pressed into ceramic or plaster of Paris moulds which slowly absorb moisture from the clay, allowing it to be removed from the mould. Large, hollow forms are supported with clay walls built on the inside of the unit. Fettling, using modelling tools or spatulas, is carried out at this stage to compress the clay and smooth the surface so as to reduce the risk of cracking during firing; greater definition can also be given to moulded ornament by fettling. On firing, a thin, partially vitrified surface layer, or fireskin, is produced, which increases the material's resistance to weathering.

Units are allowed to dry for several weeks before firing. Firing conditions influence the colour and hardness of the

Terracotta panel from the Natural History Museum, London, 1870s, showing the depth of modelling and fine detail that can be produced. The foliage in the background has been darkened by soiling.

final product. An oxygen-rich firing of a clay with a high iron oxide content produces reds, oranges and deep pinks; an oxygen-poor atmosphere results in blues and greys. In early up-draught kilns conditions were largely uncontrolled and variations in the colour and strength of pieces would occur; down-draught and continuous kilns afford more control. In some instances glazes are applied to the green, or unfired, clay. The glaze, composed of ground glass and metallic oxide colourants, is formulated to fuse tightly with the surface but without being absorbed into it. In the mid-19th century brightly coloured faience was produced by applying the glaze to fired pieces and then refiring them at a lower temperature. From the 1870s manufacturers were producing stoneware products, such as Carrara ware, made by Doulton and used on the Savoy Hotel in London, which were highly durable and less expensive as only one firing was required. A similar creamy white material was used on the Woolworth Building in New York, designed by Cass Gilbert in 1913.

Although glazed terracotta and faience are generally durable materials, they can deteriorate because of the penetration of water onto the mortar joints between the units. The mortar, typically made of a cement and sand mix harder than the terracotta and too rigid to allow for movement of the structure, often develops fine cracks. Water drawn into these cracks cannot readily evaporate and, with freezing, can put pressure on the surrounding material, leading eventually to the loss of areas of the glazed surface. These problems can be avoided by the use of a softer mortar mix.

The term terracotta is also used of red EARTHENWARE.

Terry See VELVET.

Terylene See POLYESTER.

Tesserae See MOSAIC.

Textile machinery A general term covering an enormous and diverse range of machines used in the production of textiles and characterized by the incorporation of at least one automatic action, whether worked by hand or by an auxiliary power source. All looms, for example, can be classed as textile machines since by definition they contain an automatic shedding device (see LOOM). The development of hand-powered looms and related equipment, such as the implements for spinning, goes back to ancient times and was well advanced by the 17th century; even before the widespread application of auxiliary power many automated hand-powered cloth-making devices were called engines or machines. Among these were the STOCKING FRAME, perfected for the making of solid plain-knit fabrics in 1589 and in widespread use across Europe by the 1650s, and the Swiss invention of the late 1820s known as the hand-machine; the latter, a relatively early example of developments in the embroidery machines, was related to the SEWING MACHINE.

In the early phase a symbiotic relationship existed between the evolution of textile machinery and metal-smithing, particularly wire-drawing, which produced not only pins, hooks and needles but also the equivalent holding, pulling and pushing devices needed for automatic thread manipulations; later that relationship extended to light and heavy engineering. Early textile machines, whether replicating or assisting hand operations, generally aimed to generate multiple, identical effects, and by the 1760s included a variety of treadle-operated harness (or shaft) looms, some with a flying shuttle attachment (such as John Kay's shuttle-throwing 'sling' of 1733) and drop boxes (such as the automatic shuttle-changing device invented by Kay's son Robert in 1760); the warps were measured out and pre-positioned on large rotating cages or drums called warping mills and their wefts made 16 at a time on hand-operated spinning jennies. It was the production of yarn and simple cloths with such machines that formed the basis of the industrial revolution. In addition, from c.1760 to c.1830 numerous adaptations were perfected, either to produce fabrics for which there was no handmade equivalent, such as warp-knitted fabrics (produced on a stocking frame), or to speed up the creation of threads strong enough for warps or the production of large, more complex and/or more colourful patterns. These developments were linked to the introduction of ROLLER PRINTING and the JACQUARD engine and to the latter's application in machine laces and hand- and mechanically powered cloth- and carpet-weaving.

Although industrialization is associated with the development of factories and the application of power, these did not evolve uniformly. On the one hand, in the manufacture of so-called 'fine and fancy' textiles auxiliary power was uneconomical, and on the other, factories pre-dated its introduction. It was only after warping mills were successfully mechanized in the 1840s that power looms (themselves introduced in the 1770s, successfully operating by the early 1800s and improved in the 1820s) began to outnumber hand looms. Even then, and for another century, there remained many factories that supported the work of hand-loom and hand-frame weavers, as well as sustaining hand-spinning, printing, dyeing and finishing.

Thinner A liquid added to paint to adjust the consistency and make it workable. It is generally the same fluid used to clean the brushes. Thinners (also known as diluents) have to be compatible with the binder: thus turpentine is used for oil, water for acrylics and gum, and white spirit for alkyds. Furthermore, they have to be volatile so that they evaporate once the paint has been brushed on.

Thonet furniture One of the most successful mass-produced furniture types. It was developed over a long period by the Austrian designer Michael Thonet and first made commer-

Bentwood beech chair by Michael Thonet, c.1865.

cially in 1849. Chairs, couches and small tables are the main products. Made entirely from turned and steam-bent beech, few joints are used and the individual components are joined together with steel bolts. The simplest chairs consist of only four components: the back and back legs, an open circular seat frame (the circle is secured with a long tapering 'bird's mouth' joint), and two front legs. On the best pieces the seat was completed with caning; otherwise a three-ply plywood disc was used, often ornamented with a die-pressed embossed design.

Throwing See CERAMICS.

Thuya A light brown, very hard wood from the *Tetraclinis articulata* or *Callitris quadrivalvis* species, known as thyine wood, or citron burl, found in North Africa. It is normally obtainable in Europe as a root burr and is full of small knots and curls, deliberately formed by coppicing. It is used only for fancy work and turnery. Other species of thuya include the WESTERN RED CEDAR and the ARBOR VITAE.

Tie dyeing See PLANGI.

Tiefschnitt See GLASS ENGRAVING.

Tigerwood See ZEBRAWOOD.

Tile A fired clay slab used for architectural surfacing and ornament. Ceramic tiles have been used to weatherproof and decorate architecture since the 3rd millennium BC. Unlike construction bricks, they are primarily used for surfacing, paving or roofing, and can be made from any ceramic material, although the most common is clay. They are made in moulds for consistency of size and form, then dried and fired in regular ceramic kilns (see colour plate X). Most are square in shape but roof tiles can also be circular or curvilinear. In the Near East tiles for religious buildings can be star-shaped or geometrical in form.

Tiles can be glazed and decorated like any other clay form, but several decorative techniques have been developed that are unique to tiles, such as CUENCA, CUERDA SECA and ENCAUSTIC. The decoration is usually confined to the exposed surface, which can be flat or modelled, sometimes quite deeply. This can be achieved through casting or moulding, carving and applied decoration. Other decorative techniques include impressing, which was used to decorate English Chertsey tiles of the 13th century. Most glazes can be applied to tiles, but when used for exposed surfaces the more durable glazes, such as lead or ash glazes, are desirable. In general, wall tiles are usually glazed and floor and roof tiles are often unglazed.

Tiles are made by most ceramic-producing cultures, often in the most successful ceramic technique of that culture; for example, Delftware in the Netherlands, celadon, porcelain and lead-glazed wares in East Asia, lustre ware and Isnik ware in the Near East, and terracotta in ancient Rome and modern Italy and Spain. In 19th-century England tiles were produced by mechanical methods using a dust press. The press was patented by Richard Prosser in 1840 and was originally designed for making earthenware buttons. Herbert Minton in Staffordshire applied the press to tile-making and began to mass-produce high-quality pressed tiles with relief-moulded, hand-painted, printed or tube-lined decoration (see TUBE LINING). The tile is also an increasingly popular form among modern potters, who use its wide surface as a canvas for decoration and interesting glaze effects.

Tin A soft, bluish white metal with a low melting-point. It is rarely used as a pure metal and almost always occurs in alloys such as pewter, bronze and gunmetal. Tin is also widely used as a decorative and, more importantly, protective coating because of its corrosion-resistance. This tin plating is called tinning and can be done by dipping the article in molten tin or by electroplating. Copper cooking utensils are usually tinned to protect against the poisonous effects of the copper. So-called tinplate is a thin coating of pure tin on iron or steel.

Tin glaze A white glaze opacified with tin. White tin glazes were first used extensively in the Near East in the 9th century AD. They are normally associated with Near Eastern ceramic traditions but some Chinese kilns also produced tin glazes. From the 15th century tin glazes were used extensively in European ceramics.

A traditional tin glaze is simply a lead glaze that has been opacified with tin. As they are usually white, tin glazes have often been used to disguise an unsatisfactory body material. Their whiteness also makes them ideal for painted decoration, as can be seen on lustre wares, Isnik ware, maiolica and Delftware. Tin glazes are not high-fired glazes, but they can withstand temperatures of up to 1000°C without losing opacity and are therefore normally used on earthenware or fritware bodies. As the glaze is essentially opaque, in-glaze decoration is used for painting. Tin glazes can also be stained to produce coloured grounds (see SMALTINO).

A tin-glazed earthenware food warmer consisting of four parts, probably London, c.1770.

Tinsel print See WOODCUT.

Tinsel yarn See METAL THREAD.

Tissue See LAMPAS.

Titanium white A synthetic pigment (titanium oxide) obtained from ilmenite, the principal titanium ore. It has been commercially available since the 1920s and is the main white pigment in use today, having largely replaced the toxic lead white. It is highly opaque, with a bright blue-white colour, and so inert that it can even be used in foodstuffs. It has enormous covering power and most titanium white paints contain large amounts of chalk as an extender.

Tjanting A Javanese implement for drawing with hot wax, used in the production of BATIK. It consists of a copper bowl with a narrow spout, attached to a wooden handle. Blocks embedded with copper and used to transfer wax to cloth are called *tjap*.

Togidashi-makie See MAKI-E.

Toile de Jouy See COPPERPLATE PRINTING.

Tole ware See PONTYPOOL WARE.

Toledo ware A special type of DAMASCENING practised in Spain, involving the inlay of gold and silver wire in a cross-hatched steel ground. Although there are examples of Spanish inlaid metal ware dating from as early as the 4th century BC, the most celebrated examples were produced either during the Renaissance or in the 19th century. Gold wire is mainly used, in a variety of sizes and colours, with some silver for the edges. Sometimes the inlay is decorated further with a hollow-ended punch to give a series of half-domes much like an inlaid beaded wire. An opposite effect can be achieved with a rounded punch to give a series of depressions. The whole object is either air-heated or immersed in a hot (140°C) solution of caustic soda and Chile saltpetre, after inlaying and finishing, to give the steel a contrasting black or dark blue colour. The cities of Eibar and Toledo were centres of damascening, with the Zuloaga family (active in the 19th century) the most famous makers.

Tombac See BRASS.

Tooling The process of decorating and lettering a bookbinding by hand with a variety of small tools, each with a design or numeral, letter or other decorative element in relief which is impressed into the covering material. The tools have iron or brass heads and wooden handles and are applied to slightly moistened leather with hand pressure and a rocking motion. They may be used either cold or hot, but if heated (on a finishing stove) they will darken the leather, emphasizing the design. The process is also called finishing. When used without any colouring material in the pattern, it is called blind tooling; examples can be found on Coptic bindings as early as AD 700 and the technique was in use in England by the 13th century.

If the decoration is to include gilding, the design is first 'blinded-in' or impressed with a tool. Glair is applied over the entire surface, or simply in the required areas, then gold leaf is laid down and held in place with vaseline or grease. Finally, the leaf is pressed with a heated tool, the heat activating the glair. Metal foils other than gold can also be applied to the tooled design. Gold tooling reached Europe from the Islamic world and was first practised in Italy in the mid-15th century.

Topaz A transparent gemstone composed of aluminium fluorosilicate which occurs in colours ranging from yellow, brown and orange to pale blue and has a Mohs hardness of 8. Topazes are found in eastern Germany, Brazil, Australia, Sri Lanka, Russia and a number of African countries. Pink topaz, prized in the 19th century, is produced by heating the stone to 500°C. Topaz is formed within igneous rocks and can occur in large single crystals. It is faceted for use in jewellery, which must be designed to protect the stone as it is prone to splitting.

Tortoiseshell A mottled, nutty brown shell material, with irregular patches that are much lighter in colour and which, when polished, become translucent or almost transparent. The great majority of the material described as tortoiseshell is in fact the outer, horny layer of the shell of the related marine species of turtles. The hawksbill turtle (*Chelone imbricata*), native to the Antilles in the Caribbean, was the most popular source for most British and western European craftsmen. The shell from the main area of the carapace is a brownish amber colour mottled with reddish and dark brown spots, while plates from the plastron are much paler and are referred to as 'blonde'. Shell taken from the sharply curved sides, known as 'hoofs', is usually a mixture of dark and light areas. The Seychelles variety, from the Indian Ocean, is differently coloured, the carapace being marked with black and brown spots and pale speckled patterns; the plastron often displays a reddish tint. Plates from a large specimen can be up to 10mm thick, providing material that is solid enough to carve to some depth. Most Chinese and other Far Eastern tortoiseshell is derived from the loggerhead turtle (*Thalassochelys caretta*). A third source is the green turtle (*Chelonia mydas*), considered inferior to other types; its green tinted shell tends to be used only for veneers.

Tortoiseshell has been used as both an inlay and a decorative overlay on wood, often in conjunction with contrasting materials such as ivory or mother-of-pearl. When used as an inlay or to make boxes, it was often gilded or painted red or yellow on the verso and this layer would normally be protected by a pasted paper layer. The shell is relatively soft but somewhat elastic and reasonably tough. It is easily worked with burins, gravers and files. It can be sawn and cut as screw threads. It is thermoplastic and is readily softened by hot water or steam. When the shell is soft, designs can be pressed into the surface, and it can be pressed in dies or bent around formers; it will subsequently retain its shape when cool. It is polished using graded abrasive powders lubricated with a little non-drying vegetable oil. Nowadays carborundum and aluminium oxide powders are used, but traditionally such materials as powdered bath brick, pumice or ground charcoal were used for the first polish and the final shine was produced using rottenstone, whiting or crocus powder.

The relatively small individual plates of turtleshell can be welded together to form larger continuous sheets, rings or bands. There are various welding techniques, all of which involve the use of heat, moisture and sustained pressure. One traditional method is to wrap the area to be joined in wet linen rags or paper and then crimp the join with red-hot iron tongs. The steam generated by this process softens the shell and the sustained pressure from the tongs keeps the joint faces together until cooled and set. An alternative method is first to degrease the shell by washing with a suitable detergent. The edges to be joined are prepared by skiving to as thin an edge as possible and the pieces are boiled in salted water for one hour.

Wooden tea caddy with tortoiseshell veneers and silver mounts, England, c.1760.

The softened pieces are removed from the hot solution and the joint is quickly aligned with one piece above the other, then held together using stiff wooden slips secured with stout clamps. The entire assembly is then boiled for a further 30 minutes with occasional tightening of the clamps, and then allowed to cool, after which the edges are found to be securely joined.

Tortoiseshell and turtleshell have been used as ornamental materials for several centuries and were used to produce combs, small boxes, card cases, fans and fan sticks, which were often intricately pierced or inlaid with contrasting materials. Various plastics are now used as substitutes (authentic shell fluoresces with a yellowish brown colour when exposed to ultraviolet light), and the genuine materials have become increasingly expensive and scarce owing to over-exploitation and loss of habitat. The trade in raw shell and shell artefacts is now controlled by the CITES (Convention of International Trade in Endangered Species of wild fauna and flora) regulations.

Touchmark A maker's mark found on pewter wares.

Touchstone A piece of black stone used for ASSAYING metals. A variety of stones, including tuff and chert (a form of quartz), have been used for this ancient technique, in which an object of unknown composition is drawn across the stone and the colour of the streak produced is compared with one from a known alloy. The stone basanite has often been incorrectly associated with touchstone. In fact, an analysis of 34 touchstones found that none was basanite and the association of the two may derive from the ancient Greek word for a test, βασανοσ.

Tournai marble A fine-grained black limestone, quarried from the area around Tournai in Belgium; it can be highly polished and is thus commonly termed a marble. The stone was also carved at Tournai and the exportation of fonts and grave slabs to England and other European countries began in the 12th century.

Tracing paper A thin, smooth, translucent paper used for transferring and copying a design by hand. It is also referred to by some modern designers as 'layout paper'. Tracing paper was first produced for commercial use in 1862, probably manufactured by extensive beating of the paper fibres to make them absorb water and appear semi-transparent. The same effect can also be achieved by impregnation with oils or resins.

Trailing A means of decorating glass with hot threads of glass wound around a hot vessel. The threads can be left proud of the surface or marvered smooth and combed into zigzag patterns with a pointed metal instrument. The technique was much used in the ancient world.

Transfer engraving The decoration of glass with an engraving that is stuck on the rear and then painted in polychrome colours. A thin, flat piece of glass was coated with turpentine, which was allowed to dry and harden. Then a black and white mezzotint engraving was soaked in water, drained and spread onto the prepared glass, taking great care to prevent air bubbles from being trapped beneath it. When dry, the print was soaked again and the paper rubbed away with the fingers so that only ink remained. The ink image was then painted with transparent oil colours, usually flat washes, the shading in the painting being a result of the mezzotint itself. The pictures were not varnished as this would have detracted from their translucency. The technique was used by both amateur and professional artists.

Transfer gilding See GILDING.

Transfer printing A process of decorating ceramics and glass with a printed design transferred from a thin sheet of gelatine or tissue paper. It was first recorded in Birmingham in 1751 and became popular as a means of creating repeated, standardized designs on industrially produced items. Initially, it was used for porcelain but later it was adapted to earthenwares and from around 1800 it was used for glass. Also in the 19th century tissue paper replaced gelatine.

An engraved copper plate was heated and treated with an ink prepared from one of the metallic oxides. The design was then transferred to the gelatine or onto damp paper and, while the pigment was still wet, was rubbed onto the glass or biscuit-fired ceramic. It was fixed by firing. On glassware the design could be printed in monochrome on opaque white glass, or as a black outline and infilled with polychrome painting. Ceramics were fired, decorated but unglazed, at a

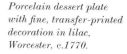

Porcelain dessert plate with fine, transfer-printed decoration in lilac, Worcester, c.1770.

low temperature (700°C) to fix the colours. They were then glazed and fired again at a higher temperature. The decoration can therefore be seen as a type of underglaze decoration. The earliest ceramic examples have monochrome designs, but by the 19th century polychrome painted decoration was in use. This required the use of separate transfers for each colour. The most popular colour was blue, and blue and white transfer-printed wares are the most common. Such wares were produced at many potteries in Staffordshire, where they are still made.

In a variation known as 'hot printing' a mixture of oil and colouring matter was added hot to a heated copper plate and a piece of tissue paper was then placed on the plate. The whole was covered with flannel and passed through a roller press, after which the printed tissue was placed on the object. The back of the tissue was rubbed with a boss to transfer the design, and the object was then fired in a low-temperature kiln.

Some examples of creamware have printed overglaze decoration. This technique is a slightly different one, called bat printing, in which a design is printed in oil on a sheet of gelatine (bat) and then pressed onto the ceramic. Pigment is then dusted onto the transferred oil design. Gold decoration can also be applied with transfers, gold powder being used to colour the copper plate or dusted onto a printed design.

Trapunto See QUILTING.

Travertine A type of limestone formed by the deposition of calcium carbonate from lime-rich hot water springs. Travertine is hard, creamy grey to yellow, red or brown in colour, and characteristically contains numerous small cavities. There are large deposits of travertine near Rome and it was used extensively by the Romans from antiquity as a building stone. It is still widely used, polished and with the cavities filled, as a modern cladding material.

Tricot A range of warp-knitted fabrics usually made with two sets of threads, characterized by vertical wales (ridges) on the face and horizontal ribs on the reverse. A variety of openwork patterns may also be incorporated. See also STOCKING FRAME.

Tripoli powder A naturally occurring silicate abrasive derived from schistose rocks.

Tri-tic A widespread and ancient RESIST DYEING method in which cloth is sewn and usually gathered before dyeing. The technique is often combined with PLANGI, when it is known by the collective term *shibori*. In Nigeria's Yorubaland the same combination of techniques is known as *adire oniko*.

Truewood See HEARTWOOD.

Tube lining A technique used to produce relief decoration on English tiles in the 19th century. As with slip trailing, lines of slip are trailed on to the surface of a tile to form a design in relief. The design is usually then filled in with coloured glazes, which are kept separate by the slip lines. Tube-lined decoration is often confused with relief-moulded designs on tiles, which are similar in appearance. Unlike moulded decoration, however, slip lines will often develop small cracks in firing.

Tudric See PEWTER.

Tufa A variety of limestone formed by the deposition of calcium carbonate from lime-rich springs and streams (see also TRAVERTINE). It can be coloured yellow or red, owing to the presence of iron oxides, and has a sponge-like texture. Tufa is lightweight and has been used to fill the spaces between the ribs of vaulted ceilings. It has also been used as a building stone, for example in Verona.

Tuff An igneous rock composed of fine-grained volcanic ash which has become solidified over time. It is generally white or grey and is soft enough to be easily worked. Tuff has been used as building stone in Italy and in Germany, where it is known locally as *trass*. Tuff is also added to lime to obtain a hydraulic set.

Tula steel Decorated steel objects made from the 18th century onwards by the Tula Arms Factory in Tula, Russia. The factory (which is still in existence) was founded in 1712 and originally produced finely decorated and inlaid arms but later went on to make furniture and decorative objects. The steel was often inlaid with precious metals and enriched with gilt bronze mounts and cut steel ornaments.

Tula work An old-fashioned term for a form of niello made in Russia. It is not synonymous with Tula steel.

Tulipwood An Australian hardwood (*Harpullia pendula*), also known as tulip lancewood. It is very hard and heavy, and is reasonably durable, with a fine grain and texture. It is variegated in colour and grain pattern, from pale yellowish brown to black and is difficult to work, but polishes well. It is available only in small sizes, and is used in turnery and high-class cabinet work. The name is also sometimes used of Rio rosewood.

Tumbaga See DEPLETION GILDING.

Tunbridge ware A type of mass-produced marquetry made from the late 17th century to the late 19th, especially in the area around Tunbridge Wells, England. Variously profiled strips and rods of dyed and natural-coloured woods were glued together to make complex pictorial and geometric designs in the form of solid blocks with the designs revealed on the ends. The blocks were then cut into thin veneers,

Tunbridge ware box, England, 19th century.

each showing the identical design. From about 1830 distinctive mosaic designs predominated. Tunbridge ware was used to decorate a variety of small wooden objects and furniture, such as work boxes, games boxes, gaming pieces, pincushions, needle cases and tea caddies.

Turkey red A bright red colour on cotton, produced by a complex method originally involving madder, olive oil, tannic acid, alum, ox-blood and potash. Known also as *rouge turc*, *rouge des Indes* and *rouge d'Adrianople*, the recipe was confined to Middle Eastern areas until the mid-18th century, when it was introduced to France, the Netherlands and Britain, where the production method was refined. It was a specialist technique producing a very fast red (sometimes known as 'morone') and often used in discharge printing. Patents for the process were taken out in Britain by James Thomson in 1813 and 1815, which led to the colour also being known as 'Thomson's red'.

Turkey work A form of hand-knotting of pile developed in Britain in the late 16th century in imitation of imported

A Swiss woodturner using a pole lathe, from J. Stumf's Chronick *(1548).*

Eastern carpets (known as 'Turkey carpets'). Used for bed and table rugs and for upholstery, the style was introduced into America by at least the mid-17th century and there retained the same type of patterns but used a needle to form a pile on a pre-woven foundation. The style was at its most fashionable between *c.*1660 and *c.*1760; its production was generally superseded in the 19th century by loom-woven pile fabrics (see CARPET-WEAVING) and hand-knotted pile rugs made with a hook.

Turning The use of a LATHE to produce items that are usually round in section. A variety of materials can be formed or decorated by turning, including ivory, horn and metal, but the technique is generally associated with wood. The wood-turner produces a wide variety of items, many of them components for use in other branches of the woodworking industry, such as chair legs or mouldings. Other products include bowls, circular boxes and goblets.

The craft of turning takes three main forms. In spindle (or between-centres) turning, the workpiece is held between the drive centre and the tailstock and is worked from the side, with waste material being removed from the circumference. This method is used to produce basically cylindrical objects such as chair legs, candlesticks, balusters and newel posts.

In faceplate turning the workpiece is held on a faceplate or in a chuck such as a cup chuck or spigot chuck, which is screwed onto the drive. The workpiece can be worked from the side or the face, and scrapers are often used. Bowls, platters, goblets and any other objects that have to be worked on the face rather than just the periphery are produced in this way. The method of working a bowl, for example, would be to fix the workpiece to the faceplate with screws or glue and work the back or underside, at the same time making the fixing which will fit into whichever type of chuck is chosen for the next process. The piece is then dismounted, refixed in the chuck and the face is worked.

Ornamental turning employs a highly developed mechanical lathe on which both the tool and the workpiece can be moved differentially to produce forms and patterns based on interlocking circles and arcs. These complex designs are generally executed on small objects made from exotic hardwoods, ivory and horn.

For the turning of ceramics, see FETTLING.

Turquoise A soft (Mohs scale 5–6), opaque, blue-green gemstone mineral, composed of hydrous copper aluminium phosphate, which forms within sedimentary rocks. The colour of turquoise can vary from a vivid blue, produced by the copper component, to a pale, and generally less prized, green, caused by the presence of iron. Its principal ancient sources were China, Persia and the Sinai peninsula, from where the Egyptians obtained it from neolithic times. It was so popular in Egypt that glazed STEATITE was used as a simulant from 4000 BC. Owing to its opacity, it is cut as cabochons or made into beads, inlays or carvings. The Aztecs made mosaics, masks and other objects by embedding small pieces of turquoise in a wax or gum, applied over a wooden support. Turquoise was widely used for jewellery and amulets by the Navaho and Hopi Indians of the south-west USA; this area is still a major source.

Turtleshell See TORTOISESHELL.

Tutenag The name under which ZINC was imported in the 18th century to Europe from Asia. It derives from the Sanskrit *tuttha* ('copper sulphate') and *naga* ('tin or lead').

Twill A weave structure in which the warp floats over more

Ritual mask inlaid with turquoise, Mexico, Mixtec–Aztec, AD 1400–1500. It was made by embedding small, precisely cut pieces of turquoise in a matrix of wax or pitch applied over a wooden support. The eyes and teeth are made of shell.

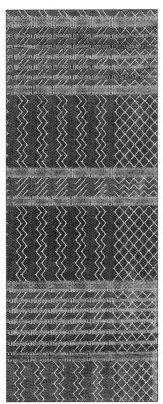

A dobby-woven two-coloured silk, showing a range of patterns based on twill weave structures, probably Britain or France, 1860s.

than one weft (in warp-faced twills) or the weft over more than one warp (weft-faced twills) to create diagonal lines. By reversing the diagonal a herringbone weave is made; four directions of diagonals create 'birds-eye' and other similar patterns. Weft-faced twills include 'old' jean (see FUSTIAN); the warp-faced equivalents are denim and 'new' jean.

Twist stem A drinking-glass stem that incorporates a spiral pattern (see colour plate VIIb). In making an air twist stem, furrows are formed in a gather of glass. The gather is then dipped in molten glass, which traps air in the indentations. As the gather is drawn and rotated into a stem, these bubbles can be manipulated into elaborate patterns. In a variation known as cotton twist, canes of opaque white or coloured glass are incorporated into the stem and twisted. The process can be repeated to make double-series and triple-series stems. The techniques were developed in England in the mid-18th century, but evolved out of *façon de Venise* work.

Typesetting The assembly of type to build up a text. The casting of movable metal type for printing began in Korea about 1400. In Europe Johann Gutenberg produced the first printed Bible in 1450–55. The design of the earliest typefaces was based on the characters formed by a pen when writing by hand; with the subsequent development of letterpress printing, new typefaces were designed to reflect different tastes and styles and to accommodate the needs of the printing process. A complete set of type of a particular face and size is called a fount. Type sizes are measured imperially in points and metrically in millimetres. Early metal type used individual letters, numbers, punctuation and spacing cast in lead by a type founder, with spaces within the characters produced by punches. A compositor assembled the pieces of metal one by one in a hand-held frame, transferring its contents to a larger frame, called a forme, to build up the text. Illustrations and decorative elements could also be set in the forme and printed simultaneously.

Despite the speed at which a skilled compositor could work, typesetting by hand was a very laborious process. At the beginning of the 20th century mechanical typesetting machines were developed. These assemble the brass matrices needed for a line of text in response to an operator working a keyboard and make a casting of them in molten metal, producing individual slugs of lead. In the case of the monotype process there is one slug for each character; with linotype a

Typesetting and printing in Germany, from Hartmannus Schopperus's De omnibus illiberalibus siue mechanicis artibus ... liber *(c.1574). The compositors work in the background while printers operate a screw press in the foreground. One inks the type and the other removes a printed sheet from the 'forme', which held the type in contact with the paper. In the foreground are two stacks of paper, one printed and the other ready for printing.*

complete line is produced as a solid piece of lead. Photocomposition now gives more flexibility than 'hot metal', as the individual characters are projected as light onto a photographic film. Electronic typesetting and editing machines use computers to select information in association with cathode ray tube typesetting machines.

Tyrian purple See SHELLFISH PURPLE.

U

Ultramarine A blue pigment obtained from LAPIS LAZULI. The stone was crushed, mixed with a paste of wax, resin and oil and kneaded in hot water. The paste retained any foreign particles, while the colouring material settled in the water. Ultramarine was extremely expensive and thus rarely used for decorative painting, except occasionally for works such as a royal commission or for touches of colour in heraldic work or arabesques.

Umber A brown earth pigment, similar to ochres but containing manganese dioxide as well as iron oxide. It is now generally produced synthetically, unless purchased from specialist suppliers. Raw umber is a cool, greenish brown, and when this is 'burnt' by heating, it is converted to a warm, reddish and more opaque brown. It is a reliable pigment in all media and on all surfaces.

Unaker See CHINA CLAY.

Underglaze decoration Decoration applied to a ceramic body under a transparent glaze. It is one of the most permanent

Porcelain flask with underglaze cobalt blue decoration, China, early 15th century.

forms of ceramic decoration and can be painted or printed (see TRANSFER PRINTING) on most body types. Underglaze painting normally uses high-temperature pigments such as cobalt, iron and copper. The earliest underglaze painted ceramics were produced in China in the 3rd century AD. These were celadons with underglaze iron brown decoration. In the 8th century underglaze cobalt blue painting was first used on porcelain in China, and underglaze copper red and green decoration was used on earthenwares and stonewares. The technique of underglaze painting is simple, in that pigments are mixed with a liquid medium and then painted on a dried or biscuit-fired surface. The ceramic is then glazed and fired.

Upsetting The process of compressing metal by FORGING. Upsetting causes the metal to thicken and is a technique often used by blacksmiths. The upsetting or thickening of edges and rims of silver hollowware is sometimes also called caulking.

Urea-formaldehyde A thermoset plastic belonging to the class of amino plastics. It was first patented in Britain in the form of a resin in 1918 by Hans John. It is made by heating urea with formalin. Moulding powders based on thiourea-formaldehyde were discovered in 1924 by a British chemist, Edmund Rossiter, while working for the British Cyanides Company (see BANDALASTA WARE). By 1929 urea-formaldehyde offered improved properties,such as increased moulding speeds and simplified moulding of deep drawn items such as beakers and cups.

Urea-formaldehyde mouldings are odourless and are cheaper and lighter in colour than phenolics. However, they are inferior in terms of heat-resistance, with a higher rate of water absorption.

Urea-formaldehyde thermos flasks, 1930s and 1940s. Urea-formaldehyde is fairly heat-resistant, does not 'taste' and is colourful, making it an attractive material for this application.

Urushi A resin used in the Far East for the production of lacquerware (see colour plate XIII). In Japan and China the principal source of urushi is the sap of the lacquer tree

Rhus vernicifera, the Japanese name for which is *urushi-no-ki*. The Chinese name is *ch'i-shu*. A related species, *Rhus succedenea*, grows in southern China and South-East Asia and was the principal source of urushi in the Ryukyu islands. In South-East Asia other species such as *Melanorrhea laccifera* and *Gluta usitata* produce a sap with similar properties to urushi. All the urushi resins are highly allergenic in the uncured state and can cause a severe skin reaction. Lacquer was first used as a decorative material in China around 5000–4000 BC and many refined techniques had been developed by the Warring States period (475–221 BC). The lacquer arts are more highly developed in Japan than in any of the other producer countries, and in recent years there has been a tendency to use Japanese terminology to describe the materials and techniques of the *urushi-gaki* ('lacquer craftsman').

The method of extraction is broadly similar to that used for collecting rubber and involves making a series of V-shaped incisions in the bark of the tree over a period of four or five weeks. Colouring is difficult, since urushi reacts with many pigments, turning grey or even black. The resin has therefore traditionally been coloured by the addition of a few finely ground pigments such as cinnabar (for red), azurite and indigo (for blue), and lampblack (for *kuro* urushi) or iron salts (for *ro-iro*) for black; in South-East Asia, particularly Burma, the natural colour of the resin is black, and no colourant is needed. Whereas most gums and resins used as varnishes require dry, warm conditions to set, urushi resins are unique in requiring high humidities in very thin layers in order to dry. A variety of means have been developed to achieve these conditions. Humidity is controlled in a specially constructed chamber or cabinet. In Japan and parts of China and Korea this consists of a slatted wooden 'stove' (known in Japan as an *urushiburo* or *muro*). Other areas, including the whole of South-East Asia, use a specially constructed underground chamber (known in Burma as a *taik*).

Urushi sets much harder than other varnishes and paint media, and is more resistant to abrasion and the effects of solvents. It has been used as a decorative and protective coating on a wide variety of decorative and utilitarian objects. The commonest support is wood but it can be applied to other materials, including metal, basketry, leather and textile, and can be built up into layers of sufficient thickness for carving.

If urushi is mixed with powdered materials such as fine sand, baked clay, diatomaceous earths, wood ash, or other vegetable matter, pastes can be made which are used to make smooth foundation layers in the manner of European gesso. The pastes are also used to produce raised designs and to cast or model small objects or small parts of larger pieces.

More than 300 different urushi finishes are recognized, each of which can be laid onto one of several different qualities of prepared grounds, ranging from a simple rubbed-in coating of *ki-urushi* to the 22 stages involved in the preparation of a *hon-kataji* ground. There are eight major divisions of technique: sprinkled urushi, incised urushi, carved urushi, inlaid urushi, painted urushi, dry urushi, moulded urushi and gilt urushi. More than one technique may be employed on the same object. For example, shell inlay may be laid into a ground sprinkled with metal powders. These techniques can be very simple, involving as few as three processes to achieve the desired finish; in the case of carved lacquer, on the other hand, up to 500 coatings may be necessary.

In a typical lacquer object the wooden ground is carefully prepared from good-quality, well-seasoned wood. A layer of raw urushi (*ki-urushi* in Japan, *ts'ao-ch'i* in China) is applied, followed by a layer of textile (usually hemp in Japan and silk or hemp in China), soaked in urushi. This may be *ki-urushi* or a mixture of *ki-urushi* and flour paste known in Japan as *mugi-urushi* when wheat flour is used, or as *nori-urushi* when rice flour is used. The next layer is a paste (called *kokuso*, *ji* or *sabi* in Japan, *htei-thayo* in parts of South-East Asia and *ni-tzu* in China) made from urushi mixed with a filler. A range of materials is used as fillers: in China wood ash and pigs' blood or finely divided riverine clays are common; in Japan special baked and ground earths, ground ceramic and shell are used; and in South-East Asia wood ash, baked teak sawdust, rice husk and cow dung are used. Once cured and smoothed, two or three coats of middle coating urushi (*naka-nuri* in Japan) are applied, followed by the decorative layers.

See also LAC BURGAUTÉ and MAKI-E.

Utrecht velvet See GAUFFERING.

Vacuum-forming See Plastics.

Valenciennes lace See Bobbin lace.

Varnish A hard, more or less transparent and glossy coating that dries and sets by evaporation of a volatile solvent, and is used to protect and enhance wood and other surfaces. Varnish finishes have been in use in Europe since the late 16th century. A unique varnish known as Urushi has been used in the Far East for at least 5000 years and the ancient Egyptians protected the painted surfaces of funerary goods with a shiny vegetable resin.

Traditionally, two main types of varnish have been used, differentiated as oil and spirit varnishes. The oil varnishes consist of resin dissolved in a vegetable oil such as linseed, which is made into a drying oil by heating with litharge (white lead oxide). This gives it the property of forming a clear film when it is exposed to the air in thin layers. Several coatings are required; the first application is often diluted with turpentine. The spirit varnishes consist of gums or resins dissolved in a volatile organic solvent. A common spirit varnish is made by dissolving Shellac in ethanol or methylated spirit. Rosin or colophony can be added to the solution to produce a harder coating with a more glassy finish.

Modern varnishes are made from a variety of synthetic polymer resins, such as polyurethane or the methylmethacrylates, dissolved in organic solvents. All of these products rely on the evaporation of a solvent to dry and should be used in a warm, dry, dust-free area. At least three applications are required to produce a satisfactory finish. The first coat is usually diluted with a suitable solvent and 'flattened' or 'cut back' with fine abrasive paper or wire wool when dry.

See also French polishing.

Vasa diatretum See Cage cup.

Vat dye See Dyeing and Indigo.

Vegetable ivory A material taken from the kernel of the nut of certain species of palm tree (principally *Phytelephas macrocarpa*) which grow in Africa and South America. About the size of a chicken egg, these nuts have a hard flesh, which is smooth and white when fresh but darkens somewhat with age. The African variety, the dum nut palm, produces a nut with a hollow centre while the South American variety, the ivory palm, has a solid nut. These nuts cut smoothly, take a good polish and are easily stained and dyed. Their small size limits their utility to the production of small objects such as salt cellars and chess pieces.

Vegetable tannage A tanning process in which a prepared skin is treated with infusions of barks, leaves, twigs, roots or fruit of specific plants. In general the skins are treated first with weak, nearly depleted, tanning liquors, and it is only when these have penetrated the surface in a uniform manner that stronger, more astringent extracts are used. Vegetable tannage dates from at least the neolithic period.

Vellum A term generally denoting a high grade of PARCH-MENT. Parchments prepared from calf- or goatskins rather than sheepskins are often termed vellums, as are parchments made from the skins of newly born animals.

Velour See VELVET.

Velvet A term that originally referred only to a silk cloth in which the pile was made by a second warp bound into the cloth at intervals between loops formed over wires. The loops are then cut to create the pile. Other terms indicate different fibres (moquette, a wool or mohair pile), cloths with uncut

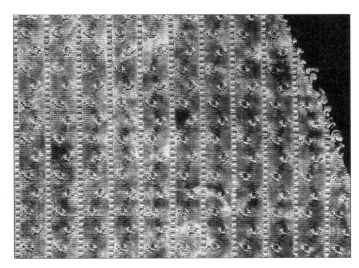

Silk velvet for men's wear, France, c. 1790. It has tiny voided (no pile) circles and a stripe created by intermittently binding down the lighter-coloured threads in the second (extra) warp, which also contains the silk for the pile areas.

loops (terry, or terry velvet if dense and of silk) or longer piles (plush, velour). Velveteen and corduroy are related structures, but made from supplementary wefts with, respectively, cut loop and uncut floats (see FUSTIAN).

Veneer Thin slices of wood cut from particularly desirable trees, or from parts of trees where the grain formations make attractive patterns. They are often applied to cheaper, less attractive or more stable timbers. Although veneers were used in the ancient world, they did not appear in Europe until the early 17th century, when Dutch craftsmen reinvented the technique to show off the exotic imported materials that were then available. Veneering allowed the more economical use of the best-figured timbers and also enabled highly figured burrs to be used for decoration. With the wide-bladed saws that had recently been invented they were also easy to produce. The broad but thin saw blades could be used in frame saws to cut thin and consistent veneers 3 mm thick.

Particular parts of a tree are often selected for veneer production. Areas of unusual growth are especially desirable, such as the burrs that are sometimes formed around areas of damage or the crotch formed where a tree trunk bifurcates and at the union of substantial branches with the tree trunk. These cuts of timber can be rare and expensive to produce,

Hand-sawing veneers using a frame saw, from André-Jacob Roubo's L'art du menuisier *(1772).*

and often the very features that make them attractive can render them prone to cracking and warping.

Veneers can be saw-cut, knife-cut or rotary-cut. Saw-cut veneers will normally be quite thick, usually in excess of 1.5 mm, and the amount of waste material produced by the saw makes this type particularly expensive. Knife-cut veneers are produced by slicing the trunk or flitch of timber with motorized knives up to 2 m long, somewhat resembling a giant plane. They are usually substantially thinner than sawn veneers, and are often paper thin. In the third method, rotary cutting, the tree trunk is peeled by being rotated against a static blade, rather like sharpening a pencil. The grain patterns produced by this method are usually uninteresting and the veneers tend to be used for plywood. Since the grain is the same throughout the flitch, matching veneers are easily made. They can be opened out to give symmetrical patterns on drawer fronts or doors.

Oyster veneers differ from most other types in that they usually display a complete section, cut at a tangent through a branch or small trunk. Usually ovoid, they are often taken from species which display an exceptionally strong colour contrast between the sapwood and the heartwood as well as between early and late banding. Laburnum is a favourite choice for veneers of this type.

See also MARQUETRY.

Verawood A variegated olive green to brown, waxy wood from the *Bulnesia arborea* species and commonly known by such names as Congo cypress, lignum vitae, maracaibo and vera amarillo. It is often used as a substitute for LIGNUM VITAE.

Veneered writing cabinet, designed by C. R. Ashbee and made by the Guild of Handicraft, England, c.1901–2. The veneer is ebony and holly on a carcass of mahogany, the feet are of carved oak, painted red, and the fittings are of wrought iron.

Vermeil A term used for gold-plated silver in general but more specifically for firegilded silver. Originally this French word was also used for firegilded bronze, brass and copper objects.

Vermilion A red pigment derived from a sulphide of mercury. It occurs as a native ore, called cinnabar, and was originally extracted from mines in Spain, but by the 9th century its manufacture, by vaporizing a mixture of sulphur and mercury, was well understood. From the 17th century the best European source of the pigment was Amsterdam. It was always expensive, a difficulty obviated, particularly on wall paintings, by underpainting it with the cheaper red lead or even mixing the two pigments together. It has now been replaced in the West by the less toxic and more reliable cadmium red, which matches it closely in colour. Vermilion can no longer be bought in the United Kingdom in tube form, but is available as a dry pigment, imported mostly from China, where it has a very important role in traditional crafts and where production has never ceased. It can blacken if used in an aqueous medium, but is generally stable in oil paint, varnishes or lacquers.

Vernis Martin A true lacquer process developed to imitate Far Eastern (principally Japanese *maki-e*) lacquerware, patented by the Martin brothers in Paris in 1748. Simon Etienne Martin had been employed by a Dutchman named Huygens, who manufactured a varnish that produced a finish very similar to oriental lacquer, and it is probable that the Martin process was developed from this. The process uses a copal varnish made by blending copal resin, Cyprus and spirit turpentine, colophony and a vegetable oil such as linseed or poppy. Amber varnish, which is a blend of powdered amber, turpentines and vegetable oil, is also used, either alone or in combination with the copal, depending on the desired result.

A vernis Martin surface is created through various techniques, depending on the timber used and the degree of finishing. In some cases the various decorative and finishing layers are laid onto the bare wood, which has previously been painted the desired colour. In others, a thin, multi-layered gesso ground is prepared and sealed, then coated with coloured varnishes in sequences suitable for the achievement of the required effect. An aventurine or MAKIE-E effect is produced by sprinkling spangles cut from rectangular silver-plated copper wire onto wet varnish grounds through a fine

Snuff box in horn, with vernis Martin decoration on the lid, France, 18th century.

sieve and then applying successive coats of varnish until the spangles are completely covered. When thoroughly dry, the surface is rubbed perfectly smooth and flat, using fine sifted pumice powder applied with a cloth rubber lubricated with water. Further coats of varnish are applied which, when dry, are rubbed down as before. After a brief further polishing with fine emery powder, a final polishing is carried out using very finely sifted rottenstone, initially applied with a cloth and finished with the palm of the hand. The final gloss is achieved by wiping over the surface with a little fine oil, which is then removed and dried using sifted wheat flour sprinkled onto the surface and removed with a soft cloth, then repeating the process with the bare hand.

Verona marble A variegated limestone, containing compact nodules of yellow to white calcium carbonate and veins of pinkish brown clay, which can be polished; it is thus commonly termed a marble. It occurs in the north of Italy, near Verona, and it was extensively used in Venice and elsewhere as a decorative stone for columns, panels and carvings, often as a contrast to the creamy grey of Istrian stone.

Verre églomisé Glass backed with engraved gold leaf, which is then protected by another layer of glass, or by varnish or paint. Although practised in antiquity (see FONDI D'ORO) and the Middle Ages, the technique is named after a French 18th-century art dealer, Jean-Baptiste Glomy, who sold prints bordered with this form of decoration. The foil was stuck to a sheet of glass with glair and then engraved with a fine needle in bold or light lines, or in dots for half-tones. A coat of black paint made the design stand out against the gold, while coloured paints made for a more naturalistic effect. See also ZWISCHENGOLDGLAS.

Vetro a fili, vetro a reticello, vetro a retorti Types of FILIGREE.

Vetro corroso See ICE GLASS.

Vicuna A fibre or yarn derived from the smallest species of the llama, *Auchenia vicugna*, native to the high Andean regions of southern Ecuador, Peru, Bolivia and north-western Argentina. The fine strands are strong, resilient, lustrous and extremely soft, and production is limited, since the animal has to be killed to obtain its hair. The term has also been used for a number of fabrics with some vicuna content, and it gives its name to a finishing process that gives a worsted fabric a fine, short, erect nap, so that it appears to be

A reliquary panel in verre églomisé, *depicting* The Nativity, *by a follower of Pietro Teutonico, Umbria, c.1320–30. In addition to the gilding, the panel is coloured with copper resinate green, red lake glazes and blue azurite. It is backed with a layer of lead or tin.*

a vicuna cloth.

Vinyl See POLYVINYL CHLORIDE.

Viridian A bright, strong green synthetic pigment with good tinting strength, made from a hydrous oxide of chromium. It has been commercially available since the mid-19th century. It is stable in all media, and because of its transparency is very useful for glazing and washes.

Viscose See RAYON.

Viscut See CELLOPHANE.

Vitrification The conversion of the raw materials from which glass is made into a vitreous substance. It takes place by heat and fusion at c.1300–1550°C, when the silica melts. Vitrification is also important to ceramic manufacture, since both glazes and clay bodies contain glass-forming materials, including silica and feldspars. As these materials melt in firing, they fuse and form glass, or vitrify, at temperatures above 800°C. The formation of the glass creates a matrix which holds the clay particles together and converts the clay to hard ceramic. Vitrification increases with temperature, and thus very high-fired ceramics such as porcelain are more vitrified than softer ceramics such as earthenware.

Vulcanite The first truly semi-synthetic plastic, known in the USA as Ebonite or 'hard rubber'. It is made from a natural material, rubber, which has been chemically altered, its composition and properties being changed by the addition of sulphur under controlled conditions, a process known as vulcanization. Thomas Hancock in Britain (1843) and Charles Goodyear in the USA (1844) patented methods for the vulcanization of rubber within a year of each other.

Self-portrait by Thomas Hancock, made from his own material, vulcanized rubber, c.1843.

The material is characteristically black. When mixed with white and red pigments, a pink substance results, which was used to make false gums for dentures. Because of its resemblance to jet, vulcanite became popular in Britain for mourning jewellery after the death of Prince Albert in 1861. Other decorative uses of vulcanite have been in pens, small boxes and musical instrument parts. Vulcanite can be distinguished from jet by its faint smell of sulphur. It is prone to oxidation, which may produce a whitish bloom on the surface.

Vyne black A pigment made from crushed charcoal. Because the particles are quite coarse, its covering power is not as good as that of lampblack. However, it has a distinctive blue-black tone and when mixed with white produces a cool grey that can be manipulated to appear almost like a true blue.

Waldglas See FOREST GLASS.

Wallpaper Printed or painted paper used as an interior wall decoration. It differs from other types of decorated paper in that the design is rarely complete on one sheet but is usually carried on over several sheets or rolls of paper which, when juxtaposed, make a repeat pattern or an extensive scene.

As the supply of paper increased in Europe at the end of the 15th century, it became possible to use it to imitate and replace more expensive wall coverings, such as leather, tapestry, wood or paintings. From the end of the 17th century sheets of handmade paper were pasted together to form rolls, making printing a repeat pattern from wooden blocks more practical (machine-made paper did not bring ready-made continuous rolls until the 19th century). Early patterned papers were applied directly to the wall, whether plaster or wood, while the elaborate productions of the 18th and 19th centuries were often lined with canvas or hessian and

A store of 19th-century wallpaper printing blocks at Cole & Son. Some are still in use.

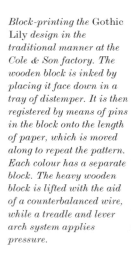

Block-printing the Gothic Lily *design in the traditional manner at the Cole & Son factory. The wooden block is inked by placing it face down in a tray of distemper. It is then registered by means of pins in the block onto the length of paper, which is moved along to repeat the pattern. Each colour has a separate block. The heavy wooden block is lifted with the aid of a counterbalanced wire, while a treadle and lever arch system applies pressure.*

mounted on wooden stretchers before hanging.

Patterns were often imitations of textile designs, and in the 18th century this was taken to extremes with the development of the richly textured FLOCK paper. The heyday of block-printed wallpaper, however, came in France and Britain between the middle of the 18th century and the end of the 19th. The blocks were made from close-grained wood such as pear or sycamore, laminated and jointed to make the size required. With the design transferred to the wood, it was cut using a range of gouges and knives. Polychrome designs required a separate block for each colour. Pins were added to the edge of the block to ensure accurate registration, and their marks can be seen on the selvedge of unused papers.

The block was inked by placing it face down on felt in a tray and then lowering it onto the paper before applying pressure with a hand- or foot-operated lever press. In Britain printing inks were bound with an animal glue medium, while in France the medium was more often oil (see also INK). Before machine-made paper became available, sheets of

handmade paper were joined to form continuous lengths which were moved through the press for each repeat. This method of printing remained fundamentally unchanged from the 16th century until machine printing was introduced around 1840. However, hand-block printing continued throughout the 19th century.

One notable style of block-printed wallpaper was the scenic paper developed from the late 18th century, printed in sets of large panels measuring 2.4–3 m in length and containing non-repeating pictorial designs. The major sets of scenic papers were produced in France by the Dufour and Zuber companies between 1800 and 1860 and may have been inspired by the painted panoramas popular at the turn of the century. Subjects depicted include scenes from classical mythology (e.g. the *Cupid and Psyche* of Dufour et Cie) and exotic locations (e.g. Zuber's *Paysage des Lointains*). Production was a complicated and skilled process, with a single design taking perhaps a year to produce. First an artist was required to draw the design, which was then transferred to a

Parts of the Monuments de Paris, *a scenic wallpaper produced by Dufour, France, c.1820. The wallpaper was printed in colour from woodblocks and forms a panorama, rather than a repeat pattern.*

full-size cartoon for the division into blocks, taking account of the different colour printings. The design was then transferred to the blocks, each measuring about 46 × 51 cm, and each motif was cut. The use of animal glue as the medium for the ink gave a matt, fresco-like surface to the image. Some papers were produced in grisaille, using a limited range of grey or buff tones; others were in colours which required up to 200 separate applications.

Block-printed paper was not the only available form of wallpaper before the introduction of mechanization. One remarkable form of wall covering developed in the 18th century was the Chinese hand-painted paper produced specifically for export to the European market (see colour plate IV). It is thought that these papers were based on the designs of indigenous hand-painted silk hangings. Two styles were popular: scenes of birds and plants, and scenes depicting human activity. The papers were painted on joined sheets of Chinese handmade (*hsuan*) paper, made of mulberry fibre and lined with two layers of bamboo fibre paper glued on with starch paste. The outlines of the design were painted over a colour-washed background in Chinese black ink made of pine soot and animal glue, and the colours added in mineral pigments with a water-soluble medium, as well as organic dyes mixed with white to form lakes. The papers were exported in

Scenes from Nursery Tales, *roller-printed wallpaper designed by Mabel Lucie Attwell and produced by C. & J. G. Potter, c.1910.*

rolls, and additional motifs were supplied to cut out and paste over the joins. The designs were suited to large rooms and, like scenic wallpapers, were hung from cornice to dado level, often on a textile backing nailed to wooden battens. Surviving Chinese wallpapers are usually seen in English country houses as part of a chinoiserie decorative scheme.

In 1839 the firm of Potters of Darwen in Lancashire adapted a calico printing machine to enable the distemper used in hand-block printing to be used on cylindrical printing blocks mounted on rollers. From the mid-19th century wallpapers began to be mass-produced by machine-printing techniques such as lithography and screen printing, while by the beginning of the 20th century a range of special-effect papers were being manufactured in Europe and America. Among these were the imitation leather wallpapers, embossed and gilded, which were fashionable in Britain from the 1870s, sometimes imported from Japan. These were made of laminated paper or paper pulp pressed into a mould to create the texture of embossed leather. Oil-based paint, gilding and varnish were then applied and the paper pasted to the wall. Other distinctive varieties introduced in the late 19th century were three-dimensional papers such as LINCRUSTA WALTON and Anaglypta, which were intended to imitate plasterwork, and a three-tier arrangement of co-ordinated patterns comprising dado, filling and frieze, in the style of wood panelling.

Although an expensive and slow method of printing wallpaper, a handful of companies still have block-printed papers in production today, because their rich effect is not reproducible by machine. Sometimes the original 19th- and early 20th-century blocks designed by artists such as William Morris, Charles Voysey and Walter Crane are used.

Walnut A hard, strong and moderately heavy timber from species such as *Juglans regia* (found in Europe and Asia minor), *J. nigra* (American black walnut) and others such as *J. australis* and *J. sieboldiana*. It is light brown to almost black, with darker markings and grain patterns. Stable when seasoned, it often displays an attractive fine, even grain pattern. Burrs, stumps, butts and crotches are highly prized for veneers.

In England walnut is recorded as a favoured timber for the manufacture of fine furniture by the late 16th century and is mentioned by Francis Bacon (*Natural Historie*, 1616) as best

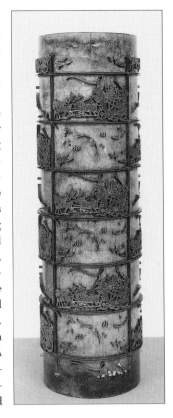

A roller for printing wallpaper by machine. The pattern is created by raised metal bands, infilled with felt for the broader areas of colour.

for tables, cupboards and desks; its durability and shock-resistance also made it well suited to the production of gun-stocks, for which it is still used. Good-quality timber was in short supply from the early part of the 17th century; a good deal was therefore imported from Europe and given names such as Grenoble wood, after its supposed place of origin. John Evelyn (*Sylva*, 1664) mentions the shortage of walnut and the use of grained beech as a substitute. The severe winter of 1709 destroyed many of the European plantations and the export of walnut from France was banned in the 1720s. In England the problem was somewhat offset by the importation of black walnut from Virginia and then by the growing popularity of mahogany. Chambers' *Encyclopaedia* of 1786 states that its use for furniture making had then almost ceased.

Well-figured Mediterranean walnut is known as ancona. Some timbers which are referred to as walnut are in fact other species, the timber of which resembles true walnut: for example, Nigerian walnut (*Lovoa klaineana*) is actually a type of mahogany.

Walrus ivory An ivory obtained from the highly modified canines of the male walrus. It is sometimes also called morse ivory. Walrus tusks average 60 cm in length but have a diameter of only 6 cm, although much larger examples have been reported. They are hollow for about 60% of their length and have a thick core of highly crystalline secondary dentine which can form up to 75% of their volume. Objects made from walrus ivory are easily identified by their generally small diameter and the presence of the distinctive secondary dentine seen on the end grain, parts of which may have been exposed on longitudinal faces by the carving process.

Wampum See BEADWORK.

Warp See WEAVING.

Warping mill See TEXTILE MACHINERY.

Water gilding A form of GILDING in which gold leaf is applied to a damp gesso surface.

Watercolour Pigment in a gum medium. Gums are collected from the wounds of a variety of plants, including fruit trees, but the most common source is the acacia tree, which produces gum arabic. Since the 20th century the paint has been sold in small tubes, but before that it was always moulded in cakes or droplets. Early users of watercolour—the manuscript illuminators, map colourers and miniature painters—

would have made up the paint from dry pigment and gums, but from the late 18th century it was increasingly sold as ready-prepared, moulded cakes. In this dry form the paint has to contain something to prevent it from becoming too brittle. Today there are many plasticizers in use, but the traditional material was sugar.

Most pigments, except those based on lead, can be used for watercolours, but the modern commercial selection tends to favour translucent lakes and synthetic, organic colours, as these are most suitable for washes. Apart from indigo, gamboge (a coloured yellow gum) and carmine (from cochineal beetles), very few natural organic pigments are still made up as watercolours, because they fade so fast. Inorganic pigments, which are heavier than organic ones, have to be ground particularly finely if they are to be successful in watercolour, because the particles must remain in suspension in the water as the paint flows off the brush.

The paint works well on paper, which is porous and counteracts the strong surface tension of water. However, heavily sized papers and smooth, impermeable surfaces are difficult to 'wet', and brushstrokes laid on these can contract to droplets unless a wetting agent such as ox-gall is added.

Watered steel See DAMASCUS STEEL.

Watermark See PAPER.

Watermark figure A stain caused by fungal infection, found in trees such as the horse chestnut. It can sometimes increase the value of the wood for decorative purposes. See also SPALTED TIMBER.

Wax A malleable, fatty substance obtained from a variety of sources. Since it is soft when warm, it is used for modelling small items that will later be cast (see CASTING and LOST WAX CASTING) and to make seals and small sculptures (which must then be kept at a cool, controlled temperature). Wax is also used as a polish and is a component of a number of lacquers, paints, coatings and varnishes. Encaustic paintings are executed in melted wax.

The natural waxes include: beeswax, which is refined by immersing bags filled with honeycomb in boiling water; carnauba wax, obtained from the Brazilian palm *Corypha cerifera*; and Japan wax, a by-product of urushi lacquer. Paraffin wax is extracted from petroleum, while stearine is a synthetic wax made by the hydrolysis of fat.

For the use of wax as a finish for wood, see WOOD.

Waxed calf A black vegetable-tanned calfskin leather finished on the flesh side to a high gloss using hard greases and waxes. It is used especially for riding boot uppers.

Weaving A general term used to denote a wide variety of processes that result in the permanent interlacing of threads at right angles (or nearly at right angles) to each other. More specifically, the term relates to the use of a tensioned vertical (the warp) and a mechanical or automatic method of creating the opening (shed) for the horizontal (weft) threads. These operations are carried out on hand- or power-driven looms (see LOOM). Permanent thread intersections made in other ways are OFF-LOOM CONSTRUCTIONS and include lace and plaiting, methods that can produce results identical to weaving. Weaving forms the basis for virtually all cloths, to such an extent that those made without interlacing, such as felt, are referred to as 'non-wovens'.

Woven patterns are always a proportion of the selvedge-to-selvedge measurement: full-width, one-half, one-quarter, one-eighth and so on. They also tend to fall into diagonal grids, to prevent uneven uptake of the warp, unless that itself is a feature of the cloth. Woven cloths can also be patterned by the addition of embroidery and stamping (see GAUFFERING) and they form the base for most printed textiles.

The names given to woven fabrics have changed over the past centuries and are still not standardized. The fabrics themselves can be classified in four different ways: by their end use, such as tapestry or carpet; by the type of loom on which they are made; by their fibre content, structure and weight or finish, as in moiré, flannel, fustian and moreen; or by their structure alone. Terms such as damask, brocade and tapestry are often used to indicate the presence of a pattern associated with these specific techniques and have been erroneously applied for at least two centuries.

Weave structures Weaves can be divided into four categories: simple, compound, supplementary and pile. The most basic is PLAIN WEAVE, in which the warp and weft threads are crossed alternately to produce a flat cloth. Changing the arrangement of intersections of warp and weft can produce a diagonal emphasis, as in TWILL, or a predominance of warp or weft on the surface (warp-faced and weft-faced, respectively), as in SATIN and DAMASK. Simple weaves continue uninterrupted across the cloth and most can be produced on any loom. Small all-over or 'spot' patterns derived

OPPOSITE *Hand-weaving silk damask on a Jacquard loom at De Vere Mill, Sudbury, Suffolk. The weaver holds the handle of a flying shuttle device, which, by yanking to the left or right, propels the shuttle through the shed; also seen are the wooden harnesses controlling the ground weave and, beyond, the cords rising up to the Jacquard above the loom. The pattern being woven is a replica of the damask ordered in 1689 from Genoa for William and Mary, for wall hangings in Hampton Court Palace.*

from these weave structures are often made on a loom with a
dobby mechanism (see DOBBY LOOM) and are therefore called
dobby weaves. Variations on simple weaves include ikat,
stripes, ginghams and plaids, created by altering the colours

of the warp and/or weft; basket weaves, made by treating two or more warp and weft yarns as one; seersuckers, with alternate bands of tight and slack warps, resulting in a 'puckered' effect; and some horizontally ribbed fabrics, including rep and poplin, which use thick and fine yarns together, the thick yarn creating the rib.

Compound weaves combine two or more weave structures and are used to create contrasting textures and the more elaborate pattern and colour effects; unlike many plain-woven fabrics, their names generally indicate their characteristic construction, regardless of their weight or fibre content (see, for example, DAMASK and TABARET). They may also have an additional warp or weft, as in brocatelle; such additions are bound into the compound cloths, which are also known, collectively, by the terms lampas, or complementary weaves.

Supplementary warps or wefts are not integral to the cloth and need not run the entire length or width of the cloth; in this case their function is ornamental rather than structural, as in brocade. A related technique is the simultaneous creation of two or more independent cloths that interlink with each other, as in doublecloth. Piled and looped constructions result from special treatment of additional warps or wefts (see VELVET and FUSTIAN).

Wedging See CERAMICS.

Weft See WEAVING.

Weld A mordant dye from the herbaceous plant *Reseda luteola*, known as dyer's rocket. It is said to be the oldest of the yellow dyes and the only one of reasonable fastness; it was the principal yellow for European dyers until their discovery of fustic and quercitron. Weld was an important dye for wool: with alum or tin it produced a lemon yellow; with iron it gave a greenish olive.

Welding The process of joining metals of similar composition in one homogeneous piece, by fusing together the edges in contact or by adding molten metal of similar composition. Any two oxide-free metal surfaces, when brought into intimate contact, should form a bond as strong as the bulk materials. Generally heat is used to achieve welding, although some metals will weld without heat. For example, when two flat pieces of gold, silver, lead or platinum are laid face to face and hammered they will fuse together. This hammer welding or forge welding is the oldest form of welding, and is the technique used in blacksmithing to join wrought iron. When two pieces of wrought iron are heated to white hot the surface is very plastic, and when the two parts are brought into contact and subsequently hammered they can be fused together. If the wrought iron is very clean no flux is needed, because the slag inclusion in the iron acts as a flux. Welding was also used by ancient sword and knife makers to weld a hard but brittle steel edge to a soft but flexible iron centre.

Another more modern form of welding involves heating the area to be joined to melting-point; often a filler metal of similar composition (called a welding rod) is added to fill the gap. The local heat needed is achieved by an electric arc, an oxy-acetylene flame or even a laser.

Western red cedar Wood from the British Columbia or Pacific red cedar (*Thuja plicata*), found in north-west America. It is reddish brown, light and soft, aromatic, very durable, and resistant to insect and fungal attack. It is strong but slightly brittle, stable, and has a very straight grain and a medium or coarse texture. Western red cedar is very easily seasoned and worked, and is used for roofing shingles, joinery, greenhouses, shelters and some cabinet work.

Wheel brace See WOODWORKING TOOLS.

Wheel cutting See CUT GLASS.

Wheel engraving See GLASS ENGRAVING.

White bronze See SPECULUM METAL.

Whitewash See LIMEWASH.

Whitework See EMBROIDERED LACE.

Whiting Crushed and purified chalk, used as a pigment and as a filler for cheap paints. It becomes transparent with oil and is therefore better suited to distemper paint. Mixed with glue, it makes gesso.

Wicker A general term for a variety of natural and artificial materials used for the construction of baskets and furniture. They include willow osiers, the inner 'reed' of the RATTAN palm and the paper-coated wire used for LLOYD LOOM furniture.

Wilton A cut-pile carpet, limited to five or six warp colours and with those not in use interwoven in the foundation. It was hand-woven in various centres from the 17th century to the mid-19th. Carpet-weavers in the English town of Wilton received a royal warrant in 1699 and made several types of carpet, including the Brussels looped-pile carpet (from 1720), the cut-pile to which the town gave its name (made on an adapted Brussels loom from *c.*1750) and hand-knotted carpets on machinery transferred from Axminster (from 1835). See CARPET-WEAVING.

Window glass See FLAT GLASS.

Windsor chair A type of chair distinguished by the fact that the legs and seat form an independent unit from the back, which (together with the arms, if present) is joined to the top of the seat, with a totally separate leg assembly being joined to the bottom. In all other chair designs the backstand and the back legs are made from a single piece of wood. The first mention of Windsor chairs dates to 1724. They were developed from various vernacular patterns of stick and

A Windsor chairmaker, from a wood engraving by Stanley Anderson. A brace bib and a howling or hollowing adze hang on the wall, below a row of centre splats, while a pair of chairmaker's braces fitted with shell bits lie on the bench.

thrown furniture made by village turners and wheelwrights. The main centre of manufacture was High Wycombe in Buckinghamshire, where a chairmaking industry was established by about 1780. Native woods readily available locally were used: beech for the legs, stretchers and sticks, elm or sometimes beech for the solid seats, and ash or yew for any bentwood components. If an ornamental backsplat was incorporated, it was often made from a well-figured fruitwood.

Numerous different designs were made, each named after the pattern of back used. The best-known are the comb back (probably the earliest pattern), the bow back (which incorporates steam-bent back bows and arm bows), the lath back and the scroll back (which became the common pattern for English kitchen chairs). Another distinguishing feature of the Windsor chair, which is sometimes used in other designs, is the use of stretchers to reinforce the leg assembly. Various types of stretcher were employed, such as the H, crinoline or cow horn, double H, X and box. From about 1750 the traditional turned front legs were often replaced with more fashionable cabrioles, especially on comb back and bow back patterns.

Wire A long filament of metal. For many centuries wire has been made by drawing thin metal rods through progressively smaller holes in a DRAWPLATE, first by hand and now mechanically. Before this, narrow strips of metal were twisted to give a hollow wire, or a square-section rod was twisted and rolled.

Woad A reduction/oxidation dye from the leaves of *Isatis tinctoria* and related plants. It gives a near black colour in a fresh dye-bath, then a blue and, when nearing exhaustion, a greenish blue. Woad is a less concentrated source of indigotin than indigo and is processed in the same way, except that the dye paste is derived by a compost method of fermentation. It was widely used in Europe until the 16th century and remained in use into the 20th century as a fermenting agent in indigo vats for dyeing wool. In France it is called *pastel*, from the term originally used for 'woad dye paste' and later for the plant itself; as woad paste mixed with calcium carbonate or gum came to be used for drawing, the name 'pastel' was given to coloured crayons and their use as a graphic medium.

Wood A hard, tough and flexible material derived from the trunks and branches of trees. It is readily available in most parts of the world, is fairly easily worked and, with care, is infinitely renewable. The unique properties of wood have led to its use as a primary material in the manufacture of houses, tools, weapons, furniture and modes of transport such as sledges, carriages and ships.

Woodworking was probably one of the first craft skills developed by mankind, and from the simple spears, clubs and throwing sticks of our remote ancestors have developed the skills of the modern cabinetmaker, joiner, woodcarver and builder. Since about the Roman period the woodworking crafts have been divided into numerous groups, each of which uses timber for a particular purpose. For example, the cooper makes barrels, the wheelwright manufactures wooden wheels and the cartwright builds wagons, while the luthier and violin maker make musical instruments and the clog maker makes shoes. Each of these crafts is highly specialized and is practised nowadays on only a small scale. CABINETMAKING, CARPENTRY, JOINERY, TURNING and WOODCARVING are more familiar branches and are still practised at an industrial and craft level. The skills, tools and materials used in the various branches of the woodworking crafts frequently overlap, and the various

The workshop shared by Ernest Gimson and the Barnsleys at Pinbury, c.1895. This is typical of the many small shops operating at the end of the 19th century.

trades are often distinguished more by their products than their techniques. For example, the techniques of the house carpenter are almost indistinguishable from those of the cartwright, which in turn are similar to those of the shipwright.

Classification and use From the point of view of the craftsman, woods are divided into two main groups: the hardwoods, which are produced by broad-leaved trees, and the softwoods, which are produced by conifers. These terms do not describe the actual hardness of the timbers and in fact some softwoods are harder than hardwoods. The softwoods in general are quite resinous and many have resin ducts running parallel to the grain; some of these resins are valuable and are extracted for use in paints, varnishes and other products. Hardwoods are generally non-resinous.

Each species of timber has its own unique characteristics of stability, durability, colour, texture, elasticity and hardness. This has led to the use of particular species for particular purposes. For example, the strength and durability of oak made it the ideal timber for house construction, shipbuilding, bridge building and cooperage; the toughness of ash makes it suitable for tool handles; and the colour, close grain, hardness and figure of walnut and mahogany make them excellent materials for furniture making; while the elasticity and resonance of certain types of spruce make that the timber of choice for musical instrument sound boards.

Deforestation and the loss of forestry reserves have meant that timber has become increasingly expensive and prime material of the type used in top-class joinery and cabinetmaking increasingly rare, so there is now increased reliance on laminates (see PLYWOOD) and particle boards or composites (see MEDIUM-DENSITY FIBREBOARD). These materials are environmentally stable, do not require seasoning and can be specially treated during production to render them fireproof and waterproof. Wide panels are easily produced and a variety of finishes such as wood veneers, lacquers or laminated sheet surfaces (including Formica or melamine) can be applied during production to enhance their appearance. With the exception of plywood, these composites are not as strong as natural wood; normal woodworking techniques are of limited use when working them and special fixings are required to join pieces together. The particular characteristics of these materials make them ideal for panelling, work surfaces and table tops, but the furniture is usually of simple panel construction and can look rather box-like.

Durability Wood is a naturally durable substance. If it is protected from the depredations of wood-boring insects and the effects of fungi, it can last for many hundreds, even thousands, of years. Wooden artefacts have been found in ancient Egyptian tombs in an excellent state of preservation. The sapwood, or living wood of all trees, which contains various nutrient substances, is particularly susceptible to decay, however, while the heartwood is more resistant and that of some species is completely immune. Cedar, mahogany and teak are just three of the most resistant. Many resistant woods are aromatic, and their durability may be due to the resins and oils that they contain.

Wood can be artificially protected against deterioration by treatment with a variety of chemical substances. The use of creosote or zinc chloride is a well-established and successful technique, but many newer methods have been introduced, a number of which are based on copper.

Conversion Before a tree trunk can be used by woodworkers it must be reduced to manageable shapes and sizes, a process known as conversion. Before the general adoption of large, two-man handsaws in the 16th century and the later development of powered circular and band saws, timber conversion was carried out by splitting or riving, using the beetle (a heavy wooden mallet) and a wedge or riving iron. The basic method was to drive hardwood or iron wedges into the end grain of a trunk, causing it to split along lines which can vary between species. As the split developed, further wedges were driven into it along the length of the trunk. The direction of the split could be adjusted to some extent by using the weight of the trunk: by changing the lie of the trunk on the ground using levers, the shearing forces acting on the split could be modified and caused to change direction. In England riving continued to be the main means of timber conversion for some trades well into the 20th century. Principal among these was the chairmaking industry, based around High Wycombe, Buckinghamshire. Here the timber used was beech, a wood that splits well and works very easily when green, with little subsequent warping. Riving is still used in Europe and North America to produce a limited amount of material for specialist craftsmen such as chairmakers.

Not all woods split well, and the value of many species was

not realized until the tools and techniques necessary for their
efficient use had been developed. Most modern conversion is
carried out at a timber mill. A number of different methods of
cutting are employed, depending on the final intended use for
the timber. Bastard or flat sawing produces the greatest
number of boards from a trunk; this cut, being tangential to
the annual rings, produces the most attractive figure in many
timbers and is known as flat grain. A trunk converted in this
way is referred to as 'cut through and through'. Boards produced in this way are prone to warping. There is an incremen-
tal reduction in the amount of sap present as the centre of the
trunk is approached, so that boards cut from the outside of a
trunk contain most sapwood and there is more sap in the outer
face than the inner; the outer face also shrinks more as the
board dries, pulling the board hollow or concave. Only the
board cut from the very centre of the trunk will resist this kind
of warping, since the quantity of sapwood is the same on both
faces. More stable timber is produced by rift or quarter sawing,
and with many timbers, such as oak or chestnut, this is the
only way of revealing the distinctive rays that produce silver
grain. The boards are cut radially and display edge, vertical

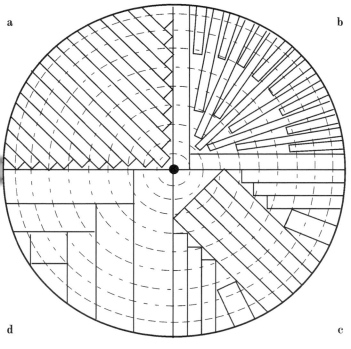

*Methods of converting
quarter-sawn timber:
(a) an economical radial
cut; (b) radial cutting
along the medullary rays,
which gives an attractive
and stable timber but is
more wasteful than other
methods; (c) a cut with a
variety of qualities and
little waste; (d) a cheap
but inferior cut.*

and straight grain. A higher proportion of waste material is produced by this method, which increases the cost of the boards.

Seasoning Freshly harvested wood contains substantial amounts of water (up to half its total weight). Before it becomes a usable product the majority of this water must be removed, a process known as seasoning. Wood is seasoned for other reasons also. As wood dries it can split and warp, especially if the drying takes place in an uncontrolled way. It is therefore important that drying occurs before the timber is prepared for use. Dry timber is also far more resistant to fungal decay and the depredations of wood-boring insects, and it is much lighter and therefore cheaper and easier to transport.

Timber can be seasoned by air drying or kiln drying. In both cases the material must be carefully stacked to allow for air circulation and to minimize warping. Air drying can take many months or even years, especially if the rough-cut boards or baulks are of substantial thickness. Kiln drying, during which the timber is exposed to controlled heat in large stoves or kilns, can be completed in a few days. If this process is carried out too rapidly the timber will become case-hardened, with a shell of dried wood being formed around an inner core with a much higher water content; such material will usually warp and split once it has been finally worked. Some craftsmen avoid using kiln-dried timber, regarding it as brittle and devoid of life.

Working and finishing Following conversion and seasoning, unless it is to be turned or carved, timber must be made true and square before it is suitable for use. Plain sawn timber is used by carpenters for structural framing, but the smooth finishes and close jointing used by joiners and cabinetmakers demand a higher degree of preparation. Today much timber is supplied 'planed all round' or 'PAR'. Most of this is not suitable for immediate use and must be refinished to remove cutter marks from machine planing and ensure that the timber is straight and true. Boards are then brought to their finished size with the use of marking gauges, trysquares and planes. The pieces of wood are joined with nails, screws, dowels and other special fixings (see WOOD FIXINGS), with glues and adhesives and with special joints (see DOVETAIL and MORTISE AND TENON). In cabinetmaking and joinery the majority of assembly is done using joints and adhesives only.

Once assembled, the work is smoothed with abrasives and

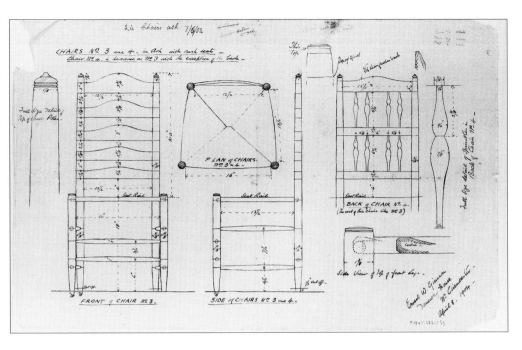

finished with various coatings to enhance its appearance and minimize the penetration of dirt. Nowadays most abrasives come in the form of paper or cloth coated with graded adhesive grits made from ground glass, garnet and carborundum. These have been available since the 19th century and can today be applied using powered tools such as belt, radial and orbital sanders. In the past a variety of natural products were employed and some still find uses today. In Europe ray skin and ground brick dust were preliminary abrasives, with the dried stems of rushes and the horsetail fern giving a smoother surface. Pumice and rottenstone (a type of naturally degraded powdered limestone) were used for final finishing, as they still are. In the Far East various abrasive leaves are used and lacquer workers in Japan, China and Korea employ various natural stones and stone powders (now largely replaced by synthetic aluminium oxide blocks) and varieties of charcoal block. In Japan the finish on high-gloss lacquer was produced with calcined and ground stags' antlers, but this has largely been superseded by titanium dioxide powder.

The coatings include waxes, varnishes, lacquers and stains. Varnish, which sets by evaporation of a volatile solvent, requires at least three applications to produce a

Design for a ladderback chair, by Ernest Gimson, 1904, showing mortise and tenon and round mortise joints.

satisfactory finish. The first coat is usually diluted with a suitable solvent and 'flattened' or 'cut back' with fine abrasive paper or wire wool when dry. FRENCH POLISHING, which uses shellac as a varnish, requires even more applications. Synthetic lacquers are mostly used on an industrial scale and are applied by spraying. They include various plastic polymers (two-part or acid-catalysed).

Waxes are usually applied as solid wax or as a paste, in which the wax is thinned with an organic solvent such as turpentine. These materials are simply rubbed into the surface of the wood, then burnished with a cloth or bundles of reeds to impart a soft sheen. Repeated application over a number of years results in a harder and deeper shine. The earliest wax finish used in Europe and North America was beeswax. Since about the 17th century a variety of other waxes and resins, such as carnauba wax, colophony and copal, have been blended to make finishes that are more easily applied and produce a deeper shine. In the 19th century paraffin waxes became available, which impart a light shine when used alone but are more usually mixed with other waxes and resins. The silicon waxes developed in the 20th century give a quick, relatively high-gloss and glassy finish when used alone, but like the paraffin waxes they are usually applied in mixtures for a more natural, softer sheen.

Oils form a strong, stain-resistant, waterproof coating that brings out and enhances the grain of the wood, but they have the disadvantage of being labour-intensive and time-consuming to apply. A number of vegetable oils are used, such as linseed, walnut and tung oil. Several applications are necessary to develop the desired sheen. Each coat must be very thinly applied and thoroughly rubbed in, then left to dry for a number of days. Four or more initial coats are required and the surface is maintained with further applications over a number of years before it is fully developed. The initial finish is more usually preserved by regular polishing with waxes. Oil finishes darken with age to present the rich patina desired in old furniture.

Alternatively, wood may be gilded, painted or lacquered (see GILDING and JAPANNING). These finishes are usually executed on a gesso foundation which fills the grain and provides a smooth surface. In ancient Egyptian times furniture was painted using tempera, on a gesso ground, probably unvarnished. In medieval Europe, painting in egg and/or glue tempera, usually on a thin gesso ground, was common. Most surviving examples are varnished; it is not known whether this is original, although some painted panels of the same period have a thin oil varnish. Later examples, from the 18th century to the early 20th, were commonly painted with oils, unvarnished, but in some cases (from the period of Louis XIV, for instance) burnished tempera seems to have been applied on a thin gesso ground. Oil and spirit varnishes have been found on some pieces from this period, but again this may not be original.

The technology of furniture making The evolution of furniture is closely linked to the development of WOODWORKING TOOLS and the availability of certain materials. The majority of the tools and techniques date back to very early times, and the first surviving furniture has been found in ancient Egyptian burials and settlement sites. Copper tools were available by the late pre-dynastic period (*c.*3000 BC) and by the time of the Middle Kingdom (*c.*2000 BC) the adze, chisel, reamer, bow drill and saw were in use. The plane was unknown in ancient Egypt and seems to have been a Roman development. The lathe also appears to have been unknown, and the earliest representation seems to be that depicted on the wall of the 4th-century BC Roman tomb of Petosiris. Before this time rounded objects or furniture parts, such as chair legs, were carved. The relatively limited range of available tools was put to good use by the Egyptians, judging by the finds from various sites and by the depictions on wall paintings and friezes of wooden artefacts such as chariots. Some tombs even contained models of woodworkers at work, so that some working methods are known. Surviving Egyptian furniture shows simple lap or peg joints reinforced with hide bindings as well as more sophisticated jointing techniques such as the mortise and tenon, dovetail, housing and dovetail housing methods. Mitre joints, dowelling and a type of flat dowel resembling the modern 'biscuit' joint have also been found. The artefacts also display the prolific use of carving, shell, stone and ivory inlay, and painting and gilding techniques. Veneering with imported exotic woods such as ebony and boxwood was used to decorate boxes made from less expensive woods.

Technological improvements in the Graeco–Roman period, such as the use of iron and

Wooden chair, Egypt, 18th dynasty, c.1400 BC. It shows the use of through and blind mortises.

steel tools and the development of the lathe and plane, led to the more widespread use of furniture and the development of new types. Few examples of furniture or woodcarving from this period have survived, but representations in wall paintings and carved stone friezes indicate a widespread use of tables, chairs, stools and couches, decorated with carving, inlay, gilding and cast metal fixtures. Turned and carved elements were incorporated, and the use of curvilinear legs and chair backs reflects both improved technology and manufacturing technique.

Little is known of European furniture and woodworking from the collapse of the Roman empire until the late medieval period. The most significant technological development of this period was the introduction in the 13th century of framed and panelled construction, which was used in the manufacture of chests, cupboards, aumbrys and panelling. The development of panelled construction led to more trade specialization. Relatively simple furniture was made by carpenters and embellished by carvers, while panelling was done by joiners or 'ceilers', but eventually all furniture would be made by joiners until the establishment of cabinetmaking in the late 17th century.

Most high-class medieval furniture was made of oak, but walnut became increasingly fashionable from the end of the 16th century. It was not until the 17th century, and increasing international trade with Africa, India and the Americas, that imported timbers such as mahogany, rosewood and ebony became available. Their expense and beauty stimulated the development of veneer, while the trade also brought new finishing materials such as the lac resins, copal and sandarac. These were essential to the new

Cabinet with floral marquetry, attributed to Jan van Mekeren, Amsterdam, c. 1690. Van Mekeren's marquetry designs were derived from contemporary flower paintings.

craft of japanning.

Advances in technology, such as new methods of making wide, thin strips of steel (*c.*1590) and later the efficient manufacture of cast tool steel (1740), led to the development of more efficient tools, in greater quantities and at lower prices. Wide-bladed saws improved the production of veneers, and with the development of finer blades for fretsaws and the fretcutter's donkey the production of fine marquetry became easier and quicker, reducing costs and expanding its use. Also, thin-bladed backsaws enabled the cutting of smaller, neater joints, which were essential in the lighter, more refined furniture of the Georgian period. Other cutting tools, such as joiner's and carver's chisels and gouges, improved in quality, and a wide range of shapes and cuts became available, enabling the more widespread production of fine work.

In the latter part of the 18th century and more rapidly in the 19th, machines were developed to carry out many of the tasks of woodworkers. Sawing and basic planing were mechanized, as were the accurate cutting of joints and very thin veneers. Turners' lathes became increasingly efficient and copy lathes were developed, although they did not become common until the 20th century. Efficient and accurate carving machines were also developed which, though expensive to produce, were used increasingly as the 19th century

Oak settle, designed by Gustav Stickley and made by the Craftsman Workshops, Syracuse, New York, c.1908. It exemplifies the functional design that derived from the English Arts and Crafts movement: the construction is plain and clear and the natural figure of the wood has been exploited. Both plain and silver grain can be seen.

advanced. All this enabled the mass production of cheap furniture, though much of it was and is poorly constructed. Through the efforts of William Morris and other exponents of the Arts and Crafts movement there was a revival of fine craftsmanship at the end of the 19th century. The next stage was for designers and makers to manufacture high-quality furniture by uniting the power of machine tools and the industrial process with the skills of the handworker for finishing and detail. Throughout the 20th century furniture manufacture in Europe and North America saw an increasing reliance on plywood and wood composites, often combined with metal and plastics.

Wood engraving A relief printing process which uses a block of end-grain wood (wood cut across the growth rings) to make the printing surface. Boxwood is particularly suitable because of its close grain, but the blocks are limited in size (since the box tree is small) and are sometimes joined. The design is cut with metal burins with a square, triangular or diamond section capable of incising fine lines, and it is the areas of the wood not cut away that carry the ink.

The technique was most skilfully exploited in the late 18th century by the English engraver Thomas Bewick in his book illustrations (see page 410) and subsequently it took hold as an illustration process for periodicals. The woodblocks soon wore out and in commercial use were replaced from about 1840 by electrotypes. To make an electrotype, a mould is taken from the original block and a copper film deposited on it. Backed with lead, this provides the printing surface.

Wood fixings Devices such as screws, nails and dowels, used to join pieces of wood. Nails are small, tapering metal rods which are driven into the wood with a hammer. They were first used as wood fixings by the Romans and were produced by forging iron rods to the desired size and shape. Their use was usually confined to heavy constructions. In later periods they were employed to secure hinges, locks and lock plates. Since the early 19th century common nails have been made from drawn wire; known as wire nails, they are round or oval in section, with or without a head. They are commonly made of mild steel, and may be plated with zinc to resist corrosion, but they may also be of brass or copper, usually for use in areas where iron would rust or have a detrimental effect on the timber. Wrought nails, fashioned by hammering, are nowadays seldom produced.

A book-plate printed in colours from a combination of cut and engraved woodblocks, by Josef Váchal, Czechoslovakia, early 20th century.

Screws are cylindrical, often tapering, fastenings made with a helical thread that engages the material into which it is screwed. They are made from, steel, brass, copper and gun metal and may be provided with a decorative or protective coating by galvanizing, japanning, oxidizing or chromium plating. Screws were first used as furniture fixings in the late 16th century, when small brass, hand-filed, tapering, slot-headed screws were used as light fixings for hinges and locks. Lathe-turned screws were first made around the middle of the 18th century and since about 1850 machine-made, gimlet-pointed, helical screws have been in general use.

Dowels are wooden pins, usually cylindrical and made of hardwood, used as a means of joining pieces of timber together, for reinforcing joints or sometimes in place of mortise and tenon joints. They can be made by hammering a piece of wood through the hole in a 'dowel plate', making it perfectly round and accurately sized. One or more grooves will normally be cut along the length of the dowel to allow air and excess glue to escape from the hole into which the piece is hammered.

Knock-down (KD) fixings are modern plastic fixings used in the construction of 'flat pack' panelled furniture. Consisting of a two-part plastic block, the halves are held together with a steel screw and kept in registration with moulded lugs. In use the halves are separated and one part is screwed to the inner side of a vertical component, while the other is screwed to the inside of a horizontal component. The parts are then fitted together and secured by tightening the locking screw.

Woodcarving The creation of wooden artefacts, ranging from free-standing three-dimensional sculptures to relief-carved and intaglio designs used to embellish objects made by other specialized woodworkers. The origins of the art of woodcarving are unknown but other carved materials such as bone, antler and ivory which have survived from palaeolithic times suggest that wood was similarly treated. There have been few technical innovations to the tools of the woodcarver since Roman times apart from the development of tool steel and an increased range of chisel and gouge shapes. The closing decades of the 20th century saw the use of power tools for the production of wood sculpture, but otherwise hand-carving tools have changed little since medieval or even ancient Egyptian times. However, while most carvers have long used a range of specialized chisels, gouges, knives and abrasives, traditional workers in Africa have achieved fine results using simple iron tools, principally various types of adze.

There are few fixed rules for the creation of a woodcarving, whether in the round or in low relief, apart from the need to keep tools razor sharp and as far as possible to cut with or across the grain of the wood. Almost any wood can be carved, and choice is largely dependent on the desired final appearance. Timbers such as sycamore are easily carved but generally lack an interesting figure or grain, while oak is harder to carve but is well coloured and its grain and figure can be

A woodcarver at work on a mirror frame for Spencer House, London. He uses a variety of carving chisels and a lignum vitae mallet. In the foreground is a swag of roses for a table. Both the frame and the swag are of limewood and will be gessoed and gilded.

exploited to enhance the work. Lime also lacks an interesting grain but has the advantage of being soft, even and environmentally stable. For small and detailed work it may be necessary to use a very hard and fine-grained wood such as boxwood or pear.

Successful work can be created working directly on the

wood, with little pre-planning or laying out. Much traditional carving is produced in just this way, with the design existing only in the mind of the craftsman or an already extant model. When it is necessary to produce or reproduce a design more or less exactly, a certain amount of preparatory work may be necessary. In the case of sculpture in the round, the design may be drawn or traced onto all six faces of the (generally square-sectioned) piece of timber. It is then usually brought roughly to shape by sawing and the fairly rapid removal of large areas of waste with broad flat-sectioned gouges. The shape can be further refined using rasps and rifflers, or selected gouges and drills are used to produce deep undercuts. The details are applied with the appropriate tools, which may include veiners, chisels or even gravers for fine detail. Broad areas such as the cheeks and neck of a portrait or the limbs of a complete figure can be smoothed and refined using abrasive papers, finer grades of which are used to polish the work, which may then be finished by waxing, oiling or varnishing. In the past the great majority of woodcarving was embellished by painting or gilding, often over a preparatory coat of gesso.

In the case of low relief or intaglio carving, the chosen design is drawn or traced onto a selected board and the design is 'set in' by tracing over the pattern with a carving tool which conforms to the shape of the line being traced. The tool is held vertically and struck once with a mallet, then moved on to the next part of the line, and the process is repeated until the entire design has been set. Waste is then removed using a tool of appropriate shape. Low relief carving can be refined by careful use of abrasives but intaglio carving is rarely, if ever, sanded.

In Japan somewhat different methods have been used for the production of three-dimensional carvings. An early understanding of the requirements of quartering and seasoning to produce stable timber was exploited throughout a long tradition of woodcarving. Early sculpture was carved from the solid, a technique knows as *ichiboku zukuri*, and was more or less limited to the size of the log, with supplementary pieces occasionally being added for arms. Initially various different hardwoods and softwoods were used but by the Nara period (645–794) cypress, with its even texture, smooth grain and inherent stability, had become the timber of choice. By the start of the Kamakura period in the late 12th century, the technique of *yosegi zukuri* had developed, in which statues were constructed from carefully joined separate pieces, each of which was hollowed out. Using this technique even a relatively small statue, for example of a seated Buddha, would be made from at least eleven separate pieces. One piece each would be used for the front and back of the head, two more for the trunk of the body, at least one more for the folded legs, two for each of the arms and one each for the hands. Besides making the finished sculpture lighter and more stable, this technique enabled the construction of monumental sculptures up to 5 m high and allowed the sculptor more expression through the use of extended limbs and flowing drapery.

Yosegi zukuri is the ultimate development of the practice of jointing pieces of wood for carving, but it is not unique. Other cultures also joined pieces together to extend the range on a figure and hollowed out solid areas to improve stability. Each culture and period tended to develop its own methods, but the basic principles were universal. For example, if a carving of a human figure required an extended arm, a flat area could be worked on both the body and the arm at the joining point and the pieces simply glued together and reinforced with nails or tree nails. Alternatively, a tenon might be worked on the end of the arm, to fit into a mortise on the body. If an extension was required, for flowing robes, a simple half-lap joint was used.

Woodcut A form of print which transfers ink from the relief areas of a carved block of wood. The wood used is long-grain, cut parallel to the trunk like a plank, which is not capable of such fine detail as the end-grain used for WOOD ENGRAVING. Cherry wood is often used, particularly in Japan; sycamore and beech are also suitable. The wood is cut with knives, chisels and gouging tools which have a U- or V-shaped section, and ink is applied to the remaining raised areas with a roller. Printing can be done by hand or mechanically in a screw press. The paper (used dry) is slightly deformed by contact with the block under pressure so that blank areas stand up, creating an impression. The wood-grain itself is sometimes visible in the inked areas.

Woodcuts were in use in China as early as the 8th century and first reached the West as a method for printing textiles. The earliest European woodcuts are playing cards and religious images dating from the end of the 14th century. When

movable type was introduced to Europe in the mid-15th century, woodcuts became the main form of book illustration, and they remained so until the end of the 16th century, when they were generally replaced by copper engraving (see PRINTING). Block books, using woodcuts for both text and illustrations, were a short-lived method of book production used in Europe between *c*.1460 and *c*.1500.

Woodcuts could be hand-coloured or stencilled, or decorated with flock. Occasional 'tinsel prints' from this early period are decorated with quartz crystals and fragments of sparkling metal foil on a base of starch paste or animal glue. Printing in colours was tried from the second half of the 15th century, separate blocks being cut for each colour, but the achievements of the woodblock printers of the Japanese Edo period (1615–1857) were never rivalled in Europe. The Japanese prints used subtle shadings of colour applied directly to the block with a brush, and several colours could be printed from the same block.

Woodworking tools The implements used by craftsmen in the various branches of the woodworking trades. A wide range of hand tools, power tools and fixing methods and materials have been developed to enable the particular qualities of wood to be exploited. Most of the hand tools currently in use have changed little in overall appearance since the Roman period. Although many early tools were made from iron, with perhaps a little steel added to the working edge,

A woodcut in three sections by Kunisada, 1857. It shows in a stylized form the production of Japanese woodblock pictures. On the left, pots of ink and inking brushes are shown, while two circular barens covered in bamboo leaf, used for smoothing the paper face down against the inked block, lie on the work surfaces. In the centre, large areas of wood are removed with a chisel from the parts of the block that are to print blank, while at the same time the paper is being prepared. On the right, a design is being transferred from paper to the woodblock, while an assistant sharpens the tools.

The tool chest of a late 18th-century English cabinetmaker. This example was given to Benjamin Seaton, then aged 21, by his father in 1796. Saws can be seen in the lid of the chest; in the foreground are bench planes, a chuck brace, a chisel and other tools. Fitted compartments inside the chest accommodated Mr Seaton's entire inventory of tools.

most modern hand tools are made of solid steel. The tools used by the individual branches of the woodworking trades are broadly similar and interchangeable from one trade to another. But each trade also uses tools that have been developed for specific purposes. These are usually variants of standard carpenters' and joiners' tools: saws, axes, planes, chisels and gouges for cutting and shaping; hammers, mallets, drills, gimlets and screwdrivers for fixing; and rules, trysquares, gauges and tape measures for measuring and marking. (For further illustrations see pages 530 and 544.)

One of mankind's oldest tools is the axe. Flint hand axes were used by our remotest ancestors. The first iron axes were produced *c.*900 BC and they developed into the variety of types used today for felling and other preliminary or secondary rough preparation and dressing of timber. Many different patterns in a variety of sizes are made, but all consist of a steel head, much wider than it is thick, tapering in thickness from the heel to a more or less flared, convex cutting edge set parallel to the haft. The head is attached to the haft, often made from ash or hickory, with a wedge. One of the major variations of type is the side axe. Usually short and light, the heads of these tools are often much thinner in section than other patterns, and the blade is offset to the left or right of the eye. Kept exceptionally sharp, the side axe can produce a very good finish and can even be used in place of the plane or adze to surface boards.

The adze is a steel cutting tool resembling an axe but with the cutting edge at a right angle to the haft. The head is made from forged steel and is more or less curved along its length. Some patterns have gouge-shaped blades for deep hollowing work. The adze is mainly used for the removal of heavy waste material, and for the trimming, shaping and levelling of timbers, but in tropical regions small domestically made patterns of adze are used to good effect as carving tools. Many different patterns were once made, identified by trade, such as the cooper's, chairmaker's (or seat), joiner's, carpenter's or shipwright's adzes. Others were named after their intended purpose, such as cleaving, hollowing, stripping and nailing, or by the location in which that pattern was favoured, such as the Brazil, Chinese and oriental (Turkish).

A saw is essentially a sheet or ribbon of steel with the edge or edges filed to form teeth which are set, that is bent alternately to the left and right of centre. Fitted with a handle, it is used for the sizing and rough shaping of timber. Saws made to the European pattern are usually made to cut when pushed through the wood. Oriental saws, which tend to be much thinner and more flexible, are made to cut when pulled. Particular types of saw are used for specific purposes. They are differentiated by size, shape and the way in which the teeth are ground. European types include the rip, cross-cut, panel, case, tenon, dovetail, gentleman's, veneer, chairmaker's, coping, piercing and frame-saw. For general purposes these are separated into three main groups: handsaws, which are long and tapering; backsaws, which are rectangular and stiffened by a heavy brass or steel strip along the back; and frame-saws (for illustration see page 514).

A chisel is a steel cutting tool fashioned to cut at one end or, in the case of some special types, the side of one end. Until fairly recently all European chisels were made from laminated steel but most are now made from a rectangular bar of cast steel. One end is reduced to a square-sectioned tapering tang or a conical socket to which a handle is fitted. The blade is usually tapered in thickness from the tang to the cutting edge. A bevel (the grinding bevel), the pitch of which varies with type, is ground at the cutting end and a secondary, very narrow, cutting bevel is produced by honing. Different trades use different patterns of chisel, the main variation being in the thickness and width of the blade.

Scrapers are used by cabinetmakers, joiners and woodcarvers. The term implies a somewhat crude tool but, properly sharpened and used, a scraper is capable of producing a very fine finish and is particularly useful on erratic or curly grain. Those used by cabinetmakers and joiners are made from a sheet of tool steel, often part of a discarded saw blade. Two patterns are used: one is a simple rectangle, usually about 15 cm × 7.5 cm when new, while the other is curvilinear and roughly kidney-shaped and is used for working concave surfaces. The tool is held in both hands, with the edge at a slight angle to the surface being worked and with the thumbs pressing firmly against the middle, causing the sides of the steel sheet to bend backwards. It is pushed across the surface taking off lines of very fine shavings. The turner's scraper is a bar of tool steel between 10 mm and 50 mm wide and 6–9 mm thick. The end is worked to the desired profile, which can be a complex moulding or a straight edge, but the common tool is worked to a radius with a steep bevel on the underside. The other end is worked to a tang which is fitted into a long turner's pattern handle. This scraper is used with the handle raised and the bevel underneath and is particularly useful for working end grain or particularly hard wood such as ebony, lignum vitae and box.

The plane is used to prepare the timber for use by bringing it square, true and smooth. Using shaped irons and soles, simple or complex mouldings can also be made. In its simplest manifestation a plane comprises a wooden stock or body pierced through from top to bottom with a sloping mortise, shaped to hold a blade or iron. The cutting edge of the blade protrudes through the bottom, or sole, of the stock, which serves to control the depth of cut. European planes are generally used by pushing the tool across the surface of the workpiece, while in most oriental countries the tool is pulled towards the operator. A great variety of types was produced until fairly recently, but many of the functions of the more specialized patterns are now carried out by power tools. Wood-bodied planes are still made in considerable numbers (in Japan a very simple pattern is still the favoured tool), but the majority of planes are now metal-bodied and often of the 'Stanley' pattern. Based on the Bailey patents of 1867, these iron-bodied planes incorporate mechanical adjustments for setting the depth of cut, the lateral set of the iron and the width of the mouth. All branches of woodworking use planes that have been specifically developed for their own purposes, but most craftsmen will have a set of 'bench' planes. The set consists of three to five planes of differing sizes. Many other patterns have been made in both wood and metal, all of which are designed to do one job. The exceptions are the so called 'Universal', 'Multi' or 'Combination' planes. The final manifestations of these tools, as the Stanley or Record 55s, were provided with 55 shaped irons and various detachable fences. They were designed to execute the functions of all planes apart from the standard bench planes. They worked fairly well but were expensive to buy and time-consuming to set up, so that most craftsmen continued to use the individual tools.

A number of devices have been used to drill holes in wood. One of the oldest is the bow or fiddle drill. In its simplest form it consists of a rod to which a cylindrical stock or bobbin is fitted. A wooden pad is attached to the upper end of the rod and serves as the head or nave. The lower, or working, end is fitted with a chuck, often a simple friction-fit pattern, which holds the drill bits. The bow (the straight form is sometimes called the sword or rapier) is a straight piece of wood or steel fitted with a loose string, fixed at one end and detachable at the other. The string is wound once around the bobbin and reattached to the bow, the nave is held in one hand or braced against the shoulder, and the bow is operated with a sawing action, imparting a reciprocating rotary motion to the rod. The parsee drill, or parser, is a special bow drill used for cutting shaped holes or recesses for inlays. A bifurcated spring-steel bit or cutter, with the working end sharpened to form two flat cutters with shoulders filed above to act as depth stops, is rotated inside a steel template of the desired shape. The eccentric reciprocating motion of the cutters within the template drills or routs out the shape.

While the bow drill was an efficient tool for drilling small holes, it could be difficult to use in confined areas or on narrow and thin stock. In 1864 a new type of brace, known as the wheel or engineer's brace or hand drill, was patented. Originally developed as an engineer's tool, specifically to use the newly developed Morse or twist drills in sizes from $\frac{1}{2}$ to $\frac{1}{32}$ of an inch, the value of the tool for drilling small holes was soon realized by woodworkers, among whom it largely superseded the bow drill. It consisted of an openwork iron pillar holding a horizontally mounted bevelled gear and fitted with a Barber screw chuck similar to that fitted to the modern joiner's brace. Rotary motion was provided through a large vertically mounted side wheel, fitted with a cranked handle which was free to rotate on its spindle.

Holes larger than about 1 cm are difficult to produce with the bow drill and are generally made using a brace, a cranked tool usually fitted with a mushroom-shaped head or nave, which is held in the left hand to steady the tool and is free to rotate on the body. The cranked centre of the tool is rotated by the right hand, imparting a rotary action to the bit or drill held in a chuck (originally a simple friction-fit socket) at the working end of the tool. The modern version of this tool is known as the yankee or joiner's brace. Patented in 1864 and later improved, it now consists of a cranked steel frame fitted with a rotating hardwood head and central handle. The chuck that holds the boring bits is formed from a hollow threaded shell, which is tapered inside and forces together the sprung jaws when the shell is screwed closed. It is used with a variety of bits. Other tools used to make holes include the awl, which is a sharp metal spike, usually mounted in a wooden handle, and the gimlet, which consists of a bit fitted with a handle to form a T shape. Both are hand tools.

In order to work efficiently woodworking tools, especially chisels and gouges, should be kept very sharp. Traditionally this has been done by carefully rubbing the edge back and forth at a preset angle on a hone or sharpening stone. Most modern hones are synthetic blocks of graded carborundum grains, known as 'India stones', lubricated with a thin mineral oil. Alternatively, Japanese synthetic waterstones made from aluminium oxide can be employed; these are soaked in and lubricated with water during use. In the past various natural stones were used (often limestone, such as the Charnley forest and Turkey stone), lubricated with neat's foot oil. In the Far East similar close-textured sedimentary rocks were employed, lubricated with water. A sharp edge can be maintained by very frequent honing with a leather strop charged with a fine abrasive, such as jeweller's rouge or valve-grinding paste. According to the kind of wood being carved, a tool may be touched up with the strop after as few as five or six cuts. Repeated honing produces a superfine cutting edge, and good-quality second-hand professional carving tools are often more expensive than new ones.

Saws also benefit from frequent sharpening, which is carried out with a special three-quarter second-cut file. Some craftsmen sharpen their own saws, but this can be difficult and specialist tradesmen are normally engaged.

See also LATHE.

Wool A fibre, yarn or cloth made principally from the coats of sheep, but also comprising (for labelling purposes) the fleece or hair of the CASHMERE or angora goat (see MOHAIR), and ALPACA, CAMEL HAIR and VICUNA. It has excellent dyeing properties, since it has a central canal that allows the dye to penetrate the fibre. As a result of its exterior scales, which interlock and (when wet) swell, it also provides excellent insulation by catching air between the fibres and absorbing 50% of its weight in moisture before it is saturated to the point at which it feels wet. These qualities, together with its strength and resilience, made wool the primary fibre for clothing, blankets and carpets until the advent of central heating, man-made fibres and synthetic fibres. Owing to its scales and a natural crimp, wool tends to felt, a characteristic exploited in the napped finishes given to fabrics such as baize and flannel.

The term 'woollen' refers to yarns made solely by carding, or cross-pulling the fibres prior to the spinning process; 'worsted' refers to those in which the fibres have been both carded and combed, or aligned, and so creating a smooth, tightly spun yarn. Fabrics made from such yarns are also distinguished as woollen or worsted; the latter include gabardine (tightly woven, warp-faced twill) and serge (a two-up, two-down twill, often dyed navy blue). The method of producing worsted or similar compact longer-fibre yarns (including mohair) is known as the Bradford system, after the town in Yorkshire where it originated.

Wootz See DAMASCUS STEEL.

Work hardening The hardening of a metal caused by deformation at a low temperature. This deformation is the result of cold working, hammering, rolling, drawing or stamping, usually done at room temperature. This increases the hardness of some metals but also reduces their ductility. Work-hardened metal can be brought back into a soft state by heat treatment or annealing.

Worsted A name given to fabrics made from worsted yarns (see WOOL), which are sometimes also called serge yarn.

Wove paper See PAPER.

Wrigglework A type of decorative metal engraving, consisting of zigzag lines formed using a flat graver. This flat chisel-like graver is gently pushed across the surface of the metal while being rocked from one corner to another, forming a zigzag line. Wrigglework decoration is usually found on 17th- and 18th-century pewter and silver work.

Wu tong Chinese decorative copper alloy wares, with a black surface layer inlaid with a contrasting silver alloy. The surface layer of copper, with small amounts of silver (1%) and gold (1%), is brazed or hard soldered to a low-zinc (4%) brass. This composite sheet is then decorated by engraving or chasing lines in the surface which are afterwards filled with silver solder and finished. The sheet is then used for making small objects such as boxes. After assembly the whole object is patinated black except for the silver inlay, which is not affected by the patination.

The origin of the technique is unknown. The oldest objects date possibly from around AD 1700, and *wu tong* wares are still made today in the Yunnan province of south-west China.

Pewter tankard with wrigglework decoration, England, 1698.

Xylonite See SYNTHETIC IVORY.

X & Y

Yellow satinwood A hard and heavy, lustrous, smooth and durable wood from the species *Distemonanthus benthamianus*, found in Nigeria. It is a lemon yellow colour, with darker stripes and roey figure. It is fairly easily worked and polished, and is used for high-class joinery, cabinet work and turnery.

Yew A hard, heavy, non-resinous and elastic wood from the species *Taxus baccata*. It has a fine grain and texture and acquires a natural polish. In colour it is brown or orangey brown, with distinctive cream or yellowish markings. Yew is used as flooring and for the production of veneers and small items of furniture. Since it is easily bent, it was much used for the back bows and arms of Windsor chairs; it is also famous as the wood from which the English longbow was made.

Ying mu A timber derived from the butt of the Chinese camphor tree (*Cinnamonum camphora*) and favoured for certain types of cabinet work.

York stone A pale brown fine-grained sandstone which occurs in the southern part of Yorkshire, England. York stone contains numerous fine layers of mica and can be split into thin sheets along these layers. It has been widely used for paving and roofing and as a building stone in Yorkshire.

Youghal lace See NEEDLE LACE.

Z

Zamak See MAZAK.

Zebrano African zebrawood, thought to derive from a species of *Brachystegia* or *Cynometra*.

Zebrawood A heavy, durable and strong wood from the species *Astronium fraxinifolium* and *Pithecolobium recemiflorum*, also known as bois serpent, Goncalo alves, kingwood, tigerwood, locustwood and zingana. It is orange to dark brown, with wide variegated stripes, and has a straight, fine grain. It is difficult to work but polishes easily and is used for veneers, turnery and good-quality joinery. It is normally available only in small sizes.

Zinc A bluish-white metal, brittle at room temperature but malleable and ductile at 150°C. Zinc is not found in nature in metallic state as native metal but only as an ore, often together with lead. The major modern source is the zinc sulphide sphalerite, but in the past the zinc carbonate smithsonite (previously known as calamine) was used extensively. The first zinc produced was as a rare by-product from silver mines, where zinc condensed as small droplets on the flue walls of furnaces. This 'contefei' or 'mock silver' was used to make the first BRASS: the oldest evidence of these brasses is found in Asia Minor and dates from 1300 BC.

The main difficulty in extracting zinc is the volatility of the metal, because it boils at 917°C, below the smelting temperature of the ore. Thus instead of flowing out of the furnace in a molten state, like most metals, zinc leaves a normal open furnace as vapour. In the 1st century BC the 'cementation process' for making brass was developed in Asia Minor, using sealed crucibles in which zinc ore (smithsonite) was mixed with fine divided copper and charcoal. When heated to 1000°C the zinc ore is reduced to metallic zinc in vapour which diffuses into the copper to form brass.

The East was capable of producing zinc much earlier than the West by using both the distillation and the cementation processes. Although zinc has been known as a metal in India for more than 2000 years, the first zinc as a pure metal appeared in Europe as late as the 16th century, when it was imported from Asia to Europe under such names as tutenag and SPELTER. It was only in 1738 that William Champion of Bristol developed and patented a process for smelting zinc on a large scale. Champion's method also used sealed crucibles, but filled only with calamine and charcoal. At the base of the crucible was an iron tube, leading to a vessel filled with water. This 'condensation chamber' cooled down the vapour from the crucible to metallic zinc.

Apart from being used in alloys such as brass and several forms of solder, zinc was also used in the 19th century for decorative castings in spelter. Nowadays zinc is mainly used as a die-casting alloy (see MAZAK) and to provide corrosion-resistant coatings (galvanization) on iron and steel.

Zinc white A synthetic pigment (zinc oxide) commercially available since the 1850s. It is less opaque than titanium white, and therefore not so much used as a pure white in oil paint, though it has often been added to coloured pigments when pale tints are required. It has always been an important pigment for watercolour, and in this context it is sometimes referred to as Chinese white.

Zingana See ZEBRAWOOD.

Zwischengoldglas A form of VERRE ÉGLOMISÉ developed in

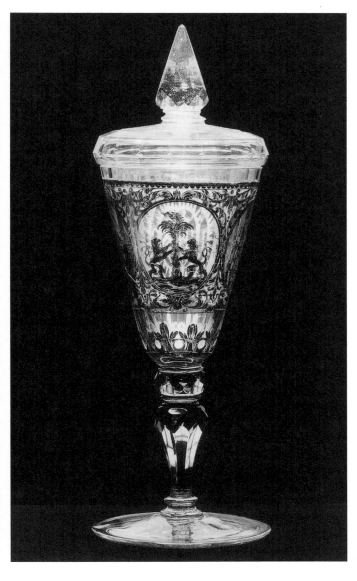

Zwischengoldglas *goblet,*
Bohemia, 1740.

Bohemia around 1730 and used for drinking glasses and
beakers; it is also sometimes called sandwich gold glass. An
inner vessel of glass was decorated with engraved gold leaf
and then protected by an outer vessel affixed with resin.
Often a projecting rim on the inner vessel concealed the gap
at the top, while the outer vessel extended below the inner
one and was filled by a disc of glass similarly decorated.

BIBLIOGRAPHY

GENERAL

Theophilus: *De diversis artibus* (1100–1150); translated with introduction by J. G. Hawthorne and C. S. Smith as *On Divers Arts: The Foremost Medieval Treatise on Painting, Glassmaking and Metalwork* (New York and London, 1979)

C. d'A. Cennini: *Il libro dell'arte* (*c.* 1390); translated by D. V. Thompson Jr. as *The Craftsman's Handbook* (New York, 1960)

G. Agricola: *De natura fossilium* (1546)

G. Agricola: *De re metallica* (1556); translated by H. C. Hoover and L. H. Hoover (New York, 1950)

J. Amman and H. Sachs: *Eygentliche Beschreibung aller Stände . . . mit kunstreichen Figuren* (1568); translated with introduction by B. A. Rifkin as *The Book of Trades (Ständebuch) by Jost Amman and Hans Sachs* (New York, 1873)

D. Diderot and J. Le Rond d'Alembert: *L'Encyclopédie, ou Dictionnaire raisonné des sciences, des arts et des métiers* (Geneva, 1754–72); English selected edition as *A Diderot Pictorial Encyclopedia of Trades and Industry*, with introduction and notes edited by C. C. Gillispie (New York and London, 1959)

G. Gregory: *The Dictionary of Arts and Sciences*, 2 vols. (London, 1806–7)

A. Rees: *The Cyclopaedia, or, Universal Dictionary of Arts, Sciences, and Literature*, 41 vols. and 6 vols. of plates (Philadelphia, 1810–24)

C. Tomlinson, ed.: *Cyclopaedia of Useful Arts, Mechanical and Chemical, Manufactures, Mining, and Engineering* (London and New York, 1854)

L. S. Maclehose: *Vasari on Technique* (London, 1907; repr. New York, 1960)

C. Singer, E. J. Holmyard and A. R. Hall, eds.: *A History of Technology*, 5 vols. (Oxford, 1954–8)

R. Mayer: *A Dictionary of Art Terms and Techniques* (London, 1969)

H. J. Plenderleith and A. E. A. Werner: *The Conservation of Antiquities and Works of Art: Treatment, Repair and Restoration* (Oxford, 1971)

H. Osborne, ed.: *The Oxford Companion to the Decorative Arts* (Oxford, 1975)

H. Hodges: *Artifacts: An Introduction to Early Materials and Technology* (London, 1976)

D. Strong and D. Brown, eds.: *Roman Crafts* (London, 1976)

M.-T. Baudry, D. Bozo, A. Chastel and J. Thirion: *La sculpture: méthode et vocabulaire* (Paris, 1978)

J. Mills: *The Encyclopedia of Sculpture Techniques* (London, 1990)

N. Penny: *The Materials of Sculpture* (New Haven and London, 1993)

J. Turner, ed.: *The Dictionary of Art*, 34 vols. (London, 1996)

AMBER

G. C. Williamson: *The Book of Amber* (London, 1932)

R. Rottlander: 'On the Formation of Amber from Pinus Resin', *Archaeometry*, 12 (1970)

R. Henderson: *The Magic of Amber* (London, 1977)

J. Grabowska: *Amber in Polish History* (Edinburgh, 1978)

D. Schlee: *Bernstein Räritaten, Farben, Strukturen, Fossilien, Handwerk* (Stuttgart, 1980)

C. W. Beck: 'Authentication and Conservation of Amber', *Washington Congress for Science and Technology in the Service of Conservation* (1982)

M. Trusted: *Catalogue of the European Ambers in the Victoria and Albert Museum* (London, 1985)

H. Fraquet: *Amber* (London, 1987)

CERAMICS

A. Brongiart: *Un Traité des arts céramiques* (Paris, 1844)

R. A. Miller: *Japanese Ceramics* (Tokyo, 1960)

H. Sanders: *The World of Japanese Ceramics* (Tokyo, 1967)

D. Rhodes: *Kilns: Design, Construction and Operation* (London, 1968)

G. Clark and M. Hughto: *A Century of Ceramics in the United States, 1878–1978* (New York, 1979)

E. Dawson: *Masterpieces of Wedgwood* (London, 1984)

A. Caiger Smith, ed.: *Lustre Pottery* (London, 1985)

G. Savage and H. Newman: *An Illustrated Dictionary of Ceramics* (London, 1985)

R. Kerr: *Chinese Ceramics: Porcelain of the Qing Dynasty* (London, 1986)

D. Kingery and P. Vandiver: *Ceramic Masterpieces* (New York and London, 1986)

R. Tichane: *Ash Glazes* (Wisconsin, 1987)

N. Wood: *Iron in the Fire: The Chinese Potters' Exploration of Iron Oxide Glazes* (London, 1988)

M. Medley: *The Chinese Potter* (London, 1989)

J. Allan: *Islamic Ceramics* (Oxford, 1991)

F. Hamer and J. Hamer: *The Potter's Dictionary of Materials and Techniques* (London, 1991)

M. Coatts and N. Wood: *Lucie Rie* (London, 1992)

R. Greene: *Interpreting the Past: Roman Pottery* (London, 1992)

R. Scott, ed.: *Chinese Copper Red Wares*, Percival David Foundation Monograph no. 3 (London, 1992)

D. H. Cohen and C. Hess: *Looking at European Ceramics: A Guide to Technical Terms* (London and Malibu, 1993)

N. Barley: *Smashing Pots: Feats of Clay from Africa* (London, 1994)

A. Dodd: *Dictionary of Ceramics*, revised and updated by D. Murfin (London, 1994)

J. Poole: *English Pottery* (Cambridge, 1995)

R. Wilson: *Inside Japanese Ceramics* (New York, 1995)

Y. H. Cuff: *Ceramic Technology for Potters and Sculptors* (Philadelphia, 1996)

S. Pierson: *Earth, Fire and Water: Chinese Ceramic Technology* (London, 1996)

R. M. Cook: *Greek Painted Pottery* (London, 1997)

I. Freestone and D. Gaimster, eds.: *Pottery in the Making: World Ceramic Traditions* (London, 1997)

J. Poole: *Italian Maiolica* (Cambridge, 1997)

R. Scott: *For the Imperial Court* (London, 1997)

N. Wood: *Chinese Glazes* (London, 1999)

GLASS AND ENAMELS

A. Neri: *L'arte vitraria*; translated by C. Merrett as *The Art of Glass* (London, 1662)

A. Pellatt: *Curiosities of Glassmaking, with Details of the Processes and Productions of Ancient and Modern Ornamental Glass Manufacture* (London, 1849)

L. E. Millener: *Enamelling on Metal*, translated by H. de Konign (1951)

G. W. Beard: *Nineteenth-Century Cameo Glass* (Newport, Monmouth, 1956)

R. G. Charleston: 'Glass', *A History of Technology*, vol. 3: *From the Renaissance to the Industrial Revolution c. 1500–1750*, ed. C. Singer and others (Oxford, 1958)

R. McGrath, A. Frost and H. E. Beckett: *Glass in Architecture and Decoration* (London, 1961)

A. Lucas: *Ancient Egyptian Materials and Industries* (London, 1962)

G. Wills: *English Looking Glasses, 1670–1820* (London, 1965)

R. J. Forbes: *Studies in Ancient Technology*, vol. 5 (Leiden, 1966)

F. Kampfer and K. G. Beyer: *Glass: A World History; The Story of 4000 Years of Fine Glass Making* (London, 1966)

R. G. Charleston: 'Some Tools of the Glassmaker in Medieval and Renaissance Times, with Special Reference to the Glassmaker's Chair', *Glass Technology*, 3 (1967), 107–11

R. Scranton: 'Glass Pictures from the Sea', *Archaeology*, 20/3 (1967), 163–73

D. B. Harden, K. S. Painter, R. H. Pinder-Wison and H. Tait: *Masterpieces of Glass* (London, 1968)

J. Burton: *Glass: Philosophy and Method* (London, 1969)

P. Hollister: *Encyclopaedia of Paperweights* (New York, 1969)

J. V. Noble: 'The Technique of Egyptian Faience', *American Journal of Archaeology*, 73 (1969), 435–9

A. L. Oppenheim, R. H. Brill, R. H. Barag and A. von Saldern: *Glass and Glassmaking in Ancient Mesopotamia* (Corning, NY, 1970)

H. Mayron: *Metalwork and Enamelling* (London, 1971)

A. Pilkington: 'Float: An Application of Science, Analysis and Judgement', *Glass Technology*, 12 (1971), 76–83

G. M. Ritz: *Hinterglasmalerei: Geschichte, Erscheinung, Technik* (Munich, 1972)

B. Schweig: *Mirrors: A Guide to the Manufacture of Mirrors and Reflecting Surfaces* (London, 1973)

M. G. Cosgrove: *The Enamels of China and Japan: Champléve and Cloisonné* (London, 1974)

L. Ibrahim, R. Scranton and R. Brill: 'The Panels of Opus Sectile Glass' in *Kenchreai: Eastern Port of Corinth*, 2 (Leiden, 1976)

A. Pilkington: 'Flat Glass: Evolution and Revolution over 60 Years', *Glass Technology*, 17 (1976), 182–93

M. Guido: *The Glass heads of the Prehistoric and Roman Periods in Britain and Ireland* (London, 1977)

H. Newman: *An Illustrated Dictionary of Glass* (London, 1977)

H. Tait: *The Golden Age of Venetian Glass* (London, 1979)

R. Hurst Vose: *Glass* (London, 1980)

L. Lee, G. Seddon and F. Stephens: *Stained Glass* ((London, 1982)

F. Mehlman: *Phaidon Guide to Glass* (Oxford, 1982)

M. S. Tite, M. Bimson and I. C. Freestone: 'Egyptian Faience: An Investigation of the Methods of Production', *Archaeometry*, 25 (1983), 17–27

E. Speel: *Popular Enamelling* (London, 1984)

T. Toninato: 'Technology and Tradition in Murano Glassmaking', *Glass in Murano* (Vicenza, 1984)

S. Wicks: *Jewellery Making Manual* (London, 1985)

C. Macleod: 'Accident or Design? George Ravenscroft's Patent and the Invention of Lead Crystal Glass', *Technology and Culture*, 28 (1987), 776–803

M. S. Tite and M. Bimson: 'Identification of Early Vitreous Materials',

Recent Advances in the Conservation and Analysis of Artefacts,
Proceedings of the Institute of Archaeology's Jubilee Conservation
Conference (London, 1987)

R. Newton and S. Davison: 'Technology of Glass Production',
Conservation of Glass (London, 1989), 54–135

G. Child: *World Mirrors, 1650–1990* (London, 1990)

C. R. Hajdamach: *British Glass, 1800–1914* (Woodbridge, Suffolk, 1991)

H. Tait, ed.: *Five Thousand Years of Glass* (London, 1991)

P. Hadsund: 'The Tin-Mercury Mirror: Its Manufacturing Technique and
Deterioration Processes', *Studies in Conservation*, 38/1 (1993), 3–16

P. T. Nicholson: *Egyptian Faience and Glass* (Haverfordwest, 1993)

E. Speel: *Dictionary of Enamelling* (Aldershot and Brookfield, VT, 1998)

K. Frankler-Balhorn: 'Historiche Spiegel in Schlossern; Plegen,
restaurieren, erganzen', *Restauro*, 4 (1999)

H. Lanz and L. Seelig, eds.: *Farbige Kostbarkeiten aus Glas:
Kabinettstücke der zürcher Hinterglasmalerei, 1600–1650* (Munich and
Zurich, 1999)

IVORY AND RELATED MATERIALS

T. K. Penniman: *Pictures of Ivory and Other Animal Teeth, Bone and
Antler*, Pitt Rivers Museum, Oxford, Occasional Papers on
Technology, 5 (Oxford, 1952)

C. I. A. Ritchie: *Ivory Carving* (London, 1969)

N. S. Baer and L. J. Majewski: 'Ivory and Related Materials', *Art and
Archaeology Technical Abstracts*, 8/2–3 (1970)

R. Silverberg: *Mammoths, Mastodons and Man* (London, 1970)

P. Hardwick: *Discovering Horn* (Guildford, 1981)

B. Burack: *Ivory and its Uses* (Rutland, USA, 1984)

A. MacGregor: *Bone, Antler, Ivory and Horn: The Technology of Skeletal
Materials since the Roman Period* (London and Sydney, 1985)

C. Chesney, N. Barley and others: *Ivory: A History and Collector's Guide*
(London, 1987)

O. Krzyszkowska: *Ivory and Related Materials*, Institute of Classical
Studies Bulletin, supplement 59 (London, 1990)

J. Chapman: *The Art of Rhinoceros Horn Carving in China* (London,
1999)

LACQUER

F. Bonanni: *Vera vernix sinica* (Rome, 1709)

J. J. Quin: *Report by Her Majesty's Acting Consulate Hacodate on the
Lacquer Industry of Japan* (London, 1882)

T. N. Mukharji: *Art Manufactures of India* (Calcutta, 1888)

'Chinese Incised Lacquer', *Burlington Magazine*, 25 (1914), 176–83,
280–86

E. F. Strange: *Chinese Lacquer* (London, 1926)

'Raden (Shell Inlaid Urushi-ware)', *Museum*, 96, 105 (March and
December 1959)

Japanese Art Lacquers, Monumenta Nipponica Monographs (Tokyo,
1961)

K. Herberts: *Oriental Lacquer Art and Technique* (London, 1962)

H. Huth: *Lacquer of the West: The History of a Craft and an Industry,
1550–1950* (Chicago and London, 1971)

Y.-K. Lee: *Oriental Lacquer Art* (London, 1972)

J. Hejzlar: *The Arts of Vietnam* (London, 1973)

B. von Rague: *A History of Japanese Lacquerwork* (Toronto, 1976)

Sir H. Garner: *Chinese Lacquer* (London, 1979)

W. Watson, ed.: *Lacquerwork in Asia and Beyond: A Colloquy Held 22–24 June 1981*, Percival David Foundation of Chinese Art (London, 1982)

J. Bourne and others: *Lacquer: An International History and Collector's Guide* (London, 1984)

S. Fraser-Lu: *Burmese Lacquerware* (Bangkok, 1985)

N. S. Bromelle and P. Smith: *Urushi: Proceedings of the Urushi Study Group, 10–27 June 1985, Tokyo* (Marina del Rey, CA, 1988)

LEATHER

A. Watt: *The Art of Leather Manufacture* (1885)

M. Nathan: *The Decoration of Leather* (London, 1905)

H. Cluzot: *Cuirs décorés* (Paris, 1925)

J. W. Waterer: *Leather in Life, Art and Industry* (London, 1946)

G. Gall: *Leder in europäischen Kunsthandwerk* (Braunschweig, 1965)

G. Moseley: *Leather Goods Manufacture* (London, 1965; repr. Walsall, 1992)

J. Sharphouse: *The Leather Technician's Handbook* (Northampton, 1971)

J. W. Waterer: *Spanish Leather* (London, 1971)

R. Reed: *Ancient Skins, Parchments and Leathers* (London, 1972)

R. S. Thomson: 'Tanning: Man's First Manufacturing Process', *Translations of the Newcomen Society* (1981)

R. Salaman: *Dictionary of Leatherworking Tools* (London, 1985)

R. S. Thomson: 'Chrome Tannage in the Nineteenth Century', *Journal of the Society of Leather Technologists and Chemists* (1985)

P. Ruck, ed.: *Pergament*, Historische Hilfswissenschaften, 2 (Sigmaringen, 1991)

C. de Hamel: *Scribes and Illuminators* (London, 1992)

E. Koldeweij: *Monumenten en landschappen* (1992), vol. 2, pp. 8–32

V. Michael: *The Leatherworking Handbook* (London, 1993)

METALS

V. Biringuccio: *De la pirotechnica* (Venice, 1540); translated with an introduction by C. S. Smith and M. T. Gnudi as *The Pirotechnica of Vannoccio Biringuccio: The Classic Sixteenth-Century Treatise on Metals and Metallurgy* (New York, 1990)

B. Cellini: *The Treatises of Benvenuto Cellini on Goldsmithing and Sculpture* (1888; repr. New York, 1967)

F. Bradbury: *History of Old Sheffield Plate* (London, 1912; repr. Sheffield, 1968)

H. H. Cotterell: *Old Pewter: Its Makers and Marks* (London, 1929; repr. 1963)

B. Cuzner: *A Silversmith's Manual* (London, 1949)

A. R. Hardy: *The Jewelry Engraver's Manual* (New York, 1954; repr. 1975)

C. Blair: *European Armour, c. 1066 to c. 1700* (London, 1958; repr. 1972, 1979)

A. Brittain, S. Wolpert and P. Morton: *Engraving on Precious Metals* (London, 1958; repr. 1975)

C. Blair: *European and American Arms, c. 1100–1850* (London, 1962; repr. 1963)

C. Oman: *English Domestic Silver*, 5th edn (London, 1962)

J. F. Hayward: *The Art of the Gunmaker*, 2 vols. (1962–3)

O. Untracht: *Metal Techniques for Craftsmen* (New York, 1968; repr. 1975)

H. J. Kaufman: *The Colonial Silversmith: His Techniques and His Products* (New York, 1969)

H.-U. Headeke: *Metalwork* (London, 1970)

G. B. Hughes: *Antique Sheffield Plate* (London, 1970)

H. J. Kauffman: *The American Pewterer: His Techniques and His Products* (London, 1970)

S. Bury: *Victorian Electroplate* (London, 1971)

H. Maryon: *Metalwork and Enamelling*, 5th edn (New York, 1971)

N. Goodison: *Ormolu: The Work of Matthew Boulton* (London, 1974)

P. Knauth: *The Emergence of Man: The Metalsmiths* (New York, 1974)

E. Turner: *Brass* (London, 1982)

O. Untracht: *Jewelry Concepts and Technology* (New York, 1982; repr. London, 1985)

R. Finegold and W. Seitz: *Silversmithing* (Radnor, PA, 1983)

C. A. Peal: *Pewter of Great Britain* (1983)

J. Wolters: *Die Granulation* (Munich, 1983)

C. Hull and J. Murrell: *The Techniques of Pewtersmithing* (London, 1984)

E. Turner: *English Silver from 1660* (London, 1985)

H. Ottomeyer and P. Pröschel: *Vergoldete Bronzen*, 2 vols. (Munich, 1986)

C. Blair, ed.: *The History of Silver* (London, 1987; repr. 1991)

E. Brepohl: *Theophilus Presbyter und die mittelalterliche Goldschmiedekunst* (Leipzig, 1987)

R. Hughes and M. Rowe: *The Colouring, Bronzing and Patination of Metals* (London, 1991)

J. Cherry: *Goldsmiths* (London, 1992)

J. Ogden: *Ancient Jewellery* (Berkeley, CA, and London, 1992)

M. Pfaffenbichler: *Armourers* (London, 1992)

R. F. Tylecote: *A History of Metallurgy*, 2nd edn (London, 1992)

S. La Niece and P. Craddock: *Metal Plating and Patination: Cultural, Technical and Historical Developments* (Oxford, 1993)

A. Williams and A. de Reuck: *The Royal Armoury at Greenwich, 1515–1649* (London, 1995)

S. J. Helliwell: *Understanding Antique Silver Plate* (Woodbridge, Suffolk, 1996)

J. D. Lavin: *The Art and Tradition of the Zuloagas: Spanish Damascene from the Khalili Collection* (1997)

K. Pinn: *Paktong: The Chinese Alloy in Europe* (Woodridge, Suffolk, 1999)

PAINT

R. Mayer: *The Artist's Handbook of Materials and Techniques* (New York, 1940; rev. edn, London, 1987)

R. J. Gettens and G. L. Stout: *Painting Materials: A Short Encyclopedia* (New York, 1942)

R. D. Harley: *Artists' Pigments, c. 1600–1835: A Study in Documentary Sources* (London, 1970; rev. edn, 1982)

B. Rhodes and J. Windsor: *Parry's Graining and Marbling* (London, 1985)

R. L. Feller, ed.: *Artists' Pigments: A Handbook of their History and Characteristics* (Cambridge, 1986)

I. C. Bristow: *Interior House Painting: Colours and Technology, 1615–1840* (New Haven and London, 1996)

PAPER AND BOOKBINDING

R. Holme: *The Academy of Armory* (1688); repr. as *The Academy of Armory: A Reprint of a Part of Book III, Concerning the Art of Printing and Typefounding* (Menston, York, 1972)

N. McClelland: *Historic Wallpapers from their Inception to the Introduction of Machinery* (1924)

D. Hunter: *Papermaking: The History and Technique of an Ancient Craft* (New York, 1947)

J. Toller: *Papier-Mâché in Great Britain and America* (London, 1962)

H. Curwen: *Processes of Graphic Reproduction in Printing* (1963)

A. M. Hind: *An Introduction to the History of Woodcut* (New York, 1963)

E. A. Entwisle: *The Book of Wallpaper: A History and an Appreciation* (Bath, 1970)

A. Gross: *Etching, Engraving and Intaglio Printing* (Oxford, 1970)

S. S. DeVoe: *English Papier-Mâché of the Georgian and Victorian Periods* (London, 1971)

N. Armstrong: *A Collector's History of Fans* (London, 1974)

J. Lowe: *Japanese Crafts* (London, 1974)

B. de V. Green: *A Collector's Guide to Fans* (London, 1975)

P. Gilmour: *The Mechanised Image: An Historical Perspective on 20th Century Prints* (London, 1978)

S. Hughes: *Washi: The World of Japanese Paper* (Tokyo, 1978)

B. Middleton: *A History of English Craft Bookbinding Technique* (London, 1978)

N. Armstrong and others: *The Book of Fans* (New Malden, Surrey, 1979)

T. Tokuriki: *Woodblock Printing* (Osaka, 1980)

R. H. van Gulik: *Chinese Pictorial Art as Viewed by the Connoisseur* (New York, 1981)

C. Oman and J. Hamilton: *Wallpapers: A History and Illustrated Catalogue of the Collection in the Victoria and Albert Museum* (London, 1982)

S. Lambert: *Printmaking* (London, 1983)

J. Banham: *A Decorative Art: 19th Century Wallpapers in the Whitworth Art Gallery* (Manchester, 1985)

P. Wills, 'Far Eastern Pictorial Art: Form and Function', *Hyogu: The Japanese Tradition in Picture Conservation*, The Institute of Paper Conservation (1985)

A. Chambers: *The Practical Guide to Marbling Paper* (London, 1986)

K. Ikegami: *Japanese Bookbinding*; translated by B. Stephen (New York and Tokyo, 1986)

L. Hoskins, ed.: *The Papered Wall* (London, 1994)

PLASTICS

Gutta Percha Company: *Gutta Percha Company Catalogue* (London, 1852)

T. Hancock: *Personal Narrative of the Origin and Progress of the Caoutchouc or India Rubber Manufacture in England* (London, 1857)

S. Hawksworth: British Patent 2345 (19 September 1861)

F. Walton: British Patent 3210 (19 December 1863)

J. W. Hyatt and I. S. Hyatt: *Improvement in Treating and Molding Pyroxyline*, United States Patent (1870)

L. Baekeland: *Journal of Industrial Engineering Chemistry*, 1 (1909), 149

J. Lawrence: *Painting from A–Z* (Manchester, 1938)

H. Mark and G. S. Whitby, eds.: *Collected Papers of Wallace H. Carothers on Polymerization* (New York, 1940)

E. Ott: *Cellulose and Cellulose Derivatives* (New York, 1943)

T. J. Fielding: *History of Bakelite Limited* (London, c. 1950)

The Telegraph Construction & Maintenance Co. Ltd: *The Telcon Story, 1850–1950* (London, 1950)

B. Parkyn: *Polyester Handbook* (London, 1953)

M. Kaufman: *The First Century of Plastics: Celluloid and its Sequel* (London, 1963)

V. E. Yarsley, W. Flavell, P. S. Adamson and N. G. Perkins: *Cellulosic Plastics* (London, 1964)

M. Kaufman: *History of PVC* (London, 1967)

J. H. Dubois: *Plastics History U.S.A.* (Boston, 1972)

S. Katz: *Plastics: Designs and Materials* (London, 1978)

J. A. Brydson: *Plastics Materials*, 4th edn (London, 1982)

R. Friedel: *Pioneer Plastic: The Making and Selling of Celluloid* (Wisconsin, 1983)

S. Katz: *Classic Plastics* (London, 1984)

C. Kennedy: *ICI: The Company that Changed our Lives* (London, 1986)

A. Coates: *The Commerce in Rubber: The First 250 Years* (Oxford, 1987)

C. Williamson: 'Bois Durci: A Plastics Antique', *Plastiquarian*, 1 (Winter 1988), 8

J. Morgan: 'Quality Control and Product Development: Erinoid, 1954–1961', *Plastiquarian*, 2 (1989), 12–13

C. Williamson: 'Shellac Union Cases', *Plastiquarian*, 3 (Summer 1989), 10

L. Edwards: 'Gutta Percha: The Plastic of its Time', *Plastiquarian*, 6 (Winter 1990), 14–15

P. J. T. Morris: *Polymer Pioneers* (Philadelphia, 1990), 28

P. Sparke, ed.: *The Plastics Age* (London, 1990)

J. Morgan: *Conservation of Plastics* (London, 1991)

J. W. Nicholson: *The Chemistry of Polymers* (Cambridge, 1991)

L. Edwards: 'Polyethylene: The New Insulating Material', *Plastiquarian*, 9 (Winter 1991–92), 12

N. S. Allen, M. Edge and C. V. Horie, eds.: *Polymers in Conservation* (London, 1992)

E. G. K. Pritchard: 'Woodflour: The Natural Filler', *Plastiquarian*, 10 (Summer 1992), 13

Canadian Conservation Insitute: *Saving the Twentieth Century: The Conservation of Modern Materials* (Ottawa, 1993)

R. G. B. Mitchell: 'History and Development of the Vinyl LP Record', *Plastiquarian*, 11 (Spring 1993), 14f.

D. Brown: 'Polymers in Dentistry', *Plastiquarian*, 13 (1994), 3–7

A. McDonach, P. T. Gardiner, R. S. McEwen and B. Culsaw, eds.: *Second European Conference on Smart Structures and Materials* (Washington, 1994)

S. T. I. Mossman: 'Parkesine and Celluloid', *The Development of Plastics*, ed. S. T. I. Mossman and P. J. T. Morris (Cambridge, 1994), 10–25

B. Parkyn: 'Fibre-reinforced Composites', *The Development of Plastics*, ed. S. T. I. Mossman and P. J. T. Morris (Cambridge, 1994), 105–14

J. Tilley: 'Versatility of Acrylics', *The Development of Plastics*, ed. S. T. I. Mossman and P. J. T. Morris (Cambridge, 1994), 95–104

T. Williams, ed.: *Collins Biographical Dictionary of Scientists* (Glasgow, 1994)

C. Williamson: 'Victorian Plastics: Foundations of an Industry', *The Development of Plastics*, ed. S. T. I. Mossman and P. J. T. Morris (Cambridge, 1994), 70–86

J. L. Meikle: *American Plastic* (New Jersey, 1995)

A. Walker: 'Decorative Laminates, 1911–1981', *Plastiquarian*, 16 (Summer 1996), 2–5

C. Friend: 'From Sensuous Aircraft to Cuddly Toasters', lecture to the Institute of Mechanical Engineers, London (20 January, 1997)

S. Mossman, ed.: *Early Plastics: Perspectives, 1850–1950* (London, 1997)

SHELL

H. K. Krauss: *Shell Art* (New York, 1965)

R. J. L. Wagner and R. T. Abbot: *Van Nostrand's Standard Catalogue of Shells* (New Jersey, 1967)

C. I. A. Richie: *Carving Shells and Cameos* (New York, 1970)

R. Tucker-Abbott: *Kingdom of the Seashell* (New York, 1972)

L. Arbale: *L'arte della tartaruga: le opera dei musei napoletani e la donazione Sbriziolo-De Felice* (Naples, 1994)

STONE AND RELATED MATERIALS

W. Millar and G. Bankart: *Plastering Plain and Decorative* (London, 1897; repr. Shaftesbury, Dorset, 1998)

J. C. Rich: *The Materials and Methods of Sculpture* (New York, 1947)

L. Salzman: *Building in England down to 1540* (Oxford, 1952)

C. Bromehead: 'Mining and Quarrying to the 17th Century', *A History of Technology*, ed. C. Singer and others; vol. 2: *The Mediterranean Civilizations and the Middle Ages* (Oxford, 1956)

W. Willets: *Chinese Art* (Harmondsworth, 1958)

N. Davey: *A History of Building Materials* (London, 1961)

A. Lucas and J. R. Harris: *Ancient Egyptian Materials and Industries*, 4th edn (London, 1962)

S. Adam: *The Technique of Greek Sculpture in the Archaic and Classical Periods* (London, 1966)

B. Cellini: *The Treatises of Benevenuto Cellini on Goldsmithing and Sculpture*; translated by B. R. Ashbee (New York, 1967)

A. Clifton-Taylor: *The Pattern of English Building* (London, 1972)

H. Mckee: *Introduction to Early American Masonry* (Washington, 1973)

A. Rainey: *Mosaics in Roman Britain* (Newton Abbot, 1973)

A. Holmes and D. Holmes: *Holmes' Principles of Physical Geology*, 3rd rev. edn (Wokingham, 1978)

G. Mitchell, ed.: *Architecture of the Islamic World* (London, 1978)

J. Gimpel: *The Cathedral Builders* (New York, 1980)

G. Beard: *Stucco and Decorative Plasterwork in Europe* (London, 1983)

A. Clifton-Taylor and A. Ireson: *English Stone Building* (London, 1983)

R. Newman: *The Stone Sculpture of India* (Cambridge, MA, 1984)

J. Ayres: *The Artist's Craft* (Oxford, 1985)

D. Cole: *Captured Heritage: The Scramble for North-west Coast Artifacts* (Seattle, 1985)

D. T. Moore and W. A. Oddy: 'Touchstones: Some Aspects of their Nomenclature, Petrography and Provenance', *Journal of Archaeological Science*, 12 (1985), 59–80

J. Alexander and P. Binski, eds.: *The Age of Chivalry* (London, 1987)

C. Woodward and R. Harding: *Gemstones* (London, 1987)

J. Ashurst and N. Ashurst: *Mortars, Plasters and Renders* (Aldershot, 1988)

C. Bertelli, ed.: *The Art of Mosaics* (London, 1988)

L. von Rosen: *Lapis Lazuli in Geological Contexts and in Ancient Written Sources* (Partille, Sweden, 1988)

J. T. Greensmith: *Petrology of the Sedimentary Rocks*, 7th rev. edn (London, 1989)

J. Montagu: *Roman Baroque Sculpture: The Industry of Art* (New Haven and London, 1989)

A. Shadmon: *Stone* (London, 1989)

J. Ashurst and F. Dimes, eds.: *Conservation of Building and Decorative Stone* (London, 1990)

R. W. Brunskill: *Brick Building in Britain* (London, 1990)

D. Collon: *Near Eastern Seals* (London, 1990)

A. Kelly: *Mrs Coade's Stone* (Upton-on-Severn, 1990)

D. Parsons, ed.: *Stone Quarrying and Building in England AD 43–1525* (Chichester, 1990)

M. Trusted: *German Renaissance Medals: A Catalogue of the Collection of the Victoria and Albert Museum* (London, 1990)

R. Zerbst: *Antoni Gaudi* (Cologne, 1990)

N. Coldstream: *Masons and Sculptors* (London, 1991)

R. Foster: *Patterns of Thought: The Hidden Meaning of the Great Pavement of Westminster Abbey* (London, 1991)

R. Keverne: *Jade* (London, 1991)

A. Wright: *Craft Techniques for Traditional Buildings* (London, 1991)

A.-M. Guisti: *Pietre dure: Hardstone in Furniture and Decoration* (London, 1992)

A. Brodrick: 'Painting Techniques of Early Medieval Sculpture', *Romanesque Stone Sculpture from Medieval England* (Leeds, 1993)

M. Davis: 'When is Jet Not Jet?', *Conservation Science in the U.K.*, ed. N. Tennent (London, 1993)

M. Farneti: *Technical-Historical Glossary of Mosaic Art* (Ravenna, 1993)

A. Kelly: 'Coade Stone in Georgian Gardens'. *Antiques* (June 1993)

P. Rockwell: *The Art of Stoneworking: A Reference Guide* (Cambridge, 1993)

G. Lynch: *Brickwork: History, Technology and Practice* (London, 1994)

Simpson & Brown, Architects: *Conservation of Plasterwork* (Edinburgh, 1994)

R. Webster: *Gems: Their Sources, Descriptions and Identification*, 5th rev. edn (Oxford, 1994)

S. Walker: *Greek and Roman Portraits* (London, 1995)

S. Butters: *The Triumph of Vulcan: Sculptors' Tools, Porphyry and the Prince in Ducal Florence* (Cambridge, MA, 1996)

A. Kelly: 'Coade Stone: Its Character and Conservation', *Architectural Ceramics: Their History, Manufacture and Conservation*, by J. Teutonico (London, 1996)

C. Phillips: *Jewelry: From Antiquity to the Present* (London, 1996)

M. Stratton: 'The Nature of Terra Cotta and Faience', *Architectural Ceramics*, ed. J.-M. Teutonico (London, 1996)

T. Tatton-Brown and J. Munby, eds.: *The Archaeology of Cathedrals* (Oxford, 1996)

W. Zwalf: *A Catalogue of the Gandhara Sculpture in the British Museum* (London, 1996)

A. Kelly: 'Coade Stone at Croome', *Apollo* (April 1997)

G. Harlow, ed.: *The Nature of Diamonds* (Cambridge, 1998)

TEXTILES

M. de Ruusscher: *Histoire naturelle de la cochenille, justifié par des documents authentiques* (Amsterdam, 1729)

M. Postlethwayt: *The Universal Dictionary of Trade and Commerce Translated from the French of the Celebrated Monsier Savary*, 2 vols. (London, 1751–5)

C. G. de Saint-Aubin: *L'Art du brodeur* (Paris, 1770); translated and annotated by N. Scheuer as *The Art of the Embroiderer* (Los Angeles, 1983)

E. Bancroft: *Experimental Researches Concerning the Philosophy of Permanent Colours; and the Best Means of Production, by Dyeing, Calico Printing, etc.* (London, 1794 and 1813)

E. Baines, Jr.: *History of the Cotton Manufacture in Great Britain* (London, 1835; repr. London, 1966)

Miss Lambert: *Hand-Book of Needlework* (London, 1842)

W. S. Beck: *The Draper's Dictionary: A Manual of Textile Fabrics* (London, 1882)

S. F. A. Caulfeild and B. Saward: *Dictionary of Needlework* (London, 1882); repr. as *Encyclopedia of Victorian Needlework* (New York, 1972)

E. E. Perkins: *A Treatise on Haberdashery and Hosiery* (London, 1833)

H. Harvard: *Dictionnaire de l'ameublement et de la décoration, depuis le XIIIe siècle jusqu'à nos jours*, 4 vols. (Paris, 1887)

T. de Dillment: *Encyclopedia of Needlework* (Mulhouse, 1890; repr. Philadelphia, 1972)

J. M. Matthews: *Application of Dyestuffs to Textiles, Paper, Leather and Other Materials* (London, 1920)

L. Hooper: *The New Draw-loom* (London, 1932)

C. W. Ashley: *The Ashley Book of Knots* (Newport News, VA, 1944; repr. London and New York, 1993)

L. G. Lawrie: *A Bibliography of Dyeing and Textile Printing* (London, 1949)

A. Albers: *On Weaving* (London, 1965)

I. Emery: *The Primary Structure of Fabrics* (Washington, D.C., 1966; repr. London, 1994)

R. J. Adrosko: *Natural Dyes in the United States* (Washington, D.C., 1968)

P. Collingwood: *The Techniques of Rug Weaving* (New York, 1968)

V. I. Harvey: *The Techniques of Basketry* (New York, 1974)

J. Storey: *Manual of Textile Printing* (London, 1974)

I. B. Wingate ed.: *Fairchild's Dictionary of Textiles*, 3rd edn (New York, 1974)

M. Straub: *Handweaving and Cloth Design* (London, 1977)

J. Storey: *Manual of Dyes and Fabrics* (London, 1978)

D. K. Burnham: *Warp and Weft: A Textile Terminology* (Toronto, 1980)

P. Earnshaw: *The Identification of Lace* (Aylesbury, 1980)

K. G. Ponting: *A Dictionary of Dyes and Dyeing* (London, Sydney and Toronto, 1980)

D. J. Jeremy: *Transatlantic Industrial Revolution* (Cambridge, MA, 1981)

C. J. Sestay: *Needle Work: A Selected Bibliography with Specific Reference to Embroidery and Needlepoint* (London and Metuchen, NJ, 1982)

G. A. Rogers: *An Illustrated History of Needlework Tools* (London, 1983)

F. M. Montgomery: *Textiles in America, 1650–1870: A Dictionary* (London and New York, 1984)

P. Earnshaw: *Lace Machines and Machine Laces* (London, 1986)

R. Rutt: *A History of Hand Knitting* (London, 1987)

J. T. Millington and S. Chapman, eds.: *Four Centuries of Machine Knitting* (Leicester, 1989)

M. Schoeser: *English and American Textiles: 1790 to the Present Day* (London and New York, 1989)

A. S. Baldinger: *Textiles: A Classification of Techniques* (Bathurst, New South Wales, 1994)

S. B. Sherrill: *Carpets and Rugs of Europe and America* (London and New York, 1996)

G. Sandberg: *The Red Dyes: Cochineal, Madder, and Murex Purple; A World Tour of Textile Techniques* (Ashville, NC, 1997)

J. Balfour-Paul: *Indigo* (London, 1998)

J. Gardiner, J. Carlson, L. Eaton and K. Duffy: ' "That Fabric Seems Extremely Bright": Non-destructive Characterization of Nineteenth-century Mineral Dyes via XRF Analysis', *North American Textile Conservation Conference 2000: Conservation Combinations*, pp. 101–15

WOOD

J. Stalker and G. Parker: *A Treatise of Japanning and Varnishing: Being a Complete Discovery of those Arts* (1688; repr. Reading, 1998)

J. Moxon: *Mechanick Exercises, or, The Doctrine of Handy-works* (London, 1703; repr. New York, 1970)

T. Chippendale: *The Gentleman and Cabinetmaker's Director* (London, 1762; repr. New York, 1966)

T. Sheraton: *The Cabinet Maker and Upholsterer's Drawing Book* (London, 1793; repr. New York, 1973)

P. Thompson: *The Cabinet Maker's Assistant: A Series of Original Designs for Modern Furniture* (Glasgow and New York, 1853; repr. New York, 1970)

J. J. Holtzapffel: *Hand or Simple Turning* (London, 1881; repr. New York, 1976)

J. J. Holtzapffel: *Ornamental or Complex Turning* (London, 1884; repr. New York, 1973)

G. Jack: *Wood Carving* (London, 1903)

P. N. Hasluck: *Manual of Traditional Woodcarving* (London, 1912)

W. Fairham: *Staining and Polishing* (London, 1932)

W. G. Desch: *Timber Technicalities* (London, 1942)

W. L. Goodman: *History of Woodworking Tools* (London, 1964)

M. Campkin: *Marquetry* (London, 1969)

J. C. Rich: *Sculpture in Wood* (New York, 1970)

E. Palutan: *Timber Monographs* (London, 1974)

H. C. Mercer: *Ancient Carpenter's Tools* (New York, 1975)

R. A. Salaman: *Dictionary of Tools, Used in the Woodworking and Allied Trades* (London, 1975)

J. Krenov: *The Fine Art of Cabinetmaking* (London, 1977)

K. Seike: *The Art of Japanese Joinery* (Tokyo, 1977)

W. L. Goodman: *British Planemakers from 1700* (Needham Market, 1978)

A. Jackson and D. Day: *The Complete Book of Tools* (London, 1978)

L. P. McDonnell: *The Use of Hand Woodworking Tools* (New York, 1978)

Y. Nakahara: *Japanese Joinery* (Washington, 1980)

J. Sainsbury and G. Chinn: *The Carpenter's Companion* (London, 1980)

F. Oughton: *The Complete Manual of Woodfinishing* (London, 1982)

W. A. Lincoln: *World Woods in Colour* (London, 1986)

W. H. Coaldrake: *The Way of the Carpenter: Japanese Tools* (Tokyo, 1990)

J. Rees and M. Rees: *The Tool Chest of Benjamin Seaton, 1797* (1994)

ACKNOWLEDGEMENTS

The Editor would like to thank Matthew Taylor for preparing the text, Julia Brown and Lisa Godson for picture research, Philip de Bay for photography and Jan Maget for the line drawings. The following have also been most helpful at various stages: Frances Halahan, Patrick Collingwood, Robert Collingwood, Gillian Craig, Martin Durrant, Mary-Jane Gibson, Victoria Lane, Katie Marsh, Martin Mortimer, Veronika Palečková, Jane Rick, Vera Ryan, Adam Sisman, Richard Trench and Alena Zapletalová.

PICTURE CREDITS

The publisher would like to thank the following for permission to use their photographs. Every effort has been made to contact the copyright owners, but if any have been inadvertently missed, the publisher would be glad to hear from them. All the line artwork is by Jan Maget, Prague.

Colour plates: © The British Museum, London, pl. I; V&A Picture Library, London, pl. II; National Trust Photographic Library, London/John Hammond, pl. III; National Trust Photographic Library, London/John Hammond, pl. IV; S. J. Phillips, London, pl. V; V&A Picture Library, London, pl. VI; © The British Museum, London, pl. VII a; National Trust Photographic Library, London/John Hammond, pl. VII b; private collection, London (courtesy Adrian Sassoon), pl. VII c; Philippe Garner, London, pl. VII d; V&A Picture Library, London, pl. VIII; private collection, New York (courtesy Adrian Sassoon), pl. IX; Pieter Jan Tichelaar, Makkum, pl. X; Rosemary Crill, London, pl. XI a; Rosemary Crill, London, pl. XI b; Jenny Balfour Paul, Crediton, pl. XI c; R. Richard Blurton, London, pl. XI d; © The British Museum, London, pl. XII; Eskenazi Ltd, London, pl. XIII abcd; National Trust Photographic Library, London/Richard Pink, pl. XIV; National Trust Photographic Library, London/Nadia MacKenzie, pl. XV; V&A Picture Library, London, pl. XVI; V&A Picture Library, London, pl. XVII; Mallett plc, London, pl. XVIII.

Black-and-white illustrations: Science Museum, London/photograph courtesy of David Watkin by Bob Cramp, p. 2; Garry Atkins, London, p. 5; V&A Picture Library, London, p. 9; Alison Kelly, London, p. 15; Science Museum, London/Science & Society Picture Library, p. 19; Nicholas Grindley, London, p. 20; Rural History Centre, University of Reading, p. 23; V&A Picture Library, London, p. 25; V&A Picture Library, London, p. 27; Adrian Sassoon, London/Matthew Hollow, p. 29; Rural History Centre, University of Reading, p. 30; Francesca Galloway, London, p. 34; Science Museum, London/Science & Society Picture Library, p. 35; Eskenazi Ltd, London, p. 36; Stapelton Collection, London, p. 39; Philippe Garner, London, p. 40 bottom; V&A Picture Library, London, p. 42; The Museum of Decorative Arts in Prague, p. 43; Rural History Centre, University of Reading, p. 46; Christopher Lloyd, Rye, p. 49; Delomosne & Son Ltd, Chippenham/Blantern & Davis, p. 50; Eskenazi Ltd, London, p. 52; T. Richard Blurton, London, p. 53; © The British Museum, London, p. 56; private collection, p. 60; private collection/Sotheby Parke Bernet & Co, p. 64; © The Hunt Museum, Limerick, Ireland, p. 67; By courtesy of the Percival David Foundation, London/Glenn Ratcliffe, p. 69; Science Museum, London/Science & Society Picture Library, p. 71; Adrian Sassoon, London/Matthew Hollow, p. 75; Science Museum, London/Science & Society Picture Library, p. 76; © The British Museum, London, p. 77; The al-Sabah Collection, Dar al-Athar al-Islamiyyah, Kuwait, p. 79; Everson Museum, Syracuse, NY/Courtney Frisse, p. 80; V&A Picture Library, London, p. 81; © The Wardens and Commonalty of the Mystery of Goldsmiths of the City of London, all rights reserved, p. 83; V&A Picture Library, London, p. 87; private collection/J. B. Archive, p. 91; V&A Picture Library, London, p. 94; private collection, p. 96; Mallett plc, London, p. 99; Jonathan Horne, London, p. 102; The Museum of Decorative Arts in Prague, p. 103; V&A Picture Library, London, p. 105; private collection, p. 107; Science Museum, London/Science & Society Picture Library, p. 108; The al-Sabah Collection, Dar al-Athar al-Islamiyyah, Kuwait, p. 110; Delomosne & Son Ltd, Chippenham/Raymond Fortt Studios, p. 111; private collection, p. 112; private collection, p. 113; Garry Atkins, London, p. 115; Christie's Images Ltd 1999, London, p. 117; © The Wardens and Commonalty of the Mystery of Goldsmiths of the City of London, all rights reserved, p. 118; V&A Picture Library, London, p. 122; © The Wardens and Commonalty of the Mystery of Goldsmiths of the City of London, all rights reserved, p. 123; Stapelton Collection, London, p. 128; private collection, p. 130; V&A Picture Library, London, p. 131; Philippe Garner, London, p. 133; The al-Sabah Collection, Dar al-Athar al-Islamiyyah, Kuwait, p. 135; Francesca Galloway, London, p. 136; private collection, p. 138; Stapelton Collection, London, p. 139; Philippe Garner, London, p. 143; © The British Museum, London, p. 146; The Museum of Decorative Arts in Prague, p. 147; The Museum of Decorative Arts in Prague, p. 148; By courtesy of the Percival David Foundation, London/Glenn Ratcliffe, p. 149; A. F. Kersting, London, p. 150; © The British Museum, London, p. 151; ©The Wardens and Commonalty of the Mystery of Goldsmiths of the City of London, all rights reserved, p. 152; Philippe Garner, London, p. 153; V&A Picture Library, London, p. 157; Josiah Wedgwood & Sons Ltd, Barlaston, p. 159; The Museum of Decorative Arts in Prague, p. 164; The al-Sabah Collection, Dar al-Athar al-Islamiyyah, Kuwait, p. 165; Science Museum, London/Science & Society Picture Library, p. 168; private collection, p. 170; private collection, p. 171; The Museum of Decorative Arts in Prague, p. 174; Wendy Ramshaw, London/Bob Cramp, p. 175; Stapelton Collection, London, p. 178; Ashmolean Museum, Oxford, p. 179; private collection, p. 181; private collection, p. 183; V&A Picture Library, London, p. 189; De Beers, London, p. 191; Arnold Wiggins & Sons Ltd, London, p. 194; Mallett plc, London/Raymond Fort Studios, p. 195; The Museum of Decorative Arts in Prague, p. 197; private collection, p. 199; The British Library, London, p. 201; Philippe Garner, London, p. 203; Delomosne & Son Ltd, Chippenham, p. 204; The al-Sabah Collection, Dar al-Athar al-Islamiyyah, Kuwait, p. 205 top; The Museum of Decorative Arts in Prague, p. 205 bottom; private collection, p. 207; private collection, p. 208; © The British Museum, London, p. 209; private collection, p. 210; The Museum of Decorative Arts in Prague, p. 211 top; The Museum of Decorative Arts in Prague, p. 211 bottom; The Museum of Decorative Arts in Prague, p. 212; The Museum of Decorative Arts in Prague, p. 213; Katz Collection, London, p. 214; Fitzwilliam Museum, Cambridge, p. 215; Science Museum, London/Science & Society Picture Library, p. 225; Delomosne & Son Ltd, Chippenham, p. 227; Verena Wriedt, Hamburg, p. 228; Colin Williamson, Shrewsbury, p. 229; The Museum of Decorative Arts in Prague, p. 231; private collection, p. 232; private collection/J. B. Archive, p. 237; private collection, p. 238; The Museum of Decorative Arts in Prague, p. 239; V&A Picture Library, London, p. 240; Philippe Garner, London, p. 241; The al-Sabah Collection, Dar al-Athar al-Islamiyyah, Kuwait, p. 242; Eskenazi Ltd, London, p. 243; Philippe Garner, London, p. 245; Science Museum, London/Science & Society Picture Library, p. 246; Eskenazi Ltd, London, p. 247; Mallett plc, London, p. 249; Stapelton Collection, London, p. 250; private collection, p. 252; Adrian Sassoon, London, p. 253; By courtesy of the Percival David Foundation, London/Glenn Ratcliffe, p. 255; private collection, p. 261; Eskenazi Ltd, London, p. 263; Rural History Centre, University of Reading, p. 265; private collection, p. 267; Winsor & Newton, Harrow, p. 268; private collection, p. 269; Delomosne & Son Ltd, Chippenham/Blantern & Davis, p. 270; Stapelton Collection, London, p. 273; Stapelton Collection, London, p. 276; Memorials by Artists, Saxmundham/Anthea Sieveking, p. 279; V&A Picture Library, London, p. 283; The Museum of Decorative Arts in Prague, p. 284; private collection, p. 286; Science Museum, London/Science & Society Picture Library, p. 287 top; Delomosne & Son Ltd, Chippenham/Blantern & Davis, p. 287 bottom; Royal Anthropological Institute Photographic Collection, London, p. 288; Alastair Lamb, Hertingfordbury, p. 289; The al-Sabah Collection, Dar al-Athar al-Islamiyyah, Kuwait, p. 293; private collection, p. 294; Mallett plc, London, p. 295; Fitzwilliam Museum, Cambridge, p. 297; V&A Picture Library, London, p. 301; Jonathan Horne, London, p. 303; Compton Marbling, Salisbury, p. 304; private collection/Stapelton Collection, London, p. 305; private collection, p. 306; private collection, p. 310; Stapelton Collection, London, p. 313; V&A Picture Library, London, p. 314; private collection, p. 315; © The Wardens and Commonalty of the Mystery of Goldsmiths of the City of London, all rights reserved, p. 317 left; David & Charles, Newton Abbot, p. 322; Caroline Dear, Southampton, p. 323; Philippe Garner, London, p. 325; The

Museum of Decorative Arts in Prague, p. 329; Reproduced by Permission of the Trustees of the Wallace Collection, London, p. 331; V&A Picture Library, London, p. 333; Elizabeth Hoare Collection at Liverpool Cathedral, George Shiffner, p. 338; The Museum of Decorative Arts in Prague, p. 339; V&A Picture Library, London, p. 341; The Knight of Glin, Glin, p. 343; private collection, p. 345; Barcham Green & Company, Maidstone, p. 346; private collection, p. 349; Barcham Green & Company, Maidstone, p. 350; Mallett plc, London, p. 352; Stad Bibliotek, Nuremberg, p. 353; private collection, p. 355; The Museum of Decorative Arts in Prague, p. 356; V&A Picture Library, London, p. 359; Stad Bibliotek, Nuremberg, p. 363; The Museum of Decorative Arts in Prague, p. 365; © The British Museum, London, p. 367; V&A Picture Library, London, p. 369; V&A Picture Library, London, p. 370; A. F. Kersting, London, p. 373; National Trust Photographic Library, London/Rupert Truman, p. 375; A. F. Kersting, London, p. 377; National Trust, Southern Region, Dorking, p. 379; Katz Collection, London, p. 381; Katz Collection, London, p. 385; Science Museum, London/Science & Society Picture Library, p. 386; By permission of the American Museum in Britain, Bath ©, p. 388; Reproduced by Permission of the Trustees of the Wallace Collection, London, p. 389; T. Richard Blurton, London, p. 391; private collection, p. 393 top; Toledo Museum of Art, Toledo, OH, gift of Mrs H. G. Duckworth, p. 393 bottom; Jenny Balfour Paul, Crediton, p. 394; Science Museum, London/Science & Society Picture Library, p. 396; private collection, p. 398; V&A Picture Library, London, p. 399; Stapelton Collection, London, p. 400; V&A Picture Library, London, p. 404; V&A Picture Library, London, p. 405; V&A Picture Library, London, p. 408; V&A Picture Library, London, p. 410; The Museum of Decorative Arts in Prague, p. 411; By courtesy of the Percival David Foundation, London/Glenn Ratcliffe, p. 412; The Museum of Decorative Arts in Prague, p. 413; The Museum of Decorative Arts in Prague, p. 415; private collection, p. 417; © The British Museum, London, p. 418; Katz Collection, London, p. 420; private collection, p. 423; V&A Picture Library, London, p. 428; Mallett plc, London, p. 429; Stapelton Collection, London, p. 430; Stead McAlpin, Carlisle, p. 431; The Museum of Decorative Arts in Prague, p. 435; Mallett plc, London, p. 437; Science Museum, London/Science & Society Picture Library, p. 439; The Museum of Decorative Arts in Prague, p. 441; Rosemary Crill, London, p. 443; Mallett plc, London, p. 444; Fitzwilliam Museum, Cambridge, p. 447; Josiah Wedgwood & Sons Ltd, Barlaston, p. 448; Fitzwilliam Museum, Cambridge, p. 449; The Museum of Decorative Arts in Prague, p. 451; Stapelton Collection, London, p. 455; Science Museum, London/Science & Society Picture Library, p. 456; Science Museum, London/Science & Society Picture Library, p. 457; Science Museum, London/Science & Society Picture Library, p. 458; Josiah Wedgwood & Sons Ltd, Barlaston, p. 459; V&A Picture Library, London, p. 461; By permission of the American Museum in Britain, Bath ©, p. 464; private collection/J. B. Archive, p. 465; V&A Picture Library, London, p. 466; private collection, p. 470; Dick Reid, York, p. 472; Jacqui Hurst, London, p. 476; V&A Picture Library, London, p. 478; A. F. Kersting, London, p. 479; private collection, p. 480; private collection, p. 482; The Edinburgh Tapestry Co. Ltd, London, p. 485; By courtesy of the Percival David Foundation, London/Glenn Ratcliffe, p. 486; Caroline Dear, Southampton, p. 489; V&A Picture Library, London, p. 492; Jonathan Horne, London, p. 495; Mallett plc, London, p. 498; Delomosne & Son Ltd, Chippenham/Raymond Fortt Studios, p. 500; private collection, p. 503; V&A Picture Library, London, p. 504; © The British Museum, London, p. 505; private collection, p. 506; Science Museum, London/Science & Society Picture Library, p. 507; By courtesy of the Percival David Foundation, London/Glenn Ratcliffe, p. 508; Katz Collection, London, p. 509; private collection, p. 513; private collection, p. 514; Cheltenham Art Gallery and Museum, Cheltenham, p. 515; V&A Picture Library, London, p. 516; Reproduced by Permission of the Trustees of the Wallace Collection, London, p. 517; Science Museum, London/Science & Society Picture Library, p. 518; Cole & Son, Rickmansworth, p. 519; Cole & Son, Rickmansworth, p. 520; V&A Picture Library, London, p. 521; V&A Picture Library, London, p. 522; Science Museum, London/Science & Society Picture Library, p. 523; The Humphries Weaving Co. Ltd, Halstead/Dennis Mansell, p. 527; private collection, p. 530; Cheltenham Art Gallery and Museum, Cheltenham, p. 532; Cheltenham Art Gallery and Museum, Cheltenham, p. 537; © The British Museum, London, p. 539; V&A Picture Library, London, p. 540; photograph © 1999, The Art Institute of Chicago, all rights reserved, gift of Mr. and Mrs John J. Evans, Jr., 1971.748, p. 541; private collection, p. 542; Dick Reid, York, p. 544; V&A Picture Library, London, p. 547; © The Tools and Trades History Society, Swanley, p. 548; V&A Picture Library, London, p. 554; The Museum of Decorative Arts in Prague, p. 557.